Political
Development
and Change

Political Development and Change

A POLICY APPROACH

EDITED BY

Garry D. Brewer
AND
Ronald D. Brunner

FP THE FREE PRESS
A Division of Macmillan Publishing Co., Inc.
NEW YORK

Collier Macmillan Publishers
LONDON

The Free Press
A Division of Macmillan Publishing Co., Inc.
866 Third Avenue, New York, N.Y. 10022

Collier–Macmillan Canada Ltd.

Library of Congress Catalog Card Number: 74-482

Printed in the United States of America

printing number
1 2 3 4 5 6 7 8 9 10

320
B847p

Library of Congress Cataloging in Publication Data

Brewer, Garry D
    Political development and change.

    Includes bibliographies.
    1. Policy sciences---Addresses, essays, lectures.
I. Brunner, Ronald D., joint author. II. Title.
H61.B644   320   74-482
ISBN 0-02-904710-2

75-4782

Contents

Preface   vii

Contributors   ix

Introduction: A Policy Approach to the Study of Political
Development and Change   1
GARRY D. BREWER and RONALD D. BRUNNER

Part I: Goals   23

1. Political Ideas in Kenya and Tanzania   31
   ELLEN B. PIRRO

Part II: Trends   89

2. Economics and History in the Study of Rebellions: The
   Argentine Case   103
   GILBERT W. MERKX

3. Supporters of the New Party of the Right: A Report and
   Discussion of the German NPD's Sources of Support   128
   KLAUS LIEPELT

Part III: Conditions   159

4. Toward a Model of the Coup d'Etat in Latin America   173
   JOHN S. FITCH III

5. The Geography of Modernization: Paths, Patterns, and
   Processes of Spatial Change in Developing Countries   197
   EDWARD W. SOJA and RICHARD J. TOBIN

6. Political Roles: Micro Analysis and Macro Process   244
   RAYMOND F. HOPKINS

v

7. Partial Order and Political Systems   268
DOUGLAS DURASOFF

Part IV: Projections   283

8. Techniques and Accuracy of Demographic Forecasting:
Predicting United States' Population Growth   303
WILLIAM ASCHER

9. Policy and the Study of the Future: Given Complexity,
Trends, or Processes?   327
RONALD D. BRUNNER and GARRY D. BREWER

Part V: Alternatives   345

10. The Israeli Policymaking System: Characteristics and Improvements   371
YEHEZKEL DROR

11. Economic Policymaking with Little Information and Few
Instruments: The Process of Macro Control in Mexico   396
JOHN E. KOEHLER

Part VI: An Afterword on Methods   435

12. Dealing with Complex Social Problems: The Potential of
the "Decision Seminar"   439
GARRY D. BREWER

13. A Modern Statistical Approach to Model Assessment   462
DONALD A. BERRY

14. Data Analysis, Process Analysis, and System Change   487
RONALD D. BRUNNER and KLAUS LIEPELT

Name Index   517

Subject Index   523

Preface

This volume presents a comprehensive approach to the study of political development and change. It is interdisciplinary. It stresses problem-identifying and problem-solving tasks associated with any intellectual endeavor: goal clarification, historical trend description, scientific investigation, detailed forecasting, and policy formulation. It strives to be contextual. It underscores the importance of using and creating appropriate methods to solve problems. And it encourages the integration of knowledge and action in systematic ways.

Being interdisciplinary risks overlooking isolated pockets of specialists, but we feel the risk is worth taking. We have attempted to select points of view representing specialized knowledge and then to relate specialities by integrating information from each with respect to central problems of development and change. For instance, if the reader is a political development specialist concerned primarily with the role of elites, then one or two of the selections will be very much related to this particular interest, and the remainder will be more or less pertinent. Another reader, say one concerned with spatial development, would have different preferences, but could incorporate several closely related selections into his teaching and thinking. An econometrician would "like" one or two of the chapters, would find several others contentious, might puzzle over several others, and so forth through an endless inventory of specialists, all concerned with pieces of the same substantive field.

To stress problem identification and problem-solving, we present lengthy bibliographic essays as introductions to each of the volume's major sections. These essays develop the main ideas associated with each of the five intellectual tasks, elaborate these general ideas with references to development-oriented literature where appropriate and available, and then indicate how the studies relate to both the general and specific ideas. Because the field is underdeveloped in significant ways, we have "cast the net" widely, but hopefully not indiscriminately, to provide tangible examples of work that could be explored with an end in view of improving the existing state of the art and practice. Fragmentation has been a major impediment to fruitful scholarship and practice, and integration and expansion are possible means to advance.

Each study presented in this collection fills only a limited number of the tasks recommended for a complete policy analysis; in effect, each is only *partially* policy relevant. Selections are strong on some points, weak on others; and we take pains to indicate each, telling the reader what pieces of the recommended framework have been filled in and what pieces of the larger "map" are not covered as well or remain to be developed. To say something about making changes in a society—the broad objective of political development policy—individual partial analytic pieces must be assembled and integrated into a comprehensive whole, and this volume is one such rendition of what this entails.

The volume emphasizes methods, but the reader may be distressed to see that we have overlooked his "favorite" method. There is no *one best* method, only a large set of realized and potential methodologies that, given a clear definition of a specific problem, may or may not be appropriately employed. A separate section on methods shows how these individual, partial insights might begin to be integrated by creating and using a variety of methods.

We hope to leave the reader with a sense of what remains and can be done in a field where much of the existing intellectual labor is specialized, fragmented, and not integrated into something of a whole. Because this holistic framework has been missing, progress in the field has been limited. It is time to get to work.

CONTRIBUTORS

WILLIAM L. ASCHER is currently an Assistant Professor in the Department of Political Science, the Johns Hopkins University. He received his A.B. degree from the University of Michigan in 1968, majoring in political science and minoring in mathematics and physics; his M. Phil. in political science was awarded by Yale University in 1970; and he is completing work toward his Ph.D. at Yale. In 1972, he was a Visiting Researcher at the Facultad Latinoamericana de Ciencias Sociales, Santiago, Chile. His current research interests focus on planning and decisionmaking, political socialization, comparative political development, and the applications of mathematical methods.

DONALD A. BERRY received his A.B. in mathematics from Dartmouth College in 1965, his M.A. and Ph.D. degrees in statistics from Yale University in 1967 and 1971. Currently he is an Assistant Professor of Statistics, University of Minnesota; he also serves as a Consultant to Operations Research Inc., of Silver Springs, Maryland; formerly he was employed by the Center for Naval Analyses in Arlington, Virginia. Berry's publications include: "A Bernoulli Two-Armed Bandit," *Annals of Mathematical Statistics*, Vol. 43 (1972); "An Improved Procedure for Selecting the Better of Two Bernoulli Populations," *Journal of the American Statistical Association*, Vol. 68 (1973), with Milton Sobel; "Optimal Sampling Schemes for Estimating System Reliability by Testing Components—I: Fixed Sample Sizes" (Minneapolis, Minn.: University of Minnesota Technical Report, 1972); and "Red-and-Black with Unknown Win Probabilities," *Annals of Statistics*, Vol. 2 (1974), with David Heath and William Sudderth. His current research interests include work on Bayesian statistical applications, sequential decision theory and design of experiments, and game theory.

GARRY D. BREWER received his B.A. in economics from the University of California at Berkeley in 1963, his M.S. in public administration from California State University at San Diego in 1966, and his M.Phil. and Ph.D. degrees in political science from Yale University in 1968 and 1970, respectively. A member of the Senior Staff of the Rand Corporation from 1970 to 1974, he is currently (1974–75) a Fellow at The Center for Advanced Study in the Behavioral Sciences, Palo Alto, California, on leave from Yale's School of Organization and Management, where he is an Associate Professor. He has also held teaching posts at U.C.L.A., U.S.C., and the Rand Graduate Institute. He is a consultant to the National Science Foundation, the Ford Foundation, and to DATUM, e.V. of Bonn-Bad Godesberg, West Germany, is the Editor of the journal *Policy Sciences*, and is a member of the editorial boards of *Simulation & Games* and *Public Policy*. His major publications include: *Organized Complexity: Empirical Theories of Political Development* (New

York: The Free Press, 1971), with R. D. Brunner; *Politicians, Bureaucrats and the Consultant: A Critique of Urban Problem Solving* (New York: Basic Books, 1973); and various articles in professional journals. Besides the research interests represented by this volume, he has worked extensively in the areas of public policy appraisal—especially with respect to health policies for children—and methodological development—particularly the creation and use of operational simulations and games.

RONALD D. BRUNNER received his B.A. and Ph.D. degrees from Yale University in political science in 1964 and 1971 respectively. Since 1968 he has been a member of the faculty of the University of Michigan, where he is presently an Associate Professor of Political Science and a Research Associate in the Institute of Public Policy Studies. He also consults for the National Science Foundation. In 1969–70 he was a Research Associate at the Center for International Affairs, Harvard University. His major publications include: *Organized Complexity: Empirical Theories of Political Development* (New York: The Free Press, 1971), with G. D. Brewer; "Simulating International Conflict: A Comparison of Three Approaches," *International Studies Quarterly,* Vol. 13 (Spring 1969), with Hayward R. Alker, Jr.; and "Government and Politics: A Fragmented Society, Hard to Govern Democratically," in *Information Technology: Some Critical Implications for Decision Makers* (New York: National Industrial Conference Board, 1972), with J. P. Crecine. Brunner's current research interests include communications theory and policy and the simulation of complex systems.

DOUGLAS DURASOFF graduated from Michigan State University in 1966 with a B.A. degree in mathematics; he is currently completing work on his Ph.D. degree in political science from Yale University. Presently employed as an Assistant Professor of Political Science at the University of Bridgeport, Durasoff was an IREX Fellow in Yugoslavia in 1970–71. His current research is concentrated on analyzing alternative models of authority-decentralized decision systems, with particular reference to Yugoslav "self-management."

YEHEZKEL DROR received his B.A. and Magister Juris degrees from the Hebrew University and his LL.M. and S.J.L. degrees from Harvard University. Since 1957 he has been affiliated with the Hebrew University, where he is a Professor and Director of Public Administration programs, and was formerly head of the Political Science Department (1967–68). He has been a guest professor and policy consultant in various countries, and a senior consultant on policymaking and planning for government agencies in Israel. In 1962–63 he was a Fellow at the Center for Advanced Study in the Behavioral Sciences in Palo Alto, California; in 1965 he was awarded the Rosolio Award for the greatest contribution to the advancement of the study and practice of public administration in Israel; in 1968–1970 he served as a Senior Staff member of the Rand Corporation; and in 1972 he received the Levi Eshkol Prize for the best study on the first twenty-five years of Israel's public administration. Dror is president of the Israeli Futures Study Association, vice-president of the Israeli Center for Policy Studies, and serves on several professional journals in editorial and review capacities. His publications include: *Public Policymaking Reexamined* (San Francisco: Chandler, 1968); *Design for Policy Sciences* (New York: Elsevier, 1971); *Ventures in Policy Sciences: Concepts and Applications* (New York: Elsevier, 1971); *Crazy States: A Counterconventional Strategic Problem* (Lexington, Mass.: Heath, 1971); *Israel: High Pressure Planning* (Syracuse, N.Y.: Syracuse University Press, 1966), co-author; and numerous publications in scholarly journals. Dror has a long-standing interest in public policymaking, policy sciences, planning and strategy.

J. S. FITCH III earned his B.A. in political science from Randolph Macon College in 1965, his M.A. in international relations from Yale University in 1967, and his M. Phil. and Ph.D. degrees from Yale in 1969 and 1973, respectively, both in political science. He is currently an Assistant Professor of Political Science at the University of Florida and formerly held a research post with Yale University's Political Data Program. His research interests focus on Latin American politics, and his most recent work is an analysis of the coup behavior of the military in Ecuador from 1948 to 1966.

RAYMOND F. HOPKINS was educated at Ohio Wesleyan University, where he earned an A.B. degree in 1960, at Ohio State University, M.A. in 1963, and at Yale University, M.A. and Ph.D. in 1965 and 1968 respectively. Currently an Associate Professor of Political Science and Director of the Center for Social and Policy Studies at Swarthmore College, he has published in a number of substantive areas, including ethics, game theory, and methodology, as well as in the area of his current research on African political development. His publications include: *Political Roles in a New State* (New Haven: Yale University Press, 1971); *Structure and Process in International Politics* (New York: Harper & Row, 1973), co-author; "Game Theory and Generalization in Ethics," *Review of Politics* (October 1965); "Aggregate Data and the Study of Political Development," *Journal of Politics* (February 1969); and "The Role of the M.P. in Tanzania," *American Political Science Review* (September 1970).

JOHN E. KOHLER, the Associate Head of the Economics Department, The Rand Corporation, was educated at Yale University, from which he received his A.B. in 1963, M.A. in 1965, and Ph.D. in 1968, all in economics. He has served as an Instructor in Economics at Yale, 1965–66, as Lecturer at El Colegio de México, 1967, and U.C.L.A., 1972, and as a faculty member of the Rand Graduate Institute. Among his publications are *The Matrix of Policy in the Philippines* (Princeton: Princeton University Press, 1971), co-author; *Indonesian Economic Issues and Options* (Santa Monica, Cal.: The Rand Corporation, R-1037, 1972), co-author; *The Philippine Family Planning Program: Some Suggestions for Dealing with Uncertainty* (Santa Monica, Cal.: The Rand Corporation, RM-6149, 1970), co-author; and *Information Systems for High Level Staffs* (Santa Monica, Cal.: The

Rand Corporation, R-840, 1970), co-author. His current research interests include studying the effects of public policy toward medical education and developing techniques for improving uncertain decisions.

KLAUS LIEPELT is Director of the Institute of Applied Social Research (Infas), a prominent German social science research organization located in Bonn-Bad Godesberg. He was educated at the Free University of Berlin and at the University of Michigan, where he received an M.A. in political science in 1954. He has served as a Visiting Lecturer in Political Science at the University of Michigan; he was co-founder and now serves as Acting Chairman of DATUM, a German public policy planning and research institute. Among his publications are numerous policy papers on the climate of public opinion in West Germany: *Thesen zur Wählerfluktuation* (Frankfurt: Europäische Verlagsanstalt, 1968), with Alexander Mitscherlich; *WAHLHANDBUCH 1965* (Frankfurt: Europäische Verlagsanstalt, 1965); "Esquisse d'une typologie des électurs allemands et autrichiens," *Revue française de sociologie* (1968); "Wider die These vom besonderen Wahlverhalten der Frau," *Politische Vierteljahreszeitschift* (1973), with Hela Riemenschnitter; and "Data Analysis, Process Analysis, and System Change," *Midwest Journal of Political Science*, Vol. 16 (November 1972), pp. 538-69, with Ronald D. Brunner.

GILBERT W. MERKX is an Associate Professor of Sociology at the University of New Mexico. He received his A.B. degree from Harvard in 1961 and his M.A. and Ph.D. degrees from Yale in 1965 and 1968, respectively. He has also been a Fulbright Scholar in Peru, held posts as Visiting Researcher at the Latin American Institute in Stockholm, Sweden, and at the Torcuato Di Tella Institute in Buenos Aires, Argentina, and has served as Bitraedande Professor at Gothenburg University in Sweden. His publications include "Sectoral Clashes and Political Change: The Argentine Experience," *Latin American Research Review,* Vol. 4, No. 3 (1969); "Revolucion, Conciencia, y Clase: Cuba y Argentina," *Revista Mexicana de Sociologia,* Vol. 33, No. 4 (1971); "Revolution in America?" *Monthly Review,* Vol. 23, No. 8 (1972), and "Recessions and Rebellions in Argentina," *Hispanic American Historical Review,* Vol. 53, No. 2 (1973).

ELLEN B. PIRRO received her A.B. degree in government from the University of New Hampshire in 1962, and her M.A. and Ph.D. in political science from Yale University in 1967 and 1968, respectively. She is presently an Associate Professor of Political Science at Drake University in Des Moines, Iowa, and has held research or teaching posts at various times at Northwestern University, the University of Minnesota, and Yale, where she did intensive work on the development of the "Lasswell Value Dictionary," reported in her contribution to this volume. Among her publications are *A Manual for Instruction in International Relations* (Boston: Little, Brown, 1972), co-author; "Foreign Policies Toward Southern Africa," in Henry J. Richardson, ed., *International Law and Development in Southern Africa* (Berkeley: University of California Press, 1972); and *Political Ideology:*

Subsaharan Africa (New Haven: Yale University Press, forthcoming). Her current research interests are wide ranging and include inquiries into the political processes of social change, conflict resolution, and community building, as well as methodological development and applications.

EDWARD W. SOJA, Associate Professor of Urban and Regional Planning, U.C.L.A., received his education at Hunter College, B.A., 1960, at the University of Wisconsin, M.S., 1961, and at Syracuse University, Ph.D., 1967, all in geography. He has held numerous posts both in the United States and in Africa, and he has published extensively. Some of his publications include: *The Geography of Modernization in Kenya: A Spatial Analysis of Social, Economic, and Political Change* (Syracuse, N.Y.: Syracuse University Press, 1968); and *The African Experience*, 3 vols. (Evanston, Ill.: Northwestern University Press, 1970), co-author. His research interests include the geographical analysis of problems of modernization and regional development, particularly in Africa, that focus on urban and communications systems development, spatial planning, and political integration.

RICHARD J. TOBIN was educated at Pennsylvania State University, where he received his B.A. degree in 1968, and at Northwestern University, where he earned his M.A. and Ph.D. degrees in political science in 1970 and 1973, respectively. He is currently a research associate at the Pennsylvania State University's Center for the Study of Environmental Policy. His publications include his contribution to this volume and "Spatial Perceptions in Northern Ghana" (University of Ghana, Institute of African Studies, 1969).

Introduction:
A Policy Approach to the Study of
Political Development and Change

GARRY D. BREWER
AND
RONALD D. BRUNNER

WHY A POLICY APPROACH?

Clearly, no one will make an exhaustive, much less definitive, list of all the questions, concepts, and procedures important in the study of political development and change.[1] Every scholar needs an approach to highlight some of his concerns, to deemphasize others, and to organize those remaining at the focus of attention so that research may proceed efficiently and effectively. But why choose a policy approach to political development and change? There are several answers.

In various degrees, a significant proportion of political scientists subscribe to the idea that part of their professional responsibility is to aid in the achievement of preferred societal outcomes through participation in the several processes related to public policy decisions. This does not mean that they must necessarily accept the goals of any set of participants in a policy process, nor does it suggest that this is their only professional responsibility or the only means of participating in politics. It does suggest, however, that the consequences of political research that *inevitably* extend beyond the discipline and into the political arena are part of their responsibility and should be explicitly taken into account.[2] One answer, then, is that with the withering of the ivory

[1] The best recent review of the state of the field is Samuel P. Huntington's excellent essay, "The Change to Change," *Comparative Politics*, Vol. 3 (April 1971), pp. 283–322.

[2] The professional responsibilities and participation of political scientists have been discussed in Harold D. Lasswell, "The Political Science of Science," *American Political Science Review*, Vol. 50 (December 1956), pp. 961–79; and *idem*, "Must Science Serve Political Power?" *American Psychologist*, Vol. 25 (February 1970), pp. 117–23.

Portions of this chapter were presented by Brewer to a conference on "Value Assumptions in the Development Process," Ladyhill Hotel, Singapore, March 22–25, 1972, and have been reported in a SEADAG Occasional Paper (New York: The Asia Society, 1972). Appreciation is extended to colleagues Harold D. Lasswell, Daniel Lerner, and Charles McVicker, and to all others who participated in that important meeting for their comments and reactions.

tower image, political scientists are beginning to take responsibility for the non-academic uses of their intellectual efforts.

A second answer is that a comprehensive set of intellectual tools for policy analysis—highlighting various questions, concepts, and procedures—has already been developed, largely through the efforts of Harold D. Lasswell, over the last forty years. These intellectual tools have not been widely or systematically applied to the study of political development and change, although they have had some influence.[3] Today's scholar need not rely on ad hoc, partial approaches reflecting the fashions of the day to achieve a productive intellectual orientation to his subject matter. The intellectual foundations for a policy approach to political development and change have already been laid, and what remains is the challenging task of building up from these foundations.

Finally, because the approach is comprehensive, its systematic use is capable of generating new insights into old problems. Previously neglected questions are emphasized; an expanded, interrelated set of variables and concepts is included; and attention is focused on a number of different methods. In each case, alternatives to conventional viewpoints are provided, giving rise to the possibility of a new burst of creativity in the field. Even if one is insensitive to the emerging norm of accountability for the nonacademic consequences of one's research, it may still be possible to respond to the possibility of realizing significant intellectual payoffs through careful application of the policy approach.

A POLICY APPROACH: OVERVIEW

A policy approach should be problem oriented in the questions asked, contextual in the consideration of any factor in the social process, and multimethod in the procedures brought to bear to help resolve its problems.[4]

Problem Orientation

Problem-oriented research generates information that explicitly considers each of the following questions:

- What *goal values* are to be sought?
- What are the *trends* in the realization of values?
- What factors *condition* trends?

[3] See the references to Lasswell's work in Gabriel Almond's introduction to the *Politics of the Developing Areas* (Princeton: Princeton University Press, 1960).

[4] Particularly, Harold D. Lasswell, *A Pre-View of Policy Sciences* (New York: Elsevier, 1971); *idem,* "Policy Sciences" in the *International Encyclopedia of the Social Sciences;* and *idem* and Allan R. Holmberg, "Toward a General Theory of Directed Value Accumulation and Institutional Development," in H. W. Peter, ed., *Comparative Theories of Social Change* (Ann Arbor, Mich.: Foundation for Research on Human Behavior, 1966).

- What *projections* characterize the probable course of future developments?
- What *policy alternatives* will bring the greatest net realization of values?[5]

The five questions and their answers are distinct, both logically and in terms of their roots in the academic division of labor. Trends and projections refer to past and possible future events, respectively, while conditions refers to causal factors and general theoretical statements that can be used to explain either. Statements about goals as *preferred* events are of course different from statements about trends, conditions, and projections. In contrast to these four kinds of information, information about policy alternatives deals with the manipulation of events to realize preferences rather than the contemplation of events.[6]

Historians and anthropologists (particularly in the developing areas) have played the major role in clarifying past trends, but there is no corresponding set of disciplinary specialists to clarify future possibilities. Social scientists as scientists in several disciplines have developed scientific information—causal theories—of the type suggested by the "conditions" questions. Political philosophers in particular and philosophers and theologians in general have specialized in the clarification of goals. Regarding policy alternatives, "Students of politics are expected to have something pertinent to offer about the probable effects of adopting one form of government or another, or one policy or another relating to power." [7] Specialists in each discipline or field have evolved relatively distinctive assumptions and procedures in pursuit of answers to each of the five questions.

While each of the five tasks is distinct, they are, taken together, also interdependent: every problem-solving activity performs each of the five tasks with various levels of insight and understanding. Without public policy alternatives, there can be no choice of solutions. Without goals, there exists no basis for ordering or choosing among possible alternatives. Characterizations of past events and possible future events in terms of goals are necessary to estimate the significance of a given problem with respect to others. Lacking such an estimate, the allocation of attention to the problem may be diversionary. Information

[5] Quoted from Harold D. Lasswell, *Politics: Who Gets What, When, How* (Cleveland and New York: Meridian, 1958 ed.), p. 187. (Emphasis added.)

See also Graham T. Allison, *Essence of Decision: Explaining the Cuban Missile Crisis* (Boston: Little, Brown, 1971), p. 278, where it is noted that analysts of foreign affairs perform the following intellectual tasks: description, explanation, prediction, evaluation, and recommendation. These categories approximate Lasswell's trends, conditions, projections, goals, and alternatives.

For a study which implicitly uses similar distinctions to appraise and improve what is known about "social action" policies in the United States, see Alice M. Rivlin, *Systematic Thinking for Social Action* (Washington, D.C.: The Brookings Institution, 1971).

[6] The contemplative–manipulative distinction is elaborated in Harold D. Lasswell and Abraham Kaplan, *Power and Society: A Framework for Political Inquiry* (New Haven: Yale University Press, 1950), pp. xi–xii; and Lasswell, *World Politics and Personal Insecurity* (New York: The Free Press, 1965 ed.), Part I.

[7] Lasswell, *Politics: Who Gets What, When, How* (Cleveland and New York: Meridian, 1958 ed.) p. 187.

about conditioning factors is necessary to estimate the future consequences of alternative courses of action. Without warranted knowledge of conditioning factors, policy is likely to be inefficient at best and counterproductive or utopian at worst. The quality of decisions depends not only on the skill with which each task is performed, but also on the performance of all five tasks. To be problem oriented is to develop habits of thought and procedure to enhance the execution of these several distinct, yet interrelated, tasks in the investigation of any social setting.

Contextuality

To be contextual is to develop habits of thought and procedure to improve understanding of the relationships between parts and wholes, emphasising past, present, and future events as they interact and change through time. This requires a comprehensive framework to direct attention to the possibly significant phenomena in a setting and a tentative conception of the whole.

The framework developed by Lasswell and others can be used to illustrate the point.[8] This framework is comprehensive in at least two senses. First, each list in the framework refers to several key categories along a dimension of the social process that has proved to be important in political and social thought over the centuries. For example, the nearly infinite number of values at stake in the social process are divided into eight categories:

- Power: Participation in decisionmaking
- Respect: Honor, status, prestige, recognition
- Rectitude: Virtue, goodness, righteousness
- Affection: Love, friendship, loyalty
- Wealth: Income, goods, services
- Well-being: Health, safety, comfort
- Skill: Proficiency in any practice, including the manipulation of symbols and resources
- Enlightenment: Knowledge, insight, information

The particular labels chosen are not as important as the function of distributing attention across the dimension.[9]

Second, by overlapping and juxtaposing the lists referring to various dimensions, an enormous number of possibly significant areas of inquiry is generated. Consider a very general list of basic elements in the social process:

- Participants: Individuals, groups, etc.
- Perspectives: Value demands, expectations, identities, etc.

---

[8] See Lasswell, *A Pre-View of Policy Sciences*; and Lasswell and Kaplan, *Power and Society*.

[9] It is no accident that at most eight categories tend to be chosen. Cognitive psychologists have shown that this is near the upper limit of the span of short-term memory, an important constraint on the number of concepts a human subject can manipulate quickly. See Herbert Simon, "The Psychology of Thinking," in his book, *The Sciences of the Artificial* (Cambridge, Mass.: The MIT Press, 1969).

- Situations: Unorganized, organized; territorial, pluralistic, etc.
- Base Values: Positive and negative assets; perspectives, capabilities, etc.
- Strategies: Coercive, persuasive, etc.
- Outcomes: Value indulgences, deprivations, decisions, choices, etc.
- Effects: Value accumulation, enjoyment, distribution; institutional change, etc.

The examples suggest direction for the elaboration of any of the seven basic categories to any desired level of detail. Considered in connection with the list of value categories, one might begin to classify participants in a particular setting: voters are participants in power processes; racial and ethnic groups shape and share respect; religious leaders are specialized to rectitude outcomes; friends and enemies are references to participants in terms of affection; and so on. Situations specialized to various value outcomes include political parties (power), ceremonies (respect), churches (rectitude), families (affection), and so forth. The point is that by use of such a framework, the classification of any detail in a setting immediately suggests alternatives to be considered and in the process clarifies the functional meaning of the detail.

This quick example by no means exhausts the creative possibilities, but it does illustrate how the framework can be used to organize observations and to estimate the significance of an event in terms of the context. The probability of misperceiving the significance of each component decreases with improvements in the breadth, depth, and accuracy of a tentatively held understanding of the whole context. If this framework or some functionally equivalent symbol system is lacking,[10] the phenomena selected for observation and analysis are likely to be chosen for reasons that do not inspire confidence that such an understanding will be developed. For example, they might be selected because they are prominent in the academic literature, in current newspaper headlines, because there exists a source of funds for studying these phenomena and not others, or because they are consistent with the latest fad. The scholar who consciously uses such a framework is a more powerful and independent thinker than one who delegates responsibility for organizing his frame of attention to someone else.

The importance of context in estimating meaning or significance has been at least partially recognized in the comparative study of political development and change. At the simplest level, most scholars recognize that the meaning of an index such as electoral turnout is contingent on other aspects of each context for which it is calculated:[11] electoral laws, the range of voting alternatives, vote-counting procedures, and anything else that might affect the individual patterns of identifications, expectations, and demands that condition the act of voting or nonvoting. At another level, the importance of context is recognized in the com-

[10] Those who downgrade the importance of symbol systems in performing simple intellectual tasks—let alone the difficult task of estimating significance—should try multiplication with roman numerals.

[11] See the discussion of index stability in Lasswell and Kaplan, *Power and Society*, pp. xx–xxi.

parative method, particularly in the belief that one country cannot be understood adequately without knowledge of others. The assumption is that un-realized possibilities in one country may have been realized in others. Sensitivi-ty to a broader range of possibilities through study of several countries enlarges and refines the framework that can be applied to each. (The limitation, of course, is that the number of realized possibilities and combinations of realized possibilities in even a large sample does not nearly exhaust the set of possibili-ties, and particularly those that may be realized only in the future.) Finally, the importance of context has also been recognized in previous approaches such as the approach introduced by Gabriel Almond and since elaborated by Almond and G. Bingham Powell.[12]

While the importance of the context has been recognized, it has been insufficiently implemented in the study of political development and change,[13] in part because the frameworks employed have not been sufficiently compre-hensive. The framework introduced by Almond, for example, is specialized to the recognition of aggregate functions and structures which perform them, but it diverts attention from the context of individual action. If the pattern of iden-tifications, expectations, and demands at the individual level which supports an aggregate pattern is changed, then so will the aggregate pattern change. The framework is also of little help in characterizing social patterns—patterns which provide inputs to the power process and over which power is exercised.

Multiple Methods

The necessity for multiple methods has been emphasized in the literature to which political scientists are typically exposed.[14] Nevertheless, two points are worth reiterating in this connection. First, every method has "blind spots," cer-tain classes or types of phenomena to which it is insensitive. For example, ob-servations generated by techniques of survey research are relatively insensitive to the organization of the perspectives of individuals, in part because the survey instrument contains an organizing scheme imposed on the individual. Further-more, mathematical modeling techniques provide much analytical power over a small number of variables, but are much less helpful in dealing with large numbers of interconnected variables. The basic problem is that an analytical solution to a system of equations becomes more difficult to find as the system be-comes large and complex. Second, the selection of problems or observations in order to apply a particular method is de facto a decision to exclude large arrays

[12] Almond, *op. cit.;* and Gabriel A. Almond and G. Bingham Powell, Jr., *Comparative Politics: A Developmental Approach* (Boston: Little, Brown, 1966).

[13] An exception is the Vicos experiment in Peru, directed by the late Allan Holmberg. See Holmberg, "The Research and Development Approach to the Study of Change," *Human Organization,* Vol. 17 (Spring 1958), pp. 12–16; and Henry F. Dobyns et al., *Peasants, Power and Applied Social Change* (Beverly Hills, Cal.: Sage Publications, 1971).

[14] Abraham Kaplan's discussion in his *Conduct of Inquiry* (San Francisco: Chandler Publications, 1964), pp. 276, 279, about the "methodological hammer" is appropriate.

of potentially significant phenomena, whether the decision is conscious or not. This criterion of selection inspires no more confidence than the ones already rejected in this discussion. An emphasis on multiple methods is a partial corrective.

About This Volume

Each of the major aspects of policy research—problem orientation, comtextuality, and multiple methods—implies principles of organization for a volume such as this. We have chosen to emphasize the five intellectual tasks of the problem orientation, to include some materials on method, and to weave in points about contextuality as best we can. Unfortunately, there is little *truly* contextual research in the study of political development and change, and this collection does little to fill the void.

Thus, within the context of a policy approach, this volume has two purposes: One is to assert and emphasize the range of distinctive kinds of questions that must be answered to improve the rationality[15] of public policy in the field of study roughly characterized as political development and change. This task is carried on throughout the remainder of this introductory chapter. The other purpose is to make available to a wider audience a set of papers which collectively span this range and individually illustrate some of these assumptions and procedures in the investigation of particular substantive problems.

This approach to the subject matter emphasizes the role or function of research in policy processes. Our hope is that it will provide a useful supplement to existing approaches which emphasize particular kinds of political phenomena. Among the latter are the cybernetic approach, emphasizing feedback and the flow of information;[16] the structural-functional approach, emphasizing structures and the functions they perform;[17] and the political-cultural approach, emphasizing the relatively stable underlying components of political behavior.[18] More specialized approaches emphasize phenomena such as elites, bureaucracy, crises of development, stages of development, and so forth. These approaches begin with the assumption that the phenomena emphasized are important, but the criteria of importance are often implicit. In contrast, the policy approach advocated here assesses the importance of political research in terms

[15] We use the term *rationality* in the sense of Robert A. Dahl and C. E. Lindblom, *Politics, Economics, and Welfare* (New York: Harper & Row, 1963 ed.), p. 38. Given goals and real word conditions, "an action is rational to the extent that it is correctly designed to maximize *net* goal achievement."

[16] See, for example, the work of Karl W. Deutsch, *The Nerves of Government: Models for Political Communication and Control* (New York: The Free Press, 1963); "Social Mobilization and Political Development," *American Political Science Review*, Vol. 55 (September 1961), pp. 483–514.

[17] A recent statement is Gabriel Almond and G. Bingham Powell, Jr., *Comparative Politics*.

[18] See Lucian W. Pye and Sidney Verba, eds., *Political Culture and Political Development* (Princeton: Princeton University Press, 1965).

of its relevance to public policy. As such, it provides a general answer to that most devastating question leveled at political research, "So what?"

Political development and change is only one of many areas of political inquiry to which the policy approach is appropriate. It is particularly appropriate because of its relatively strong emphasis on the national level of analysis, the locus in many cases of the policy processes having the largest impact on events.

THE PROBLEM ORIENTATION

The separate, yet interrelated, tasks of goal clarification, historical description, scientific investigation, forecasting, and policy invention and evaluation are insufficiently developed and in some cases largely ignored in contemporary political research. As political scientists we suffer from what our French colleagues have come to call a *déformation professionelle*—specialization in the form of a sharpened and narrowed focus that predisposes one to ignore all matters outside the focus.[19]

We have focused on the scientific and to a lesser extent historical tasks to the virtual exclusion of the others. From the viewpoint of one attempting to effect a closer approximation between societal circumstances and our ideals of a good society, scientific theory—parsimonious general assumptions about cause and effect—alone is a thin reed on which to lean. It must be particularized to a given situation, or stated differently, initial conditions must be detailed. It must be operated to generate projections for the given situations. Goals must be clarified and related to the projections. And alternative combinations of instrumental variables—policy alternatives—must be invented and evaluated.

The decision made is no better than its weakest link. Consequently, even very good theory is relatively useless unless the other four tasks are done well. Given our narrow focus of attention, it is obvious why we, as a profession, can point to few interests where we contributed to the public good through research. Given the complexity of the other three or four tasks, it is also obvious why politicians and public officials have found it convenient to ignore our theories, regardless of the quality of these theories.

Goal Values

By a goal we mean a category of preferred events, and we include both events desired in themselves and events that are instrumental to other preferred events. Thus, peace is preferred to war and productive employment is preferred to mass unemployment.[20]

[19] William Barrett, *Irrational Man* (Garden City, N. Y.: Doubleday, 1958), has written passionately and persuasively on this and related points.

[20] Lasswell and Kaplan, *Power and Society*, p. 16; and Daniel Lerner and Harold D. Lasswell, eds., *The Policy Sciences* (Stanford, Cal.: Stanford University Press, 1951), pp. 9–10.

A major point is that values influence decisions in the selection of possible events to be considered (the "agenda" so to speak), and in the preference ordering of these events.[21] It is important to determine whose values, regarding what sets of events, are at stake in any given setting. For those participating in the development process, for instance, change itself is often valued as an outcome, but done so without due regard to the full range of outcomes and effects it generates. Change, no matter how defined and measured, is a concept requiring a *net* assessment; change generates losses as well as gains in valued outcomes. Change could mean, among more obvious possibilities, the diminution of collective security and the heightening of individual tensions in the face of increased uncertainty about the future. This and many other possible combinations of outcomes are important, but how does one go about making such valued outcomes understandable objects for study?

One common assumption is that such judgments are absolute, applicable to all times and places, and derived from abstract premises. An alternative assumption is that they are relative to circumstance and grounded in experience.[22] The idealist's search for abstract principles to justify values directs attention away from the conditions and consequences of decisions and toward their religious and philosophical sources. This causes problems more adequately confronted by the realist's approach.

First, there is no necessary logical or political connection between abstract principles and the operational values and outcomes associated with a given concrete policy. Equality as a value does not depend upon a belief that men were created equal by their Maker or that men are by nature equal. The conception of liberty in the American colonies was in many respects a religious liberty, yet the weakening of Protestantism does not necessarily undermine liberty as a value, and an increase in faith is not necessarily the prescription for strengthening liberty. There is no need to deprecate absolute appeals to God or nature, whether in a formal constitution, a declaration of independence, or in a campaign platform, so long as it is clear that such appeals are normatively ambiguous: they mainly serve to conceal personal preferences and to rationalize these preferences as the logical outcomes of shared principles.[23] Second, the grounding of political ideals in religious doctrine or metaphysics tends to insulate them from daily experience, rendering them of little use as guides to policy choice and action. Values can remain ideals and absolutes only to the extent that they are divorced from real choices. The affirmation of liberty, equality, and fraternity as absolutes ignores the real problem that action to achieve one of them may undermine the others. Also, majority rule and minority

[21] See the concept of "Value," in *International Encyclopedia of the Social Sciences;* and Kenneth Boulding, "The Ethics of Rational Choice," *Management Science*, Vol. 12 (February 1966), pp. 161–69.

[22] These are the basic alternatives considered in Abraham Kaplan, *American Ethics and Public Policy* (New York: Oxford University Press, 1963). Our discussion follows Kaplan's closely.

[23] *Ibid.*, p. 9; see also Lasswell and Kaplan, *Power and Society*, pp. 22–23.

rights, as democratic theorists have emphasized, are ideals that often conflict in real situations.

The moral problem is to weigh conflicting principles and to act on a balance of probabilities on behalf of the preponderant values. We know that circumstances have the effect of altering events; concrete moral values are plainly, abstract principles aside, nothing more than circumstantial.[24] Realistically conceived, we know what is good by experience.

Let us put the matter in the context of a political scientist clarifying the normative implications of his work. It is neither an idle nor a frivolous exercise, but relates directly to key choices one makes in selecting objects for study. A common position is that a political scientist's research should contribute to the development of science, and is justified in terms of these consequences. Presumably, the benefits are enlightenment, and the beneficiaries are an institution, science, and one's circle of professional colleagues. Another position more commonly noted through reconstruction of professional behavior than in verbal justifications is that a political scientist's research should contribute to his own status, income, and security. (One wonders whether some other profession might be more productive in these terms: In our culture, social scientists are not often found at the pinnacles of the distribution of respect and income!) In this case, relative to the first, more benefits are considered, but the range of beneficiaries is restricted to the researcher and his family. A third—and more contextual position—is that research should contribute to more equitable access to power, respect, income, security, and other values in society for the many rather than for the few. This does not deny the celebration of science or any other institution as a valued outcome, but directs attention to a greater range of values and to the others who might be affected. We recognize that every scholar has the right (and obligation) to clarify the normative consequences of his own research according to the circumstances in which he finds himself. But we also recommend a contextual accounting in order that certain possibilities are not ignored because they never bridged the threshold of attention.

Let us also put the matter in the context of a political scientist clarifying the goals of those who participate in, and are affected by, policy decisions in the contexts he chooses to study. Can he justify his support for, or opposition to, these goals? Can he discern shared goals worth serving? Can he discern policy preferences in terms of which his research might be heard? Again, the exercise is not frivolous.

The relativist, realist approach provides some guidance. Moral discourse in public arenas tends to be influenced by the political advantages of reaffirming normative ideals as absolutes. This practice diverts attention from the normative bases of concrete choices and invites the public to read their own preferences into normative symbols with ambiguous referents. God, motherhood, and apple pie are more influential on the campaign platform than behind closed doors where decisions are often made. Such moralization suggests that the researcher

[24] Kaplan, *American Ethics*, p. 91.

take the connection between expressed values and values affecting decision as a matter for empirical investigation. For example, the distribution of symbols in public announcements can be compared with distributions of deeds and resources including budgets, troops, and the like. It should be possible not only to clarify operating values, but to classify the processes by which articulated values respond to and affect changing conditions. The realist approach to the clarification of the goals of others, as well as the self, is contextual.

For political scientists who take political development as a normative concept, there exists a need to move beyond the speaker's platform and public documents to the specification of preferences among the members of the public. The anthropologist's distinction between "cool" and "hot" cultures illustrates the problem rather well. Valuing stability, those in a cool culture act to reduce or dissipate forces that would lead to disruptive social changes. Such acts often take the form of creative and vigorously performed rituals and myths intended to ensure the place of the individual in a stable, dependable world. Valuing change, those in a hot culture act to increase and stimulate dynamic forces that intentionally disrupt the existing social fabric. In so doing, however, the extraordinary strains placed on individuals in the society are frequently not taken into account. Industrial societies have been more dynamic and flexible than nonindustrial ones, but in the process such societies have taken more daring and more costly risks with the psychic well-being of their people.[25] In other terms, the narrow pursuit of increases in wealth and power values frequently overlooks some significant costs in terms of other values foregone or sacrificed in the process. How much individual and collective respect, rectitude, affection, and well-being does some narrowly conceived economic development scheme entail? What are the value trade-offs associated with competing policy alternatives being considered for implementation? What are the realized and likely outcomes and longer term effects in noneconomic, as well as specifically wealth-related, terms? Surely the preferences of the public have a role in the answers to these questions. Surely the scholar has an obligation to consider a range of symbolic and material values in attempting to find answers. And surely the answers will have a bearing on the concept of development.

Trends: The Study of Recent and More Remote Events

The function of historical research is to clarify events and trends in concrete situations. As Meyerhoff put it:

The *facts* of history are peculiar, as historicism has insisted all along. They are individual, concrete, unrepeatable events and entities. . . . The *primary aim* of a historical narrative is to reconstruct these events in their unique individuality, not to

---

[25] William Barrett, *Time of Need* (New York: Harper & Row, 1972), pp. 271ff has generalized these points and related them to what he perceives to be several strong philosophical currents flowing in contemporary Western intellectual life. The points have been particularized with respect to Indonesia in a discussion contained in the introduction to Part V of this volume.

formulate general laws, to bring out particular differences rather than the common propensities of the events included in the historical portrait.[26]

Among political scientists, the assumptions of the historical method are relatively well known. On the one hand, the facts cannot be rendered intelligible in the form of a narrative without some context or theory which defines their connections and significance. On the other hand, the imposition of a context or theory on the raw materials of history frustrates the primary aim of elaborating the peculiarities of each situation. The recommended procedure is often to develop a detailed understanding of many diverse historical situations in order to expand the range of perspectives from which a given situation can be interpreted.[27]

The policy approach suggests several analytical perspectives from which historical situations can be clarified in ways that contribute to policy.

A major inherent weakness of predominantly trend-based studies is that only a very small subset of what could have and what may in the future happen has in fact already transpired. Needed are procedures to help focus collective and individual attention so as to create and illuminate choices about policy. In his *developmental construct,* Lasswell has provided us with a procedure which, among other features, gets at this weakness and helps one allocate attention in creative and potentially productive ways. Perhaps the most notable exemplification of the procedure, or at least one known to political scientists, is the "Garrison State Hypothesis," a developmental construct prompted by trend events in the immediate pre–World War II era, but one which retains relevance for the contemporary world.[28] This persistence nicely illustrates one positive operational characteristic and contribution of the policy approach to "purely" trend-based studies: Imaginative interplay between the developmental construct and data that encourages progressive modifications of the investigated trends.

Another characteristic weakness of historical work is that it is often presented so that day-by-day events are allowed to obscure longer term ones—or evolutionary sequences—and hence the specific context is disconnected from the "arrow of time" running through the immediate present on into the nearer or longer term future; the work is rarely concerned with how alternative developmental sequences to the single one being described might have been realized (a weakness of both the "stage" and "crises" schools of political–historical scholarship); and it is only aberrantly (as in the case of Marxian historians)

[26] Hans Meyerhoff, ed., *The Philosophy of History in Our Time: An Anthology* (Garden City, N. Y.: Doubleday, 1959), p. 19. (Emphasis in original.)

[27] This view is developed well in Henri Pirenne, "What Are Historians Trying to Do?" in Meyerhoff, *The Philosophy of History in Our Time,* p. 95.

[28] This example was originally presented in Lasswell, "Sino-Japanese Crisis: The Garrison State versus the Civilian State," *China Quarterly,* Vol. 3 (Fall 1937), pp. 643–49. A generalization and clarification of the construct was presented in "The Garrison State," *American Journal of Sociology,* Vol. 46 (1941), pp. 455–68. And a reappraisal and reconstruction of the idea is found, some twenty-five years later, in "The Garrison State Hypothesis Today," in Samuel P. Huntington, ed., *Changing Patterns of Military Politics* (New York: The Free Press, 1962).

concerned with the ideological or normative content and implications of the description.[29] In short, by selecting narrowly from the whole available symbolic array, trend specialists have allowed themselves to become insufficiently problem oriented.

What one might expect from trend specialists are robust descriptive narratives featuring the elaboration of specific details of a given context as they unfold and intertwine over time,[30] If the work is especially well done, it may even be possible to tease out of the verbal representation weakly explanatory and tentative causal relationships for more intensive and imaginative investigation—using procedures such as the developmental construct.

What one ultimately expects from trend-oriented specialists are time-based studies that consider in detail the significance of events and trends taken with respect to various participant's goals. What, in short, are the patterns of expectations, identifications, and demands operating through time in specific contexts?

Conditions: The Identification of Interrelated Factors

Whole and part come into the direct consideration of scientific specialists dedicated to the discovery and measurement of underlying *structural* features of a context and their specifiable interrelationships. This is in contrast with *behavioral* outcomes produced by a given structural configuration. In the former case one is concerned with the development of an abstract model, and in the latter one focuses on the time series generated by that model. This concern for determining structural characteristics by rigorously measuring behavioral data is important but may be quite diversionary if the other four intellectual tasks are not explicitly treated.

Because, as far as we know, there exist no well-defined procedures to clarify the structures of complex and organized—as contrasted with either complex and disorganized or simple—systems,[31] at least two unproductive intellectual styles are currently discernible among scientific specialists.

Often in their haste to measure, they may overlook the research or policy question with the result that simple numbers replace complex good sense. One

[29] Qualitative and quantitative observations of contexts should reflect and monitor the key normative concepts which are discerned to be operating, which implies convergence between normative conceptions of political development and the design and application of social indicators, as one practical example. See Lasswell, "How to Integrate Science, Morals, and Politics," in his *The Analysis of Political Behavior: An Empirical Approach* (London: Kegan Paul, 1948).

[30] While the study of change is by definition time dependent, e.g., change with respect to what, over what period of time, it is distressing to see how frequently this basic requirement is overlooked by students of political development and change. An unusual treatment of the difficulty is contained in Eric Nordlinger, "Political Development: Time Sequences and Rates of Change," *World Politics,* Vol. 20 (April 1968), pp. 494–520.

[31] See Warren Weaver's important article, "Science and Complexity," *American Scientist,* Vol. 36 (1948), pp. 536–44, for a concise description of these key concepts.

reason, it seems to us, that attempts to measure the dimensions of nations[32] have not been more enlightening is that insufficient attention was given to the matter of measurement of what, for what purpose, and for whom. The same comment is to some degree applicable to diverse efforts to create social indicators in several locales.

A variation of this theme is demonstrated by specialists who rely heavily on correlational statistical methods to summarize aggregate patterns in their data. What is frequently overlooked in much of this work is the need to understand the expectations, identifications, and demands that support the measured patterns.[33] If the underlying props change, as they do with distressing (to the specialists) regularity, so will the observed patterns. Without adequate forewarning and equipped with only a limited number of observational tools, the conditions specialist is hard pressed to explain these shifts over time or the differences in patterns between different observational settings.[34]. What results in the first instance are decidedly conservative "theories" or explanations of behavior, and in the second case one is occasionally treated to the sight of perplexed data analysts justifying aberrations in their data as "deviant cases"—deviant perhaps with respect to some aggregated statistical artifact, but certainly not with respect to the specific constellation of events operating in the given context.

At another extreme, scientific specialists have eschewed data in an effort to deduce formally elegant, often axiomatized, structural models.[35] However, when such structures are not related to any known empirical context, empty formalism quickly substitutes for *social* scientific explanation. This habit of thought is more prevalent among economic than political specialists,[36] but it is nonetheless a consideration to be confronted.

[32] See R. J. Rummel, "Dimensions of Conflict Behavior Within and Between Nations," *General Systems* (1963 Yearbook), for one example of the "numbers game."

[33] Cutting through some of the smoke, it seems that this is the primary point at issue in a recent critical review of one "numbers intensive" characterization of the Philippines. See B. J. Kerkvliet, "Critique of the Rand Study on the Philippines," *The Journal of Asian Studies,* Vol. 23 (May 1973), pp. 489–500. The referenced study is H. A. Averch, F. H. Denton, and J. E. Koehler, *The Matrix of Policy in the Philippines* (Princeton: Princeton University Press, 1971).

[34] As Warren Weaver hinted and as we, in our *Organized Complexity: Empirical Theories of Political Development* (New York: The Free Press, 1971), Part II, stressed, to say that X is a problem of organized complexity is to say that the context (not just its simple, tentative representation) must be understood to understand observed behavior.

[35] Talcott Parsons, "Evolutionary Universals in Society," *American Sociological Review* (June 1964), pp. 339–57, is one example that fits this characterization. In economics, J. R. Hicks, *Value and Capital: An Inquiry into Some Fundamental Principles of Economic Theory,* 2nd ed. (London: Oxford University Press, 1946), p. iii, typifies the problem. "This is a work on Theoretical Economics, considered as the logical analysis of an economic system of private enterprise, without any inclusion of reference to institutional controls. . . . For I consider the pure logical analysis of capitalism to be a task in itself, while the survey of economic institutions is best carried on by other methods, such as those of the economic historian."

[36] See Martin Shubik, "A Curmudgeon's Guide to Microeconomics," *Journal of Economic Literature,* Vol. 9 (June 1970), pp. 405–33, for some trenchant observations on the issue and its consequences.

Despite aspirations and considerable pretention, few "purely" scientific inquiries have produced results that are anymore than weakly predictive. Much social scientific work is rendered irrelevant for policymaking concerns when the scientist's choice to select according to his own discipline's imperatives takes precedence over a policymaker's, and indeed society's, preferences. Not only are policy-relevant variables often foresaken in the interests of measurement (or for other scientific reasons), but many normatively interesting features of a context are likewise overlooked. Addressing themselves to reasons why this occurs, Robert A. Dahl and C. E. Lindblom have raised several interesting points: Preferences are hard to quantify; preferences in any situation are numerous, conflicting, and often unknown; and calculation is by itself no substitute for the policymaker's visceral apparatus.[37]

A more specific illustration of the conditions orientation's weaknesses for policy purposes, weaknesses attributable in part to the scientist's objectives of producing parsimonious, generalizable, cause-and-effect explanations, is understandable when one considers the results of the systematic application of the maximization postulate—a source of much of the utility of economic theory for policy analysis. Variously referred to as the assumption of rationality or of goal-seeking, maximizing, or satisficing behavior, the postulate holds that living forms act in ways that are expected to leave the actor (and those with whom he or she identifies) better off in net value terms than if the actor had performed differently.[38] In Herbert Simon's formulation of artificial behavior,[39] it is convenient to distinguish the goals, the inner environment, and the outer environment of an actor. For some actors, behavior can be predicted from knowledge of goals and the shape of the outer environment, with few assumptions about the inner environment. The environment serves as the mold, for example, in the case of a profit maximizing firm in a competitive market. For others, behavior can be predicted from knowledge of goals and the internal environment. Variations in the outer environment are compensated to maintain a homeostatic relationship between goals and the inner environment, as in the case of a firm able to dominate the market.

The limitations of economic and other social theory as applied to policy stem in part from a failure to recognize in concrete situations the salient features of the inner and outer environments, and to consider the potential relevance of a larger number of goals in addition to wealth and power that figure in human behavior. If any salient goal or feature of the two environments is omitted in an application, then explanation or prediction of behavior is inaccurate. Put another way, explanation and prediction depend upon a comprehensive understanding of the context. Recognition of the salient features and demands in any context requires a comprehensive model to organize observations and to reduce

[37] Robert A. Dahl and C. E. Lindblom, *Politics, Economics and Welfare* (New York: Harper & Bros., 1953), pp. 77–79.

[38] See Lasswell, *A Pre-View of Policy Sciences*, p. 16.

[39] Herbert A. Simon, *The Sciences of the Artificial* (Cambridge, Mass.: The MIT Press, 1969), pp. 8–9.

dependence on partial and, therefore, less useful cues such as one's disciplinary training, the latest academic fad, or current headlines.

Scientific formulations also suffer from the deformations of specialization; they, like trend-based formulations, have been insufficiently contextual.

The study of conditions is important, obviously, because of its concern for rigorous measurement and its general desire to clarify the underlying structures responsible for behavior in a context. An area of great *potential* contribution is in the specification of alternative structural interpretations, i.e., the development of multiple theoretical explanations for contextual behavior that are capable of taking into account the related issues of goals, as well as inner and outer environments.[40] In large measure such explanations are to be expected because any single given formulation will be adequate with respect to specific space-time contexts. Indeed, there is a scientific burden to ensure that a formulation remains "chronologically pertinent to the ordering of political events as the future unfolds," [41] but this potential has not been realized to any great degree in practice.

Projections: Where We Seem to Be Headed

Projections clarify possible future events. They are important because policy is necessarily a step into the future. We can interpret the past, but we cannot otherwise change it. Projections are also important to allocate attention to gain some lead time. The distributions of problem intensities now, five years ago, and five years from now are not the same. It is important to anticipate the central problems in order to have the appropriate analyses ready when they are needed. To relate these ideas to the cybernetic approach, it is an important factor to increase lead time if one's goals are to be attained at reasonable cost, or attained at all.

Specialists in projection concentrate on sorting out what conditioning factors are going to have what important consequences for whom at specified times in the future. These efforts must be contextual if they are to aid scientific investigation and reasonable policy intervention.

Part of the "sorting out" process involves determining over a period of analysis what factors are going to be relatively constant, e.g., habits of language and culture;[42] what factors will undergo systematic change, e.g., demographic

---

[40] A rare example of the need for multiple models is contained in Robert Bush and Frederick Mosteller, "A Comparison of Eight Models," in Paul Lazarsfeld and Neil W. Henry, eds. *Readings in Mathematical Social Sciences* (Chicago: Science Research Associates, 1966), pp. 335–49.

[41] This is what Lasswell has labeled the "principle of subsumption." See Lasswell, "The Political Science of Science," *American Political Science Review,* Vol. 50 (December 1956), pp. 961–79, at p. 978.

[42] Lucian W. Pye, *Politics, Personality, and Nation Building* (New Haven: Yale University Press, 1962), provides one example of this sort of work in the political development area.

characteristics;[43] and what factors fluctuate in orderly ways, e.g., business cycles and "mood" cycles.[44]

A prime weakness of specialized projective inquiries is the innate difficulty one has in accounting for unique events such as "great men," or natural disasters.

In practice, projective specialists have been few in number and have limited themselves to one of several techniques. Representative techniques include extrapolation, model building—or one of its variants, gaming, simulation, and scenario construction—and the collection of expert opinion and judgment. Ideally, although extremely rare in practice, all of these techniques could be combined in the following or similar fashion.

One technique is to extrapolate quantified trends and distributions to locate zones of probable contradiction or conflict, and to utilize available knowledge of the inter-dependencies among conditioning factors to make an estimate of the probable outcomes. The hypotheses thus developed can be evaluated in the light of nonquantified information provided by competent observers.[45]

The raw ingredients needed for productive projective efforts are clear: quality data on important trends, some understanding of how these data are inter-related, a reasonably clear understanding and statement of individual and collective goals, and finally systematic methods and procedures by which non-quantified but expert opinion may be brought to bear on what is indicated by the projected trends.

Alternatives: Knowing Better Where We Seem to Be Headed, What Might We Do about It?

It is ultimately in the course of making collective public choices that the true importance of the policy approach is made manifest. The creation, estimation, selection, implementation, evaluation, and termination of policy alternatives are integrative tasks in that they consider all four of the previous intellectual tasks, if done well.

To specify alternatives is to know the history of a context and to understand, at even the crudest level, how key elements are interrelated to one another. To select from among possible specified alternatives is to have valued,

43 James M. Beshers, *Population Processes in Social Systems* (New York: The Free Press, 1967), provides just one example of a large literature.

44 See for instance, National Bureau of Economic Research, *Long Range Economic Projection—Studies in Income and Wealth* (Princeton: Princeton University Press, 1954); and *idem, Short Term Forecasting* (Princeton: Princeton University Press, 1955), for business cycles. Frank T. Klingberg, "The Historical Alteration of Moods in American Foreign Policy," *World Politics* (January 1952), and "Predicting the Termination of War," *Journal of Conflict Resolution* (June 1966), has treated mood cycles.

45 Lasswell, "The Future of the Comparative Method," *Comparative Politics,* Vol. 1 (October 1968), pp. 3–18, at p. 14.

preferred outcomes somewhere in mind. In short, specification of alternatives occurs at the nexus of fact and value with experience from the past and expectations about the future.

Specifying alternatives forces one to account for an assortment of operating goals existing in any context; it also focuses attention on the needs for the evaluation of the past performance of public officials: If we do not know who was successful for what reasons in the past, how can we select those capable of making reasonable choices in the future? And it forces one to confront the goals' trade-off issue: How much of one goal needs to be sacrificed to obtain another goal? At what cost? To whose account?

There are fundamental difficulties with this task. Man, to echo a continuing argument, is a limited information-processing being. Except for the most trivially simple social setting imaginable, there are just too many possible alternative courses of action to be considered. Furthermore, preferences associated with any one of these alternatives may not yet have been experienced; that is, prior to experiencing the outcomes of some novel policy, how can one actually know whether one will like it or whether it will work out as planned?

Just on the issue of implementation of a selected policy option, we have extraordinarily little information to explain how it is that even the "simplest," most "clear-cut" policies often work out in ways that are not only different from what was anticipated, but often inimical to the best interests of those affected by the policy.

Because the compass of what any one or a few policymakers know is limited, relative to either what they should know or to what the logical possibilities for knowledge are, the chances for something approaching rational selection processes to operate are also quite limited. With increased societal complexity, one learns to suffer the unexpected as a result of purposive human intervention.[46] Merely on the issue of deciding among competing goals, short-term calculations that yield slight or transitory benefits quite often obliterate serious considerations of the longer term consequences of a public act.

An Emphasis on Multiple Methods

We have repeatedly stressed the need to question and probe one's subject matter from a variety of specialized observational perspectives. As is often the case in exploring virgin terrain, we consistently find ourselves coming up short when it comes to having the right equipment to begin answering those questions. Besides raising new questions, the policy approach encourages the creation of "equipment" or methods to resolve those questions; furthermore, it stresses that

[46] Some of these matters have been considered in more detail in Garry D. Brewer, "Analysis of Complex Systems: An Experiment and Its Implications for Policymaking," in Todd R. La Porte, ed., *Organized Social Complexity: Challenge to Politics and Policy* (Princeton: Princeton University Press, forthcoming).

the research or policy question determines the range of possible analytic techniques, not the reverse, and that there is no primacy among methods.

CONTRIBUTIONS TO THIS VOLUME

Each part of this volume corresponds to one of the five distinct intellectual tasks comprising the policy approach—goals, trends, conditions, projections, and alternatives. Each is prefaced with a bibliographic essay that selects several of the major ideas related to the specific task and then presents representative literature to illustrate the main currents of intellectual activity associated with that task. Chapters begin with an editorial comment explaining their relationship to the whole contribution cast in terms of a few-word abstract and a skeleton outline of the chapter's contents. What follows here is the briefest of introductions to each of the contributions to give the readers a better sense of what the book represents.

Goals

Political goals as reflected in the political speeches of African leaders captured Ellen Pirro's attention, and the results of her exhaustive analysis of political symbols are presented in "Political Ideas in Kenya and Tanzania." The rigorous empirical study of political goals is unfortunately a relatively rare occurrence in the study of political development and change. It is so mainly because the importance of symbolic activity is not widely recognized and because the available methodological procedures are not well developed nor particularly sharp for this sort of research. As a result, we are shown an array of analytic techniques that variously selects out features of the research problem and that compositely tells us a great deal about the goals of two important political leaders: Nyerere and Kenyatta. Furthermore, efforts are made to relate these verbal materials to the distributions of goods and services, over time, in each setting.

Trends

To illustrate trends, we selected two very different, even "deviant," pieces. In Gilbert Merkx's effort to find rhyme and reason in the perplexing political events of immediately post-Peron politics in Argentina, "Economics and History in the Study of Rebellions: The Argentina Case," it was necessary to stand back, to expand the level of temporal resolution in the analysis to obtain a longer view of interrelationships between economic and political trends. Fascinatingly, he found order where little or none seemed to have existed before. Trend information was manipulated to suggest what the underlying structure, or conditioning factors, might be, and Merkx has had some qualified successes projecting Argentine political cycles; as far as we know, the normative and policy uses of this work have been few.

On the other hand, Klaus Liepelt took a much shorter range view in trying to understand the emergence of the ultra-rightist NPD Party in the Federal Republic of Germany. Historical information was used to point out where and under what conditions such a party would appear—information that proved quite useful in executing several finely detailed public opinion surveys. The study itself establishes an historical datum or point of reference against which subsequent developments might be assessed. The policy demand to know how great such a movement might become furthermore contributed to our understanding of evolutionary sequences in the German electorate.

Conditions

We have divided the study of conditioning factors into macro and micro phenomena. The divisions are not terribly precise, but they do serve to separate aggregated, relatively whole system events from disaggregated, partial, or individual level ones.

The reader will note that we have more selections in this section than in the others. This is not to lay undue stress on the conditions task; it merely reflects its extent of development relative to the other four tasks.

John S. Fitch, "Toward a Model of the Coup d'Etat in Latin America," considers what regular systematic components are involved in the Latin American coup d'etat. This effort follows constructively after Merkx's contribution and considers several problems of specifying and building formal models to study developmental processes.

Edward Soja and Richard Tobin, "The Geography of Modernization: Paths, Patterns, and Processes of Spatial Change in Developing Countries," are also concerned with aggregated activity, but their main emphasis is on the political-spatial aspects of change in several African states.

At the micro level, Raymond Hopkins "Political Roles: Micro Analysis and Macro Process," is also concerned with African political development, but his attention is concentrated on the role of decisionmaking elites at the top executive and legislative levels. Not surprisingly, his research purposes, specification of relevant problem elements, methodological techniques, and results are quite different in kind from those of Soja and Tobin.

Bureaucratic behavior has long held the political scientist's attention. However, the explanatory model Douglas Durasoff proposes, "Partial Order and Political Systems," represents a radical and quite imaginative departure from the norm. As different as the chapter is from the others in this section, it is complementary as it stresses both problems of alternatives specification and fundamental goal clarification.

Projections

One holds out hope that accurate social projections of high quality will one day be realized. However, William Ascher, "Techniques and Accuracy of Demographic Forecasting: Predicting United States' Population Growth," makes such hopes appear to be all the more problematic. One of the many important messages contained in this chapter is the need to examine clearly the underlying assumptions being made in a given projection. In making this point, we are dramatically reminded of the basic interrelatedness of each of the intellectual tasks: in this case, the strong connections among conditions, projections, and trends.

Ronald D. Brunner and Garry D. Brewer, "Policy and the Study of the Future: Given Complexity, Trends, or Processes?" examine several of the underlying theoretical and practical issues involved in making projections and interpreting these projections for policymaking purposes. In its own way, this chapter explores the "raw ingredients" needed for productive efforts that were mentioned earlier in this discussion. A small model of modernization and mass politics is used for these purposes.

Alternatives

Yehezkel Dror treats the goals issues quite differently in "The Israeli Policymaking System: Characteristics and Improvement." In describing what the present system seems to be and contrasting this with what it should become, a goals-alternative bias is nicely demonstrated.

The Mexican policymaking system has provided the basis for many diverse studies of political development and change. John Koehler has looked carefully at the system and makes some interesting observations on the levels of governmental performance where a key constraint is severely limited information: "Economic Policymaking with Little Information and Few Instruments: The Process of Macro Control in Mexico."

Methodological Views

The chapters in this collection attack their respective analytic questions using an assortment of methodological tools and data of varying amount and quality. Where appropriate, the authors have discussed why they selected the method they did, why alternatives might not have been as suitable, and what followup literature the interested reader could pursue. Additionally, we have chosen to develop the concept of multiple methods beyond the individual chapters themselves. This was done for several reasons: The primary thrust of the individual chapters was *not* the examination and demonstration of novel methods; if such appears to be the case in individual contributions, it is more a matter of trying to manage one's analytic problem and question than it is the display of technical virtuosity. Second, the particular requirements of the policy approach appear to generate rather interesting and difficult demands on the current stock of tools; it is useful to examine both the demands and some possible management strategies.

The concept of the "decision seminar" has been advanced as one such strategy. Its purpose and practice are examined in "Dealing with Complex Social Problems: The Potential of the 'Decision Seminar'."

Donald A. Berry, a statistical specialist, provides a statistical rationale for the evaluation and creation of multiple models and thereby encourages the pursuit of more sophisticated and systematic procedures such as the "decision seminar": "A Modern Statistical Approach to Model Assessment."

Ronald D. Brunner and Klaus Liepelt, "Data Analysis, Process Analysis, and System Change," call into question much of the current descriptive statistical analysis used to understand developing systems. In so doing, many of the severe limitations of the specialized scientific view are called out for detailed scrutiny. Such questioning alerts the unwary analyst to the counterproductive nature of relying on one method and indicates that we must not be satisfied with anything less than a problem-oriented, multimethod, and comprehensive, i.e., a policy, approach to our subject matter.

CONCLUSION

Several themes have been introduced and underlie much of what follows: Man, despite his magnificent facility for abstraction, is at base a limited information-processing being; the number and precision of our finest abstractions are at best insufficient to understand and manage the complexity of present-day social affairs. As part and parcel of our best efforts to cope with the full richness of society, we find ourselves dealing with ever narrowing pieces of the whole: fragmentation of the world has led to a serious problem of deformed professional vision which allows mastery over a few artificially disconnected aspects of the whole at the expense of mastery (or even perception) of the rest. A clarifying image is that of the photographer who, when confronted with capturing a complex subject, is forced to focus with great intensity on but one view, thereby omitting all but a very few possible images of the whole.

Our problem, and one that we have barely begun to recognize—much less overcome, is nothing short of figuring out ways by which the scholar may orient himself to his subject matter to be continually reminded of his severe limitations and to begin their transcendence. Snapshots of the passing development scene are no longer enough.

The intellectual challenge facing us is to provide a durable reorientation of the social science professions toward contextual, problem-oriented, and versatile concepts and methods.

Part I
Goals

INTRODUCTION

To pursue aggregate valued outcomes in a society, it is helpful to distinguish between general philosophical exercises on man's ethical-moral status and more specific analyses dealing with real operating preferences. Furthermore, it is important to distinguish between aggregate, or *mass*, and particular, or *elite*, behavior when studying concrete social preferences.

Of the five intellectual tasks, the study of goals is evidently one of the more "underdeveloped." It is not that no work has been done, rather, existing work is found in disparate disciplines, is highly specialized or technical, and has not yet been focused effectively on political development problems, an unfortunate situation.

To the extent that the interest of political development scholars is primarily on historical and scientific work and excludes normative, projective, or policy efforts, such an emphasis may be misplaced. In a real sense, accomplishing our overriding problem-solving purpose is limited by the quality of the weakest link in the chain of required information, and the paucity of work devoted to the study of normative behavior in diverse contexts points out a serious weakness indeed.

THE LITERATURE

One natural division of the existing literature is into the areas of man's general ethical-moral situation, including a small sampling from works in philosophy, social ethics, and decisionmaking; the identification and management of value-laden symbols, including mass-oriented analyses of propaganda and studies of elite verbal behavior; the relationship of political development and goals; and, finally, what methods might be used to study and measure goals in many contexts. Let us reemphasize the highly selective nature of this review; the list is representative, not exhaustive.

Ethical-Moral

Abraham Kaplan, *American Ethics and Public Policy* (New York: Oxford University Press, 1963), offers a succinct and highly readable account of the elements of moral behavior and presents an empirical model describing the role of values and statements about values in the American political process. He also articulates the general issue of "moral dualism," the insulation of absolute values, e.g., freedom, equality, equity, etc., from experience. Implications of such insulation are detailed by Gibson Winter, *Elements for a Social Ethic: Scientific Perspectives on Social Process* (New York: Macmillan, 1966); and James Gustafson, "Context versus Principles: The Misplaced Debate," *Harvard Theological Review* (April 1965). Other general works include R. L. Means, *The Ethical Imperative* (New York: Doubleday, 1969); and for a more parochial, but important, view, Paul Ramsay and Gene H. Outka, *Norm and Context in Christian Ethics* (New York: Charles Scribner, 1968). These latter two works are worth reading to indicate just how far removed much goals-related scholarship is from the desired contextual and problem-oriented approach we advocate.

On the study of mass preferences we especially recommend Robert A. Dahl and Charles E. Lindblom, *Politics, Economics, and Welfare* (New York: Harper, 1953); and Kenneth Arrow, *Social Choice and Social Process* (New York: Basic Books, 1968).

Decisionmaking or elite studies having a strong and explicitly normative component include Wayne A. R. Leys, *Ethics for Policy Decisions* (Englewood Cliffs, N.J.: Prentice-Hall, 1952); C. West Churchman, *Prediction and Optimal Decision* (Englewood Cliffs, N.J.: Prentice-Hall, 1961), which, as the title suggests, also addresses problems of projection; Robert A. Dahl and Charles E. Lindblom, *Politics, Economics, and Welfare* (New York: Harper & Row, 1963 ed.); and sections of Lindblom, *The Policy Making Process* (Englewood Cliffs, N.J.: Prentice-Hall, 1968).

Symbols and Values

One of the best and most comprehensive treatments that we know is Murray Edelman, *The Symbolic Uses of Politics* (Urbana, Ill.: University of Illinois Press, 1967). Other important initiatives in the study of symbols and symbol flows as value laden data are H. D. Lasswell, "Communications Research and Politics," in D. Waples, ed., *Print, Radio, and Film in a Democracy* (Chicago: University of Chicago Press, 1942), pp. 101–17; H. D. Lasswell, Nathan Leites et al., *Language of Politics: Studies in Quantitative Semantics*

(New York: George Stewart, 1949); C. E. Osgood, "Studies on the Generality of Affective Meaning Systems," *American Psychologist*, Vol. 17 (1962), pp. 10–28; Charles Morris, *Signs, Language, and Behavior* (New York: Prentice-Hall, 1946); Ithiel de Sola Pool, *Symbols of Democracy* (Stanford, Cal.: Stanford University Press, 1952); *idem, Symbols of Internationalism* (Stanford, Cal.: Stanford University Press, 1951); and, a definitive work, H. D. Lasswell, Daniel Lerner, and I. de Sola Pool, *The Comparative Study of Symbols* (Stanford, Cal.: Stanford University Press, 1962).

The literature on propaganda, in large part symbols designed for mass consumption, is diffuse, but several excellent general sources and specific analytic examples are known to us. Alexander George, *Propaganda Analysis* (New York: Row Peterson, 1959), is a thoroughly competent introductory work. H. D. Lasswell, *Propaganda Technique in the World War* (New York: Knopf, 1927), reports one of the earliest scientific attempts to study political values embedded in wartime propaganda. H. D. Lasswell and Dorothy Blumenstock, *World Revolutionary Propaganda* (New York: Knopf, 1939), is particularly relevant for those interested in the generation and sustenance of mass political movements. Robert Merton, *Mass Persuasion: The Social Psychology of a War Bond Drive* (New York: Harper, 1946), is an insightful and detailed case study analysis that has many generally useful implications for the study of political change. Another more specific example is J. S. Bruner, "The Dimensions of Propaganda: German Shortwave Broadcasts to America," *Journal of Abnormal and Social Psychology*, Vol. 41 (1941), pp. 311–37. R. K. White, "Hitler, Roosevelt, and the Nature of War Propaganda," *Journal of Abnormal and Social Psychology*, Vol. 44 (1949), pp. 157–74, indicates that the mass–elite distinction we have adopted to classify the literature is not as sharp as it is convenient. In fact, in all works cited both elements operate; whatever distinctions exist are more those of emphasis than of rigid definition.

One recent effort to examine changes in elite symbol behavior over one century is H. D. Lasswell and J. Zvi Namenwirth, *Changing Values in American Party Platforms* (New Haven: Yale University, Office for Advanced Political Studies, 1966). Less rigorous, but noteworthy because the literature in the area appears to be quite limited, is R. Angell, Vera Dunham, and J. David Singer, "Social Values and Foreign Policy Attitudes of Soviet and American Elites," *Journal of Conflict Resolution*, Vol. 8 (1964). Other related examples are J. W. Prothro, "Verbal Shifts in the American Presidency: A Content Analysis," *American Political Science Review*. Vol. 50 (1956), pp. 726–39; and H. L. Runion, "An Objective Study of the Speech Style of Woodrow Wilson," *Speech Monographs*, Vol. 4 (1936), pp. 75–94.

Several observations are prompted by a general perusal of this short list: the study of political symbols and values is not currently "fashionable," nor did it ever have many truly *political* scientific proponents; war appears to be the major stimulus for this kind of work, although we are not aware of major current studies of this type.

Political Development and Goals

It is important to distinguish the goals bearing on the problem of the social sciences or a particular social scientist from the goals bearing on the development problems of a particular country or region. We are primarily concerned with the latter, and the list of recommended readings that follows reflects this concern. This section on political development and goals is subdivided into parts on general studies, the study of goals operating in mass settings, and the study of goals and elite behavior.

A good general work which we regard highly is J. Roland Pennock, "Political Development, Political Systems, and Political Goods," *World Politics,* Vol. 18 (April 1966).

The interrelated issues of value trade-offs, preference recognition and specification, and decisionmaking under uncertainty in the context of social development and change are treated with varying emphases in Ralph Braibanti and Joseph J. Spengler, Jr., *Tradition, Values and Socioeconomic Development* (Durham, N.C.; Duke University Press, 1961); Bert F. Hoselitz, "Economic Policy and Economic Development," in Hugh G. J. Aitken, ed., *The State and Economic Growth* (New York: Social Science Research Council, 1959); and Jan Tinbergen, *The Design of Development* (Baltimore, Md.: Johns Hopkins University Press, 1958).

Several scholars have attempted to relate values, ideologies, and development policymaking in specific empirical settings. As with much goals related work, primary proponents are by and large *not* political scientists. See Clyde Kluckhohn, "Toward a Comparison of Value Emphases in Different Cultures," in Leonard D. White, ed., *The State of the Social Sciences* (Chicago: University of Chicago Press, 1956), pp. 116–32, for a concise overview of many of these issues. On the question of how specific cultural factors affect preferences and decisionmaking in diverse settings, a collection prepared by Paul E. Sigmund, Jr., ed., *The Ideologies of the Developing Nations* (New York: Praeger, 1963), offers many interesting descriptive examples. To illustrate one instance wherein there is no separation of the social scientist's goals and those bearing on the development problems of a region, look over Charles Wolf, Jr., *Foreign Aid: Theory and Practice in Southern Asia* (Princeton: Princeton University Press, 1960), especially Chapters 7–10; or *idem,* "National Priorities and Development Strategies in Southeast Asia," *Philippine Economic Journal,* Vol. 4 (Second Semester 1965), pp. 156–72.

We know of one truly *general* and *contextual* work that considers and relates goals concerns to the four other intellectual tasks: H. D. Lasswell and Allan R. Holmberg, "Toward a General Theory of Directed Value Accumulation and Institutional Development," in Ralph Braibanti, ed., *Political and Economic Development* (Durham, N.C.: Duke University Press, 1969), pp. 354–99.

Joseph J. Spengler, Jr., "Social Value Theory, Economic Analyses and Economic Policy," *American Economic Review*, Vol. 42 (May 1953), pp. 340–45, has many excellent ideas about the identification of collective preferences and the development and implementation of (economic) policies. Two related pieces in the same vein are Philip M. Hauser, "Cultural and Personal Obstacles to Economic Development in the Less Developed Areas," *Human Organization*, Vol. 18 (Summer 1959), pp. 78–84; and John D. Montgomery, "Public Interest in the Ideologies of National Development," in Carl J. Friedrich, ed., *The Public Interest, Logos V* (New York: Atherton, 1962).

Studies that focus on collective or mass values and are simultaneously tied to a single national or regional context are not common. However, the following are representative of this type of work: Khalid Bin Sayeed, "Religion and Nation Building in Pakistan," *Middle East Journal*, Vol. 28 (Summer 1963), pp. 279–91; Arnold Rivkin, "Incentives in African Life," *Journal of African Administration*, Vol. 12 (October 1960), pp. 224–27; and Richard Gable, "Culture and Administration in Iran," *Middle East Journal*, Vol. 13 (Autumn 1959), pp. 407–21. One quite interesting effort is Donald Rothchild, "Kenya's Africanization Program: Priorities of Development and Equity," *American Political Science Review*, Vol. 64 (September 1970), pp. 737–53.

An excellent general theoretical treatment of the relationship of goals and elite behavior using economic criteria is James Tobin, "Economic Growth as an Objective of Government Policy," *American Economic Review*, Vol. 54 (May 1964), pp. 1–27. Public administration specialists have treated this subject rather extensively. A good starting point is Joseph LaPalombara, ed., *Bureaucracy and Political Development* (Princeton: Princeton University Press, 1963): especially see the contributions of LaPalombara, "Bureaucracy and Political Development: Notes, Queries, and Dilemmas," and Fritz Morstein Marx, "The Higher Civil Service as an Action Group in Western Political Development." Elite behavior that is contrary to prescribed norms is taken up in the literature dealing with corruption. One excellent overview of the field is J. S. Nye, "Corruption and Political Development: A Cost Benefit Analysis," *American Political Science Review*, Vol. 61 (June 1967), pp. 417–27. Other works on corruption include Nathaniel Leff, "Economic Development Through Bureaucratic Corruption," *American Behavioral Scientist*, Vol. 6 (November 1964), pp. 8–14; and for one very specific description which emphasizes cultural norms and elite behavior in one setting, M. G. Smith, "Historical and Cultural Conditions of Political Corruption Among the Hausa," *Comparative Studies in Society and History*, Vol. 6 (January 1964).

Another important emphasis combines work from the intellectual tradition studying values and symbols with that interested in elite behavior. Two general articles, one by Morris Janowitz and William Delaney, "The Bureaucrat and the Public: A Study of Informational Perspectives," *Administrative Science Quarterly*, Vol. 2 (September 1957), pp. 141–62; and another by John T. Dorsey,

Jr., "A Communication Model for Administration," *Administrative Science Quarterly*, Vol. 2 (December 1957), pp. 307–24; both combine some interest in values and symbols with a heavily public administration orientation. While each has its own merits, neither addresses the question of political development as explicitly as do Charles F. Andrain, "Democracy and Socialism: Ideologies of African Leaders," in David E. Apter, ed., *Ideology and Discontent* (New York: The Free Press, 1964); and Kenneth Grundy, "Recent Contributions to the Study of African Political Thought," *World Politics*, Vol. 10 (July 1966).

This selected list of literature related to political development and goals supports our earlier comment about the literature on values and symbols: Work in the area is sparse, not usually produced by "name" scholars in political science, and we suspect, as in the case of corruption studies, is generally regarded as aberrant. On the one hand, it is unfortunate that such an important area has gone begging, so to speak; on the other hand, the field is literally wide open for serious scholarship.

Methods to Study Goals

We shall not pretend that there are any preferred methods or techniques to study goals; the field is simply too diffuse, too unsettled, and occupied by scholars of too many disciplinary stripes. It may even be a bit premature calling this assortment of work a field. Nevertheless, it occurs to us that the general mass and elite conceptual distinctions that we have so far relied on have methodological counterparts as well.

General studies on how to study ethics in concrete settings include Abraham Kaplan, *American Ethics and Public Policy*, particularly in his "Methodology of Morals"; Abraham Edel, *Method in Ethical Theory* (Indianapolis, Ind.: Bobbs-Merrill, 1963); portions of Abraham Kaplan, *The Conduct of Inquiry* (San Francisco: Chandler, 1964); portions of C. West Churchman, *Challenge to Reason* (New York: McGraw-Hill, 1968); and, for a bold attempt to rationalize and specify, Nicholas M. Smith, Jr., "A Calculus for Ethics: A Theory of the Structure of Value," *Behavioral Science*, Vol. 1 (April 1956).

Methodological treatments of collective value phenomena are contained in Kenneth Arrow, *Social Choice and Individual Values* (New York: John Wiley, 1951); Robert A. Dahl, *A Preface to Democratic Theory* (Chicago: University of Chicago Press, 1956); parts of H. D. Lasswell and Abraham Kaplan, *Power and Society: A Framework for Political Inquiry* (New Haven: Yale University Press, 1950), especially pp. 56–62 and Part III, if read carefully; and, for a rather skeptical, but balanced, view, Robert A. Dahl, "The Evaluation of Political Systems," in Ithiel de Sola Pool, ed., *Contemporary Political Science: Toward Empirical Theory* (New York: McGraw-Hill, 1967), pp. 166–81.

When we shift to consider methods for the study of values and symbols, particularly at the individual (or elite) level, the literature becomes more concrete—and in many cases more substantial. Colin Cherry, *On Human*

Communication (Cambridge, Mass.: The MIT Press, 1967 ed.), Chapters 4–6, is an excellent technical source. Besides many of the titles cited under the "Symbols and Values" section above, we also recommend G. U. Yule, *The Statistical Study of Literary Vocabulary* (London: Cambridge University Press, 1964); Ithiel de Sola Pool, ed., *Trends in Content Analysis* (Urbana, Ill. University of Illinois Press, 1959); Philip J. Stone et al., *The General Inquirer: A Computer Approach to Content Analysis in the Behavoral Sciences* (Cambridge, Mass.: The MIT Press, 1966); Abraham Kaplan, "Content Analysis and the Theory of Signs," *Philosophy of Science,* Vol. 10 (1943), pp. 230–47; and D. P. Cartwright, "Analysis of Qualitative Material," in Leon Festinger and D. Katz, eds., *Research Methods in the Behavioral Sciences* (New York: Dryden Press, 1953), pp. 421–70.

POLITICAL IDEAS IN KENYA AND TANZANIA

Ellen Pirro's contribution to this volume and to the literature on goals is basically characterized as a study of political values and symbols used by African elites in the Kenyan and Tanzanian settings. Content analysis is relied on as the primary methodology for the investigation.

The Question

There are three related questions underlying Pirro's research. The first two are descriptive and are concerned with clarification of the nature of political ideas in each of the two contexts and with a comparison of the similarities and differences between ideas in each setting. It is hypothesized that the degree of similarity will be considerable because of the common cultural and experimental elements existing in each context. Passing from the descriptive phase of the research, Pirro then questions the extent to which these political ideas square with specific realities.

Strengths of the Study

A major strength of the work is its demonstration that values can be studied rigorously: terms comprising the dictionary that forms the basis for the research are explicitly defined; reanalysis based on different or more specific research questions is possible; replication and reanalysis of the source data by other scholars are possible; and the source data are available for archival purposes and subsequent use.

The work is empirically based. Real verbal behavior is analyzed, and political values are consciously related to concrete events. The concept of "Africanization," taken as an abstract and absolute value, means very little until it is related to concrete events in a context, and to a degree, Pirro has been successful in doing this. A reasonably fair separation is made between the political values of the researcher and those operating in the context.

Weaknesses of the Study

A deficiency of the work is also a deficiency of content analysis in general. For the amount of pure labor required to prepare, manipulate, analyze, and interpret data, one must seriously wonder whether the results obtained are worth the effort. This is less a criticism of Pirro's chapter than it is an observation on content analysis as a research technique.

This is a "one-shot" study; it has not been replicated. No attempt has been made to collect and analyze data either from other related contexts or from the same two contexts at subsequent periods of time. Again, the fact that the technique is hard to execute seems to be an acceptable explanation for this situation.

We are uncertain, given the facts that the source data have not been re-examined, replicated elsewhere, or in any other way validated, about the overall quality of the data, This is a weakness more of omission than commission and points out one area requiring additional research effort.

Subsequent Developments

Several other items that deserve general attention are suggested by Pirro's chapter.

If content analysis is an important methodological technique for studying values, then we need to devote serious thought to means for making it cheaper, faster, and even more reliable. Ideally, improving data would include routinely obtaining verbal behavior over time and sampling more broadly from a variety of data-generating sources. Hopefully, more comparative work can be encouraged as well.

Chapter 1
Political Ideas in Kenya and Tanzania

Political ideas provide the scientific observer the point of entry into the operating goals of a given polity, for it is the politician who is the specialist most easily identified as primarily concerned with sensing, abstracting, articulating, and providing symbolic referents to explain and rationalize policy choices that have been made and shall be made at some time in the future. This chapter attacks the symbolic environments of Kenya and Tanzania, relates these to historical events and to key societal indicators of political and economic development, and suggests the type and form of impact that such symbolic configurations have for the making of policy choices. (In the last instance, goals articulated in political speeches are seen as "precursors to institutional innovations.") A good comparison between Kenya and Tanzania is made to highlight the many similarities and significant differences that existed in the elite political symbol systems of each. A variety of methods is demonstrated, including content analysis, regression analysis, factor analysis, and analysis of variance, all of which were employed to begin answering many of the difficult aspects of the basic research question: "How does one study symbols and goals in a policy setting in a systematic fashion?"

INTRODUCTION

Understanding the political policies of African countries has been extremely difficult due to the fluid nature of their political systems. Questions arise that create contradictions and yet, to analyze African politics, these questions must be addressed. What could be the reason that Julius Nyerere accords diplomatic recognition to Biafra? In what way does Jomo Kenyatta decide when to hold national elections? Why do both leaders emphasize "self-help" agricultural communes? These are specific policies that create practical contradictions and analytic difficulties of considerable moment. These policies are intimately tied to the political ideas articulated by African leaders, a point that comprises our central problem: How do political ideas contribute to national policy?

Appreciation is expressed to the Office of International Programs, University of Minnesota, for a travel grant and to Charles E. Cleveland, K. Belman, L. Schuman, K. Wendt, and Garry D. Brewer for assistance and comments.

Political ideas are common to all political systems. However rapidly the political system is changing, a nation's goals and objectives and the paths or means to obtain these goals are continually articulated. Examining manifest political ideas is one consistent means for determining the operation of African political systems, the trends and fluctuations in their directions, and the methods by which policy is implemented. In each case, political ideas are tied to the ongoing situations in a nation. These ideas need not be cohesive, consistent, nor provide a definite philosophical viewpoint in themselves, but they do establish the conceptualizations of the moment, providing an indication of the current situation, how it has been, and how it might be changing. Political ideas, especially those articulated by national leaders, are singled out as one entry into investigations of the political process.

Traditional Inquiry

There are two standard approaches to the analysis of African political ideas. The first approach sees in African political ideas the potential emergence of new ideologies. The second utilizes African political ideas as only one of several outputs of the political institutions.

Studies associated with the ideological approach have sought to identify a coherent, comprehensive, and persistent system of thought. For example, Grundy (1966) and Andrain (1964) trace the roots of African political thought in the works of past thinkers, from Plato to Martin Luther King. They and others approach "African Socialism" as the new philosophy of the sixties (Friedland and Rosberg, 1964). But, as Clapham (1970) notes, the ideas of African leaders have defied coherent philosophical analysis and have changed as national fortunes have changed. Popularly viewed as philosophers, African leaders have come to be more realistically regarded as politicians: mindful of the requirements of office, attentive to the assumption and maintenance of power, and conscious of the particular needs of their clientele at any one point in time. It is notable that these politicians, for the most part, do not subscribe to any coherent system of thought; on the contrary, their ideas are eclectic, reflecting divergent problems and political situations. As Clapham (1970, p. 3) suggests, "the results of treating them [political ideas] as ideologies are so slight . . . any general explanation of the one party theories as attempts to formulate a coherent ideological response to the problems facing the developing countries is left hanging in the air . . . this brings one no closer to the actual political uses of their ideas."

A second approach to the study of African political ideas is behaviorally based. Hence, African political ideas are usually linked to one or another political institution. Thus, Coleman and Rosberg (1964) see political ideas as one component of the party system. Rothchild (1970) puts political ideas within the context of bureaucratic programs. Zolberg (1966) suggests that political ideas are communication or socialization devices used for mass indoctrination. These approaches emphasize political institutions much more than political ideas. Yet, when institutions have disappeared or have been altered by governmental changes, many of the political ideas continue to exist, being adopted by the new leadership, both civil and military.

An Alternative Approach

Political ideas shall be viewed as instrumentalities, as policy initiatives, and as precursors to institutional innovation. Stressed shall be both the maintenance and innovation of the political system. While specific individuals, parties, and institutions disintegrate, political ideas are continually formed and reformed by persons holding power. In each case, political ideas are articulated within the bounds of what is necessary to run and maintain the country. Measuring these political ideas, both what they have been and what they are now, may be a first step toward more comprehensive analyses of a nation's past, present, and future.

This study has two purposes. The first is analytic—to specify the components of political ideas in two Sub-Saharan African nations, Kenya and Tanzania. The second is empirical—to measure over time the magnitudes of political ideas as expressed by indigenous national leaders while discoursing on public policy matters.

THE MEANING AND MEASUREMENT OF POLITICAL IDEAS

What are political ideas; what elements do they contain; what patterns do they form; and what policies do they promote? For most African political contexts, power is vested in a single national leader, and political ideas are translated into policy by his will. Policymaking depends on the clarity with which a leader specifies his ideas, both in terms of the goals established and the paths or procedures created to achieve these goals. Political ideas focused on a central theme can contribute to policymaking more than inchoate political ideas. Ideas focused on a theme and articulated clearly, though infrequently, appear to be easier to implement than ideas articulated frequently, but lacking a unifying theme. Moreover, one or a few ideas persistently articulated over time provide more impetus for action than manifold ideas less consistently presented.

Thus, the measurement of the contribution of political ideas to political policy within a given nation depends on several factors: (1) The relative frequency of occurrence of arrays of political ideas or concepts at a single point in time; (2) the consistency of occurrence of any single political idea or concept articulated over time; and (3) the clustering of political ideas forming thematic patterns. These can be combined in a formula in Figure 1–1.

FIGURE 1–1.   MAGNITUDE OF THE CONTRIBUTION OF A SINGLE POLITICAL
IDEA TO THE POLICY OF COUNTRY

$$\left[\left(\frac{F_{ij}/TF_j}{PB_i}\right)\left(\frac{\sum_{j=1}^{N} F_i/\sum_{j=1}^{N} TF}{PB_i}\right)\right](|L_i|) = M_{ij}$$

i = A single political idea or concept.

j = A single point in time.

M_{ij} = The magnitude of the contribution of a single political concept i to policy at a single point in time j.

$\dfrac{F_{ij}/TF_j}{PB_i}$ = The relative frequency of occurrence of a political concept at a single point in time where:

F_{ij} = Frequency of occurrence of concept i at time j.

TF_j = Total Frequency of occurrence of all ideas at time j.

PB_i = Probability of concept i occurrence in a frequency distribution B of English.

$\dfrac{\sum_{j=1}^{N} F_i/\sum_{j=1}^{N} TF}{PB_i}$ = The consistency of occurrence of a single political concept over time where:

$\sum_{j=1}^{N} F_i$ = The sum of occurrences of the single political concept over time.

$\sum_{j=1}^{N} TF$ = The sum of all occurrences of all political concepts over time.

PB_i = Probability of concept i occurrence in a frequency distribution B of English.

$|L_i|$ = The tendency of a single political idea to cluster, taken over time (absolute value).

This formula assumes that a political idea is an articulation of both a national objective, or goal, and a specified means for achieving that goal. The *frequency of occurrence* of a single political idea is a measure of a leader's expressed concern for the concept or idea. *Continuity over time* is the degree to which this political idea recurs throughout the set of articulations. *Cluster-ability* is the extent to which a single political idea co-occurs with other political ideas forming conceptual clusters. The notion of clusterability includes both structural placement and magnitude.

Each of these components is used individually to isolate relationships between the political ideas, but the utility of the data is best depicted in the integration of these elements as per the formula, to analyze governmental policies and activities both as they occur and as they have changed since independence.

The formula in Figure 1-1 suggests that the contribution of a political idea or concept to policy formation can be approximated by taking a measure of a political idea's clusterability and multiplying it by the product of the frequency of occurrence of a single political idea at a single point in time, multiplied by the degree to which the idea is used continually over time. The two components, frequency of articulation and continuity over time, are controlled by the probable frequency of that concept as it would occur in "normal" English (Kucera, 1967).

Through utilizations of these three elements—frequency of conceptualization, continuity over time, and clusterability—explanations of the degree and relationships of political ideas to policy are possible. Should one idea preoccupy the leader at one point in time, it will have a very high frequency of occurrence and will ultimately influence the formulated pattern. Another idea may persist over a period of time, but have a low frequency of occurrence at any single point. However, its contribution may be significant when integrated over the entire time span. The formulated pattern shows not only which ideas fit together, but also what their structural groupings are (Deese, 1962). Central ideas can, therefore, be distinguished from peripheral or dependent ones. Emphasis will be placed throughout this chapter on those political concepts related to governmental policy goals.

The Contexts

This study reports on selected sets of patterned themes connected with development and indicative of overriding political goals. To understand the application of political ideas, we must consider briefly the problems of development in East Africa. Whereas both Kenya and Tanzania are African and developing, they possess unique aspects distinguishing them from other African countries and from each other. Unlike the rain-forest shores of West Africa, where malarial mosquitoes and humid heat kept colonists away, Kenya and Tanzania attracted a number of permanent colonial inhabitants from European nations, especially Britain. Colonialism meant enforced taxation, cultivation of plantation crops, and forced relocation of natives away from fertile farmlands to make way for settlers. Kenya, with proportionally more settlers, had more of these elements. Colonialism also brought roads, railroads, and the concept of a single East Africa. These elements forged links among Kenya, Tanzania (then Tanganyika), and Uganda. Such colonial similiarities are in many respects superficial; the differences are notable.

Kenya

Kenya is a relatively prosperous agricultural nation possessing nascent manufacturing introduced by British firms. The fertile highlands and a rail link from the coast to Lake Victoria gave Kenya a head start in the economic affairs of East Africa. The major portion of Kenya's population lives in the southeastern band of the country stretching from the sea port of Mombasa, along the railroad to the capital, Nairobi, through the coffee and tea plantations of the highlands to the lake port of Kisumu. The northern portion of the country is largely desert, sparsely populated by nomads and herders. Two major tribal groupings, Kikuyu and Luo, dominate politics. Kenya's progress to independence was impeded slightly by the Mau Mau rebellion of the 1950's. Mau Mau has been considered elsewhere (Rosberg and Nottingham, 1966) as a major element of the fight for independence and as a nationalist or quasi-religious phenomenon. At the least, one major result of Mau Mau was the emergence of Jomo Kenyatta as the paramount national leader. Although Kenyatta was incarcerated during the worst of the difficulties, all political parties turned to him for national leadership toward independence. He controlled the Kenyan African National Union (KANU) and led the nation as its first prime minister. Through a series of crises, an army mutiny (experienced also in Tanzania), the assassination of the very popular economic minister, Tom Mboya, and an attempted coup, Kenyatta has remained a singular power in the Kenyan government.

Kenya faces continued political problems today. The partially industrialized economy is controlled largely from abroad. Outsiders, particularly the Asians, occupy many trained positions and operate retail commerce throughout the country in spite of concentrated programs of Africanization. Severe droughts in 1971 have injured the herds, imposing strains on the already tight economy. The major problem, however, is the political one of resolving ethnic differences to forge a single nation. On Independence Day in 1964, Kenyatta's government contained representatives of all major ethnic groups. Afterward, the defection of Luo leader Oginga Odinga, whose leftist leanings caused some consternation in Nairobi and abroad, provided an occasion for government reshuffling. Mboya's assassination not only struck down an able leader but eliminated another Luo and left government predominantly in Kikuyu control. Tribalism is a major problem. The 1969 elections were won by KANU, and the release of Odinga in 1970 calmed the tense tribal situation until the attempted coup in the summer of 1971. As Kenyatta ages, the question of Kenya's political future remains in doubt.

Tanzania

In many ways Tanzania is different, having distinctive problems and different political issues from those common to Kenya. Relatively less fertile than Kenya, Tanzania consists mainly of an arid, sparsely inhabited central plateau. The predominantly agricultural population lives on the borders of the country, along the coastal plains north and south of the port capital, Dar es Salaam, in the fertile coffeelands of the Kilimanjaro region, along Lake Victoria's coast, and in the forest and mining regions along the borders of Malawi and Zambia.

Ethnic diversity led to widespread use of a lingua franca, Swahili, which has developed into something like a national language. Partly as a result, no major ethnic grouping dominates national politics and tribal hostility is reduced.

Tanzanian history diverges from Kenya's. Kenya was a crown colony under the British Colonial Office, but Tanganyika was originally colonized by the Germans, who turned the colony over to the League of Nations mandate after World War I and, after World War II, to United Nations' control supervised by Britain. Neither organization had much lasting impact on national mores within the colony, but the experience is recognized as one pressure for independence.

In 1961, Tanzania gained independence under Julius Nyerere's leadership. Shortly after the 1964 Zanzibari Revolution, Tanganyika and Zanzibar became the United Republic of Tanzania. In 1962, following an army mutiny, Nyerere resigned the prime ministership and reorganized the Tanganyikan African National Union (TANU), the single party of the nation. Subsequent to joining with Zanzibar and transforming the nation into a republic, Nyerere became its first president and was reelected in 1970.

Tanzania's major problems are economic. It is very poor in mineral resources, soil, and water supplies. Droughts, such as the 1971 rain failures, are major catastrophes. The demand for sisal, a principal crop, suffered severe declines in the 1960's with the introduction of artificial rope fibers. Malnutrition and other diseases are widespread among the peasant farmers. Nyerere's efforts have been directed toward organization for attainment of economic objectives.

The Arusha Declaration is the single most significant event in recent Tanzanian political history. A statement of policy issued through the political party, the Arusha Declaration sets forth a comprehensive program for socialist development of the nation. Supplemented by other statements, the declaration urges conscious, rather than haphazard, development, encourages seeking aid without strings, and stresses investment for communal and cooperative growth. Nyerere, in an astute political move, cut his own salary, then nationalized the banks and major industries. Party members were restricted in the amounts of goods and money they could possess. Recently extended to landlords, these restrictions have created some unrest, especially in the wealthier northern regions of the country. In contrast to Kenya, where most foreign aid is welcome and investors have ready access, investments are restricted in Tanzania, and aid must conform to guidelines set forth after Arusha and to requirements of the Five-Year Development Plan.

The Contexts in Summary

We have suggested some major differences between the two countries. Kenya has two major tribal groupings that correspond to political parties divided along ethnic lines. Its structures and processes of government resemble the British or "Westminster," model. Tanzania has a multiethnic society and, though legally a single-party system, it has regular competitive electoral processes. Economic factors are also quite different. Kenya is more prosperous than Tanzania. Tanzania is less urbanized, has more people engaged in subsistence agriculture, and has poorer communications among its more scattered population.

When considering politics, several consistent conditions emerge. First, politics is clearly and unmistakably the prerogative of the national leaders in both Kenya and Tanzania. The leader's decree is tantamount to the creation of policy. Second, despite ethnic, political, and institutional upheavals in both countries, the leadership has persisted and has continued to articulate consistent political ideas. Naturally, changing situations have produced changes in political thinking; yet the basic conceptual components and political positions of the leaders have remained remarkably stable. Finally, "development" is the one overriding political goal articulated by both political leaders. Virtually all political ideas are centered on development goals and implemented procedures.

The Scope of the Research

This research centers on ideas about development and features political ideas articulated by the "official" voices of Kenya and Tanzania. Statements were sampled to determine goals, goals establishment, goal attainment activities, and the necessities to reach these goals (Lane, 1962; Putnam, 1971). Our theoretical construct includes a limited range of goal-oriented political ideas expected to occur in the articulations of African leaders (Table 1–2). Each articulation determines some of the kinds of political ideas represented. This suggests that the theoretical construct for policymaking is composed of a set of political ideas, some of which can be located empirically in the verbal behavior of each leader and in the policy contribution of each idea assessed.

Political ideas are found in the speeches and addresses of national leaders. Unlike many Western societies where policy is the resultant of complex processes involving many people, in these two countries, policy results from the direction and goal resolution of the heads of state (Zolberg, 1966). The executives of Kenya and Tanzania dominate and initiate formal and informal political activity, the former through governmental institutions, and the latter through political parties. Kenyatta and Nyerere have held power since independence. Ministers and officials have died, failed reelection, been replaced, or retired, but prevalent political ideas have remained remarkably stable. Were either leader replaced right now, their cumulative impact upon the goals and direction of the two countries would persist. Their verbalizations form the basis of our analysis.

The Sample

A sample was taken from major speeches or addresses of these two national leaders. Each set of speeches spans the period from immediately before independence to early 1970; each speech was delivered to a domestic audience. Other characteristics vary. People addressed ranged from party cadres to inhabitants of small villages; many of the addresses eventually received national publicity through the national news bureaus; and several of the speeches have been published in book form (Kenyatta, 1968; Nyerere, 1967, 1968).

TABLE 1–1.   SPEECHES BY PRESIDENTS OF TANZANIA AND KENYA

A. Julius Nyerere

September, 1959	Individual Human Rights
December 16, 1959	Responsible Self-Government Proposals
May 17, 1960	Corruption as an Enemy of the People
October 19, 1960	Africanization of the Civil Service
May 1, 1961	Broadcast on Becoming Prime Minister
July 29, 1961	Groping Forward
August 1, 1961	Functions of Leadership
October 18, 1961	The Principles of Citizenship
October 25, 1961	Education and Law
December 3, 1961	Independence Message .
December 9, 1961	Independence Message to TANU
December 9, 1961	Receiving the Instruments of Independence
January 22, 1962	Why I Resigned
March 16, 1962	Unity of the African Youth Movements
December 10, 1962	President's Inaugural Address
December 9, 1963	This is the Way Forward
January 12, 1964	President's Address to the OAU Emergency Meeting of African Foreign Ministers
May 5, 1964	Address to Parliament
August 21, 1964	Address at the Opening of Dar Es Salaam University
February 1, 1965	Arusha Declaration
February 13, 1965	Policy for the Sisal Industry
October 12, 1965	President's Address at the Opening of the National Assembly after the General Election
December 14, 1965	Address to the National Assembly
October 1, 1967	Speech to the TANU Bi-annual National Convention
October 16, 1967	Policy on Foreign Affairs
October 18, 1967	After the Arusha Declaration
December 9, 1967	Anniversary of Independence Day
January 4, 1968	Speech at the Reception for Diplomats at the State House
May 28, 1969	Speech to the TANU Conference
April 19, 1970	Opening Address at the Meeting of Non-Aligned Nations

B. Jomo Kenyatta

September 21, 1963	Speech as the Head of Kenya's Government's Delegation
October 20, 1963	Report to the Country on the Outcome of the Constitutional Mission
February 21, 1964	Speech at the Oil Refinery at Changamwe
April 12, 1964	Speech at the African Women's Seminar Kabete
May 13, 1964	State Banquet in Honor of Haile Selassie, City Hall, Nairobi
May 25, 1964	African Unity and Commonwealth Day
June 9, 1964	Reply to State Visit by Emperor Haile Selassie
June 10, 1964	Statement on Development Plan
June 11, 1964	State Banquet for Haile Selassie
June 17, 1964	Statement on South Africa
June 21, 1964	Speech at Protest Rally in Nairobi Following the Outcome of the Manela Trial

TABLE 1–1 (*continued*)

June 25, 1964	Speech at the Presentation of an Aircraft, Wilson Airport, Nairobi
August 13, 1964	Speech on Kenya's Progress Towards Becoming a One-Party State
September 2, 1964	Message to the Kenya Israel School for Rural Social Workers' Training, First Graduation Ceremonies
September 15, 1964	Kenyatta Accepts Chairmanship of the Ad Hoc Commission of the OAU
September 18, 1964	Speech to Delegates of the Ad Hoc Commission on the Congo
September 29, 1964	Speech to Businessmen at Nairobi City Hall
September 30, 1964	Speech at Kenya Agricultural Societies' Show
October 8, 1964	Kenyatta Opens Tea Factory
October 10, 1964	Kenyatta Opens School
October 10, 1964	Kenyatta Opens Coffee Factory
October 19, 1964	Broadcast to the Nation
October 20, 1964	Speech Using Radio and Television on Kenyatta Day
October 24, 1964	United Nations Day Address to Political and Diplomatic Company
November 10, 1964	Kenyatta Welcomes KADKU MPs into the Government
November 19, 1964	Statement on the Congo
November 25, 1964	Statement on the Congo Situation
December 10, 1964	Kenyatta Bids Farewell to British Troops
December 11–14, 1964	Four Speeches Given during Jamhuri Week, Including: The Swearing-in Ceremony of Kenyatta as President of the Republic of Kenya; A Farewell to the Governor General; Broadcast to the Nation; and State Opening of Parliament.
December 12, 1964	Speech at the Inauguration Ceremony
December 14, 1964	Swahili Independence Speech
December 22, 1964	Passing Out of Officer Cadets at Lenet
December 31, 1964	New Years Speech
January 27, 1965	The Opening of Kaguthu Secondary School
February 9, 1965	To the Economic Commission of Africa
February 16, 1965	The East African Institute of Social and Cultural Affairs
February 25, 1965	Speech at the Opening Session of the OAU Ad Hoc Commission on the Congo
March 5, 1965	The Inaugural Ceremony of the Seven Forks Hydro Electric Scheme, Kindaruma on the Tana River
March 26, 1965	Speech Held in the Makerere University College
April 27, 1965	Statement to the Press on the Publication of the Government Sessional Paper, *African Socialism and its Application to Planning in Kenya*
May 4, 1965	Speech on *African Socialism*
June 1, 1965	Madaraka Day Speech to the People of Kenya
June 23, 1965	Policy Statement by the President on Trade Union Development
July 28, 1965	Speech at the Foundation Stone Laying of Kisumu Hospital
July 28, 1965	Speech on the Occasion of Laying the Foundation Stone of the Textile Mills at Kisumu
July 29, 1965	Speech to the Members of the Diplomatic Corps at a Luncheon Given in his Honor in Nairobi
August 19, 1965	Speech at the Seminar for Officers Implementing Development Plans in the Kenya Institute of Administration
November 2, 1965	Address Delivered at the State Opening of Parliament
November 2, 1965	Speech at the Opening of the New Chambers of the Parliament Buildings
November 5, 1965	Speech at the Graduation Ceremony at University College
December 12, 1965	Broadcast Address to the Nation on Uhuru-Jamhuri Day
March 13, 1966	Presidential Address to KANU Delegates' Conference
March 31, 1966	Address to Heads of State of East and Central Africa at State House, Nairobi

TABLE 1–1 (*continued*)

April 20, 1966	Statement from the Office of the President on Assembly Decisions
May 5, 1966	On the Revised Development Plan 1966–70
May 10, 1966	Speech to the Central Legislative Assembly of the East African Common Services Organization Building
July 15, 1966	Speech at the Official Opening of the Starehe Boys' Center Nairobi, Read by Vice President Jmurumbi
August 28, 1966	Speech at the Presidential Parade Held at Azania Drive, Mombasa
October 16, 1966	Address to a Festival of Youth, Nairobi
November 25, 1966	Speech Presenting Certificates to Former Squatters at the Ngoliba Estates, Central and Eastern Provinces
December 2, 1966	Laying the Foundation Stone to the Pumwani Maternity Hospital, Nairobi
December 31, 1966	Speech on the Occasion of the New Year
March 14, 1967	Speech at the Official Opening of the IPS Building, Nairobi
May 1, 1967	Speech at the May Day Celebrations, Read on his Behalf by Vice President Daniel Arap-Moi
May 2, 1967	Speech Read on his Behalf by Minister of Finance, Mr. J. S. Gichuru, at the Sixth Session of African Labor Ministers' Conference
May 5, 1967	Speech at the National Tree Planting Ceremony
September 28, 1967	Speech on the Occasion of Conferring of Degrees, University College, Nairobi
November 28, 1967	Opening of the Mortgage Housing Project
March 1, 1968	Speech at the Opening of the Eldoret Show
June 3, 1968	Speech at the International Press Institute Assembly
June 7, 1968	Speech at the Opening of Kindaruma Hydro Electric Scheme
July 22, 1968	Speech at the Conference on Education and Training in Nairobi, Read on his Behalf by Vice President Daniel Arap-Moi
August 28, 1968	Speech at the Meeting of the Board of Governors of the African Development Bank, Read on his Behalf by Vice President Daniel Arap-Moi
September 26, 1968	Speech at the University College, Nairobi
October 31, 1968	Opening of the Chemelil Sugar Factory
November 1, 1968	Speech at the Official Opening of the Kitale Agricultural Show
November 19, 1968	Speech at the Opening of the First Annual Conference of the Afro American Dialog
November 27, 1968	Opening of the National and Grindlays Bank
December 1, 1968	Opening of Kenyatta Hall at Dagoratti High School
December 11, 1968	Foundation Stone Laying at Kenyatta National Hospital
February 14, 1969	Opening of the Mwea Rice Mill
March 5, 1969	Opening Pumwani Hospital Extensions
March 28, 1969	Kenyatta Opens Kenya School of Law
May 1, 1969	Address on Labor Day
May 28, 1969	Foundation Stone Laying Ceremony
June 1, 1969	Madaraka Day Speech

Table 1–1 contains a complete list of all speeches used. The set of speeches includes 250,000 words about evenly divided—125,000 each for Kenyatta and Nyerere. The leaders' speechmaking habits vary somewhat. Nyerere speaks less frequently, but makes major addresses of longer duration. Kenyatta schedules a series of events requiring speechmaking and carries on a continuing dialogue, for several days, of shorter speeches.

To capture a range of political ideas, every effort has been made to include a variety of occasions, audiences, and materials in the sample.

THE METHOD

To measure the kind and magnitude of policy relevant to political ideas, conceptual content analysis was selected as the method because content analysis provides a direct measurement of conceptualizations within verbalizations. This method allows the researcher to abstract concepts or ideas embedded within verbal materials. The researcher can then cluster, differentiate, and manipulate these ideas in various ways. Several assumptions are made in a conceptual content analysis. First, the political idea is embodied in a concept, and the concept becomes the operational unit of analysis. Second, a particular group of words forms a concept. Third, each word in a text may be part of more than one concept. These concepts can be located in political speeches by machine content analysis.

The analysis of each political speech is made using a comprehensive computer content analysis system Quester (Quester Symbolic Analysis System). It is used on CDC 6000 series machines and incorporates the associative processes of natural language analysis suggested in the theoretical work of Deese (1962), Kolers (1968), Quillan (1966), and others. Quester defines and specifies occurrences of particular concepts within natural language texts by means of a twofold process. English words are assigned to a category, and categories are assigned to a word creating nonexclusive sets of words and categories. Each category is assigned all words and phrases that connote the idea of the category. Each word is assigned to all categories that connote the ideas associated with the word. A network of words and categories results.

To operationalize the theoretical construct of political ideas, we use a conceptual dictionary, *The Pirro African Dictionary* (Pirro, 1968). It consists of over 5,000 words and 102 conceptual categories. Each concept category is a set of words and phrases embodying a possible political idea or some associated activity. One set of categories is African in nature and encompasses political processes and institutions. African self-definitions of problems and concepts, incorporating indigenous terminology, were used to the greatest possible extent. A second set deals with economic development. A third set establishes and describes action and consists of adjective and verb categories. It is important to distinguish whether an idea is used negatively or not and whether a particular policy includes favorable action references. A complete list of all concept categories can be found in Table 1–2. Selected illustrations of dictionary categories and entries are in Table 1–3.

Machine Processing

The Quester Symbolic Analysis System was used to match the dictionary with the textual material. Each word in a text is machine recognized by searching for it in the dictionary array. After a successful match is made, each conceptual

TABLE 1–2.   *THE PIRRO AFRICAN DICTIONARY:* LIST OF CATEGORIES

N	N	N
01 SELF	36 OPPOSITION	72 POLITICAL
02 WE	37 HATRED	73 PARTY
03 THEY	38 ATTACK	74 EXECUTIVE
04 INDIVIDUAL	39 EXPEL	75 GOVERNMENT
05 GROUP	40 DANGER THEME	76 LEGISLATURE
06 MASS	41 DISTRESS	77 JUDICIAL
07 QUANTITY	42 DEATH THEME	78 MILITARY
08 SPACE	43 POSITIVE	79 SOCIAL WELFARE
09 PAST TIME	44 REGULAR	80 FINANCE
10 PRESENT TIME	45 COMPETENCE	81 HEALTH
11 FUTURE TIME	46 APPROVE	82 ECONOMIC
12 STRUCTURE	47 PLEASURE	83 INDUSTRIAL-
13 OBSTACLE	48 GLORIOUS	IZATION
14 DEFENSE	49 VERY	84 AGRICULTURE
MECHANISM	50 VITAL	85 URBANIZATION
15 IF	51 STATUS	86 IGNORANCE
16 OUGHT	52 PROGRESS	87 HISTORY
17 EQUAL	53 INTERNATIONAL	88 LOCAL
18 NOT	54 IMPERIALISM	GOVERNMENT
19 SENSE	55 BRITAIN	89 LEGITIMACY
20 THINK	56 FRANCE	90 ECONOMIC
21 COMMUNICATE	57 THE WEST	DEVELOPMENT
22 CAUSE	58 THE EAST	91 INTEGRATION
23 WISH	59 NEUTRAL	92 PARTICIPATION
24 INITIATE ACTION	60 CLASS	93 PENETRATION
25 APPROACH	61 GHANA	94 KENYA
26 MOVE	62 GUINEA	95 TANZANIA
27 GET	63 AFRICA	96 NYERERE
28 POSSESS	64 NATIONALISM	97 KENYATTA
29 GUIDE	65 TRIBALISM	98 TANU
30 CONTROL	66 RACE	99 KANU
31 COMBINE	67 DIVIDE	100 OTHER KENYAN
32 INCOMPETENCE	68 UNITY	PARTIES
33 BAD	69 FREEDOM	101 SLOGANS
34 CORRUPTION	70 DEMOCRACY	102 YOU
35 AVOID	71 SOCIALISM	

category assigned to the word is checked for consistency with the central idea of words in the text surrounding it. This process of disambiguation is described by Kelly (1970) and Cleveland (1972). The most appropriate conceptual catgories, given the context of surrounding words, are determined, and counters for each are incremented.

After all words are processed, each counter is reduced as a percentage of total words in the text. Words not found in the dictionary (Pirro, 1968) are also counted. Counts represent probability statements that a conceptual category, i.e., a political idea in its operational form, has occurred in the text. When processed, each text yields a percentage figure for each conceptual category. These percentages indicate distributions of specified political ideas as theoretically operationalized in the dictionary. Used directly, they describe the magnitude of particular political ideas within a text. By manipulating these percentages, comparisons can be made both within and between texts, permitting explanations of the relationships among political ideas and their relationship to political policy. Two types of manipulations are performed here. A first series of manipulations involves the components of the function presented in Figure 1–1. Another manipulation is a short series of statistical analyses which includes

TABLE 1–3.   SELECTED DICTIONARY ENTRIES

	Category	*Selected Entries*
African categories		
	TRIBE	elder
		ceremonial
		chiefdom
		ethnic
		house of chiefs
		village
	IMPERIALISM	client state
		metropolitan nation
		exploitation
		hegemony
		neo-colonialism
		imperialist
	EXECUTIVE	head of state
		president
		presidency
		ruler
		leadership
Economic development categories	ECONOMIC	commercial
		commodity
		wealth
		seven-year plan
		business
		consumer cooperatives
	AGRICULTURE	acreage
		cultivate
		coffee
		sisal
		earth
		irrigation
		livestock
		flood control
	FINANCE	bank
		low-cost loan
		profit
		sterling zone
		payment
		debt

Table 1–3 (*continued*)

Category		Selected Entries
Adjective and verb categories on action	INITIATE ACTION	contrive begin explore inaugurate prepare introduce
	VERY	considerable extremely certainly elaborately undoubtedly
	INCOMPETENCE	untrained bumble indolent failure poorly shiftless irresponsible

Source: *The Pirro African Dictionary*, 1968.

comparison of factor structures, ANOVA, and regressions to assess the function and suggest the contributions of political ideas to policy over time.

Content Analysis of the Function

Application of the content analysis instrument results in a percentage figure for each conceptual category, the frequency of occurrence of a conceptual category in a text. The percentages for each category for all texts form a matrix input of raw scores. One part of the matrix is for Kenya and the other for Tanzania, and all entries are arranged over time. Thus, a row of the matrix tallies the occurrence of one concept category over time, in one country. A column totals, at one time point, each of the concept categories. This matrix is 102 concept categories by 86 texts for Kenya and 36 texts for Tanzania.

This matrix is manipulated according to the function described in Figure 1–1. Figure 1–2 takes the function and describes these operations. To obtain the frequency of occurrence, the percentages entered in the raw scores matrix are controlled by the frequency with which the concept categories entries occur in "normal" English usage, as presented in the Brown University analysis (Kucera, 1967). The continuity of the political ideas over time is measured by summing across the matrix and controlling again by reference to the Kucera (1967) study. The clusterability of political ideas is obtained by factor analyzing the raw scores matrix.

FIGURE 1–2.   OPERATIONALIZATION OF FIGURE 1–1

$$\left[\left(\frac{F_{ij}/TF_j}{PB_i}\right)\left(\frac{\sum_{j=1}^N F_i/\sum_{j=1}^N TF}{PB_i}\right)\right](|L_i|) = M_{ij}$$

$\dfrac{F_{ij}/TF_j}{PB_i} =$ The relative frequency of occurrence of a political concept at a single point in time where:

$F_{ij} =$ The percentage frequency of a single political idea operationalized in a concept category, within one text for one country. This is a single entry in the raw scores matrix.

$TF_j =$ The total of all political ideas, i.e., all conceptual categories, within one text for one country.

$PB_i =$ The summed frequency of occurrence of that category in the Brown University frequency distribution of English usage (Kucera, 1967).

$\dfrac{\sum_{j=1}^N F_i/\sum_{j=1}^N TF}{PB_i} =$ The continuity of occurrence of a single political concept over time where:

$\sum_{j=1}^N F_i =$ The summed frequency of occurrence of a conceptual category over all articulations within one country. This is the sum of the entire raw scores of one concept category in the matrix.

$\sum_{j=1}^N TF =$ The total appearance of all conceptual categories in all texts within one country. This includes all categorized and non-categorized words in all articulations.

$|L_i| =$ The tendency of a single political idea to cluster, taken over time. This is the score of a conceptual category formed when the matrix of standardized raw scores is factor analyzed. Each conceptual category has a loading on the principal factor of a nonrotated factor matrix for each country. The absolute value of this figure is used here.

The final result is a measure within texts and between texts of the degree to which each political idea contributes to articulated national political policy.

The generating function assumes that the more often a concept is used, the more it is used over time, and in similar ways, the greater the force of the political idea, and therefore the more it contributes to policy.

To assess the function, several statistical analyses are performed. The factor analysis of the raw scores matrix produced clusters of concept categories, which in turn yielded the central political ideas, for the clusterability variable.

At this point, distinctions between the two nations are plotted using a factor comparison formula to assess distances between points in the clusters. Comparison of the two leaders is accomplished by an analysis of variance of the conceptual categories themselves: the unrefined magnitude of political ideas.

Finally, to relate political ideas to political accomplishments and to consider the evolution of these ideas since independence, regression analysis is used.

A ratio of the articulated conceptual category frequencies and aggregate data is regressed by time to assess the degree to which policy is consistent with actual goal achievements. Comparisons can be made of time rates change of individual contributing political ideas and aggregate data. This comparison is used to predict differences in policy pronouncements and actual outputs.

RESULTS

The Factor Analysis

A principal components factor analysis was performed on the resultant conceptual content analysis raw scores matrix,[1] with the initial 102 variables reduced to 83. This removed conceptual category frequencies that were three or more standard deviations out in overall distributions. In most cases this procedure eliminated categories containing high-frequency words, such as *a, the, by, of, from*, etc., which constitute about 40% of English utterances, but add little or no "meaning" to sentences. Thus, we removed one channel of possible distortion in the factor loadings.

One factor analysis was performed on each of the two sets of data: one for Kenya and one for Tanzania. In the Kenyan analysis, 25 factors had eigenvalues over 1.0 and accounted for 87% of the variance. We concentrated on the first four factors which accounted for over 45% of the total variance. In the Tanzania analysis, 22 factors had eigenvalues over 1.0 and accounted for 96% of the variance. In this case, the first five factors accounted for 45% of the variance.

This factor analysis illustrates the complexity of African political ideas. Even after reducing our data, we could discuss coherently over 20 dimensions of each leader's political ideas; however, the first five factors seem to incorporate the major ideas. Each factor has been named based on an interpretation of the concepts underlying the dimension.

To compare results for the two countries, we used a factor comparison technique (Harman, 1967) that computes a coefficient of congruence between factor loadings. Factors are presented in pairs, and loadings and congruence coefficients measure the degree of similarity between factors.

The factor analyses presented in this section are standard F–factor non-rotated analyses. An F–factor analysis, like any small space analysis, is a measure in a (vector) space of the relationship (distance) between variables (concept categories). A visual representation of a factor analytic structure might best be couched as a three-dimensional box (cube) with some structure within the box, the shape of the structure being measured against each axis of

---

[1] Raw scores matrix percentaged by total words in text and Z-scored by text.

the box. Position and relationship between concept categories are then defined, not in actual distance from each other, but rather in terms of each of the three axes of the box. Each concept category is said to load on each factor. Each factor is a dimension or axis of the box. Factor loadings are said to be negative or positive depending on the loading of the concept categories' distance from origin either in one direction $(+)$ or to the other direction $(-)$, where origin is a point x, the mathematical mean or center of the cluster. The positive and negative signs on the factor loading provide only one distinction of direction from the mean and should not be construed in any other manner. A clustering along one of the axes of concept categories indicates the presence of some underlying commonality which can be titled or named to indicate commonality of these clustered variables (concept categories).

The primary factor explained 30% and 12% of the variance in the Kenyan and Tanzanian analyses, respectively. Of direct interest is the opposing structure of the Kenyan and Tanzanian primary factors.

Primary Factor: Kenya

Kenya's primary factor (see Table 1–4) had 36 concept categories loading $(\pm)$ .600, and could be conceptually characterized as "Means of Coping with Problems." A common dimension underlies Kenyan ideas and philosophies about means of coping with various difficulties. Loading on the positive side are

TABLE 1–4.   KENYA FACTOR 1: COPING WITH DEVELOPMENT PROBLEMS[a]

Factor Loading	Concept Category	Factor Loading	Concept Category
+.912	APPROACH	−.601	STRUCTURE
+.872	CORRUPTION	−.634	INDUSTRIALIZATION
+.869	DEATH THEME	−.641	IF
+.862	AVOID	−.672	MASS
+.855	EXECUTIVE	−.709	PAST TIME
+.854	DANGER THEME	−.717	FUTURE TIME
+.843	ATTACK	−.721	GUIDE
+.824	LOCAL GOVERNMENT	−.740	COMMUNICATE
+.813	EXPEL	−.773	COMPETENCE
+.806	NOT	−.779	OUGHT
+.796	SOCIALISM	−.832	INTERNATIONAL
+.740	KANU	−.859	THING
+.739	OPPOSITION	−.859	PRESENT TIME
+.737	DIVIDE	−.873	SPACE
+.735	MILITARY		
+.705	INCOMPETENCE		
+.704	KENYAN PARTIES		
+.696	SENSE		
+.665	DISTRESS		
+.657	BAD		
+.637	URBANIZATION		
+.611	HATRED		

a 31.132% variance explained.

major problems Kenya faces (CORRUPTION, EXECUTIVE, LOCAL GOV-
ERNMENT, SOCIALISM, KANU, OPPOSITION, MILITARY, DIVIDE,
KENYA PARTIES, URBANIZATION). Also loading positively on this first
factor is a series of negative-sense categories (DEATH THEME, AVOID,
ATTACK, EXPEL, NOT, DISTRESS, BAD, HATRED), indicating that this
portion of the factor is viewed normatively in a very bad way.

Problems include the EXECUTIVE, which is a continuing concern as
Kenyatta ages and various officials jockey for position in the event of his death.
His awareness of the matter is revealed by his off-the-record comments during
Jamhuri Day speeches in 1969, when he stressed that there is still life in him and
he still rules the nation. LOCAL GOVERNMENT also presents problems.
There are few trained officials at the local level, but it is at this level that major
political problems occur. Agricultural and other development schemes have to be
implemented over the objections of many peasants; this problem is overlaid with
the scourge of tribalism.

Both socialism and Kanu, the major party, are in this factor. Socialism
presents leadership challenges. African Socialism to a Kenyan is a mild form
of government involvement, while KANU is the scene of the national power
struggles and intertribal confrontations between Kikuyus and the Luos. OPPO-
SITION encompasses various other political parties, especially the KPU and
Oginga Odinga, and presents great obstacles to Kenyan political integration.
This element is also included in the KENYAN PARTIES category. MILITARY
threatens government; military coups have taken place in several African countries, recently in neighboring Uganda, and they could occur in Kenya. With
tribal problems rampant, the need for UNITY is strongly felt.

CORRUPTION throughout the government bureaucracy is a standard
governmental concern, so is URBANIZATION, which has become particularly
salient as great numbers of the jobless enter cities, especially Nairobi, and
reduce the rural labor force at the expense of increased demands on the government for many social welfare expenditures.

A few quotations from Kenyatta illustrate these ideas.

Many able-bodied [COMPETENCE] people come to town [URBANIZATION] and
spend many months living on relatives and friends, and being generally a nuisance
[DISTRESS]. Whereas we believe in African Socialism, we do not believe in loitering
and laziness [CORRUPTION]. (Kenyatta, September 11, 1964)

What have the KPU [KENYAN PARTIES] done for anybody? I am telling you
that these were once my friends. . . . Now I am calling upon them to change their
minds [SENSE] before it is too late. . . . I am telling you now . . . that if you see
a KPU man [KENYAN PARTIES], and some of them are here, know then that you
have seen a snake hiding in the grass [BAD]. (Kenyatta, October 29, 1967)

A series of elements loads negatively on this factor and talks about the
constraints of time and space on the resolution of difficulties (SPACE, THINGS,
PRESENT TIME, FUTURE TIME, PAST TIME). It is necessary to do the
job well and completely (GUIDE, COMMUNICATE, COMPETENCE,

OUGHT). Two interesting categories included in this factor are the INTER-NATIONAL one, indicating that Kenya looks outside for assistance and IN-DUSTRIALIZATION, indicating the means by which solutions are sought. "Urban growth and the development of manufacturing industries [INDUS-TRIALIZATION] should improve our external [INTERNATIONAL] eco-nomic position, and help build up a wage economy for our skilled labour [Kenyatta, August 19, 1965]."

This first factor summarizes how development problems are symbolized and indicates Kenyatta's preoccupation with national growth. He seems aware that underdevelopment can be defined in terms of difficulties ranging from industrialization needs to power-maintenance requirements for the regime. In-tegration is central in defining Kenyan development; the two concepts are effectively equated. Building a coherent nation and removing various political threats are equivalent.

Primary Factor: Tanzania

The Tanzanian first factor is characterized, similarly, as the "Means of Coping with Problems," but the factor's content differs considerably from Kenya's (see Table 1–5). The first Tanzanian factor also differs from other factors included in the analysis, a point demonstrated momentarily with con-gruence coefficients.

TABLE 1–5.   TANZANIA FACTOR 1: COPING WITH DEVELOPMENT PROBLEMS[a]

Factor Loading	Concept Category	Factor Loading	Concept Category
+.648	CONTROL	−.448	TRIBALISM
+.647	STRUCTURE	−.462	APPROVE
+.614	INITIATE ACTION	−.488	SLOGANS
+.451	SPACE	−.614	SELF
+.440	DISTRESS	−.667	KENYATTA
+.421	PRESENT TIME	−.687	KENYA
+.420	VITAL	−.749	SOCIALISM
		−.759	NYERERE
		−.829	TANU
		−.829	KENYAN PARTIES
		−.829	KANU

a 12.02% variance explained.

Positive loadings on this factor reflect features that constrain and shape the nation's attempts to solve problems. Among these are the limitations of SPACE, TIME, and STRUCTURE, while INITIATE ACTION, CONTROL, and VITAL are ways of defining the activity. The factor indicates that someone, presumably the government, should take over (CONTROL) or grasp the initiative (INITIATE ACTION) for expeditious and appropriate development (VITAL): "What this means [STRUCTURE] is that Tanzania has said, now [TIME] is the appropriate time [TIME] for us to secure the control [CONTROL] of our economy [Nyerere, February 28, 1967]."

Negative factor loadings include two kinds of categories: Major Tanzania referents—NYERERE, TANU, SELF, and SOCIALISM—and Kenya referents—KENYA, KENYATTA, KANU, and KENYAN PARTIES. Tanzanian referential categories are basic national elements. Politics largely revolves about Nyerere, and TANU is the major instrument of government policy, educating and mobilizing the population: "If we are to succeed in building a socialist state [SOCIALISM] in this country, it is essential that every citizen and especially every TANU leader [TANU] should live up to that doctrine [Nyerere, February 14, 1967]."

The texts show that Kenyan categories are mentioned by Tanzanians in various ways. References will often be made to the East Africa Community as a major solution to the development problems plaguing the country. Kenya, of course, is a partner in this enterprise. Furthermore, economic envy of the wealthier Kenyans enters into consideration. Tanzania has a favorable balance of trade with the rest of the world, but an unfavorable balance with Kenya. Guaranteed a large market within the community, industry's inclination has been to locate where businesses already exist, in Nairobi or Mombasa, rather than on Tanzanian sites. Nyerere (August 8, 1967) cautioned: "I do not wish to suggest to this Assembly that there will be in the future no short-term conflicts of interest between Kenya, [KENYA] Uganda and Tanzania. There may well be some."

The third section of categories, loading slightly less on the first Tanzanian factor, includes SLOGANS, the general means used to educate the masses in new government programs; TRIBALISM, an indicator of integration problems; and APPROVE, a favorable category indicating encouragement. Common themes from the 1966–67 era illustrate the categories: "Building Socialism," "Hard Work is the Root of Development," and "Socialism and Self-Reliance."

Primary Factors: A Comparison of Kenya and Tanzania

The factor in both the case of Kenya and of Tanzania deals with coping methods, but the suggested implementations differ in these nations (see Table 1–6). The factor suggests that a socialist solution can be implemented in Tanzania through the political party, through the person of the leader and leadership cadres, and through various educational devices and programs. This implies direct government involvement at all levels of the economy and a major reorganization of society. In Kenya, government involvement is taken to mean investment in, and encouragement of, industrial growth. Kenyatta stresses that private enterprise, urbanization, and a disintegrating society are the main stumbling blocks to economic advancement.

A comparison of factor structures (congruence coefficients ranging from +1.00 to −1.00) of Nyerere's and Kenyatta's speeches indicates a considerable difference in the major structures of the primary factor (congruence coefficient of −.462). This negative coefficient indicates that ideas which Nyerere tends to emphasize, Kenyatta deemphasizes, and vice versa. The negative congruence also indicates different orientations in national policies.

Tanzania's primary factor does not correspond to any Kenyan factor. The congruence coefficients of Tanzania's first factor and all other Kenyan factors are to some degree negative, indicating that they are neither directly, nor inversely, related. The factor suggests that Nyerere and Kenyatta are articulating very different methods of political action, even though the bases for action are quite similar. Kenyatta's speeches illustrate a goal orientation derived from the nation's prevalent idea structure. Nyerere's ideas seem to come from other sources. Nyerere's socialist-ideological statements are derived from diverse sources, including the ancient African communal society, the Israeli Kibbutz experiments, Swedish welfare-statism, and others; they are not typically congruent with his nation's own idea structure. New ideas have been introduced in hopes of restructuring society and solving basic problems. The factor indicates that Nyerere, to accomplish these goals, has been willing to pay a price for this incongruence in terms of increased popular hostility, opposition, and apathy.

TABLE 1–6.   FACTOR 2: ECONOMIC ADVANCEMENT VERSUS POLITICS

KENYA[a]		TANZANIA[b]	
Loading	Concept Category	Loading	Concept Category
+.447	ECONOMIC	+.756	INDUSTRIALIZATION
+.430	FINANCE	+.717	FINANCE
+.392	POSITIVE	+.674	AGRICULTURE
+.381	AGRICULTURE	+.605	GET
+.348	INDUSTRIALIZATION	+.584	ECONOMIC
		+.530	BAD
		+.449	GUIDE
		+.432	VITAL
		+.423	DEATH THEME
		+.401	PRESENT TIME
		−.411	DEMOCRACY
		−.428	UNITY
		−.434	PARTY
		−.453	NATIONALISM
−.402	POLITICAL	−.456	AFRICA
−.422	DEMOCRACY	−.483	WISH
−.488	AFRICA	−.490	SENSE
−.613	NATIONALISM	−.717	POLITICAL
−.636	FREEDOM	−.727	COMMUNICATE

a 4.653% variance explained.
b 10.475% variance explained.

Second factors are similar, indicating that despite differences of principal concern (factor one), underlying ideas are congruent. Comparison of second factor structures yields a coefficient of congruence of .565. Although the principal factors of both countries indicate differences of approach to development, the second factors indicate common underlying perceptions of the actual situation. The factor is called "Allocation of Scarce Resources," and clusters concern for political and economic development.

A typical dilemma is presented in this factor. Each nation's resources are limited, but demands for these resources are not; furthermore, there are numerous goals the regime would like to realize. Major demands load positively and include economic development benefits, problems of current economic life, and economic areas needing improvement. National goals load negatively on this factor and include maintenance of the regime, creation of a nation-state, and improvement in political unity through Pan-Africanism. Both Kenya and Tanzania are faced with the problem of optimizing economic resource allocations adequately to satisfy popular demands and to maintain popular support. A trade-off exists between economic and political requirements. Insufficient political expenditures may lead to declining support because of deficiencies in information acquisition, popular socialization, and, consequently, national integration. Insufficient economic expenditures of course have more obvious societal consequences. Leadership in developing nations consists to a large extent of attempts to adjust these precarious trade-offs in the interest of survival.

We used many different roads to independence; we shall probably need to use many different routes to reach the one goal of economic and social well-being for our peoples. It is not up to any one of us to imagine that we have a God-given answer for all places, and all circumstances, and all stages of a national struggle; each country must work these things out for itself. (Nyerere, February 4, 1963)

Both leaders subscribe to political primacy as the chief means to solve national problems, and both contend that economic demands are to some extent dependent upon resolution by the political structure. Loading positively for both nations' factors are the categories ECONOMIC, FINANCE, AGRICULTURE, and INDUSTRIALIZATION, basic economic development elements. Both are attempting to base industrialization on agricultural goods produced for the export market, and both are continuing to experience financial difficulties. Revaluation of the British pound cost heavily. Tanzania retaliated by nationalizing the banks and restructuring credit institutions. Kenya did not act as drastically, maintaining currency and credit arrangements with Tanzania and Uganda and hence with the East Africa Community. To quote Nyerere (February 5, 1967): "Land is the basis of human life and all Tanzanians should use it as a valuable investment [FINANCE] for future development. Because the land [AGRICULTURE] belongs to the nation, the Government [GOVERNMENT] has to see to it that it is used for the benefit of the whole nation. . . ." And Kenyatta (June 1, 1966):

Nation-building comprises the ability of a country and its people to sustain their independence and national integrity. . . . Through this Government [GOVERN-MENT] the African controls and directs land use [AGRICULTURE], commerce and industry [INDUSTRIALIZATION], power and communications, finance [FINANCE] and employment. If we weaken the Government, we weaken the only major force for African advancement.

Negative loadings on this factor include the categories NATIONALISM, AFRICA, DEMOCRACY, and POLITICAL. All highly political, their broad meaning is captured in their labels. Both leaders are aware of Africa's unique-ness, of nascent feelings of nationhood and patriotism, and of national primacy. The concept of DEMOCRACY, interpreted to mean including the African masses in politics as aware, or follower units, has currency. Included in the negative loadings for Kenya is FREEDOM, or the release from British hege-mony. This is a basic political factor as evidenced in the uprisings of the 1950's and in the disenchantment created by the large number of British settlers in Kenya. In Tanzania, the additional categories of UNITY and PARTY em-phasize the need for integration through major activity by the political party.

I want to say today that Kenya is built on the solid foundation of Kenya nationalism, by the love and loyalty of its own people. . . . (Kenyatta, December 12, 1966)

Africa must be free. And Africa's freedom will only come through united [UNITY] action. (Nyerere, April 9, 1967)

Besides these similarities, there are differences between the two countries shown by the second factor.

Politics is instrumental in solving difficulties and guiding a nation to devel-opment. On the other hand, both leaders realize the importance of economics; they define economic development similarly and confront approximately the same sets of allocation decisions. However, whereas Tanzania's second factor explains 10.45% of the variance, making it a central concern, Kenya's second factor explains only 4.65% of the variance, indicating that problems of political maintenance and integration, which characterized the first factor, override con-cerns captured in the other factors.

The third factors also have considerable in common (congruence coefficient of .320) (see Table 1–7). This "Political Processes" factor indicates that both nations emphasize ideas about political operations. Positive loadings encompass categories describing various actors who make demands on the political struc-tures, and negative loadings refer to structures themselves, i.e., to the formal side of government. Tension exists where, on the one side, informal actors within the political system make usually short-run demands that the regime must accommodate and where, on the other side, the formal structures try to "sell" their own longer term development programs. The issue concerns immediate versus deferred gratification.

In the Tanzanian third factor, political actors include the GROUP and the EXECUTIVE, each constrained by SPACE, as well as YOU, which often

TABLE 1–7.   FACTOR 3: DEMANDS VERSUS GOVERNMENT CAPABILITIES

KENYA[a]		TANZANIA[b]	
Loading	Concept Category	Loading	Concept Category
+.503	PLEASURE	+.606	SPACE
+.457	EQUALS	+.603	PLEASURE
+.448	GLORIOUS	+.577	YOU
+.423	TANZANIA	+.551	EXECUTIVE
+.385	REGULAR	+.548	GROUP
+.366	INDIVIDUAL	+.493	GLORIOUS
+.338	APPROVE	+.463	APPROVE
+.331	GROUP	+.442	DANGER THEME
		+.404	POSITIVE
		−.407	RACE
−.325	INITIATE ACTION	−.411	GOVERNMENT
−.353	PARTY	−.413	STATUS
−.358	GOVERNMENT	−.462	DEMOCRACY
−.408	LEGISLATURE	−.527	AVOID
−.513	POLITICAL	−.676	LOCAL GOVERNMENT

a 4.235% variance explained.
b 7.908% variance explained.

indicates the audience. PLEASURE, POSITIVE, and GLORIOUS are categories having highly favorable connotations about the way in which the structures (GROUP and EXECUTIVE) are regarded. Kenya has many of the same categories (PLEASURE, GROUP, APPROVE, REGULAR, and EQUAL). Kenya also has INDIVIDUAL, which is absent in Tanzania. Tanzanian politics is a process guided by the political party which organizes the masses into various groupings. Kenyan politics emphasizes individual achievement.

This means that the educational system of Tanzania must emphasize co-operative endeavour, not individual advancement. . . . (Nyerere, March 1967)

The land is the place where the ordinary man and woman [INDIVIDUAL] can do most to build the nation. (Kenyatta, February 15, 1967)

Loading negatively on this factor are the formal governmental structures and the political actors whose demands require attention (GOVERNMENT, LOCAL GOVERNMENT, PARTY, LEGISLATURE, POLITICAL, and DEMOCRACY); additionally, the categories INITIATE ACTION and STATUS give some idea of operating constraints.

Nyerere's (October 12, 1965) words sketch out the dilemma raised in this factor. Kenyatta might easily have said the same thing.

Members of Parliament must have the courage to follow their own consciences on basic issues even if they know the cost of doing so will be the people's displeasure and defeat at the next election. Always, of course, politicians must try to convert others when they feel strongly; always [when] a man takes an unpopular stand [he] must be prepared to explain and argue. But if he cannot convince others that he is right, or himself that his view is wrong, then his duty to our people demands that he sacrifice his personal comfort and his personal position to what he believes to be right.

The fourth factor, as Table 1–8 indicates, for both countries reveals a weak similarity (congruence coefficient of .194). The idea of unity and the concept of threat to unity exist in both contexts. This is a defensive factor indicative of concern about major threats to the nation from internal and external sources on the positive loading side and only from internal forces on the negative. Again, there is a dilemma. If the countries cope with threats of internal

TABLE 1–8.   FACTOR 4: INTERNAL VERSUS EXTERNAL THREATS

KENYA[a]		TANZANIA[b]	
Loading	Concept Category	Loading	Concept Category
+.480	KENYA	+.649	REGULAR
+.301	SOCIAL WELFARE	+.534	DANGER THEME
		+.527	UNITY
		+.511	GET
		+.508	IMPERIALISM
		+.500	COMBINE
		+.458	INCOMPETENCE
		+.452	FUTURE THEME
		+.436	FINANCE
		+.424	MILITARY
		+.450	AFRICA
−.307	DIVIDE		
−.336	HATRED		
−.340	DEMOCRACY		
−.342	IF	−.476	CORRUPTION
−.352	INCOMPETENCE	−.479	SPACE
−.386	HEALTH	−.492	HEALTH
−.452	INDIVIDUAL	−.496	IGNORANCE
−.473	CONTROL	−.504	OPPOSITION
−.486	GROUP	−.522	COMPETENCE

a 3.975% variance explained.
b 8.701% variance explained.

disorder, e.g., lack of political support or economic disintegration, they must also contend with more general national governmental problems and international interference. But, if they concentrate mainly on these broad forces, internal difficulties may grow out of control.

Loading positively on this factor for both nations were the categories UNITY, COMBINE, and AFRICA, all stressing the need for unity and cooperation among the African countries. The category AFRICA involves many ideas, including referents to other African neighbors, to Pan-African cooperation, and to the concept of Africa for the Africans.

Also loading positively on this factor for both nations are the threat categories DANGER THEME, GET, and IMPERIALISM. Imperialism or neo-imperialism is a major scapegoat theme throughout Africa. All African nations fear external control of their economies and cultures, yet economic development without foreign assistance is nearly inconceivable. Taking aid without acquiring imperialistic control is a formidable and delicate task. Two other threat themes also must be considered (INCOMPETENCE and MILITARY). Other African nations have recently experienced a succession of military takeovers. In Kenya and Tanzania, military rebellions occurred shortly after independence, but until 1972 there were no coups. However, the military poses a real threat to government. Past military coups have often been rationalized in the terms of government incapability or incompetence. Both countries had, at independence, shortages of trained personnel and routinized administrative procedures. These problems are being remedied slowly, but continuing political concern about incompetence is understandable. Experienced civil servants generally lack the training of more recent graduates. The government might remove the experienced, but inadequately trained, men, perhaps creating a group of malcontents in the process, or it might suffer the mistakes and inexperience of the new appointees. It is a difficult choice.

The Kenyan fourth factor indicates that threat ideas are less salient than those associated with the concepts of KENYA and SOCIAL WELFARE. Creating one nation—Kenya—is an overriding concern, and economic and social well-being are the main instrumentalities.

Kenyatta and Nyerere talk much about internal threats.

We must cherish our unity and be vigilant against challenge. . . . The fact of the Republic has removed traces of Colonialism from this land. (Kenyatta, December 14, 1964)

Africa must be free. And Africa's freedom will come only through united action. The unity has to come before there will be any great advance against the remaining bastions of privilege and racism. (Neyerere, April 9, 1967)

Negative loadings include the categories of CORRUPTION, HEALTH, IGNORANCE, OPPOSITION, INDIVIDUAL, and GROUP. All of these pose potential internal threats and obstacles to national unity. IGNORANCE and HEALTH are typical development problems. CORRUPTION creates problems for government efficiency and effectiveness, particularly at the local levels, where officials tend to enrich themselves, their families, and their home villages. The INDIVIDUAL is threatening when there develop cults of personality in opposition to government development plans, and both nations have had such individuals—Odinga in Kenya and Kambona in Tanzania. GROUP is another political threat. Both nations have experienced student disturbances, labor union disputes, and other group difficulties. For Kenya, DEMOCRACY is a negatively loading category. "One man, one vote," the usual definition of democracy, does not strictly apply. One tribe, not comprising 50% of the total national population, could still control the nation by virtue of its superior numbers over any other minority tribes. Coalition formation is not well established where inter-tribal feelings run high; resolving the difficulty has already imposed costs on the Kenyan government. In Tanzania, COMPETENCE has a high negative loading on this fourth factor; it is a prime governmental problem.

The fourth factor, to recapitulate, concerns both internal and external elements that threaten national unity.

Summary of the Factor Analysis

The first factor shows Kenyatta's concern with national unification and integration and Nyerere's emphasis on Tanzania's unique path toward socialism. The second factor, similar in both countries, presents a common dilemma for developing nations: trade-offs in the allocation of scarce resources among political and economic needs. The third factor illustrates the tension between those who make demands on a political system and that system's capacity to cope with these demands. The fourth factor concentrates on threats: imperial-istic, militaristic, oppositional, and self-inflicted.

The factor analysis partly elucidates research questions about political ideas in Kenya and Tanzania. The factor analysis characterizes the general political ideas orienting these nations and begins to illustrate similarities, dif-ferences, and contributions of each concept category to the factor structure.

A complex interconnected network of ideas results. Underdevelopment forces leaders of very diverse nations to have quite similar ideas because their problems are similar. In trying to find solutions to these problems, individual differences begin to appear, which in time blossom into a wide variety of pos-sibilities and behaviors. As national leaders search for better ways of solving their problems, they are often willing to incorporate ideas that have been partially or wholly successful elsewhere; and, regardless of personal orientation, they tend to adopt similar programs. For the two leaders we report on, there exist remarkably similar five- or seven-year development plans, having similar labels, schedules, and posited goals. The factor analysis distinguishes the sim-ilarities of national development problems and the differences between the individual leadership's orientations.

Analysis of Variance and Frequency of Concept Categories

Political ideas differ in Kenya and Tanzania. To examine further specific differences between the nations, the basic statistic has been subjected to an analysis of variance (ANOVA), category by category.

The mean Z-scored values from the raw scores matrices of both leaders' articulations are analyzed by a two-way analysis of variance, category by category. Values used in the analysis result from a three-step process. (1) Raw scores are percentaged by all counted categories of recognized words plus all nonrecognized words. (2) Percentaged category arrays for each text are Z scored. (3) The Z-scored values of all texts grouped into early, middle, and recent time periods are then averaged. Average Z-scored values are presented in the analysis of variance (ANOVA) tables. Several of these are essential to understand why there is so little apparent difference between the two textual samples. Indeed, distinctions made in several theoretical constructs (Coleman and Rosberg, 1963; Zolberg, 1966) were not supported by the data.

The several economic categories that appeared prominent (SOCIAL WELFARE, ECONOMIC, and INDUSTRIALIZATION) indicate that the leaders continue to hold them to be roughly equivalent in importance. Unchanging and important political variables were DEMOCRACY, INTERNATIONAL, POLITICAL, PARTY, EXECUTIVE, and LEGISLATURE, all concerns which have persisted since independence and which are similar for the two nations. In this vein, the variable SOCIALISM is also interesting. Socialism is a major category in Tanzania's first factor. This is explicable because socialism has been a cornerstone of Nyerere's public philosophy. However, examination of the texts indicates that socialist terminology appears prominent in both nations. Differences are not in terms of basic ideas about development, but in the implementation programs the leadership has created. Kenyatta speaks of government involvement, but is not vigorously implementing socialism. Nyerere, on the other hand, took several dramatic steps, including the Arusha Declaration, the nationalization of the banks, and recently the campaign against landlords.

Several categories change over time and illustrate the dynamic quality of the development concept in East Africa. The concept of development has changed considerably since independence, and so has its influence on politics. A few categories are presented to show specific national differences.

Progress is a future-oriented series of ideas. In many respects this category is biased because the operating concept of progress centers on Western-styled industrialization, production, and consumption. For example, as shown in Table 1–9, Kenya's whole development program is cast in these terms. Changes in mean standardized values from early to recent times indicate that Tanzanian development was not originally conceived of as PROGRESS (with Western

TABLE 1–9.   ANOVA OF CATEGORY PROGRESS[a]

	TIME		
	Early	*Middle*	*Recent*
Kenyatta	1.185	1.986	2.221
Nyerere	.022	.688	1.107

[a] Z-scored means averaged for set. Difference between countries, significance $p < .0005$. Difference over time, significance $p < .0005$.

connotations), although recently there is movement in this direction. PRO-GRESS in both nations is nearly synonymous with Western-oriented economic growth.

From Table 1–10, it is evident that Kenya has been considerably more concerned with opposition than Tanzania. This difference is understandable, given Kenya's two-party structure and continual difficulty with assorted opposi-tional elements. Tanzania's small opposition quickly faded after independence,

TABLE 1–10.   ANOVA OF CATEGORY OPPOSITION[a]

	TIME		
	Early	Middle	Recent
Kenyatta	−.473	−.539	−.528
Nyerere	−.260	−.316	−.528

[a] Z-scored means averaged for set. Differences between leaders, significance $p < .0005$.

and presently Tanzania is essentially a one-party state. Kenya's ethnic opposi-tions are not matched in Tanzania. However, both countries show increasing concern for potential and actual opposition. In Tanzania this is partly true, especially since Arusha, because a substantial oppostion could reduce the effec-tiveness of many new programs. In Kenya the opposition could shatter national unity. For both countries, opposition has changed, as concept and reality, from the formal "constructive" political opposition of independence days to the threatening, potentially destructive form it has recently taken.

At the time of independence, nationalism was a key concern in both coun-tries, although to a lesser degree in Tanzania. Since then, other factors have intervened: economic development and progress, for instance (Table 1–11).

TABLE 1–11.   ANOVA OF CATEGORY NATIONALISM[a]

	TIME		
	Early	Middle	Recent
Kenyatta	−.472	−.645	−.694
Nyerere	−.216	−.333	−.605

[a] Z-scored means averaged for set. Differences between leaders, significance $p < .004$. Difference over time, significance $p < .022$.

Also important is the successful creation of the East Africa Community, replac-ing, as it did, nationalistic xenophobia with the concepts of an East Africa Community and a need for cooperation.

Sharing the experience of British colonialism, leaders of Kenya and Tan-zania have been about equally vigorous in calling attention to the dangers of possible external control. The farther removed from the actual colonial experi-

TABLE 1–12.   ANOVA OF CATEGORY IMPERIALISM[a]

	TIME		
	Early	*Middle*	*Recent*
Kenyatta	−.306	−.448	−.501
Nyerere	−.295	−.367	−.453

[a] Z-scored means averaged for set. Difference over time, significance $p < .043$.

ence, the less concern they show for imperialist matters (Table 1–12) The neo-imperialistic scapegoat fails to excite, as it did during the immediate post-independence period. Concern has shifted to the more tangible problems of nation-building and economy-building. Fear has transferred to threats posed by the opposition and the military.

These are a few of the categories having significant changes over time. They portray leaders initially concerned with their nations' becoming independent, with nationalism and imperialism, who in time have become aware of their own domestic problems and shifted their emphasis to concerns about economic progress. Politics shifts from the international to the domestic arena and concern for internal operations and the internal opposition.

This analysis complements the factor analysis in several respects. The second factor in both nations concentrated on trade-offs between economic and political development. The analysis of variance suggests that political development has been supplanted in the post-independence period by economic development concerns. The fourth factor, illustrative of tension between internal difficulties and external threats, also changes over time. Less emphasis is placed on external concerns, especially imperialism, as more interest is devoted to internal, national problems.

Many categories showed significant differences between countries. In Tanzania, greater concern is afforded political variables than in Kenya. The following categories were significantly different between the two countries: JUDICIAL ($p < .0005$); FREEDOM ($p < .0005$); UNITY ($p < .0005$); GOVERNMENT ($p < .0005$); EQUAL ($p < .001$); and LEGITIMACY ($p < .0005$). Most of these categories relate to the restructuring of society, and Tanzania scored meaningfully higher on all. For Tanzania, having a long history of rebellion against colonialism, FREEDOM is a basic consideration. Concern is also evidenced for the human factors of UNITY and EQUALITY, both of which are emphasized in Nyerere's new communal society; GOVERNMENT in his socialist program is seen as one source of new policies, a guiding element for the emergent socialism to come. LEGITIMACY is of course a concern to newly independent nations, especially when government must continually justify itself to the masses of the governed. The JUDICIARY is one means to safeguard people and government, and there is great respect shown the written law and the formal processes of law enforcement.

Nyerere's political ideas revolve about several elements. He wants to restructure society; he has normative concerns evidenced in his rhetoric about the "right" way to do things; and he stresses the human condition of the population over the purely economic state of the society. Before Nyerere can move his society forward, he believes it necessary to establish institutions of government and judiciary as the legitimate means for executing his somewhat radical programs. Serious opposition and questioning are to be reduced. These concerns, so much a part of independence rhetoric, have all decreased in intensity over time. The farther from independence, the less concerned is Nyerere with these specific elements and the more he emphasizes economic needs.

Three other categories relating to foreign affairs are significantly different for each of the two leaders—Nyerere's interest on all is higher than Kenyatta's. Nyerere, an avowed neutralist at the time of independence, has become increasingly concerned with domestic matters. Through the United Nations and the Organization of African Unity, Tanzania still exercises a "positive neutralist" approach. The concept AFRICA is understandably significant; Nyerere consistently emphasizes Pan-Africanism and other African concerns. Today, furthermore, Nyerere supports the Southern African freedom-fighters by providing training sites, bases for operations, and funds. Very recently he has called for Rhodesians to take the lead in freeing themselves. Nyerere has also refused to recognize military regimes but relaxed this somewhat for Uganda—evidently to sustain a cooperative sense of an East Africa Community. Nyerere emphasizes HISTORY, the source of many elements of his own philosophy; the emphasis has decreased over time as internal matters have begun to occupy the focus of attention.

Comparison shows that Kenyatta's attention is focused on practical and operational matters. The categories HEALTH, COMMUNICATE, GUIDE, STRUCTURE, POSSESS, PRESENT TIME, and FUTURE TIME are all significantly different for the two leaders. Kenyatta has more concern with these elements than has Nyerere and, with such concern, he shows greater awareness of the structure and methods of development. HEALTH is basic: without it, development cannot proceed. COMMUNICATE and GUIDE reflect efforts to stimulate the population to greater efforts on behalf of national goals. STRUCTURE and POSSESS evidence Kenyatta's interest with material and practical things. Additionally, he is more future oriented than Nyerere and has a far different orientation toward development. Recall Nyerere's preoccupation with the concept HISTORY.

The picture the analysis of variance suggests is a very pragmatic one. Kenyatta emphasizes the here and now in terms of development, and most of the categories dominated by Kenyatta are verb categories, the action words. Kenya and Kenyatta are plunging into their work on the problems of development.

A substantial number of economic variables is of equivalent concern to both leaders. Differences are mostly those of approach to development. Kenyatta is practical, businesslike, and less concerned about society and the masses than about the implementation of development plans (GUIDE and COMMUNI-CATE). Nyerere, on the other hand, suggests that moving ahead is not "right" unless done within a proper social setting, one including freedom, equality, and socialism. For Nyerere, these are basically political concerns, and they tend to conflict with actual economic needs.

Several interaction effects were noteworthy; among these was the category IGNORANCE. Education is often thought of as a development panacea; however, Table 1–13 suggests the contrary. Immediately after independence, educa-

TABLE 1–13.   ANOVA OF CATEGORY IGNORANCE[a]

	TIME		
	Early	Middle	Recent
Kenyatta	−.659	−.428	−.393
Nyerere	−.182	−.366	−.558

[a] Z-scored means averaged for set. Differences between leaders, significance $p < .002$. Interaction significance $p < .0005$.

tion was given high priority in Tanzania. But, as education contributed to a migratory stream of unemployed, marginally trained people moving into urban areas, revisions in priority seemed necessary. Nyerere moved to adapt the dominant philosophy of education. After the Arusha Declaration, Tanzania began to restructure education by emphasizing practical subjects such as agriculture. Swahili was officially adopted as the language for use throughout the elementary schools, and it is now being implemented in secondary institutions as well. In addition, a quota system was imposed that would enable only about one-third of school-age children to progress at least through high school. Nyerere has said that the quota is necessary to conserve scarce resources and to maintain adequate agricultural productivity.

Kenya's education problems are different. Left with a British education system in need of restructuring, technical training is Kenya's major problem area because tribes tend to choose agricultural over trade and business occupations.

The concept WE is a nationalistic variable suggesting identification with a country. Interaction between cells in the ANOVA of this variable suggests what the future of East Africa might hold. Kenya at independence had national pride and unity forged during the long struggle against colonialism. Ethnic differences were set aside in the movement for freedom. After independence, differences reemerged, to the point that they now present substantial difficulties for the government. Kenyatta's personality and identification with independence have so far maintained national integrity in spite of sporadic outbreaks. Should present trends in the WE concept continue, Kenya may be faced with grave trouble, especially should Kenyatta die (Table 1–14).

TABLE 1–14.   ANOVA OF CATEGORY WE[a]

| | TIME | | |
	Early	Middle	Recent
Kenyatta	2.732	2.587	1.004
Nyerere	2.114	2.132	4.581

[a] Z-scored means averaged for set. Interaction significance $p < .0005$.

Trends in Tanzania differ. Independence was gained with less difficulty, and expectations about post-independence development were greater than in Kenya. Widespread understanding of the great economic difficulties facing Tanzania contributed to the Arusha Declaration, which in turn led to an emphasis on the people of the country. Nyerere has emphasized self-reliance, "bootstrap" operations, and collective popular action: the WE of Tanzania. Development is a matter of holding the populace together, keeping it mobilized, and achieving Tanzania's and Nyerere's stated goals.

The analysis of variance relates well to information presented in the factor analysis. Recall that the first factor suggests considerable differences in the means used to attain national development goals. Kenyatta is more concerned with practical and structural constraints on development initiatives, whereas Nyerere focuses on normative, socialist means to development.

Both leaders demonstrate about equal concern with the essence of the second factor, economic development. The ANOVA does show that Kenyatta has far less concern with political development than does Nyerere and that the latter's concern is decreasing over time. So, the second factor, which suggests a tension existing between economic and political development, is elucidated here to suggest that a choice has been made by both leaders and that their choice is identical: economic development must have first place.

The third factor emphasizes the tension between demands made by the population and the abilities of governmental structures to resolve them. Nyerere, by restructuring society, has shown that he intends to revise demands in line with his socialistic strategies. Nyerere will mobilize society to satisfy his own demands. Self-reliance is the slogan. Kenyatta has recognized the difficulties of popular development demands and, emphasizing time considerations, has undertaken action plans to satisfy these demands. The many verb categories on which Kenyatta scores higher show the action orientation of his government in coping with popular strivings.

The fourth factor deals with internal and external threats. The analysis of variance develops the point over time. Both leaders have far less concern with external threats to their nations as independence memories fade and the fears of immediate imperialism pale. But, internal concerns appear after independence, as threats arise from group demands within the society and from government weaknesses. Both Kenyatta and Nyerere fear the possibility of military coups. The ANOVA thus develops some of the specific considerations which emerge generally in the factor analysis.

The Regression Analysis: Political Ideas Compared with Aggregate Data over Time

Political articulations and political outputs rarely, if ever, match perfectly. Differences between stated policy and realized output provide one measure of governmental performance.

A series of curvilinear regressions compares relationships between Kenyatta's and Nyerere's verbal behavior and the national outputs realized over time. Generally, articulations of both leaders tend to anticipate gains in national productivity, but since independence, coincidence between articulated goals and national outputs has increased. This indicates greater control over national outputs, with leaders making more realistic appraisals of national capabilities. Within five years after independence, national outputs tend to coincide with articulated policy, there being only a few noteworthy exceptions as indicated by a decreasing curve across time.

A number of reasons is possible to explain divergences between verbal and realized behaviors. External factors, e.g., climate, weather, the fluctuations in international trade, monetary markets, and external political events are all examples. Fluctuation in the price of raw materials is rather quickly translated into either boom or bust for both nations, regardless of actual productivity. Bureaucratic misapplication of policy, especially at the local level, could account for a portion of the discrepancies; local bureaucrats have been known to misinterpret or haphazardly enforce various governmental programs. Finally, the people themselves may fail to comply with policy directives as a result of hostility, apathy, or any of a number of other reasons. All of these explanations would indicate a gap between the articulated policy goals and the eventual products of the nations.

Economic development has been a major theme in both leaders' verbal behavior, a point demonstrated by the second factor of the factor analysis. The regression analysis focuses on economic development both as verbalized in policy statements and as realized in terms of gains in productivity, exports, and earnings. Generally, articulations are statements of policy intent by the leaders. Coincidence, or its absence, between articulated intention and realized outcomes can be measured with the regression technique.

Each regression line presents a comparison of a verbal concept category with aggregate economic data, taken with respect to time. Each regression line indicates the change of frequency of articulations (concept category) with respect to economic productivity (aggregate data) over time. Three concept categories representative of economic development were chosen: ECONOMIC, AGRICULTURE, and INDUSTRIALIZATION. ECONOMIC is treated both as a ratio of Gross Domestic Product (GDP), the amounts of take-home pay for the workers, and as a ratio of the balance of trade index. AGRICULTURE is regressed as an index with agricultural production per capita. Finally, INDUSTRIALIZATION is regressed with the manufacturing index. The time period considered is the ten years from 1961 to 1970.

The shape of the curves in the regression analyses indicates the nature of the correspondence between the articulations and the aggregate data over time. The appearance of a horizontal straight line would indicate a constant ratio between the articulation and the aggregate data. A curve downward indicates decreasing frequency of the concept category and increasing levels of productivity. In the regressions, a beginning downward curve indicates a decreasing articulation and an increasing output. In Kenya these changing ratios generally stabilized about 1965, with articulation then varying with output. In Tanzania the articulation output notion has not had time to stabilize. Articulations increase with specific concerns, and outputs do not change as readily. In both countries, increases in articulated conceptualizations indicate future increases in a country's output, and a future decrease in articulation is forthcoming when output increases in lagged time to previous increased articulations. In all cases sampled, increases in articulations have coincided with lagged increases in the countries' outputs. In cases (especially Tanzania) where sudden shifts in articulation tend to increase ratios rapidly, output does not increase with the sudden shift. Articulation of policy must be seen as a gradual force on output. A little force of policy will produce the same result. The word of the moment must be considered in the context of prior pronouncements when relating verbal to actual outcome. This concern is accounted for in our analysis. Since we know from the content, factor, and ANOVA analyses that the leaders' articulations are not outstripped by productivity, the latter will be the general interpretation for a downward curve.

FIGURE 1-3. KENYA: ECONOMIC: GDP: POPULATION VERSUS TIME

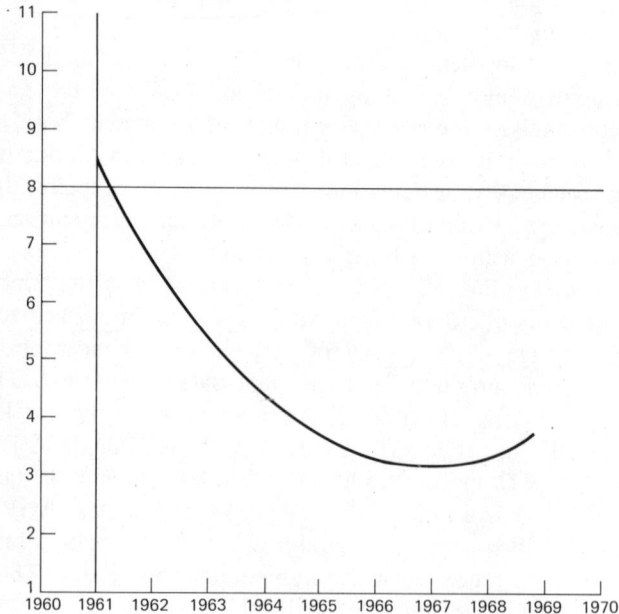

FIGURE 1-4. TANZANIA: ECONOMIC: GDP:
POPULATION VERSUS TIME

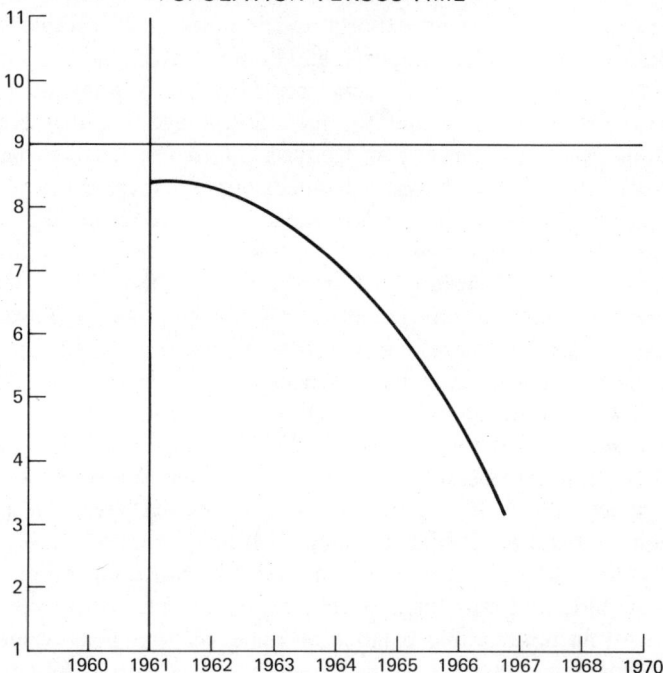

An increasing curve indicates that articulations are increasing and/or the level of productivity is not increasing rapidly. Curves which initially decrease and then turn upward and start increasing indicate that verbal emphasis continued until a policy began to show results sufficiently strong that leaders could shift their attention elsewhere. Curves which initially increase to some point and then decrease indicate that as articulations increased, production decreased proportionately. Both types of curves suggest the time lags that are required for policies to take effect. Time-lagged regressions would seem to be appropriate in Kenya and Tanzania.

In Figure 1–3 and 1–4, the concept categories ECONOMIC and Gross Domestic Product (GDP) are regressed against time. The regression lines for both nations decrease over time, indicating that as production increases and as worker contentment with higher wages increases, the articulations of the leaders on economic matters, in general, decrease.

The Kenyan economic regression (Figure 1–3) indicates that after the first five years, the ratio of ECONOMIC to GDP remains stable, in other words, the economic situation is relatively stable in relation to Kenyatta's stated policy goals. The regression line in Tanzania (Figure 1–4) indicates that economic articulations and GDP, initially rather balanced, have lately been changing, as GDP increased rapidly and articulated concern for economic matters decreased. Domestic production levels are matching articulations at an extremely rapid rate.

Figures 1–5 and 1–6 present the regressions of the articulations on ECO-
NOMIC as a ratio with the balance of trade. Balance of trade is a standard
measure of difference between exports and imports; a "favorable" balance of
trade indicates exports exceed imports, and "unfavorable" indicates the opposite
situation. The regressions for the two nations produce quite different curves.
Kenya's curve approximates that for its GDP, suggesting that Kenyatta has
decreased his economic concern as Kenya's international trade has stabilized
(Figure 1–5). On the other hand, Tanzania's curve decreases sharply, and then
increases, indicating that since independence Nyerere decreased his concern
with economic matters, international trade increased, and then something happened (Figure 1–6). Knowing East Africa suggests the coincidence of three
things. First, the agricultural raw materials market took a downward turn,
particularly for sisal because plastic fibers replaced naturally grown hemp.
Tanzania, to maintain a favorable balance of trade, has had to diversify her
domestic agricultural economy. Second, this is the period of socialism for Tanzania. Immediately after the Arusha Declaration, Nyerere began emphasizing
economic matters, particularly as socialism became fundamental Tanzanian
economic policy. Third, the signing of the East Africa Treaty in 1967 led to
the creation of the East Africa Common Market, and to a reorientation of
economic policy, which featured increased trade and cooperation within the
East African bloc and with neighboring countries. The treaty effectively left
Tanzania with an unfavorable balance of trade vis-à-vis heavily industrialized

FIGURE 1-5. KENYA: ECONOMIC: BALANCE OF
TRADE VERSUS TIME

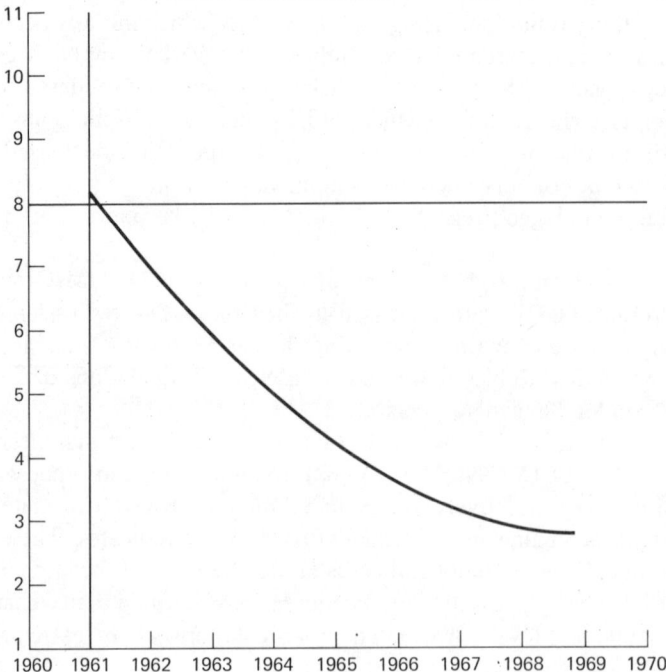

FIGURE 1-6. TANZANIA: ECONOMIC: BALANCE OF
TRADE VERSUS TIME

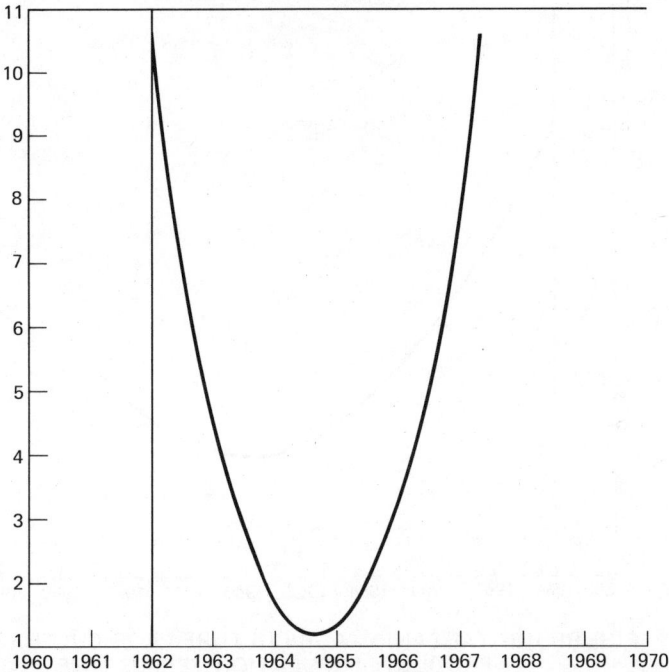

Kenya, and increased productivity was required to redress the unfavorable balance. Nyerere's recent concern for economic matters is thus made more understandable.

Regression of the articulations on AGRICULTURE as a ratio with agricultural productivity per capita (Figures 1–7 and 1–8) points out some differences. Kenya's agricultural regression curve is similar to its other economic curves. Agriculture was greatly emphasized in the initial stages of Kenyan nationhood, but concern has leveled off (Figure 1–7). Most recently, the curve seems to be turning upward, suggesting that Kenyatta has renewed his concern for matters of agricultural productivity. This is understandable given the soft raw materials markets, inflation, and the institution of international boards to improve the prices and quality of the important coffee and tea commodities.

The curve for Tanzania is a decreasing diagonal straight line, indicating that Nyerere's articulations about agriculture decrease as agricultural production increases (Figure 1–8). Apparently contradicting Nyerere's statements to the effect that agriculture is the cornerstone of Tanzania's socialism, an examination of the texts reveals there is really no contradiction at all. Nyerere is simply less concerned with specific aspects of agriculture than he is with general social restructuring. In other words, he does not talk about better livestock, new crops, and improved methods of fertilization, rather he is concerned with the cooperative efforts of the people to achieve increased production.

FIGURE 1-7. KENYA: AGRICULTURE: AGRICULTURAL PRODUCT: POPULATION VERSUS TIME

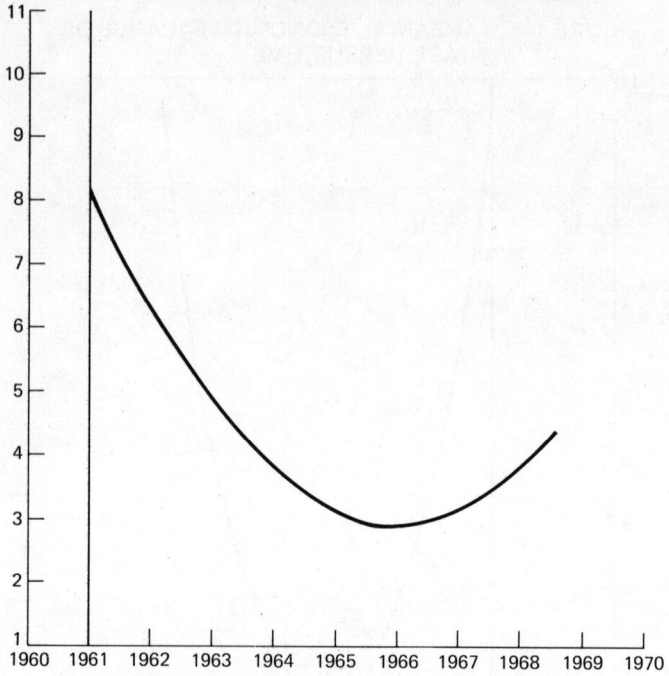

FIGURE 1-8. TANZANIA: AGRICULTURE: AGRICULTURAL PRODUCT: POPULATION VERSUS TIME

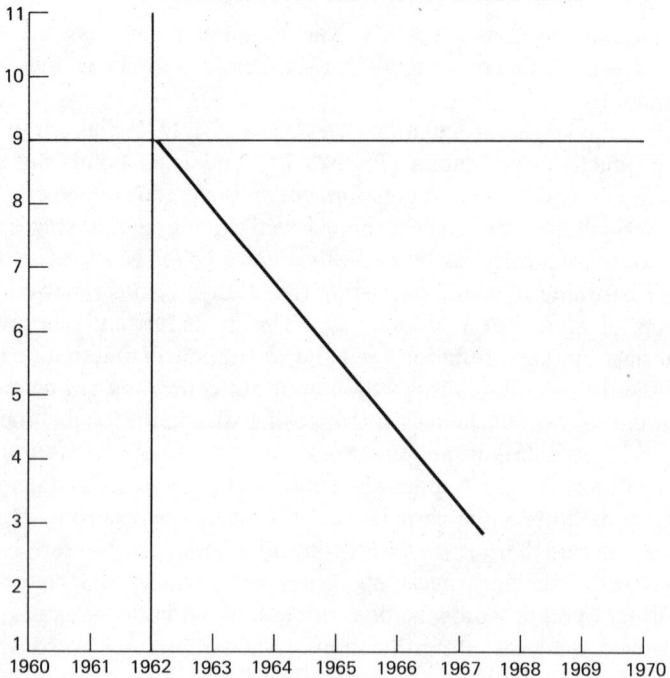

INDUSTRIALIZATION and the manufacturing index over time are presented in Figures 1–9 and 1–10. This curve is similar to Kenya's other economic curves. An initial period of concern is followed, although more slowly in this case, by a time of relative stability and then by an increase in recent verbal activity (Figure 1–9).

Tanzania's curve on INDUSTRIALIZATION reproduces its balance of trade situation. A crisis occurred just before the Arusha Declaration and the commencement of socialism when Nyerere began to degrade industrialization as the answer to Tanzania's development needs. After Arusha and the firm establishment of agriculture as the main source of economic growth, Nyerere turned his attention to industry (Figure 1–10). Recurring questions about industrialization, location, the means of creating social overhead capital, the training of support personnel, the appropriate mix of industries, and the kind and extent of foreign investment are prevalent in many of Nyerere's speeches. This means that the curve of verbal activity about industrialization has surpassed actual amounts of industrial production; therefore, it turns upward.

Interpreting the Analysis

Interpretation of these curves requires skill and caution. Their significance lies in comparisons of the Kenyan and Tanzanian situations as reflected in the

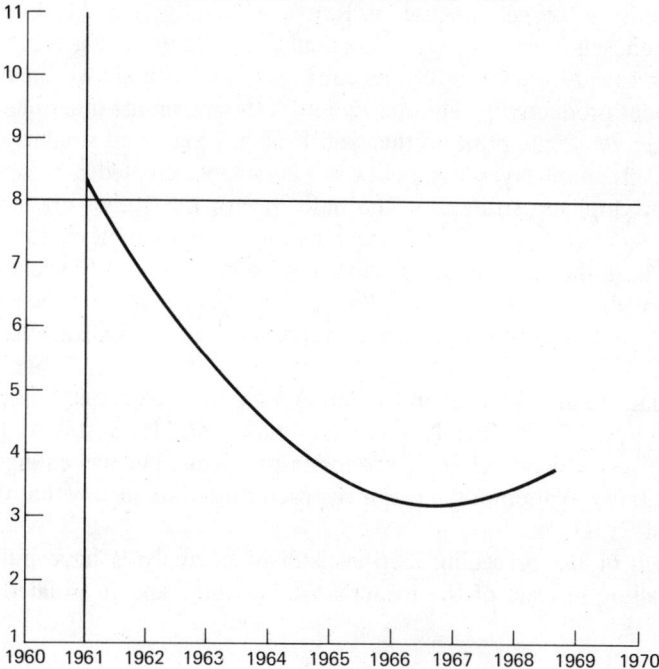

FIGURE 1-9. KENYA: INDUSTRIALIZATION: MANU-
FACTURING INDEX VERSUS TIME

FIGURE 1-10. TANZANIA: INDUSTRIALIZATION: MANU-
FACTURING INDEX VERSUS TIME

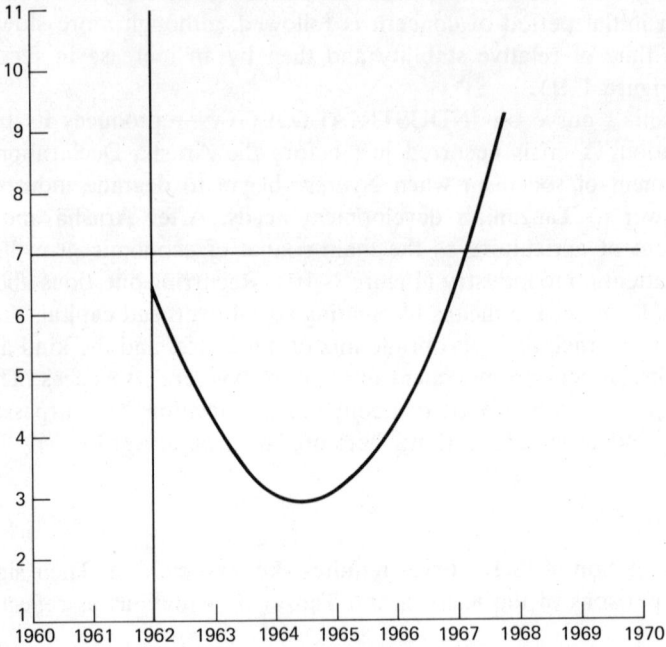

regressions. The differences in curves illustrate the differences in national goals. From the curves we get a sense of Kenya as relatively stable economically. Kenya has chosen a certain type of economic development, has stuck to it, and has realized steady growth. Only recently has Kenyatta shown an increase in concern about productivity. The Tanzanian economy, on the other hand, starting from a lower economic position than did Kenya, progressed similarly, although at lower levels, until Nyerere's policy reassessments created new sets of goals and new development strategies. The outcomes of this rather dramatic change are as yet indeterminate. With respect to the African context, the regression lines mark both the Arusha Declaration and Tanzania's turn to socialism. Likewise, we see the turmoil following Kenya's independence, at which time large numbers of settlers moved out of the nation and a major redistribution of land took place.

The data in the factor analyses and ANOVAs suggest that while Kenya is economically stable, politically there are major problems still to be solved. Tanzania gives evidence of great economic problems, but has enough inherent political stability to attempt the major restructuring of its society that the Arusha Declaration represents.

In each of the preceding sections individual analyses have indicated the ideas prevailing in each of the leader's articulations, and in isolated cases the degree of contribution of ideas to policy was indicated. The questions we will focus on now is how much does each idea relative to other ideas contribute to national policy.

THE CONTRIBUTION OF POLITICAL IDEAS TO POLICY

Figure 1–1 has provided a theoretical construct for the analytic explanation of ideas and policy in East Africa. In Figure 1–2, this function was operationalized in terms of the content analysis. The sections immediately prior to this have elaborated the elements of this function with factor analysis, ANOVA, and regressions. Putting the results of these statistical operations together, we derive a numerical value for the amount each political concept (operationalized as a category) contributes to the policy of the nation. The value is expressed as a percentage. The higher the figure, the greater the contribution to national policy. Table 1–15 lists the figures for Kenya; Table 1–16, for Tanzania.

In each of the following tables the percentage contribution is calculated on the basis of deviation from "normal" English (Kucera, 1967). Several categories (especially those referring to country, African parties, and words uniquely African) determined on this basis would automatically be expected to be high in occurrence. It should be pointed out that these percentages, while obvious, are significant. These ideas do contribute highly to the policy of each country.

In Table 1–15, on Kenya, a series of categories has high percentages. The concepts AFRICA, TANZANIA, NYERERE, TANU, KANU, OTHER KENYAN PARTIES, and SLOGANS are outstandingly high. This is expectable because the words and phrases which make up these concepts are generally unique to East Africa and to Kenya and are not used in "normal English." A similar category is SOCIALISM whose terms are not frequently used in English discourse.

A second series of categories which have high figures revolves around a problem that recurred in the factor analysis and in ANOVA—the need for integration within Kenya. The categories TRIBALISM and LOCAL GOVERNMENT are very high. There is a cluster of categories, INCOMPETENCE, BAD, CORRUPTION, AVOID, OPPOSITION, HATRED, EXPEL, DANGER, and DEATH THEME, which revolves around divisive factors and threats to the nation and government of Kenya. It is noteworthy that the category MILITARY is very high.

There are categories connected with political and economic development which illuminate the Kenyan policy position in these areas. The crucial aspects of development for Kenya are not agriculture and industry, but the problems of SOCIAL WELFARE and HEALTH, which touch the daily lives of all the population. Similarly, ideas of URBANIZATION become a major issue, as the

TABLE 1–15.   MAGNITUDE OF CONTRIBUTION OF POLITICAL IDEAS TO
POLICY: KENYATTA (KENYA)

Political Idea	Contribution	Political Idea	Contribution
SELF	.3087	VERY	.5975
INDIVIDUAL	.1905	VITAL	1.0096[a]
GROUP	.0334	STATUS	.7504
MASS	1.0948[a]	PROGRESS	.1749
SPACE	.0141	INTERNATIONAL	.3190
PAST TIME	.0208	IMPERIALISM	.6059
PRESENT TIME	.1309	AFRICA	5.2281[a]
FUTURE TIME	.5698	NATIONALISM	.1858
STRUCTURE	.0936	TRIBALISM	1.1126[a]
IF	.5601	RACE	5.6475[a]
OUGHT	.8667[a]	UNITE	.3461
EQUAL	.3838	FREEDOM	.3695
NOT	.2759	DEMOCRACY	.4569
SENSE	.3590	SOCIALISM	7.5676[a]
THINK	.1811	POLITICAL	.2820
COMMUNICATE	.1279	PARTY	.5682
CAUSE	.1428	EXECUTIVE	3.7309[a]
WISH	.8851[a]	GOVERNMENT	.1104
INITIATE ACTION	.0755	LEGISLATURE	.0659
APPROACH	.5347	JUDICIAL	1.6783[a]
MOVE	.0448	MILITARY	2.8229[a]
GET	.1410	SOCIAL WELFARE	.9276[a]
GUIDE	.3835	FINANCE	.5877
CONTROL	1.1015[a]	HEALTH	1.0905[a]
COMBINE	.0939	ECONOMIC	.4349
INCOMPETENCE	1.5577[a]	INDUSTRIALIZATION	.3762
BAD	1.1848[a]	AGRICULTURE	.1390
CORRUPTION	3.5407[a]	URBANIZATION	1.2520[a]
AVOID	1.2509[a]	IGNORANCE	.1183
OPPOSITION	3.8107[a]	HISTORY	1.3933[a]
HATRED	2.0241[a]	LOCAL GOVERNMENT	4.1213[a]
ATTACK	.3746	LEGITIMACY	.9783[a]
EXPEL	1.0157[a]	TANZANIA	1.9048[a]
DANGER	1.2880[a]	NYERERE	1.8889[a]
DISTRESS	1.5501[a]	TANU	8.6732[a]
DEATH THEME	1.3895[a]	KENYA	.2454
POSITIVE	.1092	KENYATTA	.0858
REGULAR	.3829	KANU	1.0976[a]
APPROVE	1.7666[a]	OTHER KENYAN PARTIES	5.6657[a]
PLEASURE	.1266	SLOGANS	4.6265[a]
GLORIOUS	.0035	YOU	.1019

a High-magnitude concepts. Overlay of "normal" English (Kucera, 1967) = 78.4%

rural exodus swells the cities beyond handling capacity, and have a big impact
on policy. The devolpment plans reflect these concerns with major emphasis on
expansion of education and health facilities, provision of electrical and water
supplies, and encouragement of a return to the farms.

In the political area, political ideas of several types influence policy. The fourth highest figure in Table 1–15, and the major political variable influencing policy, is RACE. Kenyatta is far more sensitive and responsive to the racial issue than other users of English in an era of racial consciousness, of school desegregation, busing, voter registration, etc. Other political ideas that carry over into Kenyan policy are LEGITIMACY, the establishment of which Kenyatta sees as a problem; EXECUTIVE, which refers to the strong position of Kenyatta in Kenyan policy; and JUDICIAL, which is an area out of Kenyatta's direct control and hence a political source of trouble for him.

The concept of MASS, which refers to the people of Kenya, ranks high in impact on policy. Kenyatta's words are directed toward measures improving conditions for the widest possible number of Kenya's population. But, Kenyatta's ideas include a continuation of strong exercise of initiative and implementation (CONTROL) from himself (EXECUTIVE) and his government (KANU). HISTORY has an effect on policy for Kenyatta, who looks back to the independence struggle. VITAL and APPROVE are high-scoring ideas conveying Kenyatta's sense of urgency and approbation of the government's stands.

Table 1–16 gives the concepts which have a great impact on policy in Tanzania. Nyerere has only 22 political ideas with an impact on policy of .80 or greater (in contrast to 35 for Kenya). An examination of these political ideas reveals their remarkable similarity to the high magnitude political ideas of Kenya.

There is a cluster of ideas concerned with East Africa, but the general concept AFRICA is not included. Yet, it is interesting that the idea of KENYATTA himself did not score highly, whereas NYERERE is the highest category, indicating the centralization of political policy in the person of the leader. SLOGANS is also extremely high, and the political slogans created by Nyerere are one major device for socializing the Tanzanian population. There is the same group of political ideas connected with divisive forces within the society—INCOMPETENCE, CORRUPTION, AVOID, OPPOSITION, HATRED, EXPEL, and DISTRESS. But, to Nyerere, the MILITARY does not have a major impact on policy, nor does TRIBALISM or LOCAL GOVERNMENT. This means Nyerere does not have these constraints on his policymaking and can rest easier about internal dissension.

Like KENYA, major political ideas are SOCIALISM, HEALTH, SOCIAL WELFARE, LEGITIMACY, and HISTORY. These have effects in the creation of development plans similar to those of Kenya. Again like Kenyatta's, Nyerere's political ideas include OUGHT, CONTROL, and APPROVE indicating similar focus on the means for achieving goals. Unlike Kenyatta's, Nyerere's ideas of SELF and PLEASURE have a high impact on policy, and MASS, VITAL, RACE, EXECUTIVE, and JUDICIARY are not of great magnitude. Nyerere is less concerned with these political ideas, and government has for him less impact on the policies. Nyerere has one high-magnitude concept, COMBINE, whose impact on policy can be seen in the post-Arusha

TABLE 1-16.   MAGNITUDE OF CONTRIBUTION OF POLITICAL IDEAS TO
POLICY: NYERERE (TANZANIA)

Political Idea	Contribution	Political Idea	Contribution
SELF	2.0696[a]	VERY	.0069
INDIVIDUAL	.3892	VITAL	.1322
GROUP	.2053	STATUS	.0726
MASS	.5472	PROGRESS	.0018
SPACE	.0963	INTERNATIONAL	.0087
PAST TIME	.1636	IMPERIALISM	.2321
PRESENT TIME	.2722	AFRICA	.0237
FUTURE TIME	.2128	NATIONALISM	.4243
STRUCTURE	.4631	TRIBALISM	.1122
IF	.1418	RACE	.1206
OUGHT	1.0914[a]	UNITE	.1488
EQUAL	.5964	FREEDOM	.0678
NOT	.0519	DEMOCRACY	.0913
SENSE	.0675	SOCIALISM	.8134[a]
THINK	.1438	POLITICAL	.0373
COMMUNICATE	.1986	PARTY	.0479
CAUSE	.2722	EXECUTIVE	.3926
WISH	.2936	GOVERNMENT	.0178
INITIATE ACTION	.3539	LEGISLATURE	.0486
APPROACH	.1683	JUDICIAL	.0000
MOVE	.0172	MILITARY	.0033
GET	.0663	SOCIAL WELFARE	.8066[a]
GUIDE	.6558	FINANCE	.0691
CONTROL	2.1611[a]	HEALTH	1.3932[a]
COMBINE	.8416[a]	ECONOMIC	.5025
INCOMPETENCE	1.8112[a]	INDUSTRIALIZATION	.0008
BAD	.5207	AGRICULTURE	.1872
CORRUPTION	2.4707[a]	URBANIZATION	.7841
AVOID	1.0181[a]	IGNORANCE	.3245
OPPOSITION	3.4018[a]	HISTORY	1.880[a]
HATRED	1.2823[a]	LOCAL GOVERNMENT	.2625
ATTACK	.3386	LEGITIMACY	1.9975[a]
EXPEL	1.4149[a]	TANZANIA	1.1028[a]
DANGER	.5392	NYERERE	19.5494[a]
DISTRESS	1.6851[a]	TANU	2.0429[a]
DEATH THEME	.2287	KENYA	.2334
POSITIVE	.0459	KENYATTA	3.1774[a]
REGULAR	.6601	KANU	.1235
APPROVE	1.9204[a]	OTHER KENYAN PARTIES	11.4926[a]
PLEASURE	4.5844[a]	SLOGANS	17.2837[a]
GLORIOUS	.2742	YOU	.7376

[a] High-magnitude concepts. Overlay of "normal" English (Kucera, 1967) = 78.4%.

campaigns urging Tanzanian citizens to cooperate and group together to achieve development goals.

The computation of this function yields the following conclusion: Political ideas voiced by Nyerere and Kenyatta differ in their primary attributes, but correspond greatly in their underlying themes. Essentially, Nyerere and Kenyatta have implemented economic development, emphasizing similar goals of well-being, health, education, and social welfare, but they have differed on the major means used to achieve these goals. Nyerere has chosen the socialist path to restructure his society with internal cooperative measures. Kenyatta has elected to expand an individualistically oriented society with concern for the potential disintegrative forces within society.

CONCLUSIONS

The analysis of political activities is extraordinarily difficult when the structures being analyzed (groups, parties, elites, etc.) are changing, or worse are ethereal. Yet, the activities of a country continue, change, and provide new activities for analysis. Our initial question asked what political ideas contribute to national policy in Kenya and Tanzania. We proposed the function which explained the magnitude of the contribution of a political idea to political policy in these two countries in terms of its frequency of occurrence, its continuity over time, and its clusterability.

Political ideas were operationalized using conceptual categories combined into a political dictionary for content analysis. Each conceptual category contained a series of words and phrases; and each word was categorized in a series of concept or idea categories creating nonexclusive sets of categories.

Two samples of speeches were collected, one for Kenyatta of Kenya, the other for Nyerere of Tanzania, spanning the time from independence to 1970. These speeches were content analyzed using the concept as the unit of analysis. A determination of the representative conceptualization was specified on a probabilistic basis using words before and following each word in a sentence. A matrix of raw scores, listing concept categories by text by country, was generated through this process. These entries in this matrix were taken individually (*frequency occurrence*), summed over the sample (*continuity over time*), and factor analyzed (*clusterability*) to assess the magnitude of each political concept's contribution to policy.

The factor analysis suggests several significant political ideas that are important to both leaders and some which are important to only one man. Nyerere, for example, sees the TANU party as the primary means to execute policy, with himself as the central focus of policymaking (NYERERE), and socialism as the coherent organizational device to attain the goals. For Kenyatta, his party, KANU, and socialism also provide some means of goal achievement. More significant to Kenyatta are the international scene, sources of aid, and threats to national integration represented by the concept categories AP-PROACH, CORRUPTION, DEATH THEME, AVOID, and DANGER THEME. The picture that emerges from this first factor differs between nations. Tanzanian policymaking is centralized and consciously and carefully executed.

Kenyatta, by contrast, is more concerned with the immediate problems that tend to disunite the country and, consequently, he operates serially from problem to problem, rather than by following some prearranged program.

Additional factors show many similar political ideas in the two nations. Nyerere considers the following variables significant:

Factor 2
INDUSTRIALIZATION, FINANCE, AGRICULTURE, COMMUNICATE, and POLITICAL

Factor 3
SPACE, PLEASURE, LOCAL GOVERNMENT

Factor 4
REGULAR, DANGER THEME, UNITY

Kenyatta's significant political ideas include the following:

Factor 2
FREEDOM, NATIONALISM, ECONOMIC

Factor 3
EQUALS, PLEASURE, LEGISLATURE, POLITICAL

Factor 4
KENYA, GROUP

There are clear similarities in these results. Politics is considered in the same way; economic development is defined using the same variables; and external dangers persist.

Yet there are differences. Nyerere emphasizes many more economic variables (AGRICULTURE, INDUSTRIALIZATION, FINANCE), as well as the structure by which economic development is to be achieved (COMMUNICATE, POLITICAL, SPACE, LOCAL GOVERNMENT, REGULAR). Kenyatta is more concerned with national integration and speaks often of nationalism and independence (FREEDOM, NATIONALISM, EQUALS, KENYA). For Kenyatta, ECONOMIC is a more general concern.

Each of these variables represents major political ideas, based on their heavy loading on the factors, and each relates to the major factor concerned with the means of goal attainment.

In the analysis of variance, many of the categories showed significant differences between countries and leaders. Nyerere was significantly concerned with FINANCE, COMMUNICATION, SPACE, UNITY, NYERERE, and TANU. Kenyatta was concerned with FREEDOM, NATIONALISM, EQUALS, and KENYA. This analysis supports the findings of the factor analysis: Nyerere is more concerned with coherent and comprehensive policymaking, centralized in the executive, and Kenyatta focuses on national independence and integration.

A significant number of concept categories was not different for the two contexts, suggesting the similarity of many political ideas. Included in this group

are concepts dealing with development goals, both economic—INDUSTRIAL-
IZATION, AGRICULTURE, and ECONOMIC—and political—POLITICAL,
LOCAL GOVERNMENT, SOCIALISM, LEGISLATURE, and GROUP.

Three significant concept categories were used in the regression analysis
to assess the relationship between verbal and national aggregate performances
taken with respect to time. Interesting differences resulted from the analysis,
suggesting that both nations see similar problems and have similar political ends,
but that each leader has developed his own style of problem management.
Policymaking in Kenya is a slow, gradual assessment process whereby political
ideas are eventually incorporated into the national fabric. Economic activity
and articulation of policy, according to this analysis, has become relatively stable
over time, after a period of turmoil immediately following independence. In
Tanzania the policymaking style is more drastic. Once Nyerere recognizes a
problem area, he attacks it head on, taking the nation along with him. As a
result, we see that Kenya is relatively stable, but Tanzania is not.

Finally, the computation of the function reinforces the findings suggested
elsewhere. Political ideas have a definite impact on political policy in these two
nations. There are great similarities in the goals and concerns of the two national
leaders with economic development, with legitimacy of their regimes, and with
internal diffculties. Differences occur in the means each leader has chosen to
achieve goals. Nyerere emphasizes cooperative socialism, whereas Kenyatta's
ideas promote an individualistic society which needs unifying factors promoting
national integration.

There are pressures operating on the two nations portending changes in
the immediate future. The East Africa Common Market, expanded to include
more nations, could have impacts on policymaking in the two nations. Kenya,
oriented toward economic development and national unity, may be expected
to work hard for the maintenance of the community. Tanzania, because
of a preoccupation with national self-interest, may conflict with the community,
although the exact sequence and probable outcomes are unclear. Tanzania may
support the community because of the industry and trade potential it represents
—this possibility is visible in the regressions, where increasing concern was
noted for economic matters. On the other hand, Tanzanian socialism, a rather
rigid ideological prescription for *the* proper way of doing things, may come into
conflict with the more profit-motivated members of the East Africa Community.
Tanzania could, for example, make major capital decisions primarily on noneconomic grounds, e.g., locating factories in the interior of the nation. Besides
this possible source of irritation, Tanzania might decide to repeat a recent performance in the case of the Uganda coup d'etat, at which point Nyerere decided
that correct socialist politics were more important than simple economic gains.

Politics itself is liable to change in both settings. Tanzanian politics is
concentrated on Nyerere; his ideas essentially alone motivate the nation. Were
severe reversals to affect the nation, he may be blamed, yet the analyses suggest
that Nyerere is capable of rapid reorientation to a changing situation. For in-

stance, the regressions pointed out several reversals in economic policy that followed close after the promulgation of the Arusha Declaration. Based on this information, one might predict that Nyerere is capable of generating adequate policies rapidly enough to manage a changing context. For Kenyatta, politics is also central; Kenyatta holds the nation together. Given Kenyatta's age, Kenya-watchers are beginning to talk about succession. It is predictable that any political system, concentrated so heavily on a single executive and having no precedents to follow, would present succession problems of considerable magnitude. However, the data suggest that Kenya has in the past approached change gradually, emphasizing stability over precipitate moves. It is conceivable that this pattern may hold at the time of succession.

This analysis suggests one way in which political ideas contributed to policymaking processes in two East African nations. Three elements are key: idea clusters isolated by the factor analysis; relative frequencies of appearance of single political ideas, operationalized with an analysis of variance between nations, over time; and sets of political ideas, explored in terms of a time-based regression analysis. The utility of content analysis for managing a research problem of this type has been developed in this chapter. These results indicate further potential for analytic prediction which needs exploration.

APPENDIX: UTILIZATION OF CONTENT ANALYSIS AS A RESEARCH METHODOLOGY

Content Analysis Problems and Decisions

In political science, as well as other fields, the volume of paper output is increasing yearly at a rapid rate. Techniques for analyzing verbal and written output have been gaining acceptance as they achieve sophistication. In this discipline, content analysis has been of great use. As the number of analysts increases and access to decisionmakers becomes limited, content analysis can be used for investigations of politics through words. This is especially true in developing areas and in Soviet studies, where research is carefully circumscribed. In most areas of political science, content analysis has shown its utility, and with the advent of newer methods, advanced statistical devices, and better theoretical understanding of language and its uses, content analysis will probably increase in applicability. It is useful, then, for us to review some of the typical problems which beset the analyst who chooses this tool, to note some of the advances which have been made, and finally to note its utility in the area of African politics.

It is wise to recall that content analysis is a tool, not a theory or a theoretical stance. As such, one must approach the tool with some definite theoretical interest in mind to achieve meaningful results. As does any tool, content analysis introduces a particular approach; it requires particular kinds of research decisions and leads to a particular structuring of the data. The simple steps involved in performing a content analysis may be easily reviewed in any of a series of manuals (see Holsti, 1968). Here we simply state a series of issues regarding the decisions one makes in performing a content analysis, to examine their implications and pitfalls.

We define content analysis very broadly as any rigorous and systematic investigation of communications. By rigorous and systematic we mean that the study uses exactly the same tools in the same manner throughout and that the study is capable of replication. It often, but not necessarily, means that results are quantifiable. Communication is construed broadly to cover the mass media, interpersonal exchanges, artistic expression, and a wide range of forms of human interaction. Most often, communication involves words, and our concern here is with this type of analysis.

A first question is when to use content analysis. If the same results are obtainable by simpler means, content analysis should not be used. This point is not always easy to determine, but a good rule of thumb is to judge whether the likely results give a description of the content which a good journalist could duplicate. If so, then perhaps a detailed analysis of that type is preferable. If a more systematic or precise description of the content is needed, then a content analysis is often desirable. Content analysis is applicable to a wide range of social science materials. However, using existing content analysis techniques it is difficult to detect irony, truth, or falsehoods. Content analysis is particularly applicable when the problem concerns the nature of structure of the communication, as is often the case in studies of propaganda or socialization. It was applicable in this chapter because the problem concerned the nature of the political ideas disseminated by two African leaders to their populations.

Thus far, content analysis has been considered as the description of the words—the manifest content. In most cases, the only material available for analysis is the text, the set of the words themselves. The question is whether inferences can be made from these words about such things as the intent of the speaker, the psychic state of the speaker, the philosophy behind his words— the latent content. Some evidence exists, particularly in psychology, that an examination of the manifest content of a series of communications can lead to a good assessment of the state of mind of the speaker. It seems there is a case for content analysis to determine latent meanings, but caution must be exercised until the extent of this procedure has been discovered and validation procedures worked out. In this chapter, care has been taken to limit the analysis to the manifest content and to avoid overgeneralizations about latent meanings.

Having determined theoretical concerns and chosen content analysis as a tool, the next decisions concern selection of a sample. How much text is sufficient to reveal content patterns? How can a random sample be selected? There is no standard answer to these questions. Where there are definite time limits, say, a five-year interval, within which to select editorials, it is not very difficult to randomize and select. It is more difficult to sample the speeches of a political leader. Taking either Kenyatta or Nyerere as an example, a search for their speeches from the time of independence yields only a partial sample. Some have been lost, others purposely destroyed. Many speeches are given far from a recording unit or even a reporter. At other times, each man speaks extemporaneously. On the other hand, the opposite problem can occur when the speeches are published in books about a leader's thought. In this case the content analysis will concern a universe of communications since these are all the speeches the leader thinks are publishable, and not a sample. Consequently, many of the statistical tests which are based on sampling will have to be used in a different form. Care must be taken in dealing with these considerations.

At an early stage in the study, a decision must be made on the unit of analysis. When we talk about the basic unit of analysis we are referring to the context unit, the unit through which meaning is conveyed. This unit varies widely, depending on what is being said in the particular study. We can choose as the basic unit a theme, a word, a sentence, a paragraph, or a longer text. Each choice has limitations. A theme as the unit of analysis is often theoretically pleasing, but its location is time consuming and difficult to mechanize. A sentence is a natural identifiable grammatical unit, but many times it contains several themes or only partial themes. Single words are often meaningless when isolated. It has been empirically shown that using the sentence as a unit of analysis generally leads to accurate contextual portrayals of various single words within it; however, it is by no means certain that an accurate picture of a theme has been obtained by using the sentence. The entire speech was used as the analysis unit in this chapter because it was felt the speech gave a world view at a single time point.

There are many types of content analysis. For ease, they are divisible into manifest and latent content analyses. One type of manifest content analysis can be termed *presence–absence*, based on the existence of particular symbols and their absence from the text. The most familiar form of manifest content analysis is word counting or frequency counting of words. Here an assumption is made that the more a word is used, the greater the significance it assumes. So, a higher count will be more important than a lower count. Often, frequency counts are made not of the total words employed, but of specifically selected lists of words. A refinement of this technique is a third form of manifest content analysis, the one used in this chapter, based on conceptual categories. In this procedure the significant words are grouped into conceptual categories based on ideas which have theoretical significance. Because these categories can be general or very specific and because they contain the operationalization of the research design, care must be exercised in construction of the categories and selection of the words which embody each concept.

There are two general kinds of latent content analysis which, while they were not used in this analysis, will be mentioned for comparison purposes. The first is called systematization and comparison and involves an analysis which takes a series of frequencies and compares them. For example, if one is trying to establish the sanity of a patient, a series of frequency categories is compared with those of individuals who are known to be insane, and deviations or similarities noted. Possibly more important is the second type, which is based on context. To some extent, contextual analysis was used in this research to establish the general climate or environment within which the two African leaders mentioned specific political ideas. More detailed analysis of this type usually employs retrieval operations based on contingencies.

In speaking of the kinds of results obtained from content analysis we would be remiss if we neglected the problems of reliability and validity. With the advent of machine content analysis it is now possible to ensure that each piece of text is dealt with in exactly the same fashion, thus achieving a high level of reliability.

Achieving validity for the categories applied is a more difficult problem. Various solutions have been advocated (Holsti, 1968). Pretesting the categories on a sample can lead to category clarification; categories can be explicitly defined and their theoretical relevance made clear; and categories can be made exhaustive so that the material has to be divided in some fashion or other. Various statistics can be computed for validity, but no clear agreement exists on what is an acceptable level of validity.

Validity can pose an even more serious problem. Face validity is fairly easy to establish in an analysis where a description of content is the object. The plausibility of the results can be checked with samples of close textual reading. Predictive validity can be similarly established. The validity of a content analysis instrument can often be established by correlation with independent data sources. Thus, in discussing African political ideas, we attempted to relate national political actions, especially those in the economic realm, to the results of the content analysis.

Establishing the validity of the theory underlying the content analysis instrument is always a problem and it is possible only with repetition, correlated results, and extensive work. For this reason, it is particularly important in content analysis for replication to take place. There has been criticism of the multiplication of content analysis "dictionaries," collections of categories based on variegated theories. The variety of these dictionaries makes it difficult to assess the work of other researchers or to make comparative statements. But, it must be recalled that the dictionaries are operationalizations of theory, and given the level of development of theory in social science, reductions to a single theoretical statement would be a tragedy. In this chapter, the dictionary (Pirro, 1968) used was one created specifically for African politics to which a series of categories derived from East African sources was added. The dictionary gains validity by virtue of its use on other African documents.

These are simply a few of the decisions and problems facing the content analyst. We turn now to the problems of machine operations.

Machine Content Analysis

In discussing the content analysis of verbal output, we have been considering three basic operations: comparison and sorting, counting, and retrieving. These operations can be performed by the analyst; however, the mechanical portions of these operations might be done by a computer. When we compare material, a list of significant words is compared with the textual material to be analyzed, and the operationalized theory is compared with the data. Then the appearance of the words is counted and tallied in frequency counts. Often the words are sorted into separate categories. Finally, the words of particular interest or significance are isolated from the mass of the text by retrievals and inspected or correlated with other words separately. All of these processes can be computer operations.

To use a computer program for content analysis, the researcher generally does the following things:

1. He makes the decisions on the rules he will use in the sorting and comparing of information. This is the establishment of categories, the dictionary creation or amendment.
2. He selects for retrieval what he believes is significant, thereby operationalizing some of his specific research hypotheses.
3. He runs tests of significance to analyze the data. This includes taking processed data and running one or more additional programs for factor analysis, regression analysis, or other forms of statistical significance.

The Quester computer content analysis system, being used at the University of Minnesota and available for CDC machines, is a general and comprehensive set of computer programs for content analysis. A series of programs is included which performs the following operations:

1. CONTENT is a dictionary comparison program which takes the categories and compares them with the text of the material to be analyzed, sorting the text into those categories and tallying frequencies on the basis of the categories.
2. SEMCONT is the same dictionary program as CONTENT, with the addition of capabilities for semantic differential, which can be used as an intensity measure, and syntactic coding.
3. WORD COUNT is a program which simply counts words. It can process massive amounts of textual material, dividing them into alphabetical lists with frequencies and percentages of appearance by various units of analysis.
4. RETRIEVE performs various retrieval operations.
5. CONTEXT is a program which performs contextual analysis.
6. There is also a series of special programs which performs specialized content analysis procedures such as handling simulation output and questionnaire responses and statistical procedures such as factor analysis and scoring or scaling of various sorts. Thus, the computer is an operational tool for carrying out the analyst's procedures.

However, the use of the computer means the introduction of additional assumptions. This has certain implications, as well as a number of advantages. Some of these will be detailed.

With Quester-like support systems, studies can be easily replicated. Also, a sample can be considerably larger. For this chapter, the sample included a quarter of a million words, which were then processed at the rate of 24,000 words per minute. Using this program, a variety of dictionaries can be used on a single set of data with varying results.

To speed the analytic process, text for Quester is punched directly onto IBM cards or onto paper tape. The analyst does not have to convert the text into coded symbols. As of yet, a certain amount of editing is desirable to eliminate obvious ambiguities with abbreviations and to add syntax if desired. From the various programs we have listed, a number of different operations can be chosen.

Included in the assumptions which must be made, however, is the notion that man thinks in the analytic unit chosen. For this study, it meant that Kenyatta's and Nyerere's ideas were contained in their speeches. There is a further assumption made that about 40% of all language is composed of words without meaning. These "N" or "nothing" words, a list of fifty or more per dictionary, are eliminating from the frequency counts and from the analysis. Incorporating them in the study can lead to lack of differentiation and distort results. Removal of these words on the basis of high frequency can lead to clarity of interpretation (Cleveland, 1970). There is a further assumption that words linearly represent what a person says. So, the more frequently a word is used, the greater significance it has for the analysis. Thus, fifteen pistols can be more significant than three submachine guns. There is an assumption that language is consistent over time. Thus, things which are repetitive are located as significant. What is sought are consistent patterns of words. This further implies that human beings tend to use language repetitively. High frequencies equate with significant findings in terms of establishment of norms of verbal behavior. This does not deny that deviations from the norm may be significant in terms of theoretical concerns. What is meant is that Quester-like routines are designed so as to establish the repetitive patterns, the normal in language, and that deviations from the normal must be plotted from this norm. In any analysis dictionary, all categories are weighted equally, meaning each division shares a similar position in terms of the final analysis.

There are some interesting implications in this form of analysis. It is assumed that the text being analyzed is an accurate portrayal of the interactions taking place, that people talk about what is uppermost in their minds, and that analyzing what they say is also determining what they consider most significant. What a man says is what he is. Communications research is still trying to establish this basic principle.

Particular words are selected as significant in terms of a theory. These words are grouped in categories and the theory is operationalized in category terms. By selecting these particular words as significant and rejecting others, we are saying that these words are indicative of particular behaviors. Thus, behavior is being examined by words concerning it. These two implications are not peculiar to Quester systems, but are applicable to most forms of content analysis.

Using the computer, particularly in retrieval operations, often means that "key" words are selected and that other words will fall into particular patterns determined by these key words. A single word can thus prove crucial for a whole area of thought. The diligence of the research analyst is sorely tried at this point.

Content analysis by computer is not concerned with patterns of recording information, but with analyzing the patterns of information. It is carried out within the context of a research design, which means that the results are relative, based on the characteristics of one text as compared with another. Thus, most computer content analysis utilizes a research design which is explicitly comparative: texts are compared over time, between individuals or nations, or compared with independent data. This chapter has illustrated instances of all three of these types of comparison.

A basic statistic used in the CONTENT subroutine of Quester is the index of percentage frequency of appearance of a category within a given document. If a category appears infrequently, it has a low index score and is often dropped from further analysis, regardless of its significance for the author of the document.

As in all research, content analysis by computer means a major role played by the intuitive understanding of the investigator in interpreting the results. As yet, there is no adequate theoretical explanation of how social science variables are related and how this relationship is expressed in language. Hence, the analyst must interpret for himself, using the program simply as a guide.

The ease and speed of computer operations has by now almost made hand content analysis obsolete. The future can see only an increase in this trend. Indications are that the existing content analytic systems will be replaced by easier, more streamlined, and generally available versions. At the same time, some exciting research is being done in communications which has great implications for the development of further content analysis studies. Questions are being asked about the nature of language, its structure, the utility of syntax, validity of intensity as a measure, and other indicators.

The application of content analytic procedures to the documents of developing nations brings with it a series of new opportunities, as well as questions. The area of cross-cultural comparison, with its many difficulties of connotation and denotation, brings a new area into question. Instability within many of the Third World nations also means instability in word usage to some extent, and this removes some of the bases of operation of the standard content analytic techniques.

As this chapter on African political ideas has suggested, content analysis can uncover various key ideas of interest. It can also provide a method of comparison for the political scientist. But, there are many questions which remain, many unexplored areas still to investigate. As both technique and Africa advance, it is hoped further work will uncover many of the answers.

BIBLIOGRAPHY

Andrain, Charles F. "Democracy and Socialism: Ideologies of African Leaders." In David E. Apter, ed., *Ideology and Discontent*. New York: The Free Press, 1964.

Clapham, Christopher. "Context of African Political Thought." *Journal of Modern African Studies*. Vol. 8, No. 1 (April 1970), pp. 1–14.

Cleveland, Charles E. *Rhetoric in Institutions*. Ph.D. dissertation, Northwestern University, 1971.

Cleveland, Charles E., McTavish, Donald, and Pirro, Ellen B. *Symbolic Information System*. University of Minnesota, Mimeo, Computation Center, computer file, 1971.

Coleman, James S., and Rosberg, Carl G. *Political Parties and National Integration in Tropical Africa*. Berkeley: University of California Press, 1964.

Deese, James E. *The Structure of Association in Language and Thought*. Baltimore, Md.: The Johns Hopkins University Press, 1965.

Foltz, William R., and Pirro, Ellen B. *Black African Leaders Speak*. In press.

Friedland, William H., and Rosberg, Carl G. *African Socialism*. Stanford, Cal.: Hoover Institute, 1964.

Grundy, Kenneth. "Recent Contributions to the Study of African Political Thought." *World Politics*. Vol. 18, No. 4 (July 1966), pp. 674–89.

Harman, Harry H. *Modern Factor Analysis*. Chicago: University of Chicago Press, 1967.

Holsti, Ole. *Content Analysis*. New York: Addison-Wesley, 1968.

Kenyatta, Jomo. *Suffering Without Bitterness*. Nairobi, Kenya: East African Publishing House, 1968.

Kolers, Paul A., and Eden, Murray, eds. *Recognizing Patterns*. Cambridge, Mass.: The MIT Press, 1968.

Kucera, Henry, and Francis, W. Nelson. *Computational Analysis of Present Day American English*. Providence, R.I.: Brown University Press, 1967.

Lane, Robert E. *Political Ideology*. New York: The Free Press, 1962.

Nyerere, Julius, *Uhuru Na Umoja*. London: Oxford University Press, 1967.

Nyerere, Julius. *Freedom and Socialism*. London: Oxford University Press, 1968.

Putnam, Robert D. "Studying Elite Political Culture: The Case of 'Ideology'." *American Political Science Review*. Vol. 65, No. 3 (September 1971), pp. 651–81.

Quillan, Ross. "Word Concepts: A Theory and Simulation of Some Basic Semantic Capabilities." Santa Monica, Cal.: System Development Corporation, Report SP-2199, 1965.

Rosberg, Carl G., and Nottingham, John. *The Myth of Mau Mau*. New York: Praeger, 1966.

Rothchild, Donald. "Kenya's Africanization Program: Priorities of Development and Equity." *American Political Science Review*. Vol. 64, No. 3 (September 1970), pp. 737–53.

Uphoff, Norman T. "Ghana and Economic Assistance: Impetus and Ingredients for a Theory of Political Development." Los Angeles: American Political Science Association, 1970.

Zolberg, Aristide. *Creating Political Order*. Chicago: Rand McNally, 1966.

BIBLIOGRAPHY

Part II
Trends

INTRODUCTION

Trend-based studies generally are characterized by their attempts to discover sequences and patterns among events both near and remote in time. As with all basic intellectual orientations, the questions and perspectives underlying any given trend-based work will vary from specialist to specialist. The information base from which relevant events are selected, and of course omitted, is substantially larger than what any one observer can capture in his interpretation of events and sequences. Despite pretentions to the contrary, trend studies are as subject to the demand for multiple observational perspectives as are normative, scientific, projective, or policy studies. One needs only recall a most famous cycle in credible, acceptable, or fashionable historical interpretation—Frederick Jackson Turner's "frontier thesis," which was supplanted by Arthur Schlesinger's "urban thesis," and in turn modified by the "class" or "interest group" thesis of Charles A. Beard—to point out the tentativeness of a single pronouncement of trend; the demand to develop multiple perspectives and interpretations of events and related sequences is clear.[1]

One needs to consider trends when carrying out a policy analysis in order to get a "sense" of the most significant descriptive events in a context. That is: What is relatively more important; how do various elements fit together and what are the temporal orderings in the context? Different observational perspectives refer both to variations among the elements selected and omitted from the analysis, and also to variations in the spatial and temporal levels of resolution used to organize the analysis. For example, with a microscope, a 10-power

---

[1] Frederick Jackson Turner, *The Frontier in American History* (New York: Holt, Rinehart & Winston, 1962 ed.), pp. 1–38; Arthur M. Schlesinger, Sr., *The Rise of the City* (New York: Macmillan, 1933), pp. 320f; and Bernard C. Borning, *The Political and Social Thought of Charles A. Beard* (Seattle, Wash.: University of Washington Press, 1962), pp. 64–138.

magnification presents a far different picture from a 500-power one, even though the general body of information, e.g., a prepared slide, is identical. So it is with the level of temporal resolution adopted by a trend specialist; it may bias the picture presented as much as do the initial selection and omission of relevant elements and events. While the clarity, even elegance, of the written presentation may "tell a story" that is plausible and, consequently, widely accepted, one must not lose sight of the fact that is just a "story," in the same way that a scientific model is a "fake," a singular, simplified, partial, and tentative representation of a context so rich and complex as to defy perfectly correct representation.

Selection of Events

The availability and selection of information with which to tell any given story about past events underlie several of the weaknesses of the trend approach if relied on exclusively.

Much historical information has been lost or was never recorded in the first place. The information used is that which exists, of course, but moreover, it is often that which is most easily obtained. In the scientific sense, this leads to suboptimization, or the solution of wrong or irrelevant problems for which no one may have even a decent question. A further manifestation of this phenomenon is an exaggerated concern for deviant, hence probably noncomparable, sequences and events. Scientific explanation naturally suffers as a result.

By concentrating on just a single sequence or a decidedly deviant set of events, the trend-oriented specialist gives up quite a bit, often unknowingly. The policy scientist is advised to consider this danger and to heed Stuart Bruchey's candid warning.

The historian perceives only sequences; it is his mind rather than his eye that determines how the facts are related to each other. In a word, the criteria by which he selects some facts and rejects others as irrelevant are not inherent in the data; they are supplied by the historian.[2]

This selecting process has made trend-oriented work only marginally useful to those interested in alternative developmental patterns or sequences. To ask the "what if" question that is a policymaker's and a policy scientist's stock in trade, is to leave very rapidly most historians behind or, to recall Meyerhoff's revealing comments, "The facts of history are peculiar, as historicism has insisted all along."[3] Efforts to project or develop normative preferences are consequently slighted as well.

[2] Stuart Bruchey, *The Roots of American Economic Growth, 1607–1816: An Essay in Social Causation* (New York: Harper & Row, 1968), p. 11.
[3] Meyerhoff, *The Philosophy of History in Our Time: An Anthology* (Garden City, N.Y.: Doubleday, 1959), p. 19.

Temporal Sequencing

To characterize the details of a specific context is important. The verbal relationships between elements provide weak explanatory hypotheses of cause and effect and time rates of change, and both of these kinds of information are useful to have if one is concerned about problem-solving and policy analysis.

Case histories are a rich and, to a distressingly great extent, overlooked source of scientifically and policy-relevant hypotheses and information. For instance, taking the period 1800–1828 in Washington, D.C., and carefully ordering events, James S. Young tells the alert reader a great deal about American political development and the possibilities for change.[4] Equally competent case studies of other national settings at comparably delicate stages in their evolution would do much for scholarship of all varieties, but for political development scholarship especially. What if the detailed sequence had proceeded at different rates or had involved slightly different elements, how might have events then taken place? Given the instability Young so richly characterizes, why was there *not* a coup d'etat or another abrupt adjustment in the actual sequence? Other questions come to mind as well, all having relevance for the orientations of goal, condition, projection, and policy.

THE LITERATURE

Because political development specialists are well acquainted with historically based scholarship, there is less demand to cite extensively from the volumes of existing literature. In fact, one imagines that the vast majority of scholarship in the field has traditionally been trend based; interest and capability to pursue scientific work, for example, are clearly less well developed and hence less evident. Because of this dominant concern, we have chosen to deemphasize trend-based work in this volume, striving to strike a better balance among *all five* orientations to problem-solving and management.

Three simple categories are suggestive of how trend-oriented work may be viewed: generalized overview or philosophical studies; theoretical and methodological works; and exemplary or illustrative cases or descriptive histories of some specific context or another.

General Works

To expand upon many of the spare comments made here and to justify the historian in somewhat more complete (and perhaps charitable) terms, we re-

[4] James Sterling Young, *The Washington Community, 1800–1828* (New York: Columbia University Press, 1966). The War of 1812 plays an interesting "intervening" role in the period considered by Young; however, why were there so few domestic repercussions in terms of significant structural changes?

commended a careful reading of Allan Bullock, "The Historian's Purpose: History and Metahistory," *History Today*, Vol. 7 (May 1951), pp. 18–21; and A. L. Rowse, *The Use of History* (London: Hodder & Stoughton, 1946). Both are standard works and will reward a careful reader many times over. For more rigid, parochial views on the trend speciality, a rapid perusal of the following works will give the policy scientist a reasonable idea of what he is up against: H. J. Muller, *The Uses of the Past* (New York: Oxford University Press, 1952); Hans Meyerhoff, *The Philosophy of History in Our Time*; and, to a lesser extent, Robin G. Collingwood, *The Idea of History* (New York: Oxford University Press, 1956). For a sweeping view of history in a scientific context, browse over Isaiah Berlin, *Historic Inevitablility* (New York: Oxford University Press, 1954).

Theories and Methods

For an urbane and highly interesting general survey of historical theory and method, we find Robin W. Winks, ed., *The Historian as Detective: Essays on Evidence* (New York: Harper & Row, 1968), to be in a class by itself. General themes developed in Winks, including the limits of historical data, the historian as a captive of data (which often do not exist or exist in bewildering disarray), and what historians do, and more important for present needs, do not do, are all in varying degrees developed in each of the following theoretically slanted treatments: Marc Bloc, *The Historian's Craft* (New York: Alfred A. Knopf, 1953); Patrick Gardiner, ed., *Theories of History* (New York: The Free Press, 1959); Robin G. Collingwood, "The Limits of Historical Knowledge," in William Debbins, ed., *Essays in the Philosophy of History* (New York: McGraw-Hill, 1966); and Morris R. Cohen, "Causation and Its Application to History," *Journal of the History of Ideas*, Vol. 3 (October 1942), pp. 386–94.

Historical method is a large subfield occupying a great deal of attention and not easily summarized into a few "most important" or "best" sources. To get a general flavor of what is involved, H. Stuart Hughes, *History as Art and Science* (New York: Harper & Row, 1964), is a very readable place to begin. More demanding and more rewarding sources are David H. Fischer, *Historian's Fallacies: Toward a Logic of Historical Thought* (New York: Harper & Row, 1970); and Homer Carey Hockett, *The Critical Method in Historical Research and Writing* (New York: Macmillan, 1955). More specific examples of the historical method in actual use, each selected to illustrate a different aspect of the topic, are Karl W. Deutsch, "Towards an Inventory of Basic Trends and Patterns in Comparative International Politics," *American Political Science Review*, Vol. 54 (March 1960), pp. 34–57, where one is treated to a virtuoso performance of a historically trained social scientist; Eric Nordlinger, "Political Development: Time Sequences and Rates of Change," *World Politics*, Vol. 20 (April 1968), pp. 494–520, is a singularly outstanding treatment of many of what we consider to be the main areas of concern; Stuart Bruchey, *The Roots of American Economic Growth,* also handles the trends–conditions nexus with rare skill and should be regarded as something of a paradigm worthy of emulation; working from a very different scientific perspective and using historical materials in a novel and powerful way is Eric H. Erikson, *Young Man Luther: A Study in Psychoanalysis and History* (New York: W. W. Norton, 1962); and finally, to cite one extremely rare instance of someone trying to address the well-known ethnocentricity problem by paying it more than lip service, see the rich collection by an able Indonesian policy scientist, Soedjatmoko, ed., *An Introduction to Indonesian Historiography* (Ithaca, N.Y.: Cornell University Press, 1965).

Cases and Descriptive Histories: Some Examples

To illustrate a range of heavily trend-oriented cases and descriptions, a small sample of the voluminous literature must be drawn. Everyone's "favorite" case or political history certainly will not be on this selective and subjectively drawn list.

Broadly concerned, general works whose durability, if nothing else, speaks well for their utility include, Robert E. Ward and Roy C. Macridis, eds., *Modern Political Systems: Asia* (Englewood Cliffs, N.J.: Prentice-Hall, 1963); Lucian W. Pye, *Cases in Comparative Politics: Asia* (Boston: Little, Brown, 1970); an old standby, for the good reason that it has several important messages and shows the importance of looking at contexts from varying perspectives and with different levels of spatial and temporal resolutions, is Karl A. Wittfogel, *Oriental Despotism: A Comparative Study of Total Power* (New Haven: Yale University Press, 1957); a solid selection of general introductory cases about African political development patterns and sequences is Gwendolyn Carter and W. O. Brown, eds., *Transition in Africa: Studies in Political Adaptation* (Boston: Boston University Press, 1958); a respectable general source on the Middle East is Kemal H. Karpat, *Political and Social Thought in the Contemporary Middle East* (New York: Praeger, 1968); and for those interested in a general overview of Latin American events, where the military is a central or important element in nearly every national context, John J. Johnston, *The Military and Society in Latin America* (Stanford, Cal.: Stanford University Press, 1964), has many useful things to say.

National studies, broadly conceived as to their levels of spatial and temporal resolution, are perhaps the most numerous sub-category of all trend-oriented work; necessarily, this short list will omit more than it includes.

Asian studies, particularly for India,[5] are overrepresented in the total available literature; however, some illustrative examples that have proven their value over the years are notable. To get a better sense of the deep roots of modern Japan—and after all, a fundamental purpose of trend-based work is

[5] In a recent *Bibliography of Asian Studies, 1970* (Ann Arbor, Mich.: Association for Asian Studies, 1972), some 145 from a total of 392 pages were devoted to Indian subjects.

to begin resolving the matter of how the world came to be what it presently is
—the thorough scholarship of Thomas C. Smith, *The Agrarian Origins of
Modern Japan* (Stanford, Col.: Stanford University Press, 1959), is recommended. A thoughtfully written and robust accounting in the traditional historical style is John F. Cady, *A History of Modern Burma* (Ithaca, N.Y.:
Cornell University Press, 1968); less well done, but valuable to orient oneself
initially to the Philippines, is O. D. Corpuz, *The Philippines* (Englewood Cliffs,
N.J.: Prentice-Hall, 1965); one of the few scholarly and competent treatments
of current Vietnamese political history which exist is John T. McAlister and
Paul Mus, *The Vietnamese and Their Revolution* (New York: Harper & Row,
1970); because of its pivotal role in modern Thai society and policymaking, the
bureaucracy has served as a primary historical focus for Fred W. Riggs, *Thailand: The Modernization of a Bureaucratic Polity* (Honolulu: East-West Center
Press, 1967); and William J. Siffen, *The Thai Bureaucracy: Institutional Change
and Development* (Honolulu: East-West Center Press, 1966).

African sources in this broadly conceived class of basically trend-oriented
studies include James S. Coleman and Carl G. Rosberg, *Political Parties and
National Integration in Tropical Africa* (Berkeley: University of California
Press, 1964); for a good in-depth portrait of a formerly dominant and persistent
class in African political history see Audrey Richards, ed., *East African Chiefs*
(London: Faber and Faber, 1960); and, for an excellent case study, it is hard
to surpass David E. Apter. *The Political Kingdom of Uganda: A Study in Bureaucratic Nationalism* (Princeton: Princeton University Press, 1961).

The Middle East has been, and will continue to be, a source of political
interest. Daniel Lerner, *The Passing of Traditional Society: Modernizing the
Middle East* (New York: The Free Press, 1958), has much to say on a variety of
essential issues; its verbal, descriptive-historical segments are extraordinarily rich
sources of sequencing and causal information. For two other competent cases,
see Leonard Binder, *Iran: Political Development in a Changing Society* (Berkeley: University of California Press, 1962); and Bernard Lewis, *The Emergence
of Modern Turkey* (London: Oxford University Press, 1961).

Latin American cases are exciting, by and large, because of the strong
personalities and passions that have traditionally operated. An interesting feature
of much of the literature, if taken compositely, comparatively, and over time, is
just how much *regularity* there is in the apparently chaotic behavioral patterns.
A concise summary of the Mexican sequence of events is Martin C. Needler,
"The Political Development of Mexico," *American Political Science Review,*
Vol. 55 (June 1961), pp. 308–12; Howard F. Cline, *Mexico: Revolution to
Evolution: 1940-1960* (New York: Oxford University Press, 1963), ably illustrates many substantive points and in so doing lends evidence to our observations
on the selectivity and interpretive limitations of standard trend-based work; an-
other fine and insightful political-historical description is Robert Gilmore, *Caudillism and Militarism in Venezuela, 1810-1910* (Athens, Ohio: Ohio University
Press, 1964); however, compare Gilmore in style, purpose, and content with

Alfred C. Stepan III, *The Military in Politics: Changing Patterns in Brazil* (Princeton: Princeton University Press, 1971).

It is instructive to review the broad historical development of the world's two super powers to see what events and sequences operated in two "successful" cases. Although a number of excellent works on the Soviet Union could be cited, we find Frederick C. Barghoorn, *Politics in the U.S.S.R.: A Country Study* (Boston: Little, Brown, 1966), Chapters 5, 7, 8, and 10, to be understandable and valuable as a point of departure; Seymour M. Lipset, *The First New Nation: The United States in Historical and Comparative Perspective* (New York: Basic Books, 1963), is a solid political history that is profitably read in conjunction with Frederick Jackson Turner, *The Frontier in American History*; and James Sterling Young, *The Washington Community, 1800–1828.*

Besides organizing the relevant scholarship according to spatial or national criteria, one could just as easily focus primarily on institutions; indeed, many of the works already cited easily lend themselves to this kind of categorization. To expand on this concept, one might consider trend-based work that favors a single institutional evolution, a general class's impact on development in a context, or the specific imprint left by a single individual.

Institutions are well developed in Myron Weiner, *Party Politics in India* (Princeton: Princeton University Press, 1964); another well-developed case description is contained in Joseph LaPalombara, *Interest Groups in Italian Politics* (Princeton: Princeton University Press, 1964). The bureaucracy has been the institutional focus of a number of commendable political-historical analyses, particularly of those nations that came from a strong British colonial tradition. See Robert O. Tilman, *Bureaucratic Transition in Malaya* (Durham, N.C.: Duke University Press, 1964), for an outstanding illustration of the genre; Morroe Berger, *Bureaucracy and Society in Modern Egypt* (Princeton: Princeton University Press, 1957); and Walter Sharp, *The French Civil Service: Bureaucracy in Transition* (New York: Macmillan, 1931). The military and the indigenous communist party, institutions of more widespread interest, clashed resoundingly in Indonesia in the late 1960's; Jerome R. Bass, "The PKI and the Attempted Coup," *Journal of Southeast Asian Studies*, Vol. 1 (March 1970), pp. 96–105, tells the tale in easy-to-follow time steps; it is quite interesting to read Bass's relatively compressed accounting of events along with Daniel S. Lev, "The Political Role of the Army in Indonesia," *Pacific Affairs*, Vol. 36 (Winter 1963–64), pp. 349–64, where the relevant elements are identified and several plausible sequential patterns are sketched out. The military has of course served as the center of institutional interest in many trend-based studies; good ones include Davis B. Bobrow, "Political and Economic Role of the Military in the Chinese Communist Movement, 1927–1959" (Unpublished Ph.D. dissertation, The Massachusetts Institute of Technology, 1962); Richard D. Robinson, *The First Turkish Republic: A Case Study in National Development* (Cambridge, Mass.: Harvard University Press, 1965); and for a much more tightly focused sequel, Walter F. Weiker, *The Turkish Revolution, 1960-1961:*

Aspects of Military Politics (Washington, D.C.: The Brookings Institution, 1963). An interesting case study that traces tribal institutions in a period of rapid change is David E. Apter, *The Gold Coast in Transition* (Princeton: Princeton University Press, 1955).

Historical works organized around class distinctions are not as common as the more straightforward institutional case study, although examples can be cited. David E. Apter, "Some Reflections on the Role of a Political Opposition in New Nations," *Comparative Studies in Society and History*, Vol. 4 (January 1962), pp. 154–68, is a place to start. Taking intellectuals as a class, Edward A. Shils spoke well of their historical importance and potential in the new states in "The Intellectual in the Political Development of the New States," *World Politics*, Vol. 12 (April 1960), pp. 329–68. Several citations have been made to the evolution of the Chinese Communist movement; however, William A. Whitson takes a forty-year frame of reference to describe the make-up and "play of the game" at the topmost levels, *The Chinese Communist High Command, 1928-1969: A Study of Military Politics* (New York: Praeger, 1970); quite parallel efforts, albeit drawn with larger brushes, are Philip Woodruff, *The Men Who Ruled India* (New York: St. Martin's Press, 1954); and Marc Raeff, "The Russian Autocracy and Its Officials," in H. McLean et al., *Russian Thought and Politics* (Cambridge, Mass.: Harvard University Slavic Studies Series #4, 1957). Remarkable expositions of the prevalent patterns of the traditional Turkish and Ecuadorian elite political games are contained in Frederick A. Frey, *The Turkish Political Elite* (Cambridge, Mass.: The MIT Press, 1965); and Martin C. Needler, *Anatomy of a Coup d'État: Ecuador 1963* (Washington, D.C.: Institute for the Comparative Study of Political Systems, 1964); the critical point to observe is how approximately comparable general information is treated when one uses an extended (Frey) versus a very contracted (Needler) level of temporal resolution.

The individual level is frequently expressed in political biographies of significant or even "great" men. A general assumption underlying the work is that nations do not make history, individual people do. Here, too it is impractical to cite exhaustively; however, a few solid examples are easily brought to mind. Eric H. Erikson's *Young Man Luther* has been roundly and deservedly praised; nonetheless, the several limitations of the approach are concisely (even brutally) summarized in Donald Meyer, "A Review of Young Man Luther," in B. Mazlish, ed., *Psychoanalysis and History* (Englewood Cliffs, N.J.: Prentice-Hall, 1963); this entire volume deserves more serious attention than political and policy scientists have heretofore given it. Another well-known and careful illustration of a trend-based but rigorous, political biography is Alexander and Juliette George, *Woodrow Wilson and Colonel House: A Personality Study* (New York: John Day, 1956); Vasily Klyuchevsky, *Peter the Great,* Archibald trans. (London: Macmillan, 1958), is fascinating, but conventional; perhaps one of the best known individual level political development works of all is Lucian W. Pye, *Politics, Personality, and Nation Building: Burma's Search for Identity* (New Haven: Yale University Press, 1962).

We have been concerned with determining how the world came to be what it presently is. This has meant browsing the historically biased corpus of scholarship to find out what it is that trend specialists routinely do and, more important, do not do. The importance of interpretive limitations caused by data availability and the historian's penchant for detailing but one sequence of events from among a much greater manifold was noted, and pertinent bibliographic references were provided. The strengths of trend-based studies, given our postulated policy interests, were several and included the explicit consideration of the selection process which operates to emphasize elements and to order them sequentially. In fact, the critical temporal dimension, commonly missing from more "scientifically" oriented social science, is perhaps the greatest single contribution of the trend specialist. It is a factor used to great and interesting advantage in Gilbert Merkx's contribution to this volume.

ECONOMICS AND HISTORY IN THE STUDY OF REBELLIONS: THE ARGENTINE CASE

Gilbert Merkx takes an unconventional position for a "regular" historian, which he is not, and returns to the basic empirical-behavioral foundations of Argentine political and economic events to understand the process of rebellions and coups d'etat. By simply respecifying the structure and greatly expanding the temporal resolution underlying his analytic model, he is able to discern rather distinct patterns in the behavioral cycles characterizing the context. In so doing, Merkx discredits the conventional wisdom which holds Argentine political fortunes to be enigmatic at best, and pathological at worst.

The Question

To understand trends predating current aggregate Argentine political behavior, the general questions Merkx poses are, approximately: What systematic relationships exist between long swings in economic and political cycles; what are the characteristic amplitude, period, and phase of each; and how are these three characteristics changing through time?

The Strengths

A most striking feature of Merkx's work is the way in which he adjusts the temporal resolution of the context to obtain a more satisfactory explanation of events. The importance of the time dimension in all development-based and development-oriented studies is resoundingly underscored.

By collecting richer, more detailed economic and political data, whose limitations may be assessed and whose importance was previously not well, nor widely, known, Merkx contributes to our general knowledge of Argentine politics. He also demonstrates the importance of working with a context from multiple perspectives, temporal in this case.

The impact of graphical displays of research results is driven home in this chapter. Until presented with a "picture" of the major arguments, the average reader is hard put to make much sense of the findings. One simple picture drastically and dramatically changes all of this. There is a very critical message here for those interested in communicating with a policymaking audience.

Hypothesis testing is a rather heretical thing for a conventional historian to do, but the chapter points out convincingly why one must move from straight descriptions of trends through hypothesis testing and other scientific efforts to explain conditioning factors, and on to projective, or forecasting, endeavors. All three habits of problem-solving thought are evident.

The Weaknesses

However, Merkx does not go far enough in this regard. While goals, both his and those constraining behavior in the context, are implicit or lightly touched upon, alternatives or policy recommendations are essentially ignored. One learns very little about how the cycles might be altered or their deleterious effects lessened. Thresholds beyond which the well-established patterns are not likely to transgress without doing permanent structural harm are also not mentioned. For example, how short can a coup cycle become (period) before chronic chaos ensues and fundamental changes have to be instituted? How great can an up or down (amplitude) cycle be before irreversible structural discontinuities occur? Or, how far out of kilter (phase) can economic and political cycles be before the rules of this special political game are irrevocably changed?

In fact, Merkx has gotten excellent mileage out of a very simply specified model. For historians, it is doubtless too simple, too general; and for social scientists, it may not be general enough—a more or less open issue because no comparative evidence is presented; in fact, the work is yet to be done.

Subsequent Developments

Other long-run, contextual, empirical political histories are required to begin resolving this last weakness. Given current predilections among historians and social scientists, the work may be a long time coming; and, in our view, that is a particular pity.

Better, more easy to use time-series data management techniques are needed to support this and related research. We are unable, given the variety of data sources, unevenness of data quality, and number of these types to manipuplate the basic information dredged up in this research. It would be particularly useful, for instance, to run a wholesale sensitivity analysis on the single model Merkx specifies to determine the relative importance of parameters governing dominant cycles. In which parameters do small adjustments provoke larger variations in amplitude or period and shifts in phase? Are they amenable to policy manipulation? If so, at what costs? With better data management it might also be possible to respecify the one model presented. Are there more persuasive or more economical structural configurations capable of reproducing the observed behavior? If so, what accounts for the differences? We are still some distance removed from being able to sensitivity analyze or respecify with economy and ease; however, these objectives are persuasively evident.

SUPPORTERS OF THE NEW PARTY OF THE RIGHT: A REPORT AND DISCUSSION OF THE GERMAN NDP'S SOURCES OF SUPPORT

The Question

The basic research questions raised by Klaus Liepelt in this clear example of applied survey research are trend related in so far as short-run phenomena are being explained with respect to the historical antecedents and prior empirical patterns or configurations as determined by surveys and historical case materials. As compared with Merkx's contribution, this chapter uses a very narrowly focused level of temporal resolution to determine where and under what socioeconomic conditions voter support for the NPD—an ultra-rightist party—can be expected.

The Strengths

The main strength of the chapter is the clear and powerful use it makes of sophisticated survey research techniques in an effort to answer the serious operational questions of where and under what conditions will what segments of the electorate be expected to support ultra conservative parties such as the NPD? This is important strategically because of international concern over the resurgence of Nazism; it is even more pressing from a tactical point of view, given the very narrow margins that traditionally separate winners from losers in Federal Republic elections.

This is an example of a serious piece of policy analysis. The responsible agency, Infas, depends for its existence on the reliability of forecasts generated by surveys such as those reported in this study.[6] It is a rare example of survey research at a very fine level of spatial detail. In fact, while the numbers generated

[6] The Institute for Applied Social Science, Infas, Bonn–Bad Godesberg, has nearly fifteen years' worth of public opinion surveys in its collection. Very little secondary or detailed reanalysis has been carried out on this considerable information stockpile. (For an exception, see Chapter 14 of this volume.)

in the survey are only a small portion of the total electorate, the political importance of the general problem—the likelihood of a neo-Nazi movement—meant that statistical niceties had to be set slightly to one side. This illustrates a very nice example of a case where the policy importance far outstrips the quality and reliability of the data, but where some information, however partial or incomplete, is better than none at all, ignoring the problem, or speculating idly about it. In this case at least, data of three distinct quality levels have been used: "hard" economic and demographic indicators, somewhat "softer" opinion data, and symbolic information gleaned from the media. These different kinds of numbers are moderated and interpreted by one who is extremely knowledgeable and sophisticated in the practical ins and outs of German politics. In effect, this is an illustration of a rare blending of data sense and common sense in the best interests of policy analysis.

Another strength of the chapter is the valuable lesson it provides us in how to go about studying minority parties, an important lesson for almost all national contexts.

The Weaknesses

Besides the various caveats listed in the author's opening disclaimer, there are several weaknesses that must be called to the reader's attention.

The most severe limitation is the methodological one of pushing and interpreting well beyond the capabilities of the data. This point has been discussed as a strength, and it is, from a policy point of view. However, it is simultaneously a weakness, from a scientific point of view. Required are continuing surveys, and surveys to sharpen the configurations that have been described and to test the adequacy of the initial formulations. Longitudinal analysis is very much needed of the times rates of change of many of the key indicators discussed in the study.

A second weakness is that the chapter is somewhat dated, The NPD "threat" of the 1960's has not yet materialized, although the potential for mobilization remains. In other words, the problem has submerged, but it remains a live issue as to under what conditions and where will the NPD resurface and become an effective political force?

Subsequent Developments

It is evident from the chapter and from our introductory discussion that much careful monitoring of the German political context is called for to sense when and if the NPD resurfaces. Such empirical investigations should in turn be linked to serious assessments of the effect such a reemergence might have for the majority parties. For instance, what might happen if the NPD gains sufficient support to swing a vote through coalition formation to one or the other of the major parties? Would coalition formation be the dominant mode of accommodation, or would one or both of the major parties elect to adopt a more conservative stance in hopes of attracting potential NPD supporters? If a conservative shift occurs, what would the implications be for foreign relations? If coalitions are formed, what would be the impact on democratic practices in the Federal Republic? What other creative possibilities exist to cope with a resurgent ultra rightist shift in political sentiment? If such a shift occurs, regardless of the political tactics adopted to manage it, what would be the effects on the German military, Germany's place in various economic and power alliances, and on Ostpolitik—to cite only three obvious concerns?

Chapter 2
Economics and History in the Study of Rebellions: The Argentine Case

GILBERT W. MERKX

Highlighting important differences between cross-sectional and longitudinal analyses in trying to unravel the "enigma" of Argentine sociopolitical behavior, this chapter presents economic and political data for one hundred years of Argentina's development, organizes the data into cyclical patterns, and finds routine where mostly chaos had been discernible before. It is shown, for example, that in "prosperous" years (economic indicators improve over previous year), 15% of the reported armed rebellions in the 1870–1970 period occurred, as compared with 39% in "downturn" years (when growth stops and decline sets in), 42% for "poor" years (indicators worsen over previous year) and only 4% for "upturn" years (decline stops and growth begins). Additional analyses indicate further the nature and extent of the relationships between economic and political instability. Much of the analysis helps us to understand some of the underlying mechanisms in large part explaining the "Permanent Crisis" in post-Peron Argentina.

The philosopher Ludwig Wittgenstein argued in his famous *Tractatus Logico-Philosophicus* that reality has a logical structure, and that whatever is sensible about language stems from the degree to which the logic of language pictures the logic of reality.[1] Everything else in language he asserted, is nonsense. He concluded that most of the debates among philosophers were meaningless, since they had no contact with reality. Wittgenstein's suspicions about the high degree of nonsense in language have been shared by almost all those who spend a good deal of time in academic circles.

Wittgenstein later came to adopt a less extreme position, recognizing that there are other kinds of meaning in language besides the picturing of reality. These meanings depend upon the context of usage, or language game, being played. Such an expanded vision of the sensibility of language was applied by Thomas Kuhn in *The Structure of Scientific Revolutions:* the languages or conceptualizations of scientists depend upon the current "paradigm" or game

---

[1] Ludwig Wittgenstein, *Tractatus Logico-Philosophicus* (London: Routledge and Kegan Paul, 1922, new trans. 1961).

that dominates a scientific community.[2] Thus, the languages scientists use vary over time, within and between disciplines.

While epistemological issues seem esoteric, they are important for the everyday work of social science. The proximity of social scientists to rich, relatively diffuse subject matter leads naturally to a wider variety of perspectives —to more competing paradigms—than are found in the natural sciences. This diversity can appear a paradigmatic Babel to the casual onlooker and active participant alike.

Yet not all perspectives are equally valid. When we think about validity it is useful to return to Wittgenstein's original formulation: The meaningfulness of a theory depends upon the degree to which it is able to reproduce the logical structure of reality. This is a very special kind of validity, not to be confused with a theory's internal elegance or current popularity.

If we are willing to make a commitment to a reality-based validity, then the starting point, as well as the final object, of a theory must be reality itself. This presents a very practical issue: How do we begin to gain insight into the structure of a process or phenomenon?

This chapter presents the history of one such attempt to make sense of reality. Out of this experience came certain methodological insights that may be valuable enough to pass along for the benefit of others.

POLITICAL DEVELOPMENT: PROBLEMS OF THEORY AND METHOD

Students of political development often concern themselves with subject areas or regional contexts well before they bother to learn organizing concepts or theory. Commitment to a set of practical problems frequently exceeds commitment to any existing paradigm.

In the early 1960's, the existing cross-national studies of Lipset, Cutright, Alker, Russett, and others provided an explicit method and implied a specific theory. Lipset's famous statement sums up much of that theory: "The more well-to-do a nation, the greater the chance that it will sustain democracy." [3] The thrust of this assertion led many scholars to dig into United Nations statistics, draw scattergrams, and run multiple correlations comparing nations on different indicators of economic development or political practice.

Nagging doubts continued to persist, however, for the theory did not provide many satisfactory interpretations of reality in specific contexts. The gap between empirical reality in Latin America (and elsewhere) and the kinds of available comparative data seemed unbridgeable. Popular theoretical generalizations based upon these data generated considerable scorn among intellectuals

[2] Thomas S. Kuhn, *The Structure of Scientific Revolutions* (Chicago: University of Chicago Press, 1962).

[3] Seymour Martin Lipset, *Political Man* (Garden City, N.Y.: Anchor Books, 1963), p. 31.

of the "developing world." The U.S. State Department nevertheless financed economic and political development, "Hearts and Minds" programs, the world over, and editors of prestigious academic journals persisted in publishing nearly all quantitative work dealing with the developing nations. But criticism of the superficiality of much cross-national data continued to rise, and was nicely articulated by Arnold Feldman's declaration that American social science needed fewer data banks and more data garbage dumps.[4]

From this adverse reaction to the quantitative cross-national studies, one key observation about the social world began to emerge. Most cross-national studies used recent data for the simple reason that the existence of cross-national data is a relatively recent occurrence. Political development is by definition a time-dependent or historical process; however, most comparative studies attempted to generalize that dynamic process from static data measured at a single point in time.

The tacit operational assumption made was that any given cross-sectional sample pictured a snapshot of different nations caught in different moments of a common and general growth process. This might be termed "the genetic fallacy." Some nations were supposed to be adults, some teenagers, some children, but all were seen as going through the same process of maturation. But what if this simple assumption is rejected? One logical alternative might be that different types of nations are like different species undergoing different patterns of growth. If this were the case, studies of development should perhaps focus upon the differences between paths of change, rather than upon their similarities. The fact that certain variables may be related at a given moment in a population of nations need not mean that these variables will be related in the history or growth process of the individual nations making up that population.[5]

What the early cross-national studies did present was some information about the typicality of certain relationships between characteristics of nations in the post–World War II period. The repeated occurrence of deviant or atypical cases, however, presented special problems of explanation to development theorists when they attempted to generalize from *the pattern found in cross-national data* to *the process operating in individual countries*.[6]

Gradually a different methodological possibility has begun to emerge. Lip-

---

[4] Comment by Arnold Feldman on a paper given at the first annual meeting of the Latin American Studies Association, New York City, 1969.

[5] The correlation coefficient and other descriptive statistics refer to the sample, not to the individual members of the sample. Statistics is a way of diverting attention from individual cases. An alternative explanation for correlations between indices of development which has not received much attention in the literature is that such correlations simply describe international patterns of stratification in the post–World War II period. They may picture a class system of nations, in which the rich, or upper-class, nations impose certain configurations of politics and economics upon their poorer, or lower-class, neighbors, either directly or through the world market. Should this be the case, it would hardly be possible to argue that this pattern of stratification represents the growth pattern of each nation (any more than a country's class system represents the social mobility pattern of each citizen).

[6] Ronald D. Brunner and Garry D. Brewer, *Organized Complexity: Empirical Theories of Political Development* (New York: The Free Press, 1971), p. 4ff.

set himself has pointed out that the comparative method is not restricted to static cross-sectional analysis of several entities.[7] One can also compare differing states of the same entity as it passes through time, i.e., historical or time-series analysis. This approach allows one to focus attention on specific causal patterns in specific contexts: present events may be influenced by prior events, but not by subsequent events.

Historical analysis also makes it possible to focus data collection efforts intensively upon a single country. Cross-sectional studies are limited in a practical way by the availability of existing data. By the time that numerous collections of national statistics are ransacked, studies often end up with data that poorly describe nations in the sample, in addition to which confidence in the validity and reliability of data sources begins to deteriorate. In contrast, historical analysis favors the assembly of richer, more detailed data whose limitations can be assessed.

Having such issues in mind, and having field experience in Latin America, I decided to undertake a historical analysis of the political development of a single Latin American nation. A preliminary examination of available data for different countries narrowed the range of possible contexts by suggesting that the best historical statistics were available for Argentina and Mexico. Argentina was chosen because its domestic politics seemed less influenced by proximity and war with the United States.

The next step was to develop a general image of the major structural changes characterizing Argentine society and politics, by the straightforward method of reading history books. All types of historical accounts were examined: conservative histories, Marxist histories, and liberal histories. Works written from different perspectives were purposely selected in order to develop as complete a picture as possible of the basic changes which all the works were trying to interpret.

During this initial stage, data sources were not examined intensively, rather searching was done broadly to find out what *kinds* of data existed. For example, the various national and local censuses, bank reports, Central Bank statistics, yearbooks of different statistical offices, materials from the business community and the labor movements, indices from Argentine scholarly journals, basic reference works of social research, and the local press were all consulted to varying degrees. The process of immersion into the local context at first seemed overwhelming, but after a while it became rare that new types of basic data would surface. There evolved a more or less comfortable sense that a working knowledge of the major Argentine data sources had been attained.

These background processes took about one year, a period that might have been considerably shortened if full-time attention had been given to these efforts.

---

[7] Seymour Martin Lipset, *Union Democracy* (Garden City, N.Y.: Anchor Books, 1962), p. 479.

METHODS

Getting a Toehold: Preliminary Variables

To explain or understand a phenomenon, one might treat it as a dependent variable. Calling it "dependent" does not mean that it is without impact, but simply that, for analytical purposes, it will allow one to examine the antecedents and context of a phenomenon. For Argentine political development, selecting a single dependent variable was an easy step.

Histories of Argentina stress one point: the Revolution of 1930 marked a turning point in Argentine political development. During the fifty years prior to the Revolution of 1930, there was not a single successful rebellion against the central government, and national politics were characterized by civilian leadership and the regular constitutional change of presidents.[8] In contrast, since 1930 no civilian elected to the presidency has successfully completed a full term of office.

Armed rebellion against the central government serves as a useful dependent variable. It is a *nominal* variable: either there is or there is not an armed rebellion underway; consensus on the matter is matter-of-fact.[9] Rebellions are important for many reasons, not the least of which is the discontinuity they cause in existing rules of political behavior. If disputes over economic or social policy lead to a rejection of the existing political rules, they may result in ideological struggles over the nature of the political system itself. Hence, rebellion seemed a good starting point from which to examine political change.

Rebellions had indeed existed in Argentina before the Revolution of 1930, even if they were unsuccessful in seizing the national government.[10] Taking 1870 as a starting point (the year following the first national census), eight instances of armed rebellion were reported prior to 1930. From 1930 until 1966 an additional 17 rebellions took place, making a total of 25. These are listed chronologically in Table 2–1.

The general state of economic activity seemed an obvious independent or explanatory variable. Most cross-national studies had, of course, found some relationship between levels of economic and political activity, however spurious.

[8] The lack of success refers to the fact that no revolutionary group took over the government between 1870 and 1930. The Revolution of 1890 was a partial success inasmuch as it led directly to the resignation of President Juarez Celman; however, the government remained in the hands of the ruling party.

[9] The criterion defining the existence of a rebellion was the use of weapons against federal troops (plots are not included). One rebellion in our list took place without the use of weapons: the October 17, 1945, occupation of downtown Buenos Aires by Peronist workers. This was considered to be a rebellion because it would have involved armed conflict had not the army hesitated at the prospect of mass bloodshed.

[10] There are numerous treatments of these rebellions by Argentine historians. Among the most useful are those by Juan Alvarez, *Las guerras civiles argentinas* (Buenos Aires: Editorial la Facultad, 1936); and Jorge Abelardo Ramos, *Revolución y contrarrevolución en la Argentina* (Buenos Aires: La Reja, 1961).

TABLE 2–1.   ARMED REBELLIONS AGAINST THE ARGENTINE
GOVERNMENT, 1870–1970

Year	Identifying Leader[a]	Year	Identifying Leader[a]
1870	López Jordán	1943	Rawson
1873	Mitre	1945 (Sept.)	Rawson
1874	Mitre	1945 (Oct.)	Perón
1876	López Jordán	1951	Menéndez
1880	Mitre	1955 (June)	Olivieri
1890	Alem	1955 (Sept.)	Lonardi
1893	Yrigoyen	1956	Valle
1905	Yrigoyen	1959	Ossorio Arana
1930	Uriburu	1960	Giovannoni
1931 (Feb.)	Toranzo	1962	Poggi
1932 (July)	Pomar	1963	Menéndez
1932 (Jan.)	Kennedy	1966	Onganía
1932 (Dec.)	Cattanéo	1970	Levingston

a The identifying leader is not necessarily the major leader or the only leader, but the man whose name is most commonly identified with the rebellion in question.

The literature about revolution devotes considerable attention to the contrasting political-economic positions: (1) the argument implied by Marx in the *Communist Manifesto* that misery leads to rebellion ("You have nothing to lose but your chains"); and (2) de Tocqueville's view that revolution reflects the rising expectations of better times ("The French found their condition the more insupportable in proportion to its improvement").[11]

In the case of the French Revolution, a gradual consensus has emerged to the effect that Marx and de Tocqueville were both right.[12] The French Revolution followed several decades of prosperity, but it was immediately preceded by intense depression and acute inflation which produced major social distress. James C. Davies has argued that a similar combination of events led up to both the Russian Revolution of 1917 and the Egyptian Revolution of 1952.[13] Davies suggests that: "Revolutions are most likely to occur when a prolonged period of objective economic and social development is followed by a period of sharp reversal." [14]

Thanks to the early start made by the Argentine government to collect trade and budgetary statistics, the nature of economic activity during the period 1870–1966 could be easily estimated. For the period 1870–1900 per capita

[11] Alexis de Tocqueville, *The Old Regime and the French Revolution* (New York: Harper and Brothers, 1856), p. 214.
[12] The debate over the French Revolution has been summarized by Ralph W. Greenlaw, ed., *The Economic Origins of the French Revolution: Poverty or Prosperity?* (Boston: Heath, 1958).
[13] James C. Davies, "Towards a Theory of Revolution," *American Sociological Review*, Vol. 27, No. 1, pp. 5–18.
[14] *Ibid.*, p. 5.

imports in gold pesos served as an index of economic conditions.[15] For the period 1900–1945 the United Nations Economic Commission for Latin America (ECLA) estimates of Argentine Gross Domestic Product (GDP) per capita were used. Subsequently similar figures from the Argentine Central Bank were used.[16]

The data were used to classify each year as one of four types, as illustrated in Figure 2–1: (1) *prosperous years* (when indicators improve over the previous year); (2) *downturn years* (a year in which growth stops and decline begins); (3) *poor years* (when indicators drop to less than the preceding year); and

FIGURE 2-1. TYPES OF YEARS IN AN
ECONOMIC CYCLE[a]

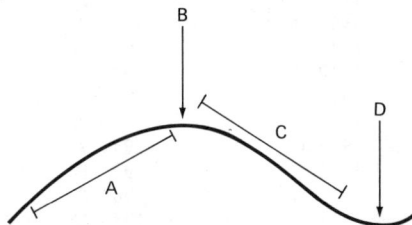

[a] A: Prosperous years. B: Downturn years. C: Poor years. D: Upturn years.

(4) *upturn years* (in which a decline stops and growth begins). Table 2–2 shows how each year is classified. Upturn and downturn years were singled out for their special significance. Thus, in 1929 Argentina's overall product was even higher than in 1928, but the crisis of 1929 completely altered the optimism of the previous year. Likewise, the upturn which began in 1933 made that year seem much better than 1932, even though gross production was about the same.

The distribution of rebellions across these four types of years is presented in Table 2–3. The findings are quite interesting: 81% of all rebellions occurred during downturn and poor years, even though these constituted only 44% of all years. Only one rebellion occurred during an upturn year, with four rebel-

[15] Import figures appear to be the best available measure of economic activity in the years before GDP estimates are available. There are three reasons: (1) For the period 1900–1930, when GDP and import–export figures are both available, the import figures show a far better year-by-year fit with GDP than do export figures. (2) Throughout most of the 1870–1900 period, Argentina was a capital-importing nation which maintained a continuous large surplus of imports over exports. (3) The impact of changes in the quantum of imports had an immediate effect upon the level of living in Argentina (which then imported most manufactures), whereas fluctuations in exports had a delayed effect of over a year or more.

[16] Figures were put in *per capita* form to control for variations in population size, which fluctuated remarkably during the years of massive immigration. The data reported in this section also appear in Merkx, "Recessions and Rebellions in Argentina, 1870–1970," *The Hispanic American Historical Review*, Vol. 53, No. 2 (May 1973), pp. 285–95.

TABLE 2–2.   ECONOMIC CONDITIONS IN ARGENTINA, 1870–1970[a]

1870 C	1896 D	1922 A	1948 A[c]
1871 C	1897 B	1923 A	1949 B
1872 D	1898 C[b]	1924 A	1950 C
1873 A	1899 C[b]	1925 B	1951 C[c]
1874 B	1900 C	1926 D	1952 C
1875 C	1901 C[b]	1927 A	1953 D
1876 C	1902 C	1928 A	1954 A
1877 C[b]	1903 D	1929 A	1955 A
1878 C[b]	1904 A	1930 B	1956 B
1879 C[b]	1905 A	1931 C	1957 D
1880 C	1906 A	1932 C	1958 A
1881 D	1907 B	1933 D	1959 B
1882 A	1908 D	1934 A	1960 D
1883 A	1909 A[c]	1935 A	1961 A
1884 A	1910 A	1936 A[c]	1962 B
1885 A[c]	1911 A[c]	1937 A	1963 C
1886 A	1912 A	1938 A[c]	1964 D
1887 A	1913 B	1939 A	1965 A
1888 A	1914 C	1940 A	1966 B
1889 A	1915 C	1941 A	1967 D
1890 B	1916 C	1942 B	1968 A
1891 C	1917 C	1943 C	1969 A
1892 C[b]	1918 D	1944 D	1970 B
1893 C[b]	1919 A	1945 B	
1894 C	1920 A	1946 D	
1895 C[b]	1921 A[c]	1947 A	

[a] A: Prosperous years. B: Downturn years. C: Poor years. D: Upturn years.

[b] Per capita imports or per capita Gross Domestic Product increased slightly, but not sufficiently to be considered an upturn.

[c] Per capita imports or per capita Gross Domestic Product decreased slightly, but not sufficiently to be considered a downturn.

lions occurring during prosperous years. There is even a possibility that three of the four rebellions occurring in prosperous years (one in 1873 and two in 1955) may actually have been linked to downturns, for the succeeding years (1874 and 1956) were years of sharp recessions which may have begun the year before without actually being reflected in the annual data.

The next question is *when* in the economic cycle did the rebellions occur? The Davies hypothesis suggests that the rebellion, if it does not occur in the

TABLE 2–3.   ECONOMIC CONDITIONS IN WHICH REBELLIONS OCCUR

	% of All Rebellions	% of All Years
Prosperous years	15% (4)	42% (42)
Downturn years	39% (10)	15% (15)
Poor years	42% (11)	29% (29)
Upturn years	4% (1)	15% (15)
	100%	101%[a]

[a] Adds up to 101% due to rounding.

year of downturn itself, should occur in the earlier, rather than the later, years of the recession. To test this hypothesis, rebellions were classified into four groups, depending upon whether they occurred in the early or late part of an expansion or contraction. *Early* was considered to be the year of upturn (or downturn) and the first two years of a subsequent expansion (or contraction); other years were considered *late* in the cycle.[17]

The findings presented in Table 2–4 offer strong support for the hypothesis that rebellions occur in the first part of an economic downturn, since 73% of the rebellions in Argentina have taken place at such a time. No rebellions took place late in an expansion. Of the five rebellions occurring during an early period of upturn, only one did not immediately precede or follow a sharp downturn, to which it may have been linked. *Rebellions in Argentina are associated historically with economic contractions, and tend to occur within two years of a downturn.*

TABLE 2–4.   THE LOCATION OF REBELLIONS IN ECONOMIC CYCLES

	% of All Rebellions	% of All Years
Year of upturn and first two years of prosperity	19% (5)	37% (37)
Later in an expansion	0% (0)	20% (20)
Year of downturn and first two years of contraction[a]	73% (19)	31% (31)
Later in a contraction	8% (2)	13% (13)
	100%	101%

a Includes 1943, 1945, 1956, 1960, and 1963.

These findings strongly suggest that if rebellions are linked to economic cycles in time, then the frequency of rebellions should be related to the frequency of economic fluctuations. This was tested by dividing the period 1870–1966 into three parts which correspond approximately to the three major divisions of modern Argentine economic history: (1) the period of export agriculture (1870–1929); (2) the period of economic transition (1930–1944); and (3) the period of import-substitution manufacturing (1945–66).[18] The length of the Argentine economic cycle grew shorter with each period. One

[17] This definition of early and late tends to overrepresent early years, given the instability of the Argentine economy, in which the *average* length of a half-cycle (a period of expansion or contraction) is only 3.4 years. However, some expansions or contractions were much larger: there were eight half-cycles lasting between 5 and 9 years.

[18] This breakdown of Argentine economic history has been made by a number of scholars, including Carlos F. Díaz-Alejandro, *Essays on the Argentine Economy* (New Haven: Yale University Press, 1971); Aldo Ferrer, *La Economía Argentina* (México: Fondo de Cultura Económica, 1963); Leopoldo Portnoy, *Análisis Crítico de la Economía* (Buenos Aires: Fondo de Cultura Económica, 1961); Arthur P. Whitaker, *Argentina* (Englewood Cliffs, N.J.: Prentice-Hall, 1964).

would expect that rebellions would also grow more frequent. The results are pictured in Table 2–5.

TABLE 2–5.   LENGTH OF CYCLES AND TIME BETWEEN REBELLIONS

Period	Total Years	Number of Downturns	Number of Rebellions	Aver. Length of Half-cycle (years)	Aver. Time between Rebellions (years)
1870–1929	60	6	8	5.0	7.5
1930–1944	15	2	6	3.8	2.5
1945–1970	26	7	12	1.9	2.2

The data in Table 2–5 do not indicate that every downturn led to a rebellion; however, the frequency of rebellions was related to that of downturns. Political instability appears to be strongly associated with economic instability in the Argentine case. The number of rebellions per downturn increased from an average of slightly more than one during the first period to about two during the last two periods. The extent of the relationship between increasing economic fluctuation and increasing rebellion is emphasized by the second part of Table 2–5, which compares the length of half-cycles (periods of expansion or contraction) with the time between rebellions.

This finding is particularly intriguing in view of the marked political instability that characterized Argentina during the last fifteen years. Lipset's observation that "the more well-to-do a nation, the greater the chance that it will sustain democracy." [19] seemed to be contradicted by the fact that Argentina has become more unstable politically as it has developed economically.[20] An explanation of this phenomenon seems to be related to the fact that the Argentine economy became more unstable at the same time that it became more developed.

Two broad methodological conclusions emerge from the data thus far presented. The first is that economic cycles and their relationship to the timing of political upheaval warrant explicit consideration. The second is that the nature of this relationship between economic and political events may alter through time, suggesting that a long time focus can be useful in establishing the direction of change.

Widening the Perspective

Having discovered systematic relationships between economic conditions and rebellions, two research strategies were suggested: (1) refine the time-series

[19] Lipset, Loc. cit.
[20] John Gunther's discussion of Argentina in his recent Inside South America (New York: Harper & Row, 1967), demonstrates a puzzlement typical of many observers who are surprised that Argentine development has not led to stable parliamentary democracy.

analysis by applying more rigorous techniques; or (2) deepen the analysis by studying intervening or linkage veriables and by taking a broader look at the economy and politics. The second approach was chosen.

There were several reasons for this choice. The simple time-series relationships that had been found hardly exhausted the possibilities for data analysis. Unfortunately, the data were uneven and certainly too crude given the rigorous demands of the available analytical techniques. Furthermore, such analyses did not appear to contribute much to understanding the rich detail of general structural change in Argentina.

The second strategy offered the possibility of suggesting *why* cycles and rebellions were linked in time. By studying such events in a more detailed social context, causal relationships between cycles and rebellions might emerge. The study also could move beyond the narrowly defined variables already treated to the overall context of political and social change.

A closer reexamination of economic and political history clearly indicated periods of distinct economic and political structure. Regardless of theoretical or ideological persuasion, economic historians described identical periods of economic activity; political and social historians agreed on periods of political structure. Although there were occasional disagreements (plus or minus a year or two) about the precise beginning of a new political or economic period, there was general agreement on the chief features and timing of periods. These are presented in Table 2–6 with my own summary labels.

TABLE 2–6. PERIODS OF ARGENTINE POLITICAL AND ECONOMIC HISTORY

Political Periods	*Economic Periods*
1. Colonial Period (to 1810)	Illegal exports (to 1810)
2. Unitarism versus Federalism (1810–52)	Economic instability (1810–52)
3. Aristocratic Liberalism (1852–1916)	Foreign investment and export expansion (1852–1914)
4. Middle-class Liberalism (the Radical Governments, 1916–30)	Economic stagnation (1914–29)
5. Conservative Reaction (the Patriotic Fraud, 1930–45)	Economic transition and industrialization (1929–45)
6. Peronism (1945–55)	Closing the economy (1945–55)
7. The Permanent Crisis (1955–70)	Economic stagnation with stop–go cycles (1955–70)

The logic of the political periods was fairly obvious: each referred to a different period of government characterized by different ruling groups, different policies, and different political practices. But what of the economic periods? Did they exist and just how were they related to the political changes?

These questions were answered by a careful collection and examination of economic evidence. Graphing time-series data was particularly helpful. It was not particularly difficult to document the transitions which Argentine writers

FIGURE 2-2. THE GROWTH OF ECONOMIC FACTORS IN
ARGENTINA, 1870–1940

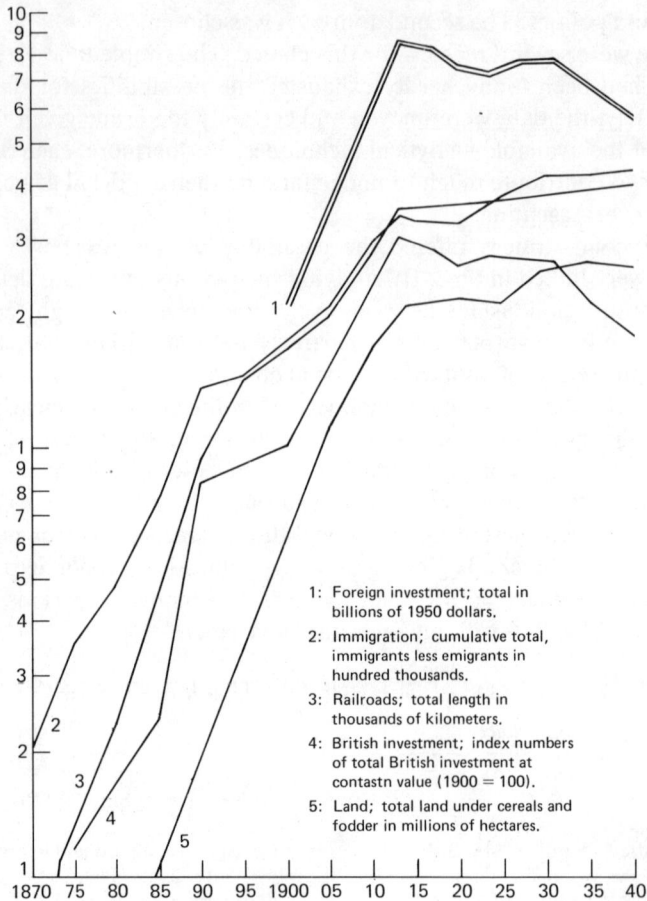

1: Foreign investment; total in
   billions of 1950 dollars.

2: Immigration; cumulative total,
   immigrants less emigrants in
   hundred thousands.

3: Railroads; total length in
   thousands of kilometers.

4: British investment; index numbers
   of total British investment at
   contastn value (1900 = 100).

5: Land; total land under cereals and
   fodder in millions of hectares.

had outlined. Figure 2–2 is representative and shows how the key elements of Argentine economic growth shifted their patterns in three economic periods.

These variables are foreign investment, particularly British investment, immigration, railroad mileage, and land area in use. Simple inspection reveals discontinuities in the trends around 1914 and 1930.

Identification of affected groups was ascertainable, knowing basic parameters of economic change in each period. During the period of trade expansion, 1852–1914, the main economic losers were the handicraft manufacturers, merchants of the interior, and the rural caudillos. The main gainers were the coastal hacendados and the Buenos Aires merchants and middle class. Just prior to the Depression, the export-linked groups began to suffer severely. The main gainers during the thirties were urban labor and entrepreneurs in the rapidly expanding industrial sector. Under Perón, the Industrial working class made strong gains at the expense of the rural landowners and the urban middle class. After Perón's fall, the working class lost many of these gains, though not all. Another group that seemed to be a conspicuous gainer during the thirties and afterwards was the military, which had suffered a decline between 1916 and 1930.[21]

To broaden the context of the rebellions, I tried to find out who the leaders of the rebellions were, what their aims were, and which social groups supported them. It became apparent that rebellions were grouped into different types according to their social character and that these types clustered in different historical periods.

The first five rebellions, occurring between 1870 and 1880, were of a type which might be called *regional rebellions*. They were carried out in the name or regional or provincial rights and were led by a regional leader, or caudillo, who usually was not a career army officer but nonetheless held the honorific title of general. Likewise, troops were local militia and personal retainers, not elements of the standing federal army. Such rebellions had been even more common in the years prior to 1870. One senator from the Argentine interior declared in 1868 that 117 rebellions had taken place in the provinces between June 1862 and September 1868, with a loss of 4,728 lives.[22]

With the 1890's a new type of rebellion appeared, which can be termed the *party rebellion*. The rebellions of 1890, 1893, and 1905 were organized in the name of the Unión Cívica Radical, the first of Argentina's modern political parties, rather than in the name of a region. Elements of the regular army were involved, but the leadership was largely civilian, and civilians were active participants in the fighting.

After the coup of 1930, a new series of party rebellions broke out. These rebellions also involved substantial military participation, but were carried out in the name of the Radical Party, not in the name of the armed forces. Likewise, the Peronist rebellions of 1945 and 1956, which involved military elements in addition to civilian, were carried out in the name of Peronism, not that of the armed forces, and thus can be considered party rebellions as well.[23]

The revolt which overthrew the Radicals in 1930, led by General Uriburu, marked the emergence of a third type of rebellion, the *military rebellion*. Like subsequent military rebellions, it was led and staffed exclusively by members of the federal armed forces. The rebellion was announced as a rebellion *of* the armed forces, not a party or region, and victory was described as a triumph *for* the armed forces. In later military rebellions, such as those of 1943, 1945, 1951, 1955, 1959, 1960, 1962, 1963, and 1966 civilian members of opposi-

[21] The evidence documenting the rise and fall of the various social groups is discussed at length throughout Gilbert W. Merkx, *Political and Economic Change in Argentina from 1870–1966* (Yale University, Ph.D. dissertation, 1968), available from University Microfilms, Ann Arbor, Michigan.

[22] Ramos, *op. cit.*, p. 189.

[23] The manifestation of October 17, 1945, did not involve the participation of specific army units, although individual army officers played an important part in bringing it about.

tion parties or groups at no time played an important role in organizing or conducting the conflict, even though they occasionally played minor roles in preliminary plotting or in voicing public support for a military takeover.

There appears to be a clear linkage between rebellions and economic changes, in addition to the impact of short-term economic cycles upon the timing of insurrection. The social groups involved in the various types of rebellions were those that had emerged as the key winners and losers in each economic period.

Regional rebellions were undertaken by the provincial groups that suffered under the impact of free trade. An examination of their manifestos supports this: the chief demand was for trade protection, followed by demands for economic equality.[24] The self-contained economy of the interior was disintegrating under the impact of foreign manufactured goods.[25] Regional rebellions represented the final but futile attempts of the interior provinces to equalize the position of Buenos Aires. The expansion of the 1880's completed Argentina's transition to an export economy, giving the central government sufficient resources to stamp out rebellions (though not the resentment of the provincianos).

The development of the export economy in turn created a new social group, the commercial middle class of Buenos Aires. Membership in urban white-collar, business, and professional occupations doubled between the censuses of 1870 and 1895, and doubled again by 1914, when it constituted 21% of the economically active population.[26] The leadership and following of the Unión Cívica Radical were drawn from this emergent middle class, and their demands were reformist in nature: political participation for all male citizens, an eight-hour working day, and so on.

The industrial transition of the 1930's created another emergent social class: the urban proletariat. The labor movement and the Socialist Party failed to organise this rapidly expanding group. After the coup of 1943, Colonel Perón encouraged first the unionization and then the politization of urban workers. His success can be seen in the fact that the Peronists remain the largest political movement in Argentina even in the 1970's.

The first military rebellion followed the drastic reductions in military budget and personal humiliation of officers by Yrigoyen's Radical government, actions contrary to those of the period of growth and professionalization begun in 1901.[27] Nevertheless, the military did not intervene until Yrigoyen, an old

---

[24] This was clearly expressed by General Varela, leader of the Catamarca rebellion of 1866–70: "The monopoly of the public treasures and the absorption of provincial revenues has come to be the patrimony of the porteños, condemning the provincianos to give them even the bread reserved for their children. To be a porteño is to be exclusive, and to be a provinciano is to be a beggar," Ramos, *op. cit.,* p. 183.

[25] The number of persons employed in the weaving trades in the interior dropped from 11% to 1% of Argentina's employed population between the census of 1869 and the census of 1914.

[26] Merkx, *op. cit.,* p. 86.

[27] Darío Cantón, "Notas sobre las Fuerzas Armadas Argentinas," *Revista Latinoamericana de Sociología,* Vol. 1, No. 3, pp. 290–313.

man in poor health, proved to be incapable of responding to the devastating economic impact of the world trade crisis. By 1930 a new generation of army officers had been trained and oriented to consider the armed forces a reference group professionally responsible for overseeing the conduct of national affairs. The overthrow of Yrigoyen was justified as an exceptional measure required by exceptional circumstances, rather than as a rejection of democracy in principle.

In subsequent years the armed forces began to develop an increasing interest in manufacturing, culminating in World War II, when Argentina was unable to purchase military supplies abroad. In 1941 the Castillo government established the Office of Military Factories, an operation that was greatly expanded by succeeding military presidents. In short, since 1941 the Argentine military has had both a general concern with economic conditions and a specific institutional interest in manufacturing.

At this stage in the research several general observations could be made. Rebellions were made by social groups that were either greatly suffering or benefiting from long-term structural changes. Rebellions were precipitated by economic crises in which groups withdrew from the existing political order, either to defend weakening economic positions or to translate new-found wealth into direct political advantage. The strongest support for parliamentary democracy seemed to come from the middle class, while both the agricultural elite and the urban workers seemed to have a more tenuous and conditional acceptance of democratic formulas. The military shifted from an upperclass orientation to an increasing concern for its own institutional interests.

Focusing the Analysis

The next step in the study was to move from questions of large-scale structural changes, reflected in the rise or decline of entire social groups, to focus upon the pattern of relationships or transactions between the social groups during each separate structural period. As before, there were two objectives: (1) to determine if such relationships could explain in detail the process whereby different groups came to alter their pattern of political behavior; and (2) to document in greater detail the impact of economic fluctuations upon the relative condition of each group. Since there were five distinct structural periods between 1870 and 1966, five distinct "case studies" were required.

These case studies turned out to be most rewarding and revealing. In actuality, these were not five separate studies, but were snapshots of the same entity at five moments in time. The genetic fallacy mentioned earlier in connection with cross-national research did not pertain. Data were adequate and supportive. Changes in political behavior, in special structure, and in economic organization stood out clearly from period to period. The specific historical events surrounding the more dramatic changes could be examined in detail. Some of the more crucial linkages between economics and politics were thus researchable.

The Permanent Crisis

It is hardly possible to discuss here each of the periods. However, findings for the final period are of the greatest current interest.[28] This period, labeled "The Permanent Crisis," began with the fall of Perón in 1955. It has featured the repeated exclusion of Peronists from electoral politics, the election and eviction of two Radical governments, and repeated military coups d'etat.

Economically, the period was marked by short-term, four-year economic cycles termed *stop–go cycles,* Beginning in the closing years of Perón's government, they are thought to be caused by a foreign exchange bottleneck, declining agricultural exports, and increasing imports of goods required by the industrial sector. The "bad" recession years have occurred every third or fourth year since 1949 and are marked by a rate of inflation that averages 38.4% per year, over twice the mean for all other years (19.1%). Bad years also typically include a fall in real wage rates, severe exchange rate devaluations, slower rates of credit expansion, and a drop in the value of cash balances.[29]

These stop–go cycles reflect the fact that Argentine exports are predominantly wage goods, the same foods and fibers that constitute 80% of the budgets of wage-earning Argentines. During recessions, as income falls off, more foods and fibers are available for export, foreign exchange is accumulated and the economy prospers. But such a prosperity benefits workers, consumption of wage goods increases, and agricultural exports are reduced. Some manufactured goods produced by the industrial sector are of course purchased by the working-class, but the bulk of such consumer goods is purchased by the upper-middle classes. A 1963 study showed that 80% of all automobiles were purchased by families in the upper 28% of the income scale.[30] Thus, Argentine entrepreneurs consume imported goods (by buying manufactures made with imported materials), whereas wage-earners consume exportable goods. A general increase in the level of prosperity doubly strains the balance of payments. The rich buy importables, and the poor consume exportables.

When foreign exchange is exhausted in this process, the government has little choice but to devalue the currency vis-à-vis foreign currencies; inflation ensues. Devaluations are also linked to recessions: sectors hurt by devaluation contract more rapidly than those sectors helped can expand.[31] Recessions then lead to a drop in the consumption of goods (real meat consumption, for example, fell by more than 22% from 1958 to 1959.)[32] Export earnings accumulate, and the cycle begins anew. Increasing agricultural exports might break

[28] A more detailed discussion of these findings can be found in Gilbert W. Merkx, "Sectoral Clashes and Political Change: The Argentine Experience," *Latin American Research Review,* Vol. 4 (Fall 1969), pp. 89–114.

[29] Carios F. Díaz-Alejandro, *Essays on the Argentine Economy* (New Haven: Economic Growth Center, 1967, mimeo), pp. 5–7.

[30] Cited by Carlos F. Díaz-Alejandro, *Exchange Rate Devaluation in a Semi-Industrialized Country* (Cambridge, Mass.: The MIT Press, 1965), p. 61.

[31] *Ibid.,* p. 168.

[32] *Ibid.,* p. 169.

the cycle, but the data show that agricultural production is impervious to government stimulation or to price increases. Since 1930 the growth of agricultural production has been outstripped by population growth.

What has happened to the various population groups throughout this process? Several facts stand out. One is that the overall distribution of the population in terms of economic activity has remained relatively stagnant. Since 1950 the relative contributions of different sectors of the ecomomy to gross domestic product have remained very much the same.[33] The stability of the social structure is apparently one of the reasons why patterns of political conflict are so repetitive. New social groups are no longer emerging to challenge the existing distribution of power.

The chief characteristics of the Argentine social structure are documented in a recent ECLA study on income distribution in Argentina.[34] Industrial employment is extremely important: one of three (36%) wage-earners is employed by industry, making up 23% of all family units. The next largest category is government and other services, which employ breadwinners from 14% of all family units. Agricultural wage-earners and entrepreneurs each constitute only 8% of all families. These figures are shown in Table 2–7. In terms of occupational structure, though not in terms of the structure of its exports, Argentina is an industrial nation.

The ECLA data were also used to estimate social class structure based upon income and occupation. The results, summarized in Table 2–8, indicate that the Argentine middle class constitutes about one-third of the population, while the skilled and white-collar working class makes up just over one-half the total population. In contrast, the two lowest socioeconomic groups make up a small minority of the population (13% combined), though not as small as the economically influential upper class (1.66%). These figures agree closely with estimates made by Gino Germani at the same time, who calculated that the middle and upper class constituted 36% of the population (compared with 35% in these figures).[35]

The importance of these figures for Argentine politics is twofold. First, they indicate the presence of two large blocks of voters, the upper-middle class, and the skilled and white-collar working class. Both groups are literate and urban. It is not surprising that the two largest political movements in contemporary Argentina are the middle-class Radicals and the working-class Peronists. Combined, the two economic classes comprise about 80% of the

[33] *Orígen del Producto y Composición del Gasto Nacional* (Buenos Aires: Banco Central, Junio de 1966), p. 19. Between 1955 and 1965 the only changes of note in the shares of different sectors were a decline of agriculture's share from 19% to 17% and a rise of manufacturing's share from 30% to 35%. This was a continuation of the pre–1950 trend, but in greatly reduced form.

[34] Alberto Fracchia and Oscar Altimir, "Income Distribution in Argentina," *Economic Bulletin for Latin America,* Vol. 11, No. 1, pp. 106–131.

[35] Gino Germani, *Estructura Social en la Argentina* (Buenos Aires: Editorial Raigal, 1955).

TABLE 2-7.   ARGENTINA—PERCENTAGES OF FAMILY UNITS IN DIFFERENT ECONOMIC SECTORS, 1961

Income types	Agriculture[a]	Industry[b]	Construction	Commerce & Finance	Transport[c]	Domestic Services	Professional Services	Government Services	Subtotal
Wage-earners	8% (444,900)	23%[d] (1,285,200)	6% (336,300)	5% (285,000)	8% (417,700)	1% (53,000)		14% (790,400)	64% (3,613,100)
Entrepreneurs	8% (475,000)	4% (244,800)	[d]	6% (337,900)	1% (72,500)		7% (387,500)	2% (100,600)	29% (1,618,600)
Pensioners									7% (395,100)
Rentiers[e]									— (25,400)
								Total	100% (5,652,000)

SOURCES and COMMENTS: Percentages do not equal all subtotals due to rounding. Compiled from data in Fracchia and Altimir, "Income Distribution in Argentina," *Economic Bulletin for Latin America*, Vol. XI, No. 1, Tables I, II, III, IV, pp. 122–131.

a Includes fisheries.
b Includes utilities and mining.
c Includes warehousing and communications.
d Included in the figure for industrial entrepreneurs.
e Income derived from property ownership.

TABLE 2–8.   ARGENTINE SOCIAL CLASSES IN 1961

Social Class	Family Income[a]	% of All Family Units	% of All Personal Income	Cumulative % of All Personal Income
I. Upper class (industrialists, major landowners, financiers, etc.)	8,000–100,000 and over	1.66	18.22	81.78–100
II. Professional and business class (entrepreneurs, independent professionals, landlords, executives, etc.)	1,300–8,000	33.24	47.42	34.36–81.78
III. Skilled and white-collar working class (government employees, factory workers, clerks, salespeople . . .)	650–1,300	51.76	30.18	4.18–34.36
IV. Unskilled working class (domestics, agricultural laborers, etc.)	455–650	10.22	3.49	0.69– 4.18
V. Marginal underclass (retired persons, unemployables, tenant farmers, etc.)	Under 455	3.19	.69	0.0– .69

SOURCES and COMMENTS: Compiled from data presented by Fracchia and Altimir, *op. cit.*, statistical appendix. The frequency distribution was obtained by matching family incomes of wage-earners and entrepreneurs in different economic sectors with the distribution of families by income levels.

[a] The numbers shown are for hundreds of pesos. During 1961 the official exchange rate was 82 pesos per U.S. dollar, but the Argentine cost of living was less than that of the United States. Thus these figures, which represent hundreds of pesos, can be increased by one-fourth to one-third for a rough U.S. dollar equivalent.

population, and the two party groupings consistently poll about 75% of the national vote.[36]

Second, the two class groupings are not linked in the same way to the structure of the Argentine economy. The working class is divided between skilled and white-collar workers. Although the white-collar workers are distributed across economic sectors, the skilled workers are concentrated in the closely-linked industrial, construction, and transportation sectors, which account for 57% of all wage and salary workers. An industrial recession strongly affects wage-earners in general, and skilled workers in particular.

The spread of the upper-middle and upper class across economic sectors means that individuals within these groups are affected differently by developments in any given economic sector. For instance, agricultural entrepreneurs and exporters may benefit in the short run from a situation which would hurt industrialists and importers.

A political conclusion to be drawn from these patterns of occupation and income distribution in Argentina is that where skilled workers should respond uniformly to factors affecting the industrial sector (such as recession), the response of white-collar workers, the upper-middle class, and the upper class

[36] Both the Peronists and the Radicals have a fragmented and fluctuating party structure with different groups claiming at different times to be the "true" Peronists or Radicals.

will be fragmented. These social groups are spread across different economic sectors and will be affected differently. Thus, we can expect the working class to unite in the face of economic crisis, and the upper-income groups to fragment.

This situation appears to characterize the recent pattern of Argentine political behavior. The celebrated Peronist election victories in 1962 and 1966, which led directly to the ousters of Presidents Frondizi and Illia, signified the reemergence of working-class unity and middle-class disunity in the face of recession. Both Frondizi and Illia were careful to test public sentiment in trial elections before allowing the Peronists to stand for office in major elections. These trial elections resulted in Peronist defeats and victories for the government parties. Unfortunately for Frondizi and Illia, their timing was bad. Trial elections took place at the tall end of the upturn part of the economic cycle, and by the time general elections came about, inflation and recession were in full swing. The workers rallied to the Peronist banner once again, and much of the middle-class vote shifted from the governing Radical Party to other Radical factions.

The socioeconomic importance of political power is illustrated by the fluctuating income shares of different groups. The Index of Discrimination in Table 2–9, for example, traces the fortunes of the agricultural sector over a

TABLE 2–9. INTERNAL AND EXTERNAL TERMS OF TRADE AND THE INDEX OF DISCRIMINATION BETWEEN RURAL AND NONRURAL GOODS (1935–39 = 100)

Period	Internal Terms of Trade (A)	External Terms of Trade (B)	Index of Discrimination (C) = 100 (A/B)
1925–29	132	111	119
1930–34	87	79	110
1935–39	100	100	100
1940–44	62	89	70
1945–46	74	120	62
1947–49	80	169	47
1950–52	68	124	55
1953–55	68	114	60
1956–58	78	93	84
1959–61	85	91	93
1962–64	93	89	104

SOURCES and COMMENTS: As the Index of Discrimination rises over 100, rural goods are in a more favored position (than in 1935–39) and as it drops below 100, nonrural goods are favored. Thus, in 1947–49 domestic rural goods earned 47% of what they would have earned had domestic prices kept the same relationship to international prices as existed in 1935–39. The data are derived from Carlos Díaz-Alejandro, *Essays on the Argentine Economy* (New Haven: Economic Growth Center, 1967), chapter 11, tables 16 (column 3), 17 (column 1) and 18 (column B). As presented here, Column *B* is based on export price indices contained in CEPAL, *El Desarrollo Económico de la Argentina, op. cit.*, Vol. 1, p. 110 (1925–49); and Ruth Kelly, "Foreign Trade of Argentina and Australia, 1930–1960, *Economic Bulletin for Latin America*, Vol. X, No. 1, p. 50 (1950–54); and Re. Argentina, Dirección Nacional de Estradística y Censos, *Boletín de Estadística,* several issues. Import price indices are based on the U.S. Wholesale Price Index excluding food and farm products, U.S. Dept. of Commerce, *Statistical Abstract of the United States,* 1965, p. 356. Column *A* is based on data from the *Anuario Geográfico Argentino,* 1941, p. 369; BCRA, *Boletín Estadístico* (Sept. 1962), pp. 51–62, and DNEC, *Boletín Mensual de Estadística,* several issues.

forty-year period. Because Argentine exports are rural goods and Argentine imports are nonrural goods, it is possible to compare their relative prices (the external terms of trade) with domestic relative prices of such goods (the internal terms of trade). Without government intervention, the internal terms of trade should reflect the international price movements shown in the external terms of trade. Any deviation between the movements of the internal and external terms of trade serves to indicate the extent of the government's discrimination in favor of either the agricultural or industrial sector. The Index of Discrimination shows that agriculture suffered severely under Perón, earning in 1947–49 only 47% of what would have been earned without government intervention. Since Perón's fall, the agricultural sector has made steady gains, finally returning in the period 1962–64 to a price relationship slightly better than that enjoyed during the base period 1935–39.

However, increased agricultural prices have been made at the expense of industrial workers, who consume the largest part of agricultural production. Comparing real wages (corrected for inflation) with changes in the Gross National Product, it is possible to construct an Index of Favoritism to Labor. Any gain in the real size of industrial wage rates relative to the nation's product should provide a rough estimate of government favoritism to workers (given the extensive government control over the wage rates during and after Perón). This index is presented in Table 2–10. The Index of Favoritism has fluctuated wildly, increasing from a base of 100 in 1943 before Perón, to a high of 156 under Perón, and back to a low of 98 under Frondizi in 1960. These data indicate that just who is in the Presidential Palace makes a great deal of difference to the working class (and presumably to everyone else).

Such data, supplemented with a number of interviews in Argentina and one in Spain with General Perón, served to document the existence of very real linkages between economic conditions and political behavior. Given the structure of Argentine income and employment, the result of high inflation and periodic economic contraction has been the maintenance of a high level of social and political conflict in Argentina since Perón's fall—the so-called "Permanent Crisis." Any income group that does not fight vigorously for its share of the economy will be left behind in the inflationary race. To stand still in terms of peso earnings is to fall rapidly behind in terms of real earnings.

It is possible to imagine such a struggle being carried out primarily on an economic front. In the Argentine case, however, it cannot avoid being political as well. Economic conflict becomes political conflict. The success of any income group in maintaining its share of national income depends upon its ability to influence government policy. Coalitions between income groups form on one issue, and then disintegrate over another. A cross-pressured government which dissatisfies too many groups at the same time will fall. It might be an overstatement to say that the lines of political conflict are drawn *only* along lines of economic interest, but as a minimum, it can be said that disagreement over economic policies has played a major part in preventing broad-based governing coalitions.

TABLE 2–10.   REAL WAGES OF MANUFACTURING WORKERS, REAL GROSS
NATIONAL PRODUCT PER CAPITA, AND THE INDEX OF
FAVORITISM TO LABOR (1943 = 100)

Year	Real Wages (A)	GNP Per Capita (B)	Index of Favoritism to Labor (C) = 100 (A/B)
1939	100	98	102
1940	97	92	105
1941	97	94	103
1942	97	99	98
1943	100	100	100
1944	111	108	103
1945	106	101	105
1946	112	112	100
1947	140	131	107
1948	173	130	133
1949	181	116	156
1950	173	113	153
1951	145	114	127
1952	135	103	131
1953	135	109	124
1954	153	111	138
1955	140	116	121
1956	164	114	144
1957	134	117	115
1958	148	124	119
1959	119	115	103
1960	120	123	98
1961	130	129	101
1962	127	123	103
1963	125	118	106
1964	131	127	103

SOURCES and METHODS: Column A is based on Table 2–4, Columns A (1939–50) and B (1950–64), in Merkx, "Sectoral Clashes and Political Change: The Argentine Experience," *Latin American Research Review,* Vol. 4 (Fall 1969), pp. 89–114. Column B is taken from Díaz-Alejandro, *op. cit.,* Table 18, Chapter 7, and is based on BCRA figures (1966 series). As the Index of Favoritism in Column C rises above 100, the wages of industrial workers improve relative to the Gross National Product per capita.

Military and civilian governments suffer alike. Time and time again, well meaning generals have taken power, confident that a firm hand is all that is needed to restore business confidence and economic growth. Each of these presidents has had to learn about the realities of international trade, about sectoral conflicts, and about the limits of import substitution. As prosperity is followed by recession, each general must face criticism from his companions in the barracks, who ask the same questions of him that he asked of the deposed civilian president. Economic failure discredits military regimes as fully as it does civilian governments.

The roots of Argentina's economic stagnation and stop-go cycles do not lie in the style or form of leadership, but rather in the structure of the Argentine economy. This fact cannot be altered by short-term policy expedients. Major policy reorientations are needed to supply what is now missing in Argentina: a *modus vivendi* between the various income groups that now struggle in the political arena.

Each group has a veto power over government. Landowners, industrialists, labor, or the generals can each destroy a development policy. Since the early days of Perón, no government has been able to command the simultaneous allegiance of enough of these interest groups to be effective. Bad faith between groups, often justified, has prevented cooperation in the making and execution of policy. The absence of trust, a pervasive *desconfianza* between social groups, has led to an intensification of the economic struggle. Each group is determined not to be exploited by the others and jealously fights alteration of the unhealthy economic status quo.

The onset of recessions brings this volatile situation to the boiling point. In an economy of shrinking real output, either all groups suffer equally, or else some groups suffer more than others. Each income group in each economic sector does all it can to minimize its own losses. The result is likely to be the eruption of open political conflict.

Argentine governments are placed in an unenviable position. They inherit a faulty economic structure in which recession inexorably follows every short period of prosperity. The room for economic maneuvering is not great, but the price of economic failure *is* great: renewed clashes within and between sectors, intensification of social and political conflict, and military intervention.

THEORETICAL IMPLICATIONS

The preceding analysis predicted the fall of President Illia in 1966, even though publication of that prediction was practically impossible. Afterwards I predicted in print the fall of President Onganía in 1969 or 1970.[37] Onganía fell in the summer of 1970. He was succeeded by General Levingston, who lasted less than a year. His successor, General Lanusse, eventually held elections that resulted in the return of Peron to power, three years after the fall of Ongania. Peron's return, which did not alter the Argentine structural crisis, does open a new political chapter that offers the possibility of a broadened popular consensus behind a fresh development effort.

It would be an abnegation of responsibility, as well as intellectually impoverishing, however, if the study were to be left in purely "Argentine" terms, located only in the time and space which was Argentine history. As such, it would be of primary interest to people concerned with Argentina. My own original interest had not been with Argentina itself, but with problems faced by all developing nations. The final task, and not the least important, to to state the findings in generalized form, so that conclusions about the logical structure of Argentine sociopolitical change become hypotheses to be tested elsewhere. If

[37] Merkx, "Sectoral Clashes and Political Change" (see note 28 above).

political changes do in fact grow out of long-term structural changes and short-term crises, mediated by each social group's definition of self-interest and ideology, the rationale for generalizing should be clear: Similar patterns of political change should occur where similar socioeconomic structures emerge.

Each of the following brief hypotheses, drawn from the Argentine findings, tries to specify both the structural development and the political result. After each hypothesis follow two other cases to which the hypothesis might apply.

HYPOTHESIS 1: The development of export trade under colonial government will lead to the emergence of local entrepreneurs who, upon finding their economic interests incompatible with those of the mother country, will demand representative government and independence (Venezuela, the United States).

HYPOTHESIS 2: The achievement of independence by a colonial region containing a dual economy (partly commercial trade oriented and partly feudal-estate mercantilism) will lead to civil war over the ideological issue of local autonomy under federalism versus strong central government (Colombia, the Congo).

HYPOTHESIS 3: A major expansion of exports under a dictator will strengthen him until his power is close to absolute, but it will also increase the size of entrepreneurial and urban elites which will attack his cult of personality and call for liberalized government (Mexico, Ghana).

HYPOTHESIS 4: As export development reaches sufficient volume, a native middle class is created, which will not challenge the existing economic order, but will demand political equality (Chile, Venezuela).

HYPOTHESIS 5: The failure of a governing middle class to cope with economic crisis will cause the previously governing elite to withdraw from support of democratic institutions by supporting military intervention. The military is likely to split, however, over whether the withdrawal from democratic mechanisms is to be temporary or permanent, resulting in a struggle between liberal and corporatist ideologies (Germany, Brazil).

HYPOTHESIS 6: The growth of an industrial sector in an export-oriented economy will result in an eventual takeover of government by a populist leader who combines appeals to the working class in the name of social justice with appeals to industrial entrepreneurs in the name of industrial development (Brazil, Egypt).

HYPOTHESIS 7: A populist leader who favors import-substitution manufacturing in a country which earns foreign exchange through primary-goods exports will eventually be faced with a foreign exchange bottleneck leading to the failure of his populist program and attacks from middle- and upper-income groups (linked to the export sector) who will call for a return to liberal principles of government. Since the populist leader possesses the means of mob violence, he is likely to be overthrown by the armed forces, which possess even more potent means of violence (Indonesia, Ghana).

HYPOTHESIS 8: The ouster of a populist leader in a nation characterized by extensive import-substitution industrialization and stop–go cycles will lead to extended political conflict characterized by the rapid alternation of governments and repeated military interventions (Turkey, Brazil).

HYPOTHESIS 9: No nation can sustain parliamentary democracy without a reasonably stable economy and a relatively constant pattern of long-term economic growth (Sweden, Australia).

HYPOTHESIS 10: (the Davies hypothesis) Long-term economic growth resulting in basic structural changes, when followed by sharp economic reversal, is likely to result in revolution (Russia, Egypt).

METHODOLOGICAL CONCLUSIONS

Because the research describes many new avenues of investigation, it is more a beginning and less a final effort. Perhaps it is appropriate to return to our initial methodological question. Reality has logical structure, as Wittgenstein posits. A fundamental problem, then, is to ascertain those aspects of structure that meaningfully explain political change. In retrospect, the chief error of the early cross-national studies was to shortcut the difficult and time-consuming task of describing socioeconomic structures. Comparative studies that describe aggregate artificial features of societies ignore the context and logic of reality.

The experience of the Argentine research reinforces the view that "harder" analysis should proceed only after painstaking historical-descriptive research has clarified important structural elements in a specific space–time context. A recent example of such research is the work of Barrington Moore on the social origins of dictatorship and democracy.[38] Moore makes little use of "hard" time-series data of the sort used in this analysis, but the methodological power of his historical descriptions is sufficent to cause the work to be recognized as deeply insightful and influential. The work of the economist Markos Mamalakis on the "Theory of Sectoral Clashes" represents another valuable attempt to analyze evolving national structures.[39] In France, the neo-Marxist sociology of Louis Althusser[40] and the anthropology of Claude Lévi-Strauss[41] represent somewhat less historically oriented, but nonetheless rigorous, attempts to focus upon structural issues.

The earlier efforts of structural-functional theorists in sociology and political science represented an attempt to define the essential features of socioeconomic structure on the basis of a priori assumptions about the functional prerequisites of system maintenance. Perhaps the social sciences are now returning to the more profitable method of generating structural inferences by examining social reality—the best way of "making sense," in Wittgenstein's words.

[38] Barrington Moore, *Social Origins of Dictatorship and Democracy* (Boston: Beacon Press, 1966).

[39] Markos Mamalakis, "The Theory of Sectoral Clashes," *Latin American Research Review,* Vol. 4 (Fall 1969), pp. 9–46.

[40] Louis Althusser, *For Marx* (New York: Vintage Books, 1970).

[41] Claude Lévi-Strauss, *Structural Anthropology* (New York: Basic Books, 1963).

Chapter 3
Supporters of the New Party of the Right: A Report and Discussion of the German NPD's Sources of Support

KLAUS LIEPELT

The specter of Nazism appeared to be materializing during the mid-1960's in the Federal Republic of Germany, manifest in the form of the ultra-rightist NPD (National Demokratische Partei Deutschlands) as this fringe party gained local success in several provincial elections. Because of the great public attention aroused by these successes, the German opinion polling and research institute—Infas of Bonn–Bad Godesberg—conducted a series of detailed empirical investigations into the characteristics of persons supporting the NPD. An effort was made to judge its vote-getting potential, to estimate the inroads and impact it was having on the major parties, to determine why the party was enjoying success, even if limited, and to speculate about its future in the German political process. In short, this is a rare, remarkable example of the policy sciences used to considerable positive effect.

The German diet (parliament) elections of April 23, 1967, once more drew public interest to the small NPD, which even today continues to make headlines. Conjecture and great concern, both in Germany and abroad, about the chances

Originally published as "Anhänger der neuen Rechtspartei: Ein Beitrag zur Diskussion über das Wählerreservoir der NPD," *Politische Vierteljahresschrift*, Vol. 8 (July 1967), pp. 237–71. This translation was made by Dolores Lofgren and edited by Garry Brewer. Liepelt is responsible for the following disclaimer.

NOTE: The original German version of this chapter proved to be extremely difficult to translate because it contained a number of parsimonious references that could easily be understood only by an audience quite familiar with German affairs. Expansion of these references for an English-speaking audience consisting primarily of Americans turned out to require more than the available resources. The editors assume responsibility for the resulting limitations of this translation and encourage the reader with purposes more specialized than ours to examine the original.

of this party continue, and data are presented in this analysis to help evaluate and understand the NPD's sources of strength.[1]

THE NPD'S POTENTIAL AND SURVEY POLLS

In 1967 new parliaments were elected in five regions of the German Federal Republic. The press and other media appeared as interested in the chances of the NPD as they were in how the major parties performed. As a result, numerous conjectures about the chances of the NPD circulated before the elections in Schleswig-Holstein (the German form of state names is used throughout) and Rheinland-Pfalz.[2] Public opinion polls were responsible for many contradictory rumors.

With such an exciting and popular topic, it is easy to understand how opinion pollsters, working under great pressure, could produce poll results that could be misinterpreted, even by other experts. Still, for other reasons, one cannot translate poll results impartially or directly into election returns. This assertion holds even for the established parties, whose bases of voter support are more numerous and stable than the NPD's.[3] With a new party, it is extremely difficult to distinguish among opinions, facts, and assertions.

Sorting out the problem means determining precisely how poll questions related to the "voter potential" of the NPD were formulated. Strikingly different results are sometimes obtained merely by wording questions differently, even in the same questionnaire.

Only a fraction of the NPD voters responded to a routine question about which party one would choose if elections were held as soon as possible. The NPD was named by only 1% of those asked this question in Hessen prior to the provincial diet election; however, on election Sunday, about 6% voted for the NPD.[4] Only one in six NPD voters had openly declared in the polls. A similar problem was observed in Niedersachsen at the end of December: only

[1] I thank Dr. Peter Hoschka and John Nagle, who compiled the data supporting this research. The analysis is based on surveys made by the Institute for Applied Social Science, Bad Godesberg, Germany, in early 1966 and at the turn of 1966–67.

[2] For Schleswig-Holstein, for example, a public opinion poll before the election is supposed to have shown that the NPD there would draw 23% of the vote. Others reported more than 40%; still others held that the NPD could realistically expect less than 10%. The actual election results of April 23, 1967, saw the NPD in Schleswig-Holstein receive 5.8%, and in Rheinland-Pfalz 4.9%, of the total votes cast.

[3] In the paper "Voter Opinion and Election Predictions," we detailed the type of problems that confound an election prediction based on public opinion polls [S. Institut für angewandte Sozialwissenschaft, "Wählermeinung und Wahlprognose. Acht Gesichtspunkte zur Lektüre von Wahlhervorsagen," *Politogramm* (Bad Godesberg: Infas, May 1966).]

[4] Of the legal votes cast in Hessen in the Federal diet election of 1965, the NPD received 2.5%, but in the 1966 provincial diet elections, it received 7.9%. In Bayern it got 2.7% in 1965, and 7.4% in 1966.

2% of persons polled indicated a preference for the NPD in the provincial diet elections. Inferring expected election returns from such figures is impossible.

This phenomenon is not peculiar to the NPD; it occurs for all small parties. When polled, many small party supporters choose to identify with a major party, or refuse to answer questions: in either case, they are obviously choosing not to be identified as minority party supporters. The problem is more pervasive, however. Even with a major party, like the FDP, voter support is often seriously underrepresented in preelection polls. It is hardly surprising that most NPD supporters choose not to be identified in polls as belonging to a minority party commonly considered to be right radical.

To circumvent this problem, it seems particularly important to reformulate party-identification questions in opinion polls. However, preliminary efforts have not been very encouraging. It may well be that for many complex reasons, polls are not a sharp enough research tool to determine precisely preelection voter preferences and identifications for minority parties.

Infas, The Institute for Applied Social Science, Bonn–Bad Godesberg, asked in several polls in the first half of 1966, "Would you personally ever vote for the NPD, or have you already done so?" Barely 7% answered affirmatively (Table 3–1). Toward the end of 1966, this number had grown to 13%, but one cannot confidently rely on so unstable an indicator.

Another polling organization, the EMNID Institute, asked in October–November 1965; "More than one-half million persons voted for the NPD in the Federal diet elections. Would you like to see such a party become stronger in

TABLE 3–1.   POLITICAL ELECTIONS OF 1966–67

Date	Total Number of Persons Interviewed	Stated Readiness to Vote for the NPD[a] (%)	PARTY PREFERENCE[b] (%)	
			CDU/CSU	SPD
April 1966	736	7	37	44
May 1966	834	4	38	43
June 1966	556	6	37	44
Provincial Elections in Hessen and Bayern: Governmental Crisis				
November 1966	761	14 ⎱ 13[c]	38	41
December 1966	841	12 ⎰	38	40
January 1967	847	10	37	42
February 1967	834	9	42	43
March 1967	764	9	39	42

SOURCE: Representative statistics from the Infas (Institute for Applied Social Science), Federal territory, random sample.

a Question: "Would you personally ever vote for the NPD, or have you ever so voted?"

b Question: "Which of the political parties do you like at present? (As far as one can say.) Which do you really think is still the best?"

c This analysis is based mainly on a synopsis of polls taken November–December 1966; these gave an average value of 13% potential NPD voters.

the future, or not?" At that time, 9.0% favored a stronger NPD, and 19.0% were undecided. Interpretations of the data produced a consistent long-term potential "estimate" of NPD strength at 15%.

Toward the end of 1966, the Institute for Demoscopy reported that 18% of the population in the Federal territory welcomed the emergence of a party such as the NPD. Even this figure has been interpreted as a measure of NPD voter strength. Finally, one might try to define the party's potential strength by singling out NPD campaign issues and then determining how many registered voters agreed with the NPD's point of view. Using this approach, for instance, one research institute obtained a figure of nearly 40%.

These examples clearly show that polling studies are not sufficiently developed to evaluate NPD election chances. For example, what does it mean when a poll taken right before the provincial diet election in Hessen indicates that about 9% will probably vote for the NPD, and then the NPD actually receives only 6% of the vote? Can one draw analogies from this experience to predict performance in subsequent elections? If 9% of the registered voters said they were for the NPD, would this mean that the party (using voter turnout rates) would surpass some 10% of the total vote in an election? In the entire Republic at the end of 1966, 13% indicated they would vote for the NPD sometime. If, as in Hessen, two-thirds of these persons actually voted for the NPD, then the party would probably receive around 9% of the total vote.

However, this conclusion is likely to be wrong because of the so-called "nominal-member effect." Generally right after an election, as numerous studies have shown, favorable popular endorsements increase for a party that has received special attention by the press. After the election in Hessen and Bayern, the NPD's unexpectedly strong showing became a popular topic of conversation. It is likely that the "nominal-member effect" contributed to this increase in the so-called "voter reservoir" of the NPD. Perhaps there were real gains underlying NPD advances in the polls, gains that could eventually be converted into votes. Still, the increases of April 23 might have been only a "nominal-member effect" with but transitory importance. This basic uncertainty about NPD strength must be emphasized, particularly in light of claims of NPD advances reported in various public opinion polls. Without more precise data and better scientific explanations, polls can say nothing specifically about the NPD; in fact, polls may confuse more than they clarify.

While public opinion polls have something to say about the NPD, the period of analysis is too short to derive measures of NPD support, and predicting election outcomes precisely is asking too much of polling techniques. Presently, only assumptions can be made regarding the trend and order of magnitude of potential NPD voter support. But polls do provide information about sources of NPD support and about supporters' attitudes on political and social problems; furthermore, this information depends far less upon the form of survey questions posed than those meant to tap voting intentions directly.

RIGHTIST VOTERS IN ELECTION STATISTICS

General agreement exists between official statistics and the data produced by various polling organizations about the social composition of potential NPD supporters.

Unlike voters belonging to traditional parties, NPD supporters have no clear group profile. They are found in all population groups, however small the overall percentage in the total population at large, while major party support is, by contrast, sharply polarized. Catholic farmers cast fewer than 10% of their votes for the SPD, while nonreligiously oriented unionized skilled workers consistently vote over 70% for the SPD. Similar contrasts hold for the CDU/CSU, and to a lesser extent for the FDP. However, for the NPD, these contrasts are essentially indistinguishable.

Nevertheless, NPD supporters have some characteristic features. Men favor the NPD more than women: 60% of the NPD voters are men, but men make up only 46% of the total electorate. Official voting statistics indicate no change in this male overrepresentation for the NPD since it was established. The NPD's age composition findings are more equivocal. Popular comments about the youthfulness of NPD rally audiences aside, official representative election statistics have shown that for both the 1965 Federal diet election and the Hessen provincial diet election, neither the youthful, nor the aged, voted for the NPD in significant numbers (Table 3–2). Quite the contrary, support came mainly from the generation that was in its prime during the Third Reich and is *now between 45 and 60 years old*. In fact, the NPD drew fewer votes from the very old and the very young than the proportion of these age groups in the voting population

TABLE 3–2.   AGE AND SEX OF NPD VOTERS

Sex	FEDERAL DIET ELECTION OF 1965[a] (%)		PROVINCIAL DIET ELECTION OF 1966 IN HESSEN[b] (%)	
	All Voters	*NPD Voters*	*All Voters*	*NPD Voters*
Men	46	60	46	60
Women	54	40	54	40
	100	100	100	100
Age group (years)				
21 to 30	18	14	16	14
30 to below 45	30	30	29	30
45 to below 60	27	33	28	34
60 and over	25	23	27	22
	100	100	100	100

a SOURCE: Data from the representative Federal diet election statistics of 1965, *Economics and Statistics* [*Wirtschaft und Statistik*], Vol. 2 (1966).

b SOURCE: Data from the representative provincial diet election in Hessen, *State and Economics in Hessen* [*Staat und Wirtschaft in Hessen*], Vol. 12 (1966).

as a whole. Furthermore, the age composition of NPD supporters remained practically constant between the 1965 Federal diet and the 1966 Hessen provincial diet elections, *despite* the sharp increase in the number of votes cast for the NPD.

Empirical studies can refute unsubstantiated rumors that the NPD is particularly attractive to young voters.

Other interesting compositional characteristics are discernible in occupational data on the NPD's supporters. Independent groups, such as farmers, industrialists, and workers are heavily overrepresented in the NPD. Polls always note the relatively high and unexpected percentage of semiskilled and unskilled workers, a percentage that obviously increased during 1966. On the other hand, pensioners supporting the NPD are underrepresented. White-collar workers and civil servants support the NPD at best only in proportion to their percentage of the general electorate. Later in the analysis we show that this difference in occupational group composition is no "class phenomenon," but rather reflects both private economic considerations and political organizational ones.

It has been said that the NPD relates most specifically to voters with higher education. In studies made at the end of 1965, evidence was found supporting this thesis. However, it appears that increases in NPD support from those in less skilled working occupations have made the "education pyramid" of NPD supporters less top-heavy, i.e., a bias toward more highly educated voters is decreasing.

Slight differences exist between refugees and immigrants who support the NPD and those in the indigenous population. Immigrants and refugees appear to support the NPD in accord with their percentage in the total population. These observations, based on polling data, have been confirmed by provincial diet election returns from Hessen and Bayern (Table 3–3). In both cases, no

TABLE 3–3.   NPD VOTE VICTORIES AND GDP VOTE LOSSES IN HESSEN AND BAYERN (1966)

GPD Losses Throughout the Preceding Provincial Diet Election (points)	Number of Districts	Average NPD Gain in Percentage Points Throughout the Federal Diet Election of 1965
Hessen	48	+5.3
0.0–1.9	24	+5.2
2.0–2.9	15	+5.2
3.0+	9	+5.4
Bayern	206	+4.7
0.0–2.9	37	+5.0
3.0–3.0	42	+4.8
4.0–4.9	27	+4.4
5.0–5.9	35	+5.3
6.0–7.9	34	+4.3
8.0+	31	+4.5

SOURCE: Official election returns, provincial diet elections, 1966.

general relationship between the gains of the NPD and the losses of the expelled GDP/BHE party can be discovered, but wherever refugees and immigrants are concentrated and have maintained the old traditions, such as in the settlement of Neu-Gablonz near Kaufbeuren, the NPD finds great sympathy. It seems that the NPD has been able to gain a firm foothold in these smaller, tightly knit, and conservative communities. Such instances seem more numerous than what seemed initially to be the case, and NPD pockets of support are not limited just to immigrants. Particularly where radical rightist positions have been tradition- ally accepted or tolerated, it is reasonable to expect the NPD to gain local sup- port and occasionally even to gain local political dominance.[5]

Such phenomena are difficult to grasp using current categories of official election statistics and standard polling data. Whole constellations of different, nearly unique, local and personal factors are simply not accounted for by these data (Table 3-4). Nevertheless, it is conjectured that NPD voters are heavily concentrated in small Protestant communities and among persons belonging to fraternities or clubs.

In the case of fraternities and groups in which potential NPD voters are active, it was possible to deal primarily with organizations that have been either

TABLE 3–4.   STRUCTURE OF THE POTENTIAL NPD VOTERS IN THE FEDERAL TERRITORY

Sociostatistical Criteria	All inter- viewees (%)	TOTAL POTENTIAL NPD VOTERS[a] (%)		Percentage of the Potential NPD Voters, November– December 1966
		April–June 1966	November– December 1966	
Professional Groups				
Independent, assistant, liberal professions	15	21	23	19
White-collar workers	20	21	14	10
Civil servants	8	8	5	10
Skilled workers	23	19	24	13
Semi-skilled and unskilled workers	16	19	21	16
Pensioners	18	12	13	9
	100	100	100	

[5] Such conditions appear in certain communities in areas where a diet has recently been elected. Thus, the NPD was able to capture 24.5% of the legal voters in the provincial diet election of 1967 in the Grumbach *Amt* in the district of Birkenfeld (Rheinland-Pfalz). This *Amt* consists of fifteen communities totaling only 3,510 legal voters. In the provincial diet election of 1963, the DRP had attained 20.0% of the votes; nevertheless, the percentage of rightist votes was greatest in the provincial diet election of 1959 (DRP = 35.27%). During the Federal diet election of 1965, the rightist voing tradition continued with the NPD gaining some 8.6% of the vote. The durability of this tradition is shown by the results of the district diet election of 1932, when the NSDAP won 62.3% of the registered vote for the Grumbach *Amt*.

TABLE 3-4 *(continued)*

Sociostatistical Criteria	All inter-viewees (%)	TOTAL POTENTIAL NPD VOTERS[a] (%)		Percentage of the Potential NPD Voters, November–December 1966
		April–June 1966	November–December 1966	
Education				
Elementary, without vocational training	35	31	36	13
Elementary, with vocational training	41	42	41	12
High or trade school	19	22	19	14
Final high school examination, or college	5	5	5	12
	100	100	101[b]	
Origin				
Member of an expelled organization	6 ⎫	24	5	12
Other expelled persons, fugitives	16 ⎬		19	15
Indigent, other	78 ⎭	76	76	13
	100	100	100	
Religion and Church Attendance				
Practicing Catholic	29	22	18	8
Other Catholics	16	14	21	17
Practicing Protestants	11	9	9	13
Other Protestants	40	52	46	14
Other or no religion	4	3	6	18
	100	100	100	
Trade Union Membership				
Trade union connections in the family	33	34	26	9
No trade union connections	67	66	47	15
	100	100	100	
Fraternal Affiliation				
Members of a fraternity	32	41	37	15
Other	68	59	63	12
	100	100	100	

SOURCE: Representative statistics of Infas in the Federal territory, April–June 1966 (2,078 interviewees, of whom 120 were potential NPD voters); November–December 1966 (1,602 interviewees, of whom 205 were potential NPD voters).

a Question: "Would you ever vote for the NPD, or have you already so voted?"
b Totals not equal to 100% because of rounding.

largely nonpolitical or that traditionally have no close political connection. The large politically oriented organization seem to have discouraged their members from extensively supporting the NPD.

It was noticed in the earliest provincial diet elections that the NPD was receiving fewer votes in Catholic areas than in primarily Protestant regions. Polls confirm that strict Catholics (the criterion here being regular attendance at mass) tend much less toward the NPD than do nominal Catholics, and Protestants prominently are represented among the NPD voter potential.

Trade unions seldom exhibit rightist tendencies, and in past provincial diet elections, opposition to the NPD seems concentrated in Catholic areas and in traditional union strongholds.

SOCIOECONOMIC PROFILE OF THE NPD RESERVOIR

Let us summarize and characterize the NPD's body of supporters: sex, age, occupation, trade unions, and church membership are obviously important socio-statistical criteria (see Table 3–4). But sex and age, taken by themselves, explain relatively little since other, stronger determinants of electoral behavior override them. For example, old women rarely vote for the NPD, not because they are old women, but because their church and occupational characteristics are greater than those for the 45–60-year old men. Sex and age can safely be omitted from our analytic considerations of old women.[6]

NPD fortunes also depend on important long-standing political-institutional ties. Close contacts with the church and trade unions are important factors for both the CDU and SPD. Even in these groups, however, there exist NPD supporters.

The vote potential of the NPD is at its lowest wherever there are close ties with the Catholic Church or trade unions (Table 3–5). Among the approximately 38.5 million registered voters in the Federal Republic, about 10.5 million men and women are trade unionists or dependents of union members. Barely two-thirds of these tend to favor the SPD, a good sixth tends toward the CDU/CSU. The NPD voter reservoir, as a result, is 10% below the overall average.[7] Corresponding to this are the nine million voting Catholic church-goers. Of these, a good two-thirds affiliate with the CDU/CSU, and barely one-sixth with the SPD. Among this group, the NPD reservoir is 8% below the

[6] The classifications in Table 3–4 were adopted after a thorough analysis indicated what a sociostatistical classification of the electorate might be which would feature high and low NPD voter potential. Relevant criteria to determine these groups are presented.

[7] Party preferences and NPD vote potential have been obtained separately. Potential NPD voters are thus included among the supporters of the traditional parties. The circles in Table 3–5 show the size of groups then and the percentages for both major parties (white field: small parties and interviewees without data); the columns show how many voters in each group have declared (independent of their behavior then; they may have voted NPD once).

average. One small group of 2.5 million Catholic unionized voters have proven to be particularly immune to the NPD. Here, where social characteristics overlap, both major parties are represented evenly, with 45% for the SPD, and 44% for the CDU, whereas the NPD's potential amounts to only 7%. However, where no ties exist with large organizations, the source of potential rightist voters is substantially larger. In this non-Catholic–nonunion portion of the electorate, the size of the NPD potential depends on the individual's occupation.

TABLE 3-5. THE NPD IN THE POLITICAL ARENA

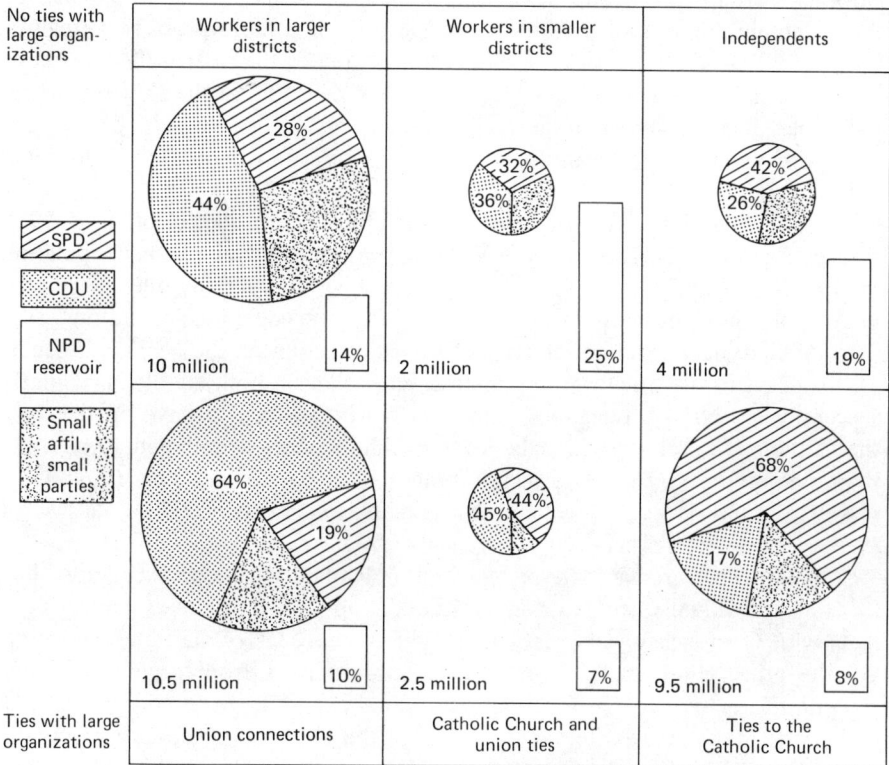

No ties with large organizations	Workers in larger districts	Workers in smaller districts	Independents
	28% / 44% / 14% / 10 million	32% / 36% / 25% / 2 million	42% / 26% / 19% / 4 million
SPD / CDU / NPD reservoir / Small affil., small parties	64% / 19% / 10% / 10.5 million	44% / 45% / 7% / 2.5 million	68% / 17% / 8% / 9.5 million
Ties with large organizations	Union connections	Catholic Church and union ties	Ties to the Catholic Church

Source: Calculations by the Institute for Applied Social Science
based on representative statistics of November 1966 to January 1967;
2,414 cases, average NPD potential = 12%.

Especially critical are two million workers who are touched neither by unions, nor by the Catholic Church, and who are active in small business. In these families, the lack of ties to the employee-type of working world seems to overlap to a large degree with middle-class consciousness; CDU and SPD preferences balance each other with a third each; and the NPD potential reaches a high level with one-quarter of the votes.

The NPD potential is lower among workers without pronounced middle-class identification than it is among freelance and independent businessmen. Of the four million farmers and independents having neither Catholic nor union ties, a good two-fifths favor the CDU/CSU, and one-quarter the SPD. The possible NPD vote amounts to nearly 19%.

Some ten million workers have no union or church ties, but come into contact with working-class ideas through participation in large industries. Two-fifths favor the SPD, and a substantial one-fourth favor the CDU/CSU. The NPD's vote potential here amounts to 14%.

As noted, the quickest to adopt NPD slogans are semiskilled and unskilled workers. Perhaps this group has unsatisfied status needs or feels threatened by the economic pressure of the business cycle (which is more probable); regardless, the NPD vote potential for this group is greater than for skilled workers. NPD vote potential among unskilled workers exceeds that of the skilled workers *only* when the unskilled are nonunionized.

NPD voter characteristics imply that the party is moving into the traditional political arena.

During the first phase of development (the Federal diet election of 1965 with 2.5% of the vote), polls show NPD support spread over various population groups (see Table 3–6). NPD voters were not attracted by the articulated interest of groups in the political process, but by a specific ideological minority.

Publicity from the first elections focused attention on the NPD and generated support for it.[8] In stage two, interest and criticism both count. Particularly susceptible to NPD propaganda were voters who seemed to have no ties with the Catholic Church or with labor unions. Those not so affiliated form more than one-quarter (28.5%) of the potential NPD voters. The CDU/CSU mobilized 17% of the socioeconomic segments, whereas the SPD only attracted 11.5%.

Political preferences derived less from individual socioeconomic status than from an individual's socioeconomic situation. Private households having contacts with Catholicism comprise about half of the CDU/CSU voter reservoir. On the other hand, half of the SPD support derives from organized labor. Despite efforts to affect its opponent's basis, neither of the two major parties has been particularly successful.[9] A full 16% of the SPD supporters are practicing Catholics, and 20% of the CDU supporters are trade unionists. It is not surpris-

---

[8] In local elections in Bayern in early 1966, the NPD (even in the Mittelfranken administrative district) sliced off no more than it had in the preceding Federal diet election. The "successes" of the radical right were lost in the general excitement of the 1965 election returns, while the insertion of NPD agents into the community parliaments was noticed everywhere; this process took place about six months later.

[9] The influence of large organizations is receding in general. The number of churchgoers among Catholics and the percentage of union members among those gainfully employed are declining in the long run. CDU/CSU victories in Protestant workers' circles and SPD gains among Catholic workers were mainly in fringe groups in which there were no close ties with church or unions.

TABLE 3–6. PARTY SUPPORT IN SOCIOECONOMIC GROUPS

Socioeconomic Groups	Percent of Potential NPD Voters	Potential NPD Voters (%)	DISTRIBUTION BY GROUP (%)		Legal Voters (%)
			SPD Supporters	CDU/CSU Supporters	
No ties to large organizations	17	59	40	37	43.5
(Of the above:)					
Independent, assistant workers	19	17	6.5	12	11
Employees, small business:	25	11.5	5	5	6
White-collar, civil servant	28				
Skilled	21				
Semiskilled, unskilled	27				
Employees, large business	14	30.5	28.5	20	26.5
White-collar, civil servant	12				
Skilled	11				
Semiskilled, unskilled	19				
Ties to large organizations	9	41	60	63	56.5
(Of the above:)					
Union ties:	10	22.5	44	14	27.5
White-collar, civil servant	7				
Skilled	13				
Semiskilled, unskilled	10				
Practicing Catholics	8	15.5	10	43	24
Union members tied to Catholic Church	7	3	6	6	5
Total legal voters	12	100	100	100	100

SOURCE: Representative statistics of Infas in the Federal territory, November 1966 to January 1967 (2,414 interviewees, random sample). See note 7 above regarding the breakdown of the legal electorate used here. The arrangement as to size is given in the table.

ing that even the absolutely smaller voter reservoirs of the minor parties are concentrated according to the weakness of organizational affiliation and other socioeconomic characteristics, where the parties are much alike. Not only is the voter reservoir of the FDP concentrated here, but so, too, is 60% of the potential NPD support. Barely two-fifths of the SPD and CDU/CSU supporters indicate no strong religious or unionist ties. Shifts in voting patterns for this segment of the voters have occurred. The CDU/CSU established itself at the expense of its smaller urban rivals; disgruntled CDU supporters siding with the SPD in recent years came mainly from these same socioeconomic groups. In this segment of the voters, the new right competes with existing parties having quite different political philosophies, a fact guaranteeing the NPD over half of its voters.

THE NPD'S RESERVOIR AND THE TRADITIONAL PARTIES

Which of the established parties loses votes because of the NPD? In other words, for what did the NPD's supporters vote when there was no NPD?

Analysis shows that the NPD's votes have (or could have) been won from all political camps because a large proportion of potential NPD voters had no fixed political identification before the NPD. Of those presently supporting the NPD, 44% changed parties since the Federal Republic was established, but our data show that only 32% crossed party lines in the overall electorate. Vote switching is clearly greater for supporters of the NPD than for others.

Since potential NPD voters do not always readily acknowledge NPD support when polled, a study is needed of NPD and non-NPD sympathies and attitudes.

It should be of little surprise that supporters of other small rightist parties, in so far as these exist, are particularly numerous among potential NPD voters. Also, the proportionate NPD potential among FDP supporters is relatively large: The average for the Federal Republic ("Federal Average") shows that 21% of the FDP's supporters could conceivably vote for the NPD, and 12% of the SPD's support, and 9% of the CDU/CSU's supporters, could also cast votes for the NPD (Table 3–7). Considering the segment of the society that supports the NPD, the figures are not surprising. The sociostatistical groups in which the NPD's potential is about average have long represented a natural source of FDP voters, too.

It is also apparent from the results of the sociostatistical analysis that the NPD's voter potential is somewhat larger for SPD supporters than for CDU/CSU supporters. Where voters are neither tied to church or union, the CDU has a clear majority among employees of large businesses. In general, the SPD is stronger among voters who are not bound to institutions: two-fifths of the electorate. Since the NPD can recruit comparatively many voters from this segment, its potential is greater among SPD than among CDU supporters.

This result is confirmed by the earlier voting behavior of potential NPD voters. Of those interviewed who said they had always voted for the SPD, a Federal (national) average of 11% belonged to the NPD voter reservoir. In the case of voters who had previously voted exclusively for the CDU/CSU, the NPD potential amounted to only 8%. The group voting for only one of the minor rightist parties is too small to be certain about, but there seems to be a tendency for this group to lean strongly toward the NPD.

Interviewees who said they had never voted expressed NPD sympathies relatively frequently. Some 16% of these "habitual nonvoters" identified themselves as potential voters for the NPD. This confirms something noticed in provincial diet election returns. It appears that the NPD gains were larger as the voter turnout rate increased over previous elections.

We already know that NPD potential is especially large among voters who

TABLE 3–7.   POLITICAL ORIGIN OF THE NPD VOTER POTENTIAL

Party Preference[a] Voter Fluctuation[b] Previous Voting Behavior[b] Never Voted for a Party Before[b]	Total Electorate (%)	POTENTIAL NPD VOTERS	
		Total (%)	Applied to the Respective Group (%)
CDU/CSU	38	26	9
SPD	41	38	12
FDP	5	7	21
Other parties	2	14	87
No data	14	15	13
	100	100	
Always votes the same	53	40	10
Changed party	32	44	18
No data, or never voted before	15	16	14
	100	100	
Consistently CDU/CSU	47	17	8
Consistently SPD	25	21	11
Consistently FDP	1	1	10
Consistently other parties	0	1	43
Voted several parties	32	44	18
Never voted	4	5	16
No data	11	11	12
	100	100	
Never voted CDU/CSU	45	46	13
Never voted SPD	53	48	11
Never voted FDP	88	78	11
Never voted for one of the major parties	17	18	14
Total number of interviewees	1,602	205	13

SOURCE: Representative statistics by Infas in the Federal territory, November–December 1966 (1,602 interviewees, random sample).

a Question: "Entirely in general this time, which of the political parties do you like best? (As far as one can say.) Which is really still the best?"

b Question: "Would you name for me all the parties you have voted for even once at any time since the end of the war (or since you became a legal voter)?"

have once changed party. Nationally, 18% of this mobile electorate rank themselves among potential NPD voters. Approximately two-fifths of this group are registered voters who had previously voted for a smaller party and then, as the political scene changed, switched over to one of the major parties. The CDU has benefited from these voter shifts about three times as much as has the SPD.

Previous small party supporters who drifted to the CDU also tend to favor the NPD more than the average; however, these voters seem to be tied more closely to the CDU than small party defectors attracted by the SPD. Nationally, 19% of those who had defected to the CDU said that they could conceivably vote for the NPD, but 31% of the same type of SPD voter said this. These relationships vary considerably from region to region (Table 3–8).

TABLE 3–8.   NPD VOTE GAINS AND INCREASE IN VOTER PARTICIPATION
IN HESSEN AND BAYERN (1966)

Increase in Vote Participation[a] (points)	Number of Districts	Average NPD Gain in Percentages[b]
Hessen	48	+5.3
0–1.9	10	+4.7
2–2.9	11	+5.0
3–3.9	16	+4.9
4.0+	11	+6.6
Bayern	206	+4.7
loss–+0.9	27	+3.3
1–2.9	71	+4.5
3–4.9	53	+5.0
5+	55	+5.4

SOURCE: Official election returns from the provincial diet elections of 1966.
a Measured in the last provincial diet election.
b Measured in the Federal diet election of 1965.

TABLE 3–9.   PARTY POLITICAL HISTORY OF THE MOBILE SEGMENT OF THE
ELECTORATE

			POTENTIAL NPD VOTERS	
Previously Voted	Present Preference	Total Mobile Voters[a] (%)	Total (%)	Related to Respective Groups (%)
SPD and CDU		27	16	11
SPD, CDU, and small parties	SPD	9	9	18
SPD and small parties		10	16	31
		46	41	
CDU and SPD and occasionally also small parties	Small parties	8	14	31
CDU and small parties		30	31	19
CDU, SPD, and small parties	CDU/CSU	12	3	14
CDU and SPD		4	10	15
		46	45	
Total (%)		100	100	18
(number)		503	92	

SOURCE: Representative statistics from Infas, November–December 1966 (1,602 interviewees).
   a Interviewees who named more than one party in response to the question: "Now name all the parties that you have voted for even once at any time since the end of the war (or since you became a legal voter)."

Three-fifths of the mobile voters have voted both for the SPD and the CDU, and some have also voted for one of the small parties (Table 3–9). If one divides these groups according to current political identification, there turn out to be no differences between SPD and CDU supporters as far as their NPD potential is concerned. But, former small party supporters, who now side more with the SPD than the CDU sympathize more with the NPD than the same type of voter who favors the CDU. On the other hand, voters whom the CDU won from the SPD seem to favor the NPD somewhat more than the SPD supporters who came from the CDU. Definitive statements are impossible to make because of the small number of interviewees in this group.

To summarize, the NPD potential is greatest among former small party voters. For SPD voters it is somewhat greater than for CDU voters (see Table 3–10). Although there are more CDU voters than SPD voters nationally, at 39%, the SPD has a somewhat greater percentage of potential NPD voters than the CDU, 37% of whose voters are included in the NPD reservoir.

The residual quarter of potential NPD voters is composed of persons who have voted exclusively for small parties or are mobile voters who now sympathize with one of the small parties (9%); those who said they had never voted (5%); and finally, those about whom nothing is known of prior party identification (10%).

Potential NPD voters include a relatively large number of the "politically

TABLE 3–10.   PRIOR ELECTION BEHAVIOR AND PARTY PREFERENCE (1966)

Previous Election Behavior[a]	Number of Cases	All Interviewees (%)	Potential NPD Voters[b] (%)
SPD voters	622	39	39
Who voted:			
Only SPD before	395	25	21
SPD and other parties, but not CDU	48	3	7
SPD and CDU (and sometimes small parties), now prefer SPD[c]	179	11	11
CDU voters	666	42	37
Who voted:			
Only CDU before	432	27	17
CDU and other parties, but not SPD	151	9	14
CDU and SPD (and sometimes small parties), now prefer SPD[c]	83	6	6
Voters from small parties only (including FDP) or who now prefer small parties[c]	70	4	9
Never voted before	63	4	5
No data	181	11	10
Total	1602	100	100

SOURCE: Representative poll by Infas in the Federal territory, November–December 1966 (1,602 interviewees, of whom 205 were potential NPD voters).

[a] Question: "Now name all parties that you have ever voted for since the end of the war (or since you have become a legal voter)."

[b] Question: "Would you ever vote for the NPD, or have you already done so?"

[c] Question: "Generally, which of the political parties do you like best at present? (As far as one can say.) Which is the best?"

homeless," persons who right after World War II voted for one of the smaller parties or did not vote at all, but then turned to one of the major parties. Voters who recently drifted over to the two major parties are also often not closely tied to the Catholic Church or to trade unions. These nonintegrated, borderline voters in both major parties are of considerable importance to the new rightist NPD.

Naturally, regional variations in voters exist. For example, in the 1950's and 1960's the CDU was able to attract many former small party supporters in Schleswig-Holstein. Among conservative Protestants in Hunsrück and Pfalz, motivated by anticlerical feelings, the SPD assumed an increased role. Thus, the NPD was able to win voters not only from the FDP in the provincial elections of April 23, 1967, but also from CDU supporters in Schleswig-Holstein. On the other hand, in Pfalz and Hunsrück, NPD support came more at the expense of the SPD.

THE NPD RESERVOIR AND ECONOMIC EXPECTATIONS

It was formerly thought that NPD political fortunes and the state of the economy were unrelated. The argument supporting this thesis held that NPD sympathizers have benefited from the growing economy as much as everyone else. NPD voters, it was said, had no special interest in economic questions. All of this is true. As Table 3–6 shows, the NPD's potential seems to be even greater among voters having high incomes than with those having lower incomes.

More decisive in the thinking of those who turn toward the NPD than a general interest in economics or even the actual economic state are philosophical or ideological ideas about economic self-determination now and in the future.

Individuals who believe themselves to be economically better off now than they were two years ago have much less use for the NPD than those who consider the present economic situation to be bad. Of the seven million or so registered voters who perceive their economic status to be improved, the NPD has 9%; however, of the nine million who felt more economically deprived at the end of 1966 than before, 19% were in sympathy with the radical NPD.

The NPD's voter reservoir varies similarly when one considers present and prospective economic situations: of persons who by the end of 1966 foresaw an improvement in their own economic position in the coming year (about six million legal voters), 12% tended toward the NPD; of the twelve million who thought things would get worse, 18% favored the NPD.

In fact, anyone who believes that his economic situation is worse today than two years ago, and that it will continue to deteriorate, is particularly susceptible to radical rightist propaganda. Nearly one-fourth (23%) of these pessimists exhibit NPD sympathies. That is to say, the percentage of persons having pessimistic expectations is significantly greater among NPD supporters than it is among the population at large. Moreover, nearly half of the potential NPD voters are "bearish" about their future economic prospects.

Thus, it is clear that the electoral successes secured by the NPD in Hessen and Bayern coincide with changes in private economic expectations.

This connection between private economic expectations and a readiness to vote for the NPD manifests itself in nearly all segments of the population. *The more pessimistic are economic expectations, the greater is NPD voter potential.*

Meanwhile, the voter groups most directly involved are those which, lacking ties to the Catholic or unionist groups, are particularly susceptible to rightist ideological propaganda. Of independents and employees in small businesses who fear economic deterioration, about two-fifths are more than twice as susceptible to NPD propaganda as those voters who view the future optimistically.

This tendency can be observed in all segments of the population, though not to the same degree in each. One exception is trade unionists for whom economics does not influence the extent to which they vote for the NPD. Apparently, trade unionism is actually strong enough to limit radical political behavior even during crises. But many skilled workers are included in trade unions. And this professional class has been favored so much in the past that far less concern is felt about their support than in the case of semiskilled or unskilled workers, or even in the case of middle-class independents. Questions about the economic future supposedly do not bother skilled workers nearly as much as they do other professional, working groups, which take economics more seriously.

Economic expectations worsened drastically during 1966.[10] In the fall of 1965, 28% still figured that their economic position would improve in the coming year, but by December 1966, this amounted to only 16%. The percentage of pessimists increased over this period from 10% to 32%.

It is insightful to determine the NPD's vote potential under economic conditions better than those existing toward the end of 1966, and under conditions that prevailed as of fall 1965. If economic expectations had been the same at the end of 1966 as in fall 1965, the following astonishing results hold: The NPD voter reservoir would have declined nationally only 3 percentage points, from 13 to 10% (see Tables 3–11 and 3–12).

Does this mean that NPD potential support is not as closely connected with changes in economic conditions as was first believed? Probably not. NPD potential and economic expectations being related as they are, even general increases in the number of potential and actual NPD voters are essentially fueled by economic deterioration.

An NPD gain of three percentage points, traceable to a deterioration in economic expectations, is an enormously high quantity, because the value is an empirically determined minimum. Therefore, one could assume that about half

[10] "Wirtschaftswunder und Wirtschaftskanzler," *Politogramm* (Bad Godesberg: Infas, November 1966).

TABLE 3–11.   NPD POTENTIAL BY INCOME AND ECONOMIC EXPECTATIONS

| | | POTENTIAL NPD VOTERS[a] | |
Income Groups—Appraisal of Private Economic Situation	Percent of Total Number Interviewed (%)	Total (%)	As Compared with Respective Groups (%)
	Family income		
Below 400 DM	10	9	12
401–800 DM	37	35	12
801–1200 DM	27	28	14
More than 1200 DM	11	14	16
No data	15	14	12
	100	100	
	Present private economic situation is . . .[b]		
Better than before	18	12	9
The same	59	59	13
Worse than before	23	29	19
	100	100	
	Future private economic situation will be . . .[c]		
Better than before	16	15	12
The same	52	40	10
Worse than before	32	45	18
	100	100	
Economic expectations pessimistic as a whole[d]	11	20	23
Total number of interviewees	1,602	205	13

SOURCE: Representative statistics from Infas in the Federal territory, November–December 1966 (1,602 interviewees, of whom 205 were potential NPD voters).

a Question: "Would you ever vote for the NPD, or have you ever done so?"

b Question: "If you compare your present economic condition with that of about two years ago, do you find that it is better, worse, or the same as it was then?"

c Question: "Do you think that your economic circumstances will improve or worsen in coming years?"

d Interviewees who defined both their present circumstances and their future prospects as bad.

of the gains in NPD sympathy can be traced back to changed economic expectations. However, population groups most susceptible to fluctuations in the business cycle are also those in which the NPD reservoir is already large, since these groups tend to lack institutional ties.

While the average percentage of potential NPD voters was nearer the population average on questions about economic expectations in the fall of 1965, economic expectations for independents worsened by about 5%, and for employees in small businesses by about 9%. This is one-third of the NPD reservoir of these groups. Among employees in larger businesses, NPD gain was only 3%. Gains associated with fluctuations in the business cycle were even lower in that segment of the population having trade union or Catholic ties. The NPD won only one or two percentage points as a result of worsening economic

TABLE 3–12.   ECONOMIC EXPECTATIONS AND THE NPD RESERVOIR

Voter Groups	Own Economic Position as Compared with Two Years Ago[a] (%)			Own Economic Position in the Future[b] (%)			Economic Position Now Is Worse and Future Expectations Are Pessimistic[c] (%)
	Better	Same	Worse	Improve	Stay the Same	Worsen	
Voters without ties to large organizations							
Independent and assistant workers	(23)[d]	23	(29)	(13)	15	42	(47)
Employees in small business	(6)	28	(40)	(14)	26	(26)	(44)
Employees in large business	8	13	25	19	9	20	27
Voters with ties to large organizations							
Union ties	10	10	9	14	7	11	(12)
Practicing Catholics	3	8	14	2	8	10	16
Union members with Catholic ties	(20)	(4)	(4)	(0)	(11)	(3)	(0)
Total population	9	13	19	12	10	18	23

SOURCE: Representative statistics from Infas in the Federal territory, November–December 1966 (1,602 interviewees, of whom 205 were potential NPD voters).

a Question: "If you compare your economic situation now with that of two years ago, do you find that it is better, worse, or the same now as it was then?"

b Question: "Do you figure that your economic circumstances will improve or worsen in coming years?"

c Combination of the first and second questions.

d The percentages give the segment of potential NPD voters in the respective group.

expectations. This is not to say that increases in the NPD voter reservoir among unionized workers and practicing Catholics is *not* caused in part by economic events. The willingness to vote radical right because of economic problems seems to be especially slight in these groups.

NPD returns in Hessen and Bayern originated essentially from pessimistic evaluations of economic conditions. A recession and governmental financial crisis combined with Economic Chancellor Ludwig Erhard's loss of authority, produced the nadir in economic expectations that made it appear that the election of an aggressive rightist opposition was the only way out. A new Federal administration buoyed hopes. As private expectations began to rise, along with public confidence in the Kiesinger–Brandt government, the NPD's voter potential slowly receded again (Table 3–13).

If the pattern in Hessen and Bayern had carried over, the NPD would certainly have received 8–9% of the registered vote, in view of the socio-economic structure of the north and southwest of the Federal Republic. Far more than the intraparty conflict—and independently of the objective data on economic developments, which have hardly changed—the optimistic expectations of private households must have been the reason why the NPD had only relatively modest success on April 23, 1967, especially in Schleswig-Holstein (Table 3–14).

TABLE 3–13.   ESTIMATE OF NPD GAINS THROUGH WORSENING OF
ECONOMIC EXPECTATIONS

Voter Groups	Potential NPD Voters at present (%)	Potential NPD Voters in the Situation of Economic Expectation of Fall of 1965 (%)	Difference in Percentage Points
Voters without ties to large organizations			
Independent and assistant workers	19	14	+5
Employees in small business	25	16	+9
Employees in large business	14	11	+3
Voters with ties to large organizations			
Union ties	10	9	+1
Practicing Catholics	8	6	+2
Union members with Catholic ties	7	6	+1
Total	13	10	+3

SOURCE: Calculation by Infas. The calculation was made so that the segments of potential NPD voters in various expectation groups reported in November–December 1966 were assigned to the distribution of economic expectations observed in the fall of 1965. On the distribution of expectations in individual voters groups, see: "Anhänger der neuen Rechtspartei [Supporters of the New Party of the Right]," *Politogramm* (Bad Godesberg: Infas, February–March 1967), p. 28.

TABLE 3-14.   NPD POTENTIAL AND ECONOMIC
EXPECTATIONS OF 1966-67

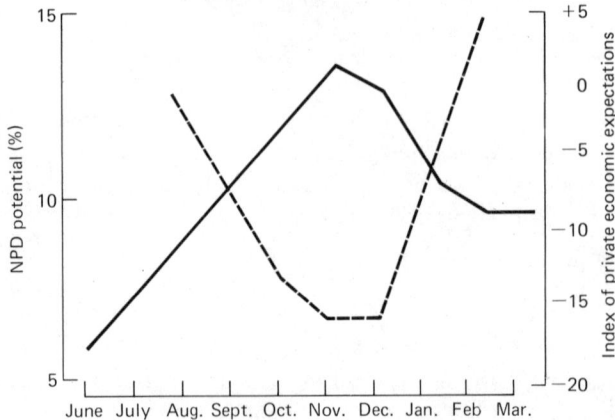

CONCEPTIONS, BEHAVIOR, AND SOCIAL CONTACTS

The idea that the economic and political difficulties confronting Bonn toward the end of 1966 together have allowed the NPD to gain in the elections of Hessen and Bayern has been popularly accepted. Two-fifths (40%) of the population think that strong NPD performances in Hessen and Bayern stem from a lack of confidence in the Bonn government. Furthermore, about 27% say that the NPD's success results primarily from economic dissatisfaction. In this appraisal, NPD supporters differ only slightly from the rest of the electorate. Abundant coverage by the media probably accounts for the agreement.

Opinions differ on two points: only 6% of the potential NPD voters—and 13% of all interviewed—mention Nazi resurgence as a reason for NPD success. Clearly, NPD sympathizers do not want their party to be identified as a Nazi party. As a result, only a minority of potential NPD voters—two-fifths (38%) —answered a direct question as to whether the NPD today has the same objectives as the NSDAP had.[11] Three-fourths (75%) of those interviewed nationally see parallels between the National Democrats and the National Socialists (see Table 3–15).

TABLE 3–15.   SUPPOSED GROUNDS FOR NPD SUCCESSES

Reason for Voting NPD[a]	Number of Cases	Percentage of Interviewees	Potential NPD Voters (%)
The NPD is the only alternative to the Bonn parties	46	6	12
Loss of confidence in the Bonn regime	344	40	39
Testing a new party	87	10	10
The SPD has no clear policy	28	4	5
Concern over the economy	234	27	28
Old Nazi sympathizers	114	13	6
Total	863	100	100

Source: Representative poll by Infas, Federal territory, November 1966.

a Question: "The NPD has been making a good showing in recent elections. What are the reasons for it?"

Another conjecture by potential NPD voters regarding the causes of the shift rightward diverges from that of the majority of the voters. Potential NPD voters consider the NPD's being the only opposition to the Bonn parties as the reason for its successes in the elections twice as much (some 12%) as do the other legal voters (6%). To overstate the point, one does not vote for the NPD if one is *for* something, but rather if one is *against* something.

This thesis is supported by the following discovery: of twenty-five voters who admitted that they had voted NPD in a poll immediately after the provincial diet election in Hessen, only two interviewees gave positive reasons for their election choice—"They have good ideas." And, "They are oriented toward law and order and austerity." All others aggressively justified their vote with argu-

[11] "Is there, or was there, a party in Germany that pursued similar goals to the NPD? Which?" Infas representative statistics in the Federal territory, April–June 1966 (random sample, 2,078 persons interviewed of whom 120 were potential NPD voters).

ments like: "The other parties are good for nothing." "One must make it clear to the others that they must try harder in everything." "The NPD is keeping its eyes on the others." "I was not satisfied with the Bonn administration." "Out of opposition. . . ."

Sentiment against the existing parties, particularly the two major ones, obviously plays a role in the symbolic world of NPD supporters. Thus, the major coalition is criticized by a majority of potential NPD (58%) partisans. It is said that the parties existing after the war distributed power poorly among themselves and impeded the formation of new parties; this may account partly for this significant NPD sentiment.

NPD sympathizers display aggressiveness besides that toward the party system. Hence, potential NPD voters favor press censorship more than the average population. NPD supporters regard an arms limitation negotiated between the United States and the Soviet Union, without German consultation, as being both more probable and reprehensible than do voters in other parties. It is evident that these attitudes are rooted in the past, when people were generally quite conforming. Only a fraction of potential NPD voters want their party to be identified as the inheritor of NSDAP (NAZI) ideas. Nonetheless, three-fourths have expressed basic agreement with NSDAP ideas, agreeing that "National Socialism has its good sides, too, since order and integrity prevailed, at least." It is evident from popular polls that certain policy preferences held throughout the general population help to explain the startling interest in the NPD's successes. Besides the majority who could conceive of the idea of voting for the NPD, more than half of the supporters of traditional parties also endorse the assertion that "National Socialism had its good sides. . . ."

Aggressive and authoritarian predispositions are not limited to radical rightists; they are everywhere latent and can be mobilized rapidly should countervailing forces weaken. In a series of interview questions whose political content was not obvious, opinions apparently differed only slightly within various political camps. For instance, these opinion polls, taken independently of vote returns, from time to time have shown about two-thirds in favor of the return of the death penalty and about one-half demanding that German policy "see to it that the foreign troops are withdrawn from our land" (Table 3–16). While aggressive predispositions to policies are often found at the extreme ends of the political spectrum, they are in no way limited to these extremes.

A real future danger is that the democratic parties might gradually slip to the extreme right both by vigorous acts and nationalistic rhetoric, coopting and making it essentially redundant for the NPD to establish itself in the society.

Studies show that while nationalistic-authoritarian attitudes are quite widespread, they become politicized only under special circumstances. Pessimism, expressed as economic expectations, is one such circumstance. When a respondent does not think that National Socialism had some virtues, economic expectations usually do not contribute to NPD support. In this case, "social protest" remains within the existing party system. But those who are still undecided about

TABLE 3-16.   OPINIONS, ATTITUDES, AND PARTY PREFERENCES

	Total Number of Interviewees	Percent of Interviewees Expressing Corresponding Opinion	Potential NPD Voters (%)	PARTY PREFERENCES (%)			
				CDU/CSU	SPD	FDP and Others	Unknown
Against a large coalition[a]	841	39	58	36	34	66	48
Against a "party cartel"[b]	2078	8	20	8	7	17	10
NPD pursues similar goals to the NSDAP[c]	2078	44	26	43	50	44	27
National socialism had its good sides[d]	764						
Arms agreement between the USA and the USSR (without consulting Germany) is ...							
possible[e]	1602	67	73	66	69	77	60
bad[f]	1602	17	26	17	15	28	17
Foreign troops should be withdrawn[g]	2082	41	56	40	43	56	36
For censoring the press[h]	2078	29	42	34	25	33	25
For the death penalty[i]	2078	67	68	69	67	69	62

SOURCE: Representative statistics from Infas, April–June 1966 (random sample, 2,078 interviewees); November–December 1966 (1,602 interviewees); December 1966 (841 interviewees); March 1967 (764 interviewees); February–March 1967 (2,082 interviewees), in Niedersachsen.

a "Is the large coalition a good solution for the Federal Republic, or is there a better solution?"
b "One sometimes hears the opinion that the popular parties, such as the CDU, the SPD, and the FDP, have divided the power among themselves and aren't letting any others emerge. Do you agree?"
c "Is there, or was there, in Germany a party that follows similar goals to the NPD? Which?"
d "Is this statement more true or false? National Socialism had its good sides. At least order and integrity prevailed."
e "Do you consider it possible for the Americans and the Russians to agree without taking Germany's opinions into account?"
f "Would this be bad for Germany, or not so bad?"
g "Do you regard this statement as more true or more false? German policy should see to it that foreign troops are withdrawn from our land."
h "From time to time articles are published in certain newspapers and journals that lack a sense of responsibility. It has been proposed that the government establish a commission of experts to check all articles and suppress a publication, if need be. Are you for or against this?"
i "It has often been said that the death penalty should be introduced for especially serious crimes. Are you for or against this proposition?"

National Socialism are especially susceptible to NPD proselytizing during actual or expected economic reverses. NPD potential support is far above average in this segment of the population, including at least one-third of the electorate.[12]

The longer the period of popular dissatisfaction, the greater are the chances that the NPD will become a more legitimate political institution in district and provincial parliaments. One can imagine conditions under which NPD membership could be declared openly without fear of sanctions. The party might be able to establish itself as a legitimate opposition, thereby winning social acceptability. A party that is so well organized, broadly distributed, and also regionally rooted does not soon nor easily disappear from the political scene.

How advanced is NPD development? What basic changes have already taken place, and what are the prospects for the 25,000 members whom the party has at its disposal?

A poll taken soon after the Hessen provincial diet election provides some indications. Only about 15% of the voters of both major parties indicate that they know people who voted for the NPD. The vast majority have no personal contact with rightist voters (see Table 3–17). The minority that know NPD voters usually do not know them very well. For instance, the emergence of the NPD has led to few family conflicts. To the extent that one knows NPD voters, they are mostly distant acquaintances whose political views are not shared.

In other words, in so far as personal contacts exist between major party and NPD voters, they are usually loose ones. For most NPD supporters the decision to vote must still be a relatively personal, private matter, carried out without the reinforcing influence of friends, colleagues, or family. Even among potential NPD voters, just under two-fifths indicated they knew someone who had voted NPD in the Hessen elections. Only this group admits to radical rightist political views, both to elicit general recognition, and to strengthen their own predispositions to vote NPD.

THE NPD'S FUTURE

Until now the NPD has just been another aggregation of fringe groups, outsiders, and the dissatisfied found in nearly all societies.

The facts that most voters have been socialized over long periods with

[12] Analysis of one set of representative statistics by the Institute for Social Science in Niedersachsen (February 1967; 1,345 interviewees, random sample), produced this result. The following percentages of potential NPD voters were found for each group:

Attitude Toward National Socialism	Estimate of One's Own Economic Position	NPD Potential (%)
Positive	Negative	32
Positive	Not negative	13
Not positive	Negative	4
Not positive	Not negative	8

TABLE 3–17.   PERSONAL CONTACTS IN THE NPD AREA (HESSEN, 1966)

	NPD VOTERS AMONG . . .[b]				DESCRIPTION OF THIS NPD VOTER[d]				
	Family (%)	Circle of friends and acquaintances (%)	Colleagues (%)	Acquainted personally with NPD voters[c] (%)	An acquaintance[a] (%)	Man[a] (%)	Protestant[a] (%)	Long-time resident[a] (%)	Has similar political opinions[a, e] (%)
Total	4	11	8	16	58	85	73	76	44
SPD voters	2	10	7	15	60	92	71	77	9
CDU voters	2	7	7	14	55	90	75	78	17
Other voters	23	27	11	30	63	63	80	63	73
Unknown	4	14	13	16	52	80	69	83	32
Potential NPD voters	23	34	17	37	56	76	70	76	64

SOURCE: Representative statistics from Infas in Hessen, November–December 1966 (1,124 interviewees).

a These percentages refer only to those interviewed who personally knew NPD voters.

b Question: "Have your relatives voted in the present provincial diet election for either the CDU or the SPD? Are there any among them who voted NPD?"

c Question: "Do you know anyone personally who voted for the NPD in the last provincial diet election?"

d A series of questions was asked by which the NPD voters with whom the interviewees had personal contact could be more carefully described.

e Question: "Do you agree with this person in all political (and other) matters fully, or only a little?"

authoritarian and aggressive means and regard their attitudes toward the environment as private, but subject to easy political change, must give us cause for some concern.

Should it one day occur to the average voter that his neighbors, friends, and colleagues are unanimously agreed to stop reparation payments to Israel, cease trying war criminals, become isolationistic in foreign affairs, seat energetic men in parliament, prescribe short hair for young men and long skirts for young women,[13] and that such opinions can be freely expressed by ballot, then the number of persons who identify themselves as rightist voters would also soon change.

Memories of the past are not limited to those remote corners of Germany that were spared war and postwar troubles and have preserved conservative traditions. The *Amt* of Grumbach in the District of Birkenfeld is no longer a curiosity since 1966. During those provincial elections, the NPD generally did well where the NSDAP had shown strength before 1933. This is no fleeting impression, it is a statistically significant observation. Of course, the percentage of votes that the NPD scored in cities of Hessen and Bayern in 1966 is absolutely smaller than the NSDAP percentages of 1932; however, the relationship be-

13 Demands of this type find consensus in public opinion polls with a great majority of the population. The sentences cited here can be added at will.

tween the NPD's votes in the 1966 provincial elections and the NSDAP votes in the Reichstag election of 1932 is expressed in a correlation coefficient of 0.71 (Table 3–18).[14]

Election returns won by the NPD in one district at the end of 1966 can be

TABLE 3–18.   INTERRELATIONSHIP OF NSDAP AND NPD IN CITIES OF BAYERN AND HESSEN

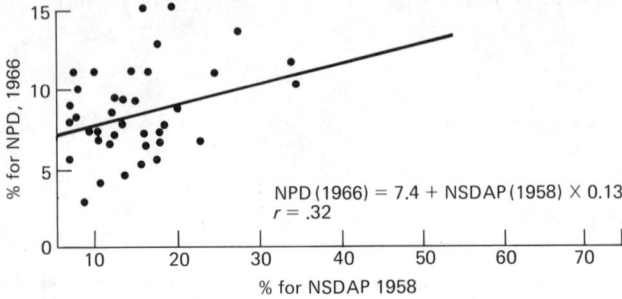

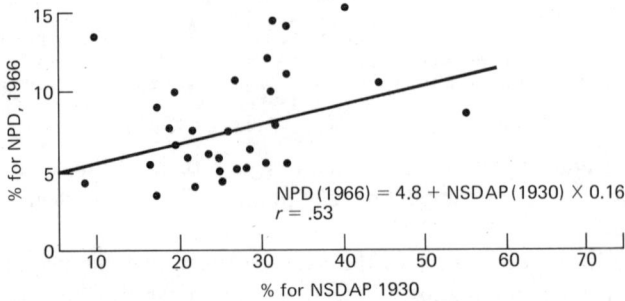

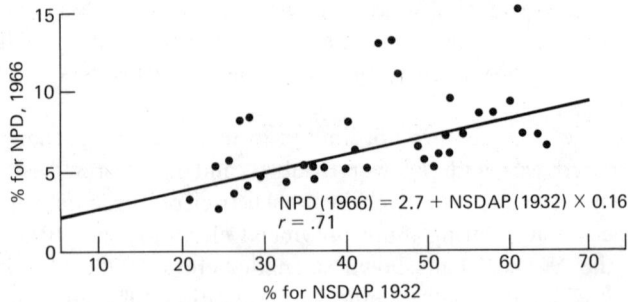

$$NPD (1966) = 7.4 + NSDAP (1958) \times 0.13$$
$$r = .32$$

$$NPD (1966) = 4.8 + NSDAP (1930) \times 0.16$$
$$r = .53$$

$$NPD (1966) = 2.7 + NSDAP (1932) \times 0.16$$
$$r = .71$$

Source: Calculations by the Institute for Applied Social Science based on official election statistics.

[14] Only the election returns from the cities form the basis for these figures, since the returns from the other districts were not all accessible. The study showed that the Reichstag election of 1932 is better adapted for evaluating the NPD returns of 1966 than was that of 1930 or 1928.

expressed as a function of the percentage of the NSDAP vote in the same district a generation ago: one need only know the NSDAP's percentage from 1932, multiply it by 0.16, and add 2.7 percentage points to the product. This simple model could have successfully reproduced the NPD vote in most of the cities of Hessen and Bayern.[15]

Despite war, destruction, population migration, and changes in the party system, the social structure that spawned National Socialism has obviously persisted or regenerated itself and could provide fertile ground, though to a lesser degree, for a rightist resurgence.

Does the existence of this traditional social structure mean that a new rightist party will develop overnight in the Federal Republic? There are few signs of this happening at present, because of four separate obstacles the radical right must overcome that appear quite formidable when taken together.

First: The Catholic Church and the trade unions provide an immunizing effect, as they did in the Weimar period. Voters associated with these organizations are also strongly integrated into one of the two major parties. A new ideology or an entirely new political organization has little apparent room to develop. Still, the influence of these organizations is gradually weakening; church and union memberships are both decreasing.

Second: Where organizational ties do not exist, for a broad segment of the blue- and white-collar classes, new and better working conditions, increased free time, and other aspects of industrial society have an important "pragmatizing effect." Nevertheless, nationalistic and aggressive attitudes encounter less rejection where middle-class consciousness conflicts with industrial society, e.g., among the smaller middle-class businessmen and farmers. Industrial concentration, even in the service sector, is occurring along with a decline in numbers in the agriculture sector. These segments of the population will continue to dwindle, thereby reducing the NPD pool of supporters.

Third: Although one encounters throwbacks to the National Socialist ideology in polls, this involves only scattered and disorganized remnants. Not totally eradicated, they still exist here and there. With the demise of NAZI ideology, the great majority have embraced behavioral patterns of Western industrial society and adopted democratic institutions, even though their meaning is not always understood. An isolated, nationalistic view of life no longer predominates. While the fragments of the past exist, there is a danger that the democratic parties might incorrectly overestimate the real strength of the new right, and yield unnecessarily to their political demands. Barring an unexpected large-scale reeducation in democratic procedures in the short run, corrosive

[15] It should be noted that a high correlation says nothing about the vote level. Naturally, the NPD percentage in 1966 is vanishingly small in comparison with the NSDAP figures of 1932 (as implied in the 0.16 coefficient). Besides, the election returns for Rheinland-Pfalz on April 23, 1967, follow the same pattern, whereas the NPD returns from Schleswig-Holstein exhibit a less close correlation with the figures from 1932. The special migrations of population in Schleswig-Holstein after the war could be the cause of this difference.

effects of time and neglect are still the best weapons against an ideological resurgence of the right.

Fourth: The most important obstacle to the resuscitation of a radical right party is still economic development. If the democratic parties succeed in achieving economic and political stability so that the common man needs to worry less about his job, income, and private way of life, then a fundamental reason for supporting the radical right will have been wiped out.

These factors, shown in Table 3–19, are all the more effective as they interact in a mutually supportive fashion. Studies show that the segment of the population most likely to be affected by crises of economic confidence is the

TABLE 3-19. OBSTACLES TO RIGHTIST RADICALISM

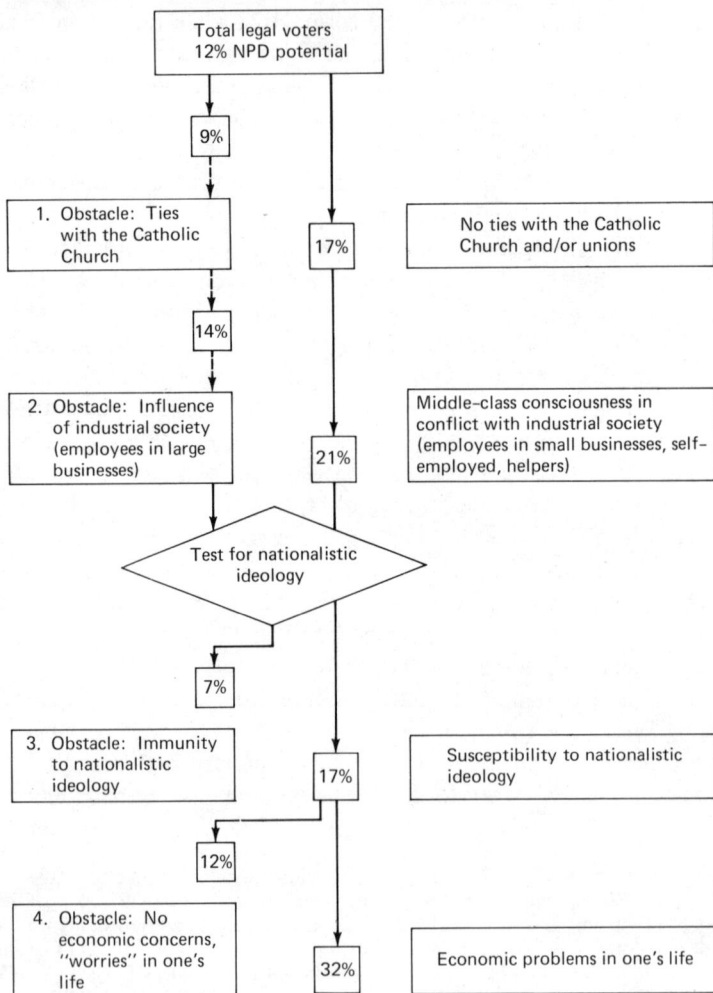

same one which a generation ago was vulnerable to rightist propaganda. Should the NPD succeed in consolidating these initial political gains before true economic stability is achieved, then it could build the "societal ties" a party needs if it is to survive. Of course, sources of prime NPD support—those voters who are not tied to the two major parties, who lack religious and union contacts, and who also have special social problems—are few in number.

Nevertheless, the middle class, encountering changes in its economic status, could evaluate its economic prospects pessimistically to supply the basis for a small radical rightist party. To capture these voters, the NPD needs time to establish itself as a viable opposition party in certain districts and regions. Alternatively, we must await either formal action from the Federal Constitutional Court, or else the disintegration process that other small parties have undergone before the NPD.

Part III

Conditions

INTRODUCTION

Studying conditions refers to the identification of factor combinations that have determined the magnitude of trends. Both trends and conditions, as distinct intellectual approaches or orientations, are concerned with generalizations and particulars; however, *trends* emphasize understanding of the sequence of events in a specific context, as interpreted through some "theory," whereas *conditions* emphasize the theoretical generalizations that are suggested by, and tested against, data from a variety of situations.

This orientation stresses the construction of theory, the development of structural descriptions by means of rigorous measurement and careful observation. As Hayward R. Alker, Jr. reminds us, the whole of any context is not only not equal to the sum of all its parts, it is basically different.[1] All too frequently, we observe, the social *scientist*, intent on measuring with great accuracy often loses sight of the fact that he is working with only a portion, not the whole.[2] Worse yet, these "rigorous" partial analyses are often carried to an extreme, decreasing one's understanding of the interconnections and important inter-relationships among a context's relevant elements.[3] In short, scientific analysis ends up destroying the wholeness of a context, the very thing it set out to measure, by allowing a researcher's focus of attention and sense of relevance to narrow excessively. A sophisticated social scientist is aware of this strong tendency to suboptimize, to borrow a term from the field of operations research, and works repeatedly back and forth between part and whole, between the

[1] See Hayward R. Alker, Jr., "The Long Road to International Relations Theory: Problems of Statistical Nonadditivity," *World Politics*, Vol. 18 (July 1966), pp. 623–55.
[2] Mario Bunge, "The Weight of Simplicity in the Construction and Assaying of Scientific Theories," *Philosophy of Science*, Vol. 28 (April 1961), pp. 120–49.
[3] Albert O. Hirschman, "The Search for Paradigms as a Hinderance to Understanding," *World Politics*, Vol. 22 (April 1970), pp. 330–43.

empirical data obtained on individual elements and the overall sequences of events in a context. In practice, such sophistication is rare.

The goal of most conditions-oriented work is, simply, to describe by inference the underlying structural processes of a given context or system through measuring the behavioral outputs of that context. However, no two social systems behave in precisely the same way, as historians eagerly point out, and no system is stagnant; consequently, the description of any given system at a point in time *must* differ from the description of the same or any other system at other times. Because one's simplifications are both gross and tentative, the need for many structural interpretations, derived from a variety of perspectives, cannot be stressed enough. There is no such thing as a final, singular, immutable theory in the social sciences; the set of possible potential simplifications is in fact logically boundless.

Conditions specialists generally try to describe a set of structural processes that are simplified—capturing a few key processes inferred to underlie complicated behavior; general—representing more than a single system; and realistic—explaining some of the important behavior of a designated context.

Often in haste to measure, conditions specialists overlook interesting and important research and policy questions. In other words, simple numbers are substituted for complex good sense. Often in haste to be formally elegant, another sort of conditions specialist eschews empirical realities. In this case, an occasional check against reality might prove either highly productive or, more likely, totally devastating; regardless, it is seldom made. The trade-off between elegant formalism and "barefooted empiricism," [4] is no trade-off at all: both styles and insights are required. Whether by a single specialist or several, raw data and raw logic must be skillfully and continually blended. Sadly, it does not happen very often.

Thorough observation, careful measurement, and astute simplification are all desirable features of conditions-oriented work and should be seized upon by those developing a contextual policy approach to their subject matter. Assorted weaknesses of the orientation must be explicitly accounted for and reduced, compensated for, or avoided. For instance, because many normatively interesting features of a context are not quantifiable, scientific specialists may elect to ignore or overlook them in their zeal to be rigorous. The ethical and policy components of such analyses are quickly diminished in the process. Because most social science produces, at best, weakly predictive structural interpretations or models, projective and policy components of an analysis tend to be slighted. And finally, because many policy interests are not susceptible to easy or ready measurement, misguided efforts to be precise may diminish the utility of an analysis for any but "academic" purposes.

Our point is the common one: the five identified intellectual tasks must be continually and carefully interrelated to solve problems.

[4] Our thanks to Joseph LaPalombara for the picturesque label.

THE LITERATURE

A handy way of categorizing the relevant literature is through considering a few broad philosophical-theoretical contributions by way of indicating the scope and purpose of the conditions orientation; models and model-building are important, and a select few sources are indicated; we end this abbreviated literature overview by citing from four discernible subspecialty fields, including structural-function, cybernetic, political culture, and systems.

Philosophical-Theoretical

A sweeping perspective is contained in Ernest Nagel's standard, *The Structure of Science: Problems in the Logic of Scientific Explanation* (New York: Harcourt, Brace, 1961); a more social scientific, and more easily comprehended, accounting of most of the fundamental issues is Abraham Kaplan, *The Conduct of Inquiry* (San Francisco: Chandler, 1964); and more directly addressed to the practical status (*c.* 1956) of science in the social disciplines, Leonard D. White, ed., *The State of the Social Sciences* (Chicago: University of Chicago Press, 1956). Two extremely important and insightful commentaries on the general issue of multiple perspectives and the need for many contextual interpretations are Thomas S. Kuhn, *The Structure of Scientific Revolutions* (Chicago: University of Chicago Press, 1962); and Albert O. Hirschman, *op. cit.* Serving as a bridge and communication link between the more exotic philosophical literature and the more pragmatic is Karl W. Deutsch, "On Theories, Taxonomies, and Models as Communication Codes for Organizing Information," *Behavioral Science*, Vol. 11 (January 1966), pp. 1–17.

Models and Model-Building

We know of very few examples of quantitative models having been built to study political development and change, a simple fact motivating the production of this volume. However, it is possible to sketch crudely what general forms such works have taken in parallel and comparable subdisciplines.

Herbert A. Simon and Allen Newall, "Models: Their Uses and Limitations," in Leonard D. White, ed., *op. cit.*, is a good place to get properly oriented; James S. Coleman, *Introduction to Mathematical Sociology* (New York: The Free Press, 1964); and Hayward R. Alker, Jr., *Mathematics and Politics* (New York: Macmillan, 1965), both have important and pertinent sections devoted to modeling issues and both warrant careful and frequent reading. Herbert A. Simon's classic, *Administrative Behavior: A Study of Decisionmaking Processes in Administrative Organizations* (New York: Macmillan, 1957 ed.), is an excellent guide to the type of empirical social science we favor and recommend; a clear application of many of Simon's lessons is J. P. Crecine, *Governmental Problem Solving* (Chicago: Rand McNally, 1969), which studies and models budget-making processes—work extended recently from the original three American urban contexts to include Dortmund, West Germany. Measurement is a key functional requisite of the conditions orientation and one well discussed in the political development setting in Phillips Cutright, "National Political Development: Measurement and Analysis," *American Sociological Review*, Vol. 61 (April 1959), pp. 200–220; specific examples of two underrated forms of measurement are Launor F. Carter, "Survey Results and Public Policy Decisions," *Public Opinion Quarterly*, Vol. 27 (1963), pp. 549–57; and for an inventive, useful, and, as far as we know, unutilized technique, William M. Evan, "Cohort Analysis of Survey Data: A Procedure for Studying Long-Term Opinion Change," *Public Opinion Quarterly*, Vol. 23 (1959), pp. 63–72. It is possible to work through a more or less continuous chain of political development models that ranges from the nearly totally verbal to the predominantly quantitative. For a good, solid verbal model of the gross structural processes underlying much observed political development behavior, see C. E. Black, *The Dynamics of Modernization* (New York: Harper & Row, 1966); still primarily verbal, but beginning to show tendencies to a simplified, generalized, and realistic structural characterization of one form of behavior, is Samuel P. Huntington's milestone piece, "Political Development and Political Decay," *World Politics,* Vol. 17 (April 1965), pp. 386–430; somewhat further along the continuum toward quantification, but relying heavily on verbal and formal theoretical works is our, *Organized Complexity* (New York: The Free Press, 1971); and finally, one of the most heavily quantitative attempts we know about that simultaneously focuses on several solid policy issues is Harvey A. Averch, F. H. Denton, and John E. Koehler, *The Matrix of Policy in the Philippines* (Princeton: Princeton University Press, 1971). Each of these four cited examples has its own peculiar strengths and several weaknesses, many, if not most of which, are traceable to the limitations inherent to the spot along the continuum at which researchers located themselves.

Political Development Subspecialty Fields

Several solid volumes written from a general conditions orientation cover a variety of political development topics in an extensive fashion, a few do the same for more circumscribed substantive areas. John D. Montgomery and William J. Siffen, eds., *Approaches to Development: Politics, Administration and Change* (New York: McGraw-Hill, 1966); S. N. Eisenstadt, *Modernization, Protest, and Change* (Englewood Cliffs, N.J.: Prentice-Hall, 1966); and Karl W. Deutsch and William J. Foltz, eds., *Nation-Building* (New York: Atherton, 1963), all handle a variety of topics well and have stood the tests of time and professional scrutiny well. The same can be said for the following intensive substance-area examples: political parties—Joseph LaPalombara and Myron Weiner, eds., *Political Parties and Political Development* (Princeton: Princeton University Press, 1966); the bureaucracy—Joseph LaPalombara, ed.,

Bureaucracy and Political Development (Princeton: Princeton University Press, 1967 ed.); the judiciary—Glendon Schubert and David J. Danelski, eds., *Comparative Judicial Behavior* (New York: Oxford University Press, 1969); and the church, considered historically and generally—S. N. Eisenstadt, "Religious Organization and Political Process in Centralized Empires," *Journal of Asian Studies*, Vol. 21 (May 1962).

Moving from these select few general treatments to one of the more developed of the subspecialties—structural-functionalism—we note Robert K. Merton, *Social Theory and Social Structure* (New York: The Free Press, 1957 rev. ed.), particularly, "Manifest and Latent Functions," as one palatable and understandable general exposition of the field's scope and intention; Gabriel A. Almond has long been an exponent, see Almond and James S. Coleman, eds., *The Politics of the Developing Areas* (Princeton: Princeton University Press, 1960); and Almond and G. Bingham Powell, Jr., *Comparative Politics: A Developmental Approach* (Boston: Little, Brown, 1966); and for one good exposition of the technique in a specific context, see David A. Apter, *The Gold Coast in Transition* (Princeton: University Press, 1955).

The cybernetic approach has been well covered generally in W. Ross Ashby, *An Introduction to Cybernetics* (London: Chapman and Hall, 1961); Karl W. Deutsch has been perhaps the prime theoretical figure in political science using the concept to advantage in his, *The Nerves of Government: Models of Political Communication and Control* (New York: The Free Press, 1966 ed.); and to a lesser extent, *idem*, "Social Mobilization and Political Development," *American Political Science Review*, Vol. 55 (September 1961), pp. 463–514. Two examples of the communications approach are represented in Daniel Lerner and Wilbur Schramm, eds., *Communication and Change in the Developing Countries* (Honolulu: East-West Center Press, 1967); and Lucian W. Pye, ed., *Communications and Political Development* (Princeton: Princeton University Press, 1963).

Political culture has been turmed "the subjective orientation to politics," [5] which has meant determining and measuring the operating norms, attitudes, and beliefs in a specific setting. Good introductions to this form of scholarship are contained in S. N. Eisenstadt, "Primitive Political Systems: A Comparative Analysis," *American Anthropologist*, Vol. 61 (April 1959), pp. 200–220; for an even clearer illustration of the anthropological perspective on these matters, see J. A. Barnes, *The Styles in the Study of Kinship* (Berkeley: University of California Press, 1972); and George M. Foster, *Traditional Cultures and the Impact of Technological Change* (New York: Harper & Row, 1962). A conventional political science treatment is contained in Gabriel A. Almond and Sidney Verba, *The Civic Culture* (Princeton: Princeton University Press, 1963); to a certain extent in Lucian W. Pye, *Aspects of Political Development* (Boston: Little, Brown, 1966); and almost entirely in Pye and Verba, *op cit*. Two quite

[5] Lucian W. Pye and Sidney Verba, eds., *Political Culture and Political Development* (Princeton: Princeton University Press, 1965), p. 513.

different examples of in-depth applications of the technique are Frederick Frey, *The Turkish Political Elite* (Cambridge, Mass.: The MIT Press, 1965); and the poignant, O. Mannoni, *Prospero and Caliban: A Study of the Psychology of Colonization*, P. Powesland, trans. (New York: Praeger, 1964 ed.).

Systems

It is really inaccurate to claim that a distinct "systems" subfield exists because all conditions-oriented work is in a real sense dealing with systems in some form or shape, or another. However, it is possible to cite David Easton, "An Approach to the Analysis of Political Systems," *World Politics*, Vol. 9 (April 1957), pp. 383–400; and Gabriel A. Almond, "A Developmental Approach to Political Systems," *World Politics*, Vol. 17 (January 1965), pp. 183–214, mostly because of the authors' self-identification, not because the articles contain any startling innovations.

TOWARD A MODEL OF THE COUP D'ETAT IN LATIN AMERICA

J. S. Fitch has boldly defined the limits of social science knowledge about the Latin American coup d'etat and has assembled much of the available scholarship, indicating not only the important areas over which there is empirical information and certain agreement, but more important, those areas where considerably more work is needed. More than just another call for research, this chapter details what kinds of research are needed, where they fit into the larger puzzle known as the coup process, and why we must not continue ignoring information and insights from other disciplines, for example, economics and anthropology.

The Question

Concisely, Fitch has set out to clarify what is known about the processes explaining the Latin American coup d'etat in an effort to delimit additional research requirements and to specify formal, symbolic, and quantitative models of the process.

The Strengths

This chapter is a vivid example of initial specification or premodeling. The processes of interest are characterized in verbal detail and relevant literature; data and theory are added to the initial characterization until one begins perceiving better what goes with what, in what sequences, and why. In this example, six contributory conditions thought to motivate a coup are condensed and sharpened from the descriptive and theoretical literature. Political histories of many of the affected nations are liberally relied on for their rich specific detail and insights. And finally, the literature and theory of several other disciplines are referred to because they improve our understanding of basic processes. In short, we are treated to a rich and carefully integrated presentation of many disciplined insights into the general problem and characteristic processes.

The importance of the research context is properly and consistently stressed. Other than political variables matter and are accounted for; timing is critical and requires detailed analysis; and the basic societal groupings and cleavages are germane and are specified.

A problem-solving orientation is evident in the work where particular emphasis is placed on conditions, or scientific explanation, and trends, or historical description. Considerably less stress is placed on goal clarification, alternative exploration, or projections, although their eventual incorporation in the research design is not excluded, but merely postponed until several more fundamental matters are treated.

One of the "cleanest" sections of Fitch's contribution is the summary assessment of model-building strengths and weaknesses. Many of the basic themes outlined in the introduction to this volume are elaborated by Fitch to good advantage.

Distinct intellectual and substantive connections exist between this chapter and Merkx's research on the coup cycle in Argentina (see Chapter 2), to the discussion of projection strategies presented by Brunner and Brewer in Chapter 9, and to Donald Berry's plea for the construction of multiple contextual interpretations (see Chapter 13).

The Weaknesses

Although Fitch succinctly summarizes a great deal of the existing scholarship by translating it into a "verbal flow chart," a great deal of formalization remains to be done. Since writing this chapter, Fitch has used these clarified theoretical concepts to guide his collection of empirical information in Ecuador.[6]

As a direct result of the field work, goals, projections, and alternatives, the three underrepresented intellectual tasks, have received more detailed treatment than they do here.

Subsequent Developments

Fitch has already taken responsibility for a major portion of the tedious and demanding field work needed to specify formal models of the coup process. Continuing efforts are being made to tie this basically political inquiry to Martin Shubik's large empirical-theoretical model of the Ecuadorian socioeconomic

---

[6] J. S. Fitch, "Toward a Model of the Coup d'Etat as a Political Process in Latin America: Ecuador 1948–1966" (Unpublished Ph.D. dissertation, Yale University, 1973).

system.[7] Finally, the work reported by other scholars of the Latin American coup d'etat requires continuous and careful consideration and incorporation into this, or any other, formal model of the process.[8]

THE GEOGRAPHY OF MODERNIZATION: PATHS, PATTERNS, AND PROCESSES OF SPATIAL CHANGE IN DEVELOPING COUNTRIES

Social scientists generally—and political scientists particularly—have inexplicably failed to confront the spatial dimension in their analyses of development paths, patterns, and processes. Not only has this glaring omission been unfortunate, it has been unnecessary. Edward Soja and Richard Tobin present a comprehensive representation of the work done by geographers and a handful of others who have been deeply concerned about the spatial dimension; in other words, useful and pertinent scholarship has existed all along, but it has not been integrated with the work of scholars from other disciplines. Hopefully, Soja and Tobin will persuade us all to take steps in a long-overdue direction.

The Question

The overriding question is how to incorporate the spatial dimension into studies of development. The question is answered by working through the relevant conceptual and theoretical ideas as applied to the tropical African experience, most particularly Nigeria and Sierra Leone.

The Strengths

This illustrative demonstration is a brief reminder of the importance and the explanatory power of the spatial dimension. Varying levels of spatial resolution are employed, and the resulting descriptive pictures are characterized vividly. The reader is introduced to a wealth of pertinent literature and scholarship, and making the required connections to well-known political development theorists such as Lerner and Deutsch should prove simple and rewarding.

Explicit concern for the spatial dimension puts communication, mobilization, and assorted development "crises" into a far more explicit and robust framework. For example, to talk about the diffusion of an innovation—be it ideological, technical, or whatever—is a rather vacuous business until one

[7] See Martin Shubik, "Simultation of Socio-Economic Systems," *General Systems*, Vol. 12 (1967), pp. 149–75.

[8] See Alfred C. Stepan III, *The Military in Politics: Changing Patterns in Brazil* (Princeton: Princeton University Press, 1971); Martin C. Needler, "Political Development and Military Intervention in Latin America," *American Political Science Review*, Vol. 60 (September 1966), pp. 616–26; and Luigi R. Einaudi, *The Peruvian Military: A Summary Political Analysis* (Santa Monica, Cal.: The Rand Corporation, RM–6048–RC, 1969).

decides on the source's location and the territory over which the innovation is diffusing at what rate of time. Soja and Tobin begin to tell us about such matters in easy-to-understand and easy-to-incorporate detail.

Trends and conditions are handled extremely well in this analysis. The emphasis is quite naturally placed on specification, to cite where in the formalization process one would locate this work.

The Weaknesses

Policy questions, normative issues, and projections are not especially stressed, but given the current state of intellectual affairs this is perfectly understandable and reasonable.

Because it is a summary survey of a considerable body of scholarship, many detailed explorations are left to the reader whose burden it is to follow up the wealth of cited material that supports the chapter.

Subsequent Developments

All social scientists would benefit by considering their research questions in richer spatiotemporal settings; in other words, we all should become more aware of the contexts surrounding our intellectual and practical affairs. Imagine how powerful a treatise on political culture would be if intranational variations were only assigned locational coordinates; and then consider what one might learn about development if time traces were kept over that spatially identified information. The fact that the work is yet undone is no excuse to leave it so.

Space and time are common unifying concepts surely and mysteriously absent in the bulk of development scholarship; Soja and Tobin are trying, hopefully with success, to tell us how we might begin to set matters aright.

Having sketched some important features of two macro system views stressing a conditioning orientation, we turn our attention to examples of micro analysis. Raymond Hopkins specifically tries to bridge the gap between the micro and macro levels in his contribution, "Political Roles: Micro Analysis and Macro Process." Douglas Durasoff is more strictly concerned with a micro view in, "Partial Order and Political Systems."

POLITICAL ROLES: MICRO ANALYSIS AND MACRO PROCESS

Social theorists have long understood the conceptual importance of *role*, but have added little empirical information either clarifying or enhancing their concepts. This is perfectly understandable: methodological and measurement problems abound in this area. Raymond Hopkins summarizes most of the theoretical arguments centering on roles—expectations, orientations, and behavior

—and reports the results of his field research in Tanzania which both clarifies and enhances general theoretical understanding. The study represents a creative departure from the norm, demonstrates a rather sensitive use of several methodological techniques, and outlines concisely research yet to be done.

The Question

The common general question posed in inquiries about political roles is usually framed in terms such as: "What are common expectations defining the behavior of individual political elites and how do they relate to the processes by which system pressures and demands are managed?" Hopkins sharpens this question and asks, in effect, "What are the 'rules of the *Tanzanian* political game'?"

The Strengths

Emphasizing a scientific orientation, the chapter demonstrates the importance of operating at several levels of resolution; in this case, making links between individual and aggregate behavior. At the same time, the actual norms or goals of a society are assessed with respect to those elite political and administrative participants who are operating on their own and the society's behalf.

Interview data are notoriously hard to collect and analyze scientifically. If scientific preferences are favored, much rich and relevant detail may be lost; however, if one settled for cozy "chats" with respondents, pretensions to perform rigorous, or even respectable, analyses may be forfeited. Most will agree that Hopkins has struck a balance between rigor and richness; furthermore, he shows what sensitive and sensible data analysis can do for the thorny research questions posed and he does so without wrecking havoc with the particulars of the Tanzanian context.

In this same vein, his honest and thorough discussion of methodological problems confronted and choices made should stand research colleagues in good stead as they execute similar studies.

The Weaknesses

Understandably, the chapter is insufficiently policy oriented. Essentially overlooked in an effort to begin the fundamental empirical tasks are concerns for historical trends and antecedents, future possibilities, and means of altering those likely outcomes.

The work reported is an improvement over prior research, but it is only a first approximation to what is required.

It is static. To be concerned about development—or in Hopkins's terms, institutionalization—means that one *must* not be satisfied with mere cross-sectional descriptions of a context. Clearly called for are repetitions of the basic, albeit amended and improved, study design to generate the necessary longitudinal information.

Because it is a "one-of-a-kind" effort, we are denied portrayals of the context from other observational perspectives. How, for instance, would a Tanzanian observer perceive and specify the problem? [9] What would an economist have to say about the effect of political role constraints on economic policymaking? What is an anthropologist's assessment of the cultural determinants of Tanzanian roles and role expectations? Would other political scientists respond to the context as Hopkins has? The list of possibilities is long and helps to reinforce our introductory arguments calling for the creation of multiple models of the same or similar contexts.

Subsequent Developments

Besides the repetition of the design to begin assessing the kinds and rates of change that are occurring, the demand to create alternative specifications of the context must be met. Referring to the model-building process characterized earlier, intentions or research purposes have been rather well determined, and initial specification has been carried out; however, no validation and only partial control is evident.

Finally, to advance comparative work and our general theoretical capabilities, this or closely related research in other settings obviously needs to be conducted.

PARTIAL ORDER AND POLITICAL SYSTEMS

In this short chapter, Douglas Durasoff presents a mathematically sophisticated attempt to restructure conventional explanations used in structural analyses and studies of organizational behavior. It is original, creative, and provocative. Hopefully, the study augurs well for a thorough rethinking of several aspects critical for scientific and systematic description, analysis, and comparison.

The Question

The general question is how one might efficiently discuss the validity of a given *style* of organization for the treatment of a particular *class* of development

---

[9] Hopkins has done much to advance the level and practice of Tanzanian social science. On several subsequent trips to that country he has led seminar groups and has trained many Tanzanian survey researchers and interviewers. In time, perhaps, one of them will repeat the initial design and begin to answer the question we pose.

problems. More specifically, the issue is the development of a language that will allow the systematic discussion of a number of organizational styles or structures in formal, comparative, cross-cultural, and scientific ways.

The Strengths

The language of set theory has provided Durasoff with a powerful analytic and descriptive tool. Not only is the language precise, it enforces a degree of logical consistency lacking in many comparable efforts. Precision, consistency, and efficiency furthermore lend themselves to those other desirable scientific outcomes underlying the research question. The set-theoretic language serves as a lingua franca having its own internal logic and clear rules of procedure. Using it enhances possibilities for comparative analyses, both intersystem and intrasystem, over time.

The chapter squarely addresses the structure–behavior distinction noted in the opening chapter of this volume. One must scrutinize real-world organizational behavior, i.e., one must learn particular contexts well to specify the structures producing the observed behavior. The possibility exists that similar behavior could be produced by quite different structural configurations; likewise, similar structures could conceivably produce disparate behavioral outcomes. The proposed language is explicitly capable of accounting for these differences in a more precise fashion than many conventional analyses. Questions such as the following are made eminently researchable:

1. When are structures qualitatively different from one another? That is, are similarly labeled institutions in fact structurally similar, or do they differ? In what ways, under what conditions, by what amounts?
2. When is organizational change in fact structural and not simply symbolic?
3. What are the propensities to change for different structural types? That is, are some structures static, others evolving slowly, and still others unstable?
4. Are certain structural arrangements "ultra-stable" and resistant to alteration efforts?

For policy purposes, this kind of work has several nice features. By concentrating on institutions controlling significant resources, an immediate policy bias is built into the research. By creating a structural representation of decision-making systems, attention is directed to the processing of information flows within the system. Liable to be indicated are structural weaknesses, overloads, blockages, patterns of communication activity, entry points in the system, and characteristic reconfigurations, given the representative symbolic content of various decisions processed from the past. By modelling in this fashion, authority conflicts and bottlenecks are explicitly displayed, thereby suggesting (in non-obvious ways) possible alterations. And by using the set-theoretic lingua franca it may turn out that certain organizational configurations, regardless of context, are inherently either highly unstable or stable in practice.

The Weaknesses

Several weaknesses in the chapter and in the recommended approach are notable. A major problem with the study is its tentativeness, its tendency to stress a priori over a posteriori argumentation. To a considerable extent this is understandable and acceptable; the ideas are relatively novel and worth consideration on their own merits. Durasoff is recently attempting to work through the described procedures to characterize Yugoslavian economic planning processes. These efforts are promising and shall be reported in a forthcoming doctoral dissertation.[10]

A related problem is that the analytic simplicity of systems characterized by set-theoretic symbols belies their actual complexity. The problem is a common one (discussed in the introduction to this volume). The modelmaker's slogan to "model simple but think complex" holds in this case. There are costs involved in trying to capture behavior in parsimonious structural models; however, we generally argue that the costs are bearable if the modelmaker keeps in intimate contact with his problem context. There is, in short, no substitute for knowing one's business.

One might accept at face value the putative strengths that have been enumerated. Even then there remains a real problem: communication among specialists. Very few social scientists have received *mathematical*, as contrasted with *statistical*, training, and in regard to this chapter at least, few political development specialists will be able to appreciate the procedures described. Full realization of the technique's potential is therefore temporarily constrained.

There is a static temporal bias evident in this work. Considerable attention must be devoted to the determination of time rates of change of various structural elements; relevant are both single contexts configured at successive periods of time and multiple comparable contexts taken singularly and collectively as they evolve over time.

Subsequent Developments

Taking a cue from the list of weakness suggests ways in which the work could be developed. A first-hand empirical test has been undertaken for the Yugoslavian setting. A next step is to make connections with other related works to assess the comparative and general strengths of the technique.[11]

Reinvestigation of the Yugoslavian, and other, contexts at subsequent periods would provide valuable information about stability, orderly change, and

[10] For the Department of Political Science, Yale University. Field work occupied the year 1970–71 and was sponsored under an IREX cooperative research grant with the Yugoslavian Government.

[11] Two potentially supportive efforts are R. W. Davies, "Economic Planning in the USSR," in M. Bornstein, ed., *Comparative Economic Systems* (Homewood, Ill.: R. D. Irwin, 1969 ed.); and J. M. Montias, "The Evolution of the Czech Economic Model, 1949–1961" (New Haven: Department of Economics, Yale University, September 1962).

discontinuity, all related to our concern for determining time rates of change of modeled elements. Implicit in this proposal is the need to use yet another type of quantitative technique, the calculus, to compute these rates.

Dissemination and acceptance of the technique are seriously hampered by the limited number of appropriately trained specialists. At the least, presentation of this chapter may serve as a reminder that quantitative techniques other than descriptive statistics exist, can be productively brought to bear on problems, and should be made more easily accessible to upcoming generations of social scientists.

With regard to the model-building process, Durasoff's effort nicely illustrates a theoretical-operational *intention* with the bulk of activity being devoted to model *specification*. Required are major efforts to *control*, by collecting additional observations on several contexts, and to *validate*, by comparing and assessing the adequacy of the technique in several applications.

Chapter 4
Toward a Model of the Coup d'Etat in Latin America

JOHN S. FITCH III

This chapter describes the Latin American coup d'etat as the culmination of two interrelated political processes: the outcome of a decision within the military to intervene and a lack of support for the existing government from the politicized sectors of society. The military submodel focuses on six situational conditions (civilian pressures, public disorders, etc.) which, where present, act as motivations for a coup d'etat, subject however to the conditioning influence of the extent of previous military intervention. The civilian politics submodel links attitudes toward the government to changes in living standards through a learning process for four socioeconomic population sectors, representing in the general case urban–rural and upper status–lower status cleavages. Possible directions for submodels of elections and economic policymaking are also discussed. The methodological emphasis is on simulation as a disciplined method for clarifying what we know and do not know about a complex problem in political analysis.

The coup d'etat is generally recognized as one of the most distinctive and enduring characteristics of Latin American political systems. My personal reading of the postwar histories of individual Latin American countries suggests two very general propositions about the process of nonconstitutional or irregular government change. These propositions, in turn, suggest the need for a dynamic and contextual approach to the study of the Latin American coup d'etat.

The first proposition is that it is difficult, if not impossible, to explain actual irregular government changes by reference to the propositions advanced to answer the question of why some countries have a higher incidence of coups than others. Despite the logical necessity of some connection between the explanation of the event and the explanation of cross-national variations in the frequency of

I wish to express my special appreciation to Professors Alfred C. Stepan III and Juan Linz of Yale University and to the members of the Yale Continuing Seminar on Political Development for their patient counsel and penetrating criticisms of earlier drafts of this chapter. The model elaborated here is tested and revised in my "Toward a Model of the Coup d'Etat as a Political Process in Latin America: Ecuador 1948–1966" (Unpublished Ph.D. dissertation, Department of Political Science, Yale University, 1973).

the event, this connection seems quite indirect. The fact that per capita income is lower in Ecuador than in Columbia may or may not explain something about why Colombia has fewer coups than Ecuador, but it does not explain why Ecuadorian President Velasco Ibarra's third nonconsecutive term lasted the full four years, yet his fourth lasted only fifteen months. Furthermore, the cross-national approach frequently leads to the "Argentina paradox" illustrated in Johnson's comment on political instability in the post-Perón era.

That such should be the case in one of the most technologically advanced, urbanized, racially homologous, and literate republics with an early record of positive middle sector participation in public affairs is somewhat surprising, but also in large part understandable when viewed historically.[1]

As Johnson suggests, explaining variations in the incidence of coups tends toward a focus on relatively stable system characteristics, whereas an explanation of the events themselves requires "a historical view," that is, an attention to the processes by which the values of the variables comprising the system change over time.

The second proposition suggested is that a Latin American coup d'etat is the outcome of the interaction over time of many elements of the social, economic, and political context of the particular country in question. If the reality being studied is relatively nondecomposable into noninteracting sets of variables,[2] then "the meaning of any detail depends on its relation to the whole context of which it is a part." [3]

Theoretically, the contextual approach requires that attention be given to the whole range of social, economic, and political processes which are indirectly related to the process of irregular government change. In particular, it would avoid the tendency, until recently common in the scholarly literature, to ignore the interaction between the military and the rest of the body politic.[4] Methodologically, a contextual approach assumes a higher degree of complexity and interrelation than can be easily dealt with by cross-national regression analysis or its derivatives, such as causal modeling.

However, the contextual approach does not require a rejection of the common assumption that the Latin American region comprises a distinctive set of relatively similar political systems.[5] Despite the wide variation in the particular configuration of initial values for relevant variables and of historically and culturally influenced parameter settings in each Latin American country,

[1] John J. Johnson, *Political Change in Latin America: The Emergence of the Middle Sectors* (Stanford, Cal.: Stanford University Press, 1958), p. 94.

[2] Franklin M. Fisher and Albert Ando, "Two Theorems on *Ceteribus Paribus* in the Analysis of Dynamic Systems," *American Political Science Review*, Vol. 55 (March 1962), p. 109.

[3] Harold D. Lasswell, *Power and Personality* (New York: Viking, 1962), p. 218.

[4] See Lyle N. McAlister, "Recent Research and Writings on the Role of the Military in Latin America," *Latin American Research Review*, Vol. 2 (Fall 1966), pp. 5–36.

[5] See Bruce M. Russett, *International Regions and the International System: A Study in Political Ecology* (Chicago: Rand McNally, 1967).

the processes by which these interact to produce individual histories seem to be sufficiently common to justify the attempt to construct a "Latin American" model. The model described in this chapter is based on propositions derived from the general literature on Latin American politics and the Latin American military; it is documented with examples from my study of the coup d'etat as a political process in postwar Ecuador. In any event, the ability of a posited regional set of variables and relationships to take account of the differences between countries in order to predict or postdict individual histories is an empirical question, as is the question of whether there will be one or several development paths for variables of interest to the student of development.

A STRATEGY OF INQUIRY

One of several possibilities for a dynamic contextual approach to the study of irregular government change is model-building through computer simulation. Like alternative methods, computer simulation models have advantages and disadvantages. One of the more unfortunate disadvantages is that simulation models are practically unknown to political scientists, while "computer simulation" evokes sometimes threatening, sometimes merely unpleasant, images of yet another esoteric technology. Neither the mystery nor the aura of "machines" is particularly well deserved. A model is an isomorphic representation of reality, the embodiment of an analogy in a highly simplified replica of the phenomenon under study.[6] A simulation model is, in the words of one professor, "an operating fake," a replica constructed so as to behave in certain salient aspects like its real-world counterpart. A simple example of a simulation model comes from Paul Samuelson's classic model of the interaction of the multiplier and the accelerator principles in economics.[7]

Samuelson's simple economic model is derived from four propositions. Gross national product (Y) for any period is by definition the sum of investment, consumption, and government expenditure. Government expenditure (G), by assumption, is fixed and, by definition of the measurement unit, equal to one. Consumption (C) in any period is a stable proportion of the gross national product of the previous period. Investment (I) is a stable multiple of the change in consumption from the last period to the present period. These propositions translate into four simple equations, where t is a time subscript.

$$Y_t = C_t + I_t + G_t$$
$$G_t = 1$$
$$C_t = a \cdot Y_{t-1}$$
$$I_t = B(C_t - C_{t-1})$$

[6] Abraham Kaplan, *The Conduct of Inquiry* (San Francisco: Chandler, 1964), pp. 258–93.

[7] Paul A. Samuelson, "Interactions Between the Multiplier Analysis and the Principle of Acceleration," *Review of Economics and Statistics,* Vol. 21 (1939), pp. 75–78.

This simple model has the intriguing property of *four qualitatively different* time paths for gross national product, depending on the values of *a* and *B*, the multiplier and the accelerator, as well as an infinite variety of quantitatively different time paths when the initial values of the four variables also vary. Although this model possesses an analytic mathematical solution, the addition of a complication such as a countercyclical government expenditure policy would require another method of calculating the consequences over time of a particular set of initial values and *a* and *B* parameters.

Tracing the interaction by computer simulation merely requires the translation of the equations into computer instructions and the input of data on the initial values and parameters. The computer then transforms the values of the four variables by successive iterations of the instructions for the desired number of time periods.[8]

In brief, simulation reduces a series of propositions, for example Lerner's urbanization-literacy-media-participation thesis,[9] to a set of instructions for changing the values of the specified variables. Computer simulation takes advantage of the computer's ability to keep track of large amounts of information, while rapidly executing and often repeating a complex set of instructions. Computer simulation is, therefore, no exception to the Iron Law of Computers, "Garbage in, garbage out." The validity of the simulation model depends entirely on the validity of the behavioral propositions of which it is composed.

It follows, then, that simulation models are a complement to, certainly no substitute for, the more familiar verbal models and theories.[10] The use of simulation involves an explicit trade-off of the capacity of verbal theories for flexibility and nuance for the precision and manipulability of a formal model. If, as we shall see, our understanding of Latin American political processes is still relatively primitive, then the value of simulation lies not in prediction, which requires both precision and accuracy in the selection of variables and the statement of relationships, but in helping us to understand better what we currently believe to be the nature of these processes.[11] Indeed, the major use of simulation here is in making it clear what we do *not* know. We do not propose to "simulate Latin American politics" or even that complex part of Latin American reality subsumed under the rubric of irregular government change. Now and for some time to come, our understanding of this process must be in terms of greatly simplified replicas with considerable abstraction, aggregation

---

[8] Lest the example be misleading, it should be noted that computer simulation does not presuppose any particular level of measurement. The choice is entirely up to the user.

[9] See Ronald D. Brunner and Garry D. Brewer, *Organized Complexity: Empirical Theories of Political Development* (New York: The Free Press, 1971), pp. 4–33.

[10] For a good example of a verbal model that is both contextual and dynamic, based on multidisciplinary historical materials, see Gilbert Merkx, *Political and Economic Change in Argentina From 1870 to 1966* (Unpublished Ph.D. dissertation, Department of Sociology, Yale University, 1968), and his contribution to this book.

[11] Jay W. Forrester, *Industrial Dynamics* (Cambridge, Mass. and New York: The MIT Press and Wiley, 1961), pp. 56–9.

of separate entities, and possibilities for error in the selection of variables and statement of relationships. Any single model will be an imperfect representation.[12]

Finally, it should be noted that model-building is an open-ended research process. One typically begins with intuitive insights and hypotheses culled from the descriptive and theoretical literature. These must be translated into specific relationships, and this imposition of discipline is generally worth the effort in construction of exploratory models. Complex propositions are demystified, and missing links are revealed in causal sequences. Generally one finds that verbal hypotheses are incompletely specified, particularly the form of the relationship, the relative impact of relevant variables, and the conditions invoking contingent relationships. Once a crude first approximation has been constructed, there must be an ongoing confrontation of the model with the reality being replicated. The macro phase of this confrontation involves crude comparisons of simulation histories with real histories to reveal those sections of the model most in need of modification or to suggest very tentatively the utility of alternative formulations of the component relations. The micro phase of the confrontation involves field research to gather the data necessary to validate component hypotheses. Only at some rather distant date will the question of validating complex whole models in some absolute sense be either relevant or feasible.

THE MODEL

The model contains six actors: four socioeconomic population groups, the government, and the military. The variables included are generally events or attributes of these actors. The model focuses on two related processes—the loss of civilian support by the government and the decision of the military to replace the existing set of authorities in a coup d'etat.

The Military

As Lieuwen and others have pointed out, military involvement in the process of irregular government change is predicated on a belief that the armed forces have a legitimate political role which supercedes loyalty to any particular government.[13] American authors, in particular, have tended to view this role as somewhat illegitimately appropriated by the military and have thus over-estimated the extent to which a coup d'etat represents military "intervention"

[12] Another use of simulation is to trace out the implications of competing verbal theories in order to compare and assess their particular strengths and weaknesses. See Ronald D. Brunner, "Some Comments on Simulating Theories of Political Development," in William Coplin, ed., *Simulation of Decision-Makers' Environments* (Chicago: Markham, 1968).

[13] Edwin Lieuwen, *Generals vs. Presidents: Neo-Militarism in Latin America* (New York: Praeger, 1964), p. 98.

or "interference." [14] Ecuador's postwar constitutions have explicitly assigned the military responsibility for maintenance of the constitutional order and for the purity of the electoral process, in addition to the external defense function. Earlier constitutions also included maintenance of internal order as a military function and contained an injunction against obeying orders contrary to the constitution and the laws.[15] Such constitutional provisions are quite common in Latin America[16] and, especially given the normal overlap in functions assigned to the president with those assigned to the military, tend to legitimize the belief common among both civilians and military men that the ultimate responsibility of the armed forces is to the "national interest," even if this requires acting against an established government.

The decision of the military to overthrow a government is probably best described as the outcome of a process of coalition-building within the officer corps. The pro-coup coalition typically begins with a hard-core group of instigators, resolutely opposed to the existing government. To these may be added, as the situation develops, a number of other officers, partial opponents of the regime with varying motivations for favoring the coup. Finally, conversions may be made among those officers whom Needler has termed the "reluctants." Some of these may have been personal supporters of the president, but, more generally, these officers oppose military intervention in politics in principle.[17] The process of coalition-building continues as more partial opponents and reluctants join the original conspirators, until some incident pushes the coalition past the intervention threshold. This threshold seems to be that minimum combination of prestigious and strategically placed officers whose agreement to intervene would prevent intramilitary fighting.[18]

Our present understanding of this process of intra-military coalition-building, and hence our ability to model it, is rather limited. Moreover, the difficulties of doing direct research in this area are such that these deficiencies are unlikely to be overcome in the near future. We have chosen, therefore, to concentrate on those situational factors which seem to be significant in motivating the formation of the pre-coup coalition, rather than modeling the coalition-

[14] See Alfred C. Stepan III, *The Military in Politics: Changing Patterns in Brazil* (Princeton: Princeton University Press, 1971).

[15] Dr. Ramiro Borja y Borja, *Las Constituciones del Ecuador* (Madrid: Ediciones de Cultura Hispánica, 1951), pp. 596–97, 634, 679.

[16] J. Lloyd Mecham, "Latin American Constitutions: Nominal and Real," *Journal of Politics,* Vol. 21, No. 2 (May 1959), p. 264.

[17] The term *reluctants* and the coalition concept come from Martin Needler, "Political Development and Military Intervention in Latin America." *American Political Science Review,* Vol. 60 (September 1966), pp. 616–26.

[18] In a perceptive insight, Needler (*ibid.,* pp. 621–24) gives some indirect evidence for the coalition-building concept. In the conspiratorial coalition of instigators, partial opponents, and reluctants, the last man to join (putting the coalition over the threshold) is usually a respected and "reluctant" senior officer, who typically emerges as the head of the new military government. Once the new government takes power, intramilitary political conflict tends to reemerge in the form of a conflict between the minimal program of the leader and the maximal program of the instigators.

building process directly. Although putting aside the coalition-building approach entails neglect of the important conspiratorial elements of the coup d'etat process, the focus on the types of situations inducing military action alerts us to the military's role as a monitor of the political scene and the ultimate judge of whether an existing government shall continue in office or be replaced.

One of the major motivations for military action is the pressure of civilian groups antagonistic to the government calling on the military "to do its duty." [19] According to Lieuwen,

The militarism of the postwar period, like that of the 1930's has been primarily a reflection of the demands made upon the armed forces by antagonistic forces—by the traditional order attempting to maintain the status quo and by new social forces attempting to alter it.[20]

The importance of civilian pressures in the coup d'etat process and the general support of civilians for a nonsubordinated military are such that Johnson, in choosing a descriptive label for Latin American civil–military relations, rejects "militarism" in favor of "civil-militarism." [21] In the Ecuadorian coup of 1963, the opposition's failure to remove President Arosemena through impeachment merely led to pressure for his removal by the armed forces. The Conservatives, in particular, called for a coup, both privately in meetings with dissident officers and publicly in the press.[22] Even the Liberal newspaper El Comercio, while not calling for a coup, editorialized that if the police are not sufficient to stop the Communist threat, "the Armed Forces are constitutionally obligated to intervene in order to preserve the laws, peace, and liberty in the Republic." [23] Consequently, in the model if hostility toward the government among upper status groups reaches a high level, civilian pressures become an important motivation for a military coup.

Similarly, high levels of hostility toward the government among either urban or rural lower status groups, if these are politically relevant, constitute an additional motivation for a coup. Such hostility is likely to lead to anti-government demonstrations, strikes, and riots by these sectors, which typically lack direct access to the military.[24] To quote Lieuwen: "If public order threatens to break down as a result of growing opposition to the policies of the incumbent government, then the military feels a constitutional duty to intervene. . . ." [25] Fossum finds that of the seventy-eight Latin American coups between 1907 and

[19] Lieuwen, op. cit., pp. 102, 104–9.

[20] Edwin Lieuwen, Arms and Politics in Latin America (New York: Praeger, 1960), p. 123.

[21] John J. Johnson, The Military and Society in Latin America (Stanford, Cal.: Stanford University Press, 1964), p. 120.

[22] Martin Needler, Anatomy of a Coup d'Etat: Ecuador 1963 (Washington, D.C.: Institute for the Comparative Study of Political Systems, 1964), p. 19.

[23] El Comercio editorial (Quito, Ecuador), June 27, 1963, p. 4.

[24] Cf. James Payne, Labor and Politics in Peru (New Haven: Yale University Press, 1965).

[25] Lieuwen, Generals, p. 98.

1966 for which he has information, there were prior public disorders in fully sixty-one cases.[26] In part this follows from the military's constitutional role, but more important, the military is forced to pass judgment on the government since the army is usually the instrument for the suppression of these disorders, a police role not popular with the military.[27] In Ecuador, "On several occasions the armed forces have been called upon to maintain internal security and the public image of the armed forces has been diminished." [28] Clearly a major factor in the 1961 coup in Ecuador was the military's unwillingness to continue supporting an unpopular government after a month of strikes and riots that had already left twenty-nine persons dead and many more wounded.

Needler also notes in his Ecuadorian study that "because people wear a uniform they do not cease to be subject to the determinants of political attitudes which act upon civilians." [29] Given the role of the military as the ultimate guardians of the national interest, how that interest will be defined in a particular situation is of crucial importance. It is likely that, in a given case, the officers corps will be recruited primarily from one or another social stratum and informed of the progovernment or antigovernment sentiments of that stratum through kinship ties. Nun argues that officers are in close contact with their civilian peers, in political and social life, thanks to the absence of wars and the large number of retired officers.[30] Therefore, although the *primary* identification of military officers is clearly with the military institution, rather than any socioeconomic group, in the model one civilian sector is specified as that with which the military most closely identifies. When this sector becomes hostile to the government, we assume that segments of the military will also feel that the government is acting "contrary to the national interest." [31] Hence, the prospects for a pro-coup coalition are enhanced.

In practice, it is also apparent that the public interest is often so defined

---

[26] Egil Fossum, "Factors Influencing the Occurrence of Military Coups d'Etat in Latin America," *Journal of Peace Research*, Vol. 3 (Fall 1967), p. 234.

[27] Liisa North, *Civil–Military Relations in Argentina, Chile, and Peru* (Berkeley: Institute of International Studies, 1966), p. 52, 37, 59.

[28] Edwin Erikson et al., *Area Handbook for Ecuador* (Washington, D.C.: U.S. Government Printing Office, 1966), p. 500. Samuel Finer points out that "In these Latin American cases, . . . the armed forces are morbidly concerned with their popularity." Samuel E. Finer, *The Man on Horseback: The Role of the Military in Politics* (New York: Praeger, 1962), p. 196.

[29] Needler, *Anatomy*, p. 44.

[30] Jose Nun, "The Middle Class Military Coup," in Claudio Veliz, ed., *The Politics of Conformity in Latin America* (New York: Oxford University Press, 1967), pp. 72–74.

[31] Despite the humble origins of some officers, most will probably identify with higher status groups to the extent that they identify with any civilian sector. Note, however, the possibility of a new wave of reformist coups in the Andean countries as recruitment patterns change, if a substantial group of officers begins to identify with the Indian population. One intuitively attractive proposition for partially explaining cross-national variations in the incidence of coups is that countries in which the sector with which the military identifies is relatively poor in electoral resources tend to be coup prone. This is a modified generalization of Nun's (*ibid.*) basic thesis.

by the armed forces that it is in large measure equivalent to the institutional interest of the military establishment. Since the military is the guardian of the national interest, the national interest requires that the military itself be diligently protected.

Perversion of the governing function includes, in the eyes of the military, any actions inimical to the interests of the armed forces, such as any humiliation, material weakening, or moral undermining of the armed forces establishment.[32]

In the model, neglect of the military in the distribution of government resources constitutes a motivation for plotting against the authorities. Conversely, increases in the military budget may act as an incentive for the military to be tolerant and thus may offset the effect of another factor motivating the military in a pro-coup direction. Replying to the president's praise for having rejected a postelection conspiracy in 1956, an Ecuadorian major replied that he had only done his duty and that furthermore the president "during his four years of government had done a great deal for the Armed Forces to give them the prestige and facilities they now enjoy." [33] The government's indulgence or deprivation of the military with the symbols of respect seems to be at least as important as its attentiveness to the military's material needs. In 1962, the participation of two Ecuadorian cabinet ministers in a student demonstration calling for more money for the universities and less for the armed forces infuriated the military and contributed to a near coup four weeks later.[34] As a first approximation, we have assumed that most governments will indulge the military materially and symbolically or deprive it in both areas.

A related motivation for military intervention is a perceived threat of a future Communist or extreme left government. In part, this is a consequence of the military's role as defender of the constitutional order and of national sovereignty. In part, it reflects the influence of U.S. anti-Communist, counterinsurgency doctrines, conveyed through military assistance and officer-training programs.[35] Nevertheless, there is mounting evidence that the military's implacable opposition to Communism is based largely on the conviction that a Communist or extreme left government would destroy the army and replace it with a civilian militia.[36] The fate of the old military in the Cuban revolution was seen as a clear indication that Castro-inspired movements presented the ultimate threat to the military institution, a challenge to its continued existence. Given the strong identification of military officers with the institution within which

[32] Lieuwen, *Generals,* p. 98.
[33] Major A. Granja, quoted in *El Comercio* (Quito, Ecuador), July 4, 1956, p. 1.
[34] "Las Fuerzas Armadas a la Nación," *El Comercio* (Quito, Ecuador), March 3, 1962, pp. 1, 3.
[35] Between 1950 and 1966, nearly 1,300 Ecuadorian officers attended U.S. military schools. Robert C. Case, "El entrenamiento de los militares latinoamericanos en los Estados Unidos," *Aportes,* Vol. 6 (October 1967), p. 55.
[36] See Stepan, *op. cit.,* pp. 156–58; Needler, *Anatomy,* p. 41.

most of them have lived since age fourteen, and given their identification of the military institution with patriotism and a whole range of "higher values," there can be little doubt of the psychological power of a threat to the institution's existence. In terms of the intramilitary coalition-building discussed earlier, the anti-Communism issue is crucial because of its appeal to those officers who otherwise would be "reluctant" to intervene because of their desire to protect the institution from the adverse consequences of military involvement in politics. In Ecuador, both civilians and soldiers seem to understand that the normally apolitical stance of the military does not imply neutrality in relation to Communists or Castroites.[37] In the model, the Communist threat is treated as an exogenous variable for sheer ignorance of the circumstances under which such a threat will be perceived.

Finally, there are several additional factors of potential significance which are essentially nonprogrammable in terms of the rest of the model:

1. Elections within a year's time in which persons or parties previously deposed might be elected, thus threatening the careers of the officers involved in the previous action, as well as reactivating their previous objections to such persons or parties.
2. Personal liabilities of the president, such as excessive corruption, a drinking problem, etc.
3. Incidents associated with the government in which the military's self-image or public image is threatened.
4. The presence of officers retired for political reasons by the government. While lacking the institutional or strategic bases for a coup attempt, such officers frequently provide the linkage between dissatisfied civilian and military groups.[38]

In a hypothetical case, these might be taken as "chance" factors. In a particular case, these influences will follow a *particular* nonpredictable pattern, and thus will be treated as exogenous inputs. With the exception of the first item, each of these factors is assumed to have a minor influence on military actions relative to other considerations, although such minor incidents often seem to be the final straw leading to a coup d'etat.

Thus far we have identified from the available evidence six situations or conditions which seem to be significant motivations for a coup d'etat:

1. pressures for military action from high-status groups antagonistic to the government
2. large-scale public disorders resulting from antigovernment sentiments among politically relevant lower status groups
3. lack of support for the government in the civilian sector with which the military most closely identifies.
4. government attention or inattention to the institutional interests of the military

[37] See Cromwell (pseud.), "Apoliticismo Bien Entendido," *El Comercio* (Quito, Ecuador), March 12, 1962, p. 4, 6.
[38] Needler, *Anatomy*, p. 22–27; Needler, "Political Development," pp. 622–24; Lieuwen, *Generals*, p. 98; Nun, *op. cit.*, p. 74; Needler, *Anatomy*, pp. 12–13.

5. the perceived threat of a future Communist or extreme left government
6. a threatening election or other nonprogrammed minor motivations[39]

These seem to be the categories within which the military will pass judgment as to whether there exists a "crisis" requiring military action. However, the tradition of military involvement in, or abstention from, irregular changes of government is an important intervening factor, conditioning the impact of the coup-motivating conditions on military judgments. This tradition varies considerably from country to country and may change substantially over time in a given country. Two aspects of this exceedingly complex factor have been included in the model as a start toward explaining why the same objective situation, defined in terms of the categories above, may lead to a coup in one country but not in another.

The first aspect of this tradition is the extent of previous military intervention. A history of abstention from military involvement in irregular changes of government seems closely linked, both as a cause and an effect, to the proportion of "reluctants" in the officer corps. Bureaucratic norms, where they exist, encourage resistance to politicization of the military. Military intervention in politics is seen as a source of chaos and inefficiency, since it inevitably leads to the introduction of political considerations into purely military affairs and particularly to presidential meddling with promotions and garrison assignments as a means of self-defense.[40] A period of abstention also allows the development of institutional pride and prestige as a professionalized non-political body and an emphasis on the role of upholders of the constitution, rather than guardians of the national interest.[41] The reverse proposition is that a coup d'etat on one occasion generally increases the probability of future coups. Bureaucratic norms are weakened, and the military's role as residual defender of the national interest is strengthened. The organizational capability for planning and executing a coup and organizing an alternative government increases, as at least a segment of the officer corps gains practical experience. Finally, the extent of previous involvement in, or abstention from, irregular government change at times of "national crisis" is also a determinant of how readily the civilian opposition perceives military intervention as an alternative to dealing with the government through constitutional procedures.[42]

[39] See the list of characteristics of twentieth-century Peruvian coups in Arnold Payne, *The Peruvian Coup d'Etat of 1962: The Overthrow of Manuel Prado* (Washington, D.C.: Institute for the Comparative Study of Political Systems, 1968), pp. 57–60.

[40] North, *op. cit.*, pp. 13, 37, 59; General Luis Larrea Alba, *La Campaña de 1941: La agresión Peruana al Ecuador y sus antecedentes históricos, políticos, y militares* (Quito, Ecuador: Casa de la Cultura Ecuatoriana, 1964), p. 234.

[41] See Johnson, *Military and Society,* p. 169, on the effects of the 1948–60 period of abstention in Ecuador.

[42] According to Rafael Caldera, "Venezuelans are so accustomed to make the army the arbiter of their political contests that at each moment the most varied groups for the most dissimilar ends attempt to involve the army . . . ," quoted in Robert Gilmore, *Caudillism and Militarism in Venezuela 1810–1910* (Athens, Ohio: Ohio University Press, 1964), p. 13.

Consequently, in the model the number of years since the last coup is one factor determining the sensitivity and receptivity of the military to the coup-motivating conditions. If there has been a relatively long period since the last coup, the impact of the operative coup-motivating conditions is lessened. If there has been a recent coup, after a short grace period, the impact is increased to reflect the difficulty of getting the military out of politics once it has become involved.[43]

The other conditioning factor is the content of the military's memory of past intervention. If that intervention was well received and relatively success-ful in accomplishing its goals, both civilians and military men are more likely to perceive future intervention as legitimate and desirable. Conversely, if the earlier experience ended in failure, the military's willingness to get involved again is lessened. The process is well illustrated in Einaudi's discussion of the 1962 and 1968 coups in Peru. In 1962 the reference point for military judgments was

the rule from 1948–56 of General Manuel Odría, which had left many officers with a bitter taste of corruption and unpopularity and made them unwilling to risk the military institution on new ventures. By 1968, however, the reference point was no longer the Odría government, but the more positive record of the 1962–3 junta.[44]

In the model, the level of support or opposition for the government at the end of the last period of military government acts to offset or reinforce the effect of the degree of recent participation in, or abstention from, irregular changes of government. Thus, in a case in which the previous intervention was both recent and well received, the military would be more inclined to act, given the same set of coup-motivating conditions, than in a case wherein the previous experience was negative and in contrast to a more recent tradition of abstention.

Here we encounter a major difficulty in that the existing literature on the Latin American military provides no indication as to how many or what combinations of the coup-motivating conditions would have to be present in order to assure the successful recruitment of a pro-coup coalition. Given the internal diversity of the military in most countries, it would seem that the arguments against the existing government would have to be strong and varied in order to put together such a coalition.[45] In the model, a more or less arbitrary threshold, varying ac-cording to the previous experience with military intervention, determines whether or not the coalition is sufficiently powerful to warrant a tentative deci-sion to act.

This tentative decision, however, is not sufficient to initiate a coup d'etat. In general, it seems to be the case that the military will not intervene as long as the government has significant support among the politically relevant sectors

[43] See Robert A. Potash, *The Army and Politics in Argentina 1928–1945: Yrigoyen to Perón* (Stanford, Cal.: Stanford University Press, 1969), pp. 283–84.

[44] Luigi R. Einaudi, *The Peruvian Military: A Summary Political Analysis* (Santa Monica, Cal.: The Rand Corporation, RM–6048–RC, 1969), p. 15.

[45] Stepan, *op. cit.*, pp. 206–8, points to the importance of "institutional interest" issues in unifying the highly factionalized Brazilian army.

of society.[46] Explaining the acquiescence of the pro-Perón officers in the 1955 coup, North writes:

By this time, the failure of Perón's economic policies, the conflicts created by his attacks on the Church, and the unpopularity of a pending [oil] contract . . . had produced a huge opposition which could have joined the rebel officers in a wider conflict. The same factors had of course also demoralized sectors that had previously supported Perón actively.[47]

It may be that intervention "in behalf of the nation" is more palatable to the "reluctants" than intervention sought only by certain groups, but the fear that civilian supporters will join with the remaining progovernment officers to resist the coup attempt seems to be more important.[48]

The converse of this proposition is that generally the government is sufficiently unpopular by the time of the coup that the new government initially enjoys widespread public support. After the overthrow of Ecuadorian President Arosemena,

The reaction of the general public to the coup was overwhelmingly favorable and the politically conscious elements of the Ecuadorian masses eagerly welcomed the new government's promise of tranquility, work, and progress.[49]

Ironically, in this case the deposed president had ridden into office on a similar wave of support after the ouster of his predecessor just two years earlier.

The Support Relationship

As we have indicated in the previous section, public support, or lack of it, for the existing set of authorities seems to play a crucial role in the process of irregular government change. There is a growing body of evidence that lack of support for the government and hence irregular changes of government are related to economic failures. In the ten countries experiencing coups between 1947 and 1963, seven of the fifteen coups occurred in years in which aggregate per capita income for that country declined, while there were twice as many years of improvement as of deterioration.[50] Another study finds that the ratio of coups per year in Latin American countries for deterioration years to improvement years is roughly fifteen to nine using national per capita income figures for the period 1951–61, and two to one using total world exports for the period 1928–38.[51]

[46] James Payne, *Patterns of Conflict in Colombia* (New Haven: Yale University Press, 1968), pp. 142–43.
[47] North, *op. cit.,* p. 44.
[48] See Merkx, *op. cit,* p. 251. The Brazilian coup of 1964 may be a counterexample as apparently the conspirators expected and were prepared for resistance which never materialized from pro-Goulart forces.
[49] Needler, *Anatomy,* p. 29.
[50] Needler, "Political Development," pp. 617–18.
[51] Fossum, *op. cit.,* p. 237.

In his study of political and economic change in Argentina,[52] Merkx also finds a strong relationship between rebellions and economic recessions (see Chapter 2 of this volume). Dividing the Argentine economic cycle into three phases yields the following:

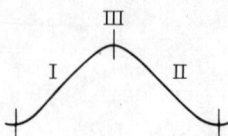

Argentine Regional, Party, and Military Rebellions (1870–1966)

	Number of Rebellions	%
I. Year of upturn	1	4
II. Year of downturn	9	39
III. Year of transition	13	57
	23	100

Dividing the economic cycle into four phases gives an even more striking result.

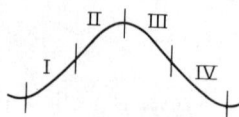

	Number of Rebellions	%
I. Year of transition plus first three years of upturn	2	8
II. Later in upturn	0	0
III. Year of transition plus first three years of downturn	19	84
IV. Later in downturn	2	8
	23	100

The available evidence may in fact understate the strength of the relationship, since it is possible for major segments of the population to experience a decreased standard of living while aggregate per capita income increases. Our own impression is that this is often the case, especially during periods of serious inflation or strong anti-inflationary efforts.

Beyond the statement that loss of support is closely tied to economic de-

[52] Merkx, *op. cit.*, pp. 29–32.

cline, there is little more which can be asserted with confidence, for the empirical evidence available sheds no light on the details of the relationship. We shall, however, try to specify an intuitively plausible relationship. The reader is cautioned that "it seems likely that" should be mentally inserted as a preface to each of the propositions detailed below.

First of all, satisfaction or dissatisfaction with the current state of affairs is probably more strongly affected by the change in one's standard of living—improvement or decline—than by one's absolute level of income or relative income position.[53] The fact that one is relatively or absolutely well off does not generally provide much compensation when one is less well off than before.

Second, changes in family income are evaluated in terms of a set of expectations defining a positive and a negative change. However, these expectations are not determined by the degree of communications exposure, as is generally the case in discussions of the "revolution of rising expectations." [54] Rather, expectations in any period are a function of past changes in income. In effect, one learns from experience what to expect.[55] In general, these two propositions are very similar to Davies's thesis that revolutionary pressures result, not from prolonged economic stagnation, but from the gap between aspirations and achievement created when a period of sharp decline follows a long period of gradual improvement in living standards.[56]

Third, the change in living standards is not perceived *in vacuo*, but will be influenced by the perceiver's existing opinions about the government. We assume that the more strongly one supports or opposes the government, the more one will distort the evidence of government performance in the direction of one's existing beliefs. Thus, the staunch supporter will discount or disregard a loss of income, while attributing exaggerated importance to any evidence of improvement in his situation, and conversely the strong opponent of the government will distort the evidence in the opposite direction. It may be that in the

[53] Cross-national studies showing a negative correlation between per capita GNP and various measures of instability, conflict behavior, violence, etc., are of dubious significance here, if only because the relationship seems to be based on differences between the developed (Western) group of nations and the underdeveloped (non-Western) group. The scattergram in Russett et al., *World Handbook of Political and Social Indicators* (New Haven: Yale University Press, 1964), p. 307, shows no discernible pattern if countries with per capita income greater than $500 are excluded from the sample.

[54] See Daniel Lerner, *The Passing of Traditional Society* (New York: The Free Press, 1958), for a statement of the argument for the role of the media in creating new wants; and Ivo and Rosalind Feierabend, "Aggressive Behavior Within Polities, 1948–1962," *Journal of Conflict Resolution,* Vol. 10 (September 1966), pp. 249–71, for an attempt to operationalize the idea of a want–get ratio. Wayne A. Cornelius, Jr., "Urbanization as an Agent in Latin American Political Instability: The Case of Mexico," *American Political Science Review,* Vol. 62, No. 3 (September 1969), pp. 833–57, presents strong evidence against the rising expectations argument.

[55] The first two propositions borrow heavily from Brunner and Brewer, *op. cit.,* pp. 22–60. Their study also contains evidence for these propositions from the descriptive literature on Turkey and the Philippines.

[56] James C. Davies, "Toward a Theory of Revolution," *American Sociological Review,* Vol. 27 (February 1962), pp. 5–19.

extreme ranges of support or opposition changes in living standards not in conformity with one's beliefs will simply not be accorded any connection with the existing set of authorities.[57]

Fourth, existing levels of support for the government from various segments of the population are determined by the initial levels of support and the government's perceived performance over time. Initial levels of support seem to depend upon one's judgment of the priority that will be accorded the interests of those like oneself by a newly elected government.[58] In the case of a government brought to power in a coup d'etat, initial levels of support seem inversely related to the level of support for, or opposition to, the previous government at the time of its overthrow. Initial levels of support are, however, only tentative evaluations. Over time, attitudes toward the government are, in effect, learned.[59] In any given period, support for the government is equal to support in the previous period, modified by the effect of the *perceived* change in living standards.[60]

Finally, we assume that extremely low levels of support will have contagion and positive feedback effects. One sector's hostility toward the government tends to produce actions—politically motivated strikes, capital flight, antigovernment propaganda—which discredit the government in the eyes of other sectors. Moreover, the same actions are likely to reinforce the attitudes of the hostile sector. For the sake of simplicity, we will ignore the possibility that a similar contagion will take place at very high levels of support or that hostility from one segment of the polity may increase support for the government in a segment in conflict with the first.

To summarize briefly, in each period the actual change in living standards for each sector is evaluated in the light of the expected change. Expectations for the next period are increased or decreased marginally, if the actual change exceeds or falls short of the expected change. Perceived government performance is a function of the change in welfare status and the perceptual distortion introduced by prior attitudes toward the government. Previous levels of support are then modified in accordance with perceived government performance. When

[57] See Daniel Lerner, "Conflict and Consensus in Guayana," in Frank Bonilla and Jose A. Silva Michelena, eds., *A Strategy for Research on Social Policy* (Cambridge, Mass.: The MIT Press, 1967), pp. 312–32.

[58] A study of the 1956 U.S. election reports the following loose classification of explanations given by voters for their presidential–party preferences: 16% gave philosophical or ideological justifications; 45% said that people like themselves would be better off with their candidate–party in power; 23% explained their preferences by asserting that these were good times or bad times which, on the basis of past experience, could be better handled by one of the parties. Angus Campbell et al., *The American Voter* (New York: Wiley, 1960), p. 249.

[59] See Daniel Goldrich, *Sons of the Establishment: Elite Youth in Panama and Costa Rica* (Chicago: Rand McNally, 1966).

[60] Survey data from many countries indicate that the overwhelming majority of respondents in almost every case are primarily concerned with the economic situation and health of themselves and their families. Hadley Cantril and F. P. Kilpatrick, *The Pattern of Human Concerns* (New Brunswick, N.J.: Rutgers University Press, 1965).

extreme levels of hostility (negative support) are reached in any sector, support decreases in all sectors.

The Support Concept

According to Easton, "We can say that A supports B either when A acts on behalf of B or when he orients himself favorably toward B." [61] Support, as we have used the term, denotes

an internal form of behavior, an orientation that takes the shape of a set of attitudes or predispositions or a readiness to act in behalf of someone or something else. . . . What such phrases share is their reference to an imputed state of feelings that will have a high probability of displaying themselves through supportive or hostile actions.[62]

Note that in the previous discussion we have assumed, for the moment, that support for the government (authorities) is unidimensional, with negative support levels equivalent to "opposition" or "hostility." The undimensional concept does imply a correlation between affect and intensity in attitudes toward the authorities, i.e., that the salience of the attitude increases as the degree of support or opposition increases.

We have also implicitly assumed that various actions tending to maintain or displace the existing government are highly probable at various levels of support for, or opposition to, the government. Thus, support is in Easton's sense a summary variable. Although this assumption is a gross oversimplification, it is useful since, in the typical Latin American case, there is no single dominant form of supportive or nonsupportive action in the government change process.[63] In another context, the key element in support may be the number of votes the government party can command in an election. In most of the countries in question here, it is uncertain whether the government will survive until the next election. In one sense, the levels of support for the government from various segments of the population may be considered as the government's stock of political currency, redeemable in such supportive acts as are appropriate to the situation and the persons involved.

Disaggregation

Clearly, not all members of a polity start with the same initial level of support for a new government, nor do they experience the same changes in living standards. Not all members are politically relevant. And, as indicated above, the

---

[61] David Easton, *A Systems Analysis of Political Life* (New York: Wiley, 1965), p. 159.

[62] *Ibid.*, p. 160.

[63] See Charles Anderson, *Politics and Economic Change in Latin America* (Princeton: Van Nostrand, 1967), pp. 87–114.

consequences of their support or nonsupport are varied. Therefore, as a simple first step toward disaggregation, the model distinguishes four socioeconomic population sectors. The two cleavages represented in the four sector disaggregation scheme are, in the general case, urban–rural and upper status–lower status.

The division of the population into upper and lower status groups, rather than upper, middle, and lower, was chosen because there seems to be no accepted distinction between the upper and middle status groups. In contrast, Beals's classic study concludes that "there is still no real break in the fundamental distinction between those who work with their hands and those who do not." [64] Adams writes:

Perhaps the major feature of our understanding of the entire structure that has emerged since the time of that [Beals's] article is that, even with the variations present, and even with the multiple effects of industrialization and urbanization, most specific locales can still be recognized as being divided into two major classes.[65]

Adams distinguishes these two classes as the power–prestige and work–wealth sectors, according to the principle of vertical mobility within each sector. He concludes that the middle sector "is definitely an expansion of the upper sector." [66]

The possibilities for the second cleavage, the criterion of horizontal differentiation, are even more varied than the two-, three- or four-strata vertical differentation schemes. Although Redfield's classic distinction between the folk and urban cultures has largely been dropped by social anthropologists in favor of finer distinctions among subcultures, the simple dichotomy is still useful as a first approximation.[67] Moreover, not all of the distinct subcultures which would thereby be lumped together in our rural lower sector category actually exist to a significant degree in every country.[68] In addition, in so far as the urban–rural distinction parallels the distinction between agricultural and nonagricultural economic activities, changes in income may be quite different between the rural and urban sectors, as they are between upper and lower status sectors.

Still, the variations among Latin American countries must be considered carefully in defining the vertical cleavage. In Ecuador, for example, the relevant

[64] Ralph Beals, "Social Stratification in Latin America," in Dwight Heath and Richard Adams, eds., *Contemporary Cultures and Societies in Latin America* (New York: Random House, 1965), p. 359. Beals continues: "It is difficult for either North Americans or Latin Americans to realize the depth of the cleavage involved. . . . Unless one occupies an impregnable social position, there are certain manual activities which may *never* be engaged in even for recreation, certain implements which must *never* be touched [*ibid*, pp. 359–60]." The argument for the distinctiveness of the middle sectors and their importance in Latin American politics can be found in John J. Johnson, *Political Change.*

[65] Richard Adams, "Introduction," in Heath and Adams, *op. cit.,* p. 266.

[66] *Ibid.,* p. 269.

[67] *Ibid.,* pp. 3–16.

[68] Charles Wagley and Marvin Harris, "A Typology of Latin American Subcultures," in Heath and Adams, *op. cit.,* pp. 42–69. The authors distinguish nine subcultures: Tribal Indian, Modern Indian, Peasant, *Engenho* Plantation, *Usina* Plantation, Town Types, Metropolitan Upper Class, Metropolitan Middle Class, and Urban Proletariat.

cleavage is less urban–rural than regional. In this largely agricultural country, the *sierra* and the coast, with their different economies and ethnic compositions, have a long history of political conflict. In the few highly urbanized countries, the relevant cleavage may be a regional one between the capital and the provincial cities. In general, the four divisions of the population should be defined so as to minimize intrasector variations in initial support levels and income changes, or conversely, defined so as to maximize intersector variations. Once the four sectors are defined, the support levels described here are assumed to be those of a "representative member" of that sector. An undoubtedly incorrect, but potentially useful, simplifying assumption may be that support levels within a sector are normally distributed around the (mean) level of the representative member.

The processes determining the level of support from the representative member are the same for all sectors, with one exception. Latin American countries differ significantly in the extent to which the lower status sectors are politically relevant. In terms of the support relationship, changes in welfare status need not be accorded any connection with the government.[69] The concept of "political relevance," distinguishing those aware of, and concerned with, government outputs, roughly parallels the distinction between "subject" and "parochial" political cultures[70] and corresponds to the "minimal politicization" discussed by Goldrich.[71] (From a different perspective, Deutsch defines the politically relevant strata as those which must be taken into account in government policy decisions.[72])

Although the propositions from the literature on social mobilization are subject to some serious qualifications,[73] urbanization seems to be a crucial factor in enlarging the politically relevant population. In addition to the greater exposure to political life and the increased difficulty of complete self-sufficiency in urban areas, the possibilities for formation of bureaucratic–corporate, patron–client hierarchies independent of the upper strata are increased. If diffuse vertical sociopolitical structures of patronage are a distinguishing characteristic of Latin American political systems,[74] then political relevance may not be a question of the extent and quality of politicization among the lower strata. Rather,

[69] In his study of political attitudes in a Venezuelan new town, Daniel Lerner ("Conflict," pp. 317–19) found that 69% of his respondents felt that the government should take the main responsibility for changing the present situation; that 78% considered economic development to be very important; and that 57% named economic items as their greatest concern in the present situation.

[70] See Robert Scott, "Mexico: The Established Revolution," in Lucien Pye and Sidney Verba, eds., *Political Culture and Political Development* (Princeton: Princeton University Press, 1965), p. 330–95.

[71] Daniel Goldrich, "Toward the Comparative Study of Politicization," in Heath and Adams, *op. cit.*, pp. 371–78. Goldrich also discusses various modes of politicization among the minimally politicized.

[72] Karl Deutsch, "Social Mobilization and Political Development," *American Political Science Review*, Vol. 55 (September 1961), pp. 493–514.

[73] Cf. Deutsch, *op. cit.*, and Lerner, *Traditional Society*, with Goldrich, "Politicization," and Cornelius, *op. cit.*

[74] Douglas Chalmers, "Parties and Society in Latin America" (Paper presented to the American Political Science Association convention, Washington, D.C., September 1968).

the political relevance of the lower strata may vary according to the difference in the market for *patrones*, from the virtual monopoly faced by the hacienda peons to the rather more open market of the big cities.

Again we note that the four-sector disaggregation scheme used in the model is only a first step. For countries like Argentina, Brazil, Chile, and Mexico, it may be inadequate even as a first approximation because of the failure to distinguish between the middle sectors and the elites. Even for a relatively under-developed country like Ecuador, the preliminary indications are that the distortions introduced by such a simple disaggregation scheme are not insignificant. Changing the number of sectors in the model would in itself be relatively simple, although the difficulty of finding disaggregated data seems to increase exponentially with the number of distinctions desired. The questions of how many socioeconomic sectors and how these shall be defined will probably have to be answered separately for each country one wishes to consider.

The inclusion of so few actors in the model is another area of oversimplification. The present insulation of the simulated system from non-national forces is admittedly artificial. Hopefully, hypotheses about the significance of the varieties of United States' presence in Latin America—diplomatic, military, and commercial—will be forthcoming as the study of national–international linkages progresses. The Catholic Church has also been excluded as an actor. Church opposition, once it emerged, seemed to be a factor in the downfall of the military dictators of Argentina, Colombia, Cuba, and Venezuela during the 1950's, but it is unclear under what conditions the church in a given country will support or oppose the government. Perhaps most serious is the omission of politicians and political parties, although at several points these are implicitly included as intermediaries between the politicized socioeconomic sectors on one hand and the government on the other. In large part, the problem is one of determining in what systematic ways the activities of parties and politicians can increase or decrease the likelihood of a coup d'etat, independently of their function as intermediaries. Here again, the omission of an actor is as much a reflection of a gap in our understanding of Latin American politics as it is an appraisal of the secondary importance of the actor in the coup d'etat process.

DIRECTIONS FOR FURTHER DEVELOPMENT

Thus far, we have attempted to describe, albeit imperfectly, the major components of the process of irregular government change in Latin America. However, the model presented is only a short-range, partial model of Latin American government change. The partial model treats the existence of a new government, the initial levels of support, and the economic outcomes as exogenous inputs. Yet even an inspection of the propositions comprising the coup d'etat model is sufficient to show that this is not acceptable. The ability of the various sectors, particularly those with favorable access to the military, to play the electoral game may in the long run critically affect the frequency of recourse to nonelectoral means of changing governments. A government's policy choices are also important factors in determining what the economic outcomes for the various sectors will be. Not only is our understanding of irregular government change impaired by the lack of a model of electoral change and of policymaking, but we are thereby severely restricted in our exploration of propositions dealing with medium and long-range change.

An Electoral Subsystem

The process of regular government change in Latin America has received little attention beyond descriptions of particular elections and a few small-scale American-style voting studies. One particularly interesting question about Latin American elections is the relationship between the changing sector composition of the population and the changing pattern of electoral coalitions. The rise of new social groups in the process of export expansion, urbanization, and industrialization is often noted, but the specific effects of these changes on electoral politics are seldom analyzed.[75]

Let us assume for a moment that those who vote will vote in accordance with their feeling that people like themselves would be better off with a particular candidate or party. (Such feelings may originate in campaign promises, the candidate's style, past favors, etc.) We further assume that such feelings are widely shared within each sector. What are the electoral possibilities? If all sectors were politically relevant, one could have a presidential candidate for each sector and each combination of sectors. Ruling out alliances across more than one cleavage, urban–rural (regional) or upper status–lower status, leaves eight possible choices. According to Riker's theory of coalition behavior, if no sector has a majority of the votes, the sectors with the minimal majority of votes will form a coalition behind a single candidate and win the election.[76]

Thus, if the urban upper sector has a near majority of votes and can ally with either the rural upper sector or the urban lower sector, it can minimize the payoffs to its ally by chosing the sector with the least number of votes. Let us assume that the urban upper sector allies with a relatively small urban lower sector against the rural upper sector. As urbanization, education, and perhaps changes in the electoral laws swell the vote of the urban lower sector, that sector will demand a larger share of the fruits of office. When the urban lower sector vote exceeds that of the rural upper sector, the urban upper sector would be better off in an oligarchic alliance.

One interesting experiment would be to trace coalition patterns in this simple model over a long period of time, holding "elections" every four or six

[75] However, see Torcuato S. DiTella, "Populism and Reform in Latin America," in Claudio Veliz, ed., *Obstacles to Change in Latin America* (New York: Oxford University Press, 1965), pp. 47–74.

[76] William Riker, *The Theory of Political Coalitions* (New Haven: Yale University Press, 1962), pp. 32–33.

years. One could start with a crude representation of a nineteenth-century society, make simple assumptions about sector growth rates and rates of increase in lower sector literacy and/or politicization, and experiment with various timings for extensions of the franchise. Such an experiment may well reveal a pattern of alliance changes corresponding in sequence, though doubtless not in detail, with the historical experience of some of the more developed countries.

However, the assumptions involved in this simple model are extremely restrictive. An election is not an abstract choice of governments. It is also to some extent a referendum on the existing government. Although presidential second terms are not common in Latin America, one of the candidates is generally a personal protégé of the president and a member of his party. Thus, the electoral coalition which backed the existing government may gain or lose votes, depending on the support levels of the sectors for the existing government at the time of the election. Nor is this political learning from experience about the coalitions offered in an election limited in time to a reaction to the current government. This is most clear when ex-presidents are running for reelection, but is also apparent in the varied reactions to the symbols of previous administrations during an election campaign. Such political memories are probably embellished, even as they fade over time.

Regardless of whether one develops a simple model or one incorporating learning processes, there is still the question of what determines how many votes a sector can muster. A sector's numerical strength and its age composition are obvious factors. Voters are likely to be some subset of the minimally politicized and in some cases a subset of the literate portion of a sector. Turnout is likely to vary with the income and education levels typical for the sector. Moreover the ability of upper status *patrones* to deliver lower sector votes for upper sector candidates may have to be taken into consideration, especially for the rural sectors. Any number of factors may be important. Yet, development of an electoral model may still be a feasible and interesting project, since crude predictions about outcomes could be made from an assessment of the relative strengths of the sectors without presuming to predict any actual vote totals.

A Policy Subsystem

Although one observer has noted that Latin American political systems have less impact on their economic systems than vice versa,[77] a government's policy choices do affect the changes in living standards for the sectors, even if not always in the manner intended by the policymakers. We have thus far given little attention to political–economic linkages through government policy options, but the political model has been designed to be compatible with Shubik's socio-economic model.[78] In that model, the government has four expenditure options

[77] Merkx, *op. cit.*, pp. 321–22, 358–63.
[78] Martin Shubik, "Simulation of Socio-Economic Systems," *General Systems,* Vol. 12 (1967), pp. 149–75.

—gross investment, health, education, and welfare, transfer payments, and other (including military) expenditures—and four revenue options—indirect business taxes, profits taxes, personal income taxes, and tariffs. Originally, values for these options were given by relatively simple behavioral equations containing no political terms. For example, "Here government investment is a simple linear function of lagged gross national product and transfers and long term capital flows from abroad." [79]

One as yet untested version of our model runs concurrently with the Shubik socioeconomic model. Per capita income and population distribution outputs from the economic model serve as inputs to the political model. On the other side, we assume that a government represents a coalition of interests or priorities reflecting the electoral or conspiratorial coalition which brought it to power.[80] Each politically relevant sector is assumed to have a policy preference for each of the twenty policy options available. For example, sector X prefers an increase or a decrease in expenditure or revenue item Y or is disinterested. Policy preferences are assigned exogenously by the analyst on the basis of whatever considerations he deems relevant.[81] In addition to economic considerations, then, government expenditures and income policies are changed marginally according to the preferences of the sector(s) accorded priority by the government. The direction and the magnitude of the increments are determined by summing the preferences of the the favored sectors. Thus, if two sectors are included in the government coalition, their preferences may be reinforcing where they agree, or self-canceling where they are contradictory. Note that Hirschman's strategy of reform-mongering[82] might be seen as one of trade-offs in areas of conflicting preferences. In the model this would require either an ordering of preferences or a set of second-order preferences.

This first effort is a crude incrementalist model, partaking of all the limitations of that view of decisionmaking. Moreover, far more relevant variables are ignored than are included. We have omitted administrative constraints, budgetary constraints, situational factors such as foreign exchange crises, and stabilization and other strings attached to foreign aid and external borrowing. Prominent among the oversimplifications is the lack of a linkage between support levels and policy changes. A politically countercyclical expenditure policy[83] is surely as plausible as its economic counterpart. The government should also have greater leeway to head off its own demise, in addition to being able to try buying off the

---

[79] *Ibid.*, p. 162.

[80] Note that we have ignored the problem of executive ability to control policy structures for the benefit of his backers.

[81] This may be a less unrealistic procedure than it seems. See Anderson, *op. cit.*, pp. 68–86, on the lack of information in the economic policymaking process.

[82] Albert O. Hirschman, *Journeys Toward Progress* (New York: Twentieth Century Fund, 1963).

[83] In effect, government attention to the preferences of sector X increases or decreases as its support declines or increases. Brunner and Brewer, *op. cit.*, pp. 19–22, argue that this seems to be the case in Turkey and the Philippines, while Joseph LaPalombara of Yale notes that the reverse seems to be true in Italy.

military. In effect, it should be credited with enough awareness of the indirect causes of coups to take evasive action, for example, by paying particular attention to the policy preferences of the sector with which the military most closely identifies. One can only hope that future studies of decisionmaking in Latin American countries will help us to begin to sort out the relevant variables. Still, the proper strategy of model-building would seem to be to start with a very simple formulation and gradually enrich it through a process of experimentation and consultation of case studies.

CONCLUSION

In view of the ample evidence that our understanding of Latin American politics is quite primitive, one is entitled to ask, "Why build complicated simulation models?" The major answer, as we indicated earlier, is that exploratory model-building has an intrinsic value as a disciplined method for answering the question, "What do we know and not know about Latin American politics?" Aside from the immediate benefits, however, simulation models may also be an important aid in the effort to make social science cumulative within and across disciplinary boundaries. Exploratory models, such as this one, by laying bare our ignorance can help identify in a more or less systematic way the data that need to be collected. Given the enormous areas of ignorance permeating the study of Latin American politics, it is imperative that our limited research resources not be expended haphazardly. Large-scale models may also be useful in integrating into a larger framework research findings on individual problem areas. Finally, by utilizing the common language of mathematics, such models may provide the practical means for bringing together the findings of several disciplines and directing research to the boundaries between them.

Chapter 5
The Geography of Modernization: Paths, Patterns, and Processes of Spatial Change in Developing Countries

EDWARD W. SOJA
AND
RICHARD J. TOBIN

The spatial level of resolution has been too long overlooked by students of political development and change. Besides providing a conceptual scheme for integrating this important dimension into routine scholarship, this chapter illustrates several trend-related and conditions-oriented features of the spatial development of both Kenya and Sierra Leone. To be truly contextual means explicitly considering space and time, and this chapter does both, as well as making many specific references to the ways in which two discrete contexts evolved over time. Kenya and Sierra Leone, the settings of the analysis, are examined for the spatial patterns that existed in the forty-year period from 1920 to 1960. In the process, important general concepts are illustrated: networks, diffusion processes, growth poles, primate city, and circulation system.

INTRODUCTION

Over the past two decades, the academic discipline of geography has experienced a conceptual and methodological transformation which rivals that of any other social science. From an essentially descriptive discipline content primarily with the collection and categorization of data about countries and regions, modern geography has become more quantitative and theoretical in orientation and technically more dependent upon mathematical and statistical modes of analysis.[1] For those who find comfort in historical precedent, it is possible to trace the roots of this transformation deeper into the history of geographic thought. But it

[1] As illustrative of these changes, see Peter Haggett, *Locational Analysis in Human Geography* (New York: St. Martin's Press, 1966); Richard J. Chorley and Peter Haggett, eds., *Models in Geography* (London: Methuen & Co., Ltd., 1967); William L. Garrison and Duane F. Marble, eds., *Quantitative Geography*, 2 vols. (Evanston, Ill.: Northwestern University Press, 1967); Brian J. L. Berry and Duane F. Marble, eds., *Spatial Analysis* (Englewood Cliffs, N. J.: Prentice-Hall, 1968); Leslie J. King, *Statistical Analysis in Geography* (Englewood Cliffs, N. J.: Prentice-Hall, 1969); and Peter Haggett and Richard J. Chorley, *Network Analysis in Geography* (New York: St. Martin's Press, 1969).

has only been since 1950 that the isolated strands of change have become interwoven and sufficiently consolidated to redirect the context and objectives of
geographical research.[2]

If one central theme can be said to have emerged from the revolutionary
changes of the last twenty years, it is *the spatial organization of human society*.
Much of contemporary geography rests upon the assumption that there exists
an inherent geographic order in human society, a spatial "anatomy" of human
behavior and societal organization which has regular and discoverable characteristics. The bulk of modern geographical research has been associated with the
search for order and regularity in spatial systems—in the distribution and size
of settlements, the patterns of industrial location and agricultural land use, the
growth and form of cities, the geometry of spatial patterns, and the structure of
communications and human interaction in space.

The fundamental purpose of this study is to explore the evolutionary
changes in the spatial organization of society brought about by the process of
modernization, to search for order and regularity in the growth and development
of spatial systems. The chapter is comprised of two parts, each distinctively
different in method and orientation, but complementary in objectives. The first
examines the spatial dynamics of modernization and attempts to outline a broad
conceptual framework for the analysis of spatial development. Avowedly tentative and exploratory, it serves to bring together several recent theoretical and
methodological statements on the development process and to structure these
statements within an explicitly geographical context and perspective.

In the second part, the concepts and themes introduced earlier are assessed
with respect to the growing literature on the geography of modernization in
tropical Africa. Empirical in focus and paradigmatic in design, it begins with a
brief discussion of the spatial structure of modernization and continues with an
attempt to trace the recurrent patterns and processes of spatial development in
Africa within the frame of a generalized historical-descriptive model. Finally, a
more detailed case study of spatial development in Sierra Leone is offered to
illustrate further both the content and techniques involved in the geographical
analysis of modernization. A primary objective here, as well as in the preceding
sections, is to suggest a methodology and direction for comparative research that
is attuned not only to contemporary social science perspectives on the modernization process, but also to the altered perspectives of modern geography.

SOME DYNAMICS OF SPATIAL DEVELOPMENT

Spatial development involves a set of processes working within a system of
regions to transform structurally the spatial organization of society. This trans-

[2] See Clyde F. Kohn, "The 1960's: A Decade of Progress in Geographical Research
and Instruction," *Annals of the Association of American Geographers,* Vol. 60 (1970),
pp. 211–19.

formation can be viewed as a consequence of innovation diffusion in which the values, attitudes, and material attributes of "modernity" are spatially disseminated through a population; differentially adopted; and eventually incorporated within a territorially defined social system as a primary basis for social, economic, political, and cultural organization.

Modernity, as it is used here, is a relative term referring to a cluster of associated innovations which, at a given point in time, represents a predominant paradigm for societal organization. Although strands of continuous change can be identified in the evolution of human society—progressive increases in the "complexity" of human relations and organization, expansion in societal scale, increases in societal differentiation—modernization is perhaps most accurately viewed as a discontinuous, but cumulative, process keyed to the dynamics of human invention.

Every historical period is thus characterized by its own prevailing form of modernity, linked to what the economist Simon Kuznets has called "epochal innovations." [3] These epochal innovations are capable of transforming social values and generating new world views to express altered norms. Examples in early human history would include the still poorly known cultural inventions which promoted sharing in human groups (e.g., the social control of sexual relations, the extension of kinship); the massive ecological revolution associated with the domestication of plants and animals; and the political and economic changes linked to the growth of cities and the emergence of the centralized territorial state.

The major epochal innovation of the contemporary period, according to Kuznets and many others, is the extended application of science to problems of economic production. More broadly viewed, this involves a variegated cluster of convergent social, political, technological, and economic innovations which have made the production and consumption of energy more efficient and produced social systems more highly adapted to continuous innovative change than any others in human history. *Twentieth-century modernization*, therefore, represents the conjoining of contemporary innovation diffusion with a series of structural transformations—the former associated with the application of modern science, technology, and organizational theory; the latter characterized by the emergence of attitudes, values, and behavior which support sustained or continuous change and innovation.

Like all societal processes, modernization has a "geography," a salient spatial component. Put most simply, spatial development refers to the *geography of modernization*, the evolutionary changes in spatial organization, behavior, and perception arising from the impress and diffusion of modernity. Moreover, it is assumed that whatever recognizable order or regularity may exist in the clustered processes of societal modernization will be associated with changing patterns and processes of human spatial organization. This view and the tasks

[3] Simon Kuznets, *Modern Economic Growth* (New Haven: Yale University Press, 1966), Chapter 1.

inherent in an attempt to construct a spatial theory of development are succinctly expressed by John Friedmann.

Society is spatially organized in the sense that human activities and social interactions are *space-forming* as well as *space-contingent*. It follows that as a society undergoes development, its spatial structure will be transformed, but the development process will also be influenced by the existing patterns of spatial relations and the dynamic tensions that will result from them. . . . In order to state a spatial theory of development, therefore, it is necessary to establish a linkage between the separate but correlative theories of social change and spatial organization.[4]

Most existing theories of regional or spatial development have been derived either from development economics or from related structural-functionalist concepts in the other social sciences. As a result, spatial systems, like economic or social systems, are usually viewed as being in a state of dynamic equilibrium. Although never fully integrated, the systems are presumed to contain built-in mechanisms which tend to assure a long-run adaptability to externally generated change and to reduce the impact of dysfunctional stress and internal deviations from equibilibrium conditions. A fully integrated equilibrium state is never reached, but the developing spatial system is viewed as moving toward such a goal in a process of gradual and self-adjusting change.

In the discussion which follows, a significantly modified perspective on the development process is introduced, one which emphasizes not the stability and structural maintenance of evolving spatial systems, but the growth and change in spatial structure, the accentuation of divergence from equilibrium, the conflict situations generated by such fundamentally inegalitarian deviations, and the irregular and nonlinear path of the development process. Conventional equilibrium theories, it is suggested, are applicable primarily at the most advanced stages of development and cannot automatically be extended backward in time to characterize the early, formative stages of modernization. Whatever empirical regularities may exist in the development process are more likely to be reflected in the sequential patterning of deviations from a presumed equilibrium state than from an inexorable, linear, and unidirectional increase in equilibrium conditions.

The Geographical Concentration of Development

The analysis of spatial development, as previously noted, is firmly rooted in the assumption that space both affects and reflects the basic processes which operate within society. These processes—migration, urbanization, industrialization, social mobilization, acculturation—assume a spatial dimension in two important ways. First, they are *space-forming* in that they work to shape and structure human interaction in space—in the development of transport and

---

[4] In "A General Theory of Polarized Development," in Niles Hansen, ed., *Growth Centers in Regional Economic Development* (New York: The Free Press, 1972), pp. 82–107. (Emphasis added.)

communications networks, in the growth of urban and administrative systems, in the territorial distribution of political authority, in the evolution of a differentiated and integrated space economy. At the same time, they are *space-contingent*. Their space-organizing influence is itself shaped by the existing spatial framework. The decision to locate a modern factory, for example, or an administrative center, both powerful and persistent forces in the organization of space, will depend in large part upon earlier locational decisions.

The interdependence of the space-forming and space-contingent properties of modernization has a profound effect on virtually all patterns of spatial development. The degree to which locational selection, for example, is channeled by past decisions, particularly when derived from similar political and economic objectives (as in a continuing colonial situation), contributes to what is perhaps the most outstanding empirical regularity of spatial development: *the tendency toward geographical concentration of the attributes of modernization.* Once initial decisions are made to locate a particular activity or institution at a specific point, a kind of self-generating momentum is established which continues to attract related enterprises and indeed "multiplies" the impact of a given social, economic, or political investment. The remarkable tenacity of initial locational decisions is evident in all stages of development, from the bulging primate cities in Africa, Asia, and Latin America to the megalopolitan giants in the northeastern United States.[5]

A primary component of any spatial theory of development, therefore, must be an explicit formulation of the dynamics of geographical concentration. In this context, the general and partial equilibrium models of traditional location theory, classical economics, and most of the derived concepts and models of modern spatial organization theory are of only limited use. Progressive development concentration is not simply the result of agglomeration economies, the indivisibility of capital inputs, or a more broadly viewed minimization of distance "costs." Nor does it appear that mechanisms automatically arise through the normal sequence of development to counteract effectively increasing development concentration and the potential diseconomies which may emerge from it. Rather, the tendency toward an increasing geographical concentration of development is part of a general pattern of *deviation-amplification,* which hinges largely upon locational advantages derived during the early stages of growth and appears to be central to the development process throughout the world.

These observations require further elaboration, for they are of critical importance to the spatial analysis of development. Much of contemporary geographical theory rests upon a "locational ideology" geared toward cost minimization or profit maximization. Locational decisionmaking is attuned to the factor of distance (e.g., in the form of transport costs) and derived from an assumption of rational and omniscient economic behavior. From this rubric have emerged

[5] See, for example, Edward Ullman, "Regional Development and the Geography of Concentration," *Papers and Proceedings of the Regional Science Association,* Vol. 4 (1958), pp. 179–98.

interlocked sets of deterministic equilibrium models postulating optimal locational patterns for industrial firms, agricultural land uses, and urban settlements.[6] Generated within a developed Western context and essentially morphostatic in that the system being dealt with is presumed to be in an integrated equilibrium state, these models have been combined with development economics into an interpretative framework for analyzing growth and change.

In many ways, most of regional development theory is an extension of the equilibrium models of economic theory and an adjunct to the fundamental tenets of structural-functionalism so pervasive in the social sciences. All concentrate on the mechanics of *deviation-counteracting systems*. Economic processes, for example, are viewed as operating to reduce deviations or inhomogeneities within the system—to pull the system toward a rational and optimal equilibrium state. Regional inequalities in income or nonoptimal ("nonrational") location patterns are presumed to iron themselves out through the normal operations and development of the economic system (e.g., through the free flow of labor and capital).

But the process of development, at least in its early and formative stages, is characterized more by deviation-amplification than by deviation-reduction, by morphogenesis (the evolution of structure) rather than by morphostasis.[7] Any evolutionary process, such as biological growth or economic development, increases structuredness and inhomogeneity through the progressive *differentiation* of the system or organism. The deviation-amplifying character of evolutionary processes severely strains the deviation-counteracting interpretations of classical economic and spatial organization theory. At the later, integrative stages of development, both the economic and political systems may work to reduce internal inequalities, but it cannot be inferred that the same processes hold true throughout all phases of development. In other words, end-state characteristics (i.e., those of fully developed systems) do not necessarily prevail during states of transition and change. Spatial development theory, therefore, must be centrally concerned with the causes and consequences of deviation-amplification within evolving spatial systems and not wholly focused upon the inexorable march toward a deviation-counteracting equilibrium.

Consider the implications for development planning. Under the traditional rubric, which can easily be associated with an economic philosophy of laissez-faire and competitive free enterprise, locational decisionmaking takes place within a deviation-counteracting system. The individual decisionmakers—governments, entrepreneurs—choose locations to minimize costs or maximize

---

[6] Walter Isard, *Methods of Regional Analysis* (Cambridge, Mass.: Harvard University Press, 1960); *idem, Location and Space-Economy* (Cambridge, Mass.: Harvard University Press, 1956). Martin Beckmann, *Location Theory* (New York: Random House, 1968); John R. Meier, "Regional Economics: A Survey," *American Economic Review,* Vol. 53 (1963), pp. 19–54; Robert D. Dean, William H. Leahy, and David L. McKee, eds., *Spatial Economic Theory* (New York: The Free Press, 1970).

[7] For a more detailed discussion of these concepts, see Magoroh Maruyama, "The Second Cybernetics: Deviation Amplifying Mutual Causal Processes," *American Scientist,* Vol. 51 (1963), pp. 164–79.

profits. Errant choices are presumably ironed out as the economic system tends ultimately toward a state of equilibrium. Initial locational choices and the advantages they may engender are assumed to be as susceptible to adjustment and equalization as any other locational choice. Through a combination of adaption (rational choice based upon locational knowledge) and adoption (a selection of the "lucky" by the economic system), locational patterns tend toward a stable and optimum ideal. It can therefore be presumed that, with a set of idealized models in mind, continued locational decisionmaking based primarily upon attempts at cost minimization and profit maximization will eventually induce a state of economic modernity. Overconcentration, should it occur, will be counterbalanced by emergent diseconomies.

But why do the rich continue to get richer while the poor get relatively poorer? Why does the population in centers of concentrated and often rapid economic growth (e.g., many of the primate cities of developing areas) increase so rapidly as to hinder the spread of development throughout the economy and population, thus delaying the structural transformations necessary for sustained growth? Why is it that apparently successful development programs often result in greater rather than reduced regional inequalities? It is no wonder that contemporary regional development theory has begun to place greater emphasis on deviation-amplifying processes. While the classical models, with their built-in assumptions of deviation-reduction, continue to demonstrate very effectively how a developed system works, a new body of theory is beginning to emerge to answer a fundamentally different question: What are the processs which characterize the evolution of developed systems?

In this latter view, which is probably best known through the works of Gunnar Myrdal, forces that create inequality and polarization are as "natural" and as much to be expected as those that lead toward economic equilibrium. Moreover, Myrdal stresses the tendency, particularly in the earlier stages of development, for the processes of change to be characterized by cycles of cumulative causation which lead to *increasing* (primarily economic) inequalities. Rather than eliciting a countervailing response to reduce deviation, development generally calls forth "supporting changes, which move the system in the same direction but much further." [8] Favored regions, once established (whether they are "rational" for the system as a whole or not), tend to generate *backwash effects*, which further amplify existing inequalities. Backwash, or polarization, involves the migration of resources (people, skills, capital) from peripheral areas to the major centers of development, where greater opportunities are perceived to exist. At whatever scale, the rich get richer and economic, social, and political gaps widen—unless the cycle is successfully reoriented toward increasing *spread effects*, the outgrowth of forces which extend the benefits of development to peripheral areas.

[8]*Rich Lands and Poor: The Road to World Prosperity* (New York: Harper & Bros., 1957), p. 26. For a review of Myrdal's ideas by a geographer, see D. E. Keeble, "Models of Economic Development," in Chorley and Haggett, *Models in Geography,* Chapter 8.

The societal transformations necessary for spread to outweigh backwash require, in Myrdal's view, massive government intervention and control. This infuses the development process with a pervasive political flavor. It also under-lines, for the development planner, the need to innovate and experiment in an attempt to control or to channel productively the deviation-amplification which dominates the development process. "Natural" forces of adjustment and equal ization are not sufficient to prevent the solidification of regional inequalities and the potential social and political turmoil they may generate at some later stages of development. Given the increasing temporal urgency of development, it is foolhardy to expect the spontaneous generation of conditions—or an invisible hand—to promote sustained and balanced growth.

In only a slightly different context, Pierre van den Berghe offers several more specific criticisms of the conventional (in this case, functionalist) dynamic equilibrium models.[9] Summarizing his arguments, he states that: ". . . while societies do indeed show a [long-run] tendency toward stability, equilibrium, and consensus, they simultaneously generate within themselves the opposites of these." [10] As a result, van den Berghe asserts that there are at least four "irreduc-ible facts" which cannot be accounted for in the conventional functionalist framework:

1. Reaction to extra-systemic change is not always adaptive;
2. social systems can, for long periods of time, go through a vicious circle of ever deepening malintegration;
3. change can be revolutionary, i.e., sudden and profound;
4. the social structure itself generates change through internal conflicts and contra-dictions.[11]

Core and Periphery Relations

One of the finest recent attempts to incorporate the concept of deviation-amplification into regional (spatial) development theory has been made by Friedmann, particularly in his work, "A General Theory of Polarized Develop-ment." [12] Development is viewed by Friedmann as a series of transformations in the institutional and organizational structures of society which, if left un-changed, would inevitably limit the system's capacity for expansion and continuous innovative change. His focus is upon the dynamics of authority-dependency relations which emerge from "the unusual capacity of certain areas

[9] "Dialectic and Functionalism: Toward a Theoretical Synthesis," *American Socio-logical Review*, Vol. 28 (1963), pp. 695–705. Reprinted in Walter L. Wallace, ed., *Sociological Theory: An Introduction* (Chicago: Aldine, 1969), pp. 202–13.

[10] In Wallace, *Sociological Theory*, p. 203.

[11] *Ibid.*, p. 204.

[12] See note 4 above. See also John Friedmann et al., "Urbanization and National Development: A Comparative Analysis," in John Friedmann, *Urbanization, Planning, and National Development* (Beverly Hills, Calif.: Sage Publications, 1973), pp. 65–90; and *idem, Regional Development Policy: A Case Study of Venezuela* (Cambridge, Mass.: Har-vard University Press, 1966).

to serve as cradles of innovation" and dominate less favored areas, i.e., from the relations between *core and periphery*.

Adopting a modified form of the Dahrendorf conflict theory model,[13] Friedmann injects the core–periphery structure into the heart of the development process.[14] From the complex interaction between core and periphery emerge the dynamic processes of spatial development.

Dominant core and dominated periphery together constitute a relatively stable spatial system in which the latter is successfully "colonized" chiefly to sustain the continued growth of the former. The further growth of core regions, however, is in the final analysis constrained by the tensions that tend to build up from the ever more visible discrepancies in the rates of expansion and modernization between core and periphery. The increasing flow of information from core to periphery, together with an aroused awareness of potentially modernizing elites in the periphery to the conditions of their own dependency, produce conflict with core region authorities over the extent of permissible autonomy.[15]

Progressive development concentration in core areas thereby becomes a major driving force for change. The periphery becomes organized into increasingly core-dependent market, supply, and administrative areas enmeshed in a feedback system characterized predominantly by backwash effects. But at the same time there is a limited extension of development impulses from the core, mobilizing the peripheral populations and creating a counter-elite, capable of challenging the social bases of integration in the spatial system.

Friedmann recognizes four possible outcomes arising from this challenge to existing authority–dependency relations between core and periphery:

1. *Suppression* of peripheral elites. This maintains the system, but may reduce the overall potential for development.
2. *Neutralization* of peripheral elites. Here there is limited, but highly selective, acceptance of peripheral demands which can encourage some modification of the authority–dependency relations. Actual access to authority by peripheral elites, however, remains highly restricted.
3. *Replacement* of core region by peripheral elites. The prospects for growth under these conditions are dependent upon the outlook of the new elite. It is likely, however, that new authority–dependency relations will emerge.
4. *Cooptation* of peripheral by core region elites. This process of accommodation leads to a more equitable sharing of powers and probably to more balanced growth

[13] Ralf Dahrendorf, *Class Conflict in an Industrial Society* (Stanford, Calif.: Stanford University Press, 1959).

[14] In many ways, Friedmann's conceptualization of core and periphery relations builds upon the work of Perroux and others on growth poles, *pôles de croissance*. An excellent review of the growth pole literature can be found in David F. Darwent, *Growth Pole and Growth Center Concepts: A Review, Evaluation and Bibliography* (Berkeley, Calif.: Center for Planning and Development, University of California at Berkeley, Working Paper No. 89, October 1968). The core-periphery concept is essentially a more explicitly spatial form of the center-periphery concept used by political scientists such as Edward Shils and Daniel Lerner. See also David F. Darwent, "Growth Poles and Growth Centers in Regional Planning—A Review," *Environment and Planning*, Vol. 1 (1969), pp. 5–32.

[15] "A General Theory," p. 30.

based upon greater economic and political decentralization and the expansion of new or already existing growth centers in the periphery.

Conflict resolution between core and periphery consequently represents a major turning point in the development process, leading either toward continued deviation-amplification or to the emergence of deviation-counteracting forces within the spatial system. Both alternatives, at least in the short run, can sustain continued growth, although in the case of increased deviation-amplification this is likely to be "growth without development"—an incremental expansion in one or more components of the societal–spatial system (e.g., regions, population groups, or sectors of the economy) without significant change or transformation of its basic structures. Continuation along this course, even when increasing the total real wealth of the whole system, most probably decreases the potential for peaceful structural transformation and increases the likelihood of greater repression and/or major revolution.

It should be noted, however, that the point at which transformation of authority–dependency relations in spatial systems becomes imperative for continued development is most difficult to identify. Moreover, the transformation is "expensive" in terms of social, economic, and political costs and may therefore curtail the short-run prospects for growth even if opportunely timed. Too little is yet known about the forms and processes of core–periphery relations, particularly the sources and intensity of conflicts and the means of conflict resolution. Deviation-amplification, for example, appears to be an essential component in the early stages of development, working effectively to mobilize the dependent periphery into the evolving societal and spatial system. Daniel Lerner contends that as long as there is a functionally selective accommodation (cooptation?) of the periphery, which maintains *political* control by the core, what he calls "difference promotion" may be the most effective development policy during the period of peripheral mobilization.[16] But how difference promotion can be prevented from leading to an overly rigid domination by the core over the periphery and how and when the core should recognize and respond to legitimate pressures from a mobilized periphery remain as unresolved challenges to the development planner and political leader.

What is being proposed here is a general perspective on the development process which is keyed to the changing patterns of authority–dependency relations between core and periphery. The essential components of this perspective and its implications for the study and planning of development can be summarized as follows:

1. The early course of development is characterized by accentuation of the differences between core and periphery. Peripheral areas increasingly become organizational dependencies of the core as the geographically concentrated impulses of development polarize space through the mechanisms of deviation-amplification. During

[16] Daniel Lerner, "Some Comments on Center-Periphery Relations," in Richard L. Merritt and Stein Rokkan, *Comparing Nations* (New Haven: Yale University Press, 1966), pp. 259–65.

this phase, regional inequalities are intensified as the transport system expands, the market economy spreads, urbanization and industrialization increase, and new ideas and technology diffuse over space.

2. This tendency toward a more pronounced concentration of modern activities and attributes in only a few areas of an organized spatial system represents a fundamental departure from the spatial equilibrium conditions postulated in conventional geographic and regional development theory. Since deviation-amplification is an inherent part of the early development process, it cannot automatically be viewed as abnormal, nor as an indicator of stagnant growth. Although centrifugal forces of development dispersal must be present in sufficient amounts for growth to continue, development can and does proceed apace under conditions in which backwash and deviation-amplification outweigh spread and equalization effects.

3. Crucial decisions are made during the early phases of development which establish a framework of locational advantage that tends to embed itself tenaciously within the developing spatial system. Despite the potential predominance of deviation-counteracting forces at later stages of development, the basic structures solidified during the period of deviation-amplification tend to maintain themselves throughout the modernization process. If only for this reason, it is of great importance to understand the causes and consequences of deviations from a presumed stable and integrated equilibrium, rather than dismissing them as temporary and patternless inconsistencies.

4. Deviation-amplifying processes, coupled with expanding social mobilization in the periphery, generates conflict situations as existing patterns of authority–dependency relations are challenged. This crucial threshold can be reached at almost any point in the development process since it typically reflects local social, economic, and political conditions (e.g., degree of cultural homogeneity, locational patterns of core and periphery, dependence upon foreign trade, the nature of the political system, fundamental ideologies). The important influence of specific local conditions makes the outcome, as well as the timing and intensity of these developmental crises, difficult to predict.

5. Expanding patterns of political participation can greatly complicate growth patterns during transitional phases of development. Given a competitive political party system and free elections, an expanding mobilized periphery is provided with a powerful avenue of expression and influence. If sufficiently organized, even at low levels of development (when, indeed, its population may greatly outnumber that of the core), it can press for increased recognition and priority either as a separate political party or (more likely to be successful) through an existing core party which needs its support. This can lead to more extensive government programs favoring balanced regional growth. Attempts at reducing the imbalance between core and periphery, however, are expensive and can limit short-run growth. Moreover, the intense competition generated in a highly compartmentalized pluralistic political system can itself contribute to the political turmoil and instability which the government seeks to avoid. To a great extent, the important role of single-party systems in many developing countries (and within socialist planned economies) reflects the desire of the dominant core to control or at least selectively accommodate the mobilized periphery during a crucial period of development.

6. Development planning during the deviation-amplification phase must seek a productive and flexible middle ground between balanced regional growth (which can

be overly expensive) and excessive core concentration (which can rigidify core periphery boundaries and encourage social and political turmoil). A major problem here is the degree to which an inherited spatial system, structured to serve significantly different goals during a period of colonial control, can or should be reorganized to serve the objectives of politically independent states.

7. Only at more advanced stages of development is there likely to be sufficient surplus capital and geographically extensive organizational structures available for the costly readjustment necessary to break the binds of core domination and move the spatial system toward a stable and integrated equilibrium. This implies that approximation to equilibrium conditions can be used as a direct gauge of development only in the most modernized societies. In the context of early development, the pace and level of modernization must be assessed with respect to the particular nature, rigidity, and pattern of change in the expected deviations from equilibrium conditions. The critical test lies in the ability of the primary decisionmakers to direct effectively the course of modernization, while simultaneously contending with and productively accommodating the pressures and tensions inherent in the development process. Herein lies the essence of what some have viewed as political development.[17]

Equilibrium, Disequilibrium, and Spatial Development

A major objective of the preceding discussion has been to illustrate the need for a more comprehensive perspective on the development process, one which builds upon and integrates existing equilibrium theory with new theoretical formulations concerning deviation-amplification, the authority–dependency relations between core and periphery, and models of conflict and irregular growth. Social and spatial systems probably do show a long-run tendency toward stability and equilibrium, but they simultaneously generate within themselves powerful forces which work in the opposite direction. These forces cannot be ignored for they represent an essential component of the development process. Rather than concentrating so heavily upon an ultimate equilibrium state, therefore, the attempt to formulate a spatial theory of development must focus greater attention on the patterns, causes, and consequences of disequilibrium within developing spatial systems.

Somewhat paradoxically, such theory-building must rest upon a fuller knowledge of the character and conditions of spatial equilibrium, for these provide a datum from which to measure and compare the salient patterns of deviation. This equilibrium state, however, has to be defined in terms broader than the purely economic, deal with systems of regions rather than the single region case, and incorporate forces leading to cumulative imbalances and disequilibrium in spatial patterns. Again we turn to Friedmann for perhaps the closest approximation to a description of such a dynamic spatial equilibrium available in the literature.

---

[17] See, for example, Ronald D. Brunner and Garry D. Brewer, *Organized Complexity: Empirical Theories of Political Development* (New York: The Free Press, 1971), pp. 1–58.

Friedmann's basic propositions concerning spatial equilibrium can be summarized as follows:[18]

1. Spatial systems in a state of integrated equilibrium are organized by an interconnected series of urban fields whose central nodes are arranged in a hierarchy according to the functions performed by each. The entire space efficiently served by this hierarchy of urban fields.

2. The spatial incidence of development is a function of distance from the central city. Troughs of relative economic backwardness thus lie in the most inaccessible areas along the intermetropolitan peripheries.

3. Development impulses are filtered in an ordered fashion from larger to smaller centers in the urban hierarchy and from them outward through their respective urban fields. Major regional variations in development are, therefore, unlikely to persist within given levels of the hierarchy.

4. A dynamic system of flows—of development impulses transmitted downward and outward through the urban hierarchy and of migration moving primarily inward and upward—maintains the system in an integrated state and sustains continued development.

The route toward this equilibrium tends to be characterized by a series of interrelated (isomorphic) transformations in four major dimensions of the developing spatial system.[19] These involve:

1. *Sociocultural patterns.* "The evolution of spatial structure proceeds from relatively isolated 'islands of innovation' via major communications corridors to a continuously [modernized] surface. However, this surface will be uneven, reflecting earlier differences in the structure of modernization as well as newly emerging (e.g., post-industrial) patterns."

2. *Locational patterns of economic activity.* "The evolution of spatial structure proceeds from a highly concentrated pattern in the location of modern economic activities to one that is spatially more deconcentrated. Agglomeration economies, however, will limit the extent to which deconcentration can occur. Of equal importance is a process of industrial dispersion into the urban fields of metropolitan areas."

3. *Settlement patterns.* "The evolution of spatial structure proceeds from primacy in urban settlements to a log-normal pattern in the hierarchy of cities. The vectors of this pattern, however, are influenced by the general structure of accessibility in the spatial system."

4. *Political organization of space.* "The evolution of spatial structure proceeds from a highly centralized to a polycentric system of decision-making characterized by polyarchical relations among a set of independent authorities."

These transformations, which are posed by Friedmann as testable hypotheses that have already received some firm empirical support in the development literature, provide an excellent prolegomenon for research into the patterns of

---

[18] The following has been adapted from Brian J. L. Berry, "Relationships Between Regional Economic Development and the Urban System—The Case of Chile," *Tijdschrift voor Economische en Sociale Geografie,* Vol. 60 (1969), pp. 283–307.

[19] From John Friedmann, "Urbanization and National Development," pp. 33–34.

deviation-amplication and disequilibrium in the spatial development process. From their very nature, they suggest a relationship between level of development and degree of disequilibrium which fits neatly with our preceding discussion of the dynamics of development. The relationship is not likely to be linear and monotonically increasing or decreasing, but appears to peak in the middle phases of development. The period of maximum disequilibrium thus separates an earlier phase of pronounced deviation-amplification from one of internal adjustment to stress (endogenous and exogenous) which either solidifies (perhaps only temporarily) the system of inequality which has emerged or begins to move the system closer to an equilibrium state.

In the second part of this study, historical patterns of spatial development are examined empirically within the African context to illustrate the prevailing paths of deviation-amplifying growth characteristic of developing countries. For the remainder of this section, however, two fundamental patterns of spatial disequilibrium will be briefly discussed with specific regard to potentially fruitful directions of future research. These include the pattern of regional development inequalities and the rank-size ordering of urban systems.

The spread of modernization throughout the world has resulted in an increasing gap between the most and least modernized regions of nearly all developing spatial systems. This pattern of regional inequality holds not only at the level of the nation-state, but is applicable as well to the global system, with the so-called Development Decade of the 1960's further accentuating the modernization gap between what might be called the global core and the global periphery. The dynamics of increasing regional economic development inequalities clearly provide a major focus for future research into problems which are among the most pressing in the world today.

Even within such relatively well-developed countries as Canada, there has yet to occur more than a small amount of convergence in regional income inequalities.[20] Friedmann summarizes the existing literature on this subject in these terms:

The best that can be said from available information is that regional income convergence is an extremely drawn-out process. It occurs, when it does, at a relatively advanced stage in the industrialization process, and it rarely changes the rank-ordering of regions by income. Core region dominance, we may conclude, is not easily challenged. And when it is, the reversal of earlier trends may require a number of genera-

[20] Alan G. Green, "Regional Inequality, Structural Change and Economic Growth in Canada—1890–1956," *Economic Development and Cultural Change*, Vol. 17 (1969), pp. 567–83. See also Jeffrey Williamson, "Regional Inequality and the Process of National Development," *Economic Development and Cultural Change*, Vol. 13 (1965); Douglas H. Graham, "Divergent and Convergent Regional Economic Growth and Internal Migration in Brazil—1940–1960," *Economic Development and Cultural Change*, Vol. 18 (1970), pp. 362–82; R. B. Hughes, Jr., "Interregional Income Differences: Self-Perpetuation," *Southern Economic Journal*, Vol. 28 (1961); J. R. Lasuen, "Regional Income Inequalities and the Problems of Growth in Spain," *Papers and Proceedings of the Regional Science Association*, Vol. 8 (1962), pp. 169–88.

tions. The continuous outward expansion of core areas may occur when subsidiary centers are drawn into the political-economic subsystem of the core, but this process is one of gradual accretion; major interregional differences in income respond considerably more slowly.[21]

Particularly relevant here is the role of transport expansion. It is generally assumed that transport investments supply a valuable planning tool for reducing regional income differences. A number of studies, however, has shown how improved transport facilities often strengthen the periphery's dependence upon the core, rather than encouraging more balanced regional growth.[22] Railways and roads can become polarizing tentacles extending outward from the core to capture isolated islands of development in the periphery, particularly when peripheral centers remain unconnected with one another and few feeder lines are constructed. Can similar conclusions be drawn concerning the expansion of the market economy? Improved educational facilities? The spread of political party organizations? What kinds of improvements are most likely to encourage self-generated peripheral growth? How is the persistence or accentuation of regional inequalities related to ethnic pluralism or to the structure of the political system?

Similar questions arise with respect to the increasing accentuation within the urban system of primate city-size distributions. It has been hypothesized that in a developed and integrated spatial system, there is a tendency for the size of a city to be a function of its rank in the urban hierarchy and the size of the largest city. Thus, the distribution of city-sizes would follow the rank–size rule in which $P_n = P_1(n)^{-1}$ where P_n is the population of a city of rank n and P_1 is the population of the largest city. It has therefore often been presumed, within conventional equilibrium theory, that rank-size (or log-normal) distributions become increasingly characteristic at higher levels of development.[23] Our modified equilibrium notions, however, would suggest that the predominant pattern is one in which primacy increases during the earlier phases of development, peaks in the middle phases, and often continues to be prominent at more advanced stages.

On the surface, the existing literature on city-size distributions seems to contradict both the conventional and modified equilibrium assertions. Brian Berry, for example, discovered very little relationship at all between the rank–

[21] "Urbanization and National Development," p. 22.

[22] Howard Gauthier, "Transportation and the Growth of the São Paulo Economy," *Journal of Regional Science*, Vol. 8 (1968), pp. 77–94; Michael McNulty, "Urban Structure and Development: The Urban System of Ghana," *The Journal of Developing Areas*, Vol. 3 (1969), pp. 159–76; Hamzah Sendut, "Patterns of Urbanization in Malaya," *Journal of Tropical Geography*, Vol. 16 (1962), pp. 114–308.

[23] George K. Zipf, *National Unity and Disunity* (Bloomington, Ind.: Principia Press, 1944); *idem, Human Behavior and the Principle of Least Effort* (Cambridge, Mass.: Addeson-Wesley Press, 1949); John Q. Stewart, "Empirical Mathematical Rules Concerning the Distribution and Equilibrium of Population," *Geographical Review*, Vol. 37 (1947), pp. 461–85.

size distribution and level of development.[24] Both primacy and log-normality were present at all points in the developmental spectrum of thirty-seven countries he investigated. But several qualifications can be made which lead to a re-evaluation of Berry's findings and lend support to our proposed relationship between primacy and development.

As Berry himself notes, for example, a powerful colonial legacy within heavily trade-dependent countries in or near the global core area explains in large part the persistence of primate distributions in many economically advanced countries. Thus, Austria, Spain, Portugal, Denmark, The Netherlands, Sweden, and France are characterized by major breaks with the log-normal city-size distribution. This results primarily from the continuing dominance of a single large city that is, or was, an important imperial capital or metropole for a significantly larger political entity in the past. This legacy of primacy reflects the powerful geographical focusing of colonial backwash effects in global core–periphery relations. Perhaps the extreme case is found in England and Wales, with primate cities grafted on to a close approximation to log-normality among the remaining smaller centers.

Similarly, Berry notes that log-normality in many less developed countries is associated with a substantial history of preindustrial urbanization. Thus, in China, India, and Korea (to which we might add Nigeria), a modern system of cities has been superimposed upon already existing traditional urban systems. Although many of the largest cities today are relatively new or have experienced their major surge of growth in the modern period, the overall effect is to produce an approximation to log-normality for the system as a whole.

This brings up another important point. The kind of primacy which is of greatest significance here takes the form of political and economic domination; and the concentration is one of communications and transactions, not necessarily of population. Hence, developmental primacy is measured most effectively in terms of such variables as decisionmaking power, political centralization, investment flows, and relative percentages of national transactions (e.g., telecommunications, postal and transport network traffic, newspaper circulation, etc.). As a result, we will find that whereas such cities as Nairobi, Lagos, Johannesburg, Seoul, or Peking may not technically be primate cities measured solely by population size, their impact on their respective spatial systems may be such that to classify them as other than primate would be grossly misleading. Unfortunately, comparative data on these variables are extremely difficult to obtain, and we are forced to leave this significantly modified analysis of primacy to future research.

But even when population figures are used alone, there appears to be evidence in support of the theory of polarized development. If the primacy indices from the *Atlas of Economic Development* are assigned to the groupings of *under-*

[24] Brian J. L. Berry, "City Size Distributions ad Economic Development," *Economic Development and Cultural Change*, Vol. 9 (1961), pp. 573–87.

developed countries discerned by Adelman and Morris, some interesting results are discovered.[25] For the countries appearing on both lists, the proportions with high primacy (the upper 50% of the *Atlas* listings) are as follows: least developed countries—42%; intermediate underdevelopment—45%; and most developed of the underdeveloped—60%. The results show a marked tendency toward increased primacy during the early phases of development.

These ad hoc reappraisals obviously do not adequately account for all the exceptions to the proposed relationship between primacy and level of development. The relative log-normality of the Indian urban system, for example, is difficult to explain. It is also recognized that clear population primacy can emerge in areas of extensive traditional urbanization, as in Egypt. The continuing exceptions, however, signal the need for further investigation of the association between population size and developmental primacy. Still greater is the need for increased attention to the causes and implications of primacy, rather than a continued emphasis on the processes underlying the rank–size rule. Primacy cannot simply be dismissed as an abberration along a developmental path to spatial equilibrium. The existence of one or more very large cities shaping and dominating the organization of space and society is an integral part of the core-periphery structure which is itself the quintessential spatial expression of the development process. The existing literature on city-size distributions represents an excellent example of how an overemphasis on general equilibrium models has led to a neglect of key processes of spatial development and change.[26]

THE GEOGRAPHY OF MODERNIZATION: EMPIRICAL PATTERNS AND PROCESSES OF CHANGE

The most fundamental expression of spatial development is the *modernization surface*, a composite map of the areal variations in development within a spatial system at a particular point in time. In much the same way that a contour map of elevation represents the product of the interplay between erosional and

[25] Norton Ginsburg, *Atlas of Economic Development* (Chicago: University of Chicago Press, 1961), Table 12, p. 36, contains a list of primacy data indices the 104 countries based upon the population of the largest city as a percentage of the total population of the four largest cities in each country. See also Irma Adelman and Cynthia Taft Morris, *Society, Politics, and Economic Development* (Baltimore, Md.: Johns Hopkins University Press, 1967), Table IV–5: Grouping of Countries by Factor Scores on Factor Representing Level of Socioeconomic Development, p. 170.

[26] Several important reevaluations of the relationship between economic development and city size distributions have been published since the writing of this chapter in 1970. Most tend to support the interpretation given here. See, for example, Saleh El-Shaks, "Development, Primacy, and Systems of Cities," *The Journal of Developing Areas*, Vol. 7, No. 1 (1972), pp. 11–36; and Brian J. L. Berry, "City Size and Economic Development: Conceptual Synthesis and Policy Problems, with Special Reference to South and Southeast Asia," in Leo Jacobson and Ved Prakesh, eds., *Urbanization and National Development* (Beverly Hills, Cal.: Sage Publications, 1971), pp. 111–43.

depositional processes on the physical landscape, the modernization surface is generated and shaped by the geographically uneven impact on the human land-scape of the forces of social, economic, and political change. Each surface has its peaks and troughs, uplands and lowlands, steep and gentle slopes. Each is also a developmental snapshot which, if viewed over a sequence of time periods, reveals a historical panorama of geographical change.[27]

A large proportion of recent development research by geographers has concentrated on the measurement and mapping of modernization surfaces (largely in Africa) and on the attempt to explain their historical evolution and contemporary implication.[28] From these studies has emerged a useful frame-work for the spatial analysis of development, particularly with regard to the core–periphery structure. The modernization surface of any spatial system reflects and highlights the patterns of geographical concentration and dispersal which underlie the organization of space into distinctive cores and peripheries. As the authority–dependency relations between dominant core and dependent periphery change through the course of development, so too will the moderniza-tion surface be reshaped.

Structural Components of the Modernization Surface

It is possible to identify several more specific components of the core–periphery structure which together comprise the most essential features of the modernization surface.

The primate city, for example, is the "Everest" of the modernization sur-face. It is the coordinative hub in which political and economic authority and influence are most heavily concentrated and from which emanate the most powerful impulses of innovative change. It is usually in the center of the most modernized region and, during the early stages of development, influences the areal patterns of development throughout the entire spatial system. Although measured primarily in terms of dominance and development, the primate city can usually be expected to be the largest city in population size as well.

Growth poles, which include the primate city, represent significant centers of concentrated development within the spatial system.[29] When there is pro-nounced functional specialization among the largest growth poles (e.g., a split

---

[27] For a more detailed view of the concept of geographical surfaces, see Peter Haggett, *Locational Analysis in Human Geography,* Chapter 6.

[28] Edward W. Soja, *The Geography of Modernization in Kenya* (Syracuse, N. Y.: Syracuse University Press, 1968); Peter Gould, "Tanzania 1920–63: The Spatial Impress of the Modernization Process," *World Politics,* Vol. 22 (1970), pp. 149–70; and J. Barry Riddell, *The Spatial Dynamics of Modernization in Sierra Leone: Structure, Diffusion, and Response* (Evanston, Ill.: Northwestern University Press, 1970).

[29] This definition is much looser and more geographically specific than Perroux's original formulation of the "growth pole" concept. It is probably more acceptable today to refer to these geographical nodes of concentrated and expanding development as major "growth centers." See the papers by Darwent noted in note 14, above.

between economic and political capitals or the inclusion of several regional primate cities within the system, as might be true in a political federation), it may not be possible to distinguish a single primate city. In general, however, one of the growth poles can usually be considered dominant.

The primary circulation system is a network of high-priority communications and transport links connecting the major growth poles and forming the interactional backbone of the spatial system. A high density of transaction flows —of people, goods, and ideas—distinguishes the primary circulation system from the remainder of the communications and transport network, just as it distinguishes the growth poles from the rest of the urban system.

The mobilized periphery consists of those areas interacting most intensively with, and generally in closest physical proximity to, the growth poles and primary circulation system. From the mobilized periphery, which has reached a minimal threshold of development, emerge the major intrasystemic pressures to change existing spatial authority–dependency relationships.

The unmobilized periphery is the least developed portion of the spatial system. If this peripheral backwater is given any attention at all, it is primarily as a reservoir of potential support for competitive core and peripheral groups or as a source of extrasystemic conflict (e.g., in relation to possible external annexation).

The modernization surface can therefore be viewed as having· a tentlike configuration peaked at the growth poles and secondarily over the major centers of the urban administrative system. Ridges of higher development exist between the major growth poles along the primary transport and communications routes, with development declining away from the major nodes and their linear connections. It can be presumed that the level or stage of development will be reflected in the particular configurative forms of the surface: the distribution of its peaks and troughs, the steepness of its slopes, and its average "elevation."

During the early stages of development, the forces leading to concentration and centralization are most narrowly focused. The core area may therefore include only the primate city and perhaps a few additional growth poles which are able to establish some degree of autonomy and influence in locational decisionmaking. For national spatial systems, these larger growth poles may be termed *national nuclei* and generally are the focal points of mobilized regions of political support and economic growth. In contrast, *secondary growth poles* are most often satellites of the core area nuclei and frequently peripheral to the primary circulation system.

As development proceeds, the regional hinterlands of the growth poles become progressively mobilized and modernized and may begin to coalesce in an areally more extensive core region. A key feature of this process of accretion is likely to be the growth of a more integrated urban subsystem within and around the core, consisting of a functionally ordered hierarchy of small, middle-sized, and large centers adequate to serve the core population efficiently. This reflects both developments within the expanding core and the extension from the core of organizational structures incorporating ever larger portions of the periphery into a system of administrative, market, and supply areas. The whole urban system, however, will tend to remain "top-heavy." The number of very large cities is likely to grow, but there will remain a pronounced paucity of middle-sized centers.

This pattern is likely to continue until a point is reached when significant changes take place in the authority–dependency relations between core and periphery, a developmental hiatus which has been discussed in greater detail earlier in this chapter. At more advanced stages of development, when spread effects outweigh backwash, and the cycle of deviation-amplification is broken, the modernization surface can be expected to mirror a trend toward a stable and integrated spatial equilibrium. The entire spatial system's population is mobilized, the core expands, and the national space becomes increasingly integrated within a hierarchically structured and functionally ordered urban, administrative, and transport system. The volume of transaction flows increases between urban centers and regions reflecting the complex territorial division of labor, functional interdependence and regional complementarity within the entire spatial system.

As Friedmann notes, there is also an associated extension throughout the system of "a common basis for social life or, more accurately, a shared frame of socio-cultural expectations, including language, cultural values, political-legal-bureaucratic institutions, and a market economy." [30] As a result, the geographical periphery is no longer so dependent upon the core, nor is physical proximity to the core as important a correlate of development. The peaks on the modernization surface will therefore be more evenly distributed and in closer accord with the overall distribution of population. Although the general elevation of the surface will be higher, with fewer deep troughs and extensive lowlands, the surface will remain uneven, reflecting, as already mentioned, the persistence of earlier locational patterns of modernization and the emergence of new, postindustrial forces of change.

To illustrate the potential insights derivable from structural analysis of modernization surfaces, we offer a brief case study of Kenya. Figures 5–1 and 5–2 represent, respectively, the generalized modernization surface and the major components of the core-periphery structure in Kenya just after independence (1963). The modernization surface was derived from a principal components analysis of 25 variables for 35 enumeration areas (districts). As has been common in most similar studies, the first unrotated component accounted for a very large proportion of the total variance (63%) and was interpreted as a composite dimension of development. Factor scores were calculated and mapped by district. This choropleth map was then transformed into a continuous surface through interpolation and a primarily nonstatistically based assessment

30 "Urbanization and National Development," p. 10.

FIGURE 5–1.   THE MODERNIZATION SURFACE OF KENYA: 1963

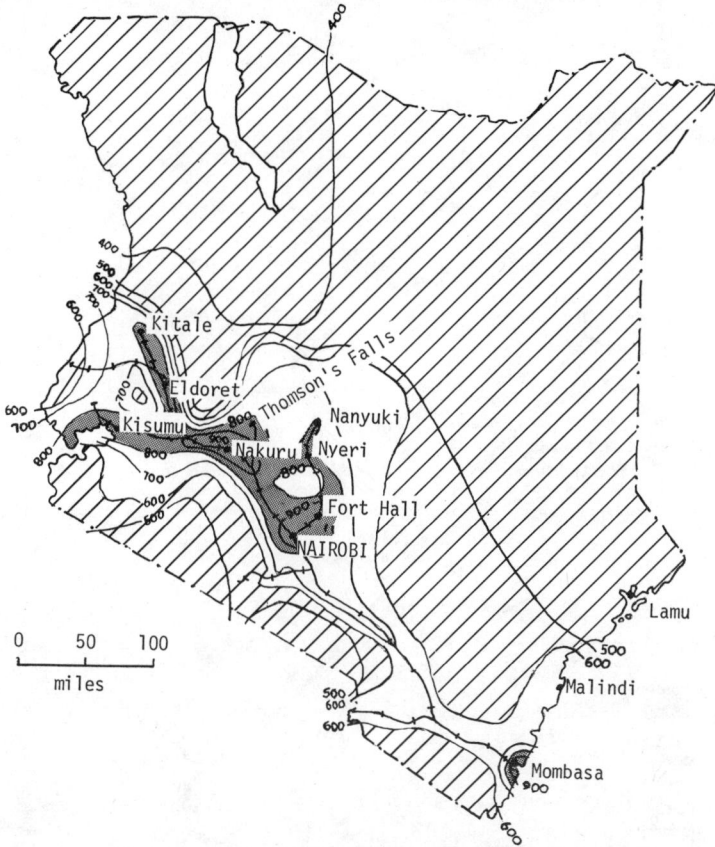

Note: Values are derived from principal components analysis of district
data in Edward W. Soja, *The Geography of Modernization in Kenya*
(Syracuse, N.Y.: Syracuse University Press, 1968).

of within-district variations to provide a more easily interpretable form of representation.[31]

A detailed analysis of the geography of modernization in Kenya has been published elsewhere.[32] Very generally summarizing this interpretation, it can be seen that modernization in Kenya has been heavily concentrated in the southwestern quadrant of the country, an area of fertile highlands and dense agricultural population and the site of extensive European settlement during the British colonial period.

The peak point of the surface clearly is Nairobi, the springboard for early

[31] The methods of analysis used here differ somewhat from those used in the case study of Sierra Leone. The variations in relative modernization scores in Kenya and in Sierra Leone are, therefore, not strictly comparable.

[32] Soja, *op. cit.* Figures 5–1 and 5–2 are derived from this study.

FIGURE 5-2.   THE SPATIAL STRUCTURE OF CORE-PERIPHERY
RELATIONS IN KENYA

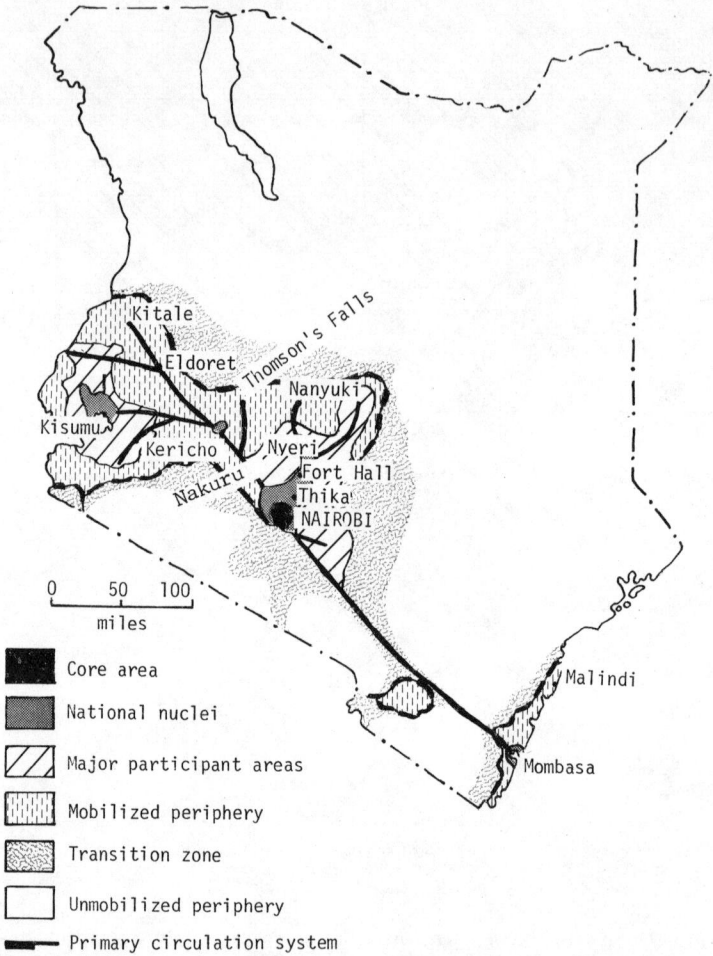

European settlement, the capital of Kenya, and major metropolis for all of East
Africa. Levels of development throughout all of Kenya are closely associated
with physical proximity to Nairobi and the intensity of interaction with the
national capital. Nairobi and its immediate environs thus constitute a core area
par excellence. Although containing only 4% of the Kenyan population, Nairobi
has close to one-half or more of the total urban population, postal traffic, radios,
television sets, English newspaper circulation, and telephones. About 17% of
the entire African labor force is employed in Nairobi and, more significant, they
receive 28% of all African wages paid. The capital is the headquarters for over
one-third of all registered political organizations and the origin or destination

for a disproportionately large share of the railway, road, and telecommunications traffic of Kenya.

Several other growth poles exist. These include the much older town of Mombasa, now the largest seaport in East Africa; Nakuru, the "capital" of the former "White Highlands"; and the important Lake Victoria port of Kisumu. As can be seen from Figure 5–2, the four growth poles are the centers for major segments of the mobilized periphery and stand as the most important nuclei for national economic and political integration.[33] It should also be noted that Kisumu has developed a larger mobilized hinterland than either Nakuru or Mombasa and stands potentially as a major competitor to the Nairobi core area and as much a source of divisive regionalism as the much larger Mombasa, focal point for the distinctive coast region.

The primary circulation system links up the national nuclei and most of the other secondary growth poles (Kericho, Eldoret, Thomson's Falls, Nyeri, Nanyuki). The major section of the mobilized periphery forms a bow-tie shaped region in the southwestern highlands, with enclaves existing along the coast and in the small Taita highlands, between Nairobi and Mombasa. Beyond these areas is a transitional zone, while the remainder of the country can be characterized as unmobilized periphery.

Politics in Kenya closely reflects the spatial–structural patterns of modernization. It was primarily from the Nairobi and Kisumu areas and their hinterlands (and secondarily from Mombasa) that the major impetus for African political development and the drive toward independence emerged. Occupied mainly by the Kikuyu, Kamba, Luo, and Luhya, these areas have acted as the most important source region for the modernized African elite of Kenya. At independence, the dominant nationalist political party, KANU (Kenya African National Union), derived most of its support from the four major ethnic groups in the hinterlands of Nairobi and Kisumu, a situation which continues with only minor modification today.

Much of the relative political stability which has characterized Kenya since independence can be attributed to the succesful neutralization of political pressures from the smaller ethnic compartments in the mobilized periphery. The major competitive political party at independence, KADU (Kenya African Democratic Union), found its support mainly among these peripheral and relatively undeveloped areas along the coast and in the Rift Valley region between Nairobi and Kisumu, as well as from the tacit—if not active—encouragement of the immigrant Asian and European communities. KADU, with this support, was successful in introducing a constitution which was specifically

[33] The category of major participant areas on the map distinguishes the most politically relevant sectors of the mobilized periphery. Here are the densely settled and most developed areas of what Soja has termed the African Subsystem, the areas which assumed pre-eminent importance in the drive toward independence and continue to provide the major sources of support in modern Kenya politics.

designed to reduce the concentration of power and development in Nairobi. This *majimbo* constitution (Swahili for regions) reorganized the administrative system of Kenya into eight new regions, with the Kikuyu and Luo—the most influential ethnic groups—homogeneously compacted into two of them and with Nairobi representing a third. Government was to be decentralized and heavy responsibilities were planned for the regional government centers.

In the years immediately after independence, through a variety of means, the regional constitution was essentially nullified, and Nairobi continued as the coordinative hub for all of Kenya. Indeed, its dominance has probably become even more pronounced in the political and economic affairs of the country. In an excellent example of selective accommodation between core and periphery, KADU was later dissolved and its membership absorbed, with promises of greater attention to their former constituencies, into the dominant KANU. The regional boundaries remain, the regional administrative centers at least have experienced significant growth, and the central government has instituted several programs to encourage a limited economic decentralization, particularly in industry. But within only seven years (1962–69), the population of Nairobi has nearly doubled (from 246,000 to 477,600), and all indicators point to an even greater piling up of development in the Nairobi core area.

Internal politics in Kenya today remain in large part a derivative of competitive relations between core and periphery, especially with respect to the increasingly dominant core elite of Kikuyu. The solidification of Kikuyu political and economic control and continued development concentration in the Nairobi area (which is adjacent to Kikuyuland) have generated renewed charges of negligence from the mobilized periphery and, significantly, from the growing pockets of economic depression and unemployment within the core area. What has complicated the situation still further, however, has been the apparent consolidation of opposition around the Kisumu nucleus and among the Luo. Unlike the KADU situation, which in many ways grew from an artificial solidarity among the smaller groups in the mobilized periphery, Luo opposition represented a challenge from part of the elite population which was regionalized around one of the major national nuclei.[34] Accordingly, the reaction of KANU was not neutralization, but direct suppression. The Luo leader, Oginga Odinga, was put in detention and his opposition party, the KPU, banned.

Several additional features of postindependence politics in Kenya are interpretable in association with the structural components of its modernization surface: the Somali claims to portions of the unmobilized periphery and attempts by the Kenya government to counter these claims and to build closer links to the Northeast Region; the Kikuyu expansion into the sections of the former "White Highlands," which have been opened to African settlement and the resistance to this expansion generated among other ethnic groups; the role of

---

[34] It should be noted that not all the Luo have rallied behind the opposition to KANU. The leadership of KANU has been, and continues to be, drawn significantly from the Luo ethnic group.

the 1969 elections in ameliorating tensions between core and periphery and absolving the suppression of KPU; the structure and tone of the recent development plan, which appears to give high priority to more balanced regional growth and reduced development concentration in Nairobi. It is not being suggested that the geography of modernization provides the only interpretative framework for the analysis of political development in Kenya or elsewhere. The application of an explicit spatial perspective, however, does supply an insightful approach and methodology which have generally been neglected in the political development literature.

The Historical Evolution of Modernization Surfaces in Tropical Africa

From the growing geographical literature on African development, and in conjunction with our preceding discussion of the dynamics and salient structural components of spatial development, it is possible to piece together a broad historical-descriptive model of the geography of modernization in Africa. Although the precise details and timing differ from country to country, sufficient regularity exists in the patterns and processes of spatial development to permit the identification of a series of distinctive historical phases beginning with the period of initial colonial contact—the springboard for the diffusion of contemporary modernization—and extending to the present.

The Early Period: Locational Selection and Structural Evolution.   In Africa and throughout most of the developing world, contemporary modernization was not indigenously generated, but derived primarily from the imposition of modern forms of social, economic, and political organization and behavior over a mosaic of predominantly small-scale traditional societies. The new systems generally encompassed much larger areas and induced greatly expanded world views. Occupational and other forms of specialization increased as the framework of exchange and interaction was extended beyond the usually parochial and largely self-subsistent traditional units. This created larger scale spatial systems that were functionally organized and structured around a network of modern transport and communications linkages, which in turn hinged upon a system of modern urban nodes. It was through this formal spatial structure that the impulses of innovative change entered and diffused over the evolving spatial system, building and shaping its modernization surface.

The external overlay of modernization became articulated with the local landscape at first in only a few areas. Nevertheless, it was during this early period of colonial contact that crucial decisions were made which established a pattern of locational advantage that tended to entrench itself tenaciously within the developing spatial system. The few favored areas built upon their initial locational advantages leading to the early emergence of dominant foci of innovative change and the progressive accentuation of differences between core and periphery. The extent to which modernization became concentrated over time in these early nuclei is one of the most outstanding features of contemporary African states.

These processes of *locational selection* and *geographical concentration* represent central components in the geography of modernization throughout the world. Although important at every stage in the development process, they are of exceptional morphogenetic significance during the early contact phase. Together they create and shape the growth of the urban, administrative, and transport systems, the basic spatial structure for the diffusion of modernization. Given the powerful impact of an initial kick on the patterns of spatial development and the accentuation of the locational advantages thus generated through the mechanisms of deviation-amplification, it is remarkable how little attention has been given to the factors which influenced decisionmaking in the early period of modernization.

Locational selection involves such elements as the spatial allocation of investment and political-administrative authority, and the choice of sites for commercial and industrial establishments, schools and hospitals, transport and communications links, and political institutions. In essence, the geography of modernization begins with the early colonial decisions which selectively imprint modern institutional and organizational structures on the traditional African landscape. Once established, the nodes of articulation between tradition and modernity become magnets for future growth, setting in motion the forces leading to geographical concentration of development.

Locational selection during the early phases of development in Africa was guided by the mode of contact and the perceived goals of the colonial powers. Growth poles were established at key points, generally coastal, which were accessible both to Europe and to retrievable interior resources. The latter included not only exportable minerals and agricultural products, but also certain human resources considered particularly attractive to the extension of Christianity and/or effective colonial control, as was the case with regard to many of the traditionally well-developed and centralized interior states of the east and west African savanna. The profound impact of this pattern of locational selection is still evident today. Almost 30% of all tropical African exports still come from within 100 miles of the coast,[35] and some of the continent's largest cities are located in coastal positions serving what were in the early colonial period important and attractive interior states: Accra re Ashanti, Lagos re Hausaland, Mombasa re Buganda.

The geography of modernization, therefore, did not begin with a totally blank map. Locational selection, like all spatial processes, is both space-forming and space-contingent. While working to structure and organize the modernizing spatial system, locational decisionmaking also reflected existing locational patterns. Knowledge of local conditions was relatively meager, but locational selection in the early contact phase became closely associated with the areal

[35] William Hance, *The Geography of Modern Africa* (New York: Columbia University Press, 1964), p. 50.

distribution of resources (material and human) as perceived by the primary decisionmakers.

In addition to the mode of contact and the pattern of perceived resources, the early patterns of spatial development were also heavily influenced by the distinctive developmental objectives of the colonial powers. The modernization surface was accordingly shaped very extensively by the colonial goals of administrative control and economic exploitation. It thus differed significantly from the surface that would have emerged had the development and integration of local economic and political systems been the primary objective. Mabogunje cogently describes this particular phenomenon with respect to the expansion of transport in Nigeria.

At the time of their advent, the British could be said to have two choices before them. One was to improve the system of internal exchange in the hope that increasing returns from this would lead to greater trading activities with Europe; the other was to concentrate on what they could profitably exploit and export from the country in the hope that this would have some incidental beneficial effect on internal exchange.

To have taken the first choice would have meant that the British colonial venture was not to serve the interest of the British people but that of the Nigerians primarily. It would also imply that any development and innovations brought by them would be undertaken or accepted within the traditional order of importance among the cities. For example, if the railway were to be introduced, it would be first to link existing important centres . . . .

However, the British did not come to Nigeria to uphold or enhance the traditional system. In their concern to exploit the resources of the country in a way most remunerative to their imperial interests, they acted . . . in such a way as would appear to a "Nigerian" at the time as entirely arbitrary. From this point of view, one can see the seventy or eighty years of British administrative control of the country between 1885 and 1960 as imposing a new but "arbitrary" spatial integration on Nigeria.[36]

Hence, the contemporary spatial patterns of modernization in Nigeria, and in nearly all former colonial areas, are largely the product of the attitudes, perceptions, and objectives of the colonial powers. Given their tenacity, it will take many years and great effort before these patterns—consisting of fragmented islands of development, mostly peripherally located to facilitate exports of primary commodities and uphold a powerful external orientation—cease to reflect the functions and requirements of a colonial territory and become restructured to serve independent governments attempting to construct cohesive and developed communities within their boundaries.

A characteristic sequence can be identified in the patterns of spatial development during the early colonial phase. This sequence revolves around the selection of nodal points for the spatial organization of colonial territories and the selection of routes to guide the diffusion of modernization through the evolving spatial system.

[36] Akin L. Mabogunje, *Urbanization in Nigeria* (New York: Africana Publishing Corporation, 1968), p. 143.

Prior to the colonial partitioning of Africa, when control over the geography of modernization moved into the hands of the European powers, there existed a series of scattered coastal ports representing the primarily peripheral interface between Europe and Africa. After the continent was colonially compartmentalized, however, development came to be concentrated in a smaller number of centers (generally one or two per compartment) which were chosen as administrative centers and/or the starting points for lines of penetration into the interior. As a result, the African coast today is dotted with abandoned or decaying ports which were at some time in the past much more important. Lamu and Malindi in Kenya, for example, have been dramatically eclipsed by the modern port of Mombasa, serving not only all of Kenya, but Uganda and parts of Tanzania as well.[37] Similar situations exist elsewhere: Dar es Salaam versus Bagamoyo and Zanzibar Town; Beira and Lourenço Marques versus Moçambique and Sofala; Port Harcourt versus Bonny; Lagos versus Badagry; Accra versus Cape Coast, Winneba, and Elmina.

The locational selection process worked in much the same way with the growth of transport lines (particularly rail lines) and the extension of colonial administration into the interior. The railway from Lagos, for example, threaded through Ibadan and Abeokuta, bypassing such important traditional centers as Ife, Oyo, Ogbomosho, Iwo, and Iseyin. While the former were significantly regenerated, most of the latter fell into relative decline despite their being connected later by road to the major circulation system. Some areas benefited simply by being "along the way"—Illorin and Zaria between Lagos and Kano, Kikuyu-land roughly midway between Mombasa and Buganda.

From these fundamental locational decisions, often made with scant knowledge of local resources and aimed primarily at economic exploitation, peacekeeping, and political control, there emerged the skeletal spatial structures of modernization. First from the selection of major contact points, then through the extension of lines of penetration into the interior, and finally through a budding off process establishing a wider mesh of modern administrative and commercial centers, chunks of African space were structured and organized to receive the pervasive impulses of modernization and change. Shaped by the perceived goals of the colonial powers and building upon the framework of initial locational advantage—which became progressively "locked in" as growth and development continued—the tentlike configuration of the modernization surface began to take form.

Polarization, Mobilization, and Regional Development. The forces of structural formation continue to shape and reshape the geography of modernization through all phases of development. But overlapping the initial formative

[37] The ports along the East African coast were initially established by Arab traders, but with the later colonial contact essentially the same pattern emerges as along the West African coast. For a more extended discussion of this subject see Edward W. Soja, "Communication and Change," in John N. Paden and Edward W. Soja, eds., *The African Experience, Volume I: Essays* (Evanston, Ill.: Northwestern University Press, 1970), pp. 359–80.

period, exemplified most typically by the impact of early locational selection and geographical concentration, is a phase of development dispersal dominated by the process of *spatial diffusion.*

Once the bare outlines of the urban, administrative, and transport systems were established,[38] more extensive forces of development dispersal operated to diffuse at least the preconditions for development beyond the primary growth poles and transport routes and to encompass a larger proportion of the population within the growing spatial system. During this phase, however, the diffusion process served primarily to solidify already existing or nascent core–periphery structures. The periphery was organized into market, supply, and administrative areas dependent upon the core and other emerging organizational nuclei. Thus, while the spatial structure for the diffusion of modernization was extended throughout the spatial system, true spread effects were geographically limited as polarization and backwash reinforced the authority–dependency relations of core and periphery. Although certain minimal levels of modernization covered a much larger area and patterns of development became more attuned to the local resource base, core concentration was intensified as the major space-linking and space-shrinking systems of urbanization, circulation, and administration expanded.

This prevailing pattern of deviation-amplification and development concentration was confined within narrow geographical limits by the highly compartmentalized political geography of the continent, the persistence of colonial objectives of economic exploitation and peacemaking control, and the relatively limited funds available for development. The initial penetration axes and the focal points they connected continued to dominate the modernization surface even as development began to spread over wider areas of colonial spatial systems. A typical feature of most African countries even today is the existence of a single dominant transport and communications corridor (occasionally two) focused on a primate city, tapping the most productive parts of the country, and functioning primarily to siphon off resources for an external market. Internal connectivity, except perhaps for the barest skeleton of a telecommunications, postal, and road network linking the major administrative centers, has been neglected in comparison. Large areas of the country thus remain only minimally affected by the diffusion of modernization.

Since each colonial power was concerned with carving out its own distinct set of territorial units, very few of the penetration lines crossed what are today international boundaries. The result was a group of compartmentalized colonies and protectorates, each with its own separate circulation system and often in closer contact with Europe than with its immediate neighbors. An interesting side effect of this tight compartmentalization was the effect that the initially artificial colonial boundaries had on the spatial incidence of modernization.

[38] This structural growth can also be viewed as a spatial diffusion process. See Peter Gould, "A Note on Research into the Diffusion of Development," *Journal of Modern African Studies,* Vol. 2 (1964), pp. 123–25.

Although bearing little relationship to traditional cultural and economic patterns, these boundaries came to enclose relatively isolated systems open primarily to the metropole. While development peaks at the zone of maximum external contact (usually the coast), the level of modernization in most African countries markedly declines toward peripheral border regions, even when they are potentially productive areas. Contemporary international boundaries thus appear as troughs of relative backwardness on the continental modernization surface and have attained a reality they never had before.

As the tenor and sequential patterning of the initial contact phase derives primarily from the process of locational selection, the phase of polarization, mobilization, and regional development is dominated by the paths and processes of spatial diffusion. Three major forms of spatial diffusion work to spread geographically the attributes of modernization. Given the fact that the majority of innovative impulses in developing countries are exogenous and locally concentrated in those locations with the highest potential for interaction, all three forms originate primarily from the core area. But whereas they tend to work almost simultaneously in developed and integral spatial systems, in the underdeveloped context there appears to be a temporal ordering of importance.

Initially most important is a primary contagious diffusion from the core area throughout the spatial system. Restrained largely by distance and accessibility, this form of innovation diffusion tends to arch or bulge the modernization surface broadly over the core and its primate city. Only slightly later, a form of hierarchical diffusion works to spread development downward through the urban administrative system, from centers of higher to centers of lower order, punctuating the modernization surface in a more widely distributed pattern of concentrated development. Finally, a secondary contagious diffusion leads to an expansion of development outward from the nodes of the urban administrative hierarchy to their respective hinterlands.

At higher levels of development, with greatly improved circulation facilities, the relative importance and strength of hierarchical diffusion comes to dominate the modernization surface, reducing large-scale regional inequalities and blurring the authority–dependency relations between core and periphery. At lower levels of development, however, the friction of distance is such that the areal blanket of diffusion is limited. As Friedmann has suggested, "cities further away from innovation generating centers will tend to receive a smaller number of innovations during a given time period than more accessible places, regardless of their hierarchical position." [39]

A similar time lag and its spatial equivalent, a marked distance decay, simultaneously tend to limit the extent of secondary contagious diffusion out from the urban nodes. The end result is the characteristic modernization surface of nearly all African countries: peaked prominently over the primate city and

[39] "Urbanization and National Development," p. 17. This hypothesis is drawn from the work of Poul Ove Pedersen on Chile, "Innovation Diffusion Within and Between National Urban Systems," *Geographical Analysis,* Vol. 2 (1970), pp. 203–54.

secondarily over a few additional national nuclei and growth poles, broadly warped upward over the core area and declining outward to the peripheral limits of the spatial system, with distinctive ridges over the primary circulation system and extensive lowlands covering most of the country.

At the same time as the core–periphery structure is being consolidated, however, the geographical foundations for the next developmental phase— particularized by patterns of conflict and adjustment between core and periphery —are being laid. A large space is functionally organized as some links are established between all the major regions. From a system of locally autonomous, externally oriented regional cells, there begins to develop a more comprehensive and interdependent regional hierarchy spanning most of the national (colonial) space. While there is further expansion of the export base, supplying the bulk of the capital needed for continued economic development, there is also a limited expansion of residentiary industries and services attuned to local markets. Educational opportunities, health facilities, and a market economy spread to larger numbers of people, while simultaneously the degree of social mobilization and participation (political and economic) increases.

It is during this period of polarization and mobilization that there usually emerge the first major pressures from the mobilized periphery against the existing authority–dependency framework. In Africa, however, these rising pressures were initially directed against the small colonial elite and led to the rise of nationalist movements and eventually to independence. Core–periphery conflict was temporarily resolved by the replacement of the colonial elite by African elites usually drawn most heavily from those groups opportunely located with regard to existing centers of development. Conflict between indigenous core and indigenous periphery elites was consequently postponed until independence and the third major phase in the geography of modernization in Africa.

Developmental Crises and Spatial Adjustment. The nature of the colonial political and economic system mitigated against a direct confrontation between indigenous elites over the geographical path of· development. Political order was maintained through a system of ethnic pluralism based in large part upon an administrative regionalization of ethnicity and an almost total concentration of decisionmaking authority in the hands of a colonial oligarchy. Whatever conflict arose between ethnic groups or between regions was resolved directly by the colonial government dealing separately with each protagonist. Under these conditions, polarized growth could and did proceed without effective challenge, progressively accentuating the authority–dependency relations between core and periphery within colonial spatial systems.

Deviation-amplifying growth did not cease with independence. Indeed, in most of Africa during the postindependence period, development has probably become even more concentrated in the primate cities and core areas. At the same time, however, new ingredients have entered the mix of forces shaping the evolution of modernization surfaces which suggest the possibility of significantly altered patterns of spatial development in the future. Although it is is too early to recognize distinctive sequences of change, it is possible to identify some of these new ingredients and to explore briefly their potential impact on the geography of modernization.

Contemporary Africa has entered a phase of early developmental crises characterized by widespread tensions between core and periphery and by the initial attempts to restructure the spatial systems inherited from the colonial period. The removal of the colonial oligarchy opened the doors, essentially for the first time, to intensive ethnic and regional competition for political power and development priority. The inherited core–periphery structure came under challenge as the egalitarian goals of the nationalist period were translated into demands for more balanced regional growth during the period of nation- and state-building. In parts of Africa, the inherent instability of this situation was contained, in some cases through the maintenance of an essentially colonial relationship between core and periphery, in others by proffered policies of African socialism and long-range designs for the reduction of regional in-equalities. The general pattern, however, was one of rising ethnic and regional tensions, threats of secession, military coups, and internal turnovers in the dominant elite.

This widespread instability, however, has not necessarily been counter-productive with respect to development. Given the enormity of the problems facing the new states of Africa, some degree of instability was to be expected. The organizational systems inherited at independence were not geared to pro-moting the growth of large-scale panethnic or national communities, nor were they particularly suitable for government by representative assembly, as opposed to centralized authority. Colonial economies were not directed as much toward serving the local population as to being raw material reservoirs for the developed world. To a great extent, the shocks and reorientations induced by coups d'etat and elite instability may be working to forestall the entrenchment of regional social and economic inequalities by providing opportunities for modification in the authority–dependency relations between core and periphery that might other-wise be made unavailable.

The central problem facing the governments of the new African states is the need to direct effectively the course of modernization, while at the same time contending with the developmental crises unleashed by it. As part of this challenge, there has emerged during the postindependence period a significantly altered set of locational and planning objectives oriented more toward the problems of *societal and spatial integration* than to the colonial objectives of economic exploitation and political control. African states are wary of the Latin American example, in which relatively unplanned growth has led to a rigidifica-tion of regional inequalities that may be unmodifiable short of wholesale societal revolution. Rather than completely accepting and building upon the develop-mental legacy of colonialism—the "arbitrary" spatial integration mentioned by Mabogunje—there are indications of a reevaluation of the inherited geographical structures and the beginnings of an attempt to adjust these structures to suit the needs of independent African-controlled states.

This process of *spatial adjustment* is a response to the pressures of development disequilibrium growing out of the deviation-amplifying growth patterns characteristic of the early stages of modernization. It has taken many forms, not the least of which has been a spatial restructuring of the administrative system. Hence, in Kenya, Uganda, Zaïre, Ghana, and, perhaps most dramatically and painfully, Nigeria, the postindependence period has witnessed significant administrative reorganizations designed in whole or in part to attain more effective control over the political organization of space, to accommodate the tensions between core and periphery, and to promote tighter societal and spatial integration at the national level. Administrative reorganization affects the modernization surface by shifting the distribution of control over such phenomena as the flow of investments, migration patterns, industrial location, and development priorities in general. New administrative centers and upgraded old ones are elevated in the stream of hierarchical diffusion from the core area, thus providing the foundation for the emergence of new growth poles and national nuclei.

The transformation of the four regions of the Federation of Nigeria into the new twelve-state structure supplies a good example of this process. The old Northern Region, with its majority population and preponderant Hausa–Fulani leadership, has been broken up into six separate states, three of which have attained a measure of autonomy from Hausa–Fulani domination which was not possible under the former regional structure. One result of these changes is likely to be a weakening of the competitive tripartite polarization of political and economic control which shattered the old federation and the accelerated growth of the relatively neglected peripheral areas in the Middle Belt, the non-Ibo fringe of what was Biafra and portions of the former Mid-West Region. Less wealthy countries probably could not afford such an administrative restructuring and the duplication of facilities and multiplication of growth centers it necessitates. The great size and resources of Nigeria, particularly its expanding petroleum production, however, should provide sufficient developmental capital and other advantages to permit at least a thorough test of its innovative administrative experiment.

Another important focus of spatial adjustment is the urban system. Like administrative reorganization, with which it is often associated, settlement planning supplies the government with a potentially powerful tool in the attempt to control and channel polarized growth productively while promoting a more equitable regional distribution of development. The continuing developmental disequilibrium in African spatial systems is largely the result of barriers to the effective diffusion of modernization through the settlement hierarchy. At the highest level, spread effects are severely curtailed by high rates of population growth and large-scale rural to urban migration which absorb virtually all the development impulses concentrated in the core area. The periphery is progressively drained of its human and material resources to feed the voracious core, maintaining or worsening traditional village life, and at the same time creating problems of unemployment and deteriorating housing conditions in the over-crowded core cities.

Another "blockage" occurs at the poorly developed middle levels of the hierarchy. Many of these centers, particularly those at some distance from the core area, serve primarily administrative, rather than economic, functions. As a result, they often tend to maintain traditional structures and culture rather than acting as transmitters of economic change.

Instead of development "trickling down" the urban size-ratchet and spreading its effects outwards within urban fields, growth is concentrated in a few large urban centers, and a wide gulf between metropolis and countryside is apparent. Rather than articulation there is polarization, in a classic "dual economy." [40]

The future role of settlement planning in the geography of modernization in Africa and elsewhere in the developing world is effectively summarized by Berry:

It might be thought that settlement planning is just a passive variable in economic development—a way to accommodate growth. Yet this is not the case. Because of the absence of any trickle-down mechanism in traditional societies, it provides a way to cut through the excessive concentration of economic and social activities in a few centers, and the maintenance of the rest of the nation as an overwhelming, stagnant traditional residual. Immediate strategies then become a combination of Lewis's de-centralizing-downward efforts—the attempt to move from metropoli to a next level of urban center in the location of larger-scale activity—and Johnson's centralizing-upward activities—attempts to urbanize the countryside by the creation of small market towns and local opportunities that will in some way help stem the tide of migration into the metropoli. Such settlement policy relies on, and exploits, the fact that the national economy is organized through its urban centers, each of which, at whatever level in the total hierarchy, has its corresponding field of influence and potentiality as a growth center. [41]

Whereas the earlier phases of spatial development in Africa have been dominated by such processes as locational selection, structural formation, geo-graphical concentration, and spatial diffusion, the geography of modernization in the contemporary period has come to revolve increasingly around the goal of spatial integration. Defined most broadly, spatial integration represents a process of articulation and adjustment which moves the spatial system toward a state of dynamic equilibrium. It involves the emergence of interdependence between the functionally specialized components of the spatial system, the systemwide accept-

---

[40] Brian J. L. Berry, "Relationships Between Regional Economic Development and the Urban System," p. 289.

[41] Ibid., pp. 289–90. The sources referred to are John P. Lewis, "The Problem of Growth Centers" (paper read at the Hyderabad, India, Seminar on Accelerating District Industrialization, 1966); and E. A. J. Johnson, Market Towns and Spatial Development in India (New Delhi: National Center for Applied Economic Research, 1965).

ance of shared institutions and fundamental value systems, and the consolidation of a hierarchically structured system of cities and city regions. The efforts to attain this goal will provide the major forces shaping the future evolution of modernization surfaces in Africa.

Modernization Surfaces in Sierra Leone

There exists an excellent study by Riddell[42] of the geography of modernization in Sierra Leone. The exercise which follows is designed only in small part to supplement this work. Its major objectives are to illustrate some of the techniques used in the analysis of modernization surfaces and to provide a more detailed empirical example of the concepts, patterns, and processes discussed in the earlier sections of this chapter.

The methodology used here essentially parallels that used by Peter Gould in his analysis of modernization surfaces in Tanzania.[43] Data for a number of variables presumed to be surrogate measures of the spatial incidence of modernization were collected for three time periods (the 1920's, 1950's, and 1960's) and assigned to a square grid of 104 cells covering Sierra Leone. Each cell is approximately 268 miles square, and the grid is located in such a way as to take maximum advantage of existing topographic maps of the country.

The purpose of the grid is threefold. First, it aids in avoiding the geographical problems arising from the use of unequal-sized enumeration units. Aggregate data for districts or provinces which vary in size by many hundreds, often thousands, of square miles can impose a restricting bias on an analysis of this kind. Equal-sized units also assure comparability over time in situations in which administrative and data collection boundaries are changing—the usual situation in most developing countries. Finally, the use of an imposed grid permits the collection of data directly from map sources, data which would otherwise be unavailable in published collections of statistics. At the same time, much published data can be disaggregated (or aggregated further) and assigned to the grid cells, thus supplying a great deal of flexibility in data collection.

Many of the variables used here were taken directly from available map sources, particularly the excellent collection in *Sierra Leone in Maps*, edited by J. I. Clarke.[44] Their selection was guided both by availability for the three different time periods and by their potential use in comparative studies in different geographical areas. The data are therefore not necessarily the best measures of modernization in Sierra Leone, but with relatively little trouble could be collected over time in almost any developing country without extensive field work.

A major effort was made to include the same variables for each time

---

[42] Riddell, *op. cit.*

[43] "Tanzania 1920–63."

[44] John I. Clarke, ed., *Sierra Leone in Maps* (London: University of London Press, Ltd., 1966).

period, a condition which was not met by Gould.[45] It was immediately discovered that comparable data for the 1930's and 1940's were simply not available outside Sierra Leone. It was possible, however, to obtain statistical information for 17 variables for the 1920's, 1950's, and 1960's, and 7 additional variables for the two later time periods in a mixture of nominal (yes–no) and interval scales.

The data were standardized in so far as possible and subjected to components analysis. This is not the place to belabor the many and formidable problems involved in the use of components analysis, particularly with such "dirty" data.[46] Its major function in this analysis was to provide a parsimonious and consistent means of clustering, ordering, and combining the data into a scaled summary index of modernization. The first principal component explained a very large proportion of the total variance, much larger than the second component, illustrating the high degree of interrelationship between most modernization variables typically found in most similar studies. Moreover, the proportion of explained variance increased over time (43.5% in the twenties, 45.6% in the fifties, 51.3% in the sixties), suggesting an increasing areal association of

TABLE 5–1.   FACTOR LOADINGS FOR 1920's, 1950's, and 1960's[a]

	FACTOR LOADINGS		
Variables Used	1920's	1950's	1960's
Government savings banks	.841	.903	.901
Range of postal services	.915	.913	.899
Administrative headquarters	.740	.812	.887
Population density		.553	.862
Medical facilities	.665	.849	.836
Primary schools	.557	.860	.835
Secondary schools		.803	.825
Post offices	.852	.845	.818
Water supply		.699	.772
Police stations	.626	.673	.765
Prisons	.556	.616	.754
Electricity supply		.648	.736
Telephone service	.556	.619	.735
Road mileage	.790	.689	.726
Petrol stations	.669	.643	.720
Commercial banks	.646	.505	.694
Teacher training colleges		.635	.690
Airports		.669	.661
Telegraph stations	.601	.642	.615
Access to railway	.622	.627	.565
Number of ethnic groups	.520	.468	.461
Accessibility to Freetown	−.472	−.484	−.387
Distance to Freetown	−.287	−.350	−.286
Marketing cooperatives		.093	.163

a Further details can be provided upon request by the authors.

45 Gould, op. cit., used 7 variables for the early twenties, 17 for the late twenties-early thirties, 12 for the late thirties, 21 for the late forties and early fifties, and 26 for the late fifties-early sixties. Data on only 4 variables were common to all the time periods.

46 See R. J. Rummel, Applied Factor Analysis (Evanston, Ill.: Northwestern University Press, 1970).

modernization variables as spatial systems develop. The variables used and their factor loadings for the three time periods are given in Table 5–1.

The components analysis yielded sets of standardized factor scores which were scaled, for comparative purposes, to Freetown = 1,000. The resulting Relative Modernization Scores (RMS) were assigned to their appropriate grid cells. Finally, to facilitate description and interpretation, a continuous modernization surface was constructed through interpolation and some subjective "wiggling" to recognize obviously important nodal (urban) components within each cell. The modernization surfaces represented in Figures 5–3 through 5–5 then provided the major basis for the historical-geographical analysis of development in Sierra Leone which follows.

Early Contact and Penetration: The Evolution of Spatial Structure. The earliest focal points for modern development in Sierra Leone were the coastal centers of Freetown and Bonthe, and secondarily in smaller coastal ports such

FIGURE 5–3.   THE MODERNIZATION SURFACE OF SIERRA LEONE: 1920's

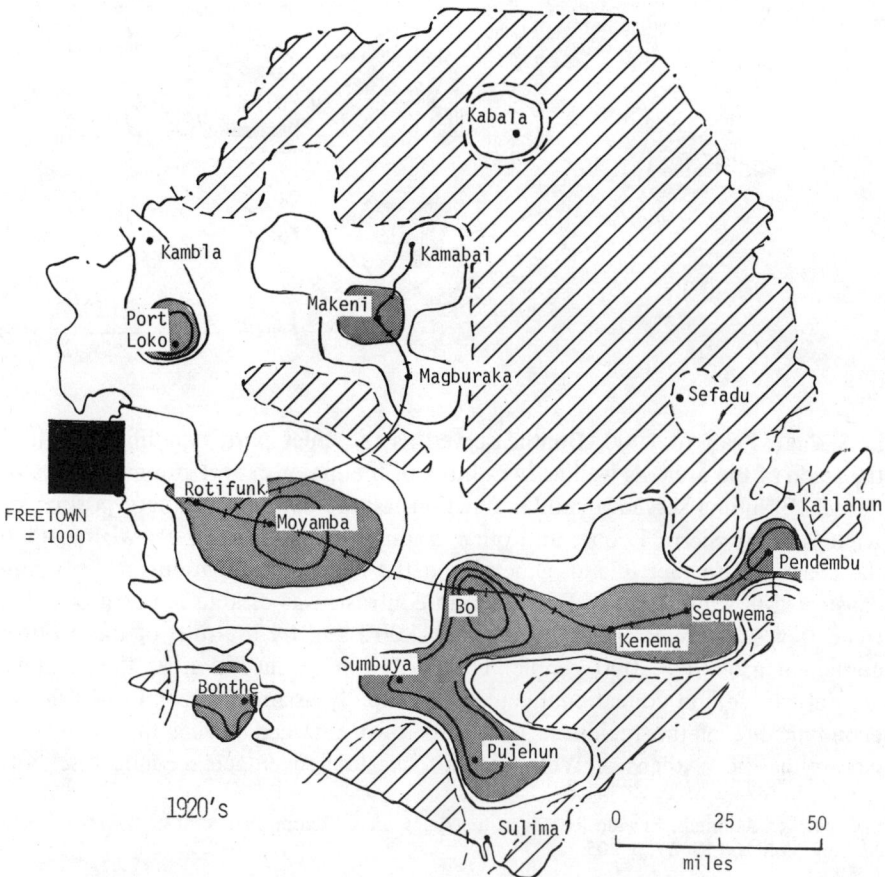

FIGURE 5-4.   THE MODERNIZATION SURFACE OF SIERRA LEONE: 1950's

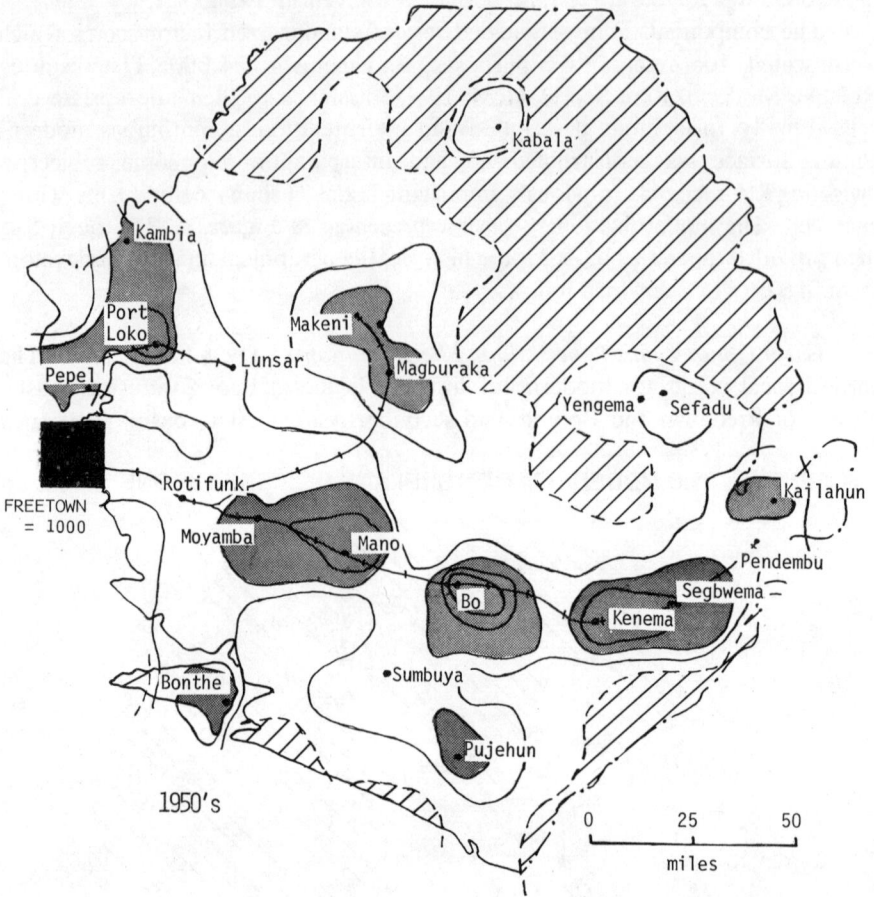

as Sulima. Prior to 1900, Bonthe served as the chief port, handling over half the trade of the area, as well as two-thirds of the major export commodity, palm kernels.[47] Sulima served a similar function for the extreme southern portion of what is today Sierra Leone, and other trading towns emerged elsewhere along the coast and further inland, generally at the head of navigation for the many coastward-flowing streams. Freetown, in contrast, was established as a base for freed slaves. It grew rapidly during the 1800's and by the turn of the century contained around 35,000 people. It stood from its inception as the primary administrative and educational center and rapidly assumed preeminence in the economic life of the region as well. Freetown emerged during the nineteenth century as the "Athens of West Africa." The first seventeen secondary schools

[47] P. K. Mitchell, "Trade Routes of the Early Sierra Leone Protectorate," *Sierra Leone Studies,* Vol. 16 (1962), p. 205.

FIGURE 5–5.   THE MODERNIZATION SURFACE OF SIERRA LEONE: 1960's

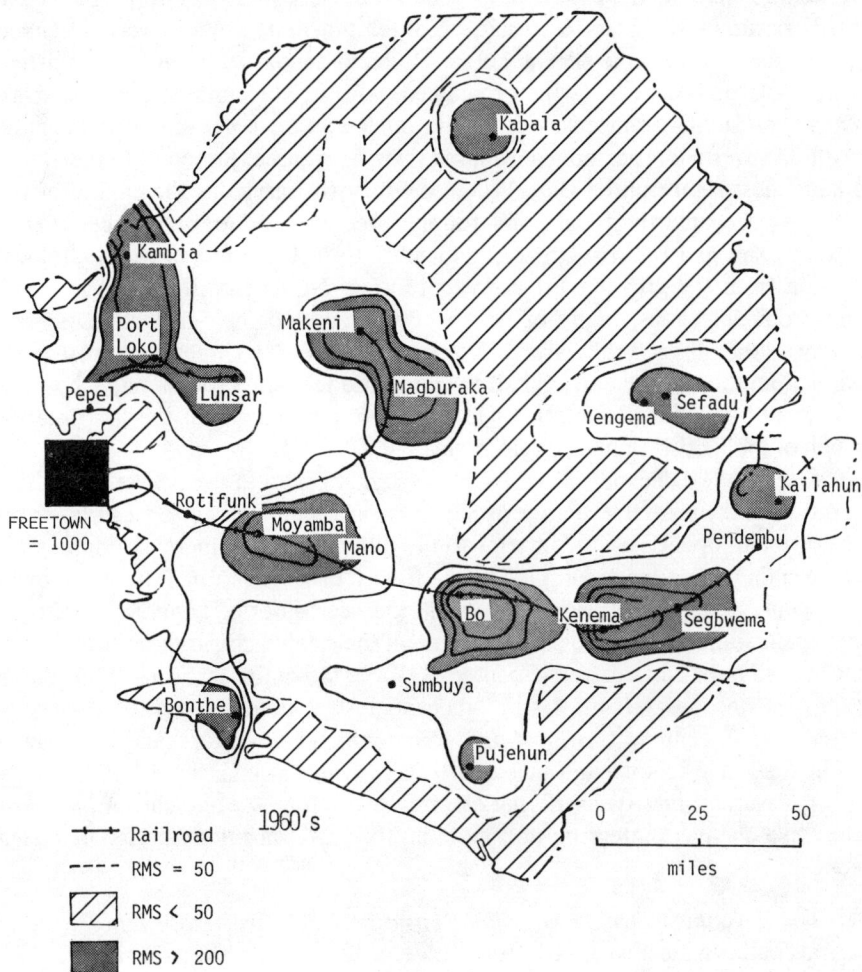

in Sierra Leone were located here as was Fourah Bay College, founded by the Church Missionary Society in 1827.[48]

From the already existing development concentration in Freetown emerged the most powerful force shaping the subsequent spatial development of the territory: the Sierra Leone Government Railway, built between 1895 and 1916. During this period, the railway created the basic spatial–structural framework for the modernization of Sierra Leone, a framework which was to have both immediate and far-reaching effects on the patterns and processes of spatial development.

[48] John I. Clarke, *op. cit.*, p. 68. See also John Peterson, *Province of Freedom: A History of Sierra Leone, 1787–1870* (Evanston, Ill.: Northwestern University Press, 1969).

The railway was explicitly constructed "as a means of opening up the interior and enabling the export of tropical products, as well as ensuring effective British occupancy." [49] As a result, a developmental tentacle was extended through the heart of the Sierra Leone Protectorate, accentuating the existing growth pole of Freetown (which remained, with its surrounding area, a crown colony), attracting trade away from the other coastal ports, and sparking the growth of several interior nodes, (among them Moyamba, Kenema, Makeni, and perhaps most significantly, Bo). Whereas Freetown served as the capital of the colony, Bo became the focal point for the protectorate. Soon after being connected by rail in 1903, Bo began significantly to feel the impact of hierarchical diffusion from the growing Freetown core area. New roads linked it to major palm-producing areas, many of which now redirected their exports along the railway, rather than southward to Bonthe and Sulima. Three years before its completion, the railway carried half the palm produce. In 1906, a major hospital and school opened in Bo and later it was chosen as the site of the first interior branch of the British Bank of West Africa.

The first two decades of the twentieth century therefore witnessed a radical alteration in the spatial structure of Sierra Leone. The railway focused flows on Freetown and opened up the interior to the diffusion of commercial, administrative, health, and educational facilities. Beads of concentrated urban growth were strung along the railway lines, while the necessities of administrative control expanded the network of change through the establishment of a more evenly spaced system of administrative centers to serve the entire territory. The spatial system became progressively structured and restructured through the interplay between the expanding transport and communications network and the system of administrative regions and headquarters. Moving through the urban administrative hierarchy and over the major circulatory routes came the impulses of innovative change, patterning and molding the modernization surface of Sierra Leone.

The Twenties: Structural Solidification and Selective Diffusion.   Several general features are revealed by the modernization surface in the 1920's: the very heavy concentration of development in Freetown, the profound influence of the railway lines, the continuing legacy of the southern coastal trade, and the very limited areal extent of modernization. Unlike Kenya, where population is highly clustered in the most favored agricultural areas, the population of Sierra Leone is more evenly distributed. The irregular patterning of modernization is consequently much more discordant with population distribution and many more densely settled areas remain isolated from the impact of development than is the case in Kenya. Table 5–2 lists the leading cells of the modernization surface of the twenties, named after the largest urban centers in each cell.

The areas of greatest development in the interior for the most part border the path of the railway. Trade formerly funneled to the southern coast has

[49] Clarke, *op. cit.*, p. 104.

TABLE 5–2.   LEADING CELLS OF THE MODERNIZATION SURFACE: 1920's[a]

Freetown	1000[a]	Port Loko	303
Bo	428[a]	Segbwema	286[a]
Moyamba	316[a]	Kenema	272[a]
Pendembu	313[a]	Bonthe	245
Sumbuya	313	Rotifunk	235[a]
Pujehun	303	Makeni	231[a]

a Denotes location along the railway.

already become reoriented by rail to Freetown. By 1928, the railway carries nearly 60% of all palm produce, although the later growth of the road network prevents the railway from ever handling this much again. Bo stands out as the preeminent interior growth pole, and from the Bo region radiate arms of development eastward along the railway line, southward through Pujehun toward the coast (although Sulima has already lost much of its former importance as a trading port), and southwestward to Bonthe. An area of relatively low development separates the Bo-dominated region from the extension of high development out of Freetown. The latter has its major interior center at Moyamba and secondarily at the end of the railway branch to Makeni, which appears to have become an important focal point for a larger region surrounding it. The northeastward bulge from Makeni reflects the early extension of the railway to Kamabai, but this link is shut down in the early thirties and fails to appear on subsequent modernization surfaces.

Although the continuing strength of the southern coastal trade is still noticeable, the relative developmental strength of Bonthe has already begun to decline. It is still the second largest town in Sierra Leone in the mid-1920's (with 5,400 people), but lags behind many interior centers in level of development. Sumbuya, however, remains relatively high, being a district headquarters in the 1920's, a major collection center near a rich belt of palm production, and accessible to cheap water transport. Pujehun, one of the three provincial headquarters in this period, plays a corresponding role as transhipment point to the port of Sulima, directly to the south.

Port Loko represents a significant concentration of development north of Freetown. In the 1920's, a road is built from Port Loko (also a district headquarters) into an important oil palm-producing area northwest of Makeni; and it has been suggested that this road, tapping a resource which would otherwise have filtered through Makeni by rail, contributes to the growth of Port Loko.[50] The biggest outlier of development is Kabala, the only administrative outpost for the undeveloped northeast. Its headquarters function accounts for the presence of a prison and a full range of postal facilities, but it will be several years before Kabala is to benefit from the impact of commercial penetration and the introduction of passable roads.

[50] *Sierra Leone Annual Report of Provincial Administration* (Freetown, 1929), pp. 3–4.

The Thirties and Forties: Administrative Adjustment and Economic Stagnation.   Although sufficient empirical data are not available to construct modernization surfaces for this period, it is possible to describe briefly the salient changes which took place. Perhaps most important was a series of administrative reorganizations which shuffled the distribution of district and provincial boundaries and headquarters. To a great extent, this reorganization represented an evolving adjustment between the administrative system and the changing locational patterns of modernization.

In the southern coastal area, Pujehun, formerly a provincial headquarters, is demoted to district headquarters. Similarly, Sumbuya and Sembehun, both near the coast, lose their status as administrative towns due largely to the continuing decline of trade and the general isolation of the southern coastal region. Bo, on the other hand, is officially elevated to provincial headquarters in accord with its important position in the interior, and after World War II it becomes the center for the Chief Commissioner of the Protectorate, the focal office for local government (moved to Bo from Freetown). The construction of new trunk roads makes it the center of a north–south transport axis in the interior, while improved telecommunications link Bo even more closely to the Freetown core.

By the end of the 1940's, the major outlines of the administrative system become stabilized and are to remain essentially unchanged up to the present day. The country was subdivided into three provinces (coinciding with the old protectorate) and the Western Area (the old colony focused on Freetown). The provinces are further subdivided into twelve districts, creating an administrative hierarchy as shown in Table 5–3.

TABLE 5–3.   ADMINISTRATIVE HIERARCHY, 1946 TO PRESENT

Territorial capital	Freetown
Provincial & District headquarters	Bo Kenema Makeni
District headquarters	Sefadu Kailahun Moyamba Bonthe Pujehun Magburaka Kabala Port Loko Kambia

Once stabilized, the administrative system was to play a powerful role channeling development in future years and solidifying a chain of hierarchical diffusion from the Freetown core.

Economically, Sierra Leone was struck by the damaging impact of worldwide depression. Earnings from Palm kernels, for example, fell nearly 50%

from their earlier levels in the 1920's. The colonial government was unable to stimulate development because of its own domestic problems, and much greater emphasis had to be placed upon local initiative. It is claimed by some that Sierra Leone actually became poorer in the period up to 1941, when the Colonial Development and Welfare Act was instituted and a more comprehensive and direct attempt at economic modernization was begun.[51]

The Fifties: Limited Spread and Further Concentration. The modernization surface of the 1950's is not greatly different from that of the 1920's, but several important changes can be identified. There is an expansion of the area of minimal modernization (arbitrarily pegged at a threshold RMS of 50 for purposes of comparison) over a larger portion of the country. There also appears to be a slight increase in development concentration in the major administrative centers and perhaps the beginnings of significant backwash effects in the areas surrounding them. Finally, new growth centers have emerged in association with the exploitation of major mineral deposits, particularly diamonds and iron ore. Table 5–5 shows the most modernized cells for the fifties.

TABLE 5–4.   LEADING CELLS OF THE MODERNIZATION SURFACE: 1950's[a]

Freetown	1000[a]	Magburaka	286[a]
Bo	487[a]	Makeni	286[a]
Mano	353[a]	Kambia	277
Port Loko	344[a]	Bonthe	248
Kenema	319[a]	Pujehun	235
Moyamba	298[a]	Pepel	218[a]

[a] Denotes location along a rail line.

The spread of the area with an RMS greater than 50, which is not particularly extensive, is due primarily to the slow but steady expansion of the road network to a position no longer subsidiary to the railway. At first, roads served almost entirely as feeders to the railway and contributed to the early growth of several strategically located interior centers. By 1939, however, nearly all the important towns, particularly those with administrative functions, were connected by road, and the circulation of goods, people, and ideas came increasingly to depend on roads rather than rails. By 1950, the road network, albeit poor and inadequate, emerges as a major force shaping the modernization surface.

The three provincial headquarters of Bo, Kenema, and Makeni each experience significant development from the 1920's, with Bo now clearly established as the major interior growth pole of Sierra Leone. In some of the cells surrounding these centers, however, there is a decline in relative modernization, suggesting the operation of limited backwash effects around some of the major interior centers. This backwash is particularly pronounced in the formerly more

[51] Michael Crowder, "£20 Million for Iron Ore," *New Commonwealth*, Vol. 35 (1958), p. 565.

developed areas south of Bo (e.g., Pujehun) and in the area between Bo and Kenema. This accords well with the notion that backwash effects tend to be influenced strongly by distance during the early stages of development and thus are likely to be noticed most clearly just beyond the immediate hinterland of important growth poles, rather than in the most backward area. Further evidence is given in the remarkably limited impact of the Freetown core on the cells to its west and southwest, although this is due in large part to the distinctive characteristics of the Freetown population (the self-imposed cultural and political isolation of the Creole population in particular).

Minerals spark the rapid development of several areas in Sierra Leone, and these areas clearly emerge in the 1950's modernization surface. The opening of the Marampa iron ore mine in 1933 represented the first large-scale industrial enterprise in Sierra Leone.[52] From a cluster of thatched huts in the 1930's, the adjacent mining town of Lunsar begins its emergence as one of the largest towns in the country. Significant development also takes place at the new ocean port of Pepel, located in the cell just north of Freetown and at the origin of a private railway line opened by the Sierra Leone Development Corporation in the 1930's to serve the Marampa mines. The port benefits from the building of bunkers, pier and loading facilities, new housing, and the creation of a deep-water shipping channel.

The whole region north of Freetown experiences more rapid development between the twenties and the fifties than any other in Sierra Leone. In addition to the activities associated with iron mining, several additional developments take place. Major improvements are made in the road network, and Sierra Leone's only international airport is built at Lungi, in the same cell as Pepel. Lungi subsequently receives such conveniences as public electricity and water, hospitals, schools, and police stations. Kambia, to the north of Port Loko, emerges as a new growth center near the border with Guinea, which it serves as the main entry point for goods coming into Sierra Leone. Kambia was elevated to district headquarters in the thirties and received an influx of government activities, postal services, primary schools, and, in the early fifties, three important medical facilities. The rapid growth of these cells supports the continuing prominence of Port Loko on the fifties modernization surface. Port Loko stands in marked contrast to other long-established trading centers such as Sumbuya and Pujehun, similarly located at the navigational heads of the country's seaward-flowing rivers, which decline significantly in RMS from the twenties.

The Sixties: The Spatial Legacy of Colonialism. The modernization surface of the sixties represents an amplification of many patterns of development initiated much earlier in Sierra Leone's history and solidified during the fifties. One of the most important of these patterns is the areal association between the

---

[52] K. Swindell, in Clarke, *Sierra Leone in Maps*, p. 98.

administrative hierarchy and the geographical incidence of modernization. As can be seen in Table 5–5, the three highest RMS after Freetown are for the three provincial headquarters of Bo, Kenema, and Makeni.[53] All nine of the remaining district headquarters are included in the next 11 cells on the list. The peak points of the contemporary modernization surface of Sierra Leone have clearly emerged in close accordance with the administrative hierarchy, which has remained virtually stable since the early fifties, and in large part as a result of hierarchical diffusion through the urban administrative system.

TABLE 5–5.   LEADING CELLS OF THE MODERNIZATION SURFACE: 1960's[a]

Freetown	1000[a] CAP	Segbwema	296[a]
Bo	451[a] PHQ	Sefadu	282 DHQ
Kenema	423[a] PHQ	Kabala	231 DHQ
Makeni	365[a] PHQ	Kailahun	226[a] DHQ
Magburaka	357[a] DHQ	Mano	226[a]
Port Loko	353[a] DHQ	Bonthe	221 DHQ
Moyamba	343[a] DHQ	Pujehan	216 DHQ
Kambia	321 DHQ	Lunsar	207

a Denotes location along a rail line.

There was very little new growth between the fifties and the sixties. If anything, the area of lowest relative modernization (RMS < 50) has increased, particularly in the extreme south and in the cells north of the Bo–Kenema axis. Even more significant, the backwash effects which began to appear in the fifties have become highly accentuated, suggesting a period of intensive deviation-amplifying growth. Almost all the major increases in RMS took place in the established urban administrative cells (see Table 5–6). Indeed, all but 23 cells experience a decrease in relative modernization from the fifties to the sixties.

TABLE 5–6.   CELLS OF GREATEST GROWTH: 1950's TO 1960's[a]

Sefadu	114	Yengema	67
Kenema	104	a	65
Kabala	97	Kambia	50
Makeni	79	Moyamba	45
Magburaka	71	Lunsar	39

a Equals cell immediately south of Pendembu.

What appears to have occurred in the last decade or so of the colonial period was a pronounced polarization of growth in the interior of Sierra Leone. Bo, the earliest major growth pole, seems to have reached a development plateau as the country's second city and experiences a relative decline in modernization from the fifties to the sixties. But such cells as Kenema, Makeni–Magburaka, Sefadu–Yengema, Moyamba, and Lunsar–Port Loko–Kambia

53 After Freetown, these are also the three largest cities in population size. The 1963 population census gives these figures: Freetown, 157,613; Bo, 26,613; Kenema, 13,246; Makeni, 12,304.

emerge as centers of concentrated growth within their respective regions, draining development in most of the surrounding areas in an excellent illustration of geographical backwash effects.

Although Freetown remains unchallenged as the core area of Sierra Leone, the pattern of polarized growth in the interior signals a significant change in the makeup of the core elite. Up to the early 1950's, the Creole population, concentrated in the Freetown area, dominated the modern social, economic, and political life of Sierra Leone, in much the same way as the small group of America-Liberians dominated Liberia. The boundary between colony and protectorate represented a powerful cultural barrier which significantly reduced the impact of primary contagious diffusion from the Freetown core. In the cell immediately east of Freetown, for example, pronounced backwash effects are evidenced in the decline in RMS from 190, in the twenties, to 105, in the sixties. The cells to the north and south of this cell also experience major decreases in RMS over this period and actually fall below 50 on the contemporary modernization surface.

The expanding development of parts of the interior, however, marks the selective entry of such groups as the Mende and the Temne into important decisionmaking positions. It is no surprise that the Mende in particular emerge at independence as the dominant political force in Sierra Leone. Numerically the largest ethnic group, the Mende are located primarily to the south of the main railway line, with especially heavy densities in the areas between Bo and Kailahun, the most highly developed area outside Freetown. The Temne, concentrated in a triangular area vertexed by Freetown, Kambia, and Masingbe (west of Yengema), and the Kono, in the region around Sefadu, also begin to play a much greater role in the modern life of Sierra Leone than they ever have before.

Since independence, the role of the Creoles has been significantly reduced, and there have been indications that Mende strength is being challenged by other groups throughout the country. In essence, Sierra Leone has entered the post-independence phase of African development, characterized by ethnic and regional jockeying for positions of decisionmaking control, political instability, and the beginnings of a reevaluation of the largely dysfunctional spatial legacy of colonialism represented in the modernization surface of the sixties.

In his excellent but brief conclusion, Riddell very effectively summarizes the spatial dynamics of modernization in Sierra Leone. At the same time, his statement stands as a perceptive overview of the fundamental patterns and processes in the geography of modernization and an appropriate epilogue to the present study.

Three dominant and tightly interwoven themes have been identified as characterizing the human geography of Sierra Leone during the last seventy years of the colonial period. It is around these themes, which illustrate the spatial dimension of the modernization process, that certain generalizations may be drawn.

A network of rail and road was imposed upon the simple, pre-existing, unimproved mesh of streams and bush paths. The evolution of this system—first as a simple, tree-like rail and feeder grid, and then as a more integrated network—was determined largely by the initial location of the rail line. It was only the construction of a wartime road to link the capital with the hinterland . . . that led to the evolution of an independent road system; as the road network gradually surpassed the rail line in areal extent and operating efficiency, the railway lost its magistral importance [and] fell into decline . . . Geographic space was structured by the emerging transport network as new and very specific avenues of movement were defined. At the same time, the emerging hierarchy of urban places also provided the nexus through which modern elements were spread and within which the new social and economic systems began to evolve. The urban system has been dominated by Freetown, the political capital and point of contact with the wider world, but it also includes at a lower level the towns which have grown up around the colonial administrative centers, the trading points at the junctions in the transport network, and the newer mining-based towns.

Together, the transportation network and the urban hierarchy provided a fabric to the geographic space of Sierra Leone. Not only was the country tied together in each of the administrative, economic, and geographic senses, but the fabric has in large part determined the pattern of diffusion of modernization. The spread of political, social, economic, and institutional change funneled through the transportation network and cascaded down the urban hierarchy. Freetown has always acted as the core area and has dominated the process of modernization, not only in its catalytic role but also by its primacy in . . . numbers of people and institutions. Freetown has been the focus of government activity, of education, of commerce, industry, and trade, and as such has always held a pre-eminent position on the modernization salient.

In Sierra Leone there is substantial evidence to indicate that the process of modernization and the present status of modernity have the same spatial expression. . . . Naturally there are a few exceptions, such as the relative historical decline of places such as Bonthe and Pujehun, which had many indicators of modernity at the beginning of the twentieth century because of their early trade role. Now these places have declined as trade has been refocused onto the railway axis and the Freetown port, while towns such as Bo, Kenema, Makeni, Lunsar, Koidu, and Yengema have become important provincial urban centers. However, other than the few exceptions, the patterns are remarkably similar and reflect the spatial continuity and recursiveness of the modernization process.[54]

[54] J. Barry Riddell, *The Spatial Dynamics of Modernization in Sierra Leone: Structure, Diffusion, and Response* (Evanston, Ill.: Northwestern University Press, 1970), pp. 129–30. Reprinted by permission.

Chapter 6
Political Roles: Micro Analysis and Macro Process

RAYMOND F. HOPKINS

*The importance of political roles as a focus for analysis is stressed in the develop-
ment setting, where routine patterns of political action and widespread understanding
of what political actors should be expected to do (and not do) are to a large extent
evolving. This emphasis on roles helps one understand a system's stability (or lack of
it) and signals when key actors are behaving in deviant ways. Besides the collection
and presentation of information on the attitudes and backgrounds of Tanzanian
elites, one perceives in this chapter a range of operating rules governing Tanzanian
political behavior. These norms are defined by describing distinct subsets of them
relevant to administrative, legislative, and other elite subgroups of the population
and by tracing out interrelationships existing among them.*

A variety of new approaches for studying comparative politics and political
development has been suggested in recent years, including ones emphasizing
political culture, changes in social and economic patterns, and structural-functional analysis.[1] Nearly all these approaches recommend a multivariate analysis
that examines a wide range of social and psychological processes such as motivations, attitudes, culture, demographic factors, social structure, technology, and

---

[1] An excellent summary of the changes in thinking about comparative politics is
Harry Eckstein, "A Perspective on Comparative Politics, Past and Present," in Harry
Eckstein and David Apter, eds., *Comparative Politics* (New York: The Free Press, 1963),
pp. 3–32.

Examples of the emphasis on political culture include G. A. Almond and Sidney
Verba, *The Civic Culture* (Princeton: Princeton University Press, 1963); and Lucian W.
Pye, *Politics, Personality and Nation-Building* (New Haven: Yale University Press, 1962).

Portions of this chapter were read as a paper at the annual meetings of the
American Political Science Association, New York City, September 2,
1969. I am grateful to Ronald D. Brunner, Robert O. Keohane, and J.
Roland Pennock who read and commented on an earlier paper. I wish to
acknowledge the Foreign Area Fellowship Program and the Yale Council
on International Relations for their research support.

individual skills and resources. A study of political roles allows us to focus on a single phenomenon that reflects the influence of many of these variables.[2]

THE INSTITUTIONALIZATION OF POLITICAL ROLES

Institutionalizing regular patterns of political action and securing the conformity of people to these patterns is an immediate problem facing newly independent nations. In Africa, nationalist leaders inherited at independence an autocratic bureaucracy and a newly established set of institutions such as a parliament, elections, and a cabinet organized according to the expectations of the metropolitan country. The task of the elite in these nascent political systems has been to create and institutionalize a set of role expectations defining the rules of politics that will accommodate the demands and pressures on the system and accord with the value patterns of the society.

Purpose and Design

This chapter describes how an analysis of political roles may be used to study more general features of a political system undergoing change and reports on the application of role analysis to research among members of the political elite in Tanzania in 1966. The study of political roles in Tanzania focused on a micro political process, but one which was directly related, in aggregate, to the macro, or system, process. The value of investigating political roles, as I hope to demonstrate, is that this approach allows us to examine political processes at more than one level of analysis and to study the interlevel connections. As such, it may both meet the demand that a comparative political study focus on units that are not tenuously connected to important political events, and the request that policy scientists examine process and context.[3]

The norms or rules shaping durable political roles involve system level, or macro, processes. These norms determine the style and stability of politics in the system. Research on roles, however, usually focuses upon individuals and what has been termed microscopic role analysis.[4] Carefully examining the role of a

[2] Roles themselves, of course, do not contain measures of these variables, but rather should *reflect their influence* in critical ways. For a study that tries to build nearly all these factors into its analysis, see Irma Adelman and Cynthia Taft Morris "An Econometric Model of Socio-economic and Political Change in Underdeveloped Countries," *American Economic Review,* Vol. 58 (December 1968), pp. 1184–1218. Their work, based on cross-national measures of 19 variables, has drawn considerable criticism for its lack of theory and its questionable attempts to reduce complexity.

[3] See Joseph LaPalombara, "Macro Theories and Micro Applications in Comparative Politics," *Comparative Politics,* Vol. 1, No. 1 (October 1968), p. 73; Harold D. Lasswell, "The Future of the Comparative Method," *Comparative Politics,* Vol. 1, No. 1 (October 1968), pp. 8–14; and Heinz Eulau, *Micro-Macro Political Analysis* (Chicago: Aldine, 1969), esp. pp. 11–19.

[4] See Neal Gross, Ward S. Mason, and Alexander W. McEachern, *Explorations in Role Analysis* (New York: Wiley, 1958), Chapters 10–12.

few major political actors allows us to combine a micro analysis of role, in which the behavior of individuals can be studied, with a macro political analysis since the norms which operate to constrain members of the political elite are major components of the political culture and constitute some of the "rules of the game." If institutionalized, they will be effective in shaping behavior and, therefore, represent "parameters" of the political system. To investigate both political rules which have emerged and the extent to which these are institutionalized, one must focus on selected aspects of a limited number of roles.[5]

A Framework of Role Institutionalization

Roles are basic analytical units of political systems. Political roles consist of a pattern of expected behavior for individuals holding particular positions in a system. These may range from the most general, such as citizen, to the fairly specific, such as president. The role concept links personality to social structure, and role expectations form the normative structure for system behavior. In a political system, role expectations contain the rules that regulate members' political actions, that is, actions involving influence, decisionmaking, or the authoritative allocation of values.

A basic assumption of this analysis is that environmental and historical constraints, cultural values, and personal predispositions acting as independent variables shape the norms and legitimize the behavior for political roles within a political system. Each role in a system has a set of boundaries or parameters which, if violated, are likely either to alter the system or to remove the role occupant from his position.

Roles mediate the impact of political culture on the overt and subjective behavior of individuals in the political process.[6] To understand how a political culture operates to regulate overt activity and to influence patterns of ideas and subjective behavior, I have focused on political roles as the key agent of translation between the broad characteristics of culture and the discrete set of acts which constitutes the political process. For example, a president, failing to satisfy the demands and expectations of those in lesser political positions, may find himself removed by coup, election, or otherwise. Similarly, lesser political figures may be forced out, probably in a more mundane fashion, for breaches of the political rules.

Whereas some role expectations are always ad hoc and issue centered,

[5] See Talcott Parsons, *The Social System* (New York: The Free Press, 1951); and David Easton, *A Framework for Political Analysis* (Englewood Cliffs, N.J.: Prentice-Hall, 1965).
[6] As defined by Lucian Pye, political culture is "the set of attitudes, beliefs and sentiments that give order and meaning to a political process, and that provide the underlying assumptions and rules that govern behavior in the political system." See Lucian W. Pye, *Aspects of Political Development* (Boston: Little, Brown, 1965), p. 104. The concept is also carefully described in Chapters 1 and 2 of Gabriel A. Almond and Sidney Verba, *op. cit.*

others are more general. The latter define general boundary rules of political roles, certain acts which are clearly wrong in the minds of most individuals. The institutionalization of roles in the political system is evidenced by a structured and interrelated set of norms for role behavior. Where such norms are weak or ambiguous, institutionalization not only of political roles, but of the political system itself, is at a low level.

Institutionalization of a political system is related to the degree of acceptance and commitment demonstrated by its participants for a set of norms orienting and guiding political acts. The kind and amount of consensus held by a political system's elite, a critical subset of participants, constitute one possible measure of system institutionalization.[7] The greater the acceptance of a compatible set of role expectations (norms) about major political roles, the more the political system may be said to be institutionalized.

The Value of the Focus on Roles

This approach allows us to combine insights from a number of political analysts. Marx, and later Mannheim, argued that "ideas" or ideology may be influenced, even determined, by a person's role or position in life.[8] Pareto and Mosca observed that there was a permanency to ruling-class behavior in spite of changes in the personalities who filled elite positions. Their observations point to the rigidity of a political structure and the roles it contains which serve to mold the ideas and behavior of people. The process of socialization into political roles ensures continuity and order to the political system.[9] Likewise, changes in a political system may be studied as a function of role conflicts caused by strains between the personality of individuals recruited to a set of

[7] It is important to distinguish the concept of institutionalization from that of political development. Political development is a normative concept. It should be an explicitly specified set of criteria which expresses the preferences of the writer. *System* development, on the other hand, is a somewhat different idea. It draws upon systems theory and the concept of a social system. Although institutionalization in a political system is empirically related to the phenomenon of political stability, it differs in two respects. First, it is not an intrinsically valued quality in itself. Second, it is a property attributed to a system but not necessarily to the individuals who are its members. The lives of individual members might be quite unstable, though the system itself were stable and institutionalized. Harold D. Lasswell, "The Emerging Policy Sciences of Development," *American Behavioral Scientist*, Vol. 17 (1965), pp. 28–33, analyzes and suggests characteristics for an adequate model of political development, reminding the reader that such models should be explicitly preferential.

[8] Marx, of course, used the concept of "class" rather than role. Mannheim and others, however, have generalized the mediating mechanism which Marx outlined, applying it to the effect of groups and roles on attitudes. See Karl Mannheim, *Ideology and Utopia*, trans. Louis Wirth and Edward Shils (New York: Harcourt, Brace, 1936), pp. 98–191.

[9] See Almond and Powell, *Comparative Politics: A Development Approach* (Boston: Little, Brown, 1966), pp. 29–30; and Talcott Parsons and Edward Shils, *Toward a General Theory of Action* (Cambridge, Mass.: Harvard University Press, 1952), pp. 190–243, especially p. 204.

political roles, roles which not only set limits on thoughts but also behavior, and the private motives and compulsions which affect the manner in which political roles are played.[10] Cultural crises and modal personality traits are also likely to influence role behavior and, consequently, system practices. Lucian Pye, for example, found in Burma a ritualization of administrative behavior among bureaucratic role occupants that was accompanied by a loss of identity and feelings of insecurity: effects of the clash between Burmese and Western cultures.[11]

Another characteristic of the approach relates to elites. The study of elites and the roles they play are relevant to understand politics in new states where leadership can have a great impact. Changes in elite composition, anxiety among elite personalities, and visions of the future held by elites have all been productive foci for studying politics in new states.[12] Thus, our analysis of the institutionalization of roles based on a study of the background and attitudes of the Tanzanian elite may provide both a test of this combination of analytical approaches, as well as some understanding of the dynamics of Tanzanian politics.[13]

THE ANALYSIS OF POLITICAL ROLES: CONSENSUS AND CONGRUENCE

The Role Process

A political role is the cluster of behavior *and* norms associated with a particular political position such as chief, policeman, or president. Several different

[10] See Harold D. Lasswell, *Power and Personality* (New York: Viking, 1948), pp. 59–93. Also, Robert E. Lane, *Political Ideology* (New York: The Free Press, 1962), examines the influence of personality on political attitudes.

[11] Lucian W. Pye, *Nation-Building*, pp. 211–43. See also the articles by Alex Inkeles and Daniel J. Levinson, "National Character: The Study of Modal Personality and Socio-cultural Systems," in Gardner Lindzey, ed., *Handbook of Social Psychology*, Vol. 2 (Cambridge, Mass.: Addison-Wesley, 1954); and Alex Inkeles, "National Character and Modern Political Systems," in Francis L. K. Hsu, ed., *Psychological Anthropology: Approaches to Culture and Personality* (Homewood, Ill.: Dorsey Press, 1961).

[12] See Marshall R. Singer, *The Emerging Elite: A Study of Political Leadership in Ceylon* (Cambridge, Mass.: The MIT Press, 1964); Wendell Bell, *Jamaican Leaders* (Berkeley: University of California Press, 1964); James A. Scott, *Political Ideology in Malaysia* (New Haven: Yale University Press, 1968); and Frederick W. Frey, *The Turkish Political Elite* (Cambridge, Mass.: The MIT Press, 1965).

[13] For the purpose of this study, the *elite* are defined as those who hold seats in the National Assembly or upper level civil service positions. Although this excludes a number of important party officials not holding government posts, as well as a few important businessmen, journalists, etc., the bulk of those who share in influencing national decisions is included in this definition. See Singer, *op. cit.*, who uses a similar rationalization and limits his elite only to parliamentarians, excluding civil servants.

distinctions and definitions of a role have been offered by other scholars.[14] Essentially, these alternative views of the role concept are based on differing operational measures. Three major types of definitions describe a role in terms of (1) role expectations, (2) role orientations, and (3) role behavior.

Role expectations refer to the demands made by society upon all individuals occupying a similar position. Individuals who frequently interact with the occupant of a position, as legislators do with a president, are the principal sources of these social norms. The concept of norm, as developed by Sherif, Newcomb, Festinger, and others, refers to communicated responses which produce conformity by prescribing behavior and by threatening sanctions.[15]

Role orientations refer to the individual role occupant's own ideas as to how he ought to behave when he is in a given situation. These ideas reflect the norms of those around him (society) which he has learned or internalized, as well as his own personality and selective perceptions.[16]

Role behavior refers to the actions of an individual as the occupant of a particular position. Sarbin, for example, suggests that a role is "a patterned sequence of learned actions or deeds performed by a person in an interaction situation." [17] The focus here is upon the empirical, rather than the normative, aspects of role. Role behavior is differentiated from other behavior by the interaction situation in which it occurs. Since it is necessary to infer the role to which an act or set of actions belongs, some external criteria for identifying roles are required. Moreover, relevant behavior theoretically includes not only actions, but also internal behavior such as motivations, beliefs, feelings, attitudes, and values.[18] This aspect of a role focuses, in practice, only on outward action

[14] See the collection of essays and extensive bibliography in Bruce J. Biddle and Edwin J. Thomas, *Role Theory: Concepts and Research* (New York: Wiley, 1966). Clarifications of the definition of role may be found in Theodore M. Newcomb, *Social Psychology* (New York: Dryden, 1950); Gross et al., *op. cit.,* pp. 11–18; Daniel J. Levinson "Role Personality and Social Structure in the Organizational Setting," in Seymour M. Lipset and Neil J. Smelser, eds., *Sociology: The Progress of a Decade* (Englewood Cliffs, N.J.: Prentice-Hall, 1961), pp. 300–302; and Lionel J. Neiman and James W. Hughes, "The Problem of the Concept of Role—A Resurvey of the Literature," *Social Forces,* Vol. 30 (December 1951), pp. 142–47.

[15] See Ragnar Rommetveit, *Social Norms and Roles* (Minneapolis, Minn.: University of Minnesota Press, 1955), pp. 18–30. Laws and courts would be examples of formal norms and sanctions: etiquette and ostracism are informal examples.

[16] Sargent, for example, uses this definition. See John H. Rohrer and M. Sherif, eds., *Social Psychology at the Crossroads* (New York: Harper Bros., 1951), p. 360. A person's role is a pattern or type of social behavior which seems situationally appropriate to him in terms of the demands and expectations of those in his group.

[17] T. R. Sarbin, "Role Theory," in Gardner Lindzey, ed., *Handbook of Social Psychology,* Vol. 1 (Cambridge, Mass.: Addison-Wesley, 1955), p. 225.

[18] Certainly role expectations contain prescriptions involving the proper attitudes or motivations for playing a given role. See David Krech, R. S. Crutchfield, and E. L. Ballanchey, *Individual in Society* (New York: McGraw-Hill, 1962), p. 311. In my own research we asked the question, "If an M.P. wished to be recognized and liked by ministers and other important people, what would he do?" Nearly 20% of those interviewed initially rejected the legitimacy of this motivation, saying that "this is wrong," or "he wouldn't care about that."

characteristics. Davis, for example, limits his use of role to "[h]ow an individual actually performs in a given position, as distinct from how he is supposed to perform." [19]

Role expectations, role orientation, and role behavior present three aspects or observational standpoints from which to analyze role events. Criticism for reifying the concept is avoided by not assuming consensus of expectations or congruence among the various aspects of role. By treating these two characteristics as variables to be examined empirically, it is possible to assess the institutionalization of a role within a political system.

Six points of possible observation for assessing a particular role are illustrated in Figure 6–1.

FIGURE 6-1. A ROLE INTERACTION PROCESS

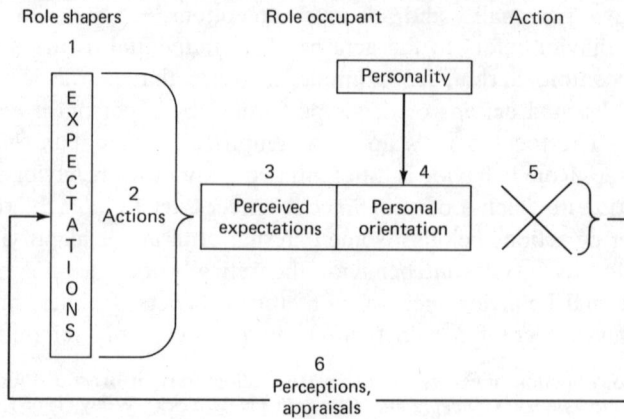

The "role process" depicted by Figure 6–1 is composed of the following six stages:

1. The expectations actually held by others with respect to the rights and duties of the role.
2. The norms sent to the role occupant by the actions, verbal and otherwise, of role shapers by means of personal interaction and also via communications media.
3. The received norms—the perceptions and ideas of the role occupant as to what "society" expects of him.
4. The definition of the situation by the role occupant and his personal views as to how the role "ought" to be played.

[19] Kingsley Davis, cited in Gross et al., *op cit.*, p. 14. Similar uses of the term may be found in Parsons, *The Social System*, p. 25. Merton also makes a twofold distinction which seems to parallel the definitions suggested here, in Robert K. Merton, *Social Theory and Social Structure* (New York: The Free Press, 1957), p. 392: "Role refers to the manner in which the rights and duties inherent in a social position are put into practice; orientation as here conceived refers to the theme underlying the complex of social roles performed by an individual."

5. Overt behavior of the role occupant relevant to the norms or prescriptions of the role held by others or himself or both.
6. The perceptions of the role behavior which will be scanned and compared with expectations by role shapers. Subsequent appraisal of the behavior will reinforce or undermine expectations and result in further actions at Stage 2 which may be either sanctions with respect to violated expectations or altered norms with respect to future role behavior. This stage completes a cycle of feedback and adjustment.

This role process is an ongoing, dynamic aspect of social life. Individuals and roles change over time, as in some cases roles become more clearly defined (and consensus increases), or they are learned better (and congruence increases), or individuals change roles—and even create new ones—by their behavior.

Role behavior performs the activities which comprise the interrelated workings of a political system and which maintain or change the system. Ideally, the actions of people are channeled into patterns which will simultaneously satisfy some of their personal motivations or drives.[20] In an actual system, however, one may expect to find roles. In appraising the "development" of a political system, therefore, it is important to examine both the attitudes and the behavior which are related to the roles in the system.

Since the institutionalization of a political system is a function of the clarity and compatibility of role expectations, the system deteriorates when expectations and behavior are incongruent and behavior loses its predictable quality.[21] Simon makes clear the importance of expectations in an analysis of power relationships.

A political regime prescribes appropriate behavior roles to its participants; these roles include appropriate actions to constrain any participant (or small group of participants) who departs from his role. But the constraints will be applied only if the remaining participants (or most of them) continue to play their roles. . . . Hence, estimates of the stability of a political structure depend not only on observation of the distribution of actual power, or of the capacity of sub-groups for coordinated action. . . . Every observation of a power relationship makes an assumption, whether explicit or implicit, as to the pattern of expectation and of group coordination. Such an observation will have predictive value, in general, only so long as this assumption holds.[22]

Thus, when political roles are unclear to role occupants, or to those who are in immediate contact with the role, or when conflicting expectations are held about boundaries of role behavior, political instability and disintegration may be ex-

[20] Melford Spiro, "Social Systems, Personality, and Functional Analysis," in Bert Kaplan, ed., *Studying Personality Cross Culturally* (Evanston, Ill.: Row, Peterson, 1961), pp. 100–104.
[21] Huntington, for example, stresses the quality of "coherence" among and within political groups as an important element in political stability. See Samuel P. Huntington, *Political Order in Changing Societies* (New Haven: Yale University Press, 1968).
[22] Herbert Simon, *Models of Man* (New York: Wiley, 1957), p. 72.

pected, in the most severe instances in the form of coups, rebellions, or revolutions.[23]

We may envision a continuum between full institutionalization of roles and its opposite, "the absence of structured complementarity of the interaction process," which Parsons at one point labels anomie.[24] Anomie occurs when discrepancies arise between role expectations and role behavior and when traditional norms no longer serve as effective guides to need-reducing role playing.[25] When anomie (or normlessness) increases, Parsons suggests, a particular system might "lose its identity, or it might be transformed into one which is drastically different." [26]

Strategies for Research

In the study of political systems in newly emergent states, examining the interrelations in the role process among role expectations, role orientations, and role behavior can provide important indications about the relative institutionalization of the system. There is a number of aspects and measures of political roles which might be investigated. I will suggest two strategies for research which I believe should yield the most economic and significant results relevant to political institutionalization. First, some boundary characteristics of a political role, that is, the limits to which the occupant of a role may publicly assert his influence, should be examined. Second, consensus among role expectations and their congruence with actual role behavior should be determined. In focusing on these two aspects of role analysis, many other aspects must be excluded or ignored.

There is a hierarchical character to the set of role expectations or norms surrounding any given role. Some "prescribed" behavior may be fairly unimportant, peripheral, or optimal. With respect to the role of legislator, for instance, attending social events may be unimportant, writing articles for magazines peripheral, and traveling among his constituents optional. Even more central expectations, such as attending legislative sessions, may be violated on occasion without being negatively sanctioned. Thus, there are norms not only for types of behavior, but also for the frequency with which it is demanded. It

[23] Chalmers Johnson, in *Revolutionary Change* (Boston: Little, Brown, 1966), proposes that disequilibrium of this sort between normative expectations and structural performance in the presence of a catalytic "accelerator" leads to revolution.

[24] Parsons, *The Social System*, p. 39.

[25] Merton, *op. cit.*, pp. 131–94, suggests that social structure may lead to anomie or "normlessness," reducing social predictability and producing neurotic personalities. He states: "It is clear that imperfect coordination of the two [the goals-and-means phases of the social structure] leads to anomie [*Ibid.*, p. 159]." See also Melvin Seeman, "On the Meaning of Alienation," *American Sociological Review*, Vol. 24, No. 6 (December 1959), pp. 783–791, who urges narrowing anomie to refer not to general feelings of normlessness, but to situations in which "there is a high expectancy that socially unapproved behavior are required."

[26] Parsons and Shils, *op. cit.*, p. 204. Parsons's analysis refers to society in general, that is "social systems," but should be equally applicable to a political subsystem.

might be conceivable to order role attributes from a pivotal attribute, the sine qua non of the role, down through less restricting and more incidental attributes contained in role expectations.[27] This latitude of behavior with respect to lesser role expectations provides a range of alternative behaviors from which individual personalities may select those behaviors most compatible with their own patterns of needs and motivations. In measuring role expectations, therefore, it will be important to avoid focusing on norms where the "ranges of permissible behavior" [28] are so wide as to have little predictable effect on behavior. Recognition of this elasticity of norms is a major reason to examine role situations which are related to public and central, or boundary, role actions.

A second area of role analysis excluded from investigation is personal roles.[29] In contrast to cultural roles, these refer to role behavior which is unique to an individual or group, and are often a differentiated subset of a major cultural role. A legislator thus may play a special aspect of his general role in relation to certain fellow legislators, a pressure group, or his constituency. This is similar to playing the role of friend a bit different depending on which friend one is with. The exposure or "public" character of the role behavior is usually an indicator of how personal it is likely to be. In general, cultural roles based on the role expectations (not necessarily in agreement) of all relevant individuals are more suited for studies of political systems, whereas personal roles may be of particular interest for investigating small subsystems such as a legislative system.[30]

Roles are usually defined in relation to other roles, such as mother–child, teacher–student, etc., and are interlocking or complementary to them.[31] The role-set depicted in Figure 6–2 focuses on a single role, that of head of government, which in Tanzania is the president. Several such interaction models, one for each political role examined, could be constructed. However, only one is necessary to illustrate propositions about the institutionalization of political roles. It should be noted that Figure 6–2 represents a limited model. The expectations of ordinary citizens have been excluded from the model both to narrow the scope of research and because the category of significant shapers is

[27] S. F. Nadel, *The Theory of Social Structure* (New York: The Free Press, 1957), pp. 31–35.

[28] Samuel A. Stouffer, "An Analysis of Conflicting Social Norms," *American Sociological Review,* Vol. 14, No. 6 (December 1949), p. 717. This conclusion is based on one of the best experiments done on norms and roles, in which it was found that a range of role expectations existed which shifted according to how "exposed" a hypothetical act was.

[29] See Roland L. Warren, "Social Disorganization and the Interrelationship of Cultural Roles," *American Sociological Review,* Vol. 14, No. 1 (February 1949), pp. 83–87; Rommetveit, *op. cit.,* pp. 35–38; and Robert K. Merton, "The Role-Set: Problems in Sociological Theory," *British Journal of Sociology,* Vol. 8, No. 2 (June 1957), pp. 110–13.

[30] John C. Wahlke, Heinz Eulau, William Buchanan, and Leroy C. Ferguson, in *The Legislative System: Explorations in Legislative Behavior* (New York: Wiley, 1962), pp. 3–28, 245–414, have done research in four state legislatures examining various subroles of legislators, both personal (as in relation to other legislators) and cultural.

[31] Merton, "The Role-Set," pp. 110–20; Newcomb, *op. cit.,* p. 285; and David Krech et al., *op. cit.,* p. 311.

exhausted once the elite have been considered. Elites in this model include what Lazarsfeld refers to as "political influentials," or what Dahl labels the "political stratum." [32] Other variables which might have been included have either been simplified or eliminated. Distinctions among the leader's perceived role expectations, role orientations, and role behavior, for instance, have been collapsed into role behavior, although his expectations and orientations could be inferred from speeches or other remarks. Likewise, the effect of social structure on expectations is not represented by, for example, ignoring possible different expectations and relationships among the elite. The role process depicted in Figure 6–2, however, serves to illustrate the major variables for analyzing the institutionalization of a major political role in new political systems.

Resources in Figure 6–2 refer to the sum, distribution, and quality of the instruments available to the role occupant for implementing role-related decisions.[33] For President Nyerere, various government agencies and the party apparatus constitute the principal instruments for executing his will. The loyalty

FIGURE 6-2. LIMITED ILLUSTRATION OF A PRESIDENTIAL ROLE MODEL

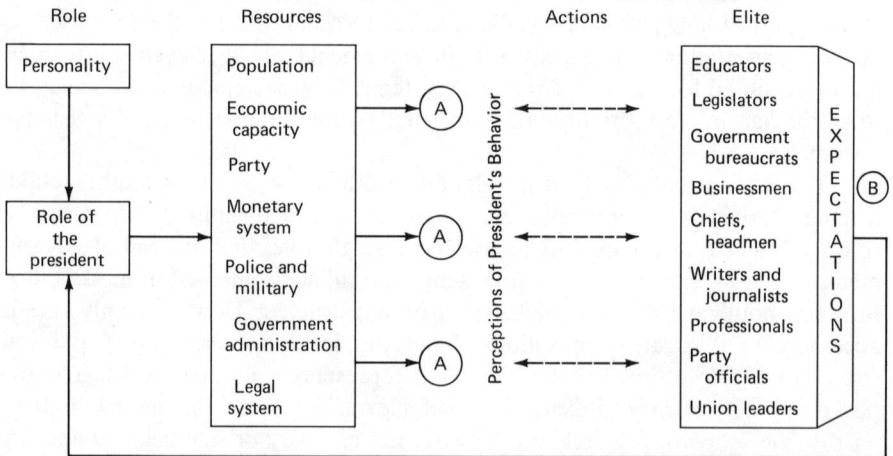

[32] See Elihu Katz and Paul F. Lazarsfeld, *Personal Influence* (New York: The Free Press, 1955) and Robert Dahl, *Who Governs?* (New Haven: Yale University Press, 1961), pp. 319–25. In describing the "two-step" flow of communication, Lazarsfeld suggests that a group of active and alert opinion leaders serves as intervening variables between political leaders and the citizenry. Dahl finds a stratum which is important for supporting the "prevailing norms" of the political system. This distinction seems even more relevant to political systems in underdeveloped areas. This is not to indicate that the problem of anomic behavior based on disjointed role relationships and ineffective socialization among "common citizens" should be ignored, except in this context. Indeed, the latent possibilities for system change by revolution or other means based on mobilizing a small but unstable portion of the citizenry is an important problem for change and stability in African politics.

[33] It should be added that resources are of an "external nature." It would be conceivable for some analytic purposes to treat the skills and personality of the leader as resources. This does not seem a very useful way of grouping variables in our case, however.

and efficiency of these instruments affect their reliability and/or usefulness. Other resources, less readily controllable by the leader, such as population, industrial capacity, and rate of social change, also circumscribe and define possible behavior for the head of government. Resources, although quite important, may be examined in analyzing role behavior in a descriptive, rather than a statistical, fashion.

Expectations should be studied both as independent and dependent variables. In the case of the president, role norms may be examined as the elite's expectations (at point B in Figure 6–2). These norms define (1) the personal attributes desirable for the role, e.g., physique, intelligence, or ancestry; (2) the political demands to which the role occupant is expected to respond; and (3) the style of behavior appropriate for the processing of these demands. In my research, only the last type of norms was studied. Expectations about procedures are particularly relevant to the style of politics which may exist in a political system. Procedural expectations affect the ability of individual actors such as legislators, administrators, or the head of government to pursue personal or group interests and they govern the channels and methods by which demands are handled. Thus, they contain the norms of the elite political culture which in part determines the "style" of the political system.[34]

FIGURE 6–3. ROLE INTERACTION

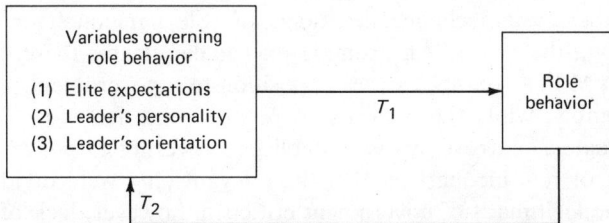

Figure 6–3 shows more clearly how rules for politics emerge from the process of role interaction. At the beginning of the process, T_1, the initial expectations of the elite create and define the role of the president. Recruitment into this role brings a second and third variable—the personality and role expectations of the leader—into the picture. As the leader begins to act, responding to the demands placed upon him with the resources at his command, a dependent variable, role behavior, emerges. At the next point in time, T_2, these actions of the president can be considered as the independent variable shaping elite expectations, his own personality, and role orientations, and the control and scope of resources available to him in his presidential role. This interacting

[34] Using role expectations may avoid measuring system "style" based on, for example, sentiments about "democratic principles," which as Prothro and Griggs have shown have a low consensus even in the United States. The focus on procedures should reveal the operational "rules of the game." See James W. Prothro and Charles M. Grigg, "Fundamental Principles of Democracy: Bases of Agreement and Disagreement," *Journal of Politics*, Vol. 22 (March 1960), pp. 276–94.

process of role behavior and role expectations may serve to strengthen or weaken consensus among elite expectations.[35] If the president's behavior is consistent with expectations, the role model presented in Figure 6–3 suggests that this will reinforce expectations, decrease variance in expectations among the elite, and lessen gaps among role expectations. On the other hand, role behavior which contravenes elite expectations would, it is predicted, lead to greater deviations, both among expectations and between expectations and basic attitudes of elites, and hence diminish the stability and institutionalization of the role.

Agreement among role expectations may generally be referred to as consensus. Consensus may be assessed among the aggregate of role shapers, such as an all-political elite, or even all citizens, or it may be examined in one or another subgroup, such as among legislators. Congruence refers to the degree of matching or similarity between two sets of role expectations. For instance, we might examine the congruence between the expectations of two groups, such as legislators and administrators, or between the expectations of an individual and a group. In the latter case we could discover how *deviant* an *individual* elite's expectations were concerning a given role compared to the pattern of expectations among all elite. Dissensus and incongruity lead to ambiguity and conflict and indicate strains upon the individuals and the system.[36] The more central the aspects of the political role and the greater the strain, the more we can expect either system change, a change of role personnel, or feelings of insecurity among the actors. An example may make clearer these distinctions. If a Tanzanian M.P. (*Mbunge*) raises opposition to a government policy in the National Assembly, while the majority of political elite felt it is his responsibility not to create a controversy over established government policy, this would be an instance of role incongruence. If the relevant elite were divided in their views about the legitimacy of government criticism, however, lack of consensus resulting in ambiguity or conflict would be indicated.

It would be possible also to analyze strains due to conflict among different elite members or with other groups, to conflict resulting from multiple roles played by the same man, to conflict endemic in competing but widely accepted roles such as traditional authority versus "modern" leader, or to discrepancies of communications among expectations, orientations, and behavior which produce incongruence. Thus, the analysis of political roles and role strain is not clear and simple; it is rather quite complex.[37]

---

[35] In the interviews, people often based their answers of expectations toward the president on Nyerere's past actions and fully expected him to continue behaving in a similar fashion.

[36] Ambiguity would describe a situation where alternative expectations are about evenly distributed. Conflict is a more serious instance in which incompatible expectations are held by important groups. When a role incumbent perceives the dissimilar expectations, he experiences role strain. On these points see Gross et al., *op. cit.*, Chapter 15; and Robert L. Kahn, *Organizational Stress: Studies in Role Conflict and Ambiguity* (New York: Wiley, 1964).

[37] For a discussion of the complex variables involved in role analysis, see Biddle and Thomas, *op. cit.*, pp. 29–45.

The existence and importance of consensus and congruence in role expectations was assessed by using the respondent's expectations. Consensus was indicated by measures of central tendencies and variance (V) and congruence (C) calculated by deviations from the "norm." While other related aspects of political role expectations could be examined, though less systematically, and other techniques to measure consensus might be employed, the data from the Tanzanian research allowed only consensus and congruence to be measured specifically.

THE TANZANIAN EXPERIENCE

A selected few of the findings from the larger Tanzanian study[38] will be presented to illustrate some basic potentialities of using a micro analysis of roles to study national politics. This section concludes with a discussion of some of the methodological problems which arose during the field research; hopefully, others who share my research and intellectual concerns will avoid some of the more obvious difficulties in pursuing their own work.

The Analysis

Since independence in 1961, Tanzania[39] has avoided serious instability. A pattern of politics which stresses unity, discipline, and national commitment has emerged. Concurrently, criticism and public discussion of policy differences have been discouraged. Politics based on the interplay of competing interests or groups has become the antithesis of the "Tanzanian way"[40] and is severely limited by both laws and informal rules. This "closed" pattern of decisionmaking evolved from the organizational procedures which TANU (the Tanganyika African National Union) developed during the drive to independence, combined with the rather authoritarian colonial structure and the formal constitutional heritage, hastily drawn up under British tutelage, which provided for parliamentary democracy.[41]

The dominance of the party and the absorption of interest groups into the party structure, however, has not completely eliminated competition and interest articulation. In September, 1965, national elections for a new National

[38] Raymond F. Hopkins, *Political Roles in a New State* (New Haven: Yale University Press, 1971).

[39] Tanzania, formally the United Republic of Tanzania, consists of the former countries of Tanganyika (which became independent on December 9, 1961) and Zanzibar (whose independence was granted on December 10, 1963). On April 23, 1964, following a revolution in Zanzibar, a union between these two countries was declared by their presidents.

[40] See Sophia Mustafa, *The Tanganyika Way* (Dar es Salaam, Tanzania: The Eagle Press, 1961). Ms. Mustafa, a former M.P., gives a personalized account of the negative attitude of leading politicians toward policies based on a balancing of interests.

[41] For a discussion of this merging of institutional practices and precedents, see Hopkins, *op. cit.*, Chapter 1.

Assembly and Presidency were held. They were generally free; participation was encouraged, and alternatives were offered the voters. A number of important party officials was defeated, including two ministers and several junior ministers.[42] The pattern of politics in Tanzania, therefore, is novel, both in rhetoric and procedure, and incorporates features of liberal democracy with an organizational structure similar to that of Lenin's "democratic centralism."

In my research, on the basis of determining consensual role expectations for ten contingency role questions, along with additional information concerning individual attitudes and recent political actions, a set of "rules" for political behavior in Tanzania was inferred. Although these rules, in absolute terms, give an exaggerated precision to the behavioral norms which they reflect, they do describe in a specific manner some of the rules that govern political activity in Tanzania, limiting conflict and ensuring unity.[43]

For instance, one rule which emerged for administrators is that they must defer to political superiors in all "policy" matters. Administrators were also expected to accept the development ethics of a socialist state. Among legislators, two important rules based on consensus of expectations were that: (1) an M.P. may not publicly oppose a policy decision of TANU's National Executive Committee; and (2) policies passed in the National Assembly must be supported in discussions with constituents.

Rules for the president included a built-in ambiguity between an expectation that the president would always act lawfully and another that the president should not be bound by any constraint other than the "people." These rules and the president's role in reinforcing norms for other roles were important in supporting a pattern of "closed" politics.

Presidential Role Expectations

A discussion of expectations about the role of the president will serve to illustrate how the analysis of roles can lead to information about the macro pattern of politics. The sample was queried about their expectations with respect to five projective role questions related to the presidency. Each question dealt with some aspect of the president's role. Responses, as with responses to similar questions dealing with the role of administrator and M.P., were collapsed into three general categories reflecting varying degrees of strength and independence of action. The first question asked: "If the president wished to change local leadership, what would he do?" The president, acting through his Ministry of Local Government, has the power to dismiss local councilors, an action which he took in 1963 against the Bukoba Council when it proved unreceptive to TANU guidance. Most responses, therefore, dealt with what consultations, if any, the president would make before taking action against local leaders. A

[42] See Lionel Cliffe, ed., *One Party Democracy* (Nairobi, Kenya: East African Publishing House, 1967).

[43] For a full discussion of these rules in some detail, see Hopkins, *op. cit.*, Chapters 4–7.

majority expected the president to engage in some consultation before he acted. But a sizable portion, 37%, expected the president simply to act. One hundred twenty Tanzanian students at all three campuses of the University of East Africa completed questionnaires containing identical items. In contrast to the elite respondents, students were more prone to expect the president to consult the public either locally or nationally before acting. This tendency among students to expect public participation in political controversies was probably due to implicit desires on their part to be more involved and consulted.

The second question probed the relationship of the president with M.P.s, focusing particularly on his expected reaction to criticism. Among legislators and students, there was a sizable number who expected the president to respond directly to a critical M.P. by criticizing him, threatening him, or, as suggested by several, even placing him in detention. Other responses, such as ignoring or accepting the criticism or responding to the criticism (rather than the critic!) were also expected by fairly large proportions of the respondents. The diversity of opinion on this question (see Table 6–1) suggests an uncertainty and flexibility of norms governing the relationship between the president and members of the National Assembly. On this point, it is particularly interesting to note the student responses. A plurality expected action directed toward the M.P., but among these only 43% approved of this behavior contrasted to 88% who approved of the president's responding only to the criticism. The gap between students' ideas of what is expected and what is desirable (as indicated by the percentage indicating approval) is greatest on this question.

The president's action in response to tribal unrest is another area of presidential behavior which was explored. The question asked: "Opposition to the government breaks out among a rural tribal group. What action would the president order to be taken?" The use of persuasion and understanding (the "weak" response, see Table 6–1) was the predominant expectation among elite respondents. Only 25% anticipated the use of force or emergency powers. Among students, however, 61% believed that the president was likely to invoke force, although they approved more highly of the president's using persuasion, rather than force, in such a situation.

The differences between student and elite expectations probably reflect two more basic differences in orientation. First, students generally were more prone to expect the president to act strongly than were members of the elite. Second, the elite, perhaps owing to their experience in dealing with various matters involving tribal loyalties, were more sensitive to the dangers of exacerbating conflict between national government regulation and tribally linked sentiments and activities. Such orientations among the elite may explain their general agreement on the desirability of persuasion, or the desirable reaction to tribal dissidence.

According to the constitution, the high court of Tanzania has the authority of constitutional interpretation. It is not inconceivable, therefore, that an action might come before it which raises the question of whether the president acted

TABLE 6–1.   PRESIDENTIAL ROLE EXPECTATIONS OF ELITE[a]

	Adminis-trators (N = 50)	Legis-lators (N = 57)	Total elite (N = 107)	Students (N = 100)	Students approving (N = 56)	X^2
Wishes to change local leadership:						
Consult public	22	19	20	58	79	
Consult advisors	44	39	41	22	93	
Will act	34	39	36	20	78	
Elite/Students						32.4[b]
Legislators/Administrators						0.2
M.P. criticizes:				(N = 103)	(N = 57)	
Accept or ignore	34	32	33	31	68	
Respond to criticism	50	25	36	30	88	
Respond to M.P.	16	40	29	39	43	
Elite/Students						2.2
Legislators/Administrators						10.2[b]
President reacts to tribal outbreak:				(N = 104)	(N = 56)	
Use persuasion	78	68	73	39	95	
Use force	16	23	20	46	78	
Use emergency powers	6	4	5	14	75	
Elite/Students						27.1[b]
Legislators/Administrators						1.2
Court declares action void:				(N = 106)	(N = 55)	
Accept	64	26	44	53	74	
Ask Parliament	26	60	44	21	71	
Override court	8	12	10	26	53	
Elite/Students						17.3[b]
Legislators/Administrators						15.9
Cabinet opposes views:				(N = 108)	(N = 61)	
Discuss, use persuasion	44	28	36	45	79	
Go to Parliament	24	35	30	4	100	
Act dramatically, alone	22	33	28	51	71	
Elite/Students						30.3[b]
Legislators/Administrators						4.1

a Percentages are given unless otherwise indicated.
b These Chi squares are significant at the $p < .05$ level.

within his constitutional powers, though a number of the elite respondents expressed doubt that such an issue would arise. Indeed, the One Party Commission specifically recommended divorcing the court from political involvement.

In order to learn about expectations regarding the president's role vis-à-vis the court, the question was asked: "A court rules the president has exceeded his authority in a particular matter and declares his action void. What would the president do?" Three types of responses to this question are reported in Table 6–1. One alternative, expected by a majority of administrators and students, is that the president would simply accept the court's action. Such expectations, I believe, reflected an acknowledgment of Nyerere's commitment to rule by law. Several respondents recited specific examples in which Nyerere stressed the necessity of accepting legal decisions, even if one did not whole-heartedly agree with their content. Legislators, in contrast to the administrators and students, were more apt to expect the president to circumvent the court's ruling. The majority (60%) suggested the president would act within constitutional bounds, asking Parliament to change the law or constitution so that he might act legally. Thus, legislators, while not expecting the president to remain passive, do expect him to remain within the legal framework. Only 10% of the elite and 26% of the students thought the president would take action directly against the court, overriding the decision or even dismissing the judges, thereby violating the independence of the judiciary as established in the constitution. The underlying notion which many respondents expressed in answering this question was that the president certainly would act lawfully on all accounts. Several answers even indicated an expectation that the president viewed the court system and legal procedure as more sacrosanct than did the respondents.

The last role question was in the area of the president's relation to his cabinet. Since the cabinet may be expected to contain, particularly in a one-party state such as Tanzania, most of the important political figures in the country, cleavages in cabinet opinion would represent an important factionalizing of politics and present a real threat to the unity of the country. Support of cabinet ministers is certainly an important source of authority and strength for presidential action.

In order to probe this sensitive area, respondents were asked: "The president finds a majority of his ministers opposing his views. What would he do?" Answers to this question range widely from an expectation that the president would yield to the cabinet majority and change his views, to the quite contrary expectation that the president would dismiss his cabinet, or would even place dissenting members in detention. The most common expectation among elite respondents was that the president would discuss the matter with cabinet members and use persuasion until some agreement was reached. It was difficult for many to conceive of a controversy being carried to a wider arena. Some of the elite, however, were prepared to acknowledge the possibility of what the question implied, namely a difference in presidential and cabinet opinion which was not resolvable by discussion. Two general alternatives were mentioned by these respondents: first, that the president would ask Parliament to resolve the disagreement, and, second, that the president would act on his own initiative, perhaps in a dramatic fashion, either to resolve the issue by dismissing dissenting cabinet members or to confront the issue broadly by taking it to the nation in a new general election. The responses suggested the degree of arena expansion which important political conflict might generate. Certainly a large number of students and elite did not expect such controversy to go beyond the more or less private discussions of cabinet members. But some did anticipate that disputes could enter wider arenas and suggested that the Parliament might be a forum for resolving political disputes between the president and a majority of his cabinet. Some elite members would not have been surprised even to find the president appealing directly to the public on such an issue. Students were rather prone to expect this third possibility, perhaps because they saw the president acting strongly in general and/or because they preferred situations in which the public, including themselves, were able to participate or voice an opinion. Since the president has broad powers of detention, even those respondents expecting the most assertive behavior by the president, such as arresting his dissenting cabinet members, were not expressing expectations that the president would act illegally or beyond the scope of his power.

Comparative Institutionalization Among Roles

The distribution of responses to all the role questions (the five regarding the president and five others) indicates that the amount of agreement among expectations differs widely. If it is assumed that differences in the amount of agreement are not simply produced by the questions, but rather reflect differences in the amount of ambiguity or conflict versus the amount of concensus surrounding each role, it is possible to assess the relative amount of consensus among the Tanzanian elite with respect to each of three roles— administrator, legislator, and president. The relative amount of consensus for each role reflects, in some sense, the degree to which these roles are institutionalized and the pressure toward conformity imposed upon a role incumbent. The statistical variance for each question has been calculated, and the average variance among questions for each of the three roles is presented in Table 6–2. Greater agreement or consensus on a role is indicated by a smaller variance.

TABLE 6–2.   COMPARATIVE ROLE CONSENSUS

AVERAGE ITEM VARIANCE BY ROLE		
Administrator	Legislator	President
.521	.394	.519

For instance, if expectations were completely ambiguous, that is, equally distributed, the variance would be .670, and if conflicting expectations were found, that is, a bimodal distribution, the variance would be .800 or above.[44]

These results indicate that the role of legislator is rather more institutionalized than that of either president or administrator. The expectations which

[44] There are statistical tests to measure differences between variances, but all such tests assume two or more independent groups, not two items from the same group. Hence, the comparative properties with respect to "significance" of differences for this measure are difficult to assess.

shape and constrain the behavior of M.P.s are less ambiguous and more con-sensual. The boundaries beyond which an M.P. is not expected to proceed in playing his role are more agreed upon by elite respondents. Expectations with respect to the administrator's role are more ambiguous and conflicting. The reason for this, I believe, is the conflict which emerged from the new role definitions assigned administrators following independence and the assumption of power by TANU. Some of the elite retained older, preindependence notions about the administrator's range of legitimate authority and decisionmaking initiative, which, however accurate in reflecting the great power exercised by the administrators in the colonial system of government, is no longer accurate nor considered desirable by the politicians who have assumed the power. The rela-tive lack of institutionalization of the administrator's role compared with that of the legislator is likely to be reduced quickly. The greatest deviance in role expectations, at least among administrators, is found among those with long careers stretching back into the colonial era. With rather rapid replacement and retirement of these older bureaucrats, it seems likely that this conflict in ex-pectations will be reduced, and institutionalization in the form of widespread agreement on the political rules for administrators will proceed smoothly.

The relatively low consensus on the role of the president is a reflection not so much of role conflict, I believe, as of role ambiguity. More so than many other "modern" political positions, the role of president is especially new to Tanzania. Although it has drawn upon traditional notions of authority, particu-larly attitudes toward chiefs, and combines, at least for the elite, ideas of authority for both a governor-general and a prime minister and in addition reflects some learned expectations produced by Nyerere's activities as head of a national movement, there is nevertheless no clear set of ideas about presidential behavior. In contrast to the administrator's role, introduction of the role of the president a year after independence did not involve narrowing or reformulating the scope of power of an older political role. Rather, it involved creating a new one out of bits and pieces culled from different traditions, cultures, and institu-tions. The consequential weakness of expectations, particularly ones deeply imbedded in an interlinking network of attitudes toward politics and the political regime, has provided President Nyerere with a wide scope of alternatives in his role.

The Cost of Deviance

If the political rules and the style of politics in Tanzania which have been described are becoming increasingly institutionalized, it seems reasonable to assume that individuals who are highly deviant in their expectations about their role are likely, in some sense, to be "punished" by the system, whereas those who are highly congruent in their expectations might be expected to be "re-warded." My research on role expectations was completed by August 1966. An examination of career changes that occurred among members of the sample between then and December 1968, a two-year period, has been undertaken.[45] For many, no change has occurred; for a few, changes have been lateral, with no noticeable movement to a more or less powerful position,[46] and information on a few was unobtainable. Table 6–3 presents the results of these investiga-

TABLE 6–3.   CHANGES IN ELITE POSITION, 1966–68[a]

	Position			
Role Congruence	Higher	About Same	Lower or None	Total[b]
High	11	41	3	55
Low	2	33	13	48
	13	74	16	103

a Chi square = 12.9, which is significant at $p < .01$.
b Information on only 103 of the 109 respondents was available.

tions. Of those of the elite with scores in the upper half on congruent expectations, 20% have moved to higher positions in the political or administrative structure, while only 5% have been demoted.

Among those with relatively noncongruent expectations, 4% have advanced, and 27% have moved to less important positions. Although this finding rests on only gross changes, it still seems significant. It indicates that whatever are the qualities that produce success or failure in the political system as presently organized in Tanzania, role expectations (as measured by this study) are related to, and possibly are even a cause of, the behavior which the system has so clearly sanctioned.

Among elite respondents who improved their position and who had high scores on role congruence were the new head of the civil service, two newly appointed ambassadors, TANU's new executive secretary, and a new minister and junior minister. Among elite respondents with low role congruence scores who were demoted was a regional commissioner who lost his job, two administrators dismissed from their posts, and several legislators and TANU officials, one of whom not only was removed from office, but also was placed in detention. This evidence suggests that the newly created political system has already acted to recognize and punish deviants and to reward conformists. In addition, it suggests that the deviance of an individual's role expectations is a good predictor of future success within a political system. The moral seems to be, if you wish to operate in the Tanzanian political system, knowing and perhaps inter-

45 I wish to thank Prof. Carl G. Rosberg, who kindly supplied information concerning the occupational status, as of December 1968, for nearly all the elite whom I had interviewed. Only six administrators were not traceable.

46 For instance, several ministers have changed ministries without any apparent change in political status.

nalizing the rules is an important prerequisite to promotion, or the avoidance of demotion, within the system.

Expectations alone, however, do not determine success or failure, even in the most institutionalized of political systems. In Tanzania, the majority of the elite did not change their status over the two-year period regardless of whether they were high or low in role congruence. Although deviant expectations only imperfectly relate to improper role performance, such behavior as perceived and assessed by others is likely to affect the role recruitment process of the system. The fact that of the twenty-nine clear changes in positional status within our sample in the years following the field research, twenty-four changes were in the direction that knowledge about role expectations would have suggested, is an impressive finding for the relevance of research on roles. This finding supports the proposition that the political system in Tanzania is developing institutional procedures to reinforce the rules, expectations, and role behavior of "closed" politics, which from the interaction of individual political actors are gradually emerging as the normative patterns and political style of the system.

Methodology

In studying the role process in Tanzania, 109 interviews with randomly selected members of the elite were conducted. Fifty-eight were with members of Parliament (out of 185 in the National Assembly) and 51 were with high-level administrators (out of 157). These interviews were conducted between April and August 1966; they averaged about two hours each; and covered a variety of topics including the individual's background, his views toward concepts such as democracy and African socialism, and his expectations about what he or others would do in a number of hypothetical role situations. Four roles were studied, that of president, M.P., administrator, and citizen.

After drawing the sample, the interview was explained briefly to each respondent either by letter or phone. Mr. E. Kapinga, a second-year law student at the University College, Dar es Salaam, assisted in the interviewing. He helped translate portions of the questionnaire into Swahili, and conducted 42 of the 109 interviews reported in this study.

Applying the rather elaborate conceptual scheme outlined in this chapter involved a number of hard methodological choices. Indeed, difficulties in measuring both role and role expectations bedeviled both the interviewing and data analysis stages of the research. In-depth interviews were used to break into the cognitive and affective network of each respondent at one point in time and to measure in a comparable fashion expectations about a small number of specified roles. My original methodological concern was to avoid the possibility of eliciting pseudoattitudes and imposing falsely structured alternatives; this led to the use of projective and open-ended techniques. However, the more open-ended the question, the less comparable were the responses and hence the more difficult it was to quantify them. This initial decision to guard against artificiality led me eventually to recategorize responses somewhat artificially along three-point continua from weak to strong role expectations in order to interpret the results. The open-ended approach also vitiated measurement of the intensity with which an expectation was held since noncomparable indications of intensity occurred during the interviews. An alternative procedure for measuring role consensus, employed in a role analysis study by Neal Gross and his colleagues,[47] would have been to suggest a particular role behavior and to ask the respondent to indicate whether such action is obligatory, irrelevant, or anathema for the role occupant. However, this procedure involves closed choices and was rejected. Are role expectations central or peripheral to the role? For instance, Muslims might feel strongly about drinking, but not transfer these attitudes to behavioral prescriptions relevant to political role occupants. Measurement techniques such as these, I now feel, would have yielded more satisfactory data than did the open-ended question approach.

A further dilemma which must be faced in measuring role expectations is whether one wishes to measure what a person predicts or what he desires. In this research, respondents were asked what they thought *would* happen. Information about what they believed *should* happen would have been valuable, but limitations of time and considerations of respondents' sensitivity prevented this type of questioning. With such information, for instance, discrepancies between what is considered likely and what is considered desirable in actions of political leaders could prove to be a useful indicator of legitimacy, perhaps even of stability.

Another dimension of role expectations not measured was that of sanctions for violations of role norms. Individuals are likely to differ in their notions about how often and how severely a role incumbent may violate expectations for his role behavior before sanctions are justified. There may also be disagreement over the nature of appropriate sanctions. Information of this sort is important for establishing what is the latitude of accepted behavior for a role occupant with respect to certain problems. Again, this study had no direct measures for this order. Role boundaries, therefore, were inferred from central tendencies in the responses and from other information.

A final consideration in creating a measurement for role expectations is the number of items required for a satisfactory measure. A considerable number of items on each role would be desirable. Moreover, where differences between roles are important to assess, equivalences among questions for each role would be needed. However, the number of items per role varied from five to two in this study, and equivalences were nearly nonexistent.

In defense of these methodological weaknesses, three points may be made. First, recognition of the complexity of variables distinguishable in any analysis of role expectations does not mean that a study which focuses upon role expectations must contain instruments sensitive to all. Indeed, no study, even one with

[47] Gross et al., *op. cit.*

a relatively high control over subjects, has elicited information relative to all the considerations and difficulties suggested in this discussion. Second, the more a researcher is concerned with contemporary social or political processes, the less likely it is that his study will be sensitive to all the dimensions of role expectations just suggested. It is more likely that one or two aspects of expectations will be selected for examination. The fewer the roles and the fewer the role expectation variables included in a study utilizing interviews, the greater the number of items possible per role and the greater the reliability the study is likely to have. Therefore, greater complexity in terms of roles and variables involves a loss in reliability if the total number of items remains constant. Furthermore, greater precision and greater complexity both decrease the possibility that the study can focus on important social and political phenomena. The third consideration is the nature of the situation in which expectations are being elicited. In this study, political elite were the subjects and they were being examined by a foreigner. Few rewards and practically no deprivations were available to me, as the researcher. Respondents were willing to cooperate largely to the extent that they felt the research might be useful to their country, or they themselves found the interview enjoyable. In addition, interviews had to be limited in duration, politically nonsensitive, and personally nonthreatening. These three points perhaps justify, though do not excuse, the methodological problems and weaknesses the study may contain.

What changes in research procedures might have been desirable? In retrospect, it seems possible that the role expectation items could have been less open-ended and utilized more forced-choice techniques. The total number of items probably could not have been expanded, but greater initial preparation of forced choices along a continuum of obligation would have been a wiser approach. This "confession" will perhaps be relevant to future researchers undertaking similar projects and provide a catharsis for other researchers whose methodological clumsiness is often a source of undisclosed frustration.

Chapter 7
Partial Order and Political Systems

DOUGLAS DURASOFF

Arguing for theoretical elegance and simplicity, this chapter demonstrates the use of a separate measurement scale, the partial order. Interestingly, the "partially ordered set," or poset, *has many abstract characteristics that correspond well with the empirical structural characteristics of a number of institutional configurations. This degree of correspondence is explored in detail by using examples of the Thai bureaucracy over three decades and a shorter term analysis of Soviet-style systems. To clarify further the concept of the poset, a "game" is presented showing the poset's main structural features and how one might go about using the concept to organize information from other settings.*

Studies of political activity and its structuring into political systems present us with the problem of a seemingly endless scope of subject matter and a great range of research approaches. The problem is not unique to political science. One might assert, for example, that physics also faces similar problems. Why then does it seem that that venerable science is so much more articulate, defined, and directed along paths of research with a foresight so far unattained by social scientists? Unable to explain and predict, we often fail to consider that the physical scientists are careful to delimit most problems. Physicists began by learning to predict the acceleration and path of a falling cannonball, not that of an autumn leaf.

Among the motivations for this chapter, perhaps primary was the belief that a great many insights and a good deal of value can be derived from basically simple concepts when these relate to common classes of real occurrences. The concept dealt with here conforms to this view.

PARTIAL ORDER

Partial order is a simple mathematical concept. Organized human activity is replete with partial orders. Studying political systems and subsystems in terms of partial order will, I believe, produce significant explanatory insights into system behavior.

The partial order is defined in most volumes devoted to basic set theory. Most simply, the partial order defines one type of ranking over a set of elements. This ranking is incomplete in two ways: the criterion used for rank need not be fully specific with respect to the positioning of each individual element (but instead, roughly, "greater than or equal to"), and not every element of the set has to be included in the ranking. Elements in the set which are not included in the ranking are defined as *incomparable* with the elements in the ranking. The *entire* set is called a partially ordered set, or *poset*. Because of the incompleteness of the ranking, such a set may contain more than one criterion for rank, each holding for either distinct subsets of elements or for subsets which have some common members (overlapping subsets). Thus, two elements ("individuals") of the poset may be comparable in one ranking and incomparable in another. These features of incomparability and overlapping of orderings within a single poset are exactly the features that appear, by extension, most commonly in political systems, and provide a basis for examining types of hierarchy in terms of set language.

An Illustration

Consider as an illustrative example the armed forces of the United States. Let the elements of a set be all individuals who belong to, or work for, the military. Within this set there exist parallel rankings which are each of the services, as well as civilians (draft boards, etc.) who are in none of these. The chain of command across services is unclear; e.g., an army colonel and naval captain may be incomparable by direct rank. Even more interesting incomparability relations arise when military leaders work outside their own ranking systems, for example, in bargaining with civilians. (Many war movies have bolstered their plots with these intrigues.) *All* these relationships occur within a conceptually unified sphere of action, a partially ordered set, which might be named *military complex*.

AN EXTENSION OF THE CONCEPT

Before advancing this analysis of particular "real-world" examples, let us explicitly develop the concept of partial order.

A relevant treatment that begins to apply the concept to behavioral science is found in "Mathematical Models and Measurement Theory," by C. H. Coombs, H. Raiffa, and R. M. Thrall.[1] The authors introduce several scales of measurement between the usually discussed nominal and ordinal scales. The partial order, as shown in Figure 7–1, is only one of a number of possible measurement scales. Furthermore, it can utilize data that do not satisfy the requirements of more common statistical procedures for interval and ordinal scales. Their article is also concerned with the nature of modeling and the relation of these scales to modeling procedures.

[1] In R. M. Thrall, C. H. Coombs, R. L. Davis, eds., *Decision Processes* (New York: Wiley, 1954).

FIGURE 7-1. TYPES OF MEASUREMENT SCALES

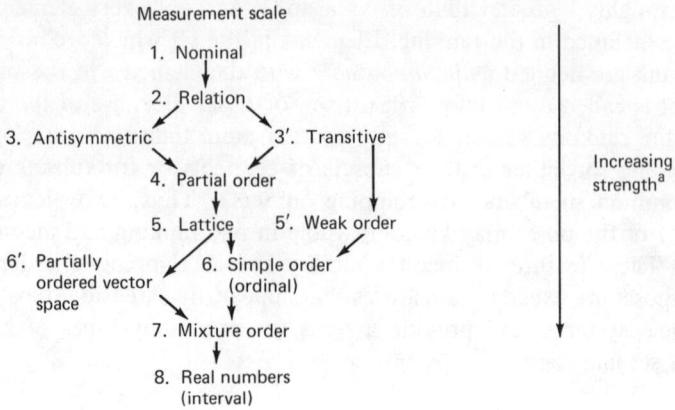

Measurement scale

1. Nominal
↓
2. Relation

3. Antisymmetric   3'. Transitive

4. Partial order

5. Lattice   5'. Weak order

6'. Partially   6. Simple order
ordered vector   (ordinal)
space

7. Mixture order
↓
8. Real numbers
(interval)

Increasing
strength[a]

KEY

1: Set of elements.

2: Introduce a relation R (set of ordered pairs)
between some pairs of elements (e.g., R = "loves").

3: R is antisymmetric. (If aRb and bRa, then $a = b$.)

3': R is transitive. (If aRb and bRa, then aRc.)

4: R is reflexive, antisymmetric, and transitive.
(If for some pair neither aRb nor bRa holds, then
a is incomparable to b for R: $a|b$.)

5, 5', and 6: Restrictions placed on R for *every* pair.

[a]Lines indicate that lower listed system is special case of one above.

Let us consider some possible uses of the concept as a basis for a language of political analysis. This extension requires explanation, hopefully provided in the following semiformal treatment.

Formalization

Let P be a set of elements, where "elements" is defined in full generality. It may, for example, refer to individuals, roles, groups, and so forth of a political system. Relations R_i from nominal to real, may be defined on P.

The *nominal* relations R_1 are formed by naming groups of elements from P. Thus, all the nominal relations on P are all the possible *subsets* of P. An "analysis" of P by nominal relations implies the problem of choosing among these, the problem of relevance. This analytical process we call *characterization*.

The *relation* relations R_2 are formed by creating sets of ordered pairs from among the elements of P (not necessarily exhaustive of P). All relation relations on P are all the possible *sets of pairs* of elements in P. Analysis of P by R_2 implies the problem of choosing among these sets. This we usually do by denoting the basis for forming the pairs ("loves," "influences," etc.). We might call this analytical process *association*.

These two scales both involve *choice* procedures on the set P: the first of subsets, the second of sets of pairs. That is, a scale might be selected algorithmically, by listing all possible subsets or pair sets and applying a given rule of choice to them. However, the magnitude of this task quickly becomes prohibitive, even using computers, as soon as P exceeds only a few elements. Hence, we normally represent a scale by definition of the naming or pairing relation and its application to elements of P. This definition is subject to no restrictions.

All further scales are derived by specific qualifications on the nature of the relation itself, qualifications which provide information about the relations among or *across* pairs.

The *antisymmetric* relation R_3 provide the property for R that, for elements a and b of P, "if aRb and bRa, then a is equivalent to b." That is, R_3 establishes equivalencies among the individual elements of P for which it holds reciprocally. Thus, we may have groups of elements in P which are equivalent to each other for a given relation R (for example, second lieutenants in the military, where P is the army and R is rank).

The *transitive* relations R_3' provide the property that "if aRb and bRc, then aRc." Given this property, we may trace out directed *chains* in P using R, where the first element stands in the same relationship to the last as to the second. We may also introduce the concept of *length* for such chains.

The *partial order* R_4 combines the properties of antisymmetry and transitivity. P is a *partially ordered set* (poset) if some of its elements are ordered by such a relation. In our description of P we have moved from such statements as "Some members of P are called N [say, army officers]," or "Some members of P relate to some others in a certain way [say, loyalty]," to statements like "*P* contains a coherent group of members organized by relation R [say, The military contains an air force which is ranked according to command authority]." It should be stressed that not all members of P need be in a given partial order. Those that are not are defined as *incomparable* (in that ordering) to those that are (*aIb* for R). As stated earlier, this inexhaustiveness means that P may contain more than one partial order, and these may overlap. Thus, analysis of P by R_4 involves the denotation of one or more roughly ranked subsets of P, and may include description of any overlapping among them. This analytical process we call *differentiation*. The word as used in this discussion does not refer to the calculus, but to the notion of development of human organization by means of increased specialization and complexity. Analysis in our terms will be particularly useful when this development is along hierarchal lines.[2]

All further scales involve the treatment of either all P together (undifferentiated), or its subsets separately, for they specify that *all* elements of the set being considered be subsumed under the given R. Hence, these are scales for

---

[2] The usage here is also related to that in certain structural-functional analytic schema. It is suggested that our definition of differentiation may provide some clarification of its use in such concepts as "structural political development." See particularly, Gabriel A. Almond and G. B. Powell, Jr., *Comparative Politics: A Developmental Approach* (Boston: Little, Brown, 1966, paper), pp. 216–17.

further specification *within* (and exhaustively to) differentiated sets, allowing no further treatment of whole sets involving different subsets and incomparables.

From this it seems that R_4 is an especially "interesting" scale for analysis of P. Higher scales are useful for more specific analysis within subsets, and lower scales treat more general categories and do not tie together the various related elements of P. Thus, R_4, the partial order, seems to be a "level" of analysis that is sufficiently general to treat whole systems which consist of a complex of parts, and sufficiently "strong" to say something about their individual parts. Since all complex political systems are neither unified completely by one ranking, nor undifferentiated into any rough hierarchies for any of the relations one might usefully consider, the concept of partial ordering could be used analytically to study these systems. Or, it might serve as the basis of a descriptive language for them.

Uses of partial ordering for political analysis appear on three distinguishable but inseparable levels. These uses are as a measurement scale (mathematical–statistical), as a more general ranking concept for whole system relations such as "power" or "influence" (situational–analytical), and as a basis for a systematic language which may free comparative studies from their culture-bound biases. All uses are demonstrated in the remainder of this chapter; attention is concentrated on the second use specifically as it contributes to the development of the third.

Illustration

Let us consider an actual case illustration of these uses to indicate areas of potential analytic development. Research of Fred W. Riggs provides the material for this example.[3] Riggs presents Thai politics as centered in the cabinet: the "apex of bureaucratic authority" and the "core of the elite." Political activity and opposition are defined in terms of rivalry for position in that major arena. Outcomes are determined by control over the three "arms of the bureaucracy," the nobility, the civilian, and the military sectors. Rivalry occurs by means of "coup groups," cliques, and factions in a process of "overturns," "realignments," "readjustments," and "consolidations." The process is essentially independent of ideology or issues, and the primary motivating factor is economic. Officials obtain lucrative positions in firms by easing legal restrictions on Chinese participants in the system of "pariah entrepreneurship." Public corporations are also sponsored and controlled by officials.

Before 1932, bureaucrats were subject to the crown; since then, they have engaged in a nearly constant shifting of alliances and dominance, apparently

---

[3] *Thailand: The Modernization of a Bureaucratic Polity* (Honolulu: East-West Center Press, 1966), particularly Chapter VIII. This illustration is not truly analytic because my knowledge of Thai politics is not extensive. However, the illustration indicates the recommended style of analysis.

without attaining any stable ordering. The actual "play" of this system is summarized in Table 7–1.[4]

TABLE 7–1.   THE "PLAY" OF THE THAI SYSTEM, 1932–63[a]

To 1932	N	1944	MBn	1951	M
1932	MB	1946	B	1955	B
1933	Bn	1947	M	1957	M
1933	Mn	1948	M	1957	M
1934	MB	1948	MB	1958	Mn
1938	M	1951	MB	1963	Mn

[a]N = Nobility; M = Military; B = Civilian bureaucracy.

This whole system may be thought of as, and the language of Riggs's description may be translated in terms of, a partially ordered set. The three bureaucratic "arms" are ordered subsets, and the participants are "incomparables" outside their own orderings. Competition may be analyzed in terms of the nature of the relations within subsets and the manner in which conflicts among incomparables occur and are dealt with.

Let P be the governmental system, containing subsets ordered by relations something like N = "Has as high or higher title than," M = [the same for rank], B = [the same for position] (variations on the theme of superiority). Before 1932, the monarch was either the head of a subset (say, for any nobleman x, monarch Nx) or was dominant over it by a superimposed superiority scale (say, for any bureaucrat b, monarch Rb, where R = "can order the demise of"). Since 1932, there has been no such single member of the set P, and the result has been competition for rule with the outcomes shown in Table 7–1.

There are several plausible reasons for this pattern. The subjection of all three subsets to the crown before 1932, none having a sense of "rule" and all having similar duties, resulted in fairly ready *comparability* of order relations *across* subsets. That is, the ordering relations N, M, and B were similar, facilitating the formation of cohesive opposition patterns among members of different subsets. Cabinet positions were limited to a number generally less than the number of contenders in any one ordering, leading to a pattern of disenchanted participants in successful coups who were willing to join forces with another group. These stimuli toward cross-subset alliances were given substance by a rough split *within* subsets between older and junior elites who were not really split along the traditional–modern continuum, but who were apparently motivated by the prospect of monetary gain. Although the military nearly became a "dominant" subset after World War II, the coup syndrome continued largely as a result of cross-subset alliances, which were bolstered by consideration for the crown and the number of viable contenders in a given ordering.

[4] This information was presented in a seminar on Southeast Asian Politics, by Robert O. Tilman, Yale University, 1968.

Thus, a system of struggle up through ranks and across different rankings, motivated by the prospect of substantial monetary gains, was facilitated by structural features of the system.

This is just an outline, but I think it is an important type of outline: a structural sketch. It indicates basic features at the center of the delimited political system. The mode of description contributes to the analysis and explanation of these features. Certain points of this analytic style appear even in this brief example, and others may be developed from it.

Extension

We begin with a description of the *structure,* defined as "patterned activity in the real world," focusing on actual arrangements of activities, rather than institutional ideal types.[5] In the Thai example, the basic structure consists of the three similarly ranked subsets converging toward a ruling cabinet. A more detailed study might describe idiosyncracies of the rankings, such as elite splits within subsets, breakdowns in the ranking relations, problems of boundary definition, and the like. The result is a state description of the poset, a delimited account that sets off explicitly political roles and activities from more diffuse sociocultural aspects of a system. For instance, the state description does not consider broad notions such as political culture. Analogously, one might call this a study of a political system's "skeleton," which might be supplemented with an analysis of the "nerves" of government and fleshed out with references to the "body" politic.

Structural description need not imply static analysis and/or deficient explanation. A feature of partial order analysis is the study of the relations already defined as "incomparable," an important feature of the Thai example. Within the poset structure, many of the Thai role-actor elements dealt with others not ranked in the same subset. These relations, such as cross-subset coup alliances and cabinet coalitions, are the "incomparable" relations of set description.

Incomparability does *not* imply incompatibility in the sense of inability to interact or to analyze such interactions. Simply, it means that because two elements do not belong to the same ranked subset of a system, there are no immediate guidelines as to relative superiority. Interaction is largely unstructured, which allows for, and even requires, innovation. Innovation occurs in a context defined by patterned behavior called structure, but is not solely a result of this pattern; more accurately, it is the resolution of a situation not defined by structure. This distinction seems to provide one way out of the common staticity criticism leveled at structure-function analysis, as related by Karl Hempel in

---

[5] This usage is meant to be related to early "structural-functional" terminology. See Marion Levy, "Some Aspects of 'Structure-Functional Analysis' and Political Science," in Roland Young, ed., *Approaches to the Study of Politics* (Evanston, Ill.: Northwestern University Press, 1958), pp. 52–66.

"The Logic of Functional Analysis." [6] Innovation in the settlement of incomparabilities provides a way to alter system structure.

A gaming model further illustrates the key concepts of our example. Using a "board," as in Figure 7–2, players could compete initially (according to any

FIGURE 7–2. STRUCTURE REPRESENTED AS GAMING BOARD

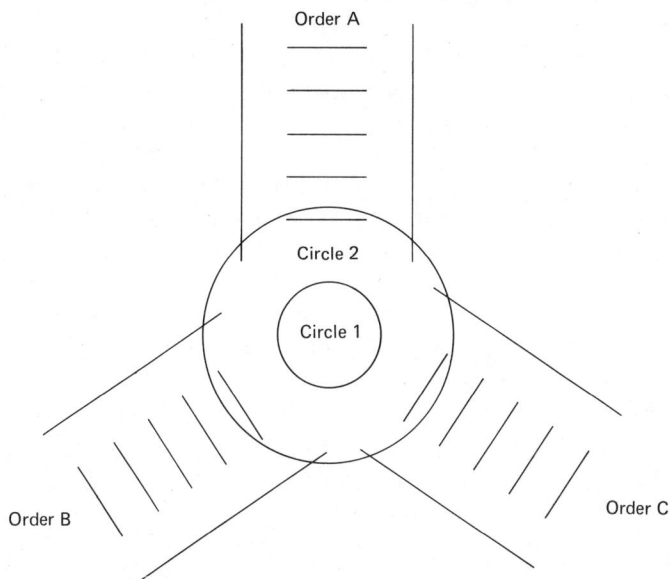

convenient procedure, say checker games, dice throws, or arm wrestling) to establish rankings. The top players in each order occupy Circle 2. Circle 1 would eventually be limited to a small number, but is left open initially. After this initial period, play proceeds in terms of challenges within orders and concentrates on broadly defined competition among players for occupation of Circle 1. Competition includes challenges, bargains, and trades; a point system is established to reward players according to their positions at the end of given periods; and major rewards go to occupants of Circle 1.

This sort of model illustrates a working system. It provides structure (board and rules) and incentive (points or money) and requires innovation. Early play provides feedback to the experiment and helps to specify the model. The model acts as an analog of a studied system and, in this case, aids in understanding possible solutions to incomparability relations among the Thai elite.

Coups, depositions, deaths, and their aftermaths provide particularly important information about systems and their structure. The coup syndrome in

[6] In L. Gross, ed., *Symposium on Sociological Theory* (New York: Harper Bros., 1959).

Thailand has been described as a structural trait, but the 1932 overthrow was something else: a system change. This discontinuity signaled the end of one structural form and the beginning of another. Alternatively, it began a "succession crisis," an important phase common to many systems (discussed in a later section).

The overthrow of a system is the ultimate form of incomparability resolution. Assuming it was not external in origin, it denotes structural weaknesses in the overthrown system, such as insufficient support for a ranking scheme. Consideration of overthrows as incomparability resolutions leads to crucial questions of *power*.

While the concept of power is fundamental, its definition and usage often present difficulties. In discussing superiority relations, "power" has not been used as an example. Using it to rank a subset would be far too limiting. "Power" is not a unidimensional concept, it is a conglomerate, derived from a variety of sources. For instance, a military man has a degree of power based solely upon his rank. He may supplement it with skill in bargaining, by amassing a following, or by cultivating friendships among superiors. If we describe a system as a poset with several rankings converging at the top, as in the Thai case, then the top elite will all have "structural power" based on their positions, and competition will tend to rest more on other sources. "Power" is difficult to define because it is that quantity by which, or scale on which, we try to compare the incomparables and to order the partially ordered.

A COMPARATIVE EXAMPLE: SOVIET-TYPE SYSTEMS

Let us consider aspects of partial order analysis to characterize Soviet-type systems, once again using our example to clarify and develop the technique.

System Characterization

The Soviet Union might be considered a "model" political system for this type of analysis. The system is hierarchically ordered and centralized, yet it contains several subsets that participate actively in the governmental process. The central political structure may be described as a poset consisting of subsets that merge toward the top in interlocking directorate fashion. One subset, the party, generally dominates in settling incomparability relations. Since this structure asserts control over the entire system, largely by controlling the sources of coercion, communications, socialization, and economics, one's attention is directed within the structure to find basic features of system operation, change, competition, and opposition. Here *opposition* is defined in terms of internal ordering procedures found at the upper levels of a system. Primarily this involves competition for overall power, in marked contrast to common definitions of opposition used for the "Western democratic" model, where distinctions are made between *the* opposition and *the* government.[7]

System Specification

To study the Soviet poset, one first describes the subsets and their mutual relations in the system. This description is done commonly, but is elaborated in different terminology.[8] Simply put, the major subsets are party, state administration, military, and police. "Lesser" subsets, such as youth organization, may under certain conditions also be relevant.

These converge as stated. Many individual elements belong to several subsets, thus increasing comparability in the orderings, but decreasing it at the top, where competition for power must be studied primarily in terms of incomparability relations.

In the second step, one describes and analyzes activity *within* the structural framework. There, while seeking to maintain the appearance of unity, competition for power and the right to set policy are intertwined, a fact causing conceptual problems for some authors who struggle to make distinctions between a "pure ideologist" and a "pure ambitionist." [9]

A Structural Treatment of System Behavior: "Succession Crises"

This competition and the incomparability relations involved become most visible in Soviet-type systems during "succession crises." During periods of Soviet leadership instability engendered by death or overthrow, many forms of incomparability resolutions become manifest. For example, Stalin used his position in the Secretariat in the 1920's as a structural power base and augmented his power by shifting between "left" and "right" ideological groups until he finally achieved personal dominance over the entire system. The process culminated in the physical elimination of possible sources of opposition.

The study of ordering procedures during succession crises is marked by several important features.

1. The ordering relations specific to the preceding period's configuration and which were dependent upon operative leadership are no longer in effect.
2. Certain more general systemic relations persist and set boundaries upon possible modes of competitive behavior.

[7] A major work in this topic is Robert A. Dahl, ed., *Political Oppositions in Western Democracies* (New Haven: Yale University Press, 1966).

[8] An excellent example of this for the full range of Soviet systems is found in Ghita Ionescu, *The Politics of the European Communist States* (New York: Praeger, 1967). Substituting *subset* for *apparat* and *poset for Apparat* results in a description nearly isomorphic to that used here.

[9] See for example, Z. Brzezinski and S. P. Huntington, *Political Power: USA/USSR* (New York: Viking, 1964), Chapter 4; and Robert Conquest, *Power and Policy in the USSR* (New York: St. Martin's Press, 1961), Chapter 2.

3. New relations result from the resolution of incomparabilities as various procedures are used to attain a new stable ordering and to achieve a favorable position within it.

Study is aided by three contrasting analyses: of the past ordering devices, of new procedures of competition, and of general ordering principles which persist over time or develop as a result of a new struggle. The final analysis is important for it concerns generalized system effects and systemic change. When such systemic change defines more clearly the patterned relations of the system and delineates more explicitly the "rules of the game," it then may be referred to as "political development," as defined by Almond and Powell, i.e., "differentiation" of the system and "secularization" of the behavior patterns.[10]

To clarify these points further, consider the Soviet succession crisis that followed Stalin's death. Because of his personal style of system control, Stalin allowed no other individual to gain any significant prominence, thereby weakening the dominance of the party subset. At his death various subsets were much more "equal" than in other eras, and there were no clear leaders. The succession struggle that resulted was not only among individuals, but among subsets as well, and so had major effects upon the entire structure. To maintain sufficient legitimacy to rule, this struggle was symbolically camouflaged by appeals for unity from the top elite. Thus, even more than usual the distinction between government and opposition was blurred. The contenders were all in "opposition," but together formed the "government."

The secret police presented a special problem for this group of successors, as Stalin had used that subset heavily to maintain control of the elite. The first "solution" in the ordering problem may well be said to be the execution of L. Beria, the chief of police. This action opened up the possibility for a general ordering principle with far-reaching implications—the abnegation of physical violence among the participants.

The ordering struggle shaped into a rough split between party and state administration subsets, with Khrushchev and Malenkov as major contenders. Beginning in 1953 in a position inferior to Malenkov's, Khrushchev slowly expanded his power position, but did not gain control until the defeat of the so-called "antiparty group" in 1957. This final victory may have come with only minority support in the Presidium, making him "the most successful oppositionist in the history of the Soviet Union." [11]

This specific mode of victory "symbolized the ascendency of the Party bureaucracy in quintessential form," [12] since it was based on strength in the Central Committee which had been gained by party appointments and was couched in terms of "antiparty" defeat. The party subset thus became truly

[10] Op. cit.
[11] F. C. Barghoorn, "Soviet Political Doctrine and the Problem of Opposition," Bucknell Review, Vol. 12, No. 2 (May 1964), p. 19.
[12] Merle Fainsod, How Russia Is Ruled (Cambridge, Mass.: Harvard University Press, 1963), Chapter 5, p. 175.

"dominant," a term we may now define: one subset is *dominant* in a poset if its members can control the *internal* ordering of the other subsets. (An alternative definition of dominance might be put in terms of the regulation of outputs of other subsets.)

Khrushchev's fall in 1964 severely curtailed the possibilities for personal rule reemerging as the basic ordering. The stability of "collective leadership," much touted in past rhetoric, seemed to have become the new ordering principle. The continued abnegation of physical violence among the elite, personified in Khrushchev's peaceful *dacha* existence after his demise, has also become a stable principle of ordering relations.

ALTERNATIVE APPLICATIONS

So far, we have been developing a way to study political systems characterized as partially ordered sets. The examples used have been systems best described as hierarchically organized. There are other systems which would be better described in other ways: a notable example is the "Western democratic party system." Yet all political systems have certain common features that can be directly treated with the analytic technique developed in this chapter. Four such applications are suggested:

1. The study of whole systems in set-descriptive terms followed by comparison of these descriptions.
2. The study of specific subsets, comparing them across systems.
3. The development of general comparative distinctions based upon such studies.
4. The development of an analytical language based in set theory.

Detailing these applications is beyond the scope of this chapter, although partial elaboration and evaluation are useful.

Whole Systems

The analysis of specific systems has already been discussed with respect to two systems, and an overall analytical pattern may now be suggested as a paradigm for the study of hierarchically organized systems as posets:

1. Identify the major subsets.
2. Study the patterns of action within them to identify the ranking scheme for each. Usually this would mean asking oneself: What is the basis for superiority? Try to distinguish the actual from the nominal.
3. Describe the manner in which subsets interact. Is there overlapping membership? Are any subsets dominant over others?
4. Study the activities and memberships at the top of the subsets. How do these top members relate across subsets? What systematization of incomparability relations exists? What happens at times of succession?

The result of these basic steps would be a "state description" of the poset. This may then be analyzed in motivational terms, and activities may be explained in dynamic terms. Detailed structural analysis of the poset leads to a more complete usage of set description as language which in turn has beneficial consequences, some of which will now be considered.

Specific Subsets

Certain subsets are common to most political systems, e.g., parties, bureaucracies, military. These might themselves be analyzed comparatively across systems, a common endeavor, as with the comparative study of bureaucracy. An ordering question for this comparison might be: What relations do such subsets usually have to the entire system as poset?

The most problematic subset with respect to this question is probably the party.[13] All parties seem to have certain common features, often described in functional terms such as "interest aggregation." These terms indicate that parties have much to do with the boundary between the political system proper and its social setting. But parties also play an active, often central, part in the bounded political system itself. This characteristic has been described in set terms. Unlike any other subset, a particular party ranking may in some systems "drop out" of the poset and later, perhaps, "reappear." That is, some parties *alternate* with others as "members" of the poset. This unique feature, coupled with the possibility that parties may be dominant subsets, could form a basis for general comparative distinctions.

General Comparison

The development of general structural distinctions across systems is a third application. Efforts could be directed toward relieving the confusion evident in various nomenclatures of "party systems." Primarily, it is essential to delineate party systems and systems that contain parties.

A political system, or poset, may have an alternating subset. This may be defined either as two or more rankings which may exchange with each other one position in the central poset according to some rule of alteration or as a "composite" subset, composed of parts, with an internal ordering rule that specifies some means for possible alternation of its leadership. Alternatively, the system may have only subsets which do not alternate, with the poset clearly defined as the juxtaposition of these subsets.

For any system we may think of a governing or controlling part which "motivates" the whole system. This would be clearly identifiable, for instance, if

---

[13] The articles contained in Section V of H. Eckstein and David E. Apter, eds., *Comparative Politics* (New York: The Free Press, 1968), illustrate many of the difficulties.

one subset were dominant. A system is a *party system* if and only if its governing part is an alternating subset. A system whose governing part is not an alternating subset may be governed either by a single, stable, dominant subset, or by alternation *among* subsets. Ionescu's usage is appropriate for the former, calling it an *Apparat* system, rather than the more common—and confusing—"one-party state." The latter type has no single dominant subset over time, as in the Thai example. We might give such a system the name *multifaceted hierarchy*.

Opposition may now be defined generally for all political systems as the struggle to control the governing part of a system.

1. In party systems, opposition occurs within the alternating subset according to its rules of ordering.
2. In Apparat systems, opposition must occur within the dominant subset. This is sometimes called "factional" opposition.
3. In multifaceted hierarchies, opposition is diffused throughout the poset. The struggle for governing control may occur among subsets, among parts of subsets, and within subsets.

An Analytic Language

Finally, it may be possible that set-theoretic descriptions can be generalized into a systematic method of study.

Partial order is a widespread de facto form of organization for human activity; the scope of application of such methodology should be great. Present usage may have been insufficiently precise by attempting to convey a sense of that scope. Starting at the whole system level to develop terminology into a precise formal language may not be an optimal strategy. A better procedure might be to concentrate on the detailed structural mapping of activities on a smaller scale, studying feedback loops, bottlenecks, short-cuts, boundary maintenance, and so forth. This in turn could lead to the analyses of system control and change and to the exploitation of theoretical insights developed in the field of cybernetics.

Starting small might facilitate the construction of formal simulation models. The greater the degree of isomorphism with actual systems, the more the analysis and manipulation of these models will reveal about actual and possible system behavior. Furthermore, initial conditions and operating parameters may be altered to simulate different environments to enable, for instance, the cross-cultural study of development alternatives.

THE PROMISE

As complicated as much of this sounds, the underlying motivation and rationale stem from the desire to simplify and delimit the technique. The language of set ordering satisfies the need for a way to study, describe, and explain fundamental modes of organization and behavior in political systems. The language enables consistent usage to replace the constant invention of analogical descriptions. The main point and the basic concept are simple and commonly applicable in areas of interest central to political science.

Part IV

Projections

INTRODUCTION

To anticipate and manage the future intelligently are desirable goals directly confounded by the complexity of most social systems. Simply extrapolating trends in complex systems may be an effective projective technique as long as system inertia is large, the number of relevant elements taken into consideration is small, the interconnections between elements are few and understood, and no untoward exogeneous or structural changes perturb the context. If any one of these contingencies does not hold, extrapolation may be quite impossible or at best may yield highly misleading information. In any case, alternative projective methods may be required; simulations, games, process models, scenario writing, group judgment techniques, planning, utopia writing, developmental constructs, and several others come to mind and should be noted in the survey of the literature.

The relationship of projection to the other aspects of the problem-solving approach is easily seen with respect to understanding conditioning factors. If the problems of political and social change are such as to violate all or nearly all of the contingencies for doing extrapolations, then the need to develop adequate scientific models and explanations of system behavior is underscored. Moreover, the prediction of future events, rather than the "postdiction" of past events, is still the preferred means of testing a theory or model, in spite of the fact that it is seldom done in the social sciences. Scientific control presumes a strong parallel interest in the identification, collection, management, and retrieval of data. Model-building and data collection are important areas that we shall identify with relevant literature.

Projection and goals are related most simply in the specification of desired and desirable future states for a given context. Planners are specialists who are charged with this task in many societies. We find, in fact, that a large portion of the projective literature has been produced by planners (including assorted "utopians") of one variety or another.

Policymaking implies that alternative versions of the future are, if even at some crude level, known. Making choices implies that valued future outcomes of one sort are preferred to others. A policy is necessarily a choice among alternative futures. To specify an alternative is to select one course and to foreclose on other, competing futures.

In a real sense, projection has been a critical missing ingredient in the study of political development and change. We are hard pressed to name research efforts or literature that set out specifically to forecast or project political events in a development setting. Indeed, projection specialists, when they can be found, are generally regarded as deviant and unorthodox by their more narrowly disposed and "serious" colleagues. Projection is a dead serious business and deserves neither scorn nor ignorance. We cite extensively from literature that appears to be, but in fact is not, far afield to encourage interest in this, the least developed orientation of all.

THE LITERATURE

There is no easy way to categorize the literature; however, we find it useful to separate general works *about* forecasting from those that are in fact political, economic, demographic, or technological projections. Much work on data control and social accounting has a distinctly projective bias; we note several prominent cases. We conclude by taking up the largest class of publications that deals with projective methods and includes works about extrapolations, model-building, data specification and control, group judgment techniques, planning, and other research methods.

General Works about Forecasting

This section is subdivided into literature that is truly general, that which is general and deals with political events, that which has a normative cast, and that which has a scientific and technological orientation.

Three excellent *overview* articles are well worth reading, regardless of one's interest or disciplinary specialization. We recommend highly, Otis Dudley Duncan, "Social Forecasting—The State of the Art," *The Public Interest,* Vol. 17 (Fall 1969), pp. 88–118; Daniel Bell, "Twelve Modes of Prediction—A Preliminary Sorting of Approaches in the Social Sciences," *Daedalus,* Vol. 93 (Summer 1964), pp. 845–80; and *idem,* "The Study of the Future," *The Public Interest,* Vol. 1 (Fall 1965), pp. 119–30. In a slightly different vein, see Bertrand de Jouvenel, *The Art of Conjecture* (New York: Basic Books, 1967), pp. 3–56; Herman Kahn and A. J. Wiener, *The Year 2000: A Framework for Speculation on the Next Thirty-Three Years* (New York: Macmillan, 1967), pp. 1–65; and H. D. Lasswell, "The Configurative Analysis of World Value Pyramids," in his *World Politics and Personal Insecurity* (New York: The Free Press, 1965 ed.), for valuable, somewhat personalized concepts and procedures for forecasting.

Several other general works that emphasize the uses and limitations of speculation about the future include Dennis Gabor, *Inventing the Future* (New York: Knopf, 1964 ed.); Geoffrey Vickers, "The Uses of Speculation," *Journal of the American Institute of Planners,* Vol. 34 (January 1968), pp. 2–10; S. Lilley, "Can Prediction Become a Science?" in B. Barber and W. Hirsch, eds., *The Sociology of Science* (New York: The Free Press, 1962); and "The Nature and Limitations of Forecasting," *Daedalus,* Vol. 96 (Summer 1967), pp.. 937–47.

General work about *political forecasting* is relatively rare, although Lasswell has been a consistent and articulate spokesman: H. D. Lasswell, *The Future of Political Science* (New York: Atherton, 1962); *idem,* "The Future of the Comparative Method," *Comparative Politics,* Vol. 1 (October 1968), pp. 8–13; *idem,* "The World Revolution of Our Time: A Framework for Basic Policy Research," in H. D. Lasswell and Daniel Lerner, eds., *World Revolutionary Elites* (Cambridge, Mass.: The MIT Press, 1966 ed.), pp. 29–96; and Lasswell, "The Political Science of Science," *American Political Science Review,* Vol. 50 (December 1956), pp. 961–79.

De Jouvenel has mounted a similar one-man campaign to capture political scientists' attention to take forecasting seriously. Bertrand de Jouvenel, "The Political Order and Foreseeability," in his *The Art of Conjecture,* pp. 237–50; *idem,* "Political Science and Prevision," *American Political Science Review,* Vol. 59 (March 1965), pp. 29–38.

Concern for integrating forecasting and forecasters into ongoing policy processes is evident throughout Lasswell's and de Jouvenel's works. It is treated primarily by Edward Shils, "The Intellectuals and the Future," *Bulletin of the Atomic Scientists*, Vol. 23, No. 8 (October 1967), pp. 7–14; H. Kahn and A. J. Wiener, "Policy Research and Social Change," in *The Year 2000,* pp. 386–413; and Benjamin Akzin, "On Conjecture in Political Science," *Political Studies,* Vol. 14 (February 1960), pp. 1–14.

General works of a distinctly *normative* cast include P. Teilhard de Chardin, *The Future of Man* (New York: Harper & Row, 1965); Kenneth E. Boulding, *The Image* (Ann Arbor, Mich.: Ann Arbor Paperbacks, 1961 ed.); and Karl Jaspars, *The Future of Mankind* (Chicago: University of Chicago Press, 1963). A normative forecast of technology's uncontrolled diffusion is Jacques Ellul, *The Technological Society,* trans. John Wilkinson (New York: Knopf, 1964).

Other general works that have a *technological* orientation include Arthur C. Clarke, *Profiles of the Future* (New York: Harper & Row, 1964); Robert Jungk and Y. Galtung, eds., *Mankind 2000* (Oslo, Norway: Norwegian Universities Press, 1968); and an excellent theoretical work on how technologies (and other innovations) are introduced and diffuse, Everrett Rogers, *Diffusion of Innovation* (New York: The Free Press, 1962).

Political Forecasts

Political forecasts are divisible into overview and philosophical-speculative works, international relations forecasts, American forecasts, and finally, development studies including general works on planning and specific projections for various contexts.

H. D. Lasswell, "The Shape of the Future," *American Behavioral Scientist,* Vol. 8 (May 1965), p. 3, is a concise treatment of why political forecasts should be made and how one might go about doing it. Herman Kahn and A. J. Wiener, *The Year 2000,* pp. 66–247; B. de Jouvenel, "Political Science and Prevision"; Yehezkel Dror, *Future in Government* (Santa Monica, Cal.: The Rand Corporation, P–3909, 1968); Frank S. Hopkins, "Looking Ahead to the Year 2001," *American Foreign Service Journal* (January 1969); John H. Herz, "The Territorial State Revisited: Reflections on the Future of the Nation-State," *Polity,* Vol. 1 (Fall 1968), pp. 11–34; T. W. Arnold et al., *The Future of Democratic Capitalism* (New York: A. S. Barnes, 1961); and Michael Maddison, "The Case Against Tomorrow," *The Political Quarterly,* Vol. 36 (April 1965), pp. 214–27, all talk about political forecasting with varying emphases and with a wide variation in guiding purposes and quality of thought. Two interesting studies of communication and politics are noted to show just how diverse the field is: Marshall McLuhan, *Understanding Media: The Extensions of Man* (New York: McGraw-Hill, 1964); and R. Gordon Kelly, "Ideology in Some Modern Science Fiction Novels," *Journal of Popular Culture,* Vol. 2 (Fall 1968), pp. 211–27.

International relations has been a fertile area for political speculation. Especially worthy of the reader's serious attention are Karl W. Deutsch, "The Future of World Politics," *Political Quarterly,* Vol. 37, No. 1 (January 1966), pp. 9–32; H. D. Lasswell, *World Politics and Personal Insecurity* (New York: The Free Press, 1962); K. W. Deutsch, "Toward an Inventory of Basic Trends and Patterns in Comparative and International Politics," *American Political Science Review,* Vol. 54 (March 1960), pp. 34–57; and H. Kahn and A. J. Wiener, *The Year 2000;* other related works of varying scope and quality include Foreign Policy Association, *Toward the Year 2018* (New York: Cowles Education Corp., 1968); Bruce M. Russett, "The Ecology of Future International Politics," *International Studies Quarterly,* Vol. 11 (March 1967), pp. 12–31; B. M. Russett, "Is There a Long-Run Trend Towards Concentration in the International System?" *Comparative Political Studies,* Vol. 1 (April 1968), pp. 103–22; and Nigel Calder, ed., *The World in 1984* (Baltimore, Md.; Penguin, 2 vols., 1965).

For some concrete examples of international relations projections whose projected contexts have already passed into history, see H. D. Lasswell, "Sino-

Japanese Crisis: The Garrison State versus the Civilian State," *China Quarterly,* Vol. 3 (Fall 1937), pp. 643–49; for a self-evaluation of the "Garrison State" forecast, *idem,* "The Garrison State Hypothesis Today," in Samuel P. Huntington, ed., *Changing Patterns of Military Politics* (New York: The Free Press, 1962); N. V. Carlisle and F. B. Latham, *Miracles Ahead—Better Living in the Post-War World* (New York: Macmillan, 1944); I. F. Clarke, *Voices Prophesying War, 1763–1984* (London: Oxford University Press, 1960); and L. P. Bloomfield, "Future Small Wars: Must the United States Intervene?" *Orbis,* Vol. 12 (Fall 1968), pp. 669–84.

Europe has been one region whose future has provided interest to political forecasters. Christoph Bertram, "Models of Western Europe in the 1970's: The Alternative Choices," *Futures,* Vol. 1 (December 1968), pp. 142–52; L. P. Bloomfield, "Western Europe to the Mid-Seventies: Five Scenarios" (Cambridge, Mass.: MIT/CIS, A/68-3, 1968), combines scenario writing and free-form gaming to develop insights about European developments; Curt Gasteyger, "Europe in the Seventies," *Atlantic Community Quarterly,* Vol. 5 (Fall 1967), pp. 317–35; Karl Jaspers, *The Future of Germany,* trans. and ed., E. G. Ashton (Chicago: University of Chicago Press, 1967); and Ronald Brech, "Britain 1984: An Experiment in the Economic History of the Future," *Humanities* (1966) have clearly specified expectations about what events will hold in the near-term future. The future relationships between the United States and the Soviet Union are found in Daniel Bell, "Ten Theories in Search of Reality: The Prediction of Soviet Behavior," in his *The End of Ideology* (New York: The Free Press, 1960); G. Paloczi-Horvath, *The Facts Rebel: The Future of Russia and the West* (London: Secker and Warburg, 1964); George Rathjens, *The Future of the Strategic Arms Race; Options for the 1970s* (New York: Carnegie Endowment for International Peace, 1969); Ernest B. Haas, *Collective Security and the Future International System* (Denver, Colo.: University of Denver Press, 1968); and K. W. Deutsch, "Outer Space and International Problems: A Look to 1988," in J. M. Goldsen, ed., *Outer Space in World Politics* (New York: Praeger, 1963).

Forecasts about the American political system are not so numerous, although Rexford G. Tugwell, "U.S.A. 2000 A.D.," *The Center Magazine,* Vol. 1 (November 1968), pp. 23–33; Robert Theobald, ed., *Social Policies for America in the Seventies: Nine Different Views* (New York: Doubleday, 1968); and R. L. Heilbroner, *The Future as History* (New York: Grove, 1959), all attack the subject with imagination and a general lack of inhibition. All three of these works are worth summary perusal to indicate how interesting a good projection can in fact be. Two more conventional accounts having a projective orientation are Todd R. LaPorte, "Politics and 'Inventing the Future': Perspectives in Science and Government," *Public Administration Review,* Vol. 27 (June 1967), pp. 117–27; and Anthony Downs, "Alternative Futures for the American Ghetto," *Daedalus,* Vol. 97 (Fall 1968), pp. 1331–78. Two technically oriented political forecasts are Arnold B. Burack, *U.S.A. and Its*

Economic Future (New York: Macmillan, 1964); and U.S. Congress, House, *Technological Trends and National Policy,* Report by the Subcommittee on Technology, Committee on National Resources, House Documents, Vol. 18, No. 360, 75th Cong., 1st sess., 1937.

Development studies run the gamut from theoretical efforts to explain the underlying events responsible for projected behavior to case studies about planning techniques in a given country for a specified period of time. Samuel P. Huntington's excellent "Political Development and Political Decay," *World Politics,* Vol. 17 (April 1965), pp. 386–430; and H. D. Lasswell, "Implications of Technological Change for Southeast Asian Administrative Systems in the Next Two Decades," *SEADAG Occasional Papers* (New York: The Asia Society, 1971), both treat theoretical matters relative to projected future states. Huntington's concern is with "negative" development, or undesirable futures, and Lasswell discusses, using a comprehensive theoretical construct, what technological factors will play a role in the future of the Southeast Asian region.

Other generally useful projective efforts concerned with development and change are United Nations, Department of Economic and Social Affairs, *Studies in Long-Term Projections for the World Economy* (E/3842, ST/ECA/80, 1964); United Nations, Department of Social Affairs, Statistical Office Population Division, *Determinants and Consequences of Population Trends* (Population Studies #17), 1953; Organization for Economic Cooperation and Development (OECD), *Employment Forecasting* (OECD, Seminar on Employment Forecasting Techniques), 1963; and H. W. Eldridge, "Futurism in Planning for Developing Countries," *Journal of the American Institute of Planners,* Vol. 34 (November 1968), pp. 382–84.

Other general pieces on planning for change include Edward S. Mason, *Economic Planning in Underdeveloped Areas: Government and Business* (New York: Fordham University Press, 1958); Everett E. Hagen, *Planning Economic Development* (Homewood, Ill.: Richard D. Irwin, 1963); and Gustav F. Papanek, "Framing a Development Program," *International Conciliation,* No. 527 (March 1960), pp. 307–72.

European examples of forecasting and planning include The French Institute of Public Opinion, "The Year 2000: The Family in France," *Ekistics,* Vol. 25 (April 1968), pp. 264–65; John Hackett and Anne-Marie Hackett, *Economic Planning in France* (Cambridge, Mass.: Harvard University Press, 1963); and Leon Lervins, "The Polish Economy: The Problems and Prospects," *Problems of Communism,* Vol. 7 (May–June 1958), pp. 14–23.

Latin American examples of forecasting and planning include E. P. Holland and R. W. Gillespie, *Experiments on a Simulated Underdeveloped Economy* [Venezuela], Part III (Cambridge, Mass.: The M.I.T. Press, 1963); and Louis J. Ducoff, *Human Resources of Central America, Panama and Mexico, 1950–1980, in Relation to Some Aspects of Economic Development* (ECLA, XIII. 1), 1960.

Asian examples are represented by these works: Han Suyin, *China in the*

Year 2001 (New York: Basic Books, 1967); Ronald Hsia, *Economic Planning in Communist China* (New York: Institute of Pacific Relations, 1955); Mahub Ul-Haq, "Planned Capital Formation in an Underdeveloped Economy: The Case of Pakistan" (Unpublished Ph.D. dissertation, Yale University, 1958); and Clifford Geertz's fine work, *Agricultural Involution: The Processes of Ecological Change in Indonesia* (Berkeley: University of California Press, 1963).

Other Social Forecasts in a Development Setting: Economics, Demography, and Technology

The literature in these three areas is quite large; however, it is important to sample selectively from it to indicate some high-quality work and to introduce the reader to different, more "off-beat" sources. A perspective of development and change is nonetheless a common attribute of each selection.

Economic forecasts have characteristically benefited from sparse, but acceptable, to copious and excellent data. Regardless of data quantity and quality, serious problems remain. On the organization and control of data (a key concern and major theme of this volume), Wassily Leontieff, "The Structure of Development," *Scientific American,* Vol. 209 (September 1963), pp. 148–66, is absolutely required reading.

Various attempts have been made to manipulate and predict from economic data bases using an assortment of techniques. Large-scale model-building is one such approach. Lawrence Klein et al., *The Brookings Quarterly Econometric Model of the United States* (Chicago: Rand McNally, 1965); G. Fromm and P. Taubman, *Policy Simulations with an Econometric Model* (Washington, D.C.: The Brookings Institution, 1968); Daniel Suits, "Forecasting and Analysis with an Econometric Model," *American Economic Review,* Vol. 52 (March 1962), pp. 104–32; and Guy H. Orcutt, Martin Greenberger, John Korbel, and Alice Rivlin, *Microanalysis of Socioeconomic Systems: A Simulation Study* (New York: Harper Bros., 1961), all with varying degrees of pretense and success attempt to project economic data using rather large-scale analytic models. These and other projects are evaluated by H. O. Stekler, "Forecasting with Econometric Models: An Evaluation," *Econometrica,* Vol. 36 (July-October 1968), pp. 437–63. Another excellent example of an economic forecast and an ex post facto evaluation is contained in Colin B. Clark, *The Economics of 1960* (London: Macmillan, 1942); and the evaluation by K. C. Kogiku, "The Economics of 1960 Revisited," *Review of Economics and Statistics,* Vol. 42, No. 4 (November 1960), pp. 398–407 where (on p. 407) he pointed out what appears to be a common characteristic weakness of economic forecasts: "The main difficulty seems to be that Clark's model is static; its structural equations do not contain time, and theoretically his model is to hold at any point in time as well as in 1960. . . . His static model does not accommodate such dynamics of growth." In this same vein is J. M. Keynes, "Economic Possibilities for Our Grandchildren," in his *Essays in Persuasion* (London:

Macmillan, 1933); and H. J. Levin, "Public Prediction in Theory and Fact," *Scottish Economic Journal,* Vol. 24 (January 1958), pp. 338–52.

Demographers, because their data are measurable with some fidelity and are relatively stable over periods of time, one might imagine, do highly accurate forecasts. Such is not the case, however. Any student of development and change does well to learn about demographic forecasting in some detail. A good starting place is L. J. Reed, "Population Growth and Forecasts," *The Annals of the American Academy of Political and Social Science,* Vol. 188 (November 1936), pp. 159–66; Stuart Mudd, ed., *The Population Crises and the Use of World Resources* (Bloomington, Ind.: Indiana University Press, 1964); E. J. Russell, *World Population and World Food Supplies* (London: Allen and Unwin, 1954); Food and Agricultural Organization, "Six Billions to Feed" (FAO *World Food Problems,* no. 5), 1962; J. Mayer, "Food and Population: The Wrong Problem," *Daedalus,* Vol. 93 (Summer 1964), pp. 830–44; and Philip Hauser, "Demographic Indicators of Economic Development," *Economic Development and Cultural Change,* Vol. 7 (January 1959), pp. 98–116.

The literature on family planning is relevant here. As public interest and the number of resultant programs increase in this area, more accurate and timely forecasts will be much in demand to measure and evaluate the outcomes of policy intervention. Ronald Freedman et al., *Family Planning, Sterility and Population Growth* (New York: McGraw-Hill, 1959); Bernard Berelson, ed., *Family Planning and Population Programs* (Chicago: University of Chicago Press, 1966); Hudson Hoagland, "Mechanisms of Population Control," *Daedalus,* Vol. 93 (Summer 1964), pp. 812–29; and S. Chandrasekhar, "The Prospect for Planned Parenthood in India," *Pacific Affairs,* Vol. 26 (1953), pp. 318–28, all treat the subject explicitly and demonstrate a heavy projective bias in their descriptions.

Measurement concerns, i.e., how to collect, control, and analyze population data, are evidenced in many technical reports from the United Nations and the United States Census Bureau. For an example of each see United Nations, Department of Economic and Social Affairs, *Provisional Report on World Population Prospects as Assessed in 1963* (ST/SO4/SER,R/7), 1964; United Nations Population Office, Statistical Office, Department of Social Affairs, *Determinants and Consequences of Population Trends* (Population Studies #17), 1953; and U.S. Bureau of Census, *Projections of the Population of the United States by Age, Sex, and Color to 1990* (Washington, D.C.: U.S. Government Printing Office, Bureau of Census Series P–25, no. 359).

Technological forecasting has burgeoned in the last decade. Here, too, we select from what is readily available those sources that illustrate general principles of technological forecasting, historical treatments, normative possibilities inherent in the growth and diffusion of technology, public policy implications, and measurement problems associated with technology.

Good general works on technological forecasting include Emmanuel G. Mesthene, "How Technology Will Shape the Future," *Science,* Vol. 161 (July

12, 1968), pp. 135–43; Hasan Ozbekhan, *Technology and Man's Future* (Santa Monica, Cal.: System Development Corporation, SP–2494, May 1966); Joshua Lederberg, *Man and His Future* (London: J. & A. Churchill and the CIBA Foundation, 1963); Erich Jantsch, *Technological Forecasting in Perspective* (Paris: Organization for Economic Co-operation and Development, OECD, 1967); Marvin J. Cetron, "Forecasting Technology," *International Science and Technology,* No. 69 (September 1967), pp. 83–92; and Olaf Helmer, *Prospects of Technological Progress* (Santa Monica, Cal.: The Rand Corporation, P–3643, 1967).

Trends in technological introduction and diffusion are important to know if one is interested in prospective innovation. Frederich Klemm, *History of Western Technology* (Cambridge, Mass.: The MIT Press, 1964), provides a solid general overview; Jeremy Bernstein, *The Analytical Engine: Computers Past, Present and Future* (New York: Random House, 1964); and for a specific and important area of application, J. C. Fisher, *Energy Input to the United States—1800–2060—History and Forecast* (Santa Barbara, Cal.: General Electric TEMPO, –6–TMP–26, 1966).

Normatively biased assessments of technology's future and present impact include Jacques Ellul, *The Technological Society;* Raymond Aron, ed., *World Technology and Human Destiny* (Ann Arbor, Mich.: University of Michigan Press, 1963); and Isaac Asimov, "Life in 1990," *Science Digest,* Vol. 58 (August 1965), pp. 63–70.

Occasionally one runs across a technological forecast intended to affect public policy rather directly. A prime example is Richard Bellman, *Science, Technology, and the Automation Explosion* (Santa Monica, Cal.: The Rand Corporation, P–2908, May 1964); Erich Jantsch, "Technological Forecasting for Planning and Its Institutional Implications," *Ekistics,* Vol. 26 (August 1968), pp. 150–61; Richard R. Nelson, *Effects of Research and Development on the Economy* (Santa Monica, Cal.: The Rand Corporation, P–2787, September 1963); Richard R. Nelson et al., *Technology, Economic Growth, and Public Policy* (Washington, D.C.: The Brookings Institution, 1967); F. S. Pardee, *State-of-the-Art Projection and Long-Range Planning of Applied Research* (Santa Monica, Cal.: The Rand Corporation, P–3181, 1965); H. H. Landsberg et al., *Resources in America's Future—Patterns of Requirements and Availabilities* (Baltimore, Md.: Johns Hopkins University Press, 1963); Todd R. La Porte, "The Context of Technology Assessment: A Changing Perspective for Public Organization," *Public Administration Review,* Vol. 31, No. 1 (January–February 1971), pp. 63–73; and Charles V. Kidd, "Technological Assessment in the Executive Office of the President," in *A Technology Assessment System for the Executive Branch* (Washington, D.C.: U.S. Government Printing Office, July 1970).

The measurement of technological changes is another distinct enterprise worth consideration. An overview of this subspecialty is F. L. Bayby et al., *A Feasibility Study of Techniques for Measuring and Predicting the State of the*

Art (Columbus, Ohio: Battelle Memorial Institute, 1959); another good summary piece is P. J. Lovewell and R. D. Bruce, "How We Predict Technological Change," *New Scientist,* Vol. 13 (1962), pp. 370–73; in a somewhat narrower substantive area see Arthur P. Lien, Paul Anton, and J. W. Duncan, *Technological Forecasting: Tools, Techniques and Applications* (New York: American Management Association, Bulletin No. 115, 1968); and, for a very detailed, technically sophisticated example, Franco Modigliani and H. M. Weingartner, "Forecasting Uses of Anticipatory Data on Investment and Sales," *Quarterly Journal of Economics,* Vol. 72 (February 1958), pp. 23–54.

Accounts, Indices, and Data Control

The "social indicators" movement has called attention to many of social science's perenniel data deficiencies. Not only are data in insufficient supply and quality to specify many formal social science models, we are finding out the large extent to which the data do not exist at all—for any purpose. Concurrently with the basic definition, measurement, and collection associated with the indicators and accounts activities, others are concerned about how to store, retrieve, and use the masses of data that eventually will be created.[1] Having one's information under control is prerequisite to doing responsible forecasting, whether the preferred method of making the forecasts is extrapolation, analytic model-building, or one of a number of conceivable alternatives.

Two very general treatments of indicators and data control, to be read as background, epistemological statements, are G. Holton, "Scientific Research and Scholarship: Notes toward the Design of Proper Scales," *Daedalus,* Vol. 91, No. 2 (Spring 1962), pp. 362–99; and Raymond A. Bauer, ed., "Forecasting the Future," *Science Journal,* Vol. 3 (October 1967).

Bertram Gross has been a leading spokesman for the national accounting movement and his work is well summarized in his *The State of the Nation: Social Systems Accounting* (London: Tavistock, 1966); the work of B. M. Russett, H. R. Alker, Jr., K. W. Deutsch, and H. D. Lasswell, *World Handbook of Political and Social Indicators* (New Haven: Yale University Press, 1964), is a major effort to be reckoned with; for one tangible example of governmental response to the needs for national accounting systems see, Senate Committee on Government Operations, *Full Opportunity and Social Accounting Act,* 3 Parts (Washington, D.C.: U.S. Government Printing Office, 1966); and finally for a less tangible, but more imaginative, extension of the main accounting concepts into the future, Kenneth E. Boulding, "A Data Collecting Network for the Sociosphere," *Impact,* Vol. 18 (April 1968), pp. 97–101.

The distinctions between accounting and index constructing are blurred by the proponents of each activity, and rightfully so. Very crudely, accounting schemes are the broad conceptual maps that define what general kinds of

---

[1] One colleague, with much experience in the data base management business, has been known to remark that data are made, not born. It seems apropos.

information are to be gathered and, if done well, what tentative theoretical interconnections exist among this information. The indicators or index-constructing efforts typically shift the emphasis to more technical measurement concerns, although this distinction is not nearly as clear in practice as this caricature would lead one to believe. Raymond A. Bauer, *Social Indicators* (Cambridge, Mass.: The MIT Press, 1966), provides a good introduction to both accounting and index constructing; a key strength of the text is that it straddles to good advantage the artificial boundary we have just created.

"Quality of life" has worked its way into official government discourse all over the world,[2] and it too may be placed somewhere between the data identification and measurement. Bertram Gross, ed., "Social Goals and Indicators for American Society," *The Annals of the American Academy of Political and Social Science,* Vols. 371 and 373 (May and September 1967)—the entire two volumes—is one standard source; and Norman Dalkey, R. Lewis, and D. Snyder, *Measurement and Analysis of the Quality of Life* (Santa Monica, Cal.: The Rand Corporation, RM–6228–DOT, August 1970), gets quickly and convincingly down to the difficult measurement problems that are created by the quality of life concept.

One very interesting amalgamation of normative—equity and distribution—concerns with social indicators construction is M. Rokeach and S. Parker, "Values as Social Indicators of Poverty and Race Relations in America," *The Annals of the American Academy of Political and Social Science,* Vol. 388 (March 1970), pp. 97–111.

Economists have much to teach us about index construction, mainly because they have been successfully doing it both as a short-term policy relevant activity and as a longer term scientific enterprise. One quickly thinks of the Bureau of Labor Statistics in the first case and the National Bureau of Economic Research (N.B.E.R.) in the second. Anyone interested in the construction and use of social indices could benefit by a careful reading of the following: Denis F. Johnston and Sophia Cooper, "Special Labor Force Report: Labor Force Projections, 1970–1980," *Monthly Labor Review,* Vol. 88, No. 2 (February 1965), pp. 129–40; Bureau of Labor Statistics, U.S. Department of Labor, *Technological Trends in 36 Major American Industries* (Washington, D.C.: U.S. Government Printing Office, 1964); for a good compendium of the N.B.E.R.'s contribution, see Arthur F. Burns et al., *Essays in Honor of Wesley C. Mitchell* (New York: Columbia University Press, 1935); N.B.E.R., *Long Range Economic Projection* (Princeton: Princeton University Press, 1954); N.B.E.R., *Short Term Forecasting* (Princeton: Princeton University Press, 1955); and two specific examples, or paradigms, that illustrate the scientific–projective nexus to good advantage, Jack L. Guttentag, "The Short Cycle in Residential Construction," *American Economic Review,* Vol. 51 (June 1961),

---

[2] We are aware of major "QOL" efforts that are in programs under O.E.C.D. auspices in Europe generally and under official German sponsorship in Bonn particularly. There are doubtless others around the world.

pp. 275–98; Sherman J. Maisel, "A Theory of Fluctuations in Residential Construction Starts," *American Economic Review,* Vol. 53 (June 1963), pp. 359–83.

Data control is a central theme of this volume, and it is an area of more general importance. Archives, data networks, and data-base management systems are all control mechanisms having importance for projective and scientific efforts. The entire issue, "Information Retrieval in the Social Sciences," edited by Ted R. Gurr and Hans Panofsky, *American Behavioral Scientist,* Vol. 7 (June 1964), is devoted to these matters; and Milton G. Weiner, *Observations of the Growth of Information Processing Centers* (Santa Monica, Cal.: The Rand Corporation, P–529, 1954), offer a general historical overview of the field. Social science applications are well reported in Philip E. Converse, "A Network of Data Archives for the Behavioral Sciences," *Public Opinion Quarterly,* Vol. 28 (Summer 1964), pp. 273–86; and Ralph L. Bisco, "Social Science Data Archives: A Review of Developments," *American Political Science Review,* Vol. 60 (March 1966), pp. 93–109.

Data-base management systems have received attention in recent years; the SPAN (Statistical Processing and Analysis) system created by Vladimir V. Almendinger and his associates at the System Development Corporation (Santa Monica, California) has been used in several large transportation studies and in census data-base management applications. See System Development Corporation, technical papers and reports, SP–2652 of November 9, 1966 and TM 4073/000/00 of August 27, 1968, for a good statement of the problems and possibilities in this critically important area. And finally, one might peruse two creative visions of where control appears to be headed in Hasan Ozbekhan, *The Idea of a "Look-Out" Institution* (Santa Monica, Cal.: System Development Corporation, SP–2017, 1967); and Harold D. Lasswell, *The Future of Political Science* (New York: Atherton, 1963), for a description of "social planetaria."

Methods to Project the Future

A great deal of literature exists that treats various projective methods. The following highly selected subset of the existing literature is meant to give the reader a flavor of the larger set and to point him in appropriate directions to pursue particular interests in greater detail. This literature is organized into sections dealing with general overview and philosophical works; extrapolations; models, simulations, and games; and other techniques including group judgment, operational code, utopias, planning, and developmental constructs.

The underlying philosophical arguments, both supporting and detracting, for projective methods in the social sciences are treated in each of the following works: Olaf Helmer and Nicholas Rescher, *On the Epistemology of the Inexact Sciences* (Santa Monica, Cal.: The Rand Corporation, P–1513, October 1958); Nicholas Rescher, *The Future as an Object of Research* (Santa Monica, Cal.:

The Rand Corporation, P–3593, 1967); S. Lilley, "Can Predictions Become a Science?" in B. Barber and W. Hirsch, eds., *The Sociology of Science* (New York: The Free Press, 1962); S. Watanabe, "Symmetry of Physical Laws: Part III. Prediction and Retrodiction," *Reviews of Modern Physics*, Vol. 27, No. 2 April 1955), pp. 179–87; and Nicholas Rescher, "Discrete State Systems, Markov Chains, and Problems in the Theory of Scientific Explanation and Prediction," *Philosophy of Science*, Vol. 30 (October 1963), pp. 325–45.

General methodological surveys and overview pieces have been cited from time to time, but the following list rounds out and collects those works. Daniel Bell, "Twelve Modes of Prediction—A Preliminary Sorting of Approaches in the Social Sciences"; B. de Jouvenel, *The Art of Conjecture,* pp. 101–213; Paul T. David, "The Study of the Future," *Public Administration Review,* Vol. 28 (March–April 1968), pp. 187–93; and Sir Geoffrey Vickers, "The Uses of Speculation," *op. cit.* More specialized treatments, but still overview or general in nature, are Warren G. Bennis, "Future of the Social Sciences," *The Antioch Review,* Vol. 28 (Summer 1968), pp. 227–55; Klaus Lompe, "Problems of Futures Research in the Social Sciences," *Futures,* Vol. 1 (September 1968), pp. 47–53; a rather demanding technical presentation that will reward careful reading is Emile Greenberg and Franco Modigliani, "The Predictability of Social Events," *Journal of Political Economy,* Vol. 62 (December 1954), pp. 465–78; and for an excellent general discussion aimed at implementation and integration questions, see Harold D. Lasswell, "The Technique of Decision Seminars," *Midwest Journal of Political Science,* Vol. 4 (August 1960), pp. 213–36.[3]

Extrapolation, completing a curve of past trends through the present and into the future, serves as a primary mode of forecasting and warrants the attention of scholars of development and change. Determining when an extrapolation is appropriate and making accurate and reliable forecasts with extrapolations are specific issues touched by much of the available literature. The first block of citations considers appropriateness and the second takes up reliability.

Everyone must read Norbert Weiner's tour de force, *Extrapolation, Interpolation and Smoothing Stationary Time Series* (Cambridge, Mass.: Technology Press, 1949), as a solid general survey of this subfield. Robert L. Heilbroner has painted a vivid descriptive extrapolation that uses trend information to excellent advantage in *The Future As History: The Historic Currents of Our Time and the Direction in Which They Are Taking America* (New York: Harper & Bros., 1960); it is a good complement to Weiner's technical treatment. Kenneth E. Boulding, "Toward a General Theory of Growth," *Canadian Journal of Political and Social Science,* Vol. 19 (August 1953), pp. 326–40, matches conditioning or scientific concerns with extrapolative methods. Two extrapolation-based forecasts are boldly, even somewhat uncritically, made in D. J. de Solla Price, *Little Science, Big Science* (New York: Columbia

[3] See "Dealing with Complex Social Problems: The Potential of the 'Decision Seminar'," for an elaboration of several of these arguments.

University Press, 1963); and Bruce M. Russett, *Trends in World Politics* (New York: Macmillan, 1965). Demographers frequently rely on extrapolated forecasts, and the results are not uniformly successful. To better understand why, see H. F. Dorn, "Pitfalls in Population Forecasts and Projections," *Journal of the American Statistical Association,* Vol. 45 (September 1950), pp. 311–34; and J. Hajnal, "The Prospects for Population Forecasts," *Journal of the American Statistical Association,* Vol. 50 (June 1955), pp. 309–22.

In working out the quantitative bases for econometric models and forecasts, Henri Theil has moved into the policy specification arena; see his *Applied Economic Forecasting* (Chicago: Rand McNally, 1966); *idem, Economic Forecasts and Policy* (Amsterdam: North Holland Press, 2nd ed., 1961). Jan Tinbergen, *Economic Policy: Principles and Design* (Amsterdam: North Holland Press, 1956), deals with many of the same issues. Three pieces that treat specific quantitative details and shed light on extrapolative methods in the process are Peter Newman, "Approaches to Stability Analysis," *Economica,* Vol. 28 (February 1961), pp. 12–29; Franco Modigliani and H. M. Weingartner, "Forecasting Uses of Anticipatory Data on Investment and Sales," *Quarterly Journal of Economics,* Vol. 72 (February 1958), pp. 23–54; and B. G. Hickman, "An Experiment with Weighted Indexes of Cyclical Diffusion," *Journal of the American Statistical Association,* Vol. 53 (March 1958), pp. 39–53. Two examples of the use of survey data to extrapolate future behavior are contained in John Dollard, "Under What Conditions Do Opinions Predict Behavior?" *Public Opinion Quarterly,* Vol. 12, No. 4 (Winter 1948–49), pp. 623–32; and William M. Evan, "Cohort Analysis of Survey Data: A Procedure for Studying Long-term Opinion Change," *Public Opinion Quarterly,* Vol. 23, No. 1 (Spring 1959), pp. 63–72. Finally, two treatments of short and medium range forecasting rely heavily on extrapolations of established trends: Robert Kirby, "A Comparison of Short and Medium Range Statistical Forecasting Methods," *Management Science,* Vol. 13B, No. 4 (December 1966), pp. B-202–B-210; and National Bureau of Economic Research, *Short Term Forecasting.*

Models, simulations, and games have all been used at one time or another for projective purposes. The literature is large and growing rapidly; however, representative works can be noted easily to give the interested reader clues to follow up at his leisure. A good place to begin is Herbert A. Simon and Allen Newell, "Models: Their Uses and Limitations," in Leonard D. White, ed., *The State of the Social Sciences* (Chicago: University of Chicago Press, 1956). A near-classic in the field is Herbert Goldhamer and Hans Speier, "Some Observations on Political Gaming," *World Politics,* Vol. 12 (October 1959), pp. 71–83. A recent survey is noteworthy for the quantity of material it contains, see Martin Shubik and Garry D. Brewer, *Models, Simulations, and Games: A Survey* (Santa Monica, Cal.: The Rand Corporation, R–1060–ARPA/RC, July 1972). Clayton J. Thomas and Walter L. Deemer provide an earlier overview in "The Role of Operational Gaming in Operational Research," *Journal of the*

Operations Research Society of America, Vol. 5, No. 1 (February 1957), pp. 1–27.

Specific forecasting models are relatively rare; however, Dwight Crane and James Crotty, "A Two-Stage Forecasting Model: Exponential Smoothing and Multiple Regression," *Management Science,* Vol. 13B, No. 8 (April 1967), pp. B-501–B-507; Torsten Hägerstrand, *The Propagation of Innovation Waves* (Lund, Sweden: Royal University of Lund, 1952); H. O. Stekler, "Forecasting and Analyses with an Econometric Model," *American Economic Review,* Vol. 56 (December 1966), pp. 1241–48; and Robert Kirby, "A Comparison of Short and Medium Range Statistical Methods," all treat the subject in interesting, different ways. Richard Bellman has been active in this area for many years and has produced two important methodological commentaries on forecasting with models. See Richard E. Bellman, *Stability Theory of Differential Equations* (New York: McGraw-Hill, 1954); and Bellman and J. M. Danskin, *A Survey of Mathematical Theory of Time-Lag, Retarded Control, and Hereditary Processes* (Santa Monica, Cal.: The Rand Corporation, R–256, 1954).

Gaming is a large, diffuse subspeciality of a number of academic disciplines. Four excellent summary pieces, couched in war or crisis gaming terms, are worth reading before one either launches his own gaming–forecasting enterprise or buys the results produced by someone else. See Milton G. Weiner, *War Gaming Methodology* (Santa Monica, Cal.: The Rand Corporation, RM–2413, July 1959); Olaf Helmer and Edward S. Quade, *An Approach to the Study of a Developing Economy by Operational Gaming* (Santa Monica, Cal.: The Rand Corporation, P–2718, March 1963); E. W. Paxson, *War Gaming* (Santa Monica, Cal.: The Rand Corporation, RM–3489–PR, February 1963); and Harvey Averch and M. M. Lavin, *Simulation of Decisionmaking in Crises: Three Manual Gaming Experiments* (Santa Monica, Cal.: The Rand Corporation, RM–4202–PR, August 1964).

An indispensable aspect of gaming and related activities is the writing of scenarios. In fact, scenarios may be one of the most underrated and important forecasting methodologies when the real problem at hand does not easily lend itself to rigorous or comprehensive quantification. For a survey of the art form by one of the two or three master scenarists living, see Harvey De Weerd, *Political Military Scenarios* (Santa Monica, Cal.: The Rand Corporation, P–3535, February 1967); and *idem, An Israeli Scenario for a Laboratory Simulation* (Santa Monica, Cal.: System Development Corporation, SP–3139, March 1968). The latter example is essentially a five-year forecast of Middle East events (1968–73) and is striking for its plausibility and the extent of its accuracy in actually "calling the shots." Other scenarios, in roughly decreasing adherence to a real-world context, include the following: Lincoln P. Bloomfield, *Western Europe to the Mid-Seventies: Five Scenarios* (Cambridge, Mass.: Massachusetts Institute of Technology, Center for International Studies, A/68–3, 1968); Nigel Hawkes, "The World in 2020," *Nature,* Vol. 218

(April 6, 1968), pp. 14–16; Herman Kahn, *Alternative World Futures* (Croton-on-Hudson, N.Y.: Hudson Institute, Paper HI–342–BIV, April 1964); Mikhail Vassiliev and Sergi Gouschev, eds., *Life in the Twenty-First Century* (New York: McGraw-Hill, 1960); C. K. Ogden, *Bentham's Theory of Fictions* (London: Kegan-Paul, 1932); and Herman Kahn, *On Escalation: Metaphors and Scenarios* (New York: Praeger 1965).

Creating utopian views of man and his world has been a durable scholarly pastime over the years. Utopian literature is similar to scenario writing in that both rely primarily on written imaginings; however, utopias are regularly *not* attached logically to the events of the here and now—proceeding from the dreary present to the dreamed-up future is left often entirely to the reader's own imagination. Scenarios, on the other hand, are tied to the past and present and concentrate particularly on the intervening processes and steps to the future. This distinction is not hard and fast, just useful. The literature is large, but we concentrate on traditional or positive utopias, negative or pessimistic utopias, and several illustrations of each.

Good surveys are contained in Lewis Mumford, *The Story of Utopias* (New York: Compass Books, 1962); Harry Ross, *Utopias Old and New* (London: Nicholson and Watson, 1938); Denis Gabor, *Inventing the Future* (New York: Knopf, 1964); Bertrand de Jouvenel, "Utopia for Practical Purposes," *Daedalus,* Vol. 94 (Spring 1965), pp. 437–53; W. E. Moore, "The Utility of Utopias," *American Sociological Review,* Vol. 31 (December 1966), pp. 765–72; and Ralf Dahrendorf, "Out of Utopia: Toward a Reorientation of Sociological Analysis," *American Journal of Sociology,* Vol. 54 (1958), pp. 116–27.

Positive utopias are evident in the writing of Karl Mannheim, *Ideology and Utopia* (New York: Harcourt, Brace, 1936); Alfred Kazin, "H. G. Wells, America, and 'The Future'," *The American Scholar,* Vol. 37 (Winter 1967–68), pp. 137–44; and Edward Bellamy's *Looking Backward: 2000–1887* (New York: Modern Library, 1951), is a classic.

Negative or pessimistic views that should be of interest both for their content and methodological insights are I. F. Clarke, *Voices Prophesying War: 1763–1984* (London: Oxford University Press, 1967); Kingsley Amis, *New Maps of Hell* (New York: Harcourt, Brace, 1960); C. Walsh, *From Utopia to Nightmare* (New York: Harper & Bros., 1962); Mark R. Hillegas, *The Future as Nightmare: H. G. Wells and the Antiutopians* (London: Oxford University Press, 1967); and finally Robert Boguslaw, *The New Utopians: A Study of System Design and Social Change* (Englewood Cliffs, N.J.: Prentice-Hall, 1965).

Group judgment procedures are being relied on to a far greater extent today than at any previous time to project into the uncertain future. Besides the impressive work done some years ago in technological forecasting using Delphi and other procedures, recent efforts have been spent examining the scientific underpinnings of group forecasting techniques. Olaf Helmer, *Social*

Technology (Santa Monica, Cal.: The Rand Corporation, P–3063, February 1965); Theodore J. Gordon and Olaf Helmer, *Report on a Long Range Forecasting Study* (Santa Monica, Cal.: The Rand Corporation, P–2982, September 1964); Norman C. Dalkey and Olaf Helmer, "An Experimental Application of the Delphi Method to the Use of Experts," *Management Science,* Vol. 9 (April 1963), pp. 458–67; and N. C. Dalkey, *Predicting the Future* (Santa Monica, Cal.: The Rand Corporation, P–3948, 1968), all chronicle the initial phases of activity. The scientific phase is reported in Norman C. Dalkey, *The Delphi Method: An Experimental Study of Group Opinion* (Santa Monica, Cal.: The Rand Corporation, RM–5888–PR, June 1969); and Dalkey and Daniel L. Rourke, *Experimental Assessment of Delphi Procedures with Group Value Judgments* (Santa Monica, Cal.: The Rand Corporation, R–612–ARPA, February 1971).

Planners have a decided predilection for projecting a defined context into the future. Because it is one of the rare few disciplines that allows itself to think comprehensively and configuratively about its varied subject matters, there are several samples of the planning literature worthy of reflection. Thomas Reiner, *The Place of the Ideal Community in Urban Planning* (Philadelphia: University of Pennsylvania Press, 1963), is midway between the utopian literature and planning; furthermore, the book is an excellent historical source for planning through the ages. Melvin Webber raises, but does not begin to resolve, many operational questions about the limits of planning as an enterprise in "The Validity and Variety of Planned Intervention," in *Planning in an Environment of Change* (Berkeley: University of California, Center for Planning and Development Research, Report #44, 1969); a few answers were provided earlier by Paul T. David, "Analytical Approaches to the Study of Change," *Public Administration Review,* Vol. 26 (September 1966), pp. 160–68; and in Hans-Georg Gadamer, "Notes on Planning for the Future," *Daedalus,* Vol. 95 (Spring 1966), pp. 572–89. More specific, better focused planning studies include George A. Morgan, "Planning in Foreign Affairs: The State of the Art," *Foreign Affairs,* Vol. 39 (January 1961), pp. 271–78; William R. Ewald, ed., *Environment for Man: The Next Fifty Years* (Bloomington, Ind.: University of Indiana Press, 1966); Donald N. Michael, *The Unprepared Society: Planning for a Precarious Future* (New York: Basic Books, 1968); and an extraordinarily solid, relevant piece of work, Roland Artle, "Planning and Growth—A Simple Model of an Island Economy: Honolulu, Hawaii," *Papers and Proceedings of the Regional Science Association,* Vol. 15 (1965), pp. 29–44. Two extremely good technical planning sources are George Steiner, ed., *Managerial Long Range Planning* (New York: McGraw-Hill, 1963); and Laurence S. Hill, *Management Planning and Control of Research and Technology Projects* (Santa Monica, Cal.: The Rand Corporation, RM–4921–PR, 1966).

The "developmental construct" is the invention of Harold D. Lasswell and is worth consideration because it is explicitly policy oriented, combining, as it does, one part expert, one part scenario, one part model-building, and a solid dash of normative specification. It is a "method" in that consistent procedures and rules underlie its execution and use. Its key objective, to allow decisionmakers to adapt rapidly to emerging conditions in changing contexts, is simple and generally worth striving for. The following reference summarizes the theory and method supporting developmental constructs and also provides several examples of the technique in use. Harold D. Lasswell, *World Politics and Personal Insecurity* (New York: McGraw-Hill, 1935), Chapter 1, pp. 3–20, is perhaps the earliest statement of the idea; and *idem,* "The Garrison State," *American Journal of Sociology,* Vol. 46 (January 1941), pp. 455–68, is an early, graphic example of the developmental construct in operation. Some twenty years after its initial formulation, Lasswell restated and refined the basic idea in "Current Studies in the Decision Process: Automation versus Creativity," *Western Political Quarterly,* Vol. 8 (June 1955), pp. 381–85.

The Marxist assertion that the principal explanation of contemporary world events is a movement from a class to a classless society, is, crudely speaking, a developmental construct. However, it lacks the scientific rigor of another construct created by Kenneth Keniston to guide his own and others' research: "How Community Mental Health Stamped Out Urban Violence (1968–1978)" (Yale University, Department of Psychology, 1968 mimeo). "Guide" in this usage means to keep key components ordered in space and time to ensure that nothing important is overlooked and that nothing trivial captures the scarce attention of the researcher. The developmental construct, it must be emphasized, serves a clarifying function for specialists interested in locating particular research, personal, and professional interests in a broader societal context. Neither scientific law nor dogmatic forecast, these constructs aid the timing and choosing of scientific work with respect to the planned observation of the future, past, and present. By helping the scientific observer to think explicitly about the real state of knowledge, exploration is narrowed to only the more relevant problem and solution spaces actually confronting decisionmakers. All of these concerns and possibilities are eloquently stated in Lasswell's 1956 presidential address to the American Political Science Association, "The Political Science of Science: An Inquiry in the Possible Reconciliation of Mastery and Freedom," *American Political Science Review,* Vol. 50 (December 1956), pp. 961–79, esp. 964–65, 977–79.

TECHNIQUES AND ACCURACY OF DEMOGRAPHIC FORECASTING

William Ascher has developed a deceptively devastating appraisal of current and past efforts to forecast with the best, most complete, and best understood social data in the world—the United States' population census. Interwoven into this survey critique are all of the five problem-solving concerns; hopefully, one gets a taste of what policy science is about after reading this chapter.

The Question

Ascher asks the simple appraisal questions: How have forecasters done over the past seventy-five years? Which methods have been reliable and accurate? Why? What are the implicit assumptions (operating theories) built into the prevalent forecasts?

The Strengths

Primarily, the chapter characterizes and evaluates several prevalent forecasting techniques most commonly applied to demographic data, but applicable to other social time series as well. The argument is concisely and systematically developed and easily convinces one of the considerable need for continuous, unrelenting appraisal and examination of the conditioning and normative factors underlying any trend-based projection into the future. In fact, the diversionary impact of supposedly "scientific" forecasts is repeatedly stressed in the chapter; it is particularly appropriate for the policy approach embraced in this volume. It is irritating to be saddled with a grossly distorted projection; irritation quickly turns to substantial societal costs when the faulty projection is uncritically relied on to plan for future contingencies.

The Weaknesses

While the appraisal of past methods is thoroughly and competently done, we are not given as much constructive help as to what alternative techniques could replace the limited ones surveyed. Several of the institutional recommendations developed in Chapter 9 may resolve this somewhat.

Subsequent Developments

Plainly the most important development that could result from the ideas set forth in this chapter would be the systematic introduction of similar appraisal standards and procedures in other social science areas.

A second development would be to create institutional alternatives to the existing ones to do more rigorous forecasting.

POLICY AND THE STUDY OF THE FUTURE

As contrasted with Ascher's contribution, Brunner and Brewer's chapter is far more abstract, although it too concentrates on several of the key problems facing those who forecast social events. The work is not so much projective as it is heuristic; but then, this is as it should be because there are essentially *no* macro political models with a strong projective bias.

The Question

The problem is the old one of whether extrapolated trends are preferable to scientifically based projections in a given context. Arguments favoring each point of view are marshaled, and a small illustrative experiment is carried out to resolve the problem, or at least to clarify its relevant dimensions.

The Strengths

Considerable attention is given to the intention and specification phases of the model-building process in an effort to clarify the conditions under which one might rely on extrapolations as a projective technique. By respecifying a simple model, the decomposability and stability assumptions implicit in an extrapolation-based forecast are tested and found wanting as the complexity of a context and the projected time horizon increase. A final contribution of the chapter is the attention it gives to possible strategies for coping with the identified problem.

The Weaknesses

The major weakness of the chapter is that it is only a preliminary effort to begin sorting out some long-standing assumptions and practices. So much additional thought needs to be expended that one scarcely knows where to begin, but begin we must.

Other weaknesses are essentially weaknesses of the method used in the example, and these are spelled out in the body of the chapter.

Subsequent Developments

Needed are other experimental tests in many settings to determine the *validity* of extrapolative and other projections. To exercise this testing or validating function we are confronted once more with the requirement to collect and otherwise *control* data. At least the two proposals suggested by Martin Shubik and Harold Lasswell, detailed in the chapter, need considerable examination and active exploration. Alternative coping strategies need to be created and tested as well.

Chapter 8
Techniques and Accuracy of Demographic Forecasting: Predicting United States' Population Growth

WILLIAM ASCHER

Accurate information is the keystone of any scientific or policy activity; however, few of us have ever explicitly evaluated the adequacy of demographic data when used for forecasting purposes—an oversight partly corrected in this account. Besides listing a number of distinct forecasting styles, including antitheoretical curve fitting, logistic curve fitting, component and cohort methods, the author evaluates each of these as to the accuracy of its projections of United States' population during the period 1900 to the present. Observations on each technique are made in light of the projection's length, the underlying theoretical and practical assumptions made about the population, and the status of evaluations made of previous forecasts and forecasters, The importance of the chapter's findings is general, although the main source of data is specifically tied to the United States—whose population data are among the most complete and reliable in the world. One is left with the gnawing question that if this is the best that can be done with U.S. data, what about the rest of the nations in the world? Hopefully, we all might be encouraged to do better in the future.

THE NEED FOR ACCURATE PROJECTIONS: PLANNING AND ANALYSIS

The prediction of future trends ought to be an integral part of the study of political and economic development because of the strong orientation of developmental studies toward *future* changes in political, social, and economic conditions. "Development" connotes this future orientation; it implies a process of change in the direction of some (usually preferred) future environment.

The most crucial *practical application* of projections of future trends is in identifying future problems and political crises originating in current trends. When crises are foreseen, attention and resources can be allocated to anticipate future resource needs. We ought to be able to anticipate, act on, and thereby defuse future crises in the supply of educational facilities (predicted by projecting school-age population), in the supply of transportation (through projections of city populations and distribution), or in pollution (through projections of waste production).

And, of course, the decisions made by policymakers trying to direct the course of political and economic development must have their impact in the context of *future* conditions. Future conditions will determine the success of today's policies, so these conditions must be taken into account *before* they come into being. For example, a future level of GNP or housing supply, which to some extent may be influenced by the present actions of policymakers, will be significant only in terms of the future number of individuals alive to share these resources.

On the political level, the survival of current political institutions will depend upon the prosperity or adversity of the future, just as political attitudes and conflicts will be generated in response to the future context. Projecting the social, demographic, and economic contexts of future political activity is as important in predicting the nature of. this activity as the present context is in analyzing current political activity.

The Costs of Inaccurate Projections

Although few would argue against the necessity of accurate predictions, there are also few who are willing to invest sufficient effort in generating projections of the future, and fewer who trust the forecasts of others. The unwillingness to make predictions has three sources: (1) traumatic experiences with inaccurate predictions made in the past; (2) lack of confidence in the particular projective techniques being used; and (3) a belief that the future is inherently unpredictable.

Pessimism concerning projections has a negative effect beyond the damage done by bad predictions themselves. An isolated inaccurate projection is damaging to the extent that resources are wasted in taking inappropriate actions different from those which would have been indicated by the accurate projections. But a succession of inaccurate projections can actually undermine the relationship between academics and policymakers.

Policymakers stand between the academic economist or political scientist and his goal to influence the course of economic and political development. Academic economists and political scientists are involved primarily in the intelligence, promotion, and appraisal phases of decisionmaking, so that the academic must depend on the policymaker to apply his advice. Since the academic must be heeded to be relevant, even a hypothetically omniscient academic is powerless without someone to listen to him. The practical-minded policymakers, who handle short-range, mundane problems as a matter of course, depend on academics for the solutions to their *long-range* problems, which are more likely to involve projections than are the short-range aspects of immediate conditions. If policymakers believe that the long-range projections generated by academics are likely to be highly inaccurate, they have no use for the academics' long-range planning efforts. The academics then will be performing within the closed circuit of their own colleagues.

The academic future-projector's position is complicated by the fact that the style of his prediction method is significant beyond the accuracy of the projections it generates. Methods must be believable whether or not they turn out to be accurate. J. K. Galbraith relates an example of R. Babson's predictions of economic crisis, ignored because of the unorthodox methods used to derive them:

The methods by which he reached his conclusions were a problem. They involved a hocus-pocus of lines and arcs on a chart. Intuition, and possibly even mysticism played a part. Those who employed rational, objective, and scientific methods were naturally uneasy about Babson, although their methods failed to foretell the crash. In these matters, as often in our culture, it is far, far better to be wrong in a respectable way than to be right for the wrong reasons.[1]

More important than the self-interest of the academic, inaccurate projections place the future orientation of the policymakers in jeopardy. If their trust in the available preconstructions of the future is lacking, they will be more likely to despair of competently preparing for the unknown future at all. They will be more resigned and content to cope with the knowable present, without regard for the unpredictable and, therefore, unknowable future, especially since policymakers are primarily accountable for their short-range performance. Policymakers need only to turn to the academic journals on something as basic as population projections to read that: "But attempts to use demographic analysis as a basis for prediction have not been very successful, and the broader the front the less successful has been the product. Nor are there grounds for believing that long-range, overall predictions are likely to be much more reliable in the future." [2] Is this obituary valid? Or are some projection methods better than others and capable of redeeming the forecasters' reputations?

THE EXAMPLE OF POPULATION PROJECTIONS

By examining the accuracy of past predictions of U.S. population, to which numerous projective techniques have been applied, it is possible to evaluate different methods of projection in terms of their accuracy in this one basic type of prediction. We shall concentrate on population predictions for several reasons. First, projecting the U.S. population has been a popular pastime, so there is a relatively large number of projections to examine. Second, the accuracy of past projections can be evaluated easily with hindsight knowledge just as soon as the actual census of the "predicted" year is carried out; the prediction accuracy can

[1] J. K. Galbraith, *The Great Crash 1929* (Boston: Houghton Mifflin, 1961), p. 90.
[2] D. V. Glass, "Demographic Prediction" (The Third Royal Society Nuffield Lecture), *Proceedings of the Royal Society*, Series B., Vol. 168 (1967), p. 119.

be evaluated in terms of the percentage error from the actual population level.[3] Third, future population levels have several qualities which ought to make them easier to predict accurately than economic, social, or political factors. There is no ambiguity in the concept of population level, as there is in the conceptions of many economic, social, and political indicators. The relative magnitudes of fluctuations in birthrates and deathrates, the major components of population change, are small compared to the shifts in economic and political indicators. Thus, if population cannot be predicted accurately, other projections are all the more suspect.

Finally, population projections are important in their own right and as components of projections of "per-capitized" indicators. The population level circumscribes the supply of human resources, determines the context of demands for territorial expansion, and defines the consumer market. Population *density* is an important factor in long-term economic and political change by virtue of its impact on the quality of living conditions, the constraints on feasible economic activity, and the behavior related to crowding. In regarding population level as a component of per-capitized indicators, we need only look at the impact of population growth on per capita income in developing countries to see how population change determines the significance of gross economic change.

To assume that the history of population projections is typical of the history of projections in general is going too far. Obviously, the prediction of a future population level is a different task from predicting the occurrence of a single "happening" such as a war or a depression. However, population projections share common characteristics with the broad class of trends with the following qualities: (1) the phenomenon is a generally increasing summation of basic human activity, affected to some extent by technological changes and by unique occurrences that are not necessarily predictable from the examination of the past trends of the phenomenon alone; but (2) future levels of the phenomenon are partially, but not totally, dependent on past levels.

Therefore, the projections of these trends, including GNP, urbanization, literacy rates, and so on, have had common qualities: the techniques applied to these phenomena have become, at least superficially, more sophisticated, beginning with the simple method of assuming that gross past trends will continue indefinitely, and later developing more complex procedures. The nature of the activities summarized by the phenomena is such that some models of their growth have incorporated ceilings, envelopes of maximum development, and sundry other assumptions about future levels which are not derived solely from past data. Thus, population projections are the same sort of enterprise as the

[3] The elegant econometric methods of computing accuracy in terms of loss from applying incorrect treatments due to the inaccuracies in projections are obviously not appropriate for evaluating population projections. It is impossible to gauge the losses resulting from public and private policies misled by inaccurate projections. For the econometric approach, see Henri Theil, *Applied Economic Forecasting* (Amsterdam: North Holland Publishing Co., 1966).

prediction of the GNP, resource utilization, urbanization, technical advancement, etc., and though the history of population projection techniques may be unique, it is certainly enlightening with respect to the problems and prospects of social forecasting in general.

Of the many formal and informal population projections appearing in scattered journals, books, and newspapers, the most important ones for this study are those with an official or semiofficial status, by virtue of their publication in government documents or their use by government officials. These are the figures known and used by government policymakers. These predictions establish the credibility of the academics responsible for generating population projections and forecasting the future in general. Since 1940 the widely used *Statistical Abstract of the United States*[4] has generally included population projections prepared by the Scripps Foundation and the Bureau of the Census, which may be considered the official projections for the post-1940 period. The *pre*-1940 projections examined here are all widely known projections generated by respected demographers: H. S. Pritchett,[5] C. S. Sloane,[6] C. E. Woodruff,[7] H. Gannet,[8] P. K. Whelpton and W. Thompson,[9] Raymond Pearl,[10] and L. I. Dublin and A. Lotka.[11] Of the twelve sets of projections prepared and published by these respected authorities, half are directly associated with the U.S. government, the others were perhaps even more widely known and used; so that the sum of the projections represents the most influential, official, and accepted forecasts of U.S. population.

[4] U.S. Department of Commerce, *Statistical Abstract of the United States* (Washington, D.C.: U.S. Government Printing Office, various years).

[5] H. S. Pritchett, "A Formula for Predicting the Population of the United States," *Quarterly Publication of the American Statistical Association,* Vol. 2, No. 14 (June 1891), pp. 278–86; *idem,* "The Population of the United States during the Next Ten Decades," *Popular Science Monthly,* Vol. 58, No. 4 (November 1900), pp. 49–53. Pritchett was president of The Massachusetts Institute of Techonology.

[6] In C. E. Woodruff, *Expansion of Races* (New York: Rebman, 1909), p. 476. Sloane was a geographer for the U.S. Bureau of the Census.

[7] Woodruff was author of *Expansion of Races* (see note 6 above), an early demographic classic. See p. 475 of this work.

[8] H. Gannet, "Estimates of Future Population," *Report of the National Conservation Commission* (Washington, D.C., 1909), Vol. 2, pp. 7–9. Gannet was a member of the National Resources Planning Board.

[9] P. K. Whelpton, "Population of the United States, 1925 to 1975," *American Journal of Sociology,* Vol. 34, No. 2 (September 1928), pp. 253–70; W. S. Thompson, *Population Problems* (New York: McGraw-Hill, 1930), p. 232 (subsequent references are to 1st ed.); also see the 2nd ed. of this volume, p. 258. Whelpton and Thompson were members of the National Resources Planning Board and the Scripps Foundation.

[10] R. Pearl and L. J. Reed, "On the Rate of Growth of the Population of the United States since 1790 and Its Mathematical Representation," *Proceedings, National Academy of Sciences,* Vol. 6, No. 6 (June 15, 1920), pp. 275–88; R. Pearl, *The Biology of Population Growth* (New York: Knopf, 1925), p. 14. Pearl was a member of the faculty, The Johns Hopkins University.

[11] L. I. Dublin and A. J. Lotka, "The Present Outlook for Population Growth," *American Sociological Society Publications,* Vol. 24, No. 2 (1930), pp. 106–14. Dublin and Lotka were employed by the Metropolitan Life Insurance Company.

They vary substantially in method and in accuracy, leading to the question of whether some methods are associated with greater accuracy than others. The evolution of projection methods is itself an interesting story of the increasing sophistication and rationality of methods, but with very limited payoffs.

The Atheoretical Curve Fitters

The early projectors, represented by Pritchett, Gannet, Sloane, and Woodruff, considered the overall population growth rate as a single, indivisible entity, rather than breaking it down to the three components of birthrate, deathrate, and rate of migration. This practice of treating the overall growth rate as a unity resulted more from a belief that the growth rate has some unifying quality about it that makes simple projections adequate, than from an inherent lack of sophistication on the part of the demographers. They were hampered, as well, by a lack of data, on birthrates in particular.

For making very short-term projections, the assumption that the current percentage increase will be repeated in the near future was (and still is) an adequate approach. For projections of more than a few years, the early projectors realized that *changes* in the percentage increase must be taken into account, even if factors such as fertility, health, mores, and economic conditions remained constant. Since the only mechanism of population increase besides immigration is the addition of not-yet-fertile children, the proportion of fertile individuals is subject to change even if the age-specific fertility and mortality rates remain constant. With a relatively large proportion of children, child mortality becomes more significant vis-à-vis geriatric mortality. As the population increases, the fixed level of migration diminishes relative to the total population. Thus, even static conditions of fertility, mortality, and migration can create a very complicated situation of population growth change.

By examining prior population levels of the United States, the early projectors concluded that "the rate of increase is steadily diminishing" because "the percentage of increase lessens as the density increases." [12] In effect, Pritchett, Gannet, Sloane, and Woodruff were ignoring the potential complexities of applying birthrates, deathrates, or migration rates to the existing population in order to generate an iterative model of growth; instead, they were simply fitting curves to the graph of previous population growth and assuming that the curve would continue into the future. Sloane, Gannet, and Woodruff described their curves verbally, rather than graphically or mathematically; Pritchett used the formula $P = A + Bt + Ct^2 + Dt^3$, solving for the the constants with old census data. Pritchett then expressed the scientific hubris of his era by claiming that his predictions "for the next hundred years will doubtless represent the growth of population within a small percentage of error." [13]

[12] Woodruff, *op. cit.,* p. 475.
[13] Pritchett, "A Formula for Predicting the Population of the United States," p. 286.

The early method of dealing with the rate of increase as a single entity was not necessarily bound up with the curve-fitting method. It could accommodate forecasts of changes in fertility, health, and migration not reflected by past trends; the net result of these changes simply would be expressed in changes within the single rate of increase. These early projectors, however, were essentially atheoretical; they avoided incorporating any theories of population growth into their projection methods and were content with observing past trends as the best indicators of future trends.

The simplicity of these early projection techniques represented the acknowledgment that the growth rate is, after all, only the manifestation of millions of discrete events—birth, deaths, and migrations—so that although the simple growth rate was the basic unit of analysis, it was recognized that this overall growth rate, reflecting three somewhat independent phenomena, was in no sense theoretically predetermined. Past trends were assumed to be the best guesses for future trends precisely because the growth rate was *not* considered to be theoretically predictable.

In the view of these projectors, theoretical predictability presumes the capacity to understand and accommodate the full complexity underlying vital processes. Their knowledge of population change mechanisms was not considered adequate at the time. Yet the projectors were confronted with easily discernible regularities in past population growth. Their consequent decision simply to extrapolate from past trends avoided the errors of incorrect theoretical formulations, but it also denied them the power to examine population characteristics other than previous growth rates to determine the extent to which past trends may not apply in future patterns of growth.

Curves from Theory

Many projectors have assumed that the entire (past, present, and future) pattern of population growth can be described by a particular type of curve. The specific parameters of the curve would be those that make the chosen type of curve fit most closely with the existing data. The crucial question is how to decide what *type* of curve is appropriate. The early projectors used existing data alone to determine what type of curve would be appropriate, and invariably the extremely uncomplicated pattern of past growth seemed to indicate an equally uncomplicated type of curve without inflection points (changes from convexity to concavity or vice versa).

In contrast to this data-supremacy approach, the biologist Raymond Pearl introduced the practice of deriving the type of curve from theoretical assumptions of the nature of population growth, then determining on the basis of past data the most appropriate specific curve of that type. Pearl advocated the logistic law of population growth, quite appropriate for describing the growth of population in the simple, controlled, fixed-parameter biological experiments where the law was generated. The logistic curve describes an initial acceleration in population increase, followed by a symmetrical deceleration in the increase, such that the population level is ultimately stable.

It is not unreasonable to assume that a small number of Pearl's fruit flies, in a fixed space with a fixed amount of food, would multiply slowly at first, then with increasing rapidity, until finally the food and space limitations would cause the increase to slacken and subsequently cause the population to level off. But is it reasonable to expect a human population, with capabilities to alter food and effective space limitations, to increase according to the same pattern?

The analogy between human being and fruit fly would seem to break down, but there are other justifications beyond resource exhaustion for expecting a logistic human population growth pattern. For example, the increasing urban proportion that usually accompanies population growth, compounded by the fact that urban fertility is generally lower than rural fertility, would result in a lower overall birthrate and therefore in a leveling off of population growth.[14] There has been a number of more general anti-Malthusian theories calling for an automatically lowered fertility rate in large populations, attributed to factors as diverse as social complexity, rational calculus, or alienation.[15] Therefore, Pearl could have justified a logistic curve for human population without invoking fruit-fly behavior.

But there is another problem, beyond the question of whether the class of logistic curves is appropriate, in using a logistic curve as a description of population growth: the difficulty of finding the inflection point in order to determine *which* logistic curve is appropriate. We cannot criticise Pearl for maintaining that U.S. population growth is logistic, because this may yet prove to be roughly the case. So far, U.S. population growth has been roughly exponential, and an exponential curve is similar to the portion of the logistic curve preceding its inflection point. We also have not yet reached the period of decreasing growth that would indicate that the population growth pattern necessarily *is* logistic, although Pearl concluded that the decreasing growth period had commenced in the 1910–20 decade.

Pearl's mistake was in overinterpreting the significance of the relatively small 1910–20 population increase, which was the first ten-year increase lower that that of the previous decade. If he had not been so rigidly committed to the "iron law" of logistic growth, perhaps Pearl would have attributed this temporary lull in the rate of increase to the absence of 2.5 million military personnel serving overseas and thus separated from their wives, and the death of one hundred thousand of these men in the prime of life. The yearly growth chart for the 1910–20 period does indicate that the decline of growth occurred within the 1917–19 period. Nevertheless, Pearl interpreted the growth rate decline as the

[14] *Statistical Abstract of the United States, 1968*, p. 54. Also see Thompson, *Population Problems*, p. 97.

[15] Thompson, *Population Problems*, pp. 25–30.

inflection point of U.S. population growth. By expecting the overall growth rate to be a single phenomenon with (almost mystical) regularity, Pearl assumed that the 1910–20 drop in the growth rate was the signal for a continual long-term decline. He chose the logistic curve with this inflection point and projected a population stabilization asymptotically approaching 197 million, with approximately 157 million in 1960. If Pearl had considered the components of the growth rate, instead of demanding so much exactness in the fit between fact and theory, he probably would have discounted the minor 1910–20 growth rate decline as a minor fluctuation.

The great irony of the history of American population projections is that Pearl's totally incorrect choice of that particular logistic curve had an enormously misleading influence on later projectors, even though his own five, ten-, and twenty-year projections were remarkably accurate. The Depression and its accompanying low birth rate saved Pearl's own projections, which were "right for the wrong reasons," though by the time of the so-called "postwar baby boom" in the late 1940's his error had become obvious.

Other demographers, even those who used completely different methods for projection, came to assume that birthrates would steadily decrease and that the overall numerical growth would also decrease. There were other reasons to believe that the birth rate was declining, but Pearl went further by assuming that: (1) the growth rate decline was an inevitable event rather than a reflection of specific, and perhaps temporary, conditions; (2) the birthrate decline would necessarily cause a decline in the successive annual numerical increase; and (3) small changes in the growth rate were inevitably indicators of major trends to come. The first assumption was disproved when the birthrate began to increase again in 1937, yet the demographers even then were assuming that future growth rates would decrease. The second assumption ignored the fact that a decreasing birthrate *per unit of population* may still produce an increasing numerical growth, since the population base to which the rate applies is steadily increasing. The third assumption reduced the capacity of Pearl's projection method to identify the major trends from among the confusing array of minor fluctuations, such as the 1910–20 decrease in growth rate.

Technical Advances in Accounting: The Component Method

The developments adding to the sophistication of projecting population immediately followed the introduction of Pearl's simplistic method, perhaps in reaction to it. When later combined, they formed the projection technique in use today.

The first advance was made in 1928 by Whelpton and Thompson, who separated the formerly undivided growth rate into its obvious components of birthrate, deathrate, and migration rate. Earlier projectors of course realized the composition of the growth rate, but Whelpton and Thompson were the first to generate separate projections of the birthrate, deathrate, and migration rate, and then combine them to reconstruct the overall growth rate. Breaking down the growth rate into its components allowed for a finer analysis of lower level trends; Whelpton and Thompson isolated the past birthrate and deathrate trends of the urban and rural, native white, foreign white, and nonwhite sectors, and extended the past numerical trend of each sector to a near-future time. Then, reweighting the sectors on the basis of their new projected proportions. Whelpton and Thompson repeated the extension process to the future time. Their iterative model enabled then not only to project fine details of population composition, but also to view the numerous potentially important trends which had balanced out or were otherwise hidden within the overall growth rate.

The component method also led Whelpton and Thompson to a much less deterministic conception of population growth—seen as only the outcome of many different trends, population growth admits of more uncertainty in its future levels, which depend on the many unpredictable social and economic background variables affecting the component rates for the various sectors. Whereas Pearl knew that his projections had to be right, Whelpton and Thompson's projections were "merely statements of what the size . . . of the population would be at specified future times if birth rates, death rates, and immigration were to follow [a] certain specified trend." [16]

In their 1935 projections, Whelpton and Thompson proved they were serious about the indeterminacy of future population levels by publishing several different series of projections to accommodate different assumptions of fertility, mortality, and migration. Though publishing several projection series does serve the purpose of keeping policymakers aware of the inherent interdeterminacy of future population levels, nevertheless to the extent that policymakers need or want a single projection, they will use the middle series of projections as if it were the only one. The middle prediction will be interpreted as the "average," or most likely, prediction. In the analysis of prediction accuracy that follows, the middle series of each set of projections is the prediction chosen for evaluation.

The Cohort Method

Whelpton and Thompson's contribution was the explicit and full use of the growth rate components which had been used only partially and implicitly in previous projection techniques. Dublin and Lotka made a similar sort of advance in 1930 by suggesting the explicit use of the population's age distribution. Their predecessors, including Whelpton and Thompson, had considered age distribution less formally in forecasting birthrate and deathrate trends for larger units of the population. It seems appropriate that Dublin and Lotka, writing for

[16] W. S. Thompson and P. K. Whelpton, *Estimates of Future Population of the United States, 1940–2000* (Washington, D.C.: National Resources Planning Board, 1943), p. 3.

the Metropolitan Life Insurance Company, would recommend taking full advantage of the actuarial breakdown of age-specific birthrates and deathrates. With a life table giving for every age the proportion of persons born who survive to that age, and an age schedule of maternity frequency, one could project the size of each age group (cohort) into each succeeding decade and determine its contribution of new births by applying the age-specific fertility rate to the size of that age group.

Dublin and Lotka's message was that the observed birthrate and deathrate, like the overall growth rate, were compound measures which could be deceptive when considered as indivisible units.[17] The women in a population with a currently high birthrate are not necessarily more fertile than other women; there simply may be relatively more women in the fertile twenty- to forty-year-old age group within the population. Similarly, a high deathrate may be explained by a large proportion of elderly, as well as by a high "natural" mortality.

Dublin and Lotka did not mention separating the population into sectors based on factors other than age, such as the white–nonwhite or urban–rural distinctions of Whelpton and Thompson. In fact, they used the fertility and mortality tables appropriate for the white population alone, maintaining that the ultimate difference between using separate tables and combined tables was negligible.

Dublin and Lotka put their technically unobjectionable method to very unorthodox use, with quite disastrous results. The assumed that the American people had acquired an inherent level of "true reproductive activity." For each age group the fertility was constant over time as was the mortality. They believed that in 1930 the true "fecundity" was actually in balance with the true "mortality" of the population, meaning that if the age distribution had been regular (i.e., if the smooth pyramidal age distribution, produced by the prolonged operations of a constant birthrate and deathrate, prevailed), the birthrate would balance the deathrate. But because our population was "overloaded" with people in midlife, due to immigration and a recently declining birthrate, more births were occurring than deaths. By assigning the constant age-specific birthrates and deathrates to each cohort for successive generations, Dublin and Lotka generated declining overall birthrates and increasing deathrates that would smooth out the bulge in the age distribution pyramid, so that the crude rate of increase would eventually (in 1970) reach the "true" rate of increase, namely zero.

Dublin and Lotka never justified their assumption that for any given age cohort the fertility and mortality will be constant; indeed, they quoted a change in the true rate of increase from 5.2 per 1,000 in 1920 to 0 per 1,000 in 1930. Perhaps they believed that once the bulk of upsetting immigration was over, the rhythm of population regeneration would return to its natural course, but it would seem that their assumption of constant age-specific birthrates and deathrates shows a blatant disregard for the social and economic factors influencing

17 Dublin and Lotka, *op. cit.*, pp. 109–10.

fertility and mortality, and their choice of zero as the true rate of increase seems to be a strained and unsubstantiated justification of the stabilizing growth theory.

Synthesis of Techniques

The official population projections of the 1940's did not adopt Dublin and Lotka's valid advance of the cohort method, perhaps because Dublin and Lotka's age-specific breakdown was hidden within such a large set of complicated methods and assumptions. Whelpton and Thompson's method of projecting birthrates and deathrates for the six combinations of urban, rural, native white, foreign white, and nonwhite was simpler and could accommodate the grosser distortions in the population age structure by incorporating their presumed effects in the projections of birthrate and deathrate trends, without using formal mathematical methods to determine just how much difference age structure would make.

The official projectors accepted Pearl's assumption of the inevitability of a decline in population increase, even though the decreasing birthrate, the main justification for predicting a logistic leveling, had reversed itself in 1937 to a small increase which even World War II could affect only slightly.[18] Pearl's assumption of imminent growth rate decline, with its aura of scientific certainty, had been around for so long that it was accepted as fact long after its justification had disappeared. Thus, the Census Bureau's estimates were formed by combining projections of constant numerical migration (hence, decreasing *rate* of migration), fairly constant deathrates, and declining birthrates for all sectors. They followed Whelpton's example[19] of publishing several series of projections based on varying assumptions which, in their diversity, tended to obscure the fact that the median assumption, the one that would generate the projection series most likely to be used as "the" projection, called for a declining growth rate. Generally the *highest* series of projections used the current birthrate as the birthrate for future years; the other two or three series assumed lower birth rates than were current.

Starting around 1953 the official projectors, perhaps stung by professional articles criticising the poor performance of prior projections,[20] developed a more elaborate projection method which combined Dublin and Lotka's cohort method with a population segment breakdown as suggested by Whelpton and Thompson. They could use the different age-specific fertility and mortality schedules

[18] R. Pearl, *The Biology of Population Growth*, p. 25.

[19] W. S. Thompson and P. K. Whelpton, *Population Trends in the United States* (New York: McGraw-Hill, 1933), p. 316.

[20] H. F. Dorn, "Pitfalls in Population Forecasts and Projections," *Journal of the American Statistical Association*, Vol. 45, No. 251 (September 1950), pp. 311–34; see also H. Hajnal, "The Prospects for Population Forecasts," *Journal of the American Statistical Association*, Vol. 50, No. 270 (June 1955), pp. 309–22.

for the white and nonwhite, rural and urban populations to follow each cohort into the future years to determine the number of its survivors and its contributions of births. Therefore, the age-specific fertility rate could be distinguished from the birthrate, which reflects the temporary population age distribution, rather than an inherent characteristic of fertility. They would abandon gross deathrates in favor of age-specific mortality rates. Yet, they would also retain the distinctions between groups within the population that would be likely to have different fertility and mortality schedules.[21] It appears that the urban–rural distinction is not being used currently to define population segments, probably because of the frequent arbitrary reclassifications of rural areas to urban status on the basis of population growth.[22]

EVALUATING PROJECTIONS

The various projection methods can be evaluated either in terms of the ultimate correctness of their underlying assumptions or in terms of how close the predicted population levels come to the actual levels. Errors of either sort are important because they both reduce the perceived expertise and reliability of the projector. In so far as future population levels are projected in order to make planning and policy decisions, however, the accuracy of the projections themselves is more important.

The inaccuracy of these projections expressed here as the percentage error of a prediction made in year X for the population in year $X + t$, equals:

$$\frac{\text{actual population in year } X + t \text{ minus predicted population in year } X + t}{\text{actual population in year } X + t} \text{ times } 100\%$$

By allowing t to equal five, ten, and twenty years, a basis for comparing projections of different lead times made in different years is provided. Since long-term projections generally are made only for decade or half-decade intervals, predictions made in other than decade or half-decade years do not usually provide estimates for precisely five, ten, and twenty years into the future. For comparability, the projections made in 1909, 1928, and 1941 are considered as if they had been made in 1910, 1930, and 1940 respectively.

The graphical representation of the accuracy of the projections, expressed in Figure 8–1, contradicts our natural tendency to assume that newer methods are necessarily more successful methods. Instead, the projections of the early curve fitters, especially Pearl, were generally more accurate in their ten-year projections than were the projections derived by the more sophisticated com-

[21] U.S. Department of Commerce, *Current Population Reports*, Series P–25, Nos. 18, 78, 187, and 212.
[22] *Statistical Abstract of the United States, 1968*, p. 2.

FIGURE 8-1. ACCURACY OF FIVE-, TEN-, AND TWENTY-YEAR
            PREDICTIONS OF U.S. POPULATION

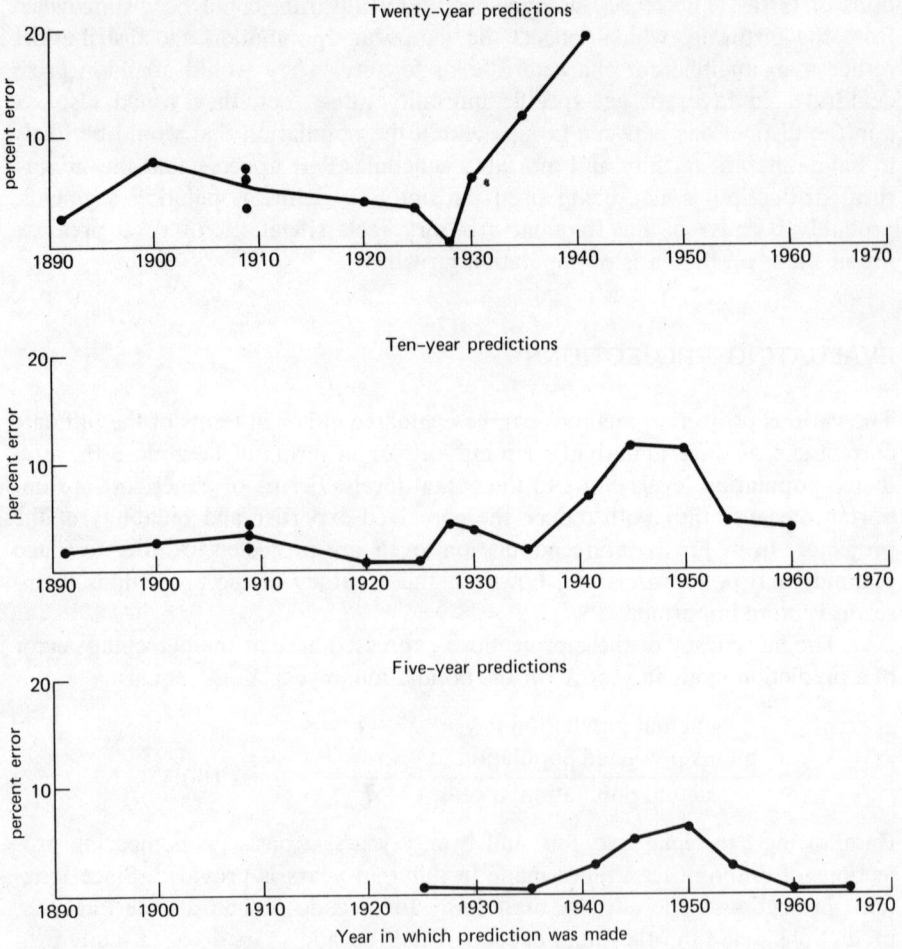

Twenty-year predictions

Ten-year predictions

Five-year predictions

Year in which prediction was made

ponent and cohort methods used later, though in the twenty-year projections, the accuracy of the curve fitters and the Whelpton–Thompson and Dublin–Lotka approaches was about the same.

The worst predictions came in the period 1940–55. The large errors are especially embarrassing in light of the prevailing faith in the progress and increasing sophistication of the methodology. Could it be that the sixty-year advance in demographic expertise from 1890 to 1950 yielded a 500% increase in error?

The first defense that comes to mind is that the accuracies of predictions made at different times are not really comparable because the more recent population growth has been more volatile and erratic, and hence is inherently more difficult to predict. Table 8–1 demonstrates one way of controlling for the alleged variability of the rates of recent population growth, by expressing the inaccuracy of ten-year predictions (not all sources provided five- and twenty-year predictions) as the percent error divided by a measure of the variation in growth rate during the ten-year period, namely the mean deviation of single-year rates from the period's overall annual rate:

$$\% \text{ error of prediction} \Bigg/ \left(\sum_{i=1}^{10} (|\text{overall annual rate minus rate in year } i|)/10 \right)$$

TABLE 8–1.   PROJECTION ERRORS STANDARDIZED
              BY GROWTH RATE VARIABILITY

Year of Prediction	% Error of 10-Year Prediction	Mean Deviation from Decade Growth Rate	% Error Divided by Mean Deviation
1900 Pritchett	1.8 (+)	.076	23.7
1909 Sloane	3.9 (−)	.353	11.0
1909 Woodruff	3.7 (−)	.353	10.5
1909 Gannet	2.3 (−)	.353	6.5
1920 Pearl	0.4 (−)	.253	1.6
1925 Pearl	0.2 (−)	.310	0.6
1928 Whelpton–Thompson	4.3 (+)	.129	33.3
1930 Dublin–Lotka	3.4 (−)	.129	26.4
1935 Whelpton–Thompson	1.5 (−)	.435	3.5
1941 *Statistical Abstract*	6.7 (−)	.291	23.0
1945 *Statistical Abstract*	11.2 (−)	.131	85.6
1950 *Statistical Abstract*	10.8 (−)	.054	200.0
1955 *Statistical Abstract*	4.3 (−)	.134	32.1

Essentially the same relative magnitudes of error differences remain. Consequently, the underestimates of the 1940–55 period cannot be attributed to more volatile or erratic population growth. Indeed, the variability in yearly growth rates during the more recent period has *not* exceeded that of earlier periods.

A more subtle defense, frequently used, maintains that projections can only be expected to forecast future conditions undisturbed by unforeseeable and unpredictable events such as wars and other catastrophes. Since the predictions made during the 1940–55 period were all too low, the "postwar baby boom" has been regarded as the occurrence responsible for the unexpected increase in birthrate and, hence, population. The argument is: The boom resulted from the occurrence of World War II, a phenomenon which population projectors could not be expected to predict from previous demographic data. Therefore, the boom itself was inherently unpredictable from demographic data, so the predictors' failing to anticipate the boom ought to be exonerated. Nonetheless, the statistics of postwar population growth betray this reasoning.

As in Figure 8–2, population growth during and after the war had the *net* effect of smooth growth as predictable linearly from the yearly growth rate from

FIGURE 8-2. U.S. POPULATION: 1920–22 AND 1940–50

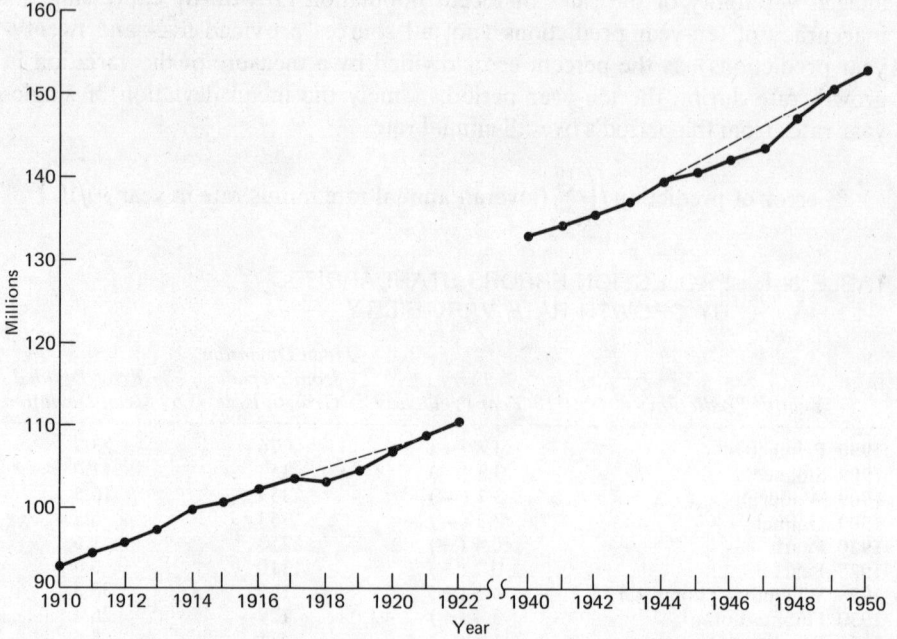

1937 to 1942. The high birthrate and growth rate of the postwar period only compensated for the births postponed because of the war. The interpretation of the growth of this period as a "boom" was a result of the unfulfilled expectation of a radical *decrease* in the pace of population growth. However, by this time there were no existing data that could justify this assumption of decreasing growth; the expectation was isolated from the available data, resulting in large prediction errors.

In the mid-1950's and the 1960's the belief in the inevitability of birthrate reduction was abandoned. However, a vestige of Pearl's thinking still remains in the bias toward lower birthrates; the *highest* projection series is based on the *current* fertility level: "Series A [the *highest* projection series] results do not differ substantially from those obtained by assuming that the average annual level of fertility in the 1962–1966 period will persist throughout the projection period." [23]

Although the most recent projections cannot yet be evaluated, it appears that projections in 1955 and 1960 were about as accurate as the curve-fitting or the simpler iterative model methods of the past, and much better than the 1940–50 projections. On the basis of the projection accuracy alone it is impossible to say whether the improvement was due to the change in method, the (partial) abandonment of the unwarranted birthrate decline assumption, or the

[23] *Ibid.*, p. 8.

charity of the population level in "accidentally" conforming to the projections.

The error magnitudes shown in Figure 8–1 reveal, as would be expected, that the shorter term predictions are in general more accurate than longer term predictions. To express this tendency more plainly, Figure 8–3 arranges the error magnitudes of predictions of 1960 and 1970 population levels in order of the date of prediction.

FIGURE 8-3. THE ACCURACY OF PROJECTIONS OF 1960 AND 1970 U.S. POPULATION[a]

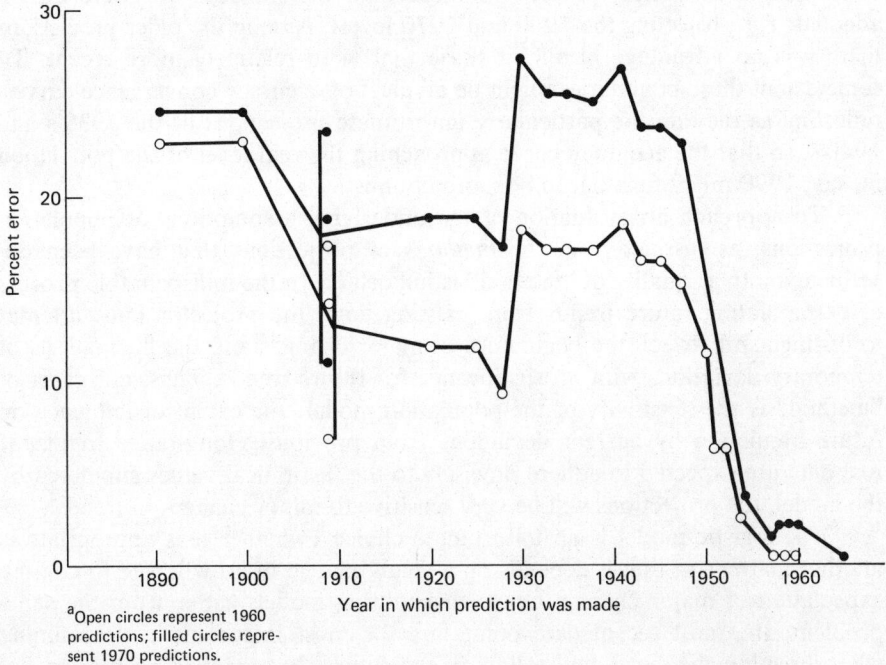

Year in which prediction was made

[a]Open circles represent 1960 predictions; filled circles represent 1970 predictions.

For both the 1960 and the 1970 projections, there is an eventual convergence of later projections toward the correct population level. The later projections, made in years closer to the date to which the prediction is made, could be expected to improve as they approach this date by virtue of the more recent data available. There is less room for error in making a short-term extrapolation than in making a long-term one. Yet, the convergence is neither smooth nor monotonic. For the 1960 population level, Gannet's sixty-year-old projection was more accurate than the official projection of 1950. And, again, the 1940–50 projections, despite their advantage of the availability of newer data, were worse than the older projections. The evidence is even more damning when one considers that since the projections are for a fixed year, the comparison of prediction accuracy cannot be attacked by the argument that differing accuracy is due to differing degrees of erratic population growth preceding the dates for which the projections were made. In comparing the accuracy of all predictions of 1960 population and all predictions of 1970 population, it is clear that the different projective techniques used over the years definitely have the same relative success that was manifested in the comparison of five-, ten-, and twenty-year projections.

The curves in Figure 8–3 allow for consideration of the lead time of good predictions. The prediction of the 1960 population level did not come close to the actual level until 1951, and the predictions of the 1970 level did not come close until 1954. Thus, predictions more than fifteen years old were all inadequate for projecting the 1960 and 1970 levels. Among the older predictions there was no advantage at all for those that were relatively more recent. To some extent these boundaries might be atypical of accuracy convergence curves, reflecting as they do the particularly unfortunate projections of the 1930's and 1940's, so that the accuracy curve approaching the real level of the population in, say, 1990 might turn out to be more optimistic.

To approach an evaluation of the underlying assumptions of population projections, as distinct from the *methods* of projections that have been described, another quality of "method" is important. In the indispensable process of extrapolating future trends from existing data, the projector must attempt to distinguish between the beginnings of major changes and the fluctuations of temporary deviations with no significance for future trends. Thus, one facet of "method" is the sensitivity of the population model: the extent of influence on future prediction by current deviations from previously long-range trends. If real data are expected to adhere precisely to the theoretical values stipulated by the model, the projections will be very sensitive to minor changes in trends.

The logistic model is an unfortunate choice (whether it is appropriate is another matter) in that it depends on a small change in growth rate to cue the expectation of major change. Other curve-fitting models suffer from the same problem: the most recent data points are the most important in determining what direction the curve will follow in the future, but there is no way to determine to what extent these points reflect temporary fluctuations, or to diffuse the effects of misleading fluctuations when they cause recent data points to deviate from the ultimately true curve of growth.

The component method provided the first means for determining the influence of temporary fluctuations; in breaking down the growth rate into birthrate, deathrate, and migration rate, a current deviation from a previous long-term trend could be attributed to change in fertility, mortality, or migration, which in turn could be attributed to a permanent or a temporary cause. For example, the drop in growth rate between 1917 and 1920 could have been explained by the unusually large decline in birthrate, easily attributed to the temporary conditions of wartime troop absence.

The cohort method has the capacity to diffuse the effects of temporary fluctuations. By determining which age cohort is experiencing a change in fertility or mortality rate responsible for an overall change in population growth, the projector can adjust his birth and death schedules for that cohort alone, thereby minimizing the overall effect of the fluctuation to the extent that it is specific to only a limited set of age cohorts.

When the component and cohort methods are combined, the projections are much less susceptible to the exaggeration of temporary fluctuations, because a more precise locus of change can be identified and adjusted. For example, if the growth rate were to decline for two years, the curve fitters would have no choice but to assume that the population was leveling off and would continue to do so. Using the component method, the projector could at least identify the cause of the growth rate decline as a decline in birthrate, deathrate, or migration rate. By using the combined component and cohort methods, the projector could discover that, for example, the source of change was confined to a marked increase in the mortality rate of the between sixty- and seventy-year-old white urban cohort. The public health records of the two years would indicate whether the mortality increase was due to a temporary cause such as an influenza epidemic. If the cause turned out to be fairly chronic, e.g., emphysema, census data will reveal the sizes of the urban white cohorts entering that age period, which may be relatively smaller or larger than the present cohort.

The mistake of "falling for" temporary fluctuations is probably not confined to the past. The declining birthrate scenario of the 1910–33 period is re-occurring, with a 1966 birthrate of 17.4 per 1,000 population, lower than the nadir of the earlier period. The projector is faced with the question of whether the birthrate will continue to decline, as it has since 1957. The official projections have opted for continued birthrate decline, in that the *highest* projection series assumes the *current* birthrate. But if childbearing is considered a human activity at least partially under human control, this blithe assumption that the birthrate will decline indefinitely simply because it has declined in the recent past is unjustified and probably invites another era of low population projections. There is the reasonable argument that needed population control will induce a lower birthrate, but the error of equating desirability with future reality has occurred before:

. . . the pre-eminent American student of future population during the 1930's and 1940's, P. K. Whelpton was persuaded of the desirability of an imminent stabilization of population size. In his 1947 report, Whelpton adduced arguments tending to show that the U.S. was not below its long run economic optimum population. He observed, moreover, that the slackening of growth would be favorable to the interests of conservationists and that it might lead to improvement in the quality of the population.[24]

Considering the past tendency of the birthrate to increase from time to time— despite the protests of demographers—the very highest projection of the 1990 population level, given officially at 300,000,0000, ought to be considered as only a medium estimate. Granting the same latitude between the official highest

---

[24] O. D. Duncan, "Social Forecasting: The State of the Art," *The Public Interest,* No. 17 (Fall 1969), pp. 88–118, at pp. 91–92.

and middle 1990 projections, the highest 1990 projection for a set of projection series *centered at* (rather than bounded by) the current birthrate, would be 321,500,000; or 21,500,000 *more* than the currently predicted *highest* level.

It is obvious, however, that a certain degree of sensitivity to fluctuations is essential since any projective method must be capable of responding to changes in the sources of population growth. Population predictions are too important for planning future facilities to allow today's projectors to ignore recent data, as Pritchett (see note 5) did when he reapplied his 1891 projections in 1900 without a single change. His ten- and twenty-year projections published in 1900 were considerably less accurate than were his 1891 projections.[25]

The error of disregarding existing data in projecting future trends is no better than the error of considering every short-term change as the precursor of major change. Along with its facilities for determining which fluctuations are likely to have temporary causes and hence temporary existence, the component–cohort method, by the same operation of identifying the course of change, can indicate which trends are likely to be long lasting. The prevailing component–cohort combination method *can* provide the projector with every opportunity to project future trends on the basis of the complete set of existing data, but the official projections have not taken full advantage of this capacity.

LENGTH OF PROJECTIONS: ACCURACY AND PLAUSIBILITY

The relationship between the eventual correctness of the projector's assumptions and the accuracy of his predictions is an odd one, providing some lessons for current forecasting projects. It would seem reasonable to expect that the more accurate the overall assumptions of a projection technique, the more accurate its projections. This is not necessarily the case for the shorter term predictions within a projection series.

The overall correctness of the assumptions of a given projection series is generally evaluated in terms of the accuracy of its longest projections. On the basis of our present knowledge we would say that Pritchett's longest estimate of 40 *billion* Americans in 2900 is so greatly exaggerated that we would conclude that his choice of growth curve was fundamentally wrong.[26] Pritchett must have realized that his curve was not expressing a universal theory of population growth when he mentioned that although his estimates within this century would be accurate, his estimate for the year 2900 was more than 200 times as large as our current population, while contemporaries were doubting the possibility of the earth's capacity to supply food to a *world* population of 40 billion.[27] And certainly Pearl's long-range assertion that the population ceiling would be 197

[25] H. S. Pritchett, "A Formula for Predicting the Population of the United States," pp. 278–86; and Pritchett, "The Population of the United States during the Next Ten Decades."

[26] H. S. Pritchett, "A Formula for Predicting the Population of the United States," p. 286.

[27] See E. M. East, *Mankind at the Crossroads* (New York: Scribners, 1928), p. 69.

million disqualifies his particular logistic curve from being correct.[28] Yet this means neither that their short- and middle-range projections were inaccurate, nor that their methods and assumptions were wrong *when confined to the shorter span of projection.*

Both Pritchett and Pearl were remarkably accurate in their five-, ten-, and twenty-year projections, even though their 1960 and 1970 projections were quite inaccurate. Their example provides two lessons. First, the worth of the short and medium predictions in a projection series is *not* best judged by the ultimate capacity of the projection method to forecast accurately the very distant future. Second, since projections *will* be judged and accepted according to their overall plausability, the projector is well advised to confine his projections to only that period for which he believes projections are useful. There will always be a temptation to allow a promising method to churn out its projections indefinitely into the future, but the very distant projections may jeopardize the credibility of the entire endeavor, as in Pritchett's case. By foregoing the satisfaction of making very distant projections, short-range and medium-range projections will stand untainted by what may be seen as ridiculous long-range guesses.

THE ACCOUNTING SYSTEM AS CONTRASTED WITH THEORIES OF GROWTH

Compared to the bold, if incorrect, assumptions of earlier projectors, today's projection methods seem somehow sterile. Indeed, the multicategory method in current use is more of an accounting system than it is an application of population growth assumptions. The current method is certainly indisputable as far as it goes, since the disaggregation of population into cohorts, and the population growth into components, "costs" nothing in terms of adding potentially unwarranted assumptions to the analysis.

From the technical point of view, demographic projection methodology has continually improved. The most significant improvement has been the progressive refinement in the choice of basic behavior upon which trend assumptions must be made. Because of the accounting methods that can convert basic information such as age-specific fertility rates into total population growth patterns for a given population structure, we can afford to focus our assumptions on the most basic behavioral indicators, namely age-specific fertility and mortality, rather than on cruder indicators such as total fertility, general birthrates, or even general growth rates.

Nevertheless, we have not eliminated the necessity of assuming a future trend in *some* factor. Even perfect accounting devices cannot fully correct the errors in the core of any projection method—the assumptions of the future

[28] R. Pearl and L. J. Reed, "On the Rate of Growth of the Population of the United States since 1790 and Its Mathematical Representation," p. 285.

trends in the basic behavior. Given age-specific fertility and mortality rates, we can generate accurate population projections out to any point in the future. But where are these fertility and mortality rates coming from? Too often they are derived from the most primitive assumptions that "all trends will continue as they are now," and then hidden by elaborate methods that convert the essentially atheoretical rates into population projections.

The cohort–component method enables careful accounting of trends, but the modern projector still must wrestle with the same demographic assumptions as his predecessors, because he must generate "mini-projections" for each of his many cohort–components. If he simply takes current fertility and mortality schedules and applies them iteratively, he is making Dublin and Lotka's very strong assumption of a constant, inherent capacity of fertility; if the projector does not assume constant fertility, he must decide which trends manifested in existing data for each cohort–component will be continued in the future. Thus, even though the modern methods are more sophisticated in their disaggregation of population growth, the projector still faces the dilemma of whether current trends are "noise" or significant changes.

A possible approach to neutralizing the ill effects of deceptive current fluctuations would be to assume that each cohort's fertility and mortality rates over the period extending t years from the prediction-making date will be the average fertility and mortality rates of the t years prior to the prediction-making year. As the prediction date is extended into the more distant future, the projected fertility and mortality rates become more reflective of their general past levels than of the most current rates.

A method that restores past levels is justified only in projecting rates that may be considered to reflect inherent capacities temporarily increased or decreased by social conditions which are far less predictable in the far distant future. This method also acknowledges that the business of making long-term predictions is not the same as the business of making short-term ones. Population growth rates of the near future are the result of current fluctuations and are, therefore, best predicted by the most current changes. However, population growth rates of the distant future will be influenced by conditions as yet unknown, so that the estimate of maximum likelihood would be the rate manifested in a period of the most recent past that is long enough to diminish the importance of temporary fluctuations—unless, of course, there are justifications beyond the demographic data to alter the expectations of fertility and mortality rates. It is reasonable to expect continued decreases in age-specific mortality rates, such that our projection of mortality rates ten years from now would not be the current ten-year average. Yet, if we were projecting distant future fertility rates without imposing social or economic theories positing either an increase or a decrease in fertility, we would do best to assume that the average fertility rate of the current *era* (as far in the past as the projected year is in the future) is virtually the "inherent" fertility rate.

PREDICTABILITY OF POPULATION GROWTH

The efforts of this chapter to classify and evaluate projective techniques would be useless if it were true that future population growth is inherently unpredictable. John Hajnal, after reviewing the disastrous projections made prior to 1954, maintained that:

These factors whose effects on future growth we can calculate are likely to be frequently outweighed by the unpredictable. It is this which accounts for the failure of more complex techniques to yield more accurate results than simple techniques and which casts doubt on the value of forecasting. We cannot hope to develop better methods which yield forecasts clustering more and more closely around the true future population. New and more complex techniques which may yet be invented are, I think, just as liable as past techniques to be fairly often upset by the unpredictablility of history. They will probably just as often—and that means rather frequently—give results which are very wide of the mark and less accurate than crude guessing.[29]

Deciding whether population is predictable is equivalent to judging the magnitudes of variations caused by demographically unpredictable events, e.g., wars or depressions. The population growth data for the periods directly before and after the world wars contradict Hajnal's impression that such major events render future population levels so hopelessly unpredictable. As Figure 8–2 shows, both World War I and World War II had little net effect on population growth. The initial lulls in growth were followed by compensating increases, as would be expected from considerations of the motives of returning servicemen to restore their life plans which had been interrupted by the wars.

Our final conclusion would be that the future *is* predictable, to a greater extent than past projections have accomplished. With careful methods and freedom from unwarranted but fashionable assumptions, this improvement may be achieved.

Each year it becomes more compelling to realize improved projections because of their increasingly crucial role in ensuring rational planning. It is easier today than ten years ago to argue that inaccurate forecasting has harmful effects on future living conditions. Instead of enjoying a gradual increase in the relative number of medical personnel and facilities, as was planned in the context of more modest population growth expectations, Americans have witnessed a stagnation in medical service accessibility, partially due to the sluggish growth of medical schools and hospitals in response to low *perceived* future demands. In housing the same problem of inadequate planning in response to population underestimates has become obvious. Our housing and medical facilities are adequate for serving the lower population level that was foreseen twenty years ago, which proves the good will of the planners, but also the inadequacy of the projection bases of the plans.

[29] Hajnal, *op. cit.*, p. 311.

As the many facets of American society become increasingly interdependent, the system loses its capacity to make successful ad hoc adjustments to correct the effects of prior errors without serious dislocations. In other words, in a complex society there is less flexibility for rectifying misplanning. Projections are, therefore, all the more important in a complex society because precise planning requires, as a start, precise conceptions of future conditions.

Chapter 9
Policy and the Study of the Future: Given Complexity, Trends, or Processes?

RONALD D. BRUNNER
AND
GARRY D. BREWER

Studying the future for policy purposes presents many important methodological choices, not the least of which is deciding whether to forecast by extrapolating trends or by using process models. This chapter argues the merits of the latter.

After introducing a minimum number of essential concepts in the formal study of political systems by way of presenting an illustrative process model, we explore the effect that complexity has on the analytical tractability of the system. Consequent implications for the scientific study of policy are sketched out as appropriate.

At this early stage in the scientific study of the future for policy purposes, many important methodological choices face social scientists. One important choice concerns the relative utility of forecasting by extrapolating trends or by using process models. The former is the most familiar method,[1] and the latter is considered to be one of the most promising.[2]

This choice and the issues rooted in it were raised at a symposium on "The Nature and Limitations of Forecasting," sponsored by the Commission on the Year 2000 of the American Academy of Arts and Sciences.[3] Wassily Leontieff pointed out the conflicting assumptions of the two methods and advocated the use of models for policy purposes.

There are predictions by models and predictions by trends. Predictions by models are based on the belief that it is possible to view the world as one whole with separate parts that are in some way interrelated. Prediction by trends gives us a view of the world

---

[1] Daniel Bell, "Twelve Modes of Prediction—A Preliminary Sorting of Approaches in the Social Sciences," *Daedalus,* Vol. 93 (Summer 1964), p. 850.

[2] *Ibid.,* pp. 872–73.

[3] *Daedalus,* Vol. 96 (Summer 1967), pp. 936–47.

Portions of this chapter were read at a conference on "Methodological Techniques and Projecting the Future," held at Santa Barbara, California, in December 1970. Some material is taken from our book, *Organized Complexity: Empirical Theories of Political Development,* copyright © 1971 by The Free Press, New York, A Division of Macmillan Publishing Co., Inc.

as if it were a handful of sand, each particle distinct from the others. . . . To discuss policies not in a deterministic way, but as a problem of choice, I think you must work with models. To build policies into trends is difficult.[4]

Using the example of stock market forecasting, Martin Shubik took the position that the "chartists" who extrapolate trends cannot be dismissed so easily because of time constraints on the decision process.

There are the chartists and the fundamentalists. The fundamentalists want to discover as much as they can about the firm—where its technology is going and so forth—while the chartists draw some linear extrapolations of what is going on and invent such phrases as "when the thing has heads and shoulders." You cannot idly dismiss the chartists, because in one sense a key to forecasting is the amount of time one has available in the decision process to make a statement about the future. A chartist can come up with some sort of fairy tale in ten or fifteen minutes. If you do not have more time, perhaps that is the best you can get.[5]

Shubik goes on to advocate the construction of,

. . . an incremental systematic process that involves among other things, linking large data-processing procedures with models or conceptual frameworks. This would give an opportunity to link the fundamentalist and chartist approaches.[6]

We reconsider this and similar proposals in the final section of this chapter.

Two lines of inquiry can be used to clarify empirical distinctions between the two methods, particularly the underlying assumption about the consequences of failing to "view the world as one whole with separate parts that are in some way interrelated." One is a small computer simulation model of modernization and mass politics developed to trace patterns of demographic, economic, and political change in two of the less developed countries.[7] Though merely a first approximation, this model is sufficiently broad in scope to serve the present purposes. The other is the Ando–Fisher theorem on the decomposability of systems, which defines some of the circumstances under which system components can be separated and studied independently.[8] We wish to explore the nature of the interdependence in social systems, to show how systems might be decomposed into their component parts for analytic purposes, and to relate the results to the choice of models in policy analysis and projection.

After introducing some essential concepts in the formal study of political systems, we provide an overview of the model and assess the degree of interdependence among its components. Then we introduce the Ando–Fisher

[4] *Ibid.*, p. 941.

[5] *Ibid.*, p. 945.

[6] *Ibid.*

[7] See the essay "Modernization and Mass Politics" in Brunner and Brewer, *Organized Complexity*, pp. 1–82.

[8] See Albert Ando, Franklin M. Fisher, and Herbert A. Simon, *Essays on the Structure of Social Science Models* (Cambridge, Mass.: The MIT Press, 1963), pp. 92–106, 108–9.

theorem and use it to assess the error involved in abstracting political trends from the rest of the model. The fourth section summarizes the limitations of the fundamentalist approach, and the final section considers some general proposals that compensate for these limitations.

FORMAL SYSTEMS

The difference between the chartist and fundamentalist approaches can be stated concisely if we conceive of a system as a state vector X_t and a set of relationships G.

$$X_t \equiv \begin{vmatrix} x_{1, t} \\ x_{2, t} \\ \vdots \\ x_{n, t} \end{vmatrix} \tag{9-1}$$

$$X_t = G(x_t, x_{t-1}, \ldots)$$

The state vector is merely the set of variables and parameters needed to describe the state of the system at any point in time. The relationships G are hypotheses about process, inferred from the observation of real-world systems, describing how the components change as a function of each other through time. (x_t is included on the right side of the equation because one component $x_{i, t}$ may be a function of some other component $x_{j, t}$ within the same time period, as in the example considered below.)

The *structure* of a class of systems (e.g., countries in a region) is the set of variables X_t and the set of relationships G. Together they constitute a theory, a temporary commitment to, and representation of, the phenomena of importance in the systems. A *model* of any one of the systems is the general structure with the magnitudes of the variables and parameters specified to represent the particular context. The *behavior* of a model is the set of time series of the $x_{i, t}$ (the individual components of X_t) which are produced as the model generates successive state descriptions.

The chartist approach to studying the future of systems assumes, at least implicitly, that the connections among different components either do not exist according to a theory, or that they are sufficiently weak in any particular system that they can be safely ignored. The value of any component $x_{i, t}$ at any time t depends only on its previous values and random disturbances u (which may or may not be included in the analysis). Thus,

$$x_{i, t} = f(x_{i, t-1}, x_{i, t-2}, \ldots) + u \tag{9-2}$$

For example, a very simple means of extrapolating rural population growth is the relationship:

$$x_{1, t} = (1 + a) x_{1, t-1} + u \tag{9-3}$$

in which $x_{1, t}$ is the size of the rural population at time t, and a is the rate of natural increase. $x_{1, t}$ is independent of the other variables in the system.

The fundamentalist approach assumes that at least some of the possible interdependencies exist in general and are sufficiently important in the specific country. The behavior of each component may depend upon its past behavior and random disturbances u, as well as on other variables in the system. Thus,

$$x_{i, t} = f\ (x_{i, t-1},\ x_{i, t-2},\ \ldots,\ x_{j, t},\ x_{j, t-1},\ \ldots) \qquad (9\text{--}4)$$

For example, the relationship (9–3) can be respecified to produce:

$$x_{1, t} = (1 + a)\ x_{1, t-1} - x_{2, t} + u \qquad (9\text{--}5)$$

where $x_{2, t}$ is the amount of urbanization at time t. The size of the rural population depends on natural increase, as well as the loss through urbanization.

Models of the fundamentalist type entail a number of problems making them difficult to evaluate and revise scientifically given the current state of the art. Two of these problems play an important role in our argument at a later point. One problem is that as the number of components and sufficiently strong connections among components increases, the links between the structure and behavior of a model become increasingly obscured by complex interactions. At some point it becomes very difficult to attribute specific errors of fit between simulated and historical time series to specific aspects of the model's structure. Consequently, it becomes increasingly difficult to evaluate and revise the structure.

The other problem is that the data used as inputs to a model (values of initial conditions and parameters) and the historical time-series data used to evaluate its outputs contain both systematic and random components. The former can be attributed to real-world processes of the kind hypothesized in the model, and the latter to variables left out of the model, to stochastic factors, and to measurement error. As the number of components and interdependencies in a model increases, increasingly long sequences of calculations are required to deduce the behavior of the model, which may result in the cumulation of the random components in the input data.[9] In any case, the larger the random components in either input data or historical time-series data, the more difficult it is to attribute errors of fit to the structure of the model and, consequently, the more difficult it is to evaluate and revise the structure.

Strategies that are at least partially effective have been devised to cope with these problems.[10] For our present purposes, however, it is sufficient to

[9] See William Alonso, "The Quality of Data and the Choice of Design of Predictive Models," in *Urban Development Models* (Washington, D.C.: Highway Research Board, Special Report 97, 1968), pp. 178–92. Alonso does not resolve the question of whether data errors cumulate in models with negative feedback mechanisms, as well as in other types of models.

[10] Aggregation, for example, tends to cumulate the systematic components of data and cancel the random ones. See G. U. Yule and M. G. Kendall, *An Introduction to the Theory of Statistics* (London: Griffin, 14th ed., 1950), p. 314. However, aggregation may increase the difficulty of choosing among alternative theories. See Guy H. Orcutt, Harold W. Watts, and John B. Edwards, "Data Aggregation and Information Loss," *American Economic Review*, Vol. 68 (September 1968), pp. 773–87.

emphasize that the problem of achieving a scientifically productive confrontation between theory and data depends in large part on the size and connectedness of the model and the accuracy of the data.

THE CONNECTEDNESS OF SYSTEM COMPONENTS

The model we use was designed to study the processes of modernization and mass politics in less developed countries, in particular Turkey and the Philippines. By *modernization* we mean primarily demographic and economic changes and changes in communications and transportation networks. By *mass politics* we mean political interactions among large aggregates of the population, not individual political actors. The aggregates defined in the model are the rural population, the urban population, the government, and (implicitly) the political opposition.

The components of this model consist of the set of variables and parameters listed and defined in Table 9–1. They are grouped into three subsystems: the demographic subsystem which is relatively specialized to the growth and distribution of the population $N_{i, t}$; the economic subsystem which is relatively specialized to the production and distribution of economic goods $Y_{i, t}$; and the political subsystem which is relatively specialized to the production of changes in the size and distribution of mass support for the government $V_{i, t}$ and the determination of the size and distribution of government expenditures $G_{i, t}$. The variables in each subsystem are denoted by uppercase letters and have time subscripts; the parameters are denoted by lowercase Latin and Greek letters, and are assumed to be constant over time. Any component with an i subscript is disaggregated into rural ($i = 1$) and urban ($i = 2$) subcomponents, and has a rural and urban aggregate ($i = 3$). Variables and parameters without i subscripts are defined only for the system as a whole, not the individual sectors.

The relationships in the model are grouped according to subsystems and presented in Table 9–2. These relationships are hypotheses about the way in which each variable changes as a function of the others, with the magnitude of the changes being determined in part by the parameters. They have been derived from Daniel Lerner's theory of political participation,[11] some general theoretical work, and case studies of Turkey and the Philippines.

Using inputs reflecting the situation in Turkey in 1950 and in the Philippines in 1951, the model was operated for ten yearly cycles to produce simulated time series of the variables for each country. A comparison of these simulated time series with the available time series from Turkey and the Philippines revealed that the maximum discrepancy between simulated and historical data (expressed as a percentage of historical data) for any variable in any individual year was about 17%. Average discrepancies were less than 5%. In short, in terms of the specification of its relationships and its behavior, the model bears

---

[11] Daniel Lerner, *The Passing of Traditional Society: Modernizing the Middle East* (New York: The Free Press, 1964), Chapter 2.

TABLE 9–1.   THE MODEL'S STATE VECTOR: VARIABLES AND PARAMETERS

a. Demographic Subsystem

U_t = The number of migrants from rural to urban areas at time t.
$N_{i, t}$ = The population of sector i at time t.
s = The proportion of the participant rural population that would urbanize when economic performance in the two sectors is the same.
a_i = The rate of natural increase in sector i.

b. Economic Subsystem

$Y_{i, t}$ = Gross product in constant currency for sector i at time t. Gross national product is the sum of gross product in the rural and urban sectors.
GR_t = Total government revenue from all revenue-generating schemes in constant currency.
$C_{i, t}$ = Consumption in constant currency in sector i at time t.
$I_{i, t}$ = Private investment in constant currency for sector i at time t.
$F_{i, t}$ = Net foreign contribution to sector i at time t, aggregating the value in constant currency of both commodity trade and monetary transfers.
τ_i = The effective tax rate in sector i.
m_i = The proportion of per capita gross disposable income consumed in sector i. Gross disposable income in sector i is $(1 - \tau_i)Y_{i, t}$.
r_i = The proportion of the change in per capita consumption which induces additions to (or deletions from) the previous level of investment.

c. Political Subsystem

$V_{i, t}$ = The proportion of sector i supporting the government at time t.
$G_{i, t}$ = Government expenditures in constant currency in sector i at time t.
$D_{i, t}$ = Government communications and transportation expenditures in constant currency in sector i at time t.
$P_{i, t}$ = The proportion of the people in sector i at time t who are participant.
$E_{i, t}$ = The expected rate of change in economic performance.
σ = The scale of fluctuations in support.
α_i = Political penetration, or the proportional extent to which responses to economic performance in sector i are channeled through the government.
β_i = The relative preference of the government for sector i.
γ_i = The ratio of government communications and transportation expenditures in sector i.
δ_i = The communications and transportation expenditures in constant currency in sector i at which the communications and transportation system can be maintained with no appreciable effect on participation.
ε = The ratio of the change in the expected rate of economic performance to the difference between the actual and expected rates.
WINVOT = The proportion of aggregate support below which the government loses the election.

enough resemblance to Turkey and the Philippines in the decade of the 1950's to be useful as a means of illustrating our methodological points. Those interested in additional information about the selection of components, the specification of relationships, and the fit between simulated and historical time series are referred to our essay on the model and its applications, "Modernization and Mass Politics" (noted above).

The degree of connectedness or interdependence implied in the relationships themselves (as opposed to the degree implied by the operation of the model in each national context) can be explored by noting the presence or

TABLE 9–2.   THE MODEL'S SET OF RELATIONSHIPS

a. Demographic Subsystem

$$U_t = s\left(\frac{C_{2,t}}{N_{2,t}}\frac{N_{1,t}}{C_{1,t}}\right)P_{1,t}N_{1,t} \tag{9-6}$$

$$N_{1,t} = (1 + a_1)N_{1,t-1} - U_{t-1} \tag{9-7}$$

$$N_{2,t} = (1 + a_2)N_{2,t-1} + U_{t-1} \tag{9-8}$$

b. Economic Subsystem

$$Y_{i,t} = C_{i,t} + I_{i,t} + G_{i,t} + F_{i,t} \tag{9-9}$$

$$GR_t = \tau_1 Y_{1,t-1} + \tau_2 Y_{2,t-1} \tag{9-10}$$

$$C_{i,t} = m_i(1 - \tau_i)Y_{i,t-1}\frac{N_{i,t}}{N_{i,t-1}} \tag{9-11}$$

$$I_{i,t} = I_{i,t-1}\frac{N_{i,t}}{N_{i,t-1}} + r_i\left(C_{i,t} - C_{i,t-1}\frac{N_{i,t}}{N_{i,t-1}}\right) \tag{9-12}$$

c. Political Subsystem

$$V_{i,t} = V_{i,t-1} + \alpha_i\sigma P_{i,t-1}[(1 - V_{i,t-1})V_{i,t-1}]^3\left[\frac{C_{i,t}}{N_{i,t}}\frac{N_{i,t-1}}{C_{i,t-1}} - E_{i,t-1}\right] \tag{9-13}$$

$$G_{i,t} = \beta_i\left[\frac{N_{i,t-1}V_{i,t-1} - \Delta(N_1 V_1)}{N_{i,t-1}V_{i,t-1} + N_{2,t-1}V_{2,t-1} - \Delta(N_1 V_1) - \Delta(N_2 V_2)}\right]GR_{t-1} \tag{9-14}$$

where $$\Delta N_i V_i = N_{i,t} V_{i,t} - N_{i,t-1} V_{i,t-1}$$

$$D_{i,t} = \gamma_i G_{i,t} \tag{9-15}$$

$$P_{i,t} = 1 - \left(\frac{\delta_i}{D_{i,t-1}}\right),\ P_{i,t} \geq P_{i,t-1} \tag{9-16}$$

$$E_{i,t} = E_{i,t-1} + \varepsilon\left(\frac{C_{i,t}}{N_{i,t}}\frac{N_{i,t-1}}{C_{i,t-1}} - E_{i,t-1}\right)P_{i,t-1} \tag{9-17}$$

$$V_{i,t} = (1 - V_{i,t})\ \text{if } t \text{ is an election year and } V_{3,t} < \text{WINVOT} \tag{9-18}$$

absence of causal links among the variables. Let us call this the structural connectedness of the model, which is summarized in Figure 9–1. The numerical entries in the cells of the matrix give the number of direct causal connections between the output (or row) variable and the input (or column) variable. Time subscripts have been ignored: Thus, for purposes of assessing the structural connectedness of the model, a variable at t is equivalent to the same variable at $t - 1$. Inspection of Figure 9–1 reveals that only 59 of 400 possible *pairs* of variables are directly connected.

This static description of the structural connectedness of the model underestimates the degree of connectedness among variables as the model operates

FIGURE 9-1. STRUCTURAL CONNECTEDNESS BY FUNCTIONAL SUBSYSTEMS[a]

Outputs		Inputs																				
		Demographic Subsystem			Economic Subsystem							Political Subsystem									
		U	N_1	N_2	Y_1	C_1	I_1	Y_2	C_2	I_2	GR	V_1	G_1	D_1	P_1	E_1	V_2	G_2	D_2	P_2	E_2
Demographic subsystem	U	0	1	1	0	0	0	0	0	0	0	0	0	0	0	0	0	0	0	0	0
	N_1	1	1	0	0	0	0	0	0	0	0	0	0	0	0	0	0	0	0	0	0
	N_2	1	0	1	0	0	0	0	0	0	0	0	0	0	0	0	0	0	0	0	0
Economic subsystem	Y_1	0	0	0	0	1	1	0	0	0	0	1	0	0	0	0	0	0	0	0	0
	C_1	0	1	1	1	1	0	0	0	0	0	1	0	0	0	0	0	0	0	0	0
	I_1	0	1	1	0	0	1	0	0	0	0	1	0	0	0	0	0	0	0	0	0
	Y_2	0	0	0	0	0	0	0	1	1	0	0	0	0	0	0	1	0	0	0	0
	C_2	0	0	1	0	0	0	1	1	0	0	0	0	0	0	0	1	0	0	0	0
	I_2	0	0	1	0	0	0	0	0	1	0	0	0	0	0	0	1	0	0	0	0
	GR	0	0	0	1	0	0	1	0	0	0	0	0	0	0	0	0	0	0	0	0
Political subsystem	V_1	0	1	1	0	1	0	0	0	0	0	1	1	0	1	1	0	0	0	0	0
	G_1	0	1	1	0	0	0	0	0	0	1	1	1	0	0	0	0	0	0	0	0
	D_1	0	0	0	0	0	0	0	0	0	0	0	1	1	0	0	0	0	0	0	0
	P_1	0	0	0	0	0	0	0	0	0	0	0	0	0	1	0	0	0	0	0	0
	E_1	0	0	0	0	1	0	0	0	0	1	0	0	0	1	1	0	0	0	0	0
	V_2	0	1	1	0	0	0	0	1	0	0	0	0	0	0	0	1	1	0	1	1
	G_2	0	1	1	0	0	0	0	0	0	1	0	0	0	0	0	1	1	0	0	0
	D_2	0	0	0	0	0	0	0	0	0	0	0	0	0	0	0	0	1	1	0	0
	P_2	0	0	0	0	0	0	0	0	0	0	0	0	0	0	0	0	0	0	1	0
	E_2	0	0	1	0	0	0	0	1	0	0	0	0	0	0	0	1	0	0	1	1

[a] $F_{i,t}$, the net exogenous contribution to the economy of sector i at time t appears in equation (9–9), but has been deleted from this figure.

through time. For example, as shown in relationship (9–10), since government revenue GR_t is merely a function of gross product in the rural and urban sectors, $Y_{1,\,t-1}$ and $Y_{2,\,t-1}$, variation in GR_t within one yearly cycle is limited to variation in these two variables. However, if the model is operated through time, the number of variables causally connected to GR_t increases. Thus, while GR_t is a direct function of $Y_{1,\,t-1}$ and $Y_{2,\,t-1}$, as we have seen, it is also an indirect function through these two variables of $C_{1,\,t-1}$, $I_{1,\,t-1}$, $G_{1,\,t-1}$, $C_{2,\,t-1}$, $I_{2,\,t-1}$, and $G_{2,\,t-1}$; and through these variables, GR_t is an indirect function of several other variables, and so on. The causal chains of one, two, and three links connecting GR_t and these variables are diagramed in Figure 9–2.

FIGURE 9-2. CASUAL CHAINS OF ONE, TWO, AND THREE LINKS
AFFECTING GOVERNMENT REVENUE GR_t

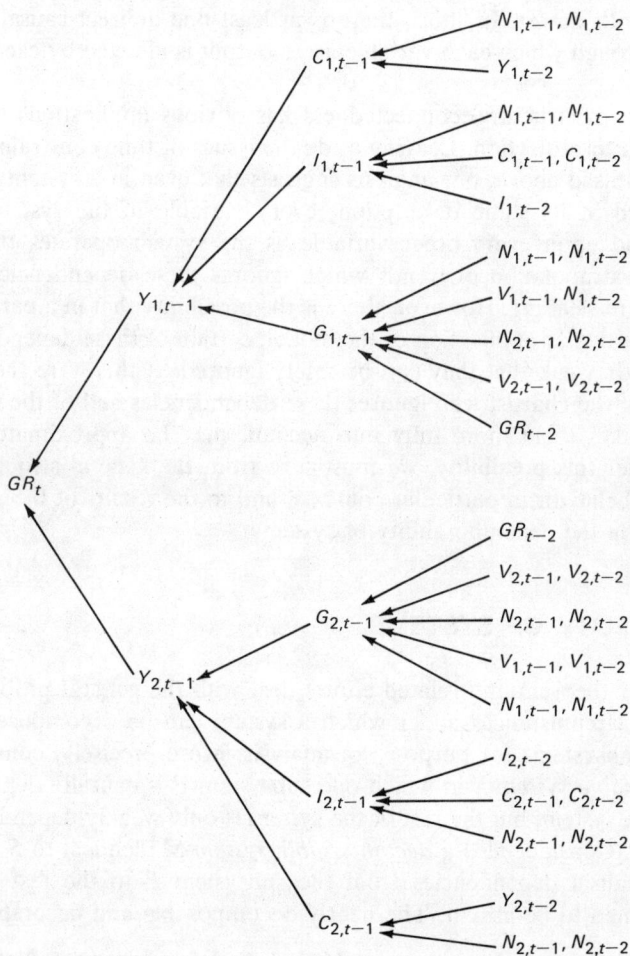

GR_t

$Y_{1,t-1}$

$C_{1,t-1}$ ← $N_{1,t-1}, N_{1,t-2}$
$C_{1,t-1}$ ← $Y_{1,t-2}$

$I_{1,t-1}$ ← $N_{1,t-1}, N_{1,t-2}$
$I_{1,t-1}$ ← $C_{1,t-1}, C_{1,t-2}$
$I_{1,t-1}$ ← $I_{1,t-2}$

$G_{1,t-1}$ ← $N_{1,t-1}, N_{1,t-2}$
$G_{1,t-1}$ ← $V_{1,t-1}, N_{1,t-2}$
$G_{1,t-1}$ ← $N_{2,t-1}, N_{2,t-2}$
$G_{1,t-1}$ ← $V_{2,t-1}, V_{2,t-2}$
$G_{1,t-1}$ ← GR_{t-2}

$Y_{2,t-1}$

$G_{2,t-1}$ ← GR_{t-2}
$G_{2,t-1}$ ← $V_{2,t-1}, V_{2,t-2}$
$G_{2,t-1}$ ← $N_{2,t-1}, N_{2,t-2}$
$G_{2,t-1}$ ← $V_{1,t-1}, V_{1,t-2}$
$G_{2,t-1}$ ← $N_{1,t-1}, N_{1,t-2}$

$I_{2,t-1}$ ← $I_{2,t-2}$
$I_{2,t-1}$ ← $C_{2,t-1}, C_{2,t-2}$
$I_{2,t-1}$ ← $N_{2,t-1}, N_{2,t-2}$

$C_{2,t-1}$ ← $Y_{2,t-2}$
$C_{2,t-1}$ ← $N_{2,t-1}, N_{2,t-2}$

More generally, since each additional power of the connectedness matrix corresponds to one additional yearly cycle of the model, it can be shown that the operation of the model through time *extends the length* of indirect causal chains connecting any two variables and *increases the number* of indirect causal chains.[12] In precise terms, the entry in the ith row and jth column of the nth power of the matrix gives the number of causal chains of n links by which variable i is indirectly connected to variable j. (The fourth power of the matrix is given in Figure 9–3 as an illustration.) For this particular model, the increases are dramatic. While there are only 59 direct causal chains, there are 163, 459, and 1,257 indirect causal chains of 2, 3, and 4 links, respectively. Furthermore, there are 3,382, 9,172, and 24,708 indirect causal chains of 5, 6, and 7 links, respectively. Of the 400 possible pairs of variables, only 16 pairs remain unconnected in the fifth power of the matrix, 2 in the sixth power, and none in the seventh power. In short, there is at least one indirect causal chain of seven links through which each variable as an output is affected by each variable as an input.

The analysis of structural connectedness has obvious implications for the chartist approach to projection. Leaving aside the issues of time constraints and policy purposes raised above, our analysis suggests that even in a system that is loosely connected in its static description, every variable in the system may ultimately depend upon every other variable as the system operates through time. A simple extrapolation of trends which ignores these dependencies may indeed be highly misleading. However, there is the possibility that in a particular system or in a particular application of the model, certain of these dependencies may be sufficiently weak that they can be safely ignored. If this were the case, the projections of the chartist who ignores these dependencies and of the fundamentalist who takes them more fully into account may be approximately the same. To consider this possibility, we must turn from the general structure of the model to its behavior in particular contexts, and to the results of the Ando–Fisher theorem on the decomposability of systems.

DECOMPOSABILITY OF SYSTEMS

The Ando-Fisher theorem and related efforts deal with the general problem of determining the circumstances under which a system can be decomposed into its component subsystems for purposes of analysis. More precisely, consider a *nearly decomposable system S* in which one subsystem P is causally dependent on the rest of the system, but the rest of the system is only weakly dependent on the subsystem P. Consider also a *decomposable system S′* identical to S except that the weak causal dependencies from the subsystem P to the rest of the system are assumed to be absent. The nearly decomposable and decomposable

[12] See James S. Coleman, *Introduction to Mathematical Sociology* (New York: The Free Press, 1964), pp. 444–47, on "connectedness" of structure.

FIGURE 9–3.   INDIRECT STRUCTURAL CONNECTEDNESS BY FUNCTIONAL SUBSYSTEMS. CAUSAL CHAINS OF FOUR LINKS: CONNECTEDNESS MATRIX TO THE FOURTH POWER

| | Inputs | | | | | | | | | | | | | | | | | | | |
| | Demographic Subsystem | | | Economic Subsystem | | | | | | | Political Subsystem | | | | | | | | | |
Outputs	U	N_1	N_2	Y_1	C_1	I_1	Y_2	C_2	I_2	GR	V_1	G_1	D_1	P_1	E_1	V_2	G_2	D_2	P_2	E_2
Demographic subsystem																				
U	8	15	15	3	5	1	3	5	1	3	3	0	2	4	0	3	0	0	0	0
N_1	7	8	7	1	4	1	1	4	1	0	0	2	1	3	0	0	1	0	0	0
N_2	7	7	8	1	4	1	1	4	1	0	0	2	1	3	0	0	1	0	0	0
Economic subsystem																				
Y_1	8	18	10	3	10	4	1	7	1	1	2	2	1	6	2	2	1	1	2	2
C_1	7	10	5	3	4	2	2	2	0	0	1	1	1	2	1	1	0	0	1	1
I_1	7	15	6	3	6	3	1	3	0	1	1	1	1	3	0	1	0	0	0	0
Y_2	8	10	18	1	7	0	3	10	4	1	2	1	1	6	2	2	2	1	2	2
C_2	7	5	10	2	2	0	3	4	2	0	1	0	1	3	1	1	1	0	1	1
I_2	7	6	15	1	3	2	3	6	3	1	1	0	1	3	0	1	1	0	0	0
GR	8	8	8	3	4	2	3	4	2	0	2	1	0	2	2	2	1	0	2	2
Political subsystem																				
V_1	11	26	8	5	11	3	1	4	0	2	3	4	4	8	4	2	0	0	0	0
G_1	14	22	22	5	9	2	5	9	2	2	3	2	4	7	3	3	2	2	3	3
D_1	4	7	7	1	5	1	1	5	1	0	1	1	1	4	2	1	1	1	2	2
P_1	2	2	2	1	1	0	1	1	0	0	1	0	0	1	1	1	0	0	1	1
E_1	7	16	7	3	6	2	1	3	0	2	2	2	2	4	1	2	0	0	0	0
V_2	11	8	26	1	4	0	5	11	3	2	3	0	1	4	0	3	4	3	4	4
G_2	14	22	22	5	9	2	5	9	2	2	3	2	4	7	3	3	2	2	3	3
D_2	4	7	7	1	5	1	1	5	1	0	1	1	1	4	2	1	1	1	2	2
P_2	2	2	2	1	1	0	1	1	0	0	1	0	0	1	1	1	0	0	1	1
E_2	7	7	16	1	3	0	3	6	2	2	2	0	1	3	0	2	2	1	1	1

FIGURE 9–4. A COMPARISON OF A NEARLY
DECOMPOSABLE SYSTEM S AND
A DECOMPOSABLE SYSTEM S'

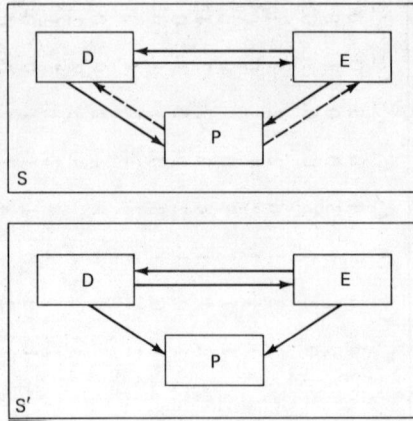

versions of S are diagramed in Figure 9–4, with the weak causal links indicated by the dotted line. Finally, let us define the *relative behavior* of the variables in P as their ratios. The result of the Ando-Fisher theorem is that for linear systems, the long-run relative behavior of the variables in P in the nearly decomposable system S and in the decomposable system S' is approximately the same, even though their behavior in terms of absolute levels and rates of change may be very different. The weaker the weak dependency in S, the better the approximation. In short, to the extent that the chartist is dealing with a system that approximates the nearly decomposable system S, he may extrapolate relative trends in P and safely ignore the rest of the system.

Let us conjecture that the model of modernization and mass politics is a nearly decomposable system in which relative behavior in the political subsystems can be explored independently of the rest of the system. Let us also conjecture that the result of the Ando-Fisher theorem holds for this model even though the model is nonlinear. If the model is nearly decomposable as applied to the Turkish case, the Philippine case, or both, the ratios of the political variables over time generated by the complete version of the model should approximate the ratios generated by the decomposable version. To specify a decomposable version, we need only replace the variable $P_{1, t}$ in relationship (9–6) and the variables $G_{i, t}$ in (9–9) by constants equal to their initial values. These are, respectively, $P_{1, 1}$ and $G_{i, 1}$. With these modifications, the urbanization and income relationships become:

$$U_t = s \left(\frac{C_{2, t} \, N_{1, t}}{N_{2, t} \, C_{1, t}} \right) P_{1, 1} N_{1, t} \qquad (9\text{–}6')$$

$$Y_{i, t} = C_{i, t} + I_{i, t} + G_{i, 1} + F_{i, t} \qquad (9\text{–}9')$$

The results are presented in Table 9–3, where the degree of approximation is calculated as the difference between the relative behavior of the complete and decomposed versions expressed as a percentage of the relative behavior of the complete version. Perhaps the best approximation is in the behavior of $G_{1,\,t}/V_{1,\,t}$ in the Philippine application. The maximum error is 15% (1961) and the errors are all less than 5% over the first ten years. The worst approximations are in $V_{1,\,t}/V_{2,\,t}$ and $G_{2,\,t}/V_{2,\,t}$ in the Turkish application. Maximum errors are, respectively, 66.9% (1965) and 25.9% (1957); the approximations are particularly poor after the eleventh year in the former and the eighth year in the

TABLE 9–3.   THE LONG-RUN RELATIVE BEHAVIOR OF A MODEL: COMPLETE VERSION (CV) AND DECOMPOSED VERSION (DV)

a. Turkey

t	$V_{1,\,t}/V_{2,\,t}$				$G_{1,\,t}/G_{2,\,t}$			
	CV	DV	Diff.	% Diff.	CV	DV	Diff.	% Diff.
1950	1.000	1.000	.000	0.0	.509	.509	.000	0.0
1951	1.007	1.007	.000	0.0	.614	.614	.000	0.0
1952	1.063	1.023	.040	3.8	.575	.599	−.024	−4.2
1953	1.096	1.048	.048	4.4	.609	.591	.018	3.0
1954	1.142	1.081	.061	5.3	.609	.589	.020	3.3
1955	.956	.885	.071	7.4	.759	.725	.034	4.5
1956	1.048	.925	.123	11.7	.488	.477	.011	2.3
1957	1.040	.972	.068	6.5	.582	.482	.100	17.2
1958	1.079	1.029	.050	4.6	.539	.490	.049	9.1
1959	1.090	1.096	−.006	−0.6	.564	.504	.060	10.6
1960	1.106	1.175	−.069	−6.2	.555	.521	.034	6.1
1961	1.110	1.267	−.157	−14.1	.561	.544	.017	3.0
1962	1.110	1.373	−.263	−23.7	.556	.573	−.017	−3.1
1963	1.102	1.494	−.392	−35.6	.552	.607	−.055	−10.0
1964	1.090	1.632	−.542	−49.7	.543	.647	−.104	−19.2
1965	1.072	1.789	−.717	−66.9	.531	.693	−.162	−30.5

t	$G_{1,\,t}/V_{1,\,t}$				$G_{2,\,t}/V_{2,\,t}$			
	CV	DV	Diff.	% Diff.	CV	DV	Diff.	% Diff.
1950	1047	1047	0	0.0	2056	2056	0	0.0
1951	1052	1052	0	0.0	1725	1725	0	0.0
1952	1155	1165	−10	−0.9	2136	1992	144	6.7
1953	1197	1236	−39	−3.3	2155	2192	−37	−1.7
1954	1250	1304	−54	−4.3	2346	2395	−49	−2.1
1955	1662	1800	−138	−8.3	2094	2197	−103	−4.9
1956	1524	1698	−174	−11.4	3271	3293	−22	− .7
1957	1583	1765	−182	−11.5	2827	3560	−733	−25.9
1958	1652	1838	−186	−11.3	3309	3855	−546	−16.5
1959	1720	1905	−185	−10.8	3326	4146	−820	−24.7
1960	1803	1965	−162	−9.0	3591	4428	−837	−23.3
1961	1898	2016	−118	−6.2	3755	4691	−936	−24.9
1962	2009	2055	−46	−2.3	4009	4925	−916	−22.8
1963	2141	2079	62	2.9	4276	5120	−844	−19.7
1964	2305	2086	219	9.5	4623	5263	−640	−13.8
1965	2508	2072	436	17.4	5059	5346	−287	−5.7

TABLE 9–3. *Continued*

b. The Philippines

	$V_{1,t}/V_{2,t}$					$G_{1,t}/G_{2,t}$			
t	*CV*	*DV*	*Diff.*	*% Diff.*	*CV*	*DV*	*Diff.*	*% Diff.*
1951	1.021	1.021	.000	0.0	.292	.292	.000	0.0
1952	.996	.996	.000	0.0	.369	.369	.000	0.0
1953	.940	.975	−.035	−3.7	.303	.318	−.015	−5.0
1954	.905	.991	−.086	−9.5	.306	.299	.007	2.3
1955	.931	1.008	−.076	−8.2	.259	.286	−.027	−10.4
1956	.912	1.024	−.112	−12.3	.266	.276	−.010	−3.8
1957	.948	.970	−.022	−2.3	.232	.267	−.035	−15.1
1958	.939	.973	−.034	−3.6	.241	.242	−.001	−0.4
1959	.990	.973	.017	1.7	.212	.232	−.020	−9.4
1960	.983	.969	.014	1.4	.227	.222	.005	2.2
1961	1.055	1.033	.022	2.1	.197	.212	−.015	−7.6
1962	1.042	1.026	.016	1.5	.220	.217	.003	1.4
1963	1.146	1.017	.129	11.3	.184	.207	−.023	−12.5
1964	1.109	1.004	.105	9.5	.222	.197	.025	11.3
1965	1.268	1.011	.257	20.3	.172	.187	−.015	−8.7
1966	1.177	.995	.182	15.5	.237	.181	.056	23.6

	$G_{1,t}/V_{1,t}$					$G_{2,t}/V_{2,t}$			
t	*CV*	*DV*	*Diff.*	*% Diff.*	*CV*	*DV*	*Diff.*	*% Diff.*
1951	335	335	0	0.0	1171	1171	0	0.0
1952	375	375	0	0.0	1011	1011	0	0.0
1953	355	357	−2	−0.6	1101	1095	6	0.5
1954	379	388	−9	−2.4	1121	1287	−166	−14.8
1955	412	423	−11	−2.7	1480	1492	−12	−0.8
1956	447	462	−15	−3.4	1535	1714	−179	−11.7
1957	478	461	17	3.6	1948	1675	273	14.0
1958	515	493	22	4.3	2002	1978	24	1.2
1959	542	543	8	1.5	2524	2232	292	11.6
1960	582	576	6	1.0	2524	2513	11	0.4
1961	602	512	90	15.0	3228	2490	738	22.9
1962	647	558	89	13.8	3065	2642	423	13.8
1963	657	597	60	9.1	4088	2931	1157	28.3
1964	711	637	74	10.4	3552	3243	309	8.7
1965	703	644	59	8.4	5179	3479	703	13.6
1966	778	689	89	11.4	3869	3779	90	2.3

latter. In general, for each comparison of relative behavior there is a tendency for the approximation to be better in the short run than in the long run.

In terms of the choice between the chartist and fundamentalist approaches, is the complete model a nearly decomposable system in which the political subsystem can be isolated from the rest of the system for purposes of studying political trends? In the absence of mathematical proof that the result of the Ando–Fisher theorem holds for this class of nonlinear model, the answer is not clear. If the result of the theorem does not hold, the errors may not be evidence of near decomposability or the lack of it, but irrelevant to the issue. If the result of the theorem does hold, then we have gained some information on its degree of near decomposability in the Turkish and Philippine cases; whether the degree of near decomposability is sufficient depends on one's time frame and margin of tolerable error. If these errors are within the limits of tolerable error for given purposes, the ceteris paribus assumption is appropriate, and the political system's behavior can be studied apart from the rest of the system. If these errors are not within acceptable limits, the ceteris paribus assumption is inappropriate, and the functional boundaries of the analysis must be expanded beyond the political subsystem to account for demographic and economic factors. For most purposes these errors seem to be rather large.

Whether complex real-world systems are less connected in a structural sense or more nearly decomposable in a behavioral sense than the model we have used remains to be seen. (We would expect the opposite.) However, to the extent that these results from the model can be generalized, they must be discouraging to those who wish to extrapolate trends as a means of studying the future of political systems. Even simple systems which are only loosely connected in their static description are highly interconnected in their dynamic behavior. Furthermore, at least in this model, these interconnections appear to be sufficiently strong that errors are likely to arise if certain trends are separated from the rest of the system for purposes of analysis. Even though we must simplify complex systems in order to understand them, the kind of simplification typical of the chartist approach does not seem to be productive in an empirical sense.

SOME LIMITATIONS

Computer simulation models, as we have seen, are relatively well suited to the investigation of the complex interdependencies underlying the behavior of social and political systems. We should not, however, underestimate the limitations of computer simulation models, and in particular the problems of developing and using them for the study of policy and the future.

To make the present model a useful tool for policy and projections, it would have to be expanded to incorporate a number of empirically or normatively important phenomena. For example, the cybernetic, structural-functional, and political-cultural approaches to the study of political systems suggest that processes producing changes in parameters are important in real-world political systems over appropriate time spans, and should be incorporated into the model. These processes would be interpreted as second-order feedback mechanisms or as socialization and recruitment processes. Normative questions about the distribution of values suggest that the model should be disaggregated beyond a simple rural–urban division to investigate, say, inequality between the few wealthy landowners and the mass of the peasantry, or between urban classes. However, as we have seen, as a model's size increases, it becomes more difficult to evaluate and revise scientifically. There is an important trade-off between the inclusion of additional phenomena to increase a model's potential realism, and the need to keep a model small for the purposes of testing it. Moreover, criteria of empirical and normative importance are apt to change over time.

Furthermore, for even a small model, such as the one considered here, data tend to be incomplete and inaccurate. For example, we have no time-series data on expected economic performance $E_{i,\,t}$ to compare with the time series generated by the model. For other variables such as consumption $C_{i,\,t}$ we have only national totals and no rural–urban disaggregation. Of the data we do have, there is reason to believe that much of it is inaccurate. Time series on Turkish government expenditures from different sources differ by as much as 33% in individual years.[13] Critics of Philippine national accounts have claimed that the level of private investment has been underestimated by as much as 40%.[14] More complete and accurate data are needed to conduct more than weak tests of the model and to increase the rate at which it can be improved.

Finally, some aspects of the behavior of real-world systems, particularly the roles of chance and individuals, cannot be adequately simulated. To be sure, we can incorporate stochastic factors into models and assess their impact on important outputs. In the final analysis, however, we cannot forecast the precise nature, magnitude, or timing of these factors. For example, in February 1959, an airplane carrying Prime Minister Menderes and fifteen other members of a Turkish delegation to London crashed. Fifteen were killed, but Menderes walked away. "As a result of this escape, he was viewed as almost superhuman by many superstitious Turkish peasants. This considerably reinforced his already large peasant support. . . ."[15] President Magsaysay of the Philippines was killed in a plane crash shortly before the election of 1957. His death drastically changed the national political situation and, among other things, reduced the level of popular support for his Nacionalista party. In each case an accident affected popular support, a variable defined in the model, but it is inconceivable that such accidents could be adequately reproduced in the behavior of the model.[16]

[13] Compare the data in the Public Finances section of several United Nations *Statistical Yearbooks* (1956, pp. 525–26; 1960, p. 535; and 1966, p. 652), with data from the Turkish State Institute of Statistics.

[14] Important contributions to the debate over Philippine national accounts are: Emmanuel Levy, *Review of Economic Statistics on the Philippines, Interim Report* (Manila: World Bank Resident Mission, 1964, mimeo.); Clarence L. Barber, "National Income Estimates in the Philippines," *The Philippine Economic Journal,* Vol. 4, No. 1 (1965), pp. 66–77; and Ruben F. Trinidad, "Some Proposed Improvements in the Estimation of Capital Formation in the Philippines," *The Statistical Reporter,* Vol. 4 (April 1960), pp. 28–40.

[15] Walter F. Weiker, *The Turkish Revolution, 1960–1961: Aspects of Military Politics* (Washington, D.C.: The Brookings Institution, 1963), p. 12.

[16] Cf. the following from Bertrand de Jouvenel, *The Art of Conjecture* (New York: Basic Books, 1967), p. 110: ". . . any systematic effort at forecasting must rest on the understanding of processes, and we would be fools not to devote ourselves to this task on the lame pretext that such understanding does not enable us to make complete predictions."

SOME CHALLENGES IMPLIED FOR THE SCIENTIFIC STUDY OF POLICY

Assuming that our scientific sensibilities prevent us from falling back on more prosaic methods of forecasting such as star gazing, gut inspection, and meditation, the importance of the trends–processes matter must be taken into account. Unfortunately, that matter is not isolated from several other related concerns, summarized here to indicate the magnitude of the challenges.

- How does one connect a model or forecasting enterprise to the concrete circumstances captured by its information base?
- How does one ease the communication burden between contingencies produced by the forecast and realities perceived by concerned decisionmakers? What observable impacts operate, in both directions?
- How does one emphasize the creative aspects of forecasting, no matter the technique employed, in hopes of expanding the attention and problem-solution spaces of policymakers? Alternatively, how does one avoid saddling policymakers with old mistakes and sterile response routines?
- How does one forecast with partial or even nonexistent data? Unless one unrealistically assumes prescience, there is no way to anticipate either a large number of potential choices or the policy instrumentalities that will in time confront and be available to decisionmakers. How then does one anticipate future data needs?
- How might forecasting be turned into an opportunity for self-observation and self-modification?

Partial answers to these difficult, though basic, questions are evolving in several settings. Present concern is more narrowly focused on citing several distinctions between the trends and process perspectives, but even here answers are far from clear-cut.

CONCLUSION

Both timeliness and accuracy are important criteria for policy analysis and forecasting. The major advantage of the chartist approach is timeliness, and the major advantage of the fundamentalist approach is greater potential accuracy. However, the empirical limitations of model-building are significant. Modeling is not a panacea, although when intelligently intermixed with other techniques, it is often better than might be anticipated.

An institutional framework is required if we are to begin the serious integrative and cumulative tasks implied in this discussion. Shubik's proposal to link large data-processing procedures with models provides a means for making quick extrapolations of trends and for the more time-consuming task of improving the quality of models and supporting data.

Lasswell's proposal to develop institutions called decision seminars is similar but more sophisticated.[17] The decision seminar is designed to track and measure social events; as a procedural matter, the experiential data collected are quickly and systematically tested against the current sets of verbal and formal models. In decision seminars, models and trend data are used to project the future course of events and to invent and evaluate alternative policies; normative judgments and scientific formulations are amended based on the mismatches that exist between them and the collected data. If we are unable to build entirely accurate scientific models, at least we can try to recognize and rectify our errors through techniques such as the decision seminar.

[17] See Harold D. Lasswell, "Technique of Decision Seminars," *Midwest Journal of Political Science*, Vol. 4, No. 3 (August 1960), pp. 213–36; and *idem*, "The Political Science of Science," *American Political Science Review*, Vol. 50 (December 1956), pp. 961–79.

Part V
Alternatives

INTRODUCTION

The alternatives approach stands at the confluence of all other approaches treated so far. It is through the invention, estimation, selection, implementation, evaluation, and termination of policy alternatives that a truly contextual, problem-oriented, and problem solving policy science will either stand or fall.

Invention: Creativity and Conceptualization

Every available method, technique, and trick must be actively employed to allow both researchers and policymakers to create and explore unheard of possibilities to solve problems. Invention refers to efforts taken to expand beyond the commonplace, trite, and outmoded conceptions of problem solution possibilities. In other terms, invention refers to explorations made to expand and redefine the problem solution space; its objective is to find more satisfactory or beneficial joint maxima—to borrow appropriate analogies from the studies of topology and game theory.

The literature on creativity contributes precious little if one is interested in a succinct description or definition of the topic concept.[1] At the very least, creativity is a little understood mechanism or process by which human beings are able to combine sense data into novel and original patterns. The process apparently proceeds by means of comparisons allowing the creative mind to see

[1] Jerome Brunner et al., *Contemporary Approaches to Creative Thinking* (New York: Atherton, 1962); Brewster Ghiselin, ed., *The Creative Process* (Berkeley: University of California Press, 1952); G. Wallas, *The Art of Thought* (New York: Harcourt, Brace, 1926); Catherine Patrick, "Creative Thought in Artists," *Journal of Psychology*, Vol. 4 (1937), pp. 35–73; and D. W. MacKinnon, "The Personality Correlates of Creativity: A Study of American Architects," *Proceedings of the XIVth International Congress of Applied Psychology*, 1962.

345

unity and order where only dissimilarity existed before. Bronowski has touched on this idea in discussing Newton's gravitational theories: "for the apple in the summer garden and the grave moon overhead are surely as unlike in their movement as two things can be. Newton traced in them two expressions of a single concept, gravitation: and the concept (and the unity) are in that sense his free creation." [2]

Creativity has served as a standard theme in the writings of man since earliest times. The notion is central in Aristotle's *Metaphysics,* Book XIII, Chapter 3; Saint Augustine's *Confessions,* Book II, Paragraph 12; Aquinas's *Summa Theologica,* Part II; Pascal's *Pensées;* and Kant's *The Critique of Judgment,* from which the following illustrative passage is taken: "The imagination (as a productive faculty of cognition) is a powerful agent for creating, as it were, a second nature out of the material supplied to it by actual nature. It affords us entertainment where experience proves too commonplace; and we even use it to remodel experience. . . ." [3] Creativity is therefore seen to be at base a universal human activity and characteristic. To the first approximation of the concept in terms of the unique combination of data, one must now add the preliminary associated notion of discovering unseen likenesses between apparently dissimilar senses or facts and data. For creation to be realized, other human beings must come to experience the process and to appreciate the beauty of the new entity "created," and we often refer to this as innovation diffusion. [4]

The development of monetary institutions presents many excellent illustrations of creative policy invention; however, these illustrations point out only a few of the myriad possibilities that exist. Just as Shubik has done in his elegant restatement of the creation and evolution of monetary institutions, [5] one could conjecture that in a coconut barter economy much pragmatic attention was devoted to the transportation of the ever-increasing numbers of those weighty counters as the economies in which they were an exchange standard developed. To be pointedly fanciful, there may have been a South Seas Islands equivalent of the modern-day military industrial complex whose consuming task was building larger, more seaworthy vessels to haul coconuts from one place to another. In time it must have occurred to someone that further refinement of outrigger design not only was an inappropriate answer to the problem, it was indeed the wrong question; monetary substitutes quickly followed. Invention refers to this fragile business of reconceptualizing a problem, redefining a range

---

[2] Jacob Bronowski, *Science and Human Values* (New York: Harper Bros., 1956), p. 15.

[3] Immanuel Kant, *The Critique of Judgment,* ed. and trans. James C. Meredith (New York: Oxford University Press, 1941), paragraph 49, "The Faculties of the Mind Which Constitute Genius."

[4] Harold D. Lasswell, "The Social Setting of Creativity," in H. H. Anderson, ed., *Creativity and its Cultivation* (New York: Harper Bros., 1959), pp. 203–21.

[5] Martin Shubik, *A Theory of Money, Prices and the Rate of Interest: Part I, The Missing Degree of Freedom: Commodity Money and Oligopoly in a General Equilibrium Model* (Santa Monica, Cal.: The Rand Corporation, P–4686, July 1971).

of appropriate solutions, and then locating a best possible choice within that range. The issue is of course more complex in present-day affairs, but the process by which fresh insights are derived and associated with a given problem probably is not.

In those areas—economic and military planning for the most part—where policy-oriented research has been useful and new concepts have been "created" that have resulted in "successful" policy, a characteristic common feature appears to be that one or two well-defined questions, the answers to which were important to policymakers, were asked early in the operational and research processes. Furthermore, those most concerned with the problem had some idea, however vague, of what an answer might look like should it happen to show up. In effect, the policy space in which the problem and the critical participants were located was initially outlined, defined, or mapped—choose your own term; and, by having some approximate idea of an answer, one knew when a departure from the routine or steady state had taken place. More important, having some vision of the connections and differences between the ordinary and the novel solution concepts facilitated relating the novel to the commonplace so that the timid, lazy, or dull might eventually see the connections for themselves and incorporate the innovation by slowly integrating it into the common routine.[6]

Estimation: Figuring out the Probabilities and Desirabilities of Options

Estimation refers to the preoutcome determination of risks, costs, and benefits associated with each of the various invented candidate policies. Probability calculation is to a large extent focused on empirical-scientific and projective issues, whereas the imputation of desirability is more clearly biased toward normative concerns.[7] The objective of estimation is to narrow the range of plausible policy solutions, by excluding the infeasible or the truly exploitative for instance, and to order those remaining options according to well-defined scientific *and* normative criteria.[8] Resource analysis, Bayesian statistics,[9] forecasting, extrapolation, model construction, and an assortment of other methods have evolved in response to the first requisite; market research, survey tech-

[6] See Garry D. Brewer, "On Innovation, Social Change, and Reality," *Technological Forecasting and Social Change,* Vol. 5, No. 1 (February 1973), pp. 19–24, for a more detailed and pragmatic discussion of the process and the ways in which it is perverted in practice.

[7] See Philip Morse and G. E. Kimball, *Methods of Operational Research* (New York: Wiley, 1950), or any other standard operations research text for a full explication of these important differences.

[8] One needs to be reminded of the demand to examine a range of diverse interpretations, orderings, and calculations. This requirement cannot be stressed enough. For a clear technical discussion, see Allen Newell, "Some Problems of Basic Organization in Problem-Solving Programs," in M. C. Yovits et al., eds., *Self-Organizing Systems, 1962* (Washington, D.C.: Spartan Books, 1962).

[9] See Donald A. Berry, Chapter 13 of this volume, for an example of Bayesian techniques.

niques, benefit analysis, and rarely, a priori social-ethical assessments have been used for the second.

Selection: Picking a Winner

Ultimately, someone must select one or a few of the "invented" and "estimated" options, and that considerable task has traditionally been the responsibility and province of policymakers, however their role is characterized.[10] Although the alternatives approach stresses rational calculation, particularly in the estimation phase, the problem of multiple, changing, and conflicting goals is seldom confronted by narrowly circumscribed analysts.[11] This problem, among others, is ultimately resolved by the politician, who "has to balance the myriad forces as he sees best, and the citizens judge him only to a limited extent by his accordance with their preconceived ideas. Rather, a great political leader is judged like a great composer; one looks to see what he has created. . . ." [12] A central part of the creative process involves the execution of the selected option —a consideration which brings us to implementation, the means by which selected policies are actually operationalized.

Implementation: The Translation of Intentions into Actualities

Implementation concerns the execution of a selected option. It is a phase of the overall alternative or decision process that is little understood, not particularly appreciated, and not well developed—either conceptually or operationally. To evaluate the performance of government policies and programs (the next logical phase in the overall process), one must understand the implementation mechanisms and structures underlying that performance. For instance, looking at the incentive systems, at both the institutional and individual levels of analysis, is one way to proceed. What is actually happening in a given setting and why is it different from what was intended or stated by those more responsible and specialized to the selection phase of the process?

And this brings us to evaluation, the means by which selected policies are

10 Bernard Crick, *In Defense of Politics* (Baltimore, Md.: Penguin, 1964 rev. ed.), captures the essence of *selection* in a disarmingly profound and important little essay. "So many problems are only resolvable politically that the politician has a special right to be defended against the pride of the engineer or the arrogance of the technologist. Let the cobbler stick to his last. We have a desperate need for good shoes—and too many bad dreams [p. 110]".

11 Critical path analysis, as only one example, is an appropriate selection device only to the extent that a desired end state is known and alternative paths are once and for all excluded. When the actual path followed is a tentative, shifting resultant of many conflicting and inconsistent norms and empirical conditions, the issues of valuation and decisionmaking responsibility are at least as important as analysis itself.

12 W. Arthur Lewis, "Planning Public Expenditures," in Max F. Millikan, ed., *National Economic Planning* (New York: National Bureau of Economic Research, 1967), pp. 201–27, at p. 207.

assessed as to their postoutcomes or longer term effects and to the general performance turned in by the responsible officials.

Evaluation: Who Got What and Who Is Responsible?

Invention and estimation are primarily forward-looking, anticipatory activities. Selection stresses the urgency of the ever-present here and now. Evaluation is backward looking, concerned with inquiries about system performance and individual responsibility. Typical topics and questions that are reflected in the literature include the following: What officials and what policies were successful or unsuccessful? How can this performance be assessed and measured? Were any criteria established to make these measurements? Who did the assessment, and what were his purposes? To what ends was the evaluation directed, and were they accomplished?

Evaluation is a necessary phase in the alternatives approach because of a variety of demands that exists in political processes everywhere. Incompetent or brutally single-purpose activities are inadequate where the real situation calls for comprehensive and competent efforts at a wide variety of places in the political and decision processes.[13]

Institutionalization of evaluation can be either internalized—in-house—or externalized—such as an audit by an inspector general or a private accounting firm. The sad matter of fact is that evaluation is carried out only sporadically[14] and then with destructiveness known well to a great number of Sicilians—the vendetta—and a smaller number of self-serving politicians—"character assassination," muckraking, "reformism," and the coup d'etat.

Termination: Closing the Loop

Termination refers to the adjustment of policies and programs that have become dysfunctional, redundant, outmoded, and unnecessary. From the conceptual and intellectual points of view, it is not a well-developed phase, but one whose importance in current affairs must not be underdevalued. For instance, how can a policy be rationally adjusted or stopped without its having had a thorough evaluative assessment? Who will suffer from the termination? What provisions of redress have to be considered? What are the costs involved to the individuals affected by the termination? Can they be met from other sources? What might be learned in the termination process that will aid the initiation and

[13] Harold D. Lasswell, "Towards Continuing Appraisal of the Impact of Law on Society," *Rutgers Law Review,* Vol. 21, No. 4 (Summer 1967), pp. 645–77.

[14] See Garry D. Brewer, *Politicians, Bureaucrats, and the Consultant: A Critique of Urban Problem Solving* (New York: Basic Books, 1973); and also Brewer and Owen P. Hall, Jr., "Policy Analysis by Computer Simulation: The Need for Appraisal," *Public Policy,* Vol. 21, No. 3 (Summer 1973), pp. 343–65, for specific examples and some general speculations about the broader implications of the problem, respectively.

invention of new policies in the same or related fields? The list of potentially relevant questions is long, but ignoring it and not making the connection to the other steps or phases in the overall sequence have mostly negative consequences for the policy and people whose lives the policy affects. "Peace with Honor," for instance, was a slogan representing a termination policy; however, there is very little indication that much thought was given to the basic set of termination questions just posed. Furthermore, there is even less indication that those responsible for the termination of American involvement in the Vietnamese war paid much attention to the pertinent historical precedents in the same and related contexts, e.g., the First Indo–Chinese War, Algeria, Malaya. On a less emotion–charged and more general level, the termination of foreign aid programs in many countries has yet to be subjected to the kinds of analyses implied in the posited set of questions—to the detriment of the programs and to the countries in which they had been operative.

THE LITERATURE

The literature on alternatives is not especially voluminous, and variations in quality are notably large, particularly for development-related works. However, it is possible to organize much of it according to our invention, estimation, selection, implementation, evaluation, and termination categories. A few interesting case examples conclude this survey.

An Elaboration of the Alternatives Approach

There are several excellent sources that refine and explicate the few concepts we have summarily sketched out. Harold D. Lasswell, "Current Studies of the Decision Process: Automation versus Creativity," *Western Political Quarterly,* Vol. 8 (September 1955), pp. 381–99; *idem,* "The Policy Orientation," in Daniel Lerner and H. D. Lasswell, eds., *The Policy Sciences* (Stanford, Cal.: Stanford University Press, 1951); and *idem, A Pre-View of Policy Sciences* (New York: American Elsevier, 1971), are all sophisticated and comprehensive treatments of the subject. Each of these documents is a basic source and will reward careful reading and reflection many times over. Another durable treatment is given by Robert S. Lynd, *Knowledge for What?* (Princeton: Princeton University Press, 1945).

Addressed primarily to the link between the estimation and selection phases are Jerome R. Ravetz, *Scientific Knowledge and Its Social Problems* (New York: Oxford University Press, 1971); and S. A. Lakoff, ed., *Knowledge and Power: Essays on Science and Government* (New York: The Free Press, 1966); and for a provocative, somewhat philosophical, treatment of the invention and selection phases, see John Rader Platt, *The Step to Man* (New York: Wiley, 1966), Part II, "Channels of Change."

Less profound, but perhaps more easily understood, general discussions are Amitai Etzioni, "Policy Research," *The American Sociologist,* Vol. 6 (June 1971), pp. 8–12; and Alvin Gouldner, "Explorations in Applied Social Science," in A. Gouldner and S. M. Miller, eds., *Applied Sociology* (New York: The Free Press, 1965), pp. 5–22.

The link between selection and evaluation is beautifully and concisely made in Alice M. Rivlin, *Systematic Thinking for Social Action* (Washington, D.C.: The Brookings Institution, 1971). Howard E. Freeman and Clarence C. Sherwood, *Social Research and Social Policy* (Englewood Cliffs, N.J.: Prentice-Hall, 1970), do much the same thing for the estimation and evaluation connection, although this volume lacks the grace, style, and compactness of the Rivlin effort.

Don K. Price has spoken eloquently and thoroughly about the personalities involved and the roles they fulfill in the policy process in his *Scientific Estate* (Cambridge, Mass.: Harvard University Press, 1965); and earlier, *idem, Government and Science* (New York: New York University Press, 1954).

Invention: Creativity, Innovation, and Diffusion

The literature on creativity has already been touched on in our introductory comments to this overview. In fact, the connection between scholarly work on creativity and topics that could be considered even remotely developmental is not often made very well. However, such is not the case for innovation and innovation diffusion materials, to which we now turn our attention.

Samuel P. Huntington, in *Political Order in Changing Societies* (New Haven: Yale University Press, 1968), defines development in terms that use the innovation concept to good and appropriate advantage; in his terms, development is the creation and incorporation of an enlarged repertoire of responses by government to phenomena and changes in its domain. In his own way, Huntington recognizes the importance of the alternatives approach to the study of political development and change, in many of the same ways that we describe here. A more generalized and solid treatment of the innovation concept is contained in W. Ross Ashby, "Variety, Constraint, and the Law of Requisite Variety," in Walter Buckeley, ed., *Modern Systems Research for the Behavioral Scientist* (Chicago: Aldine, 1968); major concepts stressed in this interesting article include the importance of information collection, communications, listening, evaluation, and the cultivation of a variety of responses to stave off legitimacy crises and loss of control. Warren G. Bennis et al., eds., *The Planning of Change* (New York: Holt, Rinehart, 1969), is becoming widely known, but for the most part is only marginally useful; for example, see Readings 2.1, 5.2, 5.3, and 7.3, but skim the rest.

Scientific work on innovation exists, but rarely is it of the quality of Thomas S. Kuhn's, *The Structure of Scientific Revolutions* (Chicago: University of Chicago Press, 1964 Phoenix ed.). The research-scientific movement has been traced reasonably well by Elihu Katz, Martin L. Levin, and Herbert Hamilton, "Traditions of Research in the Diffusion of Innovations," *American Sociological Review,* Vol. 28 (April 1963), pp. 237–52. An example of how to orchestrate innovation using a firm scientific basis is George F. Fairweather, *Methods for Experimental Social Innovation* (New York: Wiley, 1968).

To conclude this very selected list on innovation, several examples and cases may be cited of innovation-oriented work focused on levels of spatial detail beginning with the rural setting, passing through the city's budget, on to innovation processes within the American states, and concluding with a total world view. Each attacks the substantive material from a different spatial (and often temporal) point of view, but each has innovation as a common denominator. Theodore W. Schultz, *Transforming Traditional Agriculture* (New Haven: Yale University Press, 1964), is an excellent, if somewhat technically difficult, place to begin. Rufus P. Browning has looked at decisionmaking in the budgetary process to find examples of structural detail that will either induce or inhibit innovation. See his "Innovative and Noninnovative Decision Processes in Government Budgeting," in Robert T. Golembiewski, ed., *Public Budgeting and Finance* (Itasca, Ill.: Peacock, 1968), pp. 128–45. As for communication processes and the selection of topics that have served as innovations for the American states over the past few years, see Jack L. Walker's "The Diffusion of Innovations Among the American States," *American Political Science Review,* Vol. 63, No. 3 (September 1969), pp. 880–99. Between the Walker and the Browning pieces one could develop several very interesting cross-cultural companion studies; in fact, the need for comparative work is acute. For yet another perspective on the innovation concept, see Quincy Wright, William M. Evan, and Morton Deutsch, eds., *Preventing World War III: Some Proposals* (New York: Simon and Schuster, 1962). Distinguishing this work from the others cited is the fact that the authors have been concerned with the creation of innovations based on a reasonably good understanding of past trends, conditioning factors, desired goals, and probable future states of the world.

To make the transition from innovation studies to work that is concerned about the processes of innovation diffusion, one should consult a little read, unfortunately buried, but excellent piece by Lawrence Brown, "Dynamics of Innovation: A Macro-View," *Economic Development and Cultural Change,* Vol. 17 (January 1969), pp. 189–211. Besides a very competent, complete summary of much of the relevant literature, Brown develops a highly plausible quantitative model of innovation diffusion in order to investigate cost considerations at the macro level that result from either adopting or not adopting a given innovation.

The study of diffusion has been particularly advanced among European geographers, most notably the Swedes for some unclear reason. Torsten Hägerstrand has been perhaps the most visibly creative, although others have made important contributions. See Hägerstrand, *The Propagation of Innovation Waves* (Lund, Sweden: Royal University of Lund, 1952); and for a more accessible summary of the fundamental ideas, *idem* "Quantitative Techniques for Analysis of the Spread of Information and Technology," in C. Arnold Anderson and Mary Jane Bowman, eds., *Education and Development* (Chicago: Aldine, 1965), pp. 244–80. Georg Karlsson, *Social Mechanisms: Studies in Sociological Theory* (Uppsala, Sweden: Almquist and Wilksells, 1958), gives a more general overview of the Swedish innovation diffusion literature and thought; Hägerstrand is perhaps the most substantial of the lot, however. American counterparts who owe much to these earlier initiatives include many of the works cited in Elihu Katz et al., "Traditions of Research in the Diffusion of Innovations"; and Everrett M. Rogers, *Diffusion of Innovations* (New York: The Free Press, 1962).

Some experimental work exists on the underlying psychological conditioning factors explaining innovation diffusion. A fine example of the genre and a good source of references is Herbert Menzel, "Public and Private Conformity under Different Conditions of Acceptance in the Group," *Journal of Abnormal and Social Psychology,* Vol. 55 (November 1957), pp. 389–402. James S. Coleman et al., "The Diffusion of an Innovation Among Physicians," *Sociometry,* Vol. 20 (December 1957), pp. 253–70, carries many of the psychological ideas several steps further by describing the process with respect to a well-defined context and group. Jack L. Walker, "The Diffusion of Innovations Among the American States," does much the same thing, but for a larger, aggregated unit of analysis.

There is work on the diffusion of technology among less developed people, but it is spotty and not very pervasive. However, for a sampling, one might consider, Everrett M. Rogers, "Mass Media Exposure and Modernization Among Columbian Peasants," *Public Opinion Quarterly,* Vol. 29 (Fall 1965), pp. 614–25; Everrett M. Rogers and Wicky L. Meynen, "Communication Sources for 2, 4–D Weed Spray Among Columbian Peasants," *Rural Sociology,* Vol. 30 (June 1965), pp. 213–19; and Bryce Ryan and Neal C. Gross, "The Diffusion of Hybrid Seed Corn in Two Iowa Communities," *Rural Sociology,* Vol. 8 (March 1943), pp. 15–24 for three better-than-average empirical examples.

Estimation

Proving that there is considerable overlap in the six identified phases of the alternatives approach, much of the estimation literature is related directly to invention, selection, and/or evaluation. Because a given citation is noted under estimation is no reason to assume that its contents are likewise singly constrained, for this is seldom so.

A good overview of the purpose and role of estimation, generally conceived, is contained in Harold D. Lasswell and Allan R. Holmberg, "Toward a General Theory of Directed Value Accumulation and Institutional Development," in Ralph Braibanti, ed., *Political and Administrative Development* (Durham, N.C.: Duke University Press, 1971). More narrowly focused, less comprehensive works that treat a variety of estimation-related topics very well are Jerome Rothenberg, *The Measurement of Social Welfare* (Englewood Cliffs, N.J.: Prentice-Hall, 1961); and, J. R. Lawrence, ed., *Operations Research and the Social Sciences* (New York: Tavistock, 1966), has illustrative articles that cover the estimation gamut. Three other general works are worth careful reading because they are excellent social science and they show other important variations of the estimation and greater alternatives ideas. James Tobin, "Economic Growth as an Objective of Government Policy," *American Economic Review,* Vol. 54 (May 1964), pp. 1–27, illustrates a sensitive and sensible use of fundamental theoretical tools to inform the estimation and selection phases; David Braybrooke and C. E. Lindblom, *Strategy of Decision* (New York: The Free Press, 1963); and Albert O. Hirschman, *The Strategy of Economic Development* (New Haven: Yale University Press, 1958), are also excellent general sources.

The literature on probability determination can be thought of as including straight "textbook" accounts of suitable techniques for making estimates, some cost–benefit work, and a few quantitatively oriented articles on decisionmaking. An appropriate place to begin is W. Feller, *An Introduction to Probability Theory and Its Applications* (New York: Wiley, 1957); the concepts of uncertainty and decisionmaking performance are central in C. West Churchman, *Prediction and Optimal Decision* (Englewood Cliffs, N.J.: Prentice-Hall, 1961); the use of extremely sophisticated methodological techniques to make economic estimates and to inform economic planning decisions is elegantly laid out in Jan Tinbergen, *The Design of Development* (Baltimore, Md.: The Johns Hopkins University Press, 1958); and finally, one rather abstract, but provocative, attempt to relate uncertainty to the development of social theory generally is A. A. Alchian, "Uncertainty, Evolution, and Economic Theory," *Journal of Political Economy,* Vol. 58 (June 1950), pp. 211–22.

The literature on cost–benefit analysis has burgeoned in the past years, and a good place to begin finding out about these developments in a variety of substantive settings is A. R. Prest and R. Turvey, "Cost-Benefit Analysis: A Survey," *The Economic Journal,* Vol. 75 (December 1965), pp. 683–735. A classic and highly durable application of the technique is C. J. Hitch and Roland McKean, *The Economics of Defense in the Nuclear Age* (Cambridge, Mass.: Harvard University Press, 1960); a good example for the underdeveloped settings is Fred Hanssmann, "Operations Research in National Planning of Underdeveloped Countries," *Operations Research,* Vol. 9 (March–April 1961), pp. 230–48; and the normative component of benefit-cost analysis is explicitly discussed (as contrasted with "routine" applications of the technique) in J. V. Krutilla, "Welfare Aspects of Benefit-Cost Analysis," *Journal of Political Economy,* Vol. 69, No. 3 (June 1961), pp. 226–35.

Decisionmaking (selection) articles having a very high degree of concern for the determination of probabilities and estimation are not numerous, but a few respectable and interesting examples can be indicated. William J. Baumol and R. E. Quandt, "Rules of Thumb and Optimally Imperfect Decisions," *American Economic Review,* Vol. 54 (March 1964), pp. 23–46, is a particularly relevant piece; I. D. J. Bross, *Design for Decision* (New York: Macmillan, 1953); and L. Spier, "A Suggested Behavioral Approach to Cost-Benefit Analysis," *Management Science* (Applications Series), Vol. 17 (June 1971), pp. B–672 through B–693, also serve the purpose well.

The literature on determining the desirability of policies in the preoutcome or estimation phase comes from a variety of sources and is of highly variable quality. One may usefully look at a few good overview treatments before considering the issue from the researcher's point of view; that is to say, is a given policy or policy question consonant with the ethical-moral standards of a given researcher or class of researchers? More easily determined is literature treating the desirability issue with respect to specific research and policy contexts. Abraham Kaplan's *American Ethics and Public Policy* (New York: Oxford University Press, 1963), has been noted several times already because it is an excellent, thoughtful book that, here again, has great and direct applicability. So it is, too, with Gibson Winter's *Elements for a Social Ethic: Scientific Perspectives on Social Process* (New York: Macmillan, 1966). More commonly known general treatments are Kenneth J. Arrow, *Social Choice and Individual Values* (New York: Wiley, 1963 ed.); and C. West Churchman, "Decision and Value Theory," in Russell L. Ackoff, ed., *Progress in Operations Research* (New York: Wiley, 1961). The researcher's operating responsibilities and normative concerns are admirably handled in L. Wirth, "Responsibility of Social Science," *The Annals of the American Academy of Political and Social Sciences,* Vol. 249 (January 1947), pp. 143–51; and recently by Harold D. Lasswell, "Must Science Serve Political Power?" *American Psychologist,* Vol. 25 (February 1970), pp. 117–23. To shift emphasis to the policy or research context one is well rewarded by reading Wayne A. R. Leys, *Ethics for Policy Decisions* (Englewood Cliffs, N.J.: Prentice-Hall, 1952); another good, reliable source is Kenneth Boulding, "The Ethics of Rational Decision," *Management Science,* Vol. 12 (February 1966), pp. 161–69. Distributional questions among various societal sectors with respect to government expenditures, a prime issue in *all* "developing" countries provide a central thesis in Francis M. Bator, *The Question of Government Spending: Public Needs and Private Wants* (New York: Harper Bros., 1960). And finally, the connection between ethical and decision theories is concisely developed in J. V. Krutilla, "Welfare Aspects of Benefit-Cost Analysis."

Good tangible examples that combine the ideas of preoutcome estimations of probability and desirability include J. J. Spengler, "Social Value Theory, Economic Analyses, and Economic Policy," *American Economic Review,* Vol. 42 (May 1953), pp. 340-45; Robert Dorfman, ed., *Measuring Benefits of Government Investments* (Washington, D.C.: The Brookings Institution, 1965); creative appreciation for similarities in three visible streams of research and policy activity is well stated in Albert O. Hirschman and C. E. Lindblom,

"Economic Development, Research and Development, and Policymaking: Some Converging Views," *Behavioral Science,* Vol. 7 (April 1962), pp. 211–22. David Novick has edited an influential text on program budgeting that contains many specific examples worth reviewing, *Program Budgeting* (Cambridge, Mass.: Harvard University Press, 1965); two other solid texts do much the same thing, but use quite different examples, see Arthur Maas et al., *Design of Water Resource Systems* (Cambridge, Mass.: Harvard University Press, 1962), Part I; and Richard Nelson et al., *Technology, Economic Growth, and Public Policy* (Washington, D.C.: The Brookings Institution, 1967).

Selection: The Process of Decision

The literature most concerned with selection processes is divisible into theoretical and applied subsections. Presented initially are a few general treatments of selection in the context of decisionmaking; and then we point out some useful, but more narrowly defined, theoretical works on the same topic. Planning appears to be one important decisionmaking component in the developing context; hence, we note a select few planning articles in which the decisionmaking task is central. This section concludes with representative examples of development decisionmaking in a variety of spatial and temporal settings.

A good place to begin, even if one presumes to know a great deal about selection processes, is Herbert A. Simon, *Administrative Behavior* (New York: Macmillan, 1957); Robert A. Dahl and C. E. Lindblom, *Politics, Economics, and Welfare* (New York: Harper Bros., 1953), also have much excellent general material on the subject. Both of these well-known books are worth careful and thoughtful reading because so much valuable information has been condensed and well presented in each. Shading over to more straightforward development topics, but still at a very general level and focused on selection are Gunnar Myrdal, *Beyond the Welfare State: Economic Planning and Its International Implications* (New Haven: Yale University Press, 1960); S. N. Eisenstadt, "Bureaucracy and Political Development," in Joseph LaPalombara, ed., *Bureaucracy and Political Development* (Princeton: Princeton University Press, 1967 ed.); and for a well-constructed, thoroughly readable source, Albert O. Hirschman, *Journeys Toward Progress: Studies of Economic Policymaking in Latin America* (New York: Twentieth Century Fund, 1963).

Theoretical literature on decisionmaking is abundant, and we must rather ruthlessly restrict ourselves to a few selections that we have found helpful in the past. We must warn that this—and all other compiled lists—is merely suggestive of literature related to the various topics and known to have something useful to say. Rigorous technical treatments of decisionmaking theory are contained in Ward Edwards and A. Tversky, eds., *Decision Making* (Baltimore, Md.: Penguin, 1967 ed.), and we suggest that this is a good place to begin before becoming lost in less concise, usually verbal, accounting of the selection process.

It is worth pointing out that there is a great deal of decisionmaking literature that is frankly not worth reading. David Braybrooke and C. E. Lindblom, *Strategy of Decision* (New York: The Free Press, 1963), is definitely an exception to this general caveat and requires attention. The same can be said about two of Herbert A. Simon's earlier articles on decisionmaking: "A Behavioral Model of Rational Choice," *Quarterly Journal of Economics,* Vol. 69 (February 1955), pp. 99–118; and *idem,* "Theories of Decision Making in Economics," *American Economic Review,* Vol. 49 (June 1959), pp. 253–83.

More difficult theoretical treatments exist, for example, the bulk of the game theory-based explanatory work of people like Gerard Debreu and Lloyd Shapley; however, for the average reader of limited quantitative background, Fritz Machlup, "Theories of the Firm: Marginalist, Behavioral, Managerial," *American Economic Review,* Vol. 57 (March 1967), pp. 1–33, probably tells one as much as is needed to become conversant with the field. More easily understood verbal characterizations are contained in Yehezkel Dror, "Public Policymaking in Developing States," in *Public Policymaking Reexamined* (San Francisco: Chandler, 1968); Michel Crozier, *The Bureaucratic Phenomenon* (Chicago: University of Chicago Press, 1964), which is a very readable and competent general theoretical work that is admirably illustrated with appropriate French examples; and, Burton H. Klein, "The Decisionmaking Problem in Development," in National Bureau of Economic Research, *The Rate and Direction of Inventive Activity* (Princeton: Princeton University Press, 1962).

To round out this section on decisionmaking theory, we note three very different empirically based studies to give the reader a flavor of what possibilities exist in this kind of work. Aaron Wildavsky, *The Politics of the Budgetary Process* (Boston: Little, Brown, 1964), has already been used to excellent advantage by several other scholars of development problems and contexts. The early indications are such that one would predict that Graham T. Allison's *Essence of Decision* (Boston: Little, Brown, 1971), will do much the same for the field of crisis decisionmaking. And finally, to complete this list of empirically based decisionmaking studies, one might look at Merton J. Peck and Frederic M. Scherer, *The Weapons Acquisition Process: An Economic Analysis* (Cambridge, Mass.: Littauer—now the John F. Kennedy School of Government— 1962).

The planning literature that relates nicely to the selection process is also rather large, but it can be summarized without great difficulty. A reasonable starting point is Hirschman and Lindblom, "Economic Development, Research and Development, and Policymaking"; Morris Janowitz and William Delaney, "The Bureaucrat and the Public: A Study of Informational Perspectives," *Administrative Science Quarterly,* Vol. 2 (September 1957), pp. 141–62, do a very commendable job on the salient factors that must be considered in preparing a citizen participation input into program planning and implementation; the role of expert participants in the policymaking and decisionmaking processes is treated well by contributors in Robert Gilpin and Christopher Wright, eds.,

Scientists and National Policymaking (New York: Columbia University Press, 1964); political and bureaucratic impacts on the planning process and actual development decisionmaking are central themes in Everrett E. Hagen, ed., *Planning Economic Development* (Homewood, Ill.: Richard D. Irwin, 1963). Other able contributions in much the same vein are W. Arthur Lewis, "Planning Public Expenditures," in Max F. Millikan, ed., *National Economic Planning* (New York: National Bureau of Economic Research, 1967), pp. 201–27, and several other selections in the same volume; Bert F. Hoselitz, "Economic Policy and Economic Development," in Hugh G. J. Aitken, ed., *The State and Economic Growth* (New York: Social Science Research Council, 1959); and for a more narrowly focused piece having great importance for most developing contexts, Martin Rein, "Social Planning: The Search for Legitimacy," *Journal of the American Institute of Planners,* Vol. 35 (July 1969), pp. 233–44. And finally, to give one some hard pragmatic lessons learned, see Albert Waterson, *Development Planning: Lessons of Experience* (Baltimore, Md.: The Johns Hopkins University Press, 1965), is candid and to the point.

We conclude this section of the survey on selection literature with several solid case examples from a variety of development settings. Here, too, we are highly selective in compiling this abbreviated list. The Soviet Union's decision-making experience is ably captured in Zbigniew Brzezinski and Samuel P. Huntington, *Political Power: USA/USSR* (New York: Viking, 1964); for a concrete illustration of how the model functioned during a very decisive period in Soviet developmental history, see Alexander Erlich, *The Soviet Industrialization Debate, 1924–1928* (Cambridge, Mass.: Harvard University Press, 1960); an excellent "sampler" of Soviet decisionmaking is contained in Peter H. Juvilier and Henry W. Martin, eds., *Soviet Policymaking* (New York: Praeger, 1966); and a standard work is Merle Fainsod, *How Russia Is Ruled* (Cambridge, Mass.: Harvard University Press, 1963 rev. ed.).

European examples are numerous, particularly as a result of the impacts made by the Ford Foundation's Foreign Area Fellowship Program and others like it that sent hundreds of American scholars to Europe for study. Good representative works include, Yehezkel Dror, *National Planning in the Netherlands* (Syracuse, N.Y.: Syracuse University Press, 1968); Brian Chapman, *The Prefects and Provincial France* (London: Allen and Unwin, 1955); and John Hackett and Anne-Marie Hackett, *Economic Planning in France* (Cambridge, Mass.: Harvard University Press, 1963).

Latin American cases are developed in A. O. Hirschman, *Journeys Toward Progress;* and very specifically in Lynton K. Caldwell, "Technical Assistance and Administrative Reform in Columbia," *American Political Science Review,* Vol. 47 (June 1953), pp. 494–510.

Asian examples are numerous, particularly those dealing with India. Samples include Chitoshi Yanaga, *Big Business and Politics in Japan* (New Haven: Yale University Press, 1969), in which the incredible importance of Tokyo University is cited as a major determinant of who gets into positions of decisionmaking authority, what kinds and styles of decisionmaking exist, and why such flexibility of personnel between quite different, but powerful, institutions exists. A. H. Hanson, *The Process of Planning: A Study of India's Five-Year Plans, 1950–1964* (New York: Oxford University Press, 1966), makes many insightful observations and summarizes masterfully most of what one needs to know about the evolution and execution of Indian planning and policy-making; see also P. T. Bauer, *Indian Economic Policy and Development* (New York: Praeger, 1961); and Richard L. Park and Irene Tinker, eds., *Leadership and Political Institutions in India* (Princeton: Princeton University Press, 1959), for related views, but taken from different perspectives. A very nice case example from the Philippines is Frank Golay, *The Philippines: Public Policy and National Economic Development* (Ithaca, N.Y.: Cornell University Press, 1961).

Implementation: Making Policies Work

It is sad to report that very little literature exists on this phase of the process and that which does exist is either focused on basic conceptual clarification or on specific, usually American, substantive issues. The need for additional theoretical and practical work is clear, and the following few examples hopefully point the way to some much needed, difficult, but potentially rewarding scholarship. Jeffrey Pressman and Aaron Wildavsky, *Implementation* (Berkeley: University of California Press, 1973), combine case materials with a preliminary statement of the basic conceptual issues related to implementation. Confirming our suspicion about the paucity of literature, Pressman and Wildavsky searched with only slight success to find pertinent source materials (see their "Use of 'Implementation' in Social Science Literature," *ibid.,* pp. 166–75).

A few conceptual works on the organizational aspects of implementation exist, albeit in rudimentary form. James D. Thompson, *Organizations in Action* (New York: McGraw-Hill, 1967), has scattered references to the subject, as does Charles E. Lindblom, *The Intelligence of Democracy* (New York: The Free Press, 1965); however, the reader must infer far more about implementation than he should in both of these works. The matter is just not dealt with clearly. Wildavsky's interest in the issue antedates his recent joint work with Pressman, as is evident in portions of his "The Analysis of Issue-Contexts in the Study of Decision-Making," *Journal of Politics,* Vol. 24 (November 1962), pp. 717–32. In a subsequent joint work with Naomi Caiden, Wildavsky's concern is manifest, although primary emphasis is placed on the prior phases of estimation and selection. See Caiden and Wildavsky, *A Constant Quantity of Tears: Planning and Budgeting in Poor Countries* (New York: Wiley–Interscience, 1973).

Conceptual clarification focused on the individual level of analysis is likewise rare. Charles Schultze, in his "The Role of Incentives, Penalties, and Rewards in Attaining Effective Policy," in Julius Margolis and Robert Haveman, eds., *Public Expenditures and Policy Analysis* (Chicago: Markham, 1970), pp. 145–71, demonstrates a variety of monetary policies and information requirements used and needed to implement programs. The concept of incentive systems as a pre-determinant of policy outcomes is elaborated in the specific situations of flood insurance and water quality programs. At a less specific level, Philip Selznik, *Leadership in Administration* (Evanston, Ill.: Row, Peterson, 1957), Chapter 5, develops several parallel arguments and points.

Concrete examples of implementation analyses are even rarer than are conceptual ones. R. S. Rosenbloom and J. R. Russell, *New Tools for Urban Management* (Cambridge, Mass.: Harvard University Press, 1971), present a number of cases that add to our understanding of how rational analyses have failed to be implemented in any significant way in urban policy situations—a theme picked up and partially developed for the private context by James H. Batchelor in his *The Implementation of Operations Research* (New York: Wiley–Interscience, 1970). At least in part, because of the size of the investment and a steady stream of unsatisfactory reports, the field of education has provided a few implementation analyses. One of the best of these is Milbrey W. McLaughlin, *Evaluation and Reform: The Case of ESEA Title I* (Santa Monica, Cal.: The Rand Corporation, R–1292–RSR, April 1974). Another evaluation-based analysis which also touches on the implementation issue is Joel S. Berke and Michael W. Kirst, *Federal Aid to Education* (Lexington, Mass.: D. C. Heath, 1972).

The underdeveloped state of scholarship on implementation is both depressing and encouraging: depressing because the problems are rather obvious and in great need of attention and encouraging because of the vast assortment of research and operational opportunities presented.

Evaluation: Postoutcome Events and Government Performance

Evaluation has become very important in recent years as a viable field of study. There are many recent examples of evaluation work in current United States' development efforts, especially in the health, education, and welfare areas. We suspect that extensive cross-national evaluation work will not be long coming; and, to venture a small projection of our own, it seems that this might be a particularly fruitful area for research, theoretical development, and applied social science over the next five to ten years. For anyone concerned about evaluation and evaluation research, there are four essential texts that should be read and mastered. Harold D. Lasswell, *Politics: Who Gets What, When, and How* (Cleveland, Ohio: The World Publishing Co., 1958 ed.), Part III, "Results," contains most of the essential ideas and worthwhile questions; and, Francis G. Caro, ed., *Readings in Evaluation Research* (New York: The Russell Sage Foundation, 1971), provides abundant examples. Because evaluation research has a long and commendable tradition in health-related substantive areas, the tour de force produced by the late Edward A. Suchman, *Evaluative Research* (New York: The Russell Sage Foundation, 1967), Chapters 1–2,

4–7, and 10, should be read by all. Finally, to remind oneself of the potential contribution that the policy sciences can make for the improvement of policy-making generally, one need only review Alice M. Rivlin, *Systematic Thinking for Social Action* (Washington, D.C.: The Brookings Institution, 1971).

Considerations of the performance of social systems are rare; however, Robert A. Dahl, "The Evaluation of Political Systems," in Ithiel de Sola Pool, ed., *Contemporary Political Science: Toward Empirical Theory* (New York: McGraw-Hill, 1967). pp. 166–81, does a good job of working through some basic questions and a few of the more likely outcomes for the activity. Ways to evaluate systems are described in David Novick, ed., *Program Budgeting;* Michael B. Teitz, "Cost-Effectiveness: A Systems Approach to Analysis of Urban Services," *Journal of the American Institute of Planners,* Vol. 34, No. 5 (September 1968), pp. 303–11; and Peter Rossi, "Practice, Method, and Theory in Evaluating Social Action Programs," in James L. Sundquist, ed., *On Fighting Poverty: Perspectives from Experience* (New York: Basic Books, 1969), pp. 217–34. Some fine examples of evaluations done for defined contexts (or systems) include Donald Schon, "The Blindness System," *The Public Interest,* Vol. 18 (Winter 1971), pp. 25–38, a searingly bitter critique of the procedures and personnel responsible for the care and treatment of the blind; Frances Fox Piven and Richard A. Cloward, *Regulating the Poor: The Function of Public Welfare* (New York: Pantheon, 1971), Chapters 1, 6, 8–10, an attention-catching and sharp indictment of the welfare system; Ronald W. Conley, "A Benefit-Cost Analysis of the Vocational Rehabilitation Program," *Journal of Human Resources,* Vol. 4 (Spring 1969), pp. 226–52, a less emotional, more quantitative, but equally devastating evaluation of current rehabilitation practices and outcomes; and finally, Richard M. Titmus, *The Gift Relationship: From Human Blood to Social Policy* (New York: Pantheon, 1971), Chapters 1, 8–9, 12–14, which should be read particularly in light of recent revelations that commercial blood companies have been exploiting cheap sources of Haitian (and other) blood to supply American needs.[15]

Measurement is at the heart (or should be) of a well-executed evaluation, and there are several good places to look for ideas and appropriate measurement techniques. Robert Dorfman, ed., *Measuring Benefits from Government Investments,* has many excellent general examples; as does Jerome Rothenberg, *The Measurement of Social Welfare* (Englewood Cliffs, N.J.: Prentice-Hall, 1961). More specific and detailed sources of measurement ideas are R. J. Chambers, *Accounting, Evaluation, and Economic Behavior* (Englewood Cliffs, N.J.: Prentice-Hall, 1966); Bureau of the Budget, *Measuring Productivity of Federal Government Organizations* (Washington, D.C.: U.S. Government Printing Office, 1964); Eliot D. Chapple and Leonard R. Sayles, *The Measure of*

[15] This is but one striking example where an initially American-oriented evaluation study could be very easily extended and/or replicated in a foreign setting to great advantage. We trust that a few of our more imaginative colleagues will see such connections and begin doing the important cross-national and foreign work that is literally crying out for attention.

Management (New York: Macmillan, 1961); and Joseph S. Wholey et al., *Federal Evaluation Policy: Analyzing the Effects of Public Programs* (Washington, D.C.: The Brookings Institution, 1970). A good rigorous text that provides ample illustrations of how and when to measure in the interests of evaluation is Martin S. Feldstein, *Economic Analysis of Health Service Efficiency* (Chicago: Markham, 1968), Chapters 2, 5, 8, and 10.

Experimentation has become an important form of evaluating past policies and trying out recommended changes on a limited scale before subjecting masses of the population to their effects. In fact, social experimentation appears to be a rapidly emerging form of policy science activity and one that is bound to have a pervasive impact. A key spokesman over the years has been Donald T. Campbell, an experimental psychologist. See his "Validity of Experiments in Social Settings," *Psychological Bulletin,* Vol. 54 (1957), pp. 297–312, for a relatively early statement of the idea; and *idem,* "Reforms as Experiments," *American Psychologist,* Vol. 24 (April 1969), pp. 409–29, for a popular, highly regarded reformulation and expansion of the idea. The limits and potentials of the social experiment, taken from a policy perspective, are explored in Garry D. Brewer, "Social Experimentation and the Policy Process," *Twenty–Fifth Annual Report of the Rand Corporation* (Santa Monica, Cal.: The Rand Corporation, 1973), pp. 151–65.

Other evaluation examples can be cited to point out the diversity of substantive and disciplinary interests involved. At one extreme, the historian Thomas C. Smith, *Political Change and Industrial Development in Japan: Government Enterprises, 1868–1880* (Stanford, Cal.: Stanford University Press, 1955), engaged in a form of unrigorous, but insight-provoking, evaluation of a very central period and interesting aspect of Japanese societal development. The evaluation of present-day legal institutions, felt by many to be performing unsatisfactorily along a number of dimensions, is John B. Jennings, *The Flow of Clients through the New York City Criminal Court in 1967* (New York: NYC/RI, RM–6364–NYC, 1970). Another technical assessment is treated by a number of contributors in Ronald G. Ridker, ed., *Economic Costs of Air Pollution: Studies in Management* (New York: Praeger, 1966). And to conclude this short list, we note an all-to-prevalent and essentially ultimate form of evaluation, the military coup. See Fred R. von der Mehden and Charles W. Anderson, "Political Action by the Military in the Developing Countries," *Social Research,* Vol. 28 (Winter 1961), pp. 459–79. Surely better, more constructive, and timely evaluation than the coup d'etat should be the norm in the developing nations.

Termination: Ending or Redirecting Policies

There is no coherent body of literature concerned with the termination aspects of a policy's life cycle; there are bits and pieces of work that have usually been done for other basic reasons. This is not to say that termination is unimportant; it rather reflects a general lack of concern among scholars and policymakers for stopping or reframing policies that are no longer needed or that require major adjustments. A general overview of the form such efforts could assume, and a good starting point for the development of this neglected aspect of the decision sequence is contained in Harold D. Lasswell's *A Pre-View of Policy Sciences, op. cit.,* pp. 27–33, 92–93.

The key importance of contextual information is stressed in termination activities associated with changes in leadership and in significant changes in the tastes, needs, and objectives of a society. For example, in the aftermath of the 1973 coup d'etat in Chile, many substantial termination activities have been undertaken, but to date there is only the sketchiest of analytic work detailing the likely and discernible consequences of these changes. The need for such work, in Chile and elsewhere where fundamental contextual changes have occurred, is clear and great. Changes in perceived societal objectives may generate termination demands, e.g., the Alaska pipeline for the supply of oil was effectively "terminated" for a period by ecologically motivated citizens; however, the policy has been short-lived in the face of increased energy demands. The interaction of Middle East termination decisions with respect to oil production, whatever their actual motivation, and decisions to initiate resource policies throughout the world are fascinating topics; the key importance of these topics is only recently becoming evident.

Terminating policies related to unwanted technologies has proven to be largely ineffective; technologies appear to generate a momentum of their own which defies many efforts to slow, deflect, or terminate them. The creation and diffusion of technologies related to the supersonic transport, anti–ballistic missile systems, more efficient methods of killing one another, the automobile, the computer, the space shuttle, television, and on and on illustrate the contention. Even when a technology can be shown to be more costly than beneficial, we have been rather unsuccessful in devising termination strategies to reverse the situation.

Richard Neustadt's *Alliance Politics* (New York: Columbia University Press, 1970), stresses termination of technology-intensive, international defense system—SKYBOLT—and in doing so draws attention to variance in perspectives, expectations, and interpretations of partners in a decisionmaking process where a common language and heritage exist; left unsaid is the complicating effect for termination where language and heritage differ significantly.

War is a process not only associated with perceptual and expectational differences but one which increasingly has a dismal, technological inevitability associated with it. The process of war is rarely thought through from its initiation to its eventual and likely conclusions.[16] However, there has been a limited

---

[16] A more thorough and methodological treatment of this general topic is presented in Garry D. Brewer, "Gaming: Prospective for Forecasting," in Thomas Robinson and Nazli Choucri, eds., *Forecasting in International Relations* (San Francisco: W. H. Freeman, 1974), Chapter 13.

amount of scholarship on the topic which, fortunately, is of unsually high quality. For example, Fred C. Iklé, *Every War Must End* (New York: Columbia University Press, 1971), is replete with case examples, excellent research topics, and theoretical insights.

Taking a cue from Iklé and pursuing the matter a bit on our own, it appears that there are at least four distinct topics that need to be developed to improve our understanding of war termination. The first relates to understanding the characteristic styles of those thought most likely to be involved in deciding when and how to end a war; the psychological studies done by Alexander and Juliette George, *Woodrow Wilson and Colonel House: A Personality Study* (New York: John Day, 1956); Walter L. Langer, *The Mind of Adolph Hitler* (New York: Basic Books, 1972), especially pp. 209–13; and Lasswell and his associates in their *World Revolutionary Elites: Studies in Coercive Ideological Movements* (Cambridge, Mass.: The MIT Press, 1965) illustrate the kind of work referred to here. The second topic concerns systematic comprehension of negotiation strategies and tactics used by politico-military authorities, especially in a situation where termination may be considered treasonous by those determined to press on, as pointed out by Paul Kecskemeti, *Strategic Surrender: The Politics of Victory and Defeat* (Stanford, Cal.: Stanford University Press, 1958). The relationship between risk-taking behavior, perception, and negotiations is stressed in Fred C. Iklé's *How Nations Negotiate* (New York: Harper & Row, 1964); and a well-known experimental treatment of these matters is reported under the general rubric of the "risky shift," by M. A. Wallich and N. Kogan in their "The Role of Information, Discussion, and Consensus in Group Risk Taking," *Journal of Experimental Social Psychology,* Vol. 1 (1965), pp. 1–19.

The third topic focuses on the kinds of communication, command, and control apparatus that would be depended upon to wage and then terminate a war. The fourth, and clearly the most important, task is figuring out ways to end a war before it begins or, failing that, to end the war at something less than total destruction of the hostile parties. The literature on these two topics is grossly underdeveloped, which is indicative, at the least, of just how much work is yet to be done.

A Postscript on Alternatives

One major emphasis in development policymaking has been wealth related and another has concentrated on the accumulation of power in many forms. An important lesson learned through the unhappy or at least highly qualified experiences of many nations is that such single- or at best dual-purpose national objectives and their related implementation strategies and programatic schemes are not only unattainable in practice, but they may very well be self-defeating, or to recall an Indonesian colleague's vivid imagery used to characterize the Sukarno episode, "self-mutilating." What might be recommended is a fundamental reconceptualization of development, emphasizing a broadening of the policy alternatives considered as being legitimate means to achieve as yet largely untapped and potentially rewarding ends.[17]

To develop this line of thought one needs to have a few basic ideas spelled out. These include some comments on resource scarcity, "cool and hot" development strategies, and the need for a major reevaluation of what is honestly desirable and probable within a given underdeveloped setting. Reevaluation in this sense implies that one needs to consider various ways of increasing participation in the shaping and sharing of deference values unrelated for the most part to power and wealth concerns.

All nations should not be seduced into believing that it is possible to "close the gap," catch up with, or surpass the Soviet Union, the United States, Western Europe, or—for that matter—Japan in total industrial output or productivity. Every indication is that the goal is chimerical and that most policy alternatives directed exclusively to these ends wreak a malicious havoc in settings having inadequate primary resources and limited pools of skilled talent to process these resources. Such raw materials and the means to convert them into goods and services are simply *not* infinitely expandable. Chasing the phantom of economic development may well be a vacuous pastime for the vast majority of the world's people. Eating is not at issue; the view is basically one of creating modern but simple societies where material goods are in sufficient but not extravagant supply. Not every nation can hope to produce its own computers, automobiles, or nuclear weapons; these are unattainable goals that serve only to divert creative policymakers from the pursuit of more realistic and productive alternatives.

What strategies are called for then? One might think about a "cool" approach to the problem in which popular attention is directed to very simple procedures that allow individuals to derive satisfaction with life based on expressive and symbolic activities—the vision is generally relevant, not limited to the relatively materially impoverished. This approach is contrasted with the "hot" or high affect mobilization narrowly directed to the ever-increasing accumulation of power and wealth—a process shown to be self-destructive in many societies, including the United States. What is proposed is nothing short of creating a global network of people carrying a new, more humane vision of life. No one nation can do it alone, can solve its specific problems in isolation; attempts will most certainly fail. If the "cool" or symbolic approach and reorientation of man can be made to work at all, it may make the difference between surviving or not.

The underlying concept is figuring out ways to shift popular attention and the policymaking emphasis toward deference and respect concerns as distinguished from those primarily focused on power and wealth. To put the argu-

[17] The following comments reflect the thoughts and experiences of several colleagues who participated in a remarkable meeting on "Changing Value Emphases in the Development Setting," held in Singapore in March of 1972 at the invitation of the Asia Society. Signaled in these discussions was an awareness of the need for a major reorientation and a call to realistic and humane policy creation and execution for most of the world's people. Key participants were Soedjatmoko of Indonesia and Harold D. Lasswell.

ment baldly, creative attention must be devoted to means for pursuing values involving a minimum of resources and simple, unsophisticated technologies. Examples include the giving and receiving of respect, affection, or rectitude such as ceremonial participation, artistic creativeness, worship, or any activities where the resource expenditure is far outweighed by the symbolic one. What is at stake is nothing short of a respect revolution: the creation of a world distinct from the one whose main pastimes are accumulation for its own sake and production for more efficient killing. The basic policy problem is substituting symbolic for material objectives, strategies, and outcomes; the goal is to develop an awareness on a global scale of the need for an integration—not an eradication—of predominantly rural values into what at best will be only a partially "metropolitanized" world.[18]

What are the prospects, or is the task beyond reach? A flickering hope rests in observable cultural changes taking place throughout the world, as demonstrated most forcefully by many spatially disconnected, but commonly reacting, young persons. Concerns for ecology, for new personal styles to cope with technology, and for warlessness are all still incoherent, but nonetheless powerful new forces that need to be shaped and directed to achieve a better balance between a deference or respect focus as contrasted with a power- and wealth-centered one.

The underlying question, and the task that confronts us all, is how do we go about developing a vision of a world where human beings are allowed to remain human?

The studies that we have selected do not address this question, but that should not detract from the messages and questions that they contain and do in fact answer. In fact, these perceptions represent a dimly seen vision of the roughest contours of what appears to be an emerging awareness and concern for most developing societies throughout the world. Merely mentioning these ideas hopefully will bring them to a level of consciousness that may one day allow us to move ahead to their resolution and partial incorporation. We hope so.

THE ISRAELI POLICYMAKING SYSTEM: CHARACTERISTICS AND IMPROVEMENTS

Yehezkel Dror characterizes the Israeli policymaking system from a very different point of view from "normal" case study, descriptive work. Taking as a

---

[18] Recent discoveries of an untouched tribe in the wilds of the Philippines—the Tassadai—serve as an excellent case in point. Members of the expedition who have taken responsibility for the preservation of the tribe and the guiding principle of PANAMIN, the institution responsible for minority peoples throughout the Philippines, characterize, even exemplify, the importance of maintaining these tribes in part to serve as an example of what basic values man has given up in his quest for material and powerful goals. It is reported that Elizalde, the group's leader, has noted on numerous occasions that he is learning as much about himself and his society by caring for the Tassadai as he is learning about the tribe itself. The point is similar to the one we make here.

point of departure his theoretical contributions,[19] Dror analyzes the Israeli context, problems, and opportunities, all with an eye to formulating recommendations for improvement. It is a fitting exercise, for Dror has been a long-time participant observer of Israeli policymaking and a longer time practitioner theoretician of the policy sciences.

The Question

Given the very narrow margin for error and attendant penalties, how might improvements in the existing policymaking system—its structure, personnel, practices, and procedures—be effected? Exactly what are the persistent general problems and related causes hampering policymaking? What might be done to improve the present state of affairs?

The Strengths

This study is a good initial approximation of a policy science description of a system. Evident are concerns for the goals of those participating in the context, for the factors conditioning present practices, and for some rather definite alternatives recommendations. While some attention is paid the historical trends and possible future evolution and development of the system, these are less well developed than are the goals, conditions, and alternatives.

As a result of taking a problem-oriented perspective, the chapter offers a concise and rich specification of the existing system; Dror's intentions to diagnose and prescribe are likewise well done. Specifying the Israeli system in this fashion gives the reader an ample empirical illustration of several theoretical insights that Dror, and others, have been proposing over the years. Equally important, an initial reference point or datum of the Israeli system is presented. Subsequent empirical research and policy analysis could easily proceed based on this characterization, from Dror's point of departure.

The key strength of this chapter is that it is unabashedly policy relevant. Neither shy nor satisfied just to detail current deficiencies, Dror has boldly committed himself by making many tangible and plausible suggestions, proposals, and recommendations. Although one could debate the merits of each, and indeed this is *one* reason for spelling them out so unequivocally, there is no question about what policies Dror proposes and why.

The Weaknesses

We are left to our own imaginative devices to figure out the specific effects any or all of these recommendations will have; alternative future states are not

---

[19] Yehezkel Dror, *Public Policymaking Reexamined* (San Francisco: Chandler, 1968); *idem, Design for Policy Sciences* (New York: American Elsevier, 1971); and *idem, Ventures in Policy Sciences* (New York: American Elsevier, 1971).

well specified, and we are implicitly asked to take the various recommendations on the faith that they will improve matters. And here is a critical point: each and every alternative set forth *must* be carefully scrutinized from different points of view, by different specialists, and with an eye to a range of plausible results. In effect, we are presented with only the initial step of a thorough policy analysis of the Israeli system. As important and well conceived as this first step might be, it is only preliminary to the considerable supportive work that now must be done.

Consider just one example. Dror argues that top Israeli decisionmakers have generally not received sufficient formal intellectual preparation to fulfill their roles; several corrective strategies are proposed. One might counter by pointing out that one intellectual style of decisionmaking requires that as much information as possible about some problem or another be gathered and analyzed prior to making any decisions; and this takes time, certainly more time than merely relying on one's informed intuition. One might argue that most Israeli survival decisions have been, and likely will continue to be, those made rapidly and boldly. Excessive preanalysis and consequent time delay might have led to very different outcomes from those actually realized. It is an eventuality overlooked by Dror, but one among a larger list of plausible outcomes that a policy scientist absolutely must take into account.

Left to the future are appropriate efforts to validate and control. Validation refers to the rigorous development of alternative specifications of the policymaking system and to the continuous appraisal of the relative fidelity of these competing images of past, present, and future. Control concerns the assemblage and management of more detailed information about critical aspects of the system and the appraisal of all past policy recommendations in light of unfolding events.

Subsequent Developments

Because this chapter is a first approximation, much more detailed work on Israeli policymaking is needed, and Dror advocates this in several interesting ways. There are also useful possibilities he does not mention.

Comparative work might link the Israeli with other related settings. Not denying that Israel is to some degree unique, there are nonetheless other decisionmaking situations that might be compared to it to shed new light and open up as yet unimagined possibilities. What interesting and useful information might be developed were the Egyptian and Jordanian decisionmaking systems to be compared with the Israeli in times of crisis and high interaction? What about taking the Yugoslavian and Thai systems as points of comparative reference? Each is small, has a high degree of planning associated with it, and is seriously threatened by, and depends heavily upon, external events.

And, finally, because there is a large training and education component in the recommended policies, it is important that many specific initiatives be taken to appraise the outcomes, both expected and unintended, of these proposals. To imagine and implement a policy burdens researcher and practitioner alike to ensure that untoward outcomes are sensed and minimized.

POLICYMAKING WITH LITTLE INFORMATION AND FEW INSTRUMENTS: THE PROCESS OF MACRO CONTROL IN MEXICO

John Koehler's interest fastened on processes of economic policymaking in Mexico, partly because he is concerned as an economic specialist, but mainly because these processes have been remarkably accurate and beneficial for the overall development of Mexican society. To detail the structure and explain the behavior, elegant, though appropriate, econometric explorations have been carried out.

The Question

Koehler intends to inform policymaking behavior by clarifying and measuring the underlying structural features responsible for it. How, with very limited information about the context, have Mexican policymakers been able to determine when to activate, which policy options, by how much? Answers to these questions are fascinating indeed.

The Strengths

A major strength of the research is the stress it places on the evaluation of past official performance. It is a rare piece of social science that asks so explicit an evaluation question in as rigorous a fashion as this. Successes are pitifully few in development policymaking, and when one does occur, it behooves us all to figure out why: the more rigorous these probings, the better.

Illustrated is one example of how effective a policy strategy can be *if* the indicators of system performance have been well and judiciously selected. The message is an excellent one for would be compilers of social indicators: pick out measures that are accessible, reflect real policy outcomes, which are liable to manipulation by responsible parties, rather than those that might be somehow more esthetically or theoretically pleasing.

Methods are used in an extremely sophisticated way to inform the research; they did not determine either the research question or the data used to answer the question. As a result, we have a very precise description of the policymaking system and the relevant factors conditioning events in the system.

The Weaknesses

The analysis captures the essence of a relatively persistent problem and setting. As long as major structural features both within and without the Mexican system are significantly unchanged, the processes described and policy options taken will likely hold. What happens, however, when there *are* the inevitable structural realignments? In short, the long-term consequences of the described behavior are not considered either by Koehler, or the Mexicans for that matter. What main structural features are most liable to change? What will be the most likely outcomes? With what long-run effects for the system and the processes that are described? Persistent processes, and their associated analytic models, may lull policymakers and analysts into a false sense of complacency. Assuming that what was done "last time" will suffice "next time" presumes that significant shifts have not occurred in the interim to subvert or drastically alter the situation. A policy scientist must be alert to contextual changes and be prepared to recommend new appropriate policies to compensate for such shifts.

Subsequent Developments

It would be folly to make present-day policy based on the models Koehler presents without first assuring consistency and persistency of structural and contextual detail. A good general reality check is contained in the following questions: When the process breaks down or fails, why; what is done; with what outcomes; for whom?

Are there any other policy areas in the Mexican context that could benefit from such analyses? If so, we must begin the hard analytic work needed to inform these policies.

Are there other measures of the overall process that can be developed to check on those described and to serve as alternatives in the event the main indicators fail or lose relevance? If so, we must define, measure, and use them.

Can the Mexican lessons be exported to other settings? If so, we have an obligation to do so without delay. To do comparative work has more than scientific significance; it may also improve policymaking in important ways elsewhere.

Chapter 10
The Israeli Policymaking System: Characteristics and Improvements

YEHEZKEL DROR

Because it has been remarkably successful, where success is measured in terms of national survival, the Israeli policymaking system is worth in-depth analysis to determine the responsible characteristics. To do so means understanding the general contextual setting in which policies are being made and to know the specific details of who is responsible, what resources are available to these policymakers, what operational structures and institutions have been erected, and what sorts of behavioral outcomes have occurred as a result of the personnel operating in an environment with a definable array of resources.

For quite some time modernization processes and problems have occupied a focal position in the attention of social scientists. Politics of modernization, economics of modernization, comparative administration, regional studies—those are only a few of the subdisciplines or areas of interest that have developed over the last ten to twenty years and have been intensively researched by a significant number of scientists. Extensive work is also going on in the various international and national external aid units. This work also results in accumulated knowledge, even though it is more applied and practical in thrust and ideology. While interest in modernization fluctuates, depending upon international trends in the main aid-giving countries, the long-range trend is nevertheless unmistakable: The problems of modernization and the gap between the rich and the poor countries are central issues facing humanity, issues which unavoidably will become more important both to actual policy and to academic and intellectual interests. Adding to these moral and political reasons, the pure knowledge significance of modernization processes provides us with new situations in which to test knowledge and theories derived mainly from the experience of Western countries; furthermore, these new situations constitute natural laboratories to try out social designs and experiments. The combined effects of purely scientific interests and applied concerns make modernization a most important and interesting subject matter area of investigation.

Despite the urgency of modernization problems, significant investments of research resources in them, and some recognition of modernization problems of the future, available knowledge of modernization processes is very limited in

NOTE: This chapter was written prior to the Yom Kippur War.

both scope and validity. Especially striking is the absence of reliable knowledge concerning one of the most critical facets of modernization: policymaking. In so far as modernization depends on conscious human intervention and direction, policymaking is a principal means of shaping modernization processes. There may be very little that can be done to shape these processes consciously; they may depend on variables beyond control; nevertheless so far as conscious attempts to shape modernization processes must be made, both for moral and pragmatic reasons, development policymaking is critical. Understanding the realities and identifying possible means to improve development policymaking are requisites for improving the more general modernization processes.

In view of the obvious need, it is all the more surprising that contemporary behavioral and prescriptive knowledge about modernization policymaking is so meager. There are several reasons for the present underdeveloped state-of-the-art in the study and improvement of modernization policymaking,[1] including among others, the following:

- The study of policymaking, both behavioral and prescriptive, is in its infancy. The policy sciences are just emerging, and traditional intellectual disciplines have been quite unable to penetrate the realities of policymaking or to provide systematic bases for prescriptive recommendations to improve them.[2] The lack of secure disciplinary and professional bases to study policymaking, even in modern societies, means that the essential knowledge needed to study policymaking in modernizing countries is also missing.

- In addition to deficiencies in the basic paradigms of contemporary social and management sciences, the political sensitivity of policymaking and related defenses against research account for much of the meagerness in the area. Restricted access to information, political taboos, and inadequate resources to study policymaking scientifically are overt manifestations of political and social sensitivities which may be functional under some circumstances, but which actually operate to the net detriment of both science and policymaking. Most of the modernizing countries are very sensitive about their institutions and "national honor." Political elites are largely inexperienced, and many of their policymaking arrangements appear inefficient and even corrupt when evaluated by (often inappropriate) Western standards. Furthermore, many of these elites, troubled by internal turmoil and violent political strife, are extremely sensitized with respect to critical commentary. Adding the strong suspicion of foreign interference and infiltration, the near impossibility of studying policymaking in modernizing countries follows quite naturally.

Hopefully, this situation will change. When the policy sciences mature, when the elites of the modernizing countries gain more self-confidence, and when greater numbers of high-quality indigenous scholars are trained, then developing the study and practices of policymaking may proceed. In the meantime, we must be content with studying the policymaking processes in those

[1] Knowledge on policymaking in modern countries is also very inadequate, but not to the extent it is in modernizing countries.

[2] On inadequacies in policy relevance of contemporary science, see Yehezkel Dror, *Design for Policy Sciences* (New York: American Elsevier, 1971), Part I.

countries that are open for such study and where relevant information is available. Even then, it will be necessary to rely on many sources which are inadequate by the standards of social science, which is of slight consequence since these standards seldom meet the requirements of policymaking study or practice, even in the modern countries. Reliance on personal impressions, newspaper articles, informal communications, and similar secondary sources seem unavoidable because this information permits one to characterize tentatively the main features of policymaking systems and to develop some bases for further study.

This chapter studies policymaking in Israel, a country which can be regarded as a mix between the very modern and the modernizing. The study is based on the following methods and sources:

- Long-time personal immersion in Israeli politics as an observer. This permits subjective, but informed, impressions to be made about the main features of Israeli political culture and institutions.

- Intense study of policymaking by myself and groups of graduate students. This study has resulted in the preparation of case studies that, while not constituting a representative sample, do characterize some of the dynamics of actual Israeli policymaking. Furthermore, the cases serve as a reality check on more subjective impressions.

- Consultative studies and participant observation by myself and some assistants. The complete report of these studies is not available for publication; but, in most cases, revised versions including the central facts and basic ideas have been released.[3] Consultative studies and participant observation are absolutely essential sources for studying and improving policymaking. Even though nonpublication of complete versions of such studies constitutes a deviation from scientific standards, consultative studies and participant observation are essential instruments to study the policymaking phenomenon and to develop the policy sciences as a whole.

- Compilation and use of secondary information available on Israeli policymaking. One paradox of Israel is that, while many specific details of policymaking are not published, their main outlines are quite well known among certain sectors of the public, and their basic features are well reflected in published accounts. (This conclusion is supported, in principle, though not in many details, by the limited number of available case studies).

On the basis of these sources it is possible to characterize and to propose some improvements in the Israeli policymaking system. Even though these findings and recommendations are not particularly susceptible to rigorous scientific proof, their overall *gestalt* is well supported both by available information and by widely shared impressions of persons knowledgeable about the system.

Any attempt in a short chapter to characterize the policymaking system of a complex, albeit small, country like Israel suffers from all the dangers of overgeneralization. In particular, important differences between policymaking with respect to different issues, at different periods, and by various policymakers are

[3] See, for instance, Yehezkel Dror, *Ventures in Policy Sciences* (New York: American Elsevier, 1971). Chapters 12 and 23.

neglected. There *are* significant differences between policymaking on national research and development in agriculture, policymaking on immigration, policymaking with respect to protection against terrorist activities, and long-range strategic policymaking. Nevertheless, some features of the Israeli system are basic to the policymaking system as a whole, or at least to some of its more important parts, and these features are emphasized in this chapter.

THE ISRAELI POLICYMAKING CONTEXT

Examining policymaking in Israel is impossible without accounting for some of the basic conditions shaping the whole context.[4] To perceive and evaluate policymaking, we must consider the conditions and requirements that operate on it. Contextual differences make comparisons between policymaking in Israel and other countries very difficult, and, in most cases, quite misleading.

A number of basic conditions is quite unique to Israel; these conditions are critical in order to understand contemporary Israeli policymaking and they deserve special emphasis. Although we discuss them at length later in the chapter, a summary of these conditions is necessary to develop the chapter's main arguments.

Israel faces critical decisions upon which its future development and even its long-range existence depend. Even though, prima facie, this criticalness characterizes only some recent concerns dealing with possible withdrawal from parts of the occupied territories and peace arrangements with the Arab countries, the issues are so fundamental and important as to shape policymaking as a whole. Furthermore, in addition to these more visible issues, other, only slightly less critical long-range defense policy issues face Israel, along with critical economic and social issues.

The fact that Israel is in principle confronted with the threat of extermination (this, in any case, is the image of the situation as seen by major policymakers—and such images shape the reality of policy) is unique and exerts strong influence on policymaking as a whole, though unevenly for various policy issues. Possible extermination is a rather singular feature of Israeli policymaking, influenced strongly by the history of the Jewish state in ancient times and by the near extermination of European Jews. A connection with this shared sense of history is a central condition of reality, as perceived by the principal policymakers, influencing the entire policymaking context.

Policy issues are not only critical for the future of Israel, they are also not easily resolved. Alternatives seem to be few; predictions concerning the consequences of each are doubtful and ambiguous; and operational goals are unclear and seldom widely agreed upon. Policymaking with respect to the Arab states, but not confined to this issue, is particularly burdensome.

[4] For an excellent account of Israeli society as a whole, see S. N. Eisenstadt, *Israeli Society* (New York: Basic Books, 1967).

For many policy issues facing Israel, including some of the more critical ones, explicit decisions *are required*. Most of these decisions cannot be made incrementally, and easy concensus-building and simple policymaking are thus foregone to a significant extent. Because the problems are novel, past policies cannot merely be continued with minimal alterations—new policies have to be created. Without guiding precedents, a major requisite for incremental policymaking is absent in Israel.[5] This applies to economic and social, as well as to defense and foreign, policymaking. While not fully applicable to all specific policy issues, the need for novel solutions imposes a heavy burden on policymaking as a whole.

Israel's particular policymaking context results in various interpretations and evaluations of situations that, in other countries and under different conditions, may be quite useful. Coalition-building and maintenance as basic policymaking processes provide a good illustration. In every country, policymaking necessarily involves large numbers of units and individuals, most of which have different opinions, habits, and interests. Coalition-building is generally required to recruit necessary political and administrative support for policy approval and implementation. It is not only generally essential, but it often serves positive purposes: diversification of considered alternatives, elimination of extreme policy choices, reduction of power concentration, and promotion (sometimes) of an effective and efficient decision mechanism.[6] At the same time, the more broad and heterogeneous are coalitions, the more difficult is it to arrive at clear decisions, to formulate long-range operational goals, and to arrive at comprehensive and innovative policy recommendations. Given prevailing conditions in most Western, the Soviet Union, and modernizing societies, the advantages realized by coalition policymaking often may well outweigh the disadvantages. But, given the Israeli context, these disadvantages are stronger, and because of the splintered structure of political power more heterogeneous and complex coalitions than in many other countries are essential.

I return to some of these matters later in the chapter. They illustrate the unique challenge and issues faced by Israeli policymaking and, therefore, deserve special emphasis. Policymaking in Israel is hard to comprehend, and an examination of individual events may result in quite misleading conclusions unless seen within this broader context.

PRINCIPAL CHARACTERISTICS OF THE ISRAELI POLICYMAKING SYSTEM

Characteristics of the Israeli policymaking system may be examined under six classificatory headings: environment, inputs, policymakers, structure, process

[5] Yehezkel Dror, *Public Policymaking Reexamined* (San Francisco: Chandler, 1968), pp. 143–47.

[6] See Charles E. Lindblom, *The Intelligence of Democracy* (New York: The Free Press, 1965).

pattern, and aggregate characteristics. Other classifications may be more useful for different purposes; yet for the Israeli policymaking system these categories are convenient, although not mutually exclusive or exhaustive.

Environment

The three fundamental issues already discussed also belong to the policymaking environment. There are additional features, however, to be examined more closely in order to understand the impact of the various environmental features on the characteristics of the policymaking system.

The environment is dynamic and, consequently, difficult to predict. Israeli policymaking takes place in an environment which, in large part, is highly dynamic. Many changes are difficult to foresee and are not susceptible to much influence by the Israeli policymaking system because they are exogenous. Examples would include, for instance, relations between the Soviet Union and the Arab countries; the rate of immigration; relationships between the United States and China and the Soviet Union and their global perspectives; the state of the economy in the United States; and the emergence of political issues, such as the problems of underprivileged sectors of the population in Israel itself. Each example illustrates environmental facts that are very significant for policymaking but which are often difficult to predict even when elaborate forecasting methods are used.

Not only is the environment dynamic, difficult to predict and in part insensitive to Israeli policy, but it is also very critical for the development and future of Israel. In other words, possible changes in the environment, both hard to predict and insensitive, may influence significantly and even drastically the future of Israel. This situation imposes on the Israeli policymaking system very heavy burdens. It necessitates policies that increase independence from the surrounding environment and it puts into stark relief the real limitations of Israeli policy to shape a national future. This situation of course is reflected in the pragmatic tendencies of Israeli policymaking, in skepticism about the value of establishing long-range policies, and perhaps in fatalism—usually expressed in the optimistic form of "everything will be all right."

The environment places rigid constraints on what Israel can do. Perhaps the policy space is bounded even more in the images held by policymakers than in reality. If so, the space could be expanded in part by more innovative policy alternatives. Unfortunately, at least prima facie, image and reality seem to reinforce one another; feasible alternatives are few; and the policy space appears to be rigidly limited.

At the same time, the dynamics of the policy environment from time to time present exceptional opportunities. These opportunities constitute an extreme challenge for policymaking; taking advantage of them requires a combination of an advanced capacity for improvisation and a very sophisticated capability to do contingency planning. In most policy areas, the Israeli policymaking system captures such opportunities through improvisation; however, because sophisticated contingency planning is absent in many policy areas, some opportunities are not fully exploited.

As we have noted, the environment exerts very heavy pressure on the Israeli policymaking system. Problems arise and change rapidly, significant transformations occur suddenly and apparently at random, and the constrained policy space often creates a feeling of "there is no choice." Internal factors weigh heavily on policymaking, too. Israeli political life exerts intense pressure on the policymaking system and on the policymakers: There are many internal political issues, and the expected turnover among the higher political elite is high, with resulting succession struggles. The gulf between popular expectations and demands, on the one hand, and capabilities and resources, on the other, appears to be increasing in Israel, although it is absolutely smaller than in many of the modernizing countries, where the revolution of expectations is unaccompanied by any significant increase in resources and capacities. The problems represented by this gulf exert additional pressures on policymakers, causing discrepancies between what they promise and what they deliver. This hinders the establishment of realistic operational goals, inhibits longer range policymaking (which would indicate the existence of such a gulf), and introduces "sloganeering" into some of the more visible policy processes.

A harsh environment is not new to Israel: quite the opposite. From the beginnings of modern Zionism, there has been a continual expansion of the degree of independence Israel has had in policy and actions. Dependence on environmental factors has declined since the period of the Ottoman rule over Palestine, when the opportunities of the Zionist movement to influence reality were very limited; or since the period of the British mandate over Palestine and the holocaust in Europe, when most factors determining the fate of the Jewish settlement and of the Zionist movement were in the hands of others; or even since the beginning of the State of Israel, when dependence on external powers was still tremendous.

Today, the external environment is critical and the influence of Israeli policy on it is very limited; but, in comparison to earlier periods, the situation is greatly improved. (Russian involvement in the Middle East creates some especially serious problems, however). Because, in nearly all respects, the present is much better than the past, there is much self-assurance in the policymaking system, justified pride in tremendous national achievements is widespread, and the difficulties of the environment are often perceived more as challenges than as limitations. An internal contradiction exists between these common positive perceptions of the environment and certain negative implications for Israeli policymaking flowing from the environment, which have been noted. The contradiction finds expression and creates tension among the principal policymakers, and within the policymaking system and public at large. On an intellectual level it is possible to overcome this contradiction by using sophisticated concepts of policy analysis; but in Israel, as in all other countries.

such concepts are rarely utilized and have little impact on the subjective understanding of the policymaking culture. These contradictions possibly have disturbing psychological effects for some policymakers and may constitute a partial
explanation for erratic, entrenched, and other ineffective behavior. This speculation cannot be checked without psychoanalytic data and studies of senior Israeli
policymakers; however, the contradiction itself surely exists, as does a tendency
for individuals to jump occasionally from one side of the contradiction to the
the other. My personal impression is that since the Six-Day War, Israeli policymaking is in a transitional stage from extreme self-satisfaction to increasing
uneasiness. To improve Israeli policymaking, the transition is a positive development, as some feeling of uneasiness is an essential—through by itself
insufficient—requisite for directed policymaking improvements.

Inputs

On some levels of analysis, environmental variables can be regarded as inputs into policymaking. Problems, pressures, indicators of changes in the environment, all can be viewed as such. However, for the purposes of this
chapter, it is convenient to distinguish between the environmental characteristics
just discussed and policymaking inputs, in the narrower sense of this term:
scientific knowledge, current information, predictive information, and equipment. Personnel is treated separately because of its critical importance.

Since the establishment of the State of Israel, constant increases in the extent of inputs of scientific knowledge into policymaking have taken place. Thus,
senior economists are presently widespread in the policymaking system and
senior scientists—mainly from the physical and life sciences—are being appointed in most government ministries. Nevertheless, the amount of policy-
relevant knowledge from sociology, psychology, management sciences, operations research, systems analysis, and policy analysis finding its way into Israeli
policymaking is small and not really increasing. The problem is exacerbated by
the absence of channels for such inputs. There are few professional staff officers
or policymakers whose backgrounds include these disciplines, and special policy
research organizations and networks of scientific advisors are likewise scarce.
The lack of such inputs into the policymaking system is reinforced by the Israeli
academic tradition that subscribes mainly to the ideology of knowledge for its
own sake and has little regard for the use of knowledge for policymaking.

Portions of the Israeli policymaking system benefit from good information
inputs, e.g., economic and defense policy. However, information vacuums exist
in other policy areas, such as welfare and social policy. In general, much progress has been made since the establishment of central economic and demographic statistical services. More recently, attitude surveys have been undertaken by the Israeli Institute for Applied Social Research and used to inform
policy. But, compared with policymaking needs and the possibilities for information collecting, the situation is quite unsatisfactory. Less satisfactory still

is the situation of neglect that characterizes the creation and use of predictive information.

Available material indicates that Israeli policymaking suffers particularly from inadequate forecasting. Despite advances made in the past twenty years in the explicit handling of uncertainty—in the form of alternative futures, stochastic forecasts, cross-impact analyses, and so on—with the exception of some technological forecasting, very little has been done in Israel to use these new methods and tools for policymaking. Where predictive information is available, such as in demography and certain areas of economics, much of the information is presented in outdated and misleading forms, e.g., simple, linear, deterministic extrapolations. Instead of basing policymaking in part on systematic predictive information, Israeli policymakers continue to operate using personal intuition and by failing to pay systematic attention to longer range time perspectives.

Equipment is not an important policymaking input. But the scarcity of certain types of technical equipment is a good indicator of the level of sophistication of the policymaking system. The scarcity of briefing systems in many policy areas and of situation rooms, the absence of data banks of policy-relevant information in most areas and of policy-relevant model, simulation, and gaming activities all testify to the inadequacy of technical-equipment inputs into the Israeli policymaking systems.

Policymakers

Policymakers are human. It is, therefore, especially important to characterize policymakers as persons in order to characterize a policymaking system as a whole. But because great differences exist among persons and so many personalities occupy senior policymaking positions, it is difficult and misleading to generalize about the total population of policymakers. In principle, some personal characteristics are susceptible to reliable empirical investigation and to draw firm conclusion about the system or its participants without doing such studies is highly questionable. For these reasons the following characteristics of policymakers should be regarded as only tentative; they are less conclusions than impressions which constitute hypotheses for subsequent empirical study.

The number of important policymakers in Israel is very small. In most countries the number of those having significant influence on the contents of policy is small; in a small country like Israel, the number is particularly minute: for many important issues, fewer than a dozen. To expand the definition, the number of persons having significant influence on policymaking in most areas is fewer than 100. Surely, increasing the number of 250 or 300 will include nearly all actors having influential roles in policymaking.

Despite great heterogeneity in background and functional roles, there are many basic features shared by the Israeli policymaking elite. Most of the senior policymakers are older than fifty-five or even sixty, have Eastern European origins, lack formal academic educations, and have spent many years in the

Zionist movement and the prestate Jewish settlement. More important than these shared demographic features are some shared patterns of operation, to be characterized later.

Policymakers are dispersed over a wide range of formal functions, including ministers, senior civil servants, party activists, heads of public institutions, and leaders in local government, industry, agriculture, the mass media, and so on. This diversification does not reflect a real dispersal of formal roles because most senior policymakers occupy a number of different positions simultaneously. Different policymaking roles are integrated through personal ties. Strong and close interpersonal relations exist and further cohesiveness within the policymaking network.

A senior professional policymaking elite is notable in its absence, thus accounting for many weaknesses in the Israeli policymaking system. In principle, good policymaking requires a division of labor among different types and categories of policymakers, including politicians, senior civil servants, professional staff officers, scientists, etc., each elite component has unique and essential contributions to make to good policymaking, but in Israel the contribution of professional staff on the policy level is too small and so too are many of the usual professional channels to the scientific community. Israeli politicians generally fulfill their "political" policymaking responsibilities in a good and sometimes even excellent manner. But main weakness in the policymaking process is the absence of much specialized information essential to good policymaking. The absence of senior professional staff on the policymaking level is serious and means that senior civil servants either in principle operate as the politicians do, or they make only limited professional contributions. This situation is slowly improving, but it is presently one of the main defects of the Israeli policymaking system.

Senior Israeli policymakers are distinguished in many ways including, characteristically, by their strong loyalty to basic values, personal honesty, dedication, perseverance, high intelligence, and excellent political and executive skills. They exhibit other human characteristics, including the desire for power, envy, egotism, and similar qualities common to energetic and powerful persons all over the world. But, given the tentativeness of these conclusions, and in view of available material, it seems that high-level Israeli policymaking is truly distinguished by the laudible personal qualities of its politicians.

Contrasted with these personal characteristics, most senior Israeli policymakers lack formal academic training, and those few with higher education are usually trained in areas irrelevant for policymaking. This finding is moderated by the fact that senior Israeli policymakers often engage in self-study, are widely read, and have had few opportunities for formal training, devoting their lives from an early age to building Israel. Given the opportunity, doubtless many could have earned academic distinction and advanced degrees. However, the fact itself is clear and has implications—usually negative in nature—for their decision pattern, their relations with professional advisors, and their inabilities to utilize scientific contributions to policymaking.

Most policymakers seem to operate with rather unsophisticated work methods. Much work proceeds through oral discussions and meetings; there seems to be little utilization of staff papers and systematic staff work; there are underdeveloped habits of work with advisors; and the analysis of policy issues is not structured. I do not mean to imply that all senior policymakers need similarly structured work patterns. Less structure may be required from outstanding statesmen and charismatic leaders, but for the average good, even the very good, Israeli policymaker, present work patterns are not sophisticated enough and hinder use of modern tools and methods for better policymaking.

More important than, though closely related to, work patterns are decision patterns. All available material seems to indicate that the dominant decision pattern is pragmatism: policymaking is done by solving a series of immediate and short-range problems with much attachment of current decision to concrete circumstances. Pragmatic decision patterns drive out longer range considerations, reduce utilization of abstract analyses of issues, hinder accounting for intangible variables, and bar basic decisions on fundamental postures which go beyond immediate needs. This does not mean that Israeli policy does not include many long-range considerations and basic postures. But those that do exist are either the result of a priori feelings, which may be solidly based on experience, or of a series of smaller decisions. Seldom do they result from a balanced, rational, long-range analysis. Because of this pragmatism a gulf sometimes develops between immediate decisions and longer range views, which tends to reduce the consistency of Israeli policies or to introduce some rigidity in current decisions.

Everyone operates within an intellectual framework expressive of an individual's world view. Because individuals perceive, interpret, and predict reality in accordance with their world view, filtered through specific personality variables, world view is a dominant factor in understanding decisionmaking patterns and discretion. Despite their importance, it is not easy to arrive at reliable conclusions about the world view that motivates real policymakers. The possibilities for close observation over extended periods, and even for the comprehensive analysis of a series of decisions, are few. In the absence of such investigations, any diagnosis of the world views of Israeli policymakers must remain at the hypothetical level. Hedgings aside, it seems to me, as a first reasonable hypothesis based on available material, that many senior Israeli policymakers operate with outdated ideas about Israel and the forces shaping it that may not adequately reflect the present emerging reality. The separation of senior policymakers from reality, the absence of systematic feedback mechanisms, and the scarcity of systematic self-criticism of world views when combined with the tremendous reinforcements many Israeli policymakers have received through their dramatic successes in the past, result in strong attachments to ideas which may have outlived their utility and may be of doubtful validity.

As a group, the senior Israeli policymaking elite seems to be at a stage of slow turnover. This rate of turnover will increase because of age and because of the intense struggle for senior positions. Even so, it seems that the composition of the senior elite group is still quite stable, with few newcomers being accepted. At the same time, competition for entrance into this group is tough, requiring that senior policymakers devote much time and attention to preserve power and position.

There is tremendous pressure created by the work load of Israeli policymakers, pressure from both the quantity and difficulty of the work. The effect of this constant burden on overworked policymakers is a very complex issue. For most Israeli senior policymakers, work constitutes nearly *all* of their life. Based on research in work psychology, one expects permanent intensive pressure to have negative consequences for the quality of decisions, by reducing thought capacities, introducing elements of hypertension, and inhibiting elasticity and readiness to innovate. I doubt whether these findings apply directly and generally to senior policymakers—who, in large part, are extraordinary individuals. Nevertheless, there are indications that for some senior policymakers at least, the intense and permanent pressure has negative consequences.

Additional personal characteristics could be indicated, but I think that enough has been said to bring out the basic *gestalt*. Extensive detailed discussions may be more misleading than helpful. Let us now consider the structural characteristics of the Israeli policymaking system.

Structure

The structure of the Israeli policymaking system is pluralistic and decentralized, especially in view of the size of the country. Great diversity of institutions, units, government agencies, ministries, and parties exist. There are some formal integration mechanisms, including the cabinet and cabinet committees, and many informal ones, such as personal contacts and old friendships. Yet, all in all, the integration and coordination of policymaking seem weak. Common contradictions in physical planning and housing policies, in the area of welfare and social policy, and sometimes between foreign and defense policy illustrate integrative weaknesses as compared with the pluralism of the policymaking structure.

Despite a large variety of formal structures, most policymaking takes place in informal frameworks, in units formally established for other purposes, or in structures having no official basis at all. As a result certain of the formal policymaking units are preempted. This situation is not necessarily all negative; informal structures are often convenient and effective policymaking forums. Still concentrating policymaking in informal frameworks hinders efforts to improve policymaking because such frameworks are more difficult to influence and restructure by plan.

Few specialized policy analysis institutions exist. For example, there are almost no units for long-range planning and policymaking, and those that do exist have little real significance: this is certainly the case for the Economic Planning Authority and the Physical Planning Division in the Ministry of Interior.[7] There are essentially no units or institutes for policy research and very few professional staff units at the policymaking level throughout the government. Change can be discerned, as illustrated by the increasing interest shown in some government ministries for the establishment of professional policy-level staff units. The dearth of professional policy analytic staffs indicates a serious defect in Israeli policymaking. Without them, it is very difficult to develop long-range policies, to create comprehensive policies, or to utilize modern scientific knowledge and systematic analysis in order to formulate better policies.

It is not surprising that there exits no governmental evaluation institutions to facilitate learning, feedback, and policymaking improvement. The existence of such institutions depends on a high level of sophistication, which is absent at present. This is an important, through expected finding, for without such activities, it is very difficult to improve the policymaking system as a whole. Israel certainly is no worse off in this respect than most other countries, but what is more surprising and disturbing is the extent to which academic institutions have also neglected these activities. While some change is occurring, the typical situation is the one that finds subjects such as foreign policy scarcely taught in Israeli academic institutions; research and teaching on Israeli policymaking are just beginning. Even if the academic institutions encouraged research on the appraisal or evaluation aspects of the overall decision process, there is no assurance that this would have any impact on reality. The absence of such interests indicates a weakness and retards longer term improvement of Israeli policymaking.

Process Pattern

Many characteristics of the policymaking process are closely related to characteristics already discussed; nevertheless, there is a number of specific points worth mentioning.

The Israeli policymaking process is unstructured and informal. Formalized procedures exist; some are even substantive, but most are ritualistic.

The budgeting process constitutes a main mode of policymaking and is highly developed in Israel. But the bulk of the process takes place through interpersonal discussion and discourse, whose dynamics are mainly determined by the personalities and relationships of the participants. Without better structuring of the process, where policy is made nearly exclusively on an informal and interpersonal basis, necessary policymaking improvement is hindered. Not only do interpersonal relations predominate, but significant parts of the policymaking process itself seem to scramble policy and personal considerations. In other

[7] See Benjamin Akzin and Yehezkel Dror, *Israel: High Pressure Planning* (Syracuse, N.Y.: Syracuse University Press, 1965). Outdated in details, the general picture analyzed in this work is still correct today.

words, the available material seems to indicate that in Israel it may be more difficult than in some other countries to differentiate between personal relations and policy issues. The observation is not all inclusive, nor is it a condemnation of all informal interpersonal policymaking. Nonetheless, there exists extreme "personalization" of most of the Israeli policymaking process, a tendency that seems to impair overall quality. Taken together with the strong tendency toward political coalitions, the extremely informal nature of the policymaking process in Israel seems to be somewhat of a weakness.

Coalition maintenance in Israeli policymaking is important. Achieving co-operation between persons and units with different values and interests, and re-cruiting necessary support to gain approval and execute policy are general societal problems. Coalition-building is a natural policymaking process, which takes place not only between, but also within, parties and organizations. In Israel, the multiplicity of parties, diversity of interests, intensity of many public activities, and dispersal of some forms of power between a large number of units and subunits, necessitates the establishment and maintenance of very mixed coalitions to make policy. Further, traditional political activity during the pre-statehood period was quite partisan, and this has carried over to present-day maintenance. Such activities include a number of characteristics: mediacy, irrelevancy, conspiracy, and personalism. Elements of "court politics," where different factions compete for the favors of key elites, are discernible. All of these features of the coalition-building and maintenance processes shape policy-making in fundamental ways.

The stress placed on individual policymakers has been described; similar tensions overload the whole policymaking process. This overload results when the problems and demands facing policymakers are matched against the limited capacities of the policymaking process. These limitations have been detailed in terms of the absence of special professional contributions to policymaking, the scarcity of structured processes for policymaking, the small size of the policy-making elite, and so forth. The overload has important implications. The established tendency to favor a "crisis management" style increases pressure on the policymaking system and exacerbates the overload. The vicious circle caused by this positive feedback has serious consequences for the quality of policymaking.

Crisis management is a reactive style of policymaking in which elite atten-tion is narrowly focused on the needs of fire extinguishing and neglects long-range fire prevention. A crisis atmosphere permeates the entire policymaking system, and policymaking proceeds mainly by improvisation and intuition. Crisis management policymaking weakens the development of many elements of good policymaking, a problem we now examine.

The particular partisan coalition formation needed to make policy, per-sonal pressures, the dearth of predictive information, and other characteristics all result in a strong tendency to avoid elaborating operational goals for policymaking. Also, the existence of ideological values tends to reduce the necessity for clarifying operational goals: "We know what we want; we want to end the Diaspora, to have peace, to achieve social justice"; and normal organizational and political dynamics hinder the clarification of operational goals. Without clearly formulated operational goals, public evaluation of achievement is hampered, although self-congratulation over whatever successes are realized is not. As a result, few operational goals are clarified in Israeli policymaking. Occasionally, goals are presented, but these tend to be predictions of what is expected to happen or unrealistic operational goals presented for other purposes. Without operational goals, a tendency toward pragmatic and short-range policymaking is reinforced, learning is diminished, attention is diverted from system weaknesses and requirements.

In most areas, Israeli policymaking operates within a short time horizon, either in reaction to past events or with a two- or three-year time span at most. This characteristic stresses the interdependencies that exist between different characteristics of the policymaking system. A short time perspective reduces demand for predictive information, results in crisis management modes of policymaking, evokes improvisational behavior, and adds to individual and system overloads; these characteristics taken compositely, reduce the time perspective of policymaking. While Israeli conditions, especially the dynamics of the environment, mediate against the creation of good long-range policies, there is nonetheless great need for them. Not enough has been done in Israel to lengthen the time perspectives of policymakers, though it is possible and necessary to do so, even under the difficult Israeli conditions.

Creating new alternatives is a crucial factor determining the quality of policymaking. In many settings, including Israel, the inadequacy of all visible alternatives is a serious problem. Evaluating available alternatives with the help of more sophisticated analytic methods is a requisite; but, more important, new alternatives must be invented in hopes of finding one that is clearly preferable. Evaluating and creating alternatives are difficult tasks rendered more so by current organizational behavior—such as tendencies to "satisfice" and to stifle innovation by relying only on marginal change. In these respects, the quality of Israeli policymaking seems superior to that of many other countries. Innovation seems to be prevalent, as illustrated, for instance, by creative Israeli policies in foreign aid, defense, and agriculture. A number of factors encourages this kind of creative policymaking. As contributing factors one can cite, for instance, the personal quality of senior policymakers, the absence of deadening tradition in some policy areas, the challenge and difficulties of issues, which make invention an absolute necessity, the intensity of the coalition activities, which encourage free-for-all discussions where new alternatives are created, a flow of ideas from new immigrants, and a willingness to look outside Israel for novel ideas. In many respects, the Israeli policymaking system is distinguished by the extent of alternative creation and innovation that occurs. Indeed, this seems to be a main reason for many of the improvisational successes and high quality of Israeli policymaking. There are at least two constraints, however.

In most areas the search for policy alternatives is restricted to one or a few directions, and the amount of implementation of new policies is rather uneven between policy areas. These limitations stem, inter alia, from general ideological factors and from specific personality characteristics of the principal policymakers. The mere fact that an avenue of inquiry seems to contradict basic ideology or, less justifiably, contradicts the current thinking of a key policymaker, may be sufficient to restrain the search for alternatives. In some areas, innovation is scarce because nearly all policymaking proceeds incrementally. This is the case with both education and labor relations, where there are strong traditions, no life-or-death challenges, and pronounced partisan political coalitions. Whether this is a fully adequate explanation for the phenomenon or not, the situation itself is clear: there are many important areas where few creative policy alternatives occur, and there are significant policy areas where innovation is needlessly constrained.

This discussion is not only important with respect to the quality of present policymaking, but also with respect to future possibilities. The extent of alternative creation and innovation may, under certain conditions, decrease. There is no factual evidence to substantiate a decreasing trend, and there are even some encouraging signs to the contrary. Balanced against the negative influences of accumulated traditions and policies that are seldom put to the ultimate reality test of survival are the continuing pressures and threats to the existence of the State of Israel that translate into starkly positive influences to create, improvise, and innovate. However, many policy areas are not subjected to such external shocks and pressures, and for them there is a tendency to conduct "business as usual." The absence of instruments and tools specifically designed to seek alternatives and ways to implement novel policies constitutes a major potential weakness in the Israel policymaking system. In many countries the intelligentsia focuses on this political weakness; such unfortunately is not the case in Israel.

Aggregate Characteristics

Several aggregate characteristics of Israeli policymaking, merely suggested in earlier discussions, require specific consideration because they are important. These characteristics constitute a partial summary of some of the main findings of this chapter.

In so far as this discussion has characterized the Israeli reality adequately, it is clear that policymaking exhibits an imbalance between extrarationality and rationality components. Extrarationality components—still insufficiently developed—include, for instance, the policymakers' commendable personal qualifications, their devotion and commitment to their society's fundamental objectives, and their demonstrated readiness to innovate in some areas. Rationality components, which include knowledge, information inputs, the professional qualifications of policymakers, professional staff units, and more are quite underdeveloped in the Israeli policymaking system. One distinct finding appears to be the weakness of some important rationality components of policymaking.

Several characteristics taken together lead to the conclusion that Israel is weak in comprehensive and long-range policymaking, a point supported by direct observation of the policymaking process and its outputs. Because of the dynamic characteristics of the environment, comprehensive and long-range policymaking in Israel is done less than in some other countries where a more stable and predictable environment prevails. Nevertheless, the preferred and desirable amount and quality of comprehensive and long-range policymaking have not yet been achieved in Israel.

Even assuming a more positive view of Israeli policymaking than mine, there is still no doubt that there is room for improvement. Even an optimal public policymaking system would require constant effort to preserve its quality, adjustment to changing needs and conditions, and utilization of improvements supplied by advances in scientific knowledge. A fortiori, the Israeli public policymaking system could benefit from intensive improvement efforts, and some key policymakers recognize this. From time to time single improvements are introduced; for instance, there have been initiatives to introduce professional advisory services for the Knesset, study groups in the Labour Party and others have been created, and discussions and proposals for governmental reforms occur. But these are sporadic activities, initiated by individuals on a personal basis. Certainly, such initiatives are helpful, but they are inadequate. Missing are directed and systematic efforts to improve Israeli policymaking. Scholars and academics, potentially important sources of the needed information to improve policymaking, have more time to think about policymaking improvements than the established and overloaded policymakers. But, as indicated, most scholars are not fundamentally concerned with, or interested in, making the much needed inputs to the system.

THE IMPROVEMENT OF PUBLIC POLICYMAKING IN ISRAEL

Necessary scientific work supporting systematic improvements has not yet been done. Somewhat hindered by deficiencies on a theoretical level, a policy scientist nevertheless would have sufficient raw material about the Israeli system to begin making useful suggestions for its improvement. Enough progress has been made in the policy sciences to allow one to present proposals and recommendations in a systematic, even rigorous, fashion. These proposals should be directed at overcoming those weaknesses identified in our previous characterization of public policymaking in Israel. Indeed, we make several such proposals in hopes of bettering the existing system. These proposals are not conclusive; they are not magic solutions; but they do identify a few central areas of inquiry, study, and experimentation. Some of these proposals appear sufficiently well founded to justify their immediate execution; for others additional study, examination, and ultimately controlled experimentation seem more appropriate.

The feasibility of these proposals is a question underscored by the existence of a dilemma between unrealistic, overly idealized proposals, on the one hand, and trivial, but easily executed, ones, on the other. Superficially unfeasible proposals, some of which doubtless will have long-range effects on the system and its various participants, must also be taken into account. Feasibility is also tied to the scope of the proposal. Policymaking is strongly and even predominantly influenced by the political culture, institutions, *and* the general political, social, and economic infrastructure. Changing this infrastructure is one means by which the inclusive policymaking system might itself be altered. For example, one might examine the impacts of various changes in the election system on related characteristics of the public policymaking system.

For the purpose of this chapter I focus on components of the public policymaking system itself in the strict meaning of the term and do not digress into discussions of possible reforms of its infrastructure. With respect to the dilemma between feasibility and significance, effort has been made to avoid the extremes: neither easily executed, but insignificant, nor utopian proposals requiring far-reaching changes in the whole social-political infrastructure of policymaking are presented. My proposals are oriented toward a medium-range—five to seven years—time perspective and include some which are not easily executed.

All of these proposals do not have an equal, nor necessarily high, probability of realization; however, I think that the proposals have subjective realization probabilities of at least 0.1. Furthermore, the realization probabilities are susceptible to change, but questions about how these changes might be produced, either generally or specifically for Israel, are beyond the scope of this chapter.

The proposals do not presume to exhaust all possibilities for the improvement of public policymaking in Israel. The set is designed to illustrate main directions for improvement, to encourage research and study oriented toward improvement of policymaking, and to contribute to the improvement of policymaking in actuality. Surely the list requires improvements, additions, more operational elaboration, and so on.

While oriented to the specific conditions of Israel, the list of improvement suggestions is relevant to situations in other countries to the extent those countries share characteristics with the Israeli public policymaking system.[8] Many modernizing and some modern countries share a number of the characteristics of the Israeli public policymaking system, even though in some respects the situation in Israel is unique; for instance, the configuration of pressures exerted by the environment.

[8] See, for instance, Yehezkel Dror, *Ventures in Policy Sciences,* Chapters 19 and 20.

Subject to these hedgings, the following recommendations for the Israeli public policymaking system can be presented with some degree of reliability. The proposals are summarized in four general areas:

- Personnel, including politicians, policy analysts, and senior civil servants.

- Structural or systemic reconfiguration, centering on institutionalization of the policy analysis function.

- Policymaking practices and procedures, relating to information generation, management, and use; crisis decisionmaking; and administrative behavior.

- Participation, featuring increased citizen concern and involvement in governmental processes.

Personnel

The importance of developing and advancing policymaking personnel has already been emphasized. Politicians are included in this proposal as their non-improvement has two undesirable outcomes for Israeli policymaking: either a continuation of serious systematic weaknesses or a transferral of excessive policymaking power to others in the process. To improve the skills and develop the capacities of politicians, both those presently fulfilling and those who may one day occupy senior policymaking roles, is a matter of great urgency. Such proposals do not impair fundamental democratic paradigms; on the contrary, they may strengthen them as they improve the capacity of the government to cope with a very difficult environment. One should not expect immediate results in this area, but even a marginal contribution may have much importance for the improvement of policymaking. Other personnel, including policy analysis professionals and senior civil servants, must be treated much more intensively. In some ways average citizens are partners in the policymaking process, although in ways differing sufficiently from those of present interest to require separate attention. I shall return to the role of the citizen in Israeli policymaking in the final set of recommendations.

Improving policymaking personnel involves, among others, the following operational steps.

- For politicians:
Encourage parties to engage in cadre development.
Provide at public expense opportunities for specified elected officials to engage in study and self-development—for short or longer periods up to a sabbatical year. To do this requires activation of suitable study programs (something that could be accomplished by establishing a national policy college) and substitution for electees who engage in longer term studies.
Improve the flow of scientific information by designing publications in style and content for politicians, by tailoring study activities for politicians, and by encouraging personal, social, and professional contacts between politicians and scientists.

Reduce work pressure for senior elected officials by improving their personal staffs and arranging for periodic vacations and leaves of absence.

- For policy analysis professionals:

Motivate institutes of higher education to prepare professionals for staff positions in the public policymaking system, using the existing academic disciplines and establishing new educational institutions and curricula, e.g., policy sciences and policy analysis.

Organize a series of special courses to prepare professionals for new policy analysis staff positions throughout the policymaking system.

- For senior civil servants:[9]

Recognize, to a far greater extent, the critical importance of the senior civil service. Create and implement a systematic policy designed to improve the capabilities of the senior civil service.

Motivate senior civil servants to complete their academic training in appropriate areas, on the graduate level. As an intermediate stage, all senior civil servants should finish a first academic degree and participate in intensive three-month-long seminars in a national policy college.

Establish strict professional and academic criteria for entrance into the senior civil service. Establish career patterns, including time for study and periodic rotations within the civil service and outside it. The career pattern is meant to assure continuous development of the personal qualities and professional knowledge needed to improve public policymaking.

Increase the attractiveness of the senior civil service by providing a contractual option to join the senior civil service for a fixed number of years, with salary conditions competitive with the private market, but without tenure and without the other special rights enjoyed by the regular career civil service.

Institutional Reconfiguration

Creating new units is relatively easy; making structural recommendations is an apparently simple way to improve public policymaking. However, one must remember that creating new structures by itself is not necessarily useful and may even be counterproductive. For example, in the absence of a suitable staff and the capacity to engage in the real policymaking process, the mere addition of new structures will probably prove more illusory than effective. At the same time, if we are to realize the desired improvements, new units and roles obviously are needed. Some essential first steps include the following:

- Establish a series of policy analysis institutions. These units should be diversified according to location, size, and function. Possible examples follow.

A professional staff unit serving the cabinet or/and the prime minister. It should be a compact interdisciplinary unit of five to ten professionals, to prepare policy

---

[9] These proposals are based on a systematic study by myself for the Israeli Center for Policy Studies, called *Design for a Senior Civil Service Policy for Israel* (Jerusalem, Israel: The Hebrew University, 1969). (Mimeo.)

analyses of the main issues confronting the cabinet; this unit is responsible for the basic data and position papers that inform cabinet decisions. Prior to the formation, or early in the operation, of such a unit, existing information flows into cabinet discussions should be determined and recommendations proposed. As the unit settles into the process, attention would be focused on the appropriateness, timeliness, and accuracy of background analyses prepared for cabinet discussion and on the appraisal of the outcomes of cabinet decisions.

Professional staff units serving the Knesset. Professional advisors are needed for all Knesset committees not already having them, e.g., the Education Committee, the Foreign and Security Committee, the Public Services Committee, and so on. These advisors should attend all committee meetings, prepare background studies, conduct policy analyses, and draft position papers. They could select and interrogate committee witnesses and could fulfill other professional functions at the request of the committees. Together, these committee advisors serve as a Knesset policy analysis unit, which fulfills additional functions as needed. This unit will help increase effective utilization of expert witnesses in Knesset committee deliberations and will be responsible for encouraging research and keeping abreast of policy-relevant facts and opinions generated by independent scientific and professional bodies. The Knesset's policy analysis unit should be headed by a full-time senior professional.

Professional staff units serving different government ministries. Every government ministry should have a professional staff unit which is directly related to its topmost levels and helps with ministerial policymaking. This unit includes academically trained professionals in at least economics, psychology, sociology, management science, decision theory, and policy analysis; it also contains professionals who are functional specialists, expert in the operation of the ministry. Given a suitable planning and budgeting system, it may be possible to integrate these professional staffs with the planning and budgeting units.

A policy analysis institute serving the government generally but maintaining its independence from any one unit.[10] A policy analysis institute composed of about twenty-five professionals from different disciplines should be established to engage in the analysis of the main policy issues facing the government in both the intermediate period and beyond. This unit must be in close contact with the policymaking system; it must have free access to information and independence to pursue the analytical process, to formulate research questions, to develop findings, and to make necessary recommendations. The institute can also fulfill important training and guidance functions for other policy analysis units. In time, the policy analysis institute can also help to examine important current issues—on the condition that its main resources are devoted to the analysis of longer range policy issues. In all respects, the proposals to establish a policy analysis institute is most important for the improvement of public policymaking in Israel.

■ Encourage the establishment of policy analysis units throughout the policymaking system: parties, trade unions, interest groups, and so on.

Small units, they should range from one to five or six professionals. Because they are small, they will require assistance from other independent policy research and

---

[10] For a detailed proposal prepared by myself at the request of the Israeli prime minister, see Dror, *Ventures in Policy Sciences,* Chapter 27.

policy analysis organizations. To accept and diffuse policymaking innovations, such "inside" units must be dispersed throughout the public policymaking system.

■ Encourage the establishment of independent policy research and analysis organizations, both as institutions of higher learning and as independent bodies.

Independence is needed to inform and improve the public's opinion of policy matters and to study subjects where access to limited information is less necessary than is distance from current pressures. For instance, preparing alternative futures for Israel as it moves toward the year 2000 and formulating proposals for governmental reform are illustrations of suitable subjects for independent policy research organizations.

■ Establish a national planning authority.

This would combine the economic planning authority, the physical planning division of the Ministry of Interior, and a new unit for social planning. To distinguish it from the policy analysis organizations concentrating on defined policy issues, the national planning authority should focus on the preparation of systematic multiple-year plans that tie in policies to means of execution.

■ Establish a national policy college.

The professional and intellectual needs of different policymakers are not presently being satisfied. Needed is a suitable institutional framework specialized for the training of those who fulfill senior roles and are experienced. The proposed national policy college will concentrate on courses of about three months' duration that emphasize policymaking generally and major Israeli policy issues specifically. The study regimen will combine systematic study with practical, applied work. Some combination of the staffs of the national policy college and the institute for policy analysis may be mutually reinforcing.

■ Establish "brains trusts," or talent pools, to be drawn from as needed. Composed of the leading experts and scientists in Israel and abroad, these groups should be formed in such a way as to optimize their use in the service of better policymaking. Involving persons having significant policy experience in Israel and elsewhere with those having policy research and analytic proficiency is a necessary reality check for both.

Policymaking Practices and Procedures

Various proposals to improve policymaking personnel and institutions are aimed at improving practices and procedures and ultimately at improved policies. Many recommendations to improve practices and procedures are simply extensions and/or results of our earlier recommendations and need not be repeated. More and better use of policy analyses; creation, integration, and use of professional staffs; and more systematic, comprehensive national planning all have clear implications for policymaking practices and procedures. Other important recommendations are not so obvious.

■ Improve the information system, including aspects of production, storage, retrieval, distribution, and utilization.

This recommendation applies both to current and predictive information. It is necessary to collect and produce additional information, e.g., social maps and inclusive alternative futures, for Israel. All information must be stored to permit easy access, mediated by suitable permissions and codes. Infirmation should be machine-based, but with controlled access. An unrealistic advantage of Israel's small size is the possibility of having integrated information storage for the whole government.

Information utilization depends partly on the proposals we advance for policy analysis, development, and training. Of less obvious, but essential, concern are the formats in which the information is eventually presented to policymakers. Technically, instruments must be created to facilitate the use of the newly created information. This involves, for instance, equipment. Because a good policy-oriented information system should reflect and represent a wide range of differing opinions and estimates to broaden the number and scope of alternatives considered in advance of decisionmaking, positive redundancy is needed in whatever information system that evolves.

- Improve crisis management.

Because in the Israeli context it is impossible to prevent crises, all effort must be expended to improve crisis management. Planning better is one way. For instance, contingency planning might be done which addresses not only high probability events, but also low probability contingencies; hopefully, expanded will be the capacity of the system to handle unexpected and unpredictable situations. Playing crisis games is another way. With the participation of senior policymakers, such games could improve crisis management and develop the individual capacities of policymakers to handle crises.

- Introduce policymaking formats.

The development, implementation, and constant improvement of policymaking formats are important, but theoretically and practically difficult, subjects. The goal is to introduce systematic methods, patterns, procedures and doctrines that do not restrain creativity, useful improvisation, or the operational latitude of elected policymakers. Military staff procedures, planning, programing, and budgeting systems, and scientific planning are examples of what is meant by "policymaking formats." For the Israeli context, a number of more detailed, illustrated recommendations can be made; however, only careful study and experimentation are called for to detail and implement each.

The budgeting system could stand improvement by introducing an integrated planning and budgeting system based on a multiple-year plan.

Policy analysis would bridge the existing gaps between the actual system of budget allocation and the planning elements that we note.[11]

Longer time perspectives must be taken into account; all policy proposals and position papers must consider explicitly the longer range implications of what is being proposed, relating these to the alternative futures projections prepared by the central policy analysis and research institutions.[12]

National goals must be prepared on an operational level that takes into account the

[11] For a detailed discussion of some attempts to move in this direction in Israel, see Dror, *Ventures in Policy Sciences,* Chapter 12.

[12] For detailed discussions of this proposal and relevant formats, see Dror, *Ventures in Policy Science,* Chapters 5 and 6.

implications of major proposals. Efforts should be made to think through and analyze the ramifications of specific policies for the broader context and situations in which they are to be executed.

Other detailed proposals could be cited, but the scope of this particular chapter is too limited. Let the main recommendation remind us of the general intent of these and related proposals: structure policymaking, making it more systematic and creative.

Public Participation

To conclude this list of recommended improvements let us consider the importance of public participation. Important in all countries, public participation is absolutely essential in Israel because of her multicultural population, the result of successive waves of immigration from all over the globe. It is a very complex subject and includes such topics as the educational role of political leaders and the implication of technological advances for increased public participation. For instance, using modern communications equipment it is technically possible to talk about real-time referenda and constant opinion polls. Consider these three illustrations.

- Improve the amount and quality of discussion of policy issues in the mass media.

  In particular, television is underexploited as a means to present and explain policy issues to the public. For this purpose, one must figure out ways of presenting television audiences with analyses of major problems so as to explore the values, relevant facts, basic assumptions, conflicting predictions, and the main alternatives involved. This sounds complex, but it can and must be done.

- Publish a periodical devoted to policy issues and directed at a broad, not necessarily mass, audience.

  An excellent illustration is the United States' periodical *Public Interest*. Such a periodical can make a limited but important contribution to the improvement of public dicussion of policy issues and may even encourage study and research oriented toward Israeli policy issues.

- Prepare tomorrow's citizens for an expanded role in the policymaking processes of Israel.

  In the school setting, there is an urgent need for far-ranging reforms in the teaching of all civic subjects. Beyond that, it is necessary to begin teaching other subjects, e.g., history, mathematics, to develop the capacity of the pupil to consider complex issues and to arrive at individual opinions about complex subjects, opinions based on a rational analysis of facts, and an explicit and well-considered judgment about the values involved. These difficult reforms are absolutely necessary in the longer run if Israeli citizens are to contribute constructively to policies determining their descendants' fates.

Doubtless it would be possible to formulate a set of proposals preferable to the one presented in this chapter. Hopefully, the proposals that have been put forth are sufficiently interesting to illustrate, and perhaps demonstrate, some possible ways of improving the Israeli policymaking system as earlier characterized.

How to execute these proposals, how to get them approved and implemented are questions beyond the scope of this chapter. Certainly it is impossible to execute all recommendations simultaneously. At the same time, it seems that piecemeal execution is also useless. The characteristics of the policymaking system are deeply rooted in reality and result from continually operating variables. Therefore, it is doubtful whether minor changes here and there will significantly change reality. Also, many of the improvements are interdependent. Thus, for instance, there is no use setting up now units without providing professionals who can successfully operate in them; there is no use preparing personnel in policy analysis, (and such training will not succeed) in the absence of new roles for that staff; and both the preparation of such professionals and the establishment of policy analysis units may be useless unless some changes occur in the characteristics of the political policymakers and the policymaking process pattern.

There may be single changes which are significant by themselves because they may in the longer run result in the overall improvement of the policymaking system. Thus, it is possible that preparation of excellent professionals in policy analysis in the academic institutions may earlier or later assure their utilization in policymaking, and thus may finally result in improvements in policymaking. At best, this is a very long and doubtful process. Rapid improvement in policymaking requires, therefore, simultaneous realization of a series of proposals oriented toward changing basic characteristics of the public policymaking system. Such far-reaching reform of a policymaking system is difficult to achieve. But such reform is both possible and essential in respect to the Israeli public policymaking system.

Chapter 11
Economic Policymaking with Little Information and Few Instruments: The Process of Macro Control in Mexico

JOHN E. KOEHLER

Analysis of the structure of the Mexican economy indicates that information and policy instruments available to the government, although seemingly crude and inaccurate, are sufficient to achieve a reasonable degree of macroeconomic stability. Since the early 1950's, Mexico has experienced growth with respectable stability; the stability exists because public expenditure and private autonomous expenditure have moved in offsetting ways. The burden of adjustment, however, has been carried by private investment rather than by public expenditure. The level of private investment has been controlled by manipulation of the level of reserves that private financial institutions are required to deposit in the central bank, Banco de México, and this manipulation is based on the monitoring of two variables: the rate of growth of the money supply and the rate of change of foreign exchange reserves. A model is developed to measure the power of the reserve ratio to affect the level of investment and GNP.

THE PROBLEM

The world is uncertain, but decisions must be made. A policymaker rarely knows "enough" about either the structure of the world or its current state to banish serious doubt from major decisions. Compounding uncertainty about the world is ignorance of the precise consequences, direct and indirect, of the policy instruments which may be manipulated. Workable instruments may furthermore be in short supply.

The usual economists' models of the policy process pass over these inherent problems. Figure 11–1 shows the process schematically following the classifica-

Any views expressed in this chapter are my own. They should not be interpreted as reflecting the views of The Rand Corporation or the official opinion or policy of any of its governmental or private research sponsors.

FIGURE 11-1. THE STRUCTURE OF ECONOMIC POLICYMAKING[a]

Exogenous variables	System of structural relationships connecting all variables: The "model"	Endogenous variables	Utility, welfare, or "objective function"

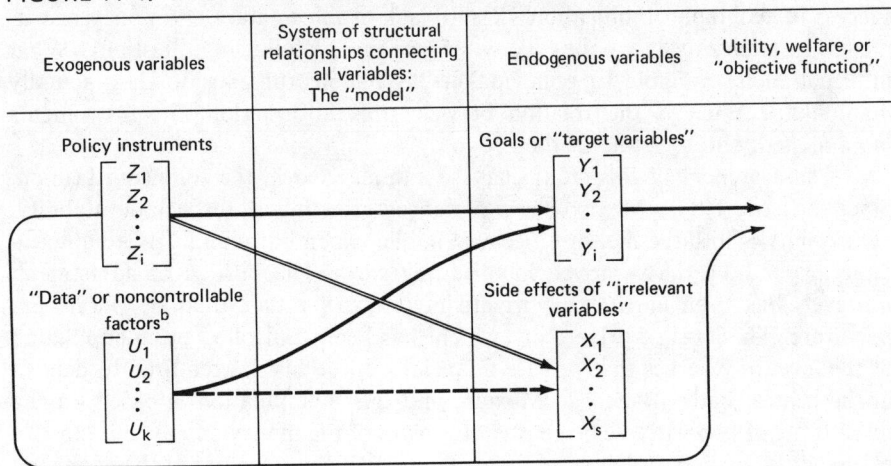

Policy instruments
$$\begin{bmatrix} Z_1 \\ Z_2 \\ \vdots \\ Z_i \end{bmatrix}$$

Goals or "target variables"
$$\begin{bmatrix} Y_1 \\ Y_2 \\ \vdots \\ Y_i \end{bmatrix}$$

"Data" or noncontrollable factors[b]
$$\begin{bmatrix} U_1 \\ U_2 \\ \vdots \\ U_k \end{bmatrix}$$

Side effects of "irrelevant variables"
$$\begin{bmatrix} X_1 \\ X_2 \\ \vdots \\ X_s \end{bmatrix}$$

[a]Adapted from K. A. Fox and E. Thorbecke, "Specification and Data Requirements in Policy Models," in B. G. Hickman, ed., *Quantitative Planning of Economic Policy* (Washington, D.C.: The Brookings Institution, 1965), p. 44.

[b]Not subject to control by the policymaker or level of government that sets the goals and uses the policy instruments in question.

tion of variables suggested by Jan Tinbergen.[1] Policy instruments are set to values such that, given the values of noncontrollable variables, the desired values of the target variables will be achieved. The outcome may be taken to be related by some function to community welfare.

In this framework a policymaker with n targets needs exactly n instruments to assume the attainment of the desired outcome. Otherwise there can be no guarantee that the equations representing the "model" of the relations between exogenous and endogenous variables will have such a solution. Given such proper algebraic properties, however, the "problem" of policymaking is not only manageable but nearly trivial.[2]

The setting for this essay is quite a different world from that described above: one in which information is so poor and policy instruments so scarce that the formal conditions for good policy performance are not met. Our concern is with the process by which "short-run" economic policy has been made in Mexico. In this realm, as we shall see, Mexico presents an interesting

[1] *On the Theory of Economic Policy* (Amsterdam: North Holland Publishing Co., 1952).

[2] Relaxing any of the stringent assumptions of certainty or perfect knowledge sharply changes all of these conclusions. For example, Brainard shows that if there is uncertainty about the effectiveness of policy instruments, "in general all instruments available should be used in pursuing one target" and "the addition of an objective requires some sacrifice in performance vis-à-vis objectives already being considered." See William Brainard, "Uncertainty and the Effectiveness of Policy," *American Economic Review Papers and Proceedings*, Vol. 57 (May 1967), p. 418.

example. In recent times at least, this country has achieved rather impressive success in economic stabilization, despite lack of information and policy instruments. In analyzing this policy we will focus on the following questions: What information is available to policymakers? What instruments do they actually manipulate? What is the relation between this information, the instruments manipulated, and the state of the economy?

The argument of this study may be summarized in the following fashion. Since the early 1950's Mexico has experienced growth with respectable stability; the stability is in large measure because public expenditure and private autonomous expenditure have moved in offsetting ways. The burden of adjustment, however, has been carried by private investment, rather than by public expenditure. The level of private investment has been controlled by manipulation of the level of reserves that private financial institutions are required to deposit in the central bank, Banco de México, and this manipulation is based on the monitoring of two variables: the rate of growth of the money supply and the rate of change of foreign exchange reserves. Because of the structure of the economy, these two data generally give consistent, meaningful, and timely signals for policy change. From time to time, however, they give contradictory signals, causing the policymaking system to fail. This system may not be optimal, but it is viable and appropriate and applicable to other countries at similar stages of development.[3]

THE GOAL OF STABILITY

Mexican real GNP per capita has grown with extraordinary constancy, suffering only three minor setbacks since 1940 (see Figure 11–2). But inflation at an average of about 13% per year marred this achievement until 1955.[4] The record is also punctuated by devaluations in 1948–49 and 1954.[5] Since 1955,

[3] On the economic record of Mexico see Sanford Mosk, *Industrial Revolution in Mexico* (Berkeley: University of California Press, 1954); Raymond Vernon, *The Dilemma of Mexico's Development* (Cambridge, Mass.: Harvard University Press, 1963); Vernon ed., *Public Policy and Private Enterprise in Mexico* (Cambridge, Mass.: Harvard University Press, 1964); William P. Glade and Charles W. Anderson, *The Political Economy of Mexico* (Madison, Wisc.: University of Wisconsin Press, 1963); Leopoldo Solís M., "Hacia un Análisis General a Largo Plazo del Desarrollo Económico de México," *Demografiá y Economía*, Vol. 1 (1967), pp. 40–91; and Clark W. Reynolds, *The Mexican Economy: Twentieth-Century Structure and Growth* (New Haven: Yale University Press, 1970).

[4] Calculated from the index of wholesale prices of 210 articles compiled by *Banco de México, Departamento de Estudios Económicos*. This index is a poor indicator of quarterly movements, but is probably reasonably accurate in the long run.

[5] The earlier devaluation is probably best seen as part of the worldwide postwar adjustment of exchange rates to the dollar, that of 1954 is still debated vigorously. See Dwight S. Brothers and Leopoldo Solís M., *Mexican Financial Development* (Austin, Texas: University of Texas Press, 1966), pp. 85–87; Walter J. Sedwitz, "La devaluación; su génesis y consecuencias," *Revista Fiscal y Financiera*, Vol. 17 (April 1957); and Clark W. Reynolds, *Changing Trade Patterns and Trade Policy in Mexico: Some Lessons for Developing Countries* (Stanford, Cal.: Food Research Institute, October 1967), Discussion Paper No. 67–4 and the ECLA works cited therein.

FIGURE 11-2. REAL GNP PER CAPITA

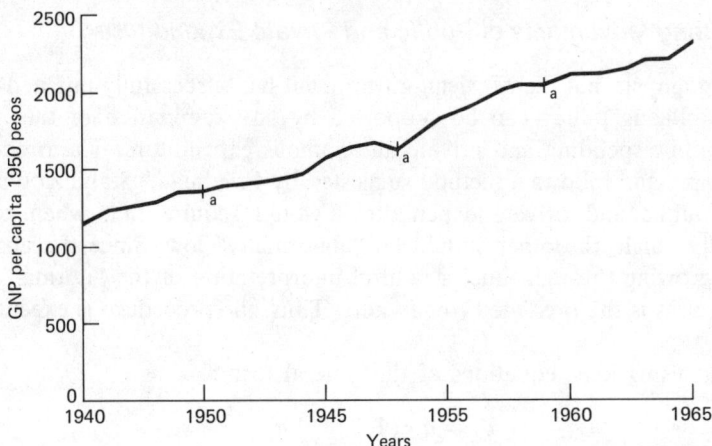

Source: Data from Nacional Financiera, S. A., *La Economía Mexicana en Cifras,*
Mexico, 1965 Table 10, except 1964 from *Banco de México,* S. A.

[a]Marks years in which GNP per capita did not grow.

however, prices have been relatively stable and the rate of exchange has been maintained. By Latin American standards this is a history of impressively stable growth.

This success is not accidental; it represents the achievement of major objectives of high-level Mexican policymakers. The Mexican government does not publish any real equivalent of *The Economic Report of the President,* so it is hard to find clear statements of official goals carefully articulated with the policies that will be adopted to achieve these goals. But from conversations with government officials, it is hard not to carry away the impression that the quite traditional goals of reasonably full use of resources, price stability, and balance of payments equilibrium are important to them. The consistency of these objectives with continuing social transformation is debated hotly, but the prevailing opinion seems to hold that inflation and recurrent devaluation would likely slow long-run progress.

The short-run aggregate-demand policy that this chapter will investigate can explain only part of Mexico's success. Achieving a satisfactory combination of employment, price increase, and balance of payments pressure requires the ability not only to adjust demand but also to maintain a satisfactory price and wage policy. Policymakers seem to be aware of this requirement. Thus, for example, the Mexican government's tepid attitude toward labor unions and the current seminal inclusion of price considerations in import-substitution policy should be seen as helping decrease the upward pressure on prices that will be felt at high levels of output. In short, appropriate structural policy and the achievement of short-run goals go hand in hand.

GOVERNMENT SPENDING AND STABILITY

The Offsetting Movements of Public and Private Expenditure

The judgment that the Mexican government has successfully pursued some kind of stabilizing policy can be supported by an examination of the movements of public spending and private autonomous expenditure. The procedure is quite simple and follows a method suggested by Friedman.[6] Stabilizing movements of public and private expenditures would require that when one is "abnormally" high, the other should be "abnormally" low. Since the absolute levels are growing through time, a natural interpretation of the "normal" level of expenditures is the predicted trend value. Thus, the procedure is executed in two steps:

1. Fit, using logs, equations of the general form:

$$Y_t = a \cdot (1 + g)^{\,t} u_t$$

where a is to be interpreted as Y_0, g is the percentage annual rate of growth, and Y_t is private autonomous expenditure, public expenditure, or some particular component of these aggregates. Calculate the predicted values of Y, $\hat{Y}_t$, from these coefficients.

2. Calculate the annual deviations from trend, $Y_t - \hat{Y}_t$, for public expenditure and for private autonomous expenditures and correlate these devia-

TABLE 11–1.   REGRESSIONS TO FIND TREND, 1948–65[a]

I. $P_t = 2120.7 \ (1.084)^t \ v_t$		$R^2 = .83$
II. $G_t = 3381.9 \ (1.056)^t \ v_t$		$R^2 = .91$
Components of G:		
A. $CG_t = 1468.1 \ (1.058)^t \ v_t$		$R^2 = .97$
B. $IPB_t = 1908.0 \ (1.055)^t \ v_t$		$R^2 = .82$
Components of IPB:		
1. $IGF_t = 860.3 \ (1.024)^t \ v_t$		$R^2 = .45$
2. $IOE_t = 879.3 \ (1.072)^t \ v_t$		$R^2 = .85$
3. $IDF_t = \ \ 77.3 \ (1.091)^t \ v_t$		$R^2 = .64$
4. $IET_t = 121.2 \ (1.026)^t \ v_t$		$R^2 = .52$

[a] Key to variables (all measured in 1950 pesos):
I: P: Private investment plus (exports minus imports).
II. G: Public sector investment plus government consumption.
  A. CG: Government consumption expenditures.
  B. IPB: Public sector investment.
   1. IGF: Investment of the federal government.
   2. IOE: Investment of autonomous organisms and state enterprises.
   3. IDF: Investment of the Federal District government.
   4. IET: Investment of the state, territorial, and municipal governments.

[6] Milton Friedman, *Essays in Positive Economics* (Chicago: University of Chicago Press, 1966), pp. 122–24.

tions. Movements that are offsetting will be revealed by a significantly negative correlation between deviations.

For this exercise we have defined private autonomous expenditure as private investment plus (exports minus imports). Total public expenditure, as well as various components of this total, were tested in the manner described above for the period 1948–65. The results of these calculations are shown in Tables 11–1 and 11–2.

These calculations seem to confirm the contention that some stabilizing policy has been successfully executed. Public and private expenditures have generally moved in offsetting ways; the regressions of the residuals of public expenditure on the residuals of private expenditure (at the bottom of Table 11–1) show that the movements of the two have been not only in contrary direction, but also of comparable magnitude. For example, a unit positive deviation of P has been·associated on the average with a .6 negative deviation of G. But this analysis cannot yet tell us whether G is adjusting to P (ordinary fiscal policy) or P to G (something else). Choosing between these possibilities is a principal concern of the analysis that follows.

The Improbability of Fiscal Policy

Assume for purposes of argument that this offsetting pattern is the result of successful fiscal policy. What information and policy capabilities would be

TABLE 11–2. CORRELATIONS BETWEEN RESIDUALS FROM THE REGRESSION

Correlation Between the Residual of P and the Residual of:	Correlation Coefficient	t^a	Significant
G	−.786	−5.081	yes
CG	−.627	−3.223	yes
IPB	−.779	−4.968	yes
IGF	−.730	−4.268	yes
IOE	−.675	−3.656	yes
IDF	−.555	−2.671	yes
IET	−.156	−.634	no

Regressions, Residuals on Residuals

Resid (G) $= 60.4 - .599$ (Resid P)	$R^2 = .61$
Resid (CG) $= 11.3 - .121$ (Resid P)	$R^2 = .39$
Resid (IPB) $= 56.8 - .478$ (Resid P)	$R^2 = .61$
Resid (IGF) $= 17.8 - .160$ (Resid P)	$R^2 = .53$
Resid (IOE) $= 40.4 - .252$ (Resid P)	$R^2 = .45$
Resid (IDF) $= 14.3 - .051$ (Resid P)	$R^2 = .31$

a Null hypothesis: $H_0 : r \geq 0$ Alternative: $H_1 : r < 0$
Test statistic: $t = r \sqrt{n-2} / \sqrt{1 - r^2}$ with $n - 2 = 16\ df$
Critical region for a one-tailed test at the .01 level is given by $t < -2.58$.
See J. Johnston, *Econometric Methods* (New York: McGraw-Hill, 1963), p. 33.

required to achieve the observed success? Are these capabilities to be found in the Mexican government? [7]

In principle, the following algorithm describes what the government must do: [8]

1. Project the level of private investment and exports and calculate the level of GNP and rate of inflation implied if government fiscal instruments are left at their present values.
2. Compare this predicted outcome with the "desired" outcome. If the two match, stop. If not, solve the economic model implicit in this exercise for values of tax rates and expenditures that *will* produce the desired outcome.
3. Change government activities so that these values of the fiscal instruments are attained.

In the Mexican system the burden of adjustment would have to be carried principally by expenditures, since tax laws are rarely changed much—and changing them substantially is politically difficult and time-consuming. The fiscal system, furthermore, is only unit-elastic with respect to gross domestic product (GDP), so the automatic stabilizer effect is nil. [9]

Several times I was in fact assured that this is the way the Mexican system works, that officials keep track of significant indicators and adjust the level of government expenditures accordingly. In such an effort the Mexican government would indeed have something of an advantage over governments with more rigid budget procedures. Although money for particular projects has been appropriated by the legislature, it need not be released by *Hacienda* (Treasury); conversely, supplemental appropriations are reliably approved whenever requested. [10] Nevertheless, the claim is not plausible.

In the first place, throughout most of the period, the information on which

[7] Since we will be considering monetary policy at some length, it is useful at this point to describe briefly the character of the Mexican financial system. The Constitution of 1917 called for the establishment of a modern banking system to replace the structure that had been largely shattered by the Revolution. It was not until 1925, however, that the central bank, *Banco de México,* was established as a dependency of the *Secretaría de Hacienda y Crédito Público* (Treasury). Until 1931 it was nearly impotent and until 1935 it was not even able to achieve a monopoly of note issue. Legislation of 1936 finally endowed it with its present powers. See Dwight S. Brothers and Leopoldo Solís M., *op cit.,* pp. 10–11, for a brief history. *Nacional Financiera,* the principal government development bank, was founded in 1934 and functioned on a modest scale until 1940. During World War II its activities grew rapidly; it has ever since played a central role in financing Mexican industrial development. For a good summary, see Calvin P. Blair, "Nacional Financiera: Entrepreneurship in a Mixed Economy," in Vernon, ed., *Public Policy,* pp. 191–240. Surrounding these two institutions are some nineteen other public financial institutions—principally specialized development banks—and over two hundred private institutions.

[8] This section draws on the common literature of quantitative economic policy: cf. Jan Tinbergen, *Centralization and Decentralization in Economic Policy* (Amsterdam: North Holland, 1952); Bert G. Hickman, ed., *Quantitative Planning of Economic Policy* (Washington: The Brookings Institution, 1965).

[9] Perhaps even perverse since taxes *this* year are collected in part on *last* year's income.

[10] For a political scientist's view of Mexican budgetary processes, see Robert E. Scott, "Budget-Making in Mexico," *Inter-American Economic Affairs,* Vol. 9 (Autumn 1955), pp. 3–20.

such adjustments would have to be based was either nonexistent, compiled too late, or inaccurate. No one makes or has made serious forecasts of private investment demand. Attempts at forecasting exports did not begin until 1958 or 1959. The wholesale and retail price indexes of the Banco de Mexico were known to be quite unreliable and have recently been thoroughly overhauled. Until recently, indexes of aggregate economic activity and national income accounts appeared with a six-month to one-year lag. Furthermore, according to new revisions of investment estimates, the private investment data available in the late 1950's and early 1960's were serious underestimates. If the government had responded "correctly" to these figures, the stimulation would have been excessive. Similarly, unemployment figures are gathered infrequently and are highly suspect. We must add to the inherent weakness of the data problems that arise from the organizational and political environment in which decisions must be made. Collection of current data is often decentralized to operating ministries—agriculture or industry and commerce, for example—and may be released only reluctantly and with some screening to the institutions responsible for macro policy. It would be most surprising if it passed through the organizational filters undistorted. The probability of distortion is increased by the keenly competitive situation in which ministers are placed. Since the president cannot succeed himself and since presidents are traditionally selected from among the ministers of the previous administration, these men have a powerful incentive to cover their failures and magnify their successes.

We must hasten to add that these are universal phenomena. Mexico is not the only country with bad data; on the contrary, Mexican statistics are surely among the best in Latin America. And the screening of information occurs in every large organization. But it does remain true that these deficiencies in available data would certainly make it impossible to use a formal Tinbergen policy model.

This does not, however, negate the possibility of any reasonably effective policy. In a system where changes are incremental and where policymakers have access to qualitative and impressionistic information—as well as some statistics—they may be able to do a quite respectable job.[11] But this leaves us with the intriguing question of exactly *how* they do it.

Even with first-rate information and the theoretical flexibility of the budgetary process, it would still be necessary that expenditures could be adjusted easily and quickly in practice. According to an official of Hacienda, because of long-term commitments, works in progress, and the difficulty of efficiently expanding activities, the maximum possible variation in public consumption expenditures is on the order of $\pm 10\%$ from their planned level; for federal government investment the figure is closer to $\pm 25\%$. If we assume a similar

[11] For example, according to Jesus Silva-Herzog, Mexican government economists in the 1930's watched the easy-to-gather figures of beer production on the theory that as long as times were good, beer consumption would continue to rise. The method was said to be reasonably successful.

flexibility in the expenditures of other levels of the public sector, then the possible deviation of the total from the planned level would be about $\pm 18\%$, the weighted average of the two. This is large enough to offset the "swing" in the residuals of P in all but five years since 1948. More formally, if we calculate

$$(\text{Resid } (P)_t - \text{Resid } (P)_{t-1})/G_t$$

we find that the absolute value of this ratio exceeds .18 in only five years. Since no one has claimed that the government does a *perfect* job of stabilization, this may be an acceptable rate of failure. So, although public expenditures are somewhat inflexible, we cannot say a priori that they are so inflexible that, *if adequate information were available,* they could not be adjusted adequately.

Yet this theoretical flexibility does not prove that the government is actually capable of deciding on and enforcing appropriate variations. The agencies primarily responsible for enforcing this required flexibility are Hacienda and the *Secretaría de la Presidencia* (equivalent to the Executive Office of the President in the United States). Presumably they could exercise rather tight control over government consumption expenditures since over 90% of these come from federal funds. Indeed, government consumption is stabilizing according to its correlation coefficient, but the magnitude of its variability is quite small. Federal investment expenditures are about one-third as large as government consumption and presumably much more flexible. They, too, are subject to the same budget controls, but they account for only 26% of the stabilizing effect. The component of public expenditure that contributes the most to stability is investment by autonomous organisms and public enterprises. But these bodies have been the hardest to control. By far the largest proportion of their investment is financed out of their own funds or by foreign loans, decreasing the control Hacienda has over their short-run activities.[12] Nominally, they are subject to control by the Investment Commission and (since 1958) the Secretaría de la Presidencia and Public Investment Bureau—successors to the Investment Commission. But, until 1959 at least, they evidently took liberties since it was necessary in that year to formulate regulations to penalize unauthorized attempts to use their resources for investment or to seek foreign loans.[13] If controls over expenditures really are exercised with appropriate wisdom, it is puzzling indeed to find that the best-behaved expenditures are those least subject to control.

The Political Cycle in Public Expenditure

To this point we have examined the proposition that the government is pursuing ordinary Keynesian countercyclical policy and found that the absence of data and the inability to control expenditures effectively cast some, but not

[12] See the data on financing of their investment in México, Secretaría de la Presidencia, *México, Inversión Pública Federal, 1926–1963* (Mexico: Talleres Gráficos de la Nación, 1964).
[13] Miguel S. Wionczek, "Mexico: Incomplete Formal Planning," in E. E. Hagen, ed., *Planning Economic Development* (Homewood, Ill.: Richard D. Irwin, 1963), pp. 166–67.

decisive, doubt on the notion. Suppose, however, that we could find an internal cycle in the behavior of public expenditures whose only plausible explanation effectively excluded the possibility that the movements represented a response to private sector demand. Then, the hypothesis of stabilizing behavior would have to be discarded. Such a cycle exists.

The outline of the following description seems to be part of the "conventional wisdom" of Mexican government economists, but it has never been tested before. In the first year of a six-year presidential term government activity coasts on its previous momentum. The administration takes office in December, but the budget for its first year has already been prepared in September. The outgoing president is reluctant to encumber his successor with large new programs, so this budget will likely be somewhat small. The new administration will be passing time getting organized and planning its particular "style," rather than spending money, so actual first-year expenditures will be low. By the second year, the government will have found its stride and be undertaking its new projects, so expenditures will rise with exceptional speed. For the third, fourth, and fifth years expenditure growth will taper off somewhat. The final year of the administration will be marked by a rush to complete as many of the projects as possible before the end of the term, in part to assure that one's monuments will in fact be finished, in part to give the next president a freer hand.[14]

Thus, the hypothesis is that the rate of growth of expenditures will be relatively high from the first to the second year, lower from the second to the fifth, and high again from the fifth to the sixth. If we plot the logarithm of government expenditure in constant pesos against year of presidential term and connect the first and last years by a straight line, the other years should appear as plotted below.

Hypothetical Pattern of Government Expenditures

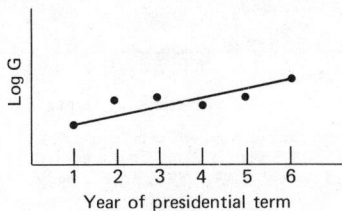

Year of presidential term

Year 2 should lie above the trend and year 5 below it. Years 3 and 4 are less clear, so we will simply lump 3 with 2, and 4 with 5. We will consider only public sector investment expenditure for two reasons: first, it seems to be carrying the major burden of adjustment (if we accept the adjustment hypothesis)

[14] The tradition that most projects will be finished within the presidential term and the frantic increase in project dedications toward the end of a presidential term implied by this tradition are noted by James W. Wilkie, *The Mexican Revolution: Federal Expenditure and Social Change Since 1910* (Berkeley: University of California Press, 1967), p. 107.

and, second, to get statistically significant results we need the longest series possible. Good constant-peso public investment data go back to 1926. The data are shown in Figure 11–3.

FIGURE 11–3. PUBLIC INVESTMENT BY PRESIDENTIAL TERM 1929–64

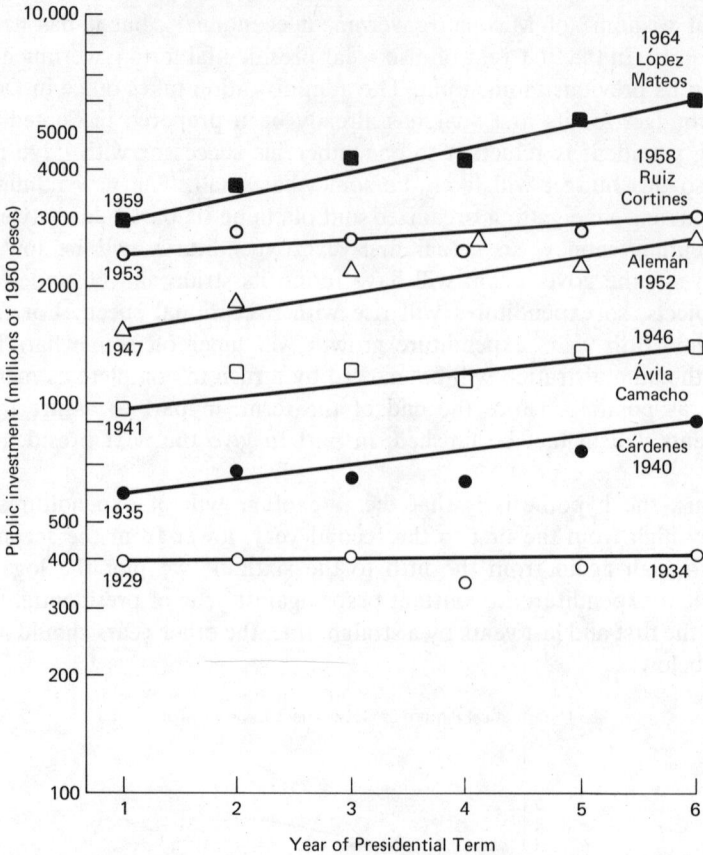

Sources: 1929–'52 from México, Secretaría de la Presidencia, *México: Inversión Pública Federal, 1925–1963,* Table 6; 1953–'64 from *Banco de México, Dpto. de Estudios Económicos.*

Since the hypothesis is basically qualitative and simply involves a four-way exhaustive classification of observations (years 2 and 3, years 4 and 5; above trend, below trend), the appropriate method is a contingency table:

	Above Trend	Below Trend	
Years 2 and 3	3	9	$\Sigma = 12$
Years 4 and 5	11	1	$\Sigma = 12$
	$\Sigma = 14$	$\Sigma = 10$	$\Sigma = 24$

The null hypothesis is that the two classifications should be independent and the observations distributed randomly in response to random movements in private autonomous expenditure.

H_0: Classifications independent

H_1: Classifications not independent

The appropriate test statistic is a one-tailed X^2,

$$X^2 = \sum_{i=1}^{a} \sum_{j=1}^{b} \frac{[x_{ij} - n(x_i./n)(x._j/n)]^2}{n(x_i./n)(x._j/n)},$$

with $(a-1)(b-1) = 1$ degree of freedom.[15] At the 99% level of confidence the critical region is given by $X^2 \geq 6.63$. Calculations yield $X^2 = 20.16 > 6.63$. Thus, the null hypothesis is rejected.

Public expenditures *do* move in some nonrandom way over presidential terms. Furthermore, inspection of the data reveals no obvious alternative to the particular cycle suggested here. This makes it highly unlikely that public expenditure can be adjusting to fluctuations in private outlays. If this is so, the next step is to investigate the mechanism by which the private sector is forced to offset the rhythm of government expenditures.

THE FRAMEWORK FOR POLICY

Excess Demand for Investable Funds

Economists often characterize monetary policy as a string which can be pulled but not pushed, capable of restraining aggregate demand, but not of stimulating the economy if investors are pessimistic. This metaphor would not apply, however, in a world in which investors' desires for funds are always unsatisfied. This is why the assumption of excess demand for investable funds is crucial to the present argument; without it we cannot explain the Mexican government's "success" in countercyclical policy. We have seen that government expenditures follow their own distinctive pattern and thus are not used to stimulate the economy if private aggregate demand should prove insufficient. Even if private investment were responsive to changes in the interest rate, this reveals nothing about policy since the Banco de México has not used the rate of interest for purposes of domestic stabilization. We have left only quantitative controls over credit. These are used vigorously, but are obviously effective only to suppress *excess* demand; if private investors are unwilling to invest more, simply making credit available will not increase investment. But if they are always unsatisfied, then releasing more credit will increase effective demand; the one instrument the government manipulates will be adequate. Thus, the assumption of excess demand is crucial.

---

[15] See Robert V. Hogg and Allen T. Craig, *Introduction to Mathematical Statistics* (New York: Macmillan, 1965), pp. 304–5.

It is difficult to prove conclusively that there is such excess demand.[16] The idea of an excess of demand over supply at the going price is really a static concept; we can see the "excess" on a graph of supply and demand schedules, but the concept becomes less clear-cut when market adjustment is viewed over time. Shifts of the supply and demand schedules and stickiness in adjustment imply that a market will be out of equilibrium most of the time. But the concept still has an operational meaning. If we surveyed "creditworthy" investors and found a substantial number of them willing to borrow and invest at the going rate of interest or higher, but unable because banks were loaned up, then we could say there was excess demand. Unfortunately, the opportunity to take such a survey in, say, 1956 has now passed forever, so we must rely on inferences from the evidence available now.

We can infer from the structure of the Mexican financial system that equilibrium in the loanable-funds market is not likely to be achieved. Most financial institutions are organized into combines composed typically of a commercial bank, one or more *financieras* (a unique Mexican institution that borrows from the public and lends to firms), and a group of associated industrial firms.[17] Resources are shifted within the group, for example from savings and trust departments of the banks to the financieras and from there channeled into the "filial" industries and other investments. Naturally, these financieras tend to concentrate their investments in the small number of industries associated with the combine. At the end of 1959, for example, the eight largest financieras had concentrated 79% of their investments in the stocks of only twenty enterprises, four banks, and one insurance company.[18] The explosive growth of financieras in the last six years has undoubtedly broadened the range of firms to which they lend, but this market structure leads one to suspect that there are probably outsiders who would like to borrow but cannot because of the exclusiveness of the arrangement. If we can assume that they are not abnormally risky businesses, they would qualify as "excess demand."

A further a priori argument can proceed from the fact that a substantial proportion of banks' legal reserves are in the form of "directed investments." Under Mexican law, financial institutions are often given the choice between depositing a portion of legal reserves in cash with the Banco de México and lending the same funds to private borrowers in approved branches of production.[19] This is obviously an attempt by the central bank to shift the composition of bank loan portfolios from their "natural" composition and should imply that

[16] However, the men who manage the Mexican banking system believe that the assumption is true. See Shelton, "The Banking System," p. 187, and "Private Sector Liquidity and Output Growth in Post-War Mexico," *Southern Economic Journal*, Vol. 34 (July 1967), p. 39. This was also clear to me from conversations with these officials.

[17] A description of these combines can be found in Antonio Campos Andapia, *Teoría de la Intermediación Financiera y las Sociedades Financieras Privadas, Mexicanas* (Tesis profesional, Escuela Nacional de Economía, UNAM, 1962). A condensed version was published by CEMLA under the title, *Las Sociedades Financieras Privadas en México*.

[18] *Ibid.*, p. 182.

[19] Cf. *Banco de México* circulars 1605, 1420, and 1589.

certain borrowers receive fewer funds than they would if the financial system were in uncontrolled equilibrium. These unsatisfied borrowers, too, would classify as excess demand. Since banks appear to have no trouble meeting these portfolio requirements, there is no evidence of an offsetting deficiency of demand in the approved branches of production.

Another essentially a priori argument is simply this: given the observed very high marginal profitability of private investment, it would be surprising if demand for investable funds were not quite high. This, coupled with movements of the interest rate that are inconsistent with equilibrium behavior, constitutes an argument that demand and supply are not equilibrated at the going interest rate charged by financial institutions and that the disequilibrium is in the direction of excess demand.

The interest rate r can be calculated as the gross rate of return on financial system assets, excluding required reserves. Thus, it represents an average of the cost of loans to private borrowers. This is the appropriate concept for our purposes. The measurement of the rate of profit is more difficult. We have only a direct measure of profits accruing to corporations, and even that is a bit rough, so P_t has been estimated as $\Delta U_t/Ip_{t-1}$, where ΔU_t is the change in corporate profits (profits $_t$ — profits $_{t-1}$). This implicitly assumes an average one-year gestation lag. Since U includes only *corporate* profits, whereas Ip is corporate *plus* noncorporate private investment, P underestimates the average rate of profit. However, P also includes the profits of government enterprises, whose investment is excluded from Ip. Thus, P *overestimates* the average rate of profit made by *private* businesses.

These defects are not correctable, but we can get some idea of the size of the biases involved, deriving an upper bound for P by removing inappropriate quantities from the denominator of P and a lower bound by adding everything possible to the denominator.

1. If we take private investment in housing out of the figure for private investment, we will move to a figure that is 80–90% *corporate* private investment. Since the numerator still includes profits of public corporations, the P^* calculated from these data is very likely an overestimate of P.
2. Alternatively, using the original figures for ΔU and dividing by private investment plus public enterprise investment, we should get a P^{**} that lies below the true P, at least until the 1960's, since net public enterprise profits were probably negligible until then.

The justification for using the raw value of P rests on the facts that it is available for the entire period (whereas P^* is not) and that it is so closely related to both that if it does not help explain private investment, neither will the alternative measures (see Table 11–3).[20]

[20] P would perhaps be more precisely labeled if we called it the "marginal private profit–capital ratio," but the shorthand used here will not be misleading so long as the temptation to identify this with the internal rate of return or marginal efficiency of capital is resisted. If we are willing to make some assumptions, however, the relation between

TABLE 11-3.　ALTERNATIVE ESTIMATES
OF P

Year	P	$P*$	$P**$
1950	1.169		.763
1951	3.035		1.738
1952	.829		.607
1953	−.581		−.437
1954	1.066		.798
1955	1.300		.930
1956	.743		.566
1957	.527		.434
1958	.429		.349
1959	.075		.059
1960	.530	.842	.418
1961	.224	.384	.159
1962	.298	.438	.205
1963	.434	.648	.290
1964	1.106	1.522	.709
1965	.228	.358	.149

$P** = .05443 + .60172\ P$　　$R^2 = .976$
$P* \ = .076828 + 1.3235\ P$　$R^2 = .994$

Over the entire period the marginal profitability of capital, as defined here, has exceeded the rate of interest by a great margin (see Figure 11–4). However, the appropriate concepts for our analysis are the marginal profitability of *investment* and the interest rate charged by the marginal lender. In a developed economy like the United States we expect the marginal efficiency of investment to decline as the flow per year of investment increases, other things being equal. As the rate of investment rises, the capital goods industries encounter their capacity limits and prices of capital goods rise; also the labor force may not

---

these concepts and our P may be specified. For example, in a smoothly growing Cobb–Douglas world, if the production function is

$$Q_t = AK^\alpha\ L_t^{1-\alpha},\ \text{we know that}$$
$$\pi_t = \alpha\ (Q_0\ \beta^t/K_0\ \lambda^t) \tag{1}$$

where π_t is the rate of return and Q and K are growing at rates $(\beta - 1)$ and $(\lambda - 1)$. Our definition of P can be specified as

$$P_t = \alpha\ (\Delta\ Q_t/I_{t-1}) \tag{2}$$

Here investment is gross; in (1) capital should be net, so if σ is the rate of depreciation, $I_{t-1} = K_{t-1} - (1 - \sigma)\ K_{t-2}$. Thus:

$$P_t = \alpha\ [\beta\ Q_{t-1}/(\lambda + \sigma)\ K_{t-2}]. \qquad \text{Since}\ Q_{t-1} = \pi_{t-1}\ K_{t-1}/\alpha, \tag{3}$$
$$P_t = \pi_{t-1}\ [\beta\ K_{t-1}/(\lambda + \sigma)\ K_{t-2}]. \tag{4}$$

But $K_{t-1}/K_{t-2} = \lambda$ and $\pi_{t-1} = r_t\ \lambda/\beta$, so

$$P_t = \pi_t\ (\lambda/\beta)\ (\beta\ \lambda/\lambda + \sigma) = \pi_t\ (\lambda^2/\lambda + \sigma). \tag{5}$$

Using Cossío's figures for the net capital stock and his assumption of depreciation at the rate of 2.5%, we find that $P_t = 1.028\ \pi_t$ for the period 1950–62. See Luís Cossío, *Alternativas de Estimación de la Inversión Bruta Fija en México, 1939–1962* (México: Banco de México, Dpto. de Estudios Económicos, 1965). Note that the data we have used for profits are consistent with the definition of national income and are therefore already net of capital consumption allowances.

FIGURE 11-4. RATE OF INTEREST AND RATE OF PROFIT

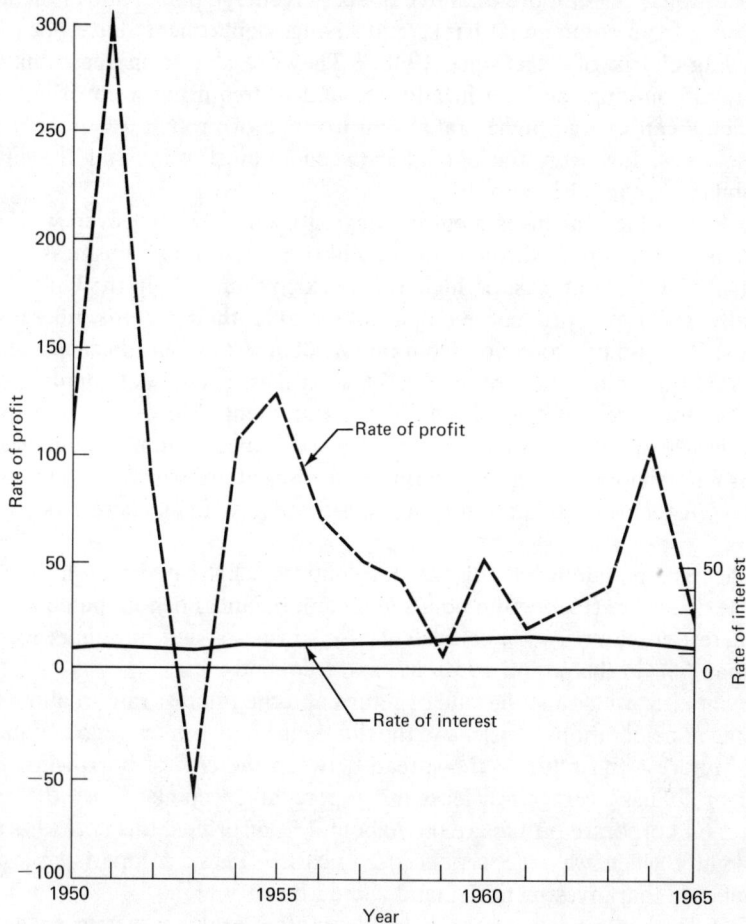

Source: Rate of interest from *Banco de México,*
S. A., *Dpto. de Estudios Económicos.* The Rate
of Profit is *P,* defined with Model I.

expand rapidly enough, forcing wages to rise faster than productivity. In the
Mexican economy these price and wage increases should be mild, if they occur
at all. A large portion of capital goods is imported from the United States; no
conceivable Mexican investment boom could ever strain U.S. capacity. And the
domestic construction industry uses extremely labor-intensive techniques, so
expansion of activity implies little expansion of capital, simply hiring more of
the pool of part-time farmers available. Thus, its elasticity of supply should be
very high. Neither is the finished plant likely to encounter rising wages as a
result of pressure on the labor market. So the figures for the marginal profitability of capital should be very close to the marginal profitability of investment.

Similarly, the marginal interest rate (if we ignore black-market and informal operations) is not more than five or six percentage points above the average rate. Loans from commercial banks and savings departments have been limited to a ceiling charge of 12% since 1948.[21] They are able to increase that somewhat by discounting the loan in advance and by requiring a covering deposit. Financieras can charge higher rates—an average of around 14 or 15%. Even at these rates, however, the spread between interest rates and the marginal profitability of capital is very large.

Is it possible that investment in Mexico is so risky that even with such a spread investors can be brought to equilibrium? Ordinary business risks are objectively lower, or at least no higher, in Mexico than, say, in the United States, especially for firms prudent enough to sprinkle their boards liberally with politicos. Because of protection from import competition and because nearly all industrial firms enjoy a secure monopoly, or at least friendly oligopoly, position, risks of failure are small. And if failure is imminent, *Nacional Financiera* and Banco de México will often rescue even a quite incompetently managed company or financial institution. Furthermore, firms that are part of a combine incur no risk of foreclosure by creditor banks. Objectively, then, these risks are very low.

The risk remaining is that of devaluation. This can be easily evaluated since Mexicans are free to hold bonds and bank balances denominated in dollars. The interest spread between equivalent assets in pesos and in dollars was never more than 6% in the period 1950–67, and frequently less.

Even after we adjust the rate of return and the interest rate to allow for the foregoing considerations—risks and the difference between average and marginal rates of interest and return—the spread between the cost of borrowing and the rate of profit has averaged at least thirty percentage points. Since the realized tax rates on corporate profits are only about 4% of profits, this spread is altered only slightly when we take profits *after* taxes.[22] These comparisons establish a strong case that investment demand should be very high.

Two further aspects of the behavior of the banking system suggest that demand for funds has often been unsatisfied at the going rate of interest. First, from time to time, deposit banks, savings banks, and financieras have been forced to adjust increases in their loan portfolios to a higher composition of "approved" activities.[23] This implies that on the margin they have to seek out new borrowers. Particularly sharp changes were imposed in January 1955, July 1959, and May 1960, the first two applying to deposit banks and the last to financieras. If the

---

[21] The ceiling was set by *Banco de México* circular 1092.

[22] The equation relating *impuesto sobre la renta* (corporate profits tax) to corporate profits is $T^\pi = 103.8 + .0412\,\pi_{t-1} + 861.1\,D$ $R^2 = .99$. This is fitted using profits lagged one year since this year's tax is collected on last year's profits. The dummy variable captures the effect of the tax reforms of 1962 and 1965.

[23] For a list of these changes see Brothers and Solís, *op. cit.*, pp. 59–64. For a summary of changes in legal reserve requirements, see Arturo Ruiz Equihau, *El Encaje Legal* (Tesis profesional, Escuela Nacional de Economía, UNAM, 1963), esp. Ch. 4.

market were in equilibrium both before and after these changes were imposed, we would expect the interest rate to fall because, by the definition of equilibrium, the borrowers who had to be included after the change were unwilling to borrow at the previous rate. In 1955 the interest rate fell slightly. In 1959, 1960, and 1961 it rose slightly; so there is no reason to suppose that banks had to cut their lending rates to lend to the new borrowers.[24]

A second indication of unsatisfied demand in the capital market is provided by the behavior of interest rates before and after the break from the period of inflation to the period of price stability. Between 1954 and 1962 the interest rate adjusted for price changes (the "real" rate) rose from near zero to 12% and the average ratio of private investment to GDP also rose. If we assume the market to have been close to equilibrium throughout the period, we must also assume that the marginal efficiency of investment schedule shifted sharply upward. Were investors' expectations unusually optimistic in the last half of the 1950's? According to Vernon, quite the contrary. "The slow-up of growth of the latter 1950's and the near-standstill of 1961 has obviously shaken that [optimistic] state of mind considerably." [25] Also the Cuban Revolution and nationalization of some foreign-held properties in Mexico "created occasional flurries of anxiety and alarm among the business groups." However, such flurries were short lived.[26] Thus, there appears to be no good reason to assume that the marginal efficiency of investment increased greatly. If it did not, how was equilibrium achieved at rising real rates of interest?

We have seen that demand for investable funds *should* have been high because of the large spread between the profitability and the cost of borrowing. We have also seen that the price in this market, the interest rate, has not behaved as we would expect it to. These facts, plus the observation that interest rates have moved in the neighborhood of the legal maximum, argue for the assumption that equilibrium has not been achieved and that the market is characterized by excessive, rather than deficient, demand for investable funds.

These arguments are not conclusive in a thoroughly satisfying way. If we were willing to complicate the equilibrium model sufficiently, all of these inconsistencies could doubtless be rationalized. But the addition of Ptolemaic epicycles is subject to sharply diminishing returns. Rather than seeking a complex structure that is consistent with both neoclassical equilibrium assumptions and the Mexican data, we will discard these assumptions and test the performance of another, simpler set against the data.

---

[24] There is a problem with this argument in that the new requirements may be met by shifting around resources within a combine or by buying bonds of quasi-public agencies; for example "credit to agriculture" may be loans to CONASUPO, the government price-support agency.

[25] Raymond Vernon, *Dilemma*, p. 14. Some of Vernon's concern for Mexico's future was undoubtedly based on the current statistics, which showed a decline in the average rate of investment. The figures have since been adjusted upward. The tone of his arguments, however, suggests that he found other, independent evidence of investors' pessimism.

[26] *Ibid.*, p. 180.

The Model

Mexican data have been inadequate and the instruments of fiscal policy have been manipulated perversely. How then do we explain the offsetting movements of public and private expenditure observed earlier? The preceding section indicates the direction we should take. The excess demand that characterizes the loanable-funds market implies that restriction or expansion of the supply of credit will be sufficient to restrict or expand private investment directly, without any intervening changes in the interest rate. Thus, we should focus on the policy instruments that change the supply of credit. Central bank open-market operations in government bonds are irrelevant—in fact, nearly nonexistent since Mexican federal government securities typically earn far below the prevailing rate of interest. The one instrument that *is* used, frequently and powerfully, is the ratio of reserves private banks are required to deposit with the Banco de México.[27] The reserve regulations have been adjusted more than thirty times since 1950, on occasion to 100% for certain liabilities and institutions. Furthermore, the information on which manipulation of the reserve ratio is based is timely and accurate; the two indicators, the supply of money and Banco de México holdings of gold and foreign exchange, are known precisely with negligible lags—twenty-eight days at most in the case of the money supply, a few hours in the case of foreign exchange.

If the hypothesis is correct that regulation of the reserve ratio is the Mexican government's principal tool of stabilization policy, then we should be able to construct a model of the economy that embodies this hypothesis, show that the model has reasonable predictive power, measure the power of the reserve ratio to affect the level of investment and GNP, and deduce the way in which policymakers have responded to the information available to them. This is the task remaining.

The two innovations that will be incorporated in this analysis of the Mexican economy are disequilibrium assumptions about the market for loanable funds and the market for imported goods. We consider first the way in which funds are rationed.

The domestic economy and the foreign sector each generate some quantity of savings, claims over resources that are not spent on consumption. Part of this saving is done by the public sector—the current-account government surplus and the net profits of government enterprises. We assume that this will be retained by the public sector. Part of private saving is invested directly without being reallocated by the banking system; the rest is channeled through banks, at which point the government can take a "cut" via required reserves and other arrangements. Foreign borrowing and direct foreign investment are the last sources of savings.

Given excess private demand for investable funds, by definition, any funds

[27] Strictly speaking, the *marginal* reserve ratio. Changing the average ratio might require the banks to recall loans, so it is avoided.

available to the private sector will be transformed into "desired" investment. Stabilization policy then requires simply the following process: The government estimates the level of its own expenditures and calculates expected tax and profit income at the desired level of GNP. The resulting deficit minus the part that will be financed by public borrowing abroad must be financed by capturing part of domestic savings. The residual of domestic saving will be invested by the private sector.

This analysis slights the variety of the ways in which the public sector can capture resources, but will serve for the present. The various instruments available will be described at greater length in the next section.

It follows from this analysis that within the framework of an aggregative model, private investment can be represented as the following identity:

Private investment = total saving − public sector saving − (financial system "reserve ratio") × (savings channeled through the financial system) − public foreign borrowing − "forced" private saving.

Two comments are required. First, the "reserve ratio" is the outcome of the relative growth of different types of financial institutions, as well as regulations that change frequently. Therefore, it can only be estimated ex post. Second, the item "forced" private saving is principally payments to contractors that are delayed after the projects have been completed and purchases by banks of bonds above their reserve requirements. Delayed payment is quite common and has been important in some years, for example, 1964. Unfortunately, the data needed for the detail shown in this identity are unavailable, so a simpler form must be used in the following model; the sum of public enterprise profits, public foreign borrowing, and "forced" private saving must be obtained as a residual. But this is not a major defect. Since expenditures of the public sector must equal financing received in one way or another by the public sector, the answer must be the same whether we obtain it as a residual or by aggregation of other series.

The other innovation in the model is the form of the import function. Fitting the reduced form of Model I revealed that exports are very closely related to imports. Normal trade theory suggests such a relation and explains the income and price adjustment mechanisms by which the balance of payments is equilibrated, without suggesting that it is proper to use one in order to explain the other. In this model, exports will be used to determine imports, but the mechanism by which imports are equilibrated with exports is primarily the explicit policy of import substitution.

It has been shown that, in general, Mexican imports are better explained by "capacity to import" than by GDP.[28] Frontier imports and imports of services, which are generally free from controls and tariffs, do depend on income,

[28] Andrei Maneschi and Clark W. Reynolds, *The Effect of Import Substitution on Foreign Exchange Needs, Savings Rates and Growth in Latin America* (Economic Growth Center, Yale University, Discussion Paper #18, December 20, 1966).

but the other components and the aggregate are more closely related to capacity to import, especially in the period 1951–62. Maneschi and Reynolds propose an essentially long-run explanation for this observation: it is evidence of a successful policy of import substitution.[29] This is the only adequate explanation since the close relation between imports and exports is primarily a correspondence of their trends, rather than of fluctuations around the trends.

Whatever mechanism we offer as an explanation, the conclusion for our purposes is the same. Since many would-be importers are refused import licenses and because there are others who do not apply for licenses because they know refusal is certain, we can infer that given the tariff rates and the rate of exchange there is excess demand for imports that is suppressed by the licensing authorities, or, in the case of public sector importers, by the commissions that oversee public investment and public sector imports. Thus, the relevant explanatory variable should not be GDP or some other that we expect to be a determinant of demand; rather, it should be the criterion (or a proxy for the criterion) used by the import control authorities or those promoting import substitution. We would expect them to be motivated to avoid, among other things, serious losses of foreign exchange reserves. If the capital account is small relative to trade, or not subject to sharp changes, then the "equilibrium" level of imports will move with the observed value of exports; *equilibrium* in this sense being the value that satisfies the government, but surely not importers.

Having explained the only two points about this model that are the least bit bizarre, we are now ready to write the equations that incorporate these disequilibrium assumptions.

Behavioral Equations

$$Cp = a_1 + b_1\, GDP - b_1\, T + Tr \tag{1}$$

$$T = a_2 + b_2\, GDP + b_3\, D \tag{2}$$

$$Sc = a_3 + b_4\, GDP \tag{3}$$

$$M = a_4 + b_5\, X \tag{4}$$

Identities

$$GDP = cp + Ip + Cg + Ig + X - M \tag{5}$$

$$S = GDP - Cg - Cp + M - X \tag{6}$$

$$Ip = S - R_0\, Sc - R^*\, Sc_0 - (T - Tr - Cg) - F \tag{7}$$

[29] In the early 1950's however, the relation may have been more circular. Izquierdo argues that "much of import-replacement . . . has been a by-product of import prohibitions and quotas used to handle balance-of-payments difficulties, of tariffs levied for revenue purposes, and of devaluations." Rafael Izquierdo, "Protectionism in Mexico," in Vernon, ed., *Public Policy*, p. 287.

Definitions of Variables

GDP Gross domestic product at factor cost.
Cp Private consumption expenditures.
Ip Private investment expenditures.
Cg Government consumption expenditures.
Ig Public investment expenditures.
X Total exports of goods and services.
M Total imports of goods and services.
T Total taxes collected by all levels of government.
Tr Federal government expenditures on "transfers to consumption."
S Total savings of the economy.
D A dummy variable equal to zero until 1963, one thereafter.
Sc The increase in private banking system liabilities to the public.
R·Sc This is defined as the increase in banking system liabilities to the public times the reserve ratio. This is linearized to $R_0 \, Sc + R^* \, Sc_0$, where R_0 is the mean of R, Sc_0 the mean of Sc, R^* is interpreted as a policy variable (the "reserve ratio") calculated as $R^* = (R \, Sc - R_0 \, Sc)/Sc_0$. $R·Sc$ is measured by the change in the quantity of federal securities held by financial institutions.
F Calculated as a residual.

The form of the *Ip* and *M* equations has already been discussed. The other equations are "standard." The equation for *Sc* is given the simplest possible form; it is the least satisfactory of the lot. The equations are fitted to annual data in current prices for the period 1950–1965.

Model I

Two-Stage Estimates

$$GDP = Cp + Ip + G + X - M \tag{1}$$

$$Cp = 3303 + .8442 \, GDP - .8442 \, T + Tr \qquad F = 21846; \; 1, 4 \; df \tag{2}$$
$$ (.00461) \qquad (.00461)$$

$$T = -109.5 + .09575 \, GDP + 2007 \, D \qquad F = 752; \quad 1, 3 \; df \tag{3}$$
$$ (.00388) \qquad\quad (725)$$

$$M = -157.4 + 1.0506 \, X \qquad\qquad R^2 = .97 \tag{4}$$
$$ (.0501)$$

$$Ip = GDP - Cp - T + M - .11805 \, Sc - X + Tr - 5418.72 \, R^* - F \tag{5}$$

$$Sc = -1900 + .05781 \, GDP \qquad\qquad F = 90.4; \quad 1, 4 \; df \tag{6}$$
$$ (.00552)$$

Equations (2), (3), (6): Figures in parentheses are asymptotic standard errors. *F* is Phoebus Dhrmyes's *F*. See Dhrmyes, *Econometrics* (New York: Harper &

Row, 1970), p. 276. The equations were also fitted using LIML with almost identical results.

Equation (5): The equation for S has been eliminated by substitution into the private investment equation, also eliminating Cg from Eq. (5) so that Cg and Ig could be combined.

The problem remaining is to define criteria by which we may evaluate this model. Such an evaluation is not a routine problem. The structural equation implies sets of restrictions on the coefficients: which are zero in a particular equation and which are not. Each restriction implies a larger residual for any particular fitted equation. Therefore, a useful standard of comparison is the goodness of fit of the more general model which includes all of the interesting exogenous variables in all its equations, that is, Model II.

Model II

$$GDP = f\,(Cg, Ig, X, Tr, D, R^*, F, P, r) = g\,(E) \qquad (1)$$

$$Cp \;\;= c\,(E) \qquad (2)$$

$$T \;\;= t\,(E) \qquad (3)$$

$$M \;\;= m\,(E) \qquad (4)$$

$$Ip \;\;= i\,(E) \qquad (5)$$

These reduced-form equations should have smaller sample-period residuals than the structural equations of Model I, the differences being a measure of the price of including the overidentifying restrictions on the structural models. Note that the rates of interest and profit (P and r) are included in Model II.

Three criteria appear desirable:

A. Goodness of fit: We would like the sample-period residuals to be small.
B. Freedom from autocorrelation of the residuals: We would prefer a structure that exhibits little autocorrelation.
C. Predictive power: We would prefer a structure that does a good job of predicting values of the endogenous variables that were not used in the fitting of the equations.

Testing Models I and II.   We can now proceed to test the models. Since all of the tests involve analysis of the differences between observed and predicted values of the jointly determined variables, we first solve the structural equations for their implied reduced forms. Setting B equal to the matrix of coefficients of jointly determined variables and C equal to the matrix of coefficients of predetermined variables, we write Model I as:

$$y = By + Cx$$

Solving,

$$y = (I - B)^{-1} Cx$$

the matrix $[(I - B)^{-1} C]$ is equivalent to the solved reduced form of the fitted structural equations. Given the vector x for each period, we can calculate y, the corresponding predicted endogenous vector.

Criterion A, goodness-of-fit, has been examined, in effect, by the standard errors and F statistics shown with the model. As a further test, for each endogenous variable we calculate $e'e^{\mathrm{I}}$ and $e'e^{\mathrm{II}}$, where the typical element of e is $y_t - \hat{y}_t$ and the superscript refers to the model from which the prediction comes. For all endogenous variables $e'e^{\mathrm{II}}$ should be the smallest, as explained above, so the sums of squared residuals from the other models will be presented as a proportion of $e'e^{\mathrm{II}}$.

CRITERION A.   GOODNESS-OF-FIT

Variable	$e'e^{\mathrm{I}}/e'e^{\mathrm{II}}$
GDP	16.9
Cp	13.2
T	3.5
M	2.1
Ip	4.8

To clarify what these ratios of squared residuals imply in terms of coefficients of determination, consider the equation for Cp. In Model II the consumption function had an R^2 of .99987. If we calculate the analogous statistic from the values predicted by the models, we find that for Model I, the thirteenfold increase in $e'e$ is equivalent to decreasing R^2 to .984. So these large differences in $e'e$ imply quite small differences in the proportion of explained to unexplained variance.

This criterion produces ambiguous results. For GDP and Cp the cost of the identifying restrictions may seem high. For the rest of the variables it seems quite low.

By Criterion B, lack of autocorrelation in the errors, Model I performs somewhat better. Here the test statistic is the ordinary Durbin–Watson d calculated from the same residuals used above. The appropriate confidence interval for d used in this manner is unknown, but it is still reasonable to desire values to be close to 2.[30] The presence of autocorrelated residuals would suggest that the structural relations were misspecified.

CRITERION B.   VALUES OF DURBIN–WATSON d

Variable	Model I	Model II
GDP	1.189	2.20
Cp	1.072	2.30
T	1.614	2.25
M	1.702	1.90
Ip	1.536	1.82

[30] For a discussion of some of the problems of using the Durbin-Watson statistics within the context of a simultaneous equation model, see Carl F. Christ, *Econometric Models and Methods* (New York: Wiley, 1966), pp. 528–29.

This criterion is also ambiguous: The equations of the general reduced form are all good; two of the equations of Model I show some autocorrelation.

The final criterion is predictive power. Data for 1966 were not included in the regressions, so the ability of the two models to project the 1966 values is an independent test of each model's overidentifying restrictions.[31] Here Model I is clearly superior.

CRITERION C.   1966 PROJECTIONS

		MODEL I		MODEL II	
Variable	Observed	Predicted	Percent error	Predicted	Percent error
GDP	275734	281707	2.2	310992	12.8
Cp	214800	221411	3.1	253952	18.2
T	28680	28828	0.5	28441	−.8
M	27100	27894	2.9	22359	22.7
Ip	31200	31056	−0.5	33173	6.3

In light of the test statistics and the predictive test, Model I appears to fit the data reasonably well. None of these tests is, however, satisfyingly decisive.[32]

It is now a simple matter to show the power of the reserve ratio as a tool of policy using the matrix $[(I - B)^{-1} C]$ from Model I.[33] The relationship between particular pairs of exogenous and endogenous variables can be read directly from the cells of the matrix $[(I - B)^{-1} C]$ (see Table 11–4). In fact,

TABLE 11–4.   MATRIX $[(I - B)^{-1} C]$ FOR MODEL 1

	[1] G	[2] X	[3] Tr	[4] D	[5] R*	[6] F	[7] Constant
(1) GDP	9.75	0	9.75	−19568	−52825	−9.75	3254
(2) Cp	7.44	0	8.44	−16630	−40320	−7.44	5879
(3) T	.93	0	.93	134	−5058	−.93	202
(4) M	0	1.051	0	0	0	0	−157
(5) Ip	1.31	.051	1.31	−2938	−12505	−2.31	−2783
(6) Sc	.56	0	.56	−1131	−3054	−.56	−1712

the coefficients are similar to partial derivatives; for example, the value of 9.75 in element (1,1) shows that if everything else remained constant, a unit increase in public expenditure would be associated with an increase in GDP of 9.75. Thus, it is akin to the derivative of GDP with respect to Ig. It is only a *partial* derivative, however. In this case, an increase in Ig would change some other equation since the expenditure would have to be financed. The act of financing

[31] *Ibid.*, pp. 570–71.

[32] More elaborate testing of an appropriate null hypothesis may be found in John E. Koehler, *Economic Policy-making with Limited Information: The Process of Macro-Control in Mexico* (Santa Monica, Cal.: The Rand Corporation, RM–5682–RC, August 1968).

[33] As defined on pp. 417–18.

the expenditure would have some other effect on the system depending on how it was accomplished. Thus, the *total* impact of a policy change can be derived from the model only after all the identities have once again been brought to equality. To continue the example, suppose that the unit increase in Ig is financed by a unit increase in F, by persuading banks to buy extra bonds, for example. By reading down the second and seventh columns of $[(I - B)^{-1} C]$, we see that these two changes will exactly offset each other, except in row 5. Here the difference in coefficients reveals that private investment will decrease by one unit. Hence, government expenditures financed in this manner will have a net multiplier of zero since the increase in Ig is exactly offset by a decrease in Ip.

To investigate the trade-offs among policy instruments implied by the model, we can perform a small exercise: projecting the 1967 values of the major economic aggregates and developing a policy mix to adjust the outcome to different values. Assume that government expenditures and exports are given at the values shown in Table 11–5. With policy instruments D, R^*, and F maintained at their 1966 levels, the model predicts an extremely large increase in *GDP* (see Table 11–6). This increase in *GDP*—17.2%—would obviously

TABLE 11–5.   EXOGENOUS VECTORS, 1966 AND 1967

	1966 (Observed)	1967 (Estimated)
G	30434	34300
X	26700	28700
Tr	4567	5000
D	1	1
R*	.3248	.3248
F	2726	2726
K	1	1

TABLE 11–6.   OBSERVED 1966 VALUES OF ENDOGENOUS VARIABLES AND 1967 PREDICTIONS ASSUMING D, R*, F CONSTANT

	Observed 1966	Predicted 1967	Percent Increase
GDP	275743	323074	17.2
Cp	214800	253295	17.9
T	28680	32834	14.5
M	27100	29995	10.7
Ip	31200	36774	17.9
Sc	15549	16776	7.9

entail substantial inflation. Taking 300,000 as a plausible target value of *GDP* and solving for values of the policy instruments, we find that any one of the following moves by itself would be sufficient to move the level of *GDP* to this target:

1. Reduce G from 34,300 to 31,933, a decline of 6.9%. As we saw before, this step is not likely to be taken promptly and may be hard to enforce.
2. Raise D from 1 to 2.179. This represents imposing a tax increase larger than the sum of those enacted in 1962 and 1964. Since the previous increases required three years of political maneuvering, this is not likely to be done in time.
3. Raise R^* from .3248 to .7616. Recall from the definition of R^* that it is part of the linearization of R^*Sc. Raising R^* by this amount is equivalent to increasing R, the real measure of required reserves, from .23 to .38. As Figure 11–5 reveals, this is a smaller increase than that registered in 1964 and leaves R below its 1965 level.

We conclude from this exercise that manipulation of the reserve ratio is quite powerful enough to compensate for the absence of fiscal policy. Thus, Model I not only fits the data, but also demonstrates that our assertion that the reserve ratio has been the principal tool of short-run policy is perfectly plausible. The only problem remaining is to examine the conjecture that monitoring of the money supply and foreign exchange reserves would have provided the appropriate information and to determine how Mexican monetary authorities responded to the signals these data give.

INFORMATION AND POLICYMAKING

The Adequacy of the Information Available

What is the relation between the data available with a short lag and the state of the Mexican economy? Do the signals received by policymakers from movements of the money supply and foreign exchange reserves and the immediate goals they pursue combine in such a way that sensible policy is likely to result? In the absence of detailed current data on the level of GNP, employment, the rate of increase of prices, and the like, the directors of the Banco de México appear to have settled on a strategy that circumvents these deficiencies: They attempt to keep the supply of money from growing either "too rapidly" or "too slowly" and to maintain the level of their foreign exchange reserves without allowing the economy to contract "too much" short-term foreign debt. These terms defy precise definition, but this is not surprising; neither is it particularly troublesome. These simple rules ignore the full richness of the nonquantitative and impressionistic information which also influences decisions, just as they suppress the complexity of the decisions themselves. Nonetheless, they are a fair description.

The efficiency of this strategy stems from the way in which the public deficit, changes in the money supply, and movements in the balance of payments are related. The money supply cannot be found explicitly in the model of the economy presented earlier, but the conditions under which the money supply will expand rapidly or slowly are intimately related to the structure of the model. If $(G + Tr - T - F) > R^* Sc$, then the central bank must be absorbing government bonds it cannot slough off onto private banks as required reserves, and the money supply will be increasing as a result. The opposite is true if the inequality is reversed. This is, of course, quite orthodox.

The nature of the Mexican economy and the behavior of Mexican wealth-holders are such that rapid expansion or contraction of the money supply will quickly appear in the capital account of the balance of payments. The demand for cash balances by Mexicans appears to be a markedly constant fraction of money national income, implying that any "speculative demand" for cash is negligible.[34] Since even the respectability of the concept is doubtful, the empirical absence of speculative demand should not trouble us unduly. But for the sake of buttressing the point, we can offer two observations. The first is that the notion of speculative demand for cash balances that vary with changing expectations of future movements in the interest rate presupposes that the interest rate indeed varies and that there is a securities market of respectable size. Both of these points are doubtful in the Mexican case. Short-run movements in the interest rate have been less than dramatic and the securities markets are quite thin, especially so since by far the greater part of government securities is locked in as required reserves of various financial institutions. The second observation is simply that the ratio of money supply to money national income has been quite constant[35] (see Figure 11–5). So, even if there is such a thing as speculative demand for peso balances, such balances could not ever have shifted greatly, which for our purposes is equivalent to their nonexistence.

However, the impact of changes in the money supply on the balance of payments does appear as a result of portfolio choice considerations. We would

FIGURE 11-5.   MONEY SUPPLY AS A PROPORTION OF NATIONAL INCOME

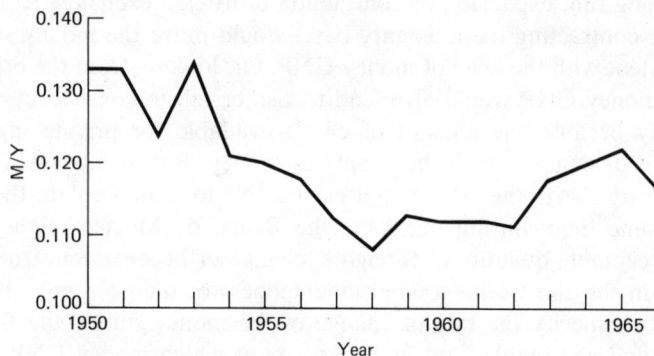

Source: Data from *Banco de Mexico*, S. A.,
Dpto. de Estudios Económicos.

[34] Brothers and Solís cite the Korean crisis year of 1950 and the recession year of 1953 as the only two instances of shifts in liquidity preferences observed. See Brothers and Solís, *op. cit.*, p. 122.
[35] Quasi-money, however, is an increasing function of national income.

expect that balances for transactions needs would be a simple function of income. If, given the customary arrangements for payments to suppliers and workers, the money supply were too small to support the current level of expenditures, those who had access to foreign sources of credit would be willing to pay some interest premium and run some foreign exchange risk for the sake of increasing their liquidity. Thus, short-term capital would flow into Mexico. In the opposite situation, with an excess of money above transactions needs, a utility maximizer would shift some of his balances into dollar assets, thereby diminishing his expected losses in the event of a devaluation of the peso, and causing a capital outflow. Since foreign central banks do not hold peso balances in their reserves, these capital movements will be immediately reflected in changes in Mexico's foreign exchange reserves.

This analysis is a bit too neat and symmetric when stated so baldly and needs to be amended somewhat. First, the argument that those who are short of working capital will borrow abroad obviously applies only to those who *can* borrow abroad—chiefly the largest firms and subsidiaries of foreign companies. Second, those who will lend their surfeit of working balances abroad must be those who cannot currently find a profitable investment project in Mexico beyond financiera bonds at 10%. Surely, some wealth-holders are always in this position; in fact, they may very well be the same subsidiaries, often plagued with excess capacity and unwilling to branch out into new lines. Nonetheless, it is plausible to argue that the capital outflow resulting from an excess above transactions demand would probably be less sharp than the inflow resulting from a shortage of the same magnitude. This asymmetry, however, is matched by a corresponding asymmetry in the responsiveness of the monetary authorities, as we shall see.

In the long run, expansion or contraction of foreign exchange reserves, by expanding or contracting the monetary base, would move the money supply to a level consistent with the level of money GNP. Or, looking from the other side, the level of money GNP would also tend to rise or fall to consistency with the money supply because the amount of credit available for private investment would expand or contract with the supply of money. But, if movements in the public deficit are sharp, the GNP might not be able to "catch up" to the money supply for some time; during that time the Banco de México might lose an entirely unacceptable quantity of foreign exchange or become concerned about the increase in the short-term foreign indebtedness of the economy. Thus, the simplest way to specify the rate of change of the money supply the Banco de México will find acceptable is to find that rate at which money GNP can still remain in step.

In the manner described, inconsistency between demands for money balances and the stock of money will be signaled through foreign exchange and gold holdings. But now we have a surfeit of signals—the money supply and reserves, in effect, more equations than unknowns, and no guarantee of perfect consistency between them—especially so when we remember that short-term capital movements may be set off by entirely exogenous events like devaluations or revolutions in Cuba. On the horns of the dilemma thus created, the Banco de México has been impaled once or twice. However, considering the experiences of other, less fortunate countries, perhaps we should shift the emphasis of this statement by rewording it as *"only* once or twice."

Using the Information

The dilemma posed above seems less serious when we discard the hope that policymaking will be flawless and when we realize that the balance of payments and the money supply will both generally be indicating a policy move in the same direction. The situation remains too ambiguous to be described by some simple decision rule, but there are, nonetheless, reasonable things we can say about the way in which Mexican monetary authorities have responded to these signals.

Some problems appear more compelling and urgent than others. In the category of problems likely to stimulate a quick response we must surely place rapid loss of foreign exchange reserves. Accumulation of reserves may indicate a disequilibrium that is just as large and real, but somehow it is less worrisome; disaster is more remote, and accumulation may even be viewed as desirable. Thus, we would expect policymakers to respond asymmetrically to loss and accumulation of reserves. In 1954 and 1955, for example, faced with large capital inflows following the devaluation, vigorous public demand in the early years of a presidential term, and fairly rapid inflation, the authorities did not move the reserve ratio to unprecedented levels. Sharp response waited until 1956 (see Figure 11–6). On the other hand, in 1959, when confronted with capital outflow, sluggish public demand associated with a change in the presidency, and relatively stable prices, they increased the reserve ratio sharply and repeated the measure in 1960. They thus behaved asymmetrically as we expected.[36]

When we look at some of the shadings of policy, it is clear that the pattern of response has not been constant over the period. One change is obvious from Figure 11–6. The average reserve ratio has drifted upward markedly since 1950.

[36] It is important to realize that the Mexican government *can* act directly to increase capital inflows. For example, in response to balance of payments pressure, private and public banks and *Nacional Financiera* may be encouraged to draw more on their lines of credit in New York. It appears that this was done in 1960 and 1964. Naturally, the supply of credit thus tapped is finite, and a prudent government will not push it too far. Thus, it has always been accompanied by monetary stringency—useful in the short run. Presumably the government could also increase the rate of inflow of direct foreign investment by relaxing the regulations governing Mexican participation, simplifying import licensing, etc., but lags make this a questionable policy for solving short-term problems. And it is politically dangerous. The government of López Mateos is still condemned for losing its nerve in negotiations with Ford and General Motors in 1959–60 and permitting the establishment of subsidiaries that are basically wholly owned. On this point, see Johnson's introductory essay in Harry G. Johnson, ed., *Economic Nationalism in Old and New States* (Chicago: University of Chicago Press, 1967).

FIGURE 11-6. RESERVE RATIO AND CHANGES
IN MONEY SUPPLY

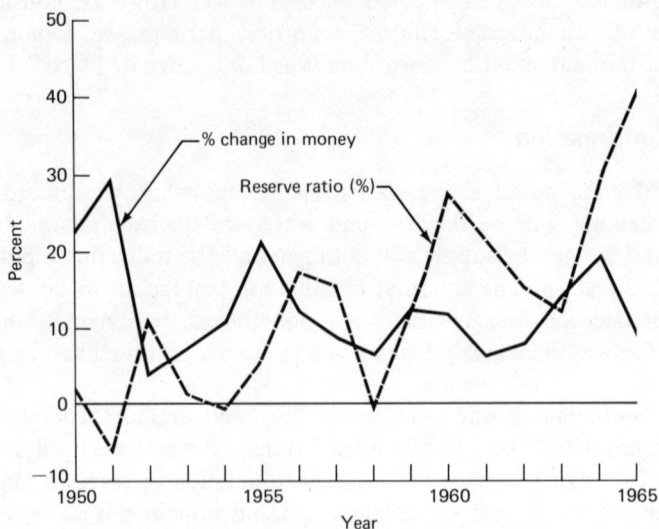

Source: Money supply from *Banco de México,*
S. A., *Dpto. de Estudios Económicos.* Reserve
ratio is *R*, defined in Model I.

This movement is partly a result of the extension of reserve requirements to nonbank institutions—financieras and *hipotecarias* (mortgage banks)—but mainly it reflects an increasing willingness to sacrifice the interests of private bankers who, naturally enough, would rather lend their assets at 12% than buy 5% government bonds.

Another significant change in capability that does not show up in the aggregate ratio has been the attempt to break free of possible balance of payments versus money supply dilemmas by subjecting peso and foreign-currency liabilities to sharply different reserve requirements, in some cases requiring 100% reserves on dollar accounts. Thus, the single instrument has become increasingly potent and more elaborate; in a real sense it has become a set of instruments that can be manipulated to pursue more than one objective. This is especially so when we remember that reserve requirements have been written so as to influence not only the level of private investment, but also its composition.[37]

So capabilities have not remained constant. The Banco de México has learned and adapted. But to phrase it this badly is to anthropomorphize the institution excessively; monetary policy is not set by a rational unitary decision-maker. The process really involves bargaining and adjustment among the directors of the Banco de México, the Secretaría de Hacienda, the Secretaría de Presidencia, and the private bankers; perhaps in a less central role, Nacional

[37] On this see Brothers and Solís, *op. cit.* p. 61.

Financiera. But who bargains for what and with what counters? Unfortunately, no ex-insider has yet written his memoirs detailing how decisions were reached, so the following brief description must admit to being based fundamentally on conjecture; proper conjecture hopefully, but not documentable.

Recall that our earlier projection for 1967 predicted a too-sharp increase in gross domestic product unless some policy changes were made. This result was derived in June 1967; the Banco de México had already taken the proper policy steps in October and November of 1966, shortly after the outline of the 1967 federal budget became clear. Between March and September of 1966, Banco de México holdings of gold and foreign exchange had fallen from $545 to $494 million.[38] The signal was somewhat ambiguous: A midyear dip in reserves is the common seasonal pattern, and the money supply did not move sharply upward until after September 1. So the directors of the bank temporized until the fourth quarter, when they sharply raised reserve requirements for both deposit banks and financieras—the neighborhood of 100% for foreign-currency liabilities.[39] The financial sector was not *too* roughly handled, though, since reserves were stipulated to be primarily in 9% bonds, rather than the more customary 3–5%, and financieras could borrow back some of their reserves.

This solicitousness for the welfare of the private bankers hints at the nature of the bargaining counters they bring to the decision process. It is not the Banco de México's job to put them out of business; furthermore, their voluntary co-operation may be needed at some future time, say, in the form of shifting dollar balances to the central bank to conceal a temporary embarrassment or chipping in from time to time with a credit to the government above their reserve requirement.[40] The bargaining strength of the banks is enhanced by the predominance of the two giants, Banco Nacional de México and the Banco de Comercio system, putting the bargaining into a bilateral monopoly framework rather than the comfortable monopoly position enjoyed by the U.S. Federal Reserve.[41] And the strength of the private bankers is enhanced when the reserve ratios have been high in the previous period—as was the case in 1966.

The position of the Banco de México vis-à-vis Hacienda and Presidencia is harder to unravel. The Banco is formally a dependency of Hacienda, so in any real showdown we would expect its directors to yield. Nonetheless, it is not without some independent power, based largely on its prestige as practically the only "nonpolitical" institution in the country, on the acknowledged technical competence of its staff, and on the fact that many of its alumi hold high positions

[38] The total includes Mexico's IMF gold tranche, which increased from $77 to $86 million. Figures from *International Financial Statistics*, Vol. 21 (March 1968), p. 215.

[39] See *Banco de México* circulars 1589 and 1591 of October 31 and November 19, 1966.

[40] The appropriateness of taking the long view in relations between the government and the banks is increased by the long tenure of the secretary of *Hacienda* and the director of *Banco de México*. The present Secretary and Director (as of 1968) had held their positions for nine and fifteen years respectively.

[41] Or oligopoly, considering the traditional independence of the New York Federal Reserve Bank.

elsewhere in the government. If, for example, the Banco argued that a projected deficit were so large as to run a real risk of inflation and devaluation, Hacienda would take the contention seriously. In turn, Hacienda could bargain more strongly with the operating ministries for budget cuts using this argument as a club, or, more probably, consider increased borrowing abroad.

Before leaving this point, it would be wise to recall a truism from beginning political science: Conflict makes politics necessary; agreement makes it possible. Although we have stressed the way in which the actors try to shift the outcome of the process in their favor—the conflicts among them—the making of policy rests upon their mutual interest in maintaining reasonable stability and rapid growth. The different actors will compromise their own specific interests for the sake of the larger goal; each possesses ultimate weapons that cannot be used without making the conflict visible to outsiders and moving to an Armageddon from which all would return badly battered. How serious a foreign exchange crisis would occur if the director of the Banco Nacional de México walked out in a huff and wrote an embittered letter to the *Times* denouncing the antiprivate-enterprise nature of government monetary policy?

Agreement among the actors is easier, too, because the proper response is in the finest tradition of "sound policy." Educating the U.S. Congress and public to accept the prescriptions of Keynesian policy took more than twenty years. Why? Surely much of the reason is that there was another, quite respectable set of macroeconomic policy prescriptions that were older, intuitively appealing, and perhaps more "moral" since they exorcised "spending beyond our means." No "sound" monetary theorist has ever suggested that the proper response to balance of payments difficulties and inflation should be looser money. Thus, agreement among policymakers is not hampered by possible disagreements as to how the instruments actually work; agreement extends beyond goals to strategy, leaving the only possible disputes to the realm of tactics and judgments of fact.

If everyone agrees on general goals and the proper direction of response to signals from the economy, and if these signals are not deceptive—and we have seen that these two points are true—then perhaps it is not surprising that the record of Mexican policy is very good.

Short-Run Policy as an Aid to Growth

The success of Mexican short-run policy cannot be explained simply as a result of the efficiency of the institutions of monetary control. If supply responses had been sluggish, cost-push endemic, export growth nil, it is inconceivable that the ability to control the level of aggregate demand would, by itself, have been able to move the economy to desirable combinations of growth, inflation, and balance of payments pressure. To explain why these problems have been avoided in Mexico would require lengthy consideration of a broad range of issues beyond the scope of this chapter, but it is worth noting quickly that avoiding these problems has not been the result of simple good fortune. The responsiveness of agricultural output to growing demand must surely be attributed in large measure to public investments in irrigation and roads; the absence of uncontrollable cost-push must be due in part to the manner in which union demands for higher wages have been restrained by the government; export growth has been based on the same public investment, on active promotion of tourism, and, perhaps, on the ability of the Mexican government to make a devaluation stick.[42]

Thus, the success of short-run policy is based on the achievement of appropriate structural change. But the relation is circular, and the ability to avoid gross errors in policy may rest in part on the possession of the appropriate short-run policy tools. All economies are subject to various shocks that will cause the level of GNP to fluctuate. Fluctuations, because they hurt the interests of one group or another and because they are now generally perceived as being curable, will elicit demands for policy measures. But will the policy measures be appropriate? What will be their cost in terms of distortion of the price mechanism and of allocation of resources away from output-increasing uses?

Monetary and fiscal policy are not neutral in their effect on the allocation of resources, but both (and especially monetary policy) are easily reversible. They offer the possibility of responses that can be easily liquidated when no longer relevant. It is much more difficult to liquidate subsidies to consumers and inefficient producers, exchange control, promonopoly measures, and so on. To give some empirical content to these abstract statements, consider the U.S. response to the Great Depression: In the absence of effective countercyclical tools, one government response was the establishment of the National Recovery Administration. What would have been the long-run efficiency cost of NRA's cartelization provisions had the organization not been struck down by the Supreme Court? How difficult would it have been to eliminate after five years' operation? This is not a farfetched analogy. The experience of Colombia, for example, can be interpreted in terms of the accretion of layer upon layer of controls in response to balance of payments crisis—controls that have not been totally liquidated when devaluation finally occurred.

Mexico seems to have avoided introducing really gross distortions into the domestic price structure. This is not to argue that the country can be characterized as one where perfect competition, free trade, and the gold standard are the dominant modes of organization; rather, it simply seems to have exercised

[42] On the Mexican policy toward labor unions see descriptions of the handling of petroleum, railroad, and telegraphers' strikes cited in Robert E. Scott, *Mexican Government in Transition* (Urbana, Ill.: University of Illinois Press, 1964, rev. ed.), pp. 165–68, and p. 254. The proportion of the labor force unionized peaked at 14.5% in 1940 and has not yet regained that level. See the figures in Nacional Financiera, S.A., *La Economiá Mexicana en Cifras* (Mexico, 1966), p. 264. Suggestive, but inconclusive, evidence is offered by the behavior of income shares. The data show a very small proportion going to labor—a high of 37.0% in 1964 and a low of 23.8% in 1950. The figures may be found, among other places, in Diego G. López Rosado, *Problemas Económicos de México* (México: Instituto de Investigaciones Económicos, UNAM, 1966), p. 213. On the devaluation issue, see Clark W. Reynolds, *Changing Trade Patterns,* pp. 41–44.

somewhat more restraint. If it is plausible to argue that this restraint flows in part from the ability of the country to solve short-run problems with short-run instruments, then these instruments are contributing importantly to long-run growth.

CONCLUSIONS AND SPECULATIONS

The principal conclusion of this study is quite simple: Because of the structure of the Mexican economy, the information and policy instruments at the disposal of the government, although seemingly inaccurate and crude, are sufficient to achieve a reasonable degree of macroeconomic stability. We have identified the information actually used and the general outline of the decision rule by which it is processed. Finally, we were at least able to speculate on the nature of the bargaining process from which observed changes in the value of the principal instrument variable emerge. This leaves several concluding questions. How general is this result? Is the Mexican solution wise? Is it viable?

Is the Structure General?

The success of the reserve ratio as a policy tool depends on three special conditions. The first is that the financial system must be developed to a stage where it is able to capture a significant portion of society's savings, but not developed to the point where the broadness of the securities market and the variety of types of financial institutions make it possible for enterprises to raise substantial funds outside the institutions that can be controlled by reserve requirements.[43] The second requirement is that demand for investable funds must be so high at the going interest rate that only restraint, rather than stimulation, of the private sector is required. This may be a rather general phenomenon in rapidly growing countries. On one side of the investment-demand equation we find that interest rates are usually controlled by usury laws. On the other, we expect rates of profit to be high for two reasons: shortage of capital relative to labor and quasi-rents that will be large when output is growing rapidly.[44] The third condition for the usefulness of the reserve ratio is that other policy tools must be able to avoid situations in which the appropriate response with respect to aggregate demand is different from that dictated by the balance of payments.

[43] The literature on "insulation" is relevant to this point. Cf. James R. Schlesinger, "Insulation of the Government Securities Market," in *Fiscal and Debt Management Policies, a Series of Studies Prepared for the Commission on Money and Credit* (Englewood Cliffs, N.J.: Prentice-Hall, 1963), pp. 219–66.

[44] The quasi-rent argument holds in a world where development involves a shift from less to more productive technology. See Richard R. Nelson, *International Productivity Differences in Manufacturing Industry: Problems with Existing Theory and Some Suggestions for a Theoretical Restructuring* (Santa Monica, Cal.: The Rand Corporation, P–3720–1, November 1967), esp. p. 25.

Thus, reliance on the reserve ratio is not a strategy that will be useful in all places and times. However, one suspects that at some point in their evolution many developing countries will pass through a stage at which the conditions are met and the strategy would be appropriate.

Is the Mexican Strategy Wise?

If economic policy capabilities need not—and probably should not—be established once and forever, we must confront the issues of choice, timing, and order of institutional reform. Mexico has implicitly resolved these issues by developing and elaborating the information-processing and execution capabilities of the Banco de México while leaving control over fiscal instruments in a comparatively backward state. The argument of the preceding paragraphs implies that the timing of this decision was proper. Was the choice itself wise?

The answer to this question has two facets: first, why is it necessary to choose one type of reform *or* another and, second, if choice is necessary, why choose to develop monetary-policy capabilities?

Economists who advise the governments of developing countries frequently ignore the fact that reforms can be achieved only by the expenditure of political resources and that these resources may be distinctly limited. But political scientists are well aware that "power" is generally limited and when spent in one way may not be available to pursue other goals.[45] We readily acknowledge this in statements like "The President can't get both a tax cut and tax reform out of Congress this year." If power is a resource to be economized like any other resource, then choosing to establish either a monetary or a fiscal control capability, but not both, may be a perfectly rational, even optimal, choice.

When the choice is put in these terms, "buying" a monetary control capability seems to be a very wise choice. In circumstances like those of Mexico it appears adequate to achieve reasonable stability. It is, furthermore, likely to make possible quick responses undelayed by a requirement to work through legislation. Perhaps most important, monetary policy is likely to present a relatively low "profile," to be nearly invisible in its impact on the typical citizen, and to offer an unsatisfying target for criticism. Furthermore, the manipulation of credit is likely to be seen as a vaguely arcane art, somehow beyond the ken of ordinary mortals. Thus, it should be difficult to build a mass movement protesting the machinations of the central bank—although not impossible, as the history of "free Silver" in the United States demonstrates. People may go to the barricades to fight a tax increase, but will they shed blood over an increase in the marginal reserve ratio coupled with interest rate penalty provisions for excessive

---

[45] Cf. Richard E. Neustadt, *Presidential Power: The Politics of Leadership* (New York: Wiley, 1960). This must be qualified by the possibility of using power in a way that restructures the system to make subsequent changes easier—replacing hostile officials with friendly ones, for example.

allocation of credit to retail trade? And keeping people away from the barricades is a significant consideration in policymaking in many countries.

Is the Strategy Viable?

However, this one-note policy song will not be adequate forever. In Mexico, as we mentioned above, short-run success depends on maintaining a high rate of return to investment. It also depends on avoiding any long-run balance of payments deficit, but on these counts no important change seems imminent. Another problem does, however. The effectiveness of the reserve ratio to combat future crisis can be eroded by relying on it too heavily to capture resources for a public sector. As Figure 11–5 shows, the ratio has drifted upward as a consequence of increasing government expenditures unmatched by tax increases. If this process continues, Mexico will one day find itself without the ability to use even *this* instrument of control to fight excessive aggregate demand. In effect, the need for some kind of fiscal reform arising from rapidly increasing public expenditures has been postponed, but not forever.

However, history teaches us that such predictions are dangerous. American economists have frequently argued that Mexico has worked itself into a difficult impasse. The usual outcome is that these predictions were falsified by measures undertaken somewhat before the hapless American's book went on sale. How can one be pessimistic about a country with a record like that?

BIBLIOGRAPHY

Bennett, Robert L. *The Financial Sector and Economic Development: The Mexican Case.* Baltimore, Md.: The Johns Hopkins Press, 1965.
Blair, Calvin P. "Nacional Financiera: Entrepreneurship in a Mixed Economy." In Raymond Vernon, ed., *Public Policy and Private Enterprise in Mexico.* Cambridge, Mass.: Harvard University Press, 1964.
Campos Andapia, Antonio. *Teoría de la Intermediación Financiera y las Sociedades Financieras Privadas Mexicanas.* Tesis profesional, Escuela Nacional de Economía, Universidad Nacional Autónoma de México, 1962.
Christ, Carl F. *Econometric Models and Methods.* New York: Wiley, 1966.
Cossío, Luís. *Alternativas de Estimación de la Inversión Bruta Fija en México, 1939–1962.* Documento del Departamento de Estudios Económicos, Banco de México, S.A., 1965 (mimeo).
Friedman, Milton. *Essays in Positive Economics.* Chicago: University of Chicago Press (Phoenix Books), 1966.
Glade, William P., Jr., and Charles W. Anderson. *The Political Economy of Mexico.* Madison, Wisc.: The University of Wisconsin Press, 1963.
Goldsmith, Raymond W. *Mexican Financial Development.* Paris: Organization for Economic Cooperation and Development, 1966.
Hogg, Robert V., and Allen T. Craig. *Introduction to Mathematical Statistics.* 2nd ed. New York: Macmillan, 1965.

Izquierdo, Rafael. "Protectionism in Mexico." In Raymond Vernon, ed., *Public Policy and Private Enterprise in Mexico*. Cambridge, Mass.: Harvard University Press, 1964.

Johnston, J. *Econometric Methods*. New York: McGraw-Hill, 1963.

Jorgensen, Dale W. "The Theory of Investment Behavior." In National Bureau of Economic Research, *Determinants of Investment Behavior*. New York: Columbia University Press, 1967.

López Rosado, Diego G. *Problemas Económicos de México*. 2nd ed. Mexico: Instituto de Investigaciones Económicos, Universidad Nacional Autónoma de México, 1966.

Mexico, Secretaría de la Presidencia. *México: Inversión Pública Federal, 1925–1963*. Mexico: Talleres Gráficos de la Nación, 1964.

Mosk, Sanford, A. *Industrial Revolution in Mexico*. Berkeley: University of California Press, 1954.

Nacional Financiera, S.A. *La Economiá Mexicana en Cifras*. Mexico, 1966.

Nelson, Richard R. *International Productivity Differences in Manufacturing Industry: Problems with Existing Theory and Some Suggestions for a Theoretical Restructuring*. Santa Monica, Cal.: The Rand Corporation, P-3720-1, January 1968.

Neustadt, Richard E. *Presidential Power: The Politics of Leadership*. New York: Wiley, 1960.

Reynolds, Clark W. *Changing Trade Patterns and Trade Policy in Mexico*. Stanford, Cal.: Food Research Institute, Stanford University, Discussion Paper no. 67-4, October 1967 (mimeo).

Ruiz Equihau, Arturo, *El Encaje Legal*. Tesis profesional, Escuela Nacional de Economía, Universidad Nacional Autónoma de México, 1963.

Schlesinger, James R. "Insulation of the Government Securities Market: Objectives, Techniques, and Implications." In *Fiscal and Debt Management Policies, A Series of Studies Prepared for the Commission on Money and Credit*. Englewood Cliffs, N.J.: Prentice-Hall, 1963.

Scott, Robert E. "Budget-Making in Mexico." *Inter-American Economic Affairs*, Vol. 9 (Autumn 1955), pp. 3-20.

———. *Mexican Government in Transition*. rev. ed. Urbana, Ill.: University of Illinois Press (Illini Books), 1964.

Sedwitz, Walter J. "La Revaluación; su Génesis y Consecuencias." *Revista Fiscal y Financiera*, Vol. 17 (April 1957).

Shafer, Robert J. *Mexico: Mutual Adjustment Planning*. Syracuse, N.Y.: Syracuse University Press, 1966.

Shelton, David H., "The Banking System: Money and the Goal of Growth." In Raymond Vernon, ed., *Public Policy and Private Enterprise in Mexico*. Cambridge, Mass: Harvard University Press, 1964.

———. "Private Sector Liquidity and Output Growth in Post-War Mexico." *Southern Economic Journal*, Vol. 34 (July 1967), pp. 27-39.

Solís M., Leopoldo. "Hacia un Análisis General a Largo Plazo del Desarrollo Económico de México." *Demografiá y Economía*, Vol. 1 (1967), pp. 40-91.

Vernon, Raymond. *The Dilemma of Mexico's Development*. Cambridge, Mass.: Harvard University Press, 1963.

Wilkie, James W. *The Mexican Revolution: Federal Expenditure and Social Change Since 1910*. Berkeley: University of California Press, 1967.

Wionczek, Miguel S. "Incomplete Formal Planning: Mexico." In Everett E. Hagen, ed., *Planning Economic Development*. Homewood, Ill.: Richard D. Irwin, 1963.

Part VI

An Afterword
on Methods

INTRODUCTION

A major purpose of this volume has been to explicate the problem-oriented aspect of the policy approach for studying political development and change. Primary emphasis has been placed on showing the relative advantages of observing a context from distinct perspectives labeled goals, trends, conditions, projections, and alternatives. So, enlarging the routine research framework and enriching the nature and content of topics needing systematic attention has created and exposed special problems that are to a large degree methodological in nature. These problems have been anticipated, but not too much has been done about them. "The gradual creation of a sense of wholeness, and of assurance in the discovery of interdetail connections within the all-encompassing totality, also requires new methods of formal exposition." [1]

How do we integrate the information generated by diverse specialists? To conclude without suggesting constructive ways of "putting the pieces" back together again would be leaving an important job undone, and it would contribute, rather than help, to resolve a major deficiency of much current social science research and policymaking practice.

What are some specific reasons for creating multiple scientific models or representations of a given problem context? A persistent argument that multiple analytic models must continually be built is reinforced by an excursion into Bayesian statistics, which provides ample graphic evidence in support of the basic argument.

What are some reasons why descriptive statistics has been of so little help,

[1] Harold D. Lasswell, *World Politics and Personal Insecurity* (New York: The Free Press, 1965 ed.), p. 12.

and indeed has often been diversionary, in trying to understand complex contexts where many significant elements interact and evolve over time? To suggest what might be a fundamental reorientation of methodological perspective and style, distinctions between routine, cross-sectional statistical and longitudinal, process forms of analysis are drawn. It is emphasized that the latter is a far more persuasive and plausible way of managing policy contexts—a finding that should be of interest to those concerned not only with political development and change, but with social systems more generally.

The following three chapters are directed to the formidable task of creating a sense of wholeness, noted by Lasswell so many years ago. Each treats a distinct aspect of the problem; hopefully, each raises issues that are worthy of much continuing debate and professional attention.

DEALING WITH COMPLEX SOCIAL PROBLEMS: THE POTENTIAL OF THE "DECISION SEMINAR"

Several attempts have been made to integrate specialized skills and perspectives in systematic ways; a few of these efforts have been directed to development problems and have been called "decision seminars." A summary description of the underlying theory of the seminar and an assessment of past experiences with its use to date are offered to inform the reader of the nature of the fragmentation problem and of the prospects for managing it. Progress is being made in a number of distinct areas, and a prognosis is sketched out that is hopeful but qualified, given the enormity of the task at hand. At least, the decision seminar is a unique methodological creation designed from the ground up to be policy oriented, contextual, and multimethod. As spotty as are the results with its use to date, we know of no more promising way to attack the problem, and hence we pursue the development of the decision seminar diligently, hoping to resolve the many difficulties that have impeded progress in the past and trying to enlist other concerned policy scientists to use the seminar methodology for their own research and policy responsibilities.

A MODERN STATISTICAL APPROACH TO MODEL ASSESSMENT

The prevalence of efforts to erect "once-and-for-all" theories of this or that social setting or process is distressing. The debilitating effects of this penchant for thinking simply about inherently complex phenomena has been emotionally and colorfully underscored by Albert O. Hirschman in his review of two contemporary works on Latin American development.[2] A more rigorous, general treatment of

<hr>

[2] Albert O. Hirschman, "The Search for Paradigms as a Hinderance to Understanding," *World Politics,* Vol. 20 (April 1970), pp. 330–43.

the problem is provided in Chapter 13. Adopting a more moderate evaluation of the utility of formal models than does Hirschman, Donald A. Berry spells out graphically and quite persuasively the need for both the creation of multiple explanations of a context, and also the need for continuing information collection to keep one's several abstractions attuned to evolving patterns and sequences within that context. The chapter complements and reinforces many of the major arguments and prescriptions contained in Chapter 12.

DATA ANALYSIS, PROCESS ANALYSIS, AND SYSTEM CHANGE

Calling for a more sensitive and sensible use of method than what one commonly encounters in quantitative studies of political development and change, Ronald Brunner and Klaus Liepelt stress the contextuality theme in arguing for a major rethinking of the prevalent use of descriptive statistical methods. Concentrating on a comparison of cross-sectional and process styles of analyses, it is shown that statistical regularities in the first instance may either divert or confuse the analyst, whereas information generated by the second style of analysis opens up quite different and potentially more productive avenues of scientific understanding and of potential policy creation. The chapter gives one much to think about, particularly so if great reliance and faith have been placed in the more conventional methodological style of analysis. At a minimum, the chapter should give one pause to reconsider just what is involved in the "discovery of interdetail connections within the all-encompassing totality," the basic task that Lasswell spelled out for us so many years ago.

Chapter 12
Dealing with Complex Social Problems: The Potential of the "Decision Seminar"

GARRY D. BREWER

The "decision seminar," a creation of Harold Lasswell, is designed to permit a group of specialists to integrate their knowledge in order to deal with a complex policy problem. Its overriding purpose is to translate a decisionmaking context into terms that make it understandable and that suggest ameliorative action. Specific procedures are prescribed. Starting with simple, relatively abstract games and verbal-visual scenarios of plausible policy innovations, seminar members move to "field tests" and controlled experimentation, finally arriving at policy recommendations. Participants represent diverse area specialities, methodological skills, and viewpoints (academic, policymaking, and so forth). Emphasis is on the use of critical imagination, methodological flexibility, and orientation to the future. Decision seminars typically extend over several years, and the experiences with several of them devoted to the study of political and social development are recounted. The chapter concludes with a look at strategies to sharpen insights, narrow the problem, assign institutional responsibility, and manage data.

INTRODUCTION

The social problems that demand the attention of the policymaker and the scientific analyst are characterized by complexity. To the lone observer, the complexity may be overwhelming; the mind is essentially incapable of processing all the information necessary to make more than partial sense of a human situation. Thus confronted with complexity, the analyst often resorts to simplifying—emphasizing some things, ignoring some things—according to his temperament, percep-

Any views expressed in this chapter are my own. They should not be interpreted as reflecting the views of The Rand Corporation or the official opinion or policy of any of its governmental or private research sponsors.

Sincere appreciation is extended to the James K. Pollock Research Program for support in preparing this chapter. Particular thanks are due colleagues Klaus Liepelt, DATUM e.V., Bonn-Bad Godesberg, and Harold D. Lasswell, The Policy Sciences Center, Inc., New York, for their assistance. Christine D'Arc Sakaguchi read and greatly improved upon the form and style of presentation.

tions, and academic specialty. Often, far from reducing and managing the complexity in the situations they confront, they end up only creating bigger and more complicated theoretical and analytic structures. What is worse, their approach may blind them to the broader implications of their efforts. Let us look more closely at some of the distorting ways in which scientific researchers and policymakers deal with complexity.

Researchers' Approaches[1]

Normative scholars, for example, hold out hope for the improvement of mankind, but seldom does their work seem relevant to any tangible segment of humanity, nor does it suggest methods that would really be effective in improving mankind. Historians write lucid prose, but their tales rarely appear useful to policymakers in dealing with actual and potential problems. Political scientists and anthropologists each look at the world quite differently, and the formulations of neither are likely to hold the interest of an economist or psychologist.

Policymakers' Approaches

As a policy problem increases in complexity, naturally it becomes less and less susceptible of clear and direct resolution. Ways of interpreting and handling it proliferate.[2] One simplifying way is to deal with a problem just as some prior, presumedly analogous problem was dealt with, though the presumption of analogy may be incorrect. Munich 1938 really has had scant relevance to Vietnam of the 1960's, but some policy was made as if it did. Another way of dealing with a complex problem is to make small, incremental changes. While such measures may be all right for routine, steady-state matters, they may be ineffective or dangerous if basic changes in structure or setting have occurred. No action at all is a third response to multiple conflicting interpretations of a problem.[3]

[1] These points are elaborated in Garry D. Brewer, "Analysis of Complex Systems: An Experiment and Its Implications for Policymaking," in Todd R. LaPorte, ed., *Organized Social Complexity: Challenge to Politics and Policy* (Princeton, N.J.: Princeton University Press, 1974).

[2] John G. Kemeny, "A Philosopher Looks at Political Science," *Journal of Conflict Resolution*, Vol. 4, No. 3 (September 1960), pp. 292–302, at pp. 295–96, has made similar remarks. See also K. Back, "The Game and the Myth as Two Languages of Social Science" *Behavioral Science*, Vol. 8 (January 1963), pp. 66–71, for a lengthy and sage treatment of differential orientations and perspectives. Modelmakers and researchers stress rigorous control, definition, and management; operational personnel appear to operate with an intuitional basis for inference about a context's structure and process. The ideal social scientist, according to Back, must be able to think rigorously *and* be able to imagine and intuit; he should "not be a mongrelizer, but he should be bilingual." Harold D. Lasswell also spoke about these matters in his "From Fragmentation to Configuration," *Policy Sciences*, Vol. 2 (December 1971), pp. 439–46.

[3] Harvey Averch and M. M. Lavin, *Simulation of Decisionmaking in Crises: Three Manual Gaming Experiments* (Santa Monica, Cal.: The Rand Corporation, RM–4202–PR, August 1964), provides an incisive glimpse into these matters, comparing decisionmaking in games and in real-world situations. They deal particularly with the escalation of violence, the impacts of information flows, and associated research questions. They believe that games are a cheap way to confront potential problems in the real world.

A Problem

It is not that analysts or policymakers are malicious or sloppy, but that there are simply limits on what an individual mind, or several minds shaped by common training and outlook can comprehend. What seems to be needed, thus, is not to do away with specialists, but to use and *integrate* their specialized knowledge.

The emergent discipline of policy science, which attempts to integrate many methods and many disciplines, holds much promise for filling this need, even though its accomplishments to date have not yet been impressive.[4] One of the most promising efforts that falls within its scope is the "decision seminar," an attempt at context-specific, disciplined, integration of diverse perspectives and purposes to solve problems.[5] The remainder of this discussion is devoted to the theory underlying decision seminars, examples of some that have been conducted, and an estimate of the technique's future utility.

THEORY OF DECISION SEMINARS

The decision seminar is a creation of Harold Lasswell,[6] and, like many of his ideas, has had a considerable gestation period. Based on the assumption that for most individuals the complexity of a given problem will be overwhelming, it is an institution designed to permit a group to deal with a problem, designed to organize and control a group's attention.

While the seminar has many specific objectives, its overriding purpose is to translate a decisionmaking context into workable, understandable terms for the benefit of all participants in that context. This translation is made "by sampling the decision process as a whole, by adapting all available means to the presentation of the problem." [7] Building abstract models is the means of accomplishing the first prerequisite,[8] and bringing various media to bear on the problem ad-

4 See Harold D. Lasswell, *A Pre-View of Policy Sciences* (New York: American Elsevier, 1971); and *idem,* "Policy Sciences," *International Encyclopedia of the Social Sciences* (New York: The Free Press, 1968), Vol. 12, for up-to-date accountings.

5 J. L. Bower, "Group Decision Making: A Report of an Experimental Study," *Behavioral Science,* Vol. 10 (July 1965), pp. 277–89. The interaction among search, analysis, information structure, and decision rules is more important than has been thought in the past. This is one of a series of much-needed experimental works on these matters.

6 Harold D. Lasswell recalls the origin of the idea in his "Technique of Decision Seminars," *Midwest Journal of Political Science,* Vol. 4, No. 2 (August 1960), pp. 213–36; an amended version is contained in "Decision Seminars: The Contextual Use of Audio-visual Means in Teaching, Research, and Consultation," in Richard L. Merrit and Stein Rokkan, eds., *Comparing Nations* (New Haven: Yale University Press, 1966), pp. 499–524.

7 Lasswell, "Technique of Decision Seminars," *Midwest Journal of Political Science,* p. 222. Subsequent references to this article are to the 1960 version.

8 The need both to simplify and keep the richness of an empirical setting in mind is stressed well in H. W. Kuhn, "Game Theory and Models of Negotiation," *Journal of Conflict Resolution,* Vol. 6, No. 1 (March 1962), pp. 1–4. Game theory abstracts out essential aspects of a context; assumptions made in the interests of theoretical tractability may produce results that are insufficiently detailed. Therefore, one needs to combine the different perspectives with respect to a specific problem context. A model-builder needs an extensive form, to describe a setting; a theory of preferences to account dynamically for

dresses the second. The two activities overlap to the extent that analysts must be willing to search out equivalent and not only specialized points of view, composed of words and word surrogates, to enable a comprehensive perspective or map of the problem to emerge. Much of what makes the decision seminar interesting is the explicit procedures prescribed for these matters.

The decision seminar differs from the more familiar forms of seminar in the following ways.

All public and private decisionmaking institutions having a bearing on the problem are considered in the seminar. Also, the process by which decisions are made is considered both as a whole and over time. For instance, study of problems of national planning in country X would entail the identification of many policymaking bodies; comprehension of how each impinges on the initiation, formulation, execution, and evolution of plans; and creation of several alternative processes that might improve existing planning. The central questions are, Who is currently making choices about the problem under consideration? How are these choices made? And under what circumstances might they be improved?

At the heart of any decision seminar is a core group of ten to fifteen concerned analysts, each of whom contributes a particular set of intellectual skills and a specific outlook on the problem and all of whom are willing to devote several years of their attention to the problem under consideration. Commitment and continuity are essential to the successful manning of the seminar. This does not exclude the occasional participation of outsiders; on the contrary, expert and specialized information is critical and is to be sought whenever it can be useful.[9] The key problem is to prevent the seminar from becoming merely a fancy eating, drinking, and debating occasion for distinguished personnel; the undertaking is too important to allow such frivolities.

A problem-solving orientation is explicitly adopted by all core members. That is, each member frequently presents verbal or written assessments of the underlying goals of relevant individuals and groups in the context, past trends, factors conditioning these trends, probable future outcomes, and possible methods to deflect, encourage, or otherwise alter these outcomes for collective appraisal. Such assessments are scheduled according to a predetermined agenda designed to control the collective focus of attention, much as the problem-solving orientation is meant to organize it.

Since "policy is choice about future events," [10] participants are encouraged to make independent estimates about probable outcomes for elements in the problem. Independent judgments are compared, discrepancies are considered,

---

participants' objectives (goals) as they evolve and are modified in the course of experiencing the setting; and solution concepts that are not static, but correspond to the changing setting and changing goals and objectives of the various participants.

[9] S. W. Becker and N. Baloff, "Organization Structure and Complex Problem Solving," *Administrative Science Quarterly,* Vol. 14, No. 2 (June 1969), pp. 260–71, provides some experimental evidence supporting a division of labor form of organization to improve group problem-solving capabilities. The issue is still a lively one.

[10] Lasswell, "Technique of Decision Seminars," p. 221.

and common expectations about the future are clarified. As events unfold and new information is brought to bear, the initial estimates are reconsidered. Appropriate appraisals of past estimates are made, not to place personal credit or blame, but to determine what estimating techniques yielded which results and why.[11]

The seminar stresses the use of multiple methods; literally any method that can shed light on the problem at hand is liable to be used. In fact, individual members may take it upon themselves to modify or devise entirely new methods as the context demands.

Because the activity is supposed to produce a decision, the proceedings work toward increasingly operational applications of group ideas and recommendations. Starting with simple, relatively abstract games and verbal-visual scenario representations of plausible policy inventions, the seminar moves to field tests and "shake-down" exercises, limited innovations, controlled experimentation, and finally assigns full operational responsibility for policy applications.[12]

To store, and recall information, and to stimulate imagination, audio-visual aids are employed to a far greater degree than in conventional seminars. Because the group does not meet continuously, but periodically, it is important to maintain a visual record of group activities.[13] Analogous groups include the "Situation Room" of the U.S. National Security Council, "war rooms" as used in many army staff headquarters, and the "combat information center" found on vessels of the U.S. Navy. The specific applications of their activities differ, but they share the general purpose of collecting, evaluating, presenting, and disseminating pertinent information about specific spatial and temporal contexts. The created environment becomes the group institutional memory.

To summarize, the distinguishing features of the decision seminar include the construction, orientation, attitude, and style of the participants. Core participants are relatively few in number, active in their involvement, and pledged to try, over a fairly long time, to master a given problem and decision context.

[11] The following describe the reconsideration of two such forecasts: Harold D. Lasswell, "Sino-Japanese Crisis: The Garrison State Versus the Civilian State," *China Quarterly*, Vol. 3 (Fall 1937), pp. 643–49; and *idem*, "The Garrison State Hypothesis Today," in Samuel P. Huntington, ed., *Changing Patterns of Military Politics* (New York: The Free Press, 1962), pp. 51–70, and Colin B. Clark, *The Economics of 1960* (London: Macmillan, 1942); and K. C. Kogiku, "The Economics of 1960 Revisited," *Review of Economics and Statistics*, Vol. 4 (November 1960), pp. 398–407.

[12] See A. Blaquiere, F. Gerard, and G. Leitmann, *Quantitative and Qualitative Games* (New York: Academic Press, 1969), for a general technical treatment of games used as a problem-solving tactic. Also consider Alex M. Mood, *War Gaming as a Technique of Analysis* (Santa Monica, Cal.: The Rand Corporation, P-899, 1954), for some thoughts on problem analysis and management. Gaming may be used as technique to solve unfactorable problems because it allows the analysis and explicit consideration of problem elements. More significantly, it requires that the pieces be reassembled and set into operation as a whole.

[13] See Harold D. Lasswell, "Sharing the Experience of Permanent Reconstruction: A Policy Science Approach," in A. R. Desai, ed., *Essays on Modernization of Underdeveloped Societies* (Bombay: Thacker and Co., 1971), Vol. 1, pp. 536–46, for a note on the use of social observatories in the development setting.

Their dominant *orientation* is toward the future. Forecasting based on knowledge about past trends, conditioning factors, and operating goals is a central seminar activity. Forecasts are updated and evaluated as events unfold.

The characteristic *attitude* is what might be called critical imagination. Blatant speculation based on "exposure to incomplete or inconsistent contours in a general map of reality," [14] is encouraged. Ego and public reputation are protected because all members engage in speculation and appreciate its importance. However, wild speculation untempered by critical judgment is frowned on. Such judgment derives from the reexamination of one's own ideas, from the criticisms and questions of colleagues, and from the sternest source of all, the reality of the decision context. [15]

And finally, the prevalent operating *style* can best be described as purposively eclectic. Given a problem and a setting, no piece of information, no means of communication or representation, and no method of inquiry is a priori excluded from consideration. Here, too, critical judgment plays an important tempering role.

"It will be a great step forward when a great many seminars dealing with similar subject matter or using the same methods are linked together." [16] We have yet to reach this potential, but a few first steps in the desired direction have been taken. Let us examine several of them.

SOME DECISION SEMINARS OF POLITICAL DEVELOPMENT

Decision seminars have been conducted on a range of topics running from secular contemplations about the past, present, and future of a great religious order to systematic observations of a remote and relatively insignificant Andean village. This discussion is limited to seminars that pertained to political development.

Vicos Project

In the late 1940's and 1950's, under the leadership of the late Allan Holmberg, Cornell University's Department of Anthropology undertook systematic monitoring and policy-advising responsibility for Vicos, a Peruvian hacienda. [17] In 1954, Holmberg spent the year assessing the project and planning for its future. To help in this task, he presented data to a small interdisciplinary seminar

---

[14] Lasswell, *A Pre-View of Policy Sciences,* p. 150.

[15] H. Kaufmann and G. M. Becker, "The Empirical Determination of Game-Theoretical Strategies," *Journal of Experimental Psychology,* Vol. 61 (1961), pp. 462–68. The authors develop a normative game theory solution and then see how players actually perform. A datum is established in the context of game play, and a standard to evaluate performance is generated based on predictions of outcomes.

[16] Lasswell, "Technique of Decision Seminars," p. 230.

[17] Allan R. Holmberg, "The Research and Development Approach to the Study of Change," *Human Organization,* Vol. 17 (Spring 1958), pp. 12–16.

whose members also visited Vicos.[18] Some of them kept in contact, and Holmberg applied the decision seminar format in various ways to involve colleagues at Cornell, scholars and government officials in Lima, and local leaders in Vicos.

It was by continual assessment of the Vicos experience that many of the ideas for the theory and procedures of the decision seminar were formulated. Vicos became a sort of prototype.

The Vicos project has been summarized in ways that emphasize the "contextual, problem-oriented, and multimethod" point of view, and suggest how the policy advisor can adapt the decision seminar technique to groups of varied composition. An effort was made to provide visual material that would remind participants of the Vicos situation *before* the Cornell intervention, *during* the period of active Cornell participation, and *afterward*. During the active phase, regular projections were made of the probable and desirable changes in the near and more remote future. Several creative policy innovations seem to have resulted from the Vicos study, although they were not implemented for one reason or another.

Assessments of the Vicos Project, now more or less officially terminated, can be summarized as follows.[19]

1. The effort was durable, extending over a decade and involving a large number of scholars, officials, and Viscosinos: Persistence, commitment.
2. Policy changes were thought out in advance of their actual execution; changes in "obvious," but potentially costly, options were made as a result: Policy relevant, future oriented.
3. The entire procedural apparatus was given a fairly thorough "shake-down"; lessons were learned and mistakes were recorded: Procedures checked out.
5. Maps and charts were used, but the media were not fully exploited: Insufficient use of audio-visual materials.
6. The core group participated periodically rather than continuously: Discontinuity of core participation.

Vicos was an important first approximation of a real policy scientific approach to the study and control of political and social change at the micro level. Valuable experiences were acquired, and the feasibility and importance of the decision seminar concept were illustrated.

SEADAG

Not exactly designed as a decision seminar, a group (Southeast Asia Development Advisory Group) regularly met during the years 1970–72 to consider alternative development strategies and the future of cooperative assistance policies in Southeast Asia. Members included fairly high-level planning and ad-

---

[18] Other members of the core group included John L. Kennedy, a psychologist, C. Edward Lindblom, a political economist, and Harold D. Lasswell, a social scientist.

[19] A basic evaluation was made by Henry F. Dobyns, *Peasants, Power, and Applied Social Change* (Beverly Hills, Cal.: Sage Publications, 1971).

ministrative personnel and distinguished scholars and analysts from Indonesia, Malaysia, Thailand, Vietnam, Laos, Korea, and the United States. Supported by the Asia Society and led by Harold D. Lasswell and Daniel Lerner, the symposia served several important functions, including the fostering of professional and personal ties, the evaluation and respecification of a number of independently initiated social indicators projects, the consideration of regional communication and media policies, and the concentration of attention on means of developing mass participation in the shaping and sharing of values not solely associated with wealth and power.

A detailed appraisal of the group's progress and promise has been made, and the following general points summarily indicate the strengths and weaknesses of the group's activities:

1. At the conclusion, the group demonstrated extraordinary candor and an eagerness to discuss substantial matters: Commitment.
2. Results of prior sessions became inputs for subsequent ones; an agenda was set and adhered to; there was continuous participation of members: Continuity.
3. High-quality intellectual effort was shown in many of the papers presented to the group. The policymaker participants showed surprising sophistication: Concern.
4. No permanent facility was created; no provision was made for the creation of "institutional memory"; uncertainty about continuance of funds prevailed: Institutional fragility.
5. Rather broadly focused to cover a wide geographic region, the group had no visible regional policymaking body to relate its activities to: Indirect decision access.
6. The group probably did not project enough into the future: Insufficiently contextual.

Development Decision Seminar

A very modest undertaking was begun at Yale University in 1969 to test further procedures and methods for decision seminars and to provide a focal point for several research projects on development. The core group was initially composed of six members, which grew to nine by the end of the first year. Area specialities included Argentina, Kenya, Tanzania, Turkey, the Philippines, Ecuador, Chile, Yugoslavia, and the Soviet Union. Besides this geographic variation, there was variation in methodological skills, a factor that shaped many of the early agendas. All agreed that studies of development could benefit from decision seminar procedures, and each member was more or less assured that his research efforts would get a full, enthusiastic, and critical hearing from his colleagues.

Meetings were held about every other month during the academic years 1969–70 and 1970–71. Financial support was minimal because members were either located at Yale or could arrange periodic visits without great hardship. Yale's Council on Comparative and International Studies supplied $2,000–$3,000 each year to meet travel and other expenses. Initially, meetings concentrated on determining the participants' professional and personal interests, shaping individual research proposals, and evaluating the results of several ongoing projects. By the middle of the first year, outside specialists were being invited to talk on specific topics. Hayward R. Alker, Jr. and Martin Shubik spoke on the state of social science model-building and the prospects for improved quantitative techniques, Harold D. Lasswell presented a draft of a paper on decision seminars that helped direct subsequent group activities.[20] J. P. Crecine ended the year by discussing his research on the budgeting process and the problems and opportunities represented in an interdisciplinary research institution such as the Institute for Public Policy Studies at the University of Michigan, which he directed.

The second year featured more individual work by group members. Four dissertation proposals were hammered out in several separate sessions. All were successfully funded, and are in various stages of completion. The volume *Organized Complexity*[21] was read in manuscript form, and several interesting additions and important revisions resulted from the group's criticism. The theme of the second year's activities was methodology and theory, that is, the discovery of theoretical constructs and research techniques that would be appropriate for studying political development.

As of the academic year 1971–72, the group became dormant. Several members left to do field work in Argentina, Chile, Ecuador, and Yugoslavia, and several left Yale to take jobs elsewhere. Contacts have still been maintained, however. As of this writing, members are professionally settled, and plans are being made to resume group activities. The enterprise will continue, and members will bring each other up to date on extensive field investigations.

To appraise the Yale group's activities so far would require a detailed statement from each member. That being infeasible, let the following comments broadly summarize one participant's assessment.

1. A marked degree of commitment was exhibited by members. There was constant, constructive interplay on most important matters. Moreover, the group continues: Commitment.
2. Many basic methodological questions were sufficiently resolved that a major field enterprise in Argentina was planned and is being carried out. This is a significant point. Each member was trained rather differently, but they were able to reach agreement on an appropriate research design for the Argentine context. Thus, the problem, as stated by the two principal field researchers, led to the selection of methods, not the reverse: Multimethod and problem oriented.
3. Each member at one time or another expressed satisfaction with the group enterprise. Personally rewarding.
4. Meeting every other month for two or three days was probably insufficient. The pressure of one's regular routine tended to attenuate the stimulation obtained in

---

[20] Later published as Harold D. Lasswell, "The Continuing Decision Seminar as a Technique of Instruction," *Policy Sciences,* Vol. 2, No. 2 (March 1971), pp. 43–57.

[21] Ronald D. Brunner and Garry D. Brewer, *Organized Complexity: Empirical Theories of Political Development* (New York: The Free Press, 1971).

intense group exchanges. A better schedule might call for semi-monthly meetings, but then the travel and scheduling constraints on more distant members would be prohibitive. An optimal schedule is still forthcoming: Discrete not continuous events.

5. A related problem was the discontinuity caused by the lack of a permanent facility. Rather than beginning with a brief review of past activities and an updating by audio-visual displays, each session essentially began anew. Good audio-visual resources should resolve this; if nothing else, experiences have reinforced the need for such aids: Not permanent.

6. Funding sources were not responsive to proposals of longer term and more detailed field work, especially when it was identified as part of a larger collective activity. However, when such parts were separated and represented singly, funding was readily given: Financial problems.

The renewed Development Decision Seminar will concentrate on two basic issues: elaboration of the Argentine research; and development of methods for appraising policies of various types. In the first instance, rather detailed quantitative models are being constructed to characterize many aspects of Argentine development and societal processes; and in the second instance, the question of how to measure government performance in health and economic policymaking is being addressed.

ADVANTAGES AND DISADVANTAGES

Reconceptualization of "Development"

Although Mannheim first associated development with the *reconstruction* process[22] common in all societies, many analysts still presume that development is something that happens only in remote or backward locales. In fact, the concept is comprehensive, and analysts must begin to monitor decision processes in many contexts to measure and interpret different outcomes that result from analogous processes. For example, the evaluation of public policies cuts across the line between developed and developing societies: How well are policy intentions carried out? Who is responsible? What differences show up between stated goals, expectations, and actual outcomes? Answers will naturally vary from context to context and from problem to problem; however, the appraisal method will be valid for all. It is to the formulation of an appraisal method and other processes, taken comparatively across many contexts, that a decision seminar could be directly useful. It is a research and policy-applicable opportunity of great importance.[23]

[22] Karl Mannheim, *Man and Society in an Age of Reconstruction* (London: Routledge & Kegan Paul, 1940).

[23] These points are elaborated in Garry D. Brewer, "On Innovation, Social Change, and Reality," *Technological Forecasting and Social Change*, Vol. 5, No. 1 (1973), pp. 19–24.

Appreciation for Reality

Indications are that social scientists are becoming increasingly aware of how limited their world views have been. With increased theoretical understanding of social complexity, both knowledge and action should improve. Herbert Simon set forth some basic ideas about complex systems; Todd LaPorte and his colleagues examined several contexts in which simple analysis and the derivative policies yielded quite unexpected and often undesired results.[24] The point is that to recognize the special structural character of most social contexts is to open up a new range of analytic and policy possibilities. The idea of the decision seminar which antedated these developments, is both benefiting, and being benefited by them.

Not the least of these benefits is a reemphasis of the need to observe social events from multiple perspectives, not limiting methodologies. Practically, this calls for increased cooperation among technical specialists, the sharing of skills to meet common problems. Here again, the decision seminar's design is well adapted to the exploitation of may specific talents.

Demand for Comprehensive Treatment

The decision seminar idea supports the reemergence of concern for the whole or comprehensive aspects of a context. The emphasis on social indicators is one symptom; no longer do policymakers find economic accounting sufficient. Thus, more than economic motivations are discernible in the ecology fad; here, too, a major message is the importance of taking complex whole systems into account. The idea of appraisal is demonstrated by several citizen-action organizations. While "Nader's Raiders" may not appreciate certain of the subtleties handed down by the Marquis of Queensberry, they have demonstrated the importance of appraisal for any policy or decision process. And finally, one must not underestimate the consequence of the "environmental impact" provision in recent federal U.S. legislation. Decisionmakers are now *required* to list the most likely outcomes of any public policy *before* it is implemented. In other words, a simple law makes many officials aware of the interconnected nature of the world by compelling them to project events into the future. Such a projective orientation is required in a decision seminar, and one can imagine that may a harried official may come to appreciate the help that a seminar could give in formulating "impact" statements. Matching the needs of the one with the capability of the other seems both plausible and desirable.

Conventional Attitudes

There are several factors complicating this rather optimistic view. The seminar idea runs counter to conventional academic mores, institutional in-

[24] Herbert A. Simon, "The Architecture of Complexity," *General Systems Yearbook,* Vol. 10 (1965), pp. 63 ff; and Todd R. LaPorte, *op. cit.,* to name only two examples.

centives, and professional reward structures. Interdisciplinary shibboleths aside, most scholars are trained and rewarded by a single specific discipline. Unless and until it can be demonstrated that professional benefits accrue from active seminar participation, chances are somewhat lessened that the seminar idea will attract many of the conservative or less imaginative of the intellectual brotherhood. The lack of publicized examples of successful seminars also makes funding sources reluctant to support the enterprise. Both drawbacks will diminish as more people get a sense of the usefulness of the approach in their problem-solving.

Temporal Constraints

The seminar demands a major commitment of time, a scarce resource. Not only is there lead time before a seminar settles down to work, after major problems and opportunities have been identified, and the first information collected and analyzed, but there is a continuing demand on participants to "make time" for similar activities. These demands are considerable, but it is hoped that the problems considered are so interesting and important that this expenditure is quickly compensated.

Accessibility of Decisionmakers

One of the thorniest problems is getting policymakers to see the importance of the seminar and consequently to participate regularly. Besides the obvious need to "sell" the idea, several subtle considerations deserve attention.

Put yourself in a policymaker's place. Why should you open yourself or your agency to scrutiny? What really is to be gained by the disclosure of operating data or policy intentions? Would you not prefer to control as much of the data and analysis as possible in order to avoid potential embarrassment, to prevent competitors from gaining an advantage, and to ensure that any successes redound to your own credit? There questions illustrate a real dilemma confronting those who try to implement decision seminars: how to attain official cooperation without suffering cloying cooptation. No satisfactory solution has yet been worked out.

On balance, taking desired outcomes, past experiences, and present constraints into account, the future viability and usefulness of the decision seminar seems assured.

STRATEGIES TO MANAGE COMPLEXITY

Several plausible scenarios of the decision seminar's future could be postulated, but outlining the simplest contours of one developmental sequence is suggestive. Individual components of the sequence are first considered to elaborate strategies for attacking and managing complex problems and to detail how a decision seminar could fit into these strategies.

Perceptual Insights

It is important that the level of resolution at which a policy scientist is conceiving of a problem context match with the corresponding images engaging a policymaker's attention.[25] To illustrate, consider the dimensions of Figure 12–1.

FIGURE 12–1. LEVEL OF RESOLUTION AND
FOCUS OF ATTENTION

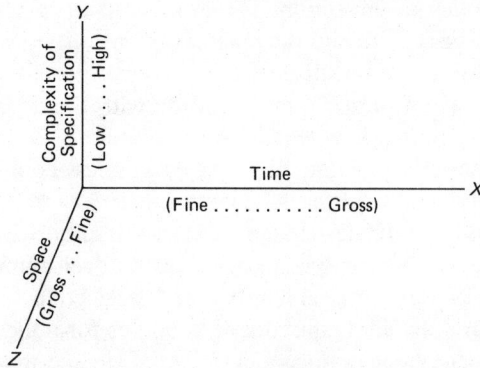

The X dimension corresponds to the basic time unit taken into account. As an expedient, time may be held constant, as in a cross-sectional analysis; however, timing is so important for policy recommendations that except for preliminary descriptive work, temporal invariance is to be avoided. Time units can be as small as a microsecond or as great as a century or a millennium. For many social phenomena, the annual increment is used, corresponding to periods of data collection. For policymakers, the appropriate unit of temporal resolution varies from issue to issue and context to context. It may be as short as an hour, or perhaps a day, a week, or a month; it depends utterly on the decision and problem at hand. The policy scientist must determine what unit of resolution the decisionmaker is using (or should be using) and must be able to communicate his analytic results and policy recommendations in other units as well. This translation and reresolution of time for the benefit of a decisionmaker is an underlying feature of many successful consultants' recommendations; the importance of re-

[25] The notion of "image" is treated in a general way in Kenneth E. Boulding, *The Image: Knowledge in Life and Society* (Ann Arbor, Mich.: University of Michigan Press, 1956). A recent and dramatic illustration of the perceptual difficulties created by the construction of inappropriate and oversimplified images is contained in Ralph E. Strauch, "Winners and Losers: A Conceptual Barrier in our Strategic Thinking," *Air University Review*, Vol. 23 (July–August 1972), pp. 33–44; also available under the same title from The Rand Corporation (P–4769, June 1972)—subsequent references to Strauch are to this edition.

solving the mismatch in time perceptions has been lost on many conventional analysts.

The Z dimension corresponds to the geographic, or spatial, unit considered. At the fine extreme, one could, for example, think of the space occupied by a single household, or, slightly greater, by a single census tract. Larger levels could include a nation, continent, or international region. For convenience and dimensional consistency, one might prefer to assign a standard measure such as miles or kilometers squared to the spatial dimension. As with time, space is variously considered by decisionmakers, and the policy scientist must be able to discuss his analytic results and policy recommendations in terms that are appropriate to those having policy responsibility. Geographers and cartographers, for example, are trained to be sensitive to the spatial dimension; however, few social and behavioral scientists are so sensitized.[26]

Specification, the Y dimension, has to do with the degree of complexity of the image, or conception, with which one operates. A 2- or 3-variable, linear, deterministic model of a phenomenon is generally less complexly specified than a 20- or 30-variable, higher order, stochastic one.[27]

Again, evidence indicates that insufficient attention is being given to determining what degree of simplification is used by decisionmakers in given contexts.[28] Researchers tend to oversimplify and neglect to specify their analytic formulations accurately, with consequent liabilities for policy use.[29]

Thus, it is incumbent upon policy scientists to see that the levels of time, space, and degree of analytic and conceptual detail in their research accord with their clients' needs and perceptions. Mismatches along all three dimensions are to be expected, and measures to resolve them should be developed.[30] Other im-

[26] Edward Soja, The Geography of Modernization in Kenya (Syracuse, N.Y.: Syracuse University Press, 1968), has contributed the geographer's perspective to our understanding of political and social development. It is a good first approximation of the sort of work that should be routinely carried out. See also Walter Isard, Location and Space-Economy (Cambridge, Mass.: Technology Press, 1956); and Brian J. L. Berry and Duane F. Marble, eds., Spatial Analysis: A Reader in Statistical Geography (Englewood Cliffs, N.J.: Prentice-Hall, 1968), for more general treatments and examples.

[27] G. Arthur Mirham, Simulation: Statistical Foundations and Methodology (New York: Academic Press, 1972), Chapter 1, has an excellent discussion of this matter. It is a rare blending of a statistical discussion with an understanding of the practical problems of modeling complex settings, and it should be required reading for the policy scientist. Jerome R. Ravetz, Scientific Knowledge and Its Social Problems (New York: Oxford University Press, 1971), treats the subject more generally.

[28] Strauch, op. cit., p. 7, notes: "It is sometimes argued that . . . assumptions . . . made for 'analytic conveniences,' and the results must, of course, be interpreted in a larger context. This argument would be valid if, in fact, the problems of interpretation in a larger context were regularly considered and addressed; but they seldom are."

[29] Martin Shubik and Garry D. Brewer, Models, Games and Simulations—A Survey (Santa Monica, Cal.: The Rand Corporation, R–1060–ARPA/RC, June 1972), assert that inadequate specification may sometimes result from inadequate data, but more often because it is a hard, nasty, boring business.

[30] "To be any good, . . . a scientist has to think of one thing, deeply and obsessively, for a long time. An administrator has to think of a great many things, widely in their interconnections, for a short time. There is a sharp difference in the intellectual and moral temperaments." C. P. Snow, Science and Government (New York: Mentor Books Edition, 1962), pp. 64–65.

plications of varying levels of analytic resolution and policy attention for the decision seminar and policy science in general can also be sketched out.

- Emphasis should be given to collecting and analyzing time-series data at relatively fine but "aggregatable" levels of resolution.[31]

- Policy scientists must continue efforts to determine the operating images held by decisionmakers.[32]

- Analyses must be conducted at varying degrees of spatial and temporal resolution.[33]

- Policy scientists must pay more attention to respecification and continuous verification and validation of research constructs.[34]

- It would be beneficial to construct alternative models of the same context to account for perceptual and operational differences among policymakers.[35]

Problem Identification

A fundamental task in identifying and defining a problem is to narrow systematically and explicitly the social context so as to consider elements within the problem solution space that are both scientifically manageable and policy relevant. No single strategy will accomplish this, but an example will suggest one possibility.

An initial step is to ask a broad question such as: What are the most important problems facing X? One might use survey techniques to sample responses

[31] Methodological improvements, such as spectral analysis, are clearly called for. See George S. Fishman and P. J. Kiviat, "The Analysis of Simulation-Generated Time Series," *Management Science,* Vol. 13 (March 1967), pp. 525–57, for an exemplary treatment. Better data-base management procedures and techniques must also be created to provide much-needed flexibility, both for the purposes of analysis and for the presentation of results and recommendations in appropriate dimensions for policymaking. Vladimir V. Almendinger addressed the data-base management concern in a series of technical papers: Almendinger et al, TM(L) 4269/000/00, April 10, 1969; TM 1563/010/02, December 1, 1965; TM 1563/014/03, July 29, 1966; TM 1563/021/02, December 1, 1965; SP–2652, November 9, 1966; TM 4073/000/00, August 27, 1968; all available from the System Development Corporation, Santa Monica, California.

[32] One of the many strengths of J. P. Crecine's work on problem-solving and municipal budgets is the attention he gives to this matter. *Governmental Problem-Solving* (Chicago: Rand McNally, 1969). Another Carnegie-trained researcher develops these procedures to advantage in another context, G. P. S. Clarkson, *Portfolio Selection: Simulation of Investment Trust* (Englewood Cliffs, N.J.: Prentice-Hall, 1962).

[33] See Peter R. Gould, "Structuring Information in Spacio-Temporal Preferences," *Journal of Regional Science,* Vol. 7 (Winter 1967), pp. 259–74, for a general discussion of the problem.

[34] Thomas Naylor and J. M. Finger, "Verification of Computer Simulation Models," *Management Science,* Vol. 14 (October 1967), pp. B-92–B-101; and Richard L. Van Horn, "Validation of Simulation Results," *Management Science,* Vol. 17, No. 5 (January 1971), pp. 247–57.

[35] Robert P. Bush and Frederick Mosteller, "A Comparison of Eight Models," in Paul Lazarsfeld and Neil W. Henry, eds., *Readings in Mathematical Social Science* (Chicago: Science Research Associates, 1966), pp. 335–49, concisely demonstrate why this is imperative. See also Earl B. Hunt, "The Evaluation of Somewhat Parallel Models," in Fred Massarik and Philbun Ratoosh, eds., *Mathematical Exploration in Behavioral Science* (Homewood, Ill.: Dorsey Press, 1965), for a supporting view.

from a variety of "target populations." For a general policy area, information from an exploratory survey could be sorted out by distinct groups, e.g., disaggregated by age cohort, geographic location, socioeconomic status, race, political affiliation, and so on; within the group, replies could be ordered according to the prevalence or intensity of the cited issues (see Figure 12–2).

FIGURE 12-2. PROBLEM-RECOGNITION SURVEYS: STEP 1

Groups

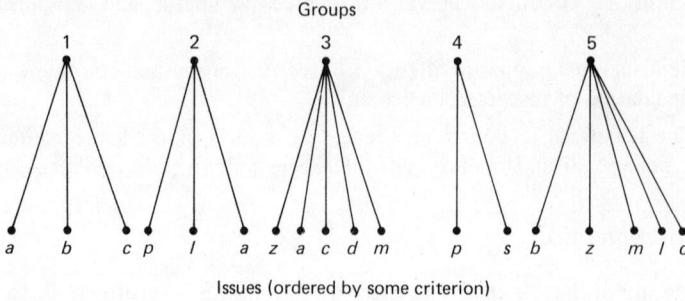

Issues (ordered by some criterion)

Any node with its attached branches defines the problem space for a group at a given time, e.g., $PS_{j,t}$, where the *problem set* (*PS*) is defined by those issues (*a,b,c,...z*) found to be most frequently and/or intensely held by a given group *j*, where $j = 1,2,3, ...n$, and stands for groups sharing a common set of characteristics.

At time $t = 0$, an initial survey is carried out primarily to establish a datum, or reference point, against which subsequent measurements may be compared. At some later time a resurvey is made to check the stability of datum or initial characterizations of groups and to calculate changes in the definition, ordering, and intensity of the issues ascribed to each group. Periodic additional surveys are made to verify the amended configurations and to measure the changes that occur over time. By splitting a sample into time phases, as is proposed, the imprecision of information generated in initial rounds is reduced over time as measurement sharpens and observations "flesh out" the groups sampled. More important, such a technique develops information about rates of change that is unobtainable in more conventional, single, cross-section samples. This information is likely to be useful also in assessing the affected groups' reactions to the outcomes of various policies implemented to reduce the problems identified and monitored by the surveys.

Reducing the Problem Space

The use of surveys as described above helps identify the portions of the problem space that are important for significant affected groups. Figure 12–3 illustrates how the surveys abstractly relate to institutional maps defining the

FIGURE 12-3. NARROWING THE PROBLEM SPACE BY PARTICIPANT SURVEY

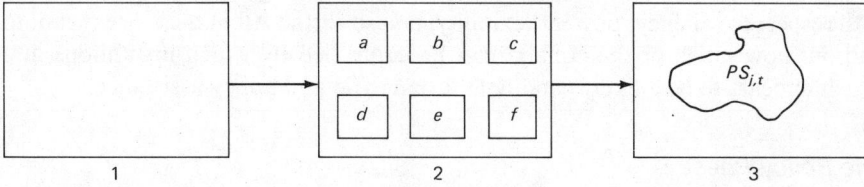

problem space. Block 1 is some roughly defined sector of society. For the sake of discussion, let us call it public safety in Malaysia. Moving right to Block 2 suggests that public safety in Malaysia is conceptually divisible: there are jails; courts; national, state, local, and private police forces; criminals, rehabilitation, and parole; welfare; and many other definable elements in the broad concept of public safety. The policy scientist's task is to locate the problem space adequately in the broader contextual map. Again, for discussion's sake, assume we are interested in crimes against persons (Box c in Block 2). Surveys of the type described would be instituted to determine how various groups in society viewed the general issue of personal crimes. Block 3 superimposes the problem set of Group j at time t on the field of personal crimes. Group differences are expected; for instance, rural Malays will probably differ from urban Chinese in their identification of a problem set, and both will likely change over time as levels of personal insecurity vary in response to events in the context.

The next task in mapping the context and reducing the problem space is to determine all institutions having responsibility for matters in each block, as shown in Figure 12-4.

FIGURE 12-4. INSTITUTIONAL RESPONSIBILITY
IN THE CONTEXTUAL MAP

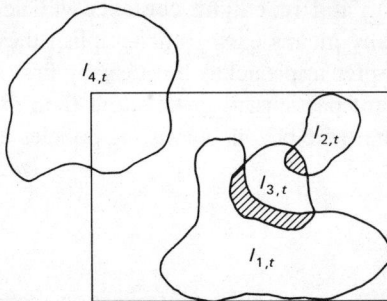

Besides providing clues as to functional overlaps, omissions, and contradictions, one obtains a picture of how many institutions are in fact responsible for policy in the specified context and which among them may be appropriate clients for the analysis. Questions that might be asked about each institution at this stage include: What are its resource constraints? How well can it manage the context, i.e., is it effective or not? Is there an ordering among all institutions with respect to saliency, power, flexibility, and so forth? All of these are meant to find out how much of the context can be controlled by which institutions and which appears to be a likely candidate for analytic and policy assistance.

The Policy Phase

After we have mapped out the context, identified participant groups, ordered and measured a range of problems, and characterized existing institutional responsibilites, the next step is to analyze the areas of overlap between problem sets and institutional responsibility (see Figure 12–5).

FIGURE 12-5. MATCHING PROBLEMS
AND INSTITUTIONS

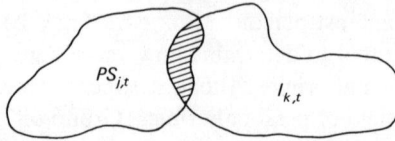

$PS_{j,t}$ $I_{k,t}$

Initially, this overlap points up an area where current problems and existing ameliorative policies match, and it may signal inadequacies in current policy or implementation procedures. In the future, new policy may be conceived of as means to increase the amount of overlap through time; to reduce the size of problem sets such as $PS_{j,t}$; or to orchestrate existing institutions to increase the overlapping area, refocus attention on aspects more important to the affected groups, or create new institutions where the old are inadequate.

Systematically narrowing and redefining contexts will be central tasks of future decision seminars. Many means exist to accomplish these purposes. The strategy proposed in this chapter approaches the task by first *surveying* to find out salient issues for important participant groups and then *identifying* institutional responsibilities to estimate the effects of existing policies and to suggest the needs for new policy.

Measurement and Display

A major constraint on this, or any other, information-management strategy is the present inadequacy of social measurement. As noted, both the Yale and SEADAG decision seminars concentrated on measurement development. They were partially able to differentiate and carefully reintegrate objective, subjective, and symbolic data sets; create data-base management procedures and software; and more effective and efficient means to portray data and analytic results.

Many social indicators and economic accounting schemes fail to make distinctions between fundamental qualitative differences in data:[36] decision seminars of the future should address this problem.

It is useful to make distinctions among objective, subjective and symbolic data. Each type is important for policy analysis, but the large discrepancies among them in precision, methods and costs of collection, and reliability ought to make the analyst wary about their indiscriminant recombination and un-qualified use. Engineering specialists refer to a "mismatch of impedances" in communication hardware, where a great deal of design skill is devoted to the specification and matching of components to balance a system and to avoid having signals distorted or destroyed. The analogy is appropriate.

The task is roughly this: to separate relatively "hard," precise, reliable in-formation, such as that compiled for a census of population or for economic accounting purposes, from moderately "soft," less precise and less reliable in-formation, such as that collected in public opinion surveys. More challenging yet is the need to assess the measurement and use of even "softer" symbolic and other data such as is found in newspapers, political speeches, and expert specula-tion on the future.[37]

Recombination and integration of different qualities of information are to some extent reducible to data-base management problems; however, the major differences among data types must not be overlooked or assumed away prior to the construction of indicator and data-management systems. The essential design requirements for such support systems are the following:

- They must be flexible. Premature "hardening" of data definitions and reducing pos-sibilities for reconfiguration are to be avoided.

- Because all policy contingencies cannot be anticipated, data must be kept in rel-atively "primitive" formats that may be easily recombined as problems or questions occur.

- Spatial considerations are important; data must be identified by location.

- Temporal considerations are important; data must be longitudinal to the greatest extent possible.

- Presentation and display are important; powerful graphical and other audio-visual output features must be part of the system.

Display: "A Picture Is Worth . . ."

In physics or astronomy, "hard" numbers and quantitative representations of research results and policy recommendations usually suffice. The audience for such information is typically small in number, shares a common orientation to the problems addressed, and, most important, is trained to converse in these

---

[36] Daniel Bell, "Toward a Social Report," *The Public Interest,* Vol. 15 (Spring 1969), pp. 98–105.

[37] We are not ignoring important—but even more speculative—classes of information, e.g., psychic, physiological, olfactory, and so on, still first things first.

technical languages. Such is not the case in the "softer" sciences, where information comes from a variety of sources in many different forms and in much disarray. Communication is not a trivial problem among the large number of "relevant participants" in social affairs. Deficiencies in communication are both serious and surprising:

- Detailed technical analyses are frequently condensed into one or a few summary indices.[38]

- Analyses are occasionally publicized by distinguished specialists in such a way that nonspecialists are asked to buy the results and the recommendations on faith alone.[39]

- Less frequently, efforts are made to translate results into consumable, easy-to-understand forms.[40]

The policy sciences have rather special data requirements. As compared with the physical sciences, they have more data of varying degrees of quality; less agreement and hence less certainty about which data to collect; a greater need to keep data in simple, easily reconfigured formats; and more complex problems in the communication of analyses, results, and recommendations. Two examples should help to characterize these matters and illustrate ways in which policy information might be communicated.

Pictured in Figure 12–6 is an envelope describing the maximum, minimum,

FIGURE 12-6. ENVELOPE DISPLAY OF INDEX VALUES FOR A GROUP

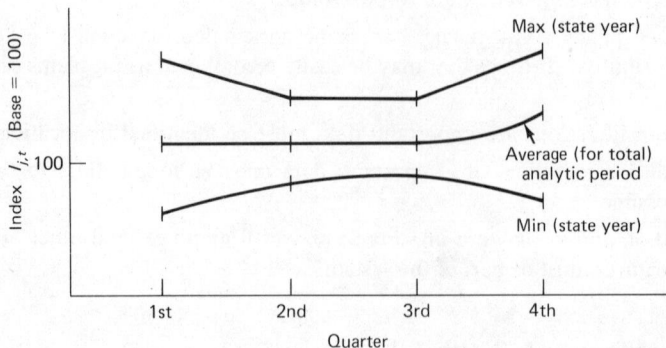

[38] Economic indices such as the consumer price index, inflation rate, and stock market average are good examples. Few, save a handful of technical specialists, really understand these indices although they receive much publicity.

[39] The "Coleman Report" on racial segregation in schools is a well-known, recent example. James S. Coleman et al., *Equality of Educational Opportunity, Report in Response to Section 402 of the Civil Rights Act of 1964* (Washington, D.C.: U.S. Department of Health, Education and Welfare, July 1966.)

[40] Jay Forrester's visceral sense has served him extremely well in this regard. Whatever the technical and theoretical deficiencies of his analysis of industry, cities, and the world, he has succeeded in capturing public attention. His extensive use of graphical outputs, "pretty pictures," ranks as a major reason.

and average values for an index I_j defined for a group $_j$, where index values are known to fluctuate periodically and where the group could be defined according to characterictics such as age, class, location, party affiliation, and so forth. Besides giving one a visual sense of whether or not "business is progressing as usual," such a scheme, kept up-to-date, shows the policymaker at a glance when current levels either exceed or undershoot past levels.

To the extent that expectations are not met, policy intervention may be called for. Because the index is disaggregated along several dimensions, intergroup distinctions are readily made. One can find out what people are pleased or discontent about, for example, equibility of distribution, and governmental performance. A decision seminar should collect and display such information as a routine matter of early warning and detection.

Longer term trends are somewhat more conventionally represented, as in Figure 12–7. Disaggregating the index according to groups j and time t enables

FIGURE 12-7. TREND INDICES FOR A GROUP

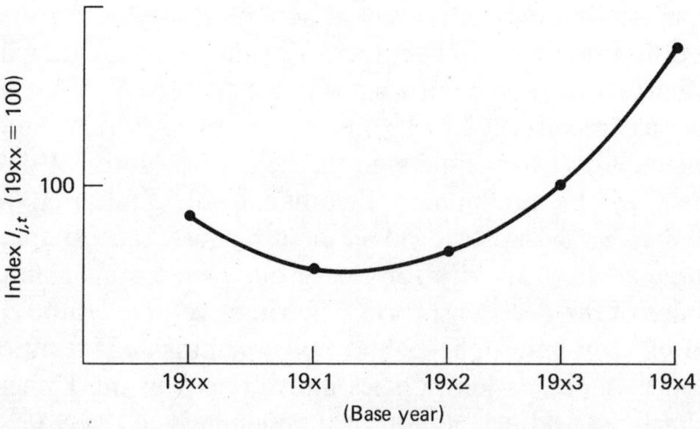

one to take the measure of such important policy matters as the location, age specificity, and class affiliation of those tending to polarize or coalesce on an issue. Combining information presented in Figure 12–6 with longer term matters summarized in this graph would help us sort out chronic from transient phenomena and, because the indices are specified by groups, might help us to understand more precisely for whom and where certain trends have what kinds of impacts. Because time is given as a standardizing measure, other indices may be superimposed to provide intergroup or other comparisons. Finally, this sort of display facilities, even encourages, simple extrapolations into the future.

A major technical bottleneck—data-base management—has nearly been overcome. Almendinger's pioneering work with the SPAN system has been cited,[41] and others are nearly as well developed.[42] Many, if not most, of the design

[41] See note 31 above. SPAN operates as an integral segment of a large regional information system project currently undergoing early design and implementation at DATUM e.V., Bonn-Bad Godesberg. This project and system are known by the acronym, ROLAND.

[42] The ADMINS system developed by Stuart McIntosh and associates at the Massachusetts Institute of Technology is one notable example.

requirements already noted are either contained in, or are well within the reach of, each of these systems. What remains is to begin the tedious but necessary process of implementation. A second, related technical problem has been well handled in the TROLL time-series data analysis package of routines developed at M.I.T., and in the BIOMOD programs recently completed by E. C. DeLand and associates at The Rand Corporation.[43] A third area of interest, graphics and display, has not been fully exploited, although the BIOMOD package, work recently completed at the Harvard Laboratory for Computer Graphics and Spatial Analysis, and other graphics activities are making strides.[44]

PROGNOSIS

These are all important items on the agenda of future decision seminars. As regards the prognosis for the decision seminar as an institution, let us consider current and prospective developments in several settings.

Four separate development-oriented activities suggest the emergence of a network of decision seminars. While the work is in progress and will be reported from time to time, let us sketch out what is going on. The Yale Development Decision Seminar has reconvened to begin the task of processing information on Argentina collected by two members in the field work during 1970–72. Besides extending some of the preliminary theoretical work reported by two other members,[45] the group hopes to produce better, more context-specific formulations. A complementary activity for this group will be an elaboration of the evaluation phase of the decision process. Substantive areas to be considered are a comparison of economic policies and policymaking in Argentina and Chile, and health and communication policies and services in the United States. The common background and orientation of the members of the Yale group should enable diverse substantive interests to be represented under a directorate that is in intellectual and professional accord. A large working bibliography and a

[43] BIOMOD is a very elegant, operational, interactive computer-graphics system. See G. F. Groner et al., *BIOMOD: A User's View of an Interactive Computer System for Biological Modeling* (A Preliminary Report) (Santa Monica, Cal.: The Rand Corporation, RM–6327–NIH, August 1970); G. F. Groner, R. L. Clark, R. A. Berman, and E. C. DeLand, *BIOMOD: An Interactive Computer Graphics System for Modeling* (Santa Monica, Cal.: The Rand Corporation, R–617–NIH, July 1971); and G. A. Beckey and E. C. DeLand, *Interactive Simulation of Continuous Systems: Progress and Prospects* (Santa Monica, Cal.: The Rand Corporation, P–4503, January 1971).

[44] See Keith W. Uncapher, *The Rand Video Graphic System—An Approach to the General User—Computer Graphic Communication System* (Santa Monica, Cal.: The Rand Corporation, R–753–ARPA, April 1971); T. O. Ellis, J. F. Heafner, and W. L. Sibley, "The GRAIL Project: An Experiment in Man-Machine Communication," *Proceedings of the Society for Information Display*, Vol. 11, No. 3 (Third Quarter, 1970), pp. 121–29; H. B. Baskin and S. P. Morse, "A Multilevel Modeling Structure for Interactive Graphic Design," *IBM Systems Journal*, Vol. 7, Nos. 3 and 4 (1968); and Richard Saul Wurman, *Making the City Observable: Design Quarterly 80* (Cambridge, Mass.: The MIT Press, 1971).

[45] Brunner and Brewer, *Organized Complexity*.

software system have been developed to manage the group's reference literature, and plans are underway to implement the BIBLIO system on the Michigan MTS computational system.

Ann Arbor is the proposed site for two decision seminars.[46] The staff of the University of Michigan's Institute of Public Policy Studies is setting up the facilities and procedures for an effort that will involve official and citizen participation, student training, development of comprehensive maps and charts of the Ann Arbor policy environment, and faculty contributions in local problem-solving and policymaking.

The second Ann Arbor initiative is still being planned and will capitalize on the experiences deriving from the first effort. Emphasizing research, it is expected to concentrate the attention of faculty and policymakers on decision-making and the U.S. federal budget, both research interests of several University of Michigan staff members.

In the summer of 1972, a German-sponsored decision seminar located at DATUM e.V., Bonn-Bad Godesberg, was begun. Participants in the planning and early development stages included representatives from the Yale and Ann Arbor groups, DATUM professional staff members, and several German officials. The seminar will focus on the elaboration and integration of objective, subjective, and symbolic time-series data.[47] the comparative examination of policies on pollution, housing, and bureaucratic decisionmaking;[48] the construction of social indicators of the German quality of life;[49] and electoral and party behavior.

The decision seminar as a means of dealing with complex sociopolitical issues is on the point of bearing real fruit, as a "critical mass" of competent and committed professionals is being approached. The problems being scrutinized are diverse and important. Technical constraints on data availablitiy, management, and display that impeded earlier decision seminars have been, or are being, resolved. Theoretical and conceptual problems remain, although work is in progress to solve many of them; at least, many appropriate questions are being raised, and people are beginning to become aware of the type and magnitude of the limitations. Funding resources are beginning to flow in support of the undertakings. The decision seminar's time appears to have arrived and with it the vision of a truly contextual, problem-oriented, policy science.

---

[46] Ronald D. Brunner, *The Ann Arbor Decision Seminar: A Summary* (Ann Arbor, Mich.: Institute of Public Policy Studies, May 1972).

[47] DATUM-infas has collected public opinion data throughout Germany on a monthly basis since the late 1950's; official German agencies maintain comprehensive statistics; and work is underway to monitor the German press using a version of the General Inquirer content analysis routines.

[48] Under the auspices of the James K. Pollock Research Program.

[49] A series of meetings was held in June 1972 with German officials. Preliminary indications are excellent that substantial government support and individual participation will be forthcoming.

Chapter 13
A Modern Statistical Approach to Model Assessment

D O N A L D   A .   B E R R Y

Everyone distorts or dismembers reality in the process of selecting and abstracting for the purposes of constructing theoretical and quantitative models. Taking a cue from several elementary ideas underlying the philosophy and practice of statistics —especially of the Bayesian variety—this chapter raises and begins to answer questions such as when does the distortion in a model exceed acceptable limits, how does one compare and evaluate alternative models—and the methods used to construct them, how much information is "enough," and what difference does repeated observation make for model development, use, and acceptability? Numerous easy-to-understand examples are provided to characterize and illustrate these matters. The overriding theme and basic argument of the chapter is that models or sets of models can and should be discarded as new information is collected and new empirical questions present themselves for solution.

INTRODUCTION

A central concept of scientific endeavor is the use of mathematical models (or, theories) to describe processes, be they physical, chemical, biological, or social. No mathematical model can precisely describe any such process. The scientist visualizes an *ideal* process that can be so described and that reasonably approximates the unknown *actual* process. Doing the mathematics in the *ideal* enables him to draw inferences about the *actual*. He can act as though there were no difference between the ideal and the actual, and for some kinds of actions this is appropriate. Typically, however, the inferences depend in a substantial way on this difference.

He may consider part of this difference explicitly by appending an "error term" to his model and making an assumption about the probabilistic form of the "error." For example, he may suspect that the very many variables not explicitly considered, but that nevertheless affect the process, add together in such a way that no small subset (for example, one) of the variables dominates the others. When stated slightly more rigorously, this justifies—according to the central limit theorem of probability—the assumption implicit in regression analysis, etc., that observational error (where the actual process is observed and compared with an ideal) behaves according to the normal, or Gaussian, probability distribution. He may be able, and certainly should want, to examine the validity of his assumptions by making scatter plots, for example. He may also be able to relax his assumptions. In the case of regression analysis, Anscombe (1967) does this by treating error as having a Student t distribution. This is a genuine relaxation since it includes the normal assumption as a special case.

Of course, any assumption about the error term may be far from the truth, and error may be present in other than an additive way. Regardless of the form of his error assumption, the scientist can never be certain that his model adequately reflects reality. In this respect, however, a deterministic, or nonstochastic, model is essentially different from a stochastic model, one in which one or more of the variables (the error term, for example) has a probability distribution. For a deterministic model, the first few observations will indicate that the model is not precisely correct. For a stochastic model, no finite amount of observation can counterindicate the model—unless the assumed distributions assign probability zero to possible outcomes. Be that as it may, one stochastic model may be indicated by data over other stochastic models. Considering a wider class of models in order to make inferences based on the model or subclass of models indicated by data is essentially the same as relaxing the assumptions of the model.

A central point made in this chapter is that the *only* way a stochastic model can be indicated or counterindicated using empirical evidence is by comparing it to other models. To fulfill this purpose, let us introduce the concept of a *model universe*, or more simply, *universe*. With each process the scientist associates a universe that includes all the models he wishes to consider. Therefore, a universe is itself a model, and as such it cannot be indicated or counterindicated except by comparing it to other models or universes. We can increase relative confidence in a universe by increasing the number of models it includes, but a universe cannot logically encompass every possible model. This limitation must be lived with (see Halmos, 1960, p. 6, for a discussion of the logical existence of a "universe"). (In treatises on probability, what we call a *universe* is called a *sample space*; for this reason, "model space" may be more suggestive to some readers than "model universe.")

The logic of the indication process for stochastic models is the concern of statistics, where the probabilistic nature of the universe is used to associate probabilities with the "correctness" of the component models. Deterministic models do not lend themselves to this kind of analysis (or to any scientific indication process), except when one or more variables are suitably "stochasticized." The following two sections of this chapter describe and illustrate the process of statistical reasoning as it relates to the social scientist. The purpose of these sections is not to present and compare the statistical and quasi-statistical methods used by social scientists; for the interested reader there are people who do this—Alker (1969), Dollar and Jensen (1971), Kossack (1966), and Morrison (1967), among others. Rather, a purpose is to provide the reader with some ability to compare statistical methods and models for himself. Social scientists who use statistics or statistical methods should now and then be exposed to statistical philosophy; these two sections will provide such an exposure.

The chapter is intended for statistically unsophisticated readers (except perhaps for Example 5), but mathematical examples are inevitable. The approach taken in the second and third sections will be new to many readers, even some of the most quantitatively inclined readers. Sets of examples will, therefore, be given which are somewhat redundant. These sections can serve as an introduction to a different kind of statistical thinking than most texts present, one that is intuitively appealing, and, I think, more relevant than the older kind. There is, or at least there should be, the feeling that this older kind of statistics is complicated and statisticians come up with numbers that are not easy to understand (but are used nonetheless). I point to "significance level" and "sizes of errors of Types I and II" as examples. This state of affairs is sad because it is unnecessary.

A word of caution about using statistics and statisticians is in order here. Two statisticians can easily view the same problem in two different ways. Individual statisticians (and scientists in general) are better equipped in certain directions than in others and tend to fit problems into molds that they best understand. A consulting statistician who is an expert in rank order statistics has been heard to say: "Amazing, I've seen ten problems in rank order statistics so far this week!" Anyone who uses the services of a statistician should be careful to ask the questions to which he is interested in answers, and not those which the statistician is best prepared to answer. Not so doing has made life relatively easy for some statisticians. They teach courses and write textbooks that indoctrinate their prospective clients into thinking that the most natural kind of statistical question to ask is: "How do I test the hypothesis that . . . ?" I have never heard such a question that did not seem more contrived than natural. What the client usually wants to ask is: "What is the probability that this hypothesis is true on the basis of the following evidence?"—a question that a test of the hypothesis does not address, though some clients think it does. Given such widespread indoctrination, a statistician can live a successful professional life knowing only how to test hypotheses (which may not make for an easy life since testing hypotheses can involve very sophisticated mathematics). If his client does not formulate precise questions, the hypothesis tester can always answer by testing a hypothesis, one of his own.

The fourth section addresses a different kind of question, and does so in a different way. Suppose that no model of any kind is assumed, can anything be done, and if so, what? The approach is one of "just looking," looking for something in the data which might indicate the nature of the actual process. Two increasingly popular methods of "just looking" will be described and illustrated by example.

STATISTICAL REASONING

In my view, statistical reasoning uses available information to assess the validity of a statement (or hypothesis) by assigning a probability, or measure of truth, to it. Statistics indicates how that assessment changes as information accrues. In a sense, it says how quantitative learning takes place under uncertainty. For example, we suspect that a coin that has just been tossed five times yielding five heads is not a fair coin. The probability that a fair coin would show five heads in any five independent tosses is $1/32$. There is a nonsensical tendency to say that $1/32$ is the probability that the coin is a fair coin, a tendency that lives in the hearts of some statisticians and nonstatisticians alike. The probability that the coin is fair is of course related to the evidence at hand (a relationship given by Bayes's theorem), but the problem cannot be addressed unless alternative hypotheses (or models) are specified.

Bayes's theorem is an immediate consequence of the definition of conditional probability and is the essential tool of statistics. (Most statisticians will dispute the latter point, in part because it represents such a simple-minded— but not narrow-minded—view of statistics.) Stated simply, the theorem says that the probability that any statement is true given some new evidence E is proportional to the probability that it was considered true before obtaining E times the probability that E would obtain if the statement were true. [Bayes's theorem pushes many authors to a personalistic view of probability, for example, Edwards et al. (1963). The point is that if the probability that a hypothesis is true or that a model is valid is desired, then Bayes's theorem must be applied and, therefore, "prior" probabilities assessed.]

In the above example, suppose that prior to tossing a coin we consider it to be fair with probability .95 and, say, two-headed with probability .05. Given the new evidence, the probability that the coin is fair is proportional to $(.95)(1/32)$ and the probability that the coin is two-headed is proportional to $(.05)(1)$; since the corresponding probabilities must sum to 1 they are approximately .37 and .63, changed from .95 and .05. In this example the model universe consists of two models: (1) the coin is fair, and (2) the coin is two-headed. The output of Bayes's theorem is a "posterior" probability assessment of the truth of the individual models.

In general, let U be a model universe and M_i an individual model in U. Assume temporarily that U contains a finite (or a countably infinite) number of models. The probability that model M_i is the correct model, given that the correct model is in U, is $P[M_i|U]$ or, more briefly, $P[M_i]$—the *prior probability* of M_i. $P[E|M_i]$ is the *likelihood function* of M_i, the probability that model M_i would produce evidence E if it were the correct model. The probability that model M_i is the correct model given evidence E and given that the correct model is in U is $P[M_i|E, U]$, or more briefly, $P[M_i|E]$—the *posterior probability* of M_i. We can now state Bayes's theorem formally:

$$P[M_i|E] = KP[E|M_i]P[M_i], \qquad (13\text{--}1)$$

where K is determined by the requirement that the total probability be 1; that is,

$$K^{-1} = P[E|M_1]P[M_1] + P[E|M_2]P[M_2] + \ldots$$

Example 1

To illustrate the use of formula (13–1), consider an election between two candidates, a Republican and a Democrat. Suppose that it is known before the election that the winner will receive 60% of the votes, each has the same chance of winning, but it is not known which candidate will emerge victorious. (This is certainly artificial and is used for illustration only—a more realistic supposition will be made shortly. It is, however, more complicated than the coin example.) A random sample of seven people is selected from the electorate and polled for candidate preferences. (While assuming that the sample is random makes theoretical treatment easy, to sample without some bias is impossible in actuality; more about the effects of this assumption later.) Suppose that five of the people polled prefer the Republican and two prefer the Democrat. What do we conclude about the Republican's chances? Let p denote the proportion of the vote the Republican will receive: according to our assumptions p has only two possible values—.4 and .6—each of which corresponds to a model in our universe. According to Bayes's theorem, the probability that p is .4 conditional on evidence E, five of seven prefer the Republican, is

$$P[p = .4 \mid E] = KP[E \mid p = .4] \, P[p = .4]. \tag{13–2}$$

In equation (13–2), K is a constant which does not depend on p; $P[E \mid p = .4]$ is the probability that $p = .4$ would generate evidence E and is given by the binomial probability function; and $P[p = .4]$ is the probability that $p = .4$ using evidence other than E. The latter is 1/2 since the candidates are deemed to have equal chances a priori. Evaluating (13–2) we find:

$$P[p = .4 \mid E] = K \frac{7!}{5! \, 2!} (.4)^5(.6)^2(1/2) = .0387K.$$

Likewise, the probability that p is .6 given evidence E is

$$P[p = .6 \mid E] = KP[E \mid p = .6]P[p = .6]$$

$$= K \frac{7!}{5! \, 2!} (.6)^5(.4)^2(1/2) = .1306K.$$

The constant K can be found easily since the total probability must be 1:

$$K = \frac{1}{.0387 + .1306} = 5.905.$$

Therefore, the (posterior) probability of a Republican victory, of the Republican receiving 60% of the vote, is .77, increased from .50. A larger sample which generates evidence E', say, will likely make $P[p = .6 \mid E']$ either close to

0 or close to 1, in the sense that the probability of any value other than 0 or 1 decreases to zero as the sample size increases. On the other hand, a model in which we can be 77% confident may be sufficient for our purposes.

Example 2

As a further illustration, consider a continuous version of Example 1— now any value of p between 0 and 1 is possible. (Readers who have not been introduced to probability density functions can skip this example without loss of continuity.) Each value of p corresponds to a different model. Suppose that before a poll is taken we consider values of p between .4 and .5 more likely than other values (it may be that in recent elections an average of 45% of the electorate voted Republican and the current election is not obviously different from recent elections), though values of p markedly different should be entertained. This thinking can be quantified into a (prior) probability density function $f(p)$; Figure 13–1 shows the graph of one possible $f(p)$. This $f(p)$ means that, for example, we regard the probability that the Republican wins to be:

$$P[p > .5] = \int_{.5}^{1} f(p)dp \doteq .35.$$

In order to be mathematically precise suppose that

$$f(p) = Cp^9(1 - p)^{11}, \qquad \text{for } 0 < p < 1, \tag{13-3}$$

(a so-called beta density function) where C is independent of p and serves only to ensure that the total probability is 1. $f(p)$ given in (13–3) coincides closely with the graph in Figure 13–1.

Suppose that a random sample of 100 people are polled, and 60 are found to prefer the Republican candidate. Letting E now denote this evidence, and modifying $f(p)$ by E, we obtain the posterior probability density function of p:

$$g(p \mid E) = KP[E \mid p]f(p), \tag{13-4}$$

FIGURE 13-1.

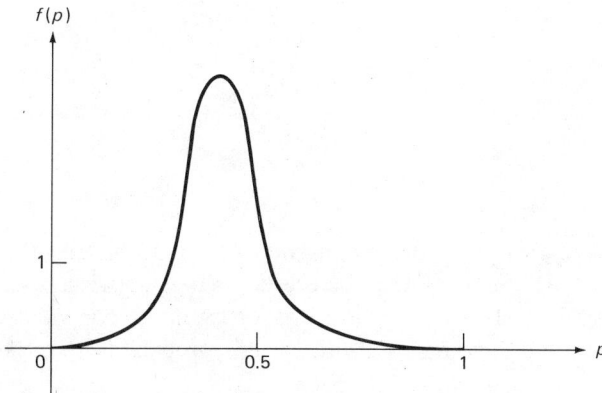

which is the continuous version of (13–1). In equation (13–4), K is a constant determined by the condition that

$$\int_0^1 g(p \mid E)dp = 1;$$

$P[E \mid p]$ is the probability that a particular p would generate evidence E—the likelihood function of p—and $f(p)$ is given by (13–3). As in the previous example, the likelihood function is given by the binomial probability function, so that (13–4) becomes

$$g(p \mid E) = Kp^{60}(1 - p)^{40}p^9(1 - p)^{11} = Kp^{69}(1 - p)^{51}, \qquad \text{for } 0 < p < 1.$$
$$(13\text{–}5)$$

It happens that $K = 121!/(69!51!)$. The graph of $g(p \mid E)$ is shown in Figure 13–2.

Comparing $g(p \mid E)$ with $f(p)$ indicates how the poll has affected our assessment of the individual models. Now we expect the Republican to receive about $70/122 = 57.4\%$ of the vote (the posterior expected value of p) and, more important, to win the election; the probability he wins is

$$P[p > .5 \mid E] = K \int_{.5}^1 p^{69}(1 - p)^{51}dp \doteq .91. \qquad (13\text{–}6)$$

This conclusion rests strongly on the assumption that the sample is random.

FIGURE 13-2.

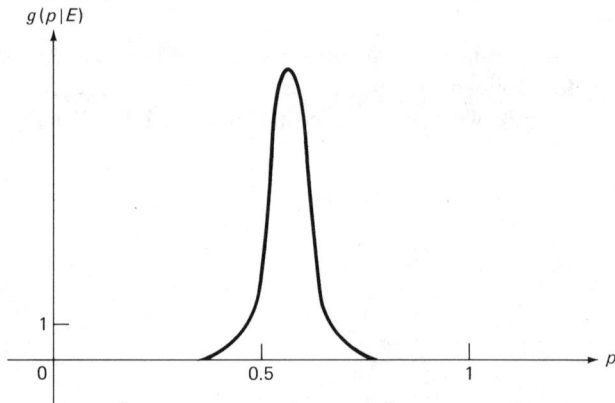

We had some idea prior to sampling that we would be led to a conclusion as strong as (13–6). Suppose that before sampling we wished to assess the effect that a sample of 100 would have on, for example, our ability to predict the winner. We would have required the (prior) probability that the candidate indicated to be the favorite (on the basis of our total information) would actually win; that is, the expected value of

$$\max \{P[p < .5 \mid E], P[p > .5 \mid E]\} = \max \left\{ \int_0^{.5} g(p \mid E)dp, \int_{.5}^1 g(p \mid E)dp \right\},$$

averaging over the possible states of evidence E. The mathematically inclined reader may wish to verify that the answer is

$$\frac{21!}{9! \, 11!} \left[\int_0^{.5} p^9(1 - p)^{11} \sum_{r=0}^{51} \frac{100!}{r! \, (100 - r)!} p^r(1 - p)^{100-r}dp \right.$$

$$\left. + \int_{.5}^1 p^9(1 - p)^{11} \sum_{r=52}^{100} \frac{100!}{r! \, (100 - r)!} p^r(1 - p)^{100-r}dp \right] \doteq .85,$$

indicating that our prediction will likely be right, though the number .91 given by (13–6) is a little larger than expected.

For the purpose of predicting a winner, a smaller sample may be sufficient or a larger sample may be required. If a one-time sample is to be taken, an optimal sample size can easily be found as a function of the costs (in time and resources) of sampling and of making a wrong prediction. Such problems are part of the realm of statistical decision theory not discussed further in this chapter. See Raiffa and Schlaifer (1961), for example, for such a discussion.

Discussion of Examples 1 and 2

In discussing the foregoing examples we asked questions that are somewhat tangential to our central purpose: we are primarily concerned with the role of a model—or more precisely, a model universe—in statistical analysis. The examples are particularly simple ones, but they indicate how *all* statistical reasoning takes place: a universe is specified and assessments of the validity of the component models change according to Bayes's theorem. The examples allow us to investigate more fully the character of a particular universe and the problems involved in selecting a universe.

The universe in Examples 1 and 2 is binomial, which is to say that the individual models are binomial and indexed by a value of p—we could not specify a more detailed class of models in the binomial universe. The two models in Example 1 have $p = .4$ and $p = .6$; each of the uncountable number of models in Example 2 is associated with a different value of p between 0 and 1. The following set of assumptions would justify using such a universe: (1) the sample is a true sample of the voting population, so that everyone in the sample will vote; (2) everyone in the sample prefers either the Republican or the Democrat, specifies which, and will vote accordingly; (3) the sampling is random, that is, every possible subset of the voting population having the same size as the sample could equally well have been selected; and (4) the fact that a person is in the sample does not influence his preference.

It would be nice, of course, to be able to relax some of these assumptions, and theoretically we can. For example, if we suspect that some people lie about their preferred candidate, violating assumption 2, then we could introduce this possibility into our universe. If we do not have some way of checking up on some of the people in the sample (by taking a sample within the sample, say, and exposing them to more intensive questioning) to get some additional idea of how many are lying (and who they are), our prior assessment of this effect would have to carry the day. In the latter case, unless we know either that everyone is lying or that everyone is telling the truth, the sample will provide less information than otherwise. In the other extreme, if our prior probability on the proportion of people lying is distributed symmetrically about 1/2, then the sample may have no information value whatever. (Actually, the issue is complicated by all sorts of interactions, but there are situations when it would be wise to sample even though it is known that half of the population are liars.) In practice, when a sample is suspected of badly violating one of the above assumptions the sample is usually discarded, which may be more efficient than trying to extract from it something of value.

The validity of the universe can clearly affect the validity of the conclusions. It is now generally recognized that most of the polls taken before the Truman–Dewey election in 1948 were not based on random samples, thereby violating assumption 3. Most pollsters had unconsciously sampled too little from large segments of the voting population that overwhelmingly preferred Truman, causing themselves eventual embarrassment and dealing the profession a blow from which it still has not recovered.

It is easy to see from Bayes's theorem that the validity of a universe is independent of prior information, but the validity of conclusions depends directly on the quality of prior information. As long as the prior assessment reflects some degree of openmindedness, conclusions will likely be valid if the universe is no more than mildly incorrect (see Edwards et al., 1963, for an analysis of the effect of prior distributions that reflect "openmindedness"). If, however, the universe is wildly incorrect, they will likely be valid only if they are deemed sufficiently reasonable a priori.

INDICATING (SELECTING) MODELS AND SETS OF MODELS

Suppose that a universe is specified and that one particular model in that universe is to be selected for some special purpose. Naturally, the model which should be selected depends on this purpose. (See the subject of estimation in statistics texts.) If it is desired that the model be that which is most likely correct (relatively speaking) on the basis of the data and other information, then the model that maximizes the posterior probability function should be selected. Using this selection criterion in Example 1, the indicated model would be binomial with parameter $p = .6$, since $P[p = .6 \mid E] = .77$, while $P[p = .4 \mid E] = .23$. In Example 2, the indicated model would be binomial with parameter

$p = 59/120 \doteq .558$, since this value maximizes (13–5). Though it is appropriate only for the stated purpose, this criterion will be used in this section, thus trading generality for simplicity.

A related approach to model selection, which is particularly important historically, is provided by *maximum likelihood estimation*; the indicated model is the one most likely to have produced the data—the likelihood function is the only selection indicator. In Example 1, the maximum likelihood value of p is .6, since $P[E \mid p = .6] = .2612$, while $P[E \mid p = .4] = .0774$. In Example 2, the maximum likelihood value of p is again .6, since this value of p maximizes $p^{60} (1 - p)^{40}$.

These related approaches, maximizing the posterior probability distribution and maximizing the likelihood function, indicate different models in general since posterior probabilities depend on prior probabilities and the likelihood function does not. However, they indicate the same model when prior probability is distributed uniformly among the various models; that is, when the individual models are considered equally likely a priori. In order to be general we would not want to assume a particular prior distribution; nevertheless, it would be a pity not to be able to draw on the enormous literature which deals with the maximum likelihood method. Therefore, uniform prior distributions will be assumed in most of the remainder of this section. An additional advantage of this assumption is that the maximum likelihood method is undoubtedly familiar to many readers. In his own problem the reader would use whatever prior distribution is appropriate.

Most of the remainder of this section will be concerned with relating two particular universes, those of Examples 3 and 4.

Example 3

As an example process, consider the growth of the population of the United States since 1790, which is shown in Table 13–1. As a model (more accurately,

TABLE 13–1.   THE POPULATION OF THE UNITED STATES[a]

Year	Population	Year	Population
1790	3,929	1890	62,980
1800	5,308	1900	76,212
1810	7,240	1910	92,228
1820	9,638	1920	106,022
1830	12,866	1930	123,203
1840	17,069	1940	132,288
1850	23,192	1950	151,718
1860	31,443	1960	180,007
1870	39,818	1970	208,615[b]
1880	50,189		

SOURCE: *1970 World Almanac.*
[a] Population is given in thousands.
[b] Estimated.

a model universe) of this process, suppose that population increases exponentially, with a constant but unknown rate of increase. Letting $X(t)$ denote the population of the United States at time t, for $t = 1790, 1800, \ldots, 1970$, we propose that

$$X(t) = \alpha \exp(\beta t), \qquad (13\text{–}7)$$

for (unknown) positive constants α and β. The universe specified by (13–7) is deterministic, the individual models indexed by the pair (α, β). Suppose further that error enters multiplicatively in our model by way of a positive random variable $\varepsilon(t)$ thus:

$$X(t) = \alpha \exp(\beta t) \, \varepsilon(t), \qquad (13\text{–}8)$$

or equivalently:

$$\log X(t) = \log \alpha + \beta t + \log \varepsilon(t).$$

For a complete specification of the universe we need to say how $\varepsilon(t)$ is distributed. Assume that $\log \varepsilon(t)$ is normally distributed (i.e., $\varepsilon(t)$ is log-normally distributed) with zero mean and constant variance, and that the values of $\varepsilon(t)$ are independent. Strictly speaking, this variance is another parameter to worry about, but we shall ignore it whenever we can. We will eventually examine this universe; our immediate objective is to use our criterion to select a model from the universe.

Implicit in what has been said thus far is that we are interested in a model for population growth and not one for predicting U.S. population in the year 2000, say. If we were interested in the latter we would surely make some effort to ensure at least that for the α and β we settle on

$$X(1970) = \alpha \exp(1970 \, \beta),$$

so that our model would agree with the latest information.

It is well known that the maximum likelihood values $\hat{\alpha}$ and $\hat{\beta}$ of α and β are the least squares estimates (regression coefficients), those which minimize

$$\sum_{t=1790}^{1970} (\log X(t) - \log \alpha - \beta t)^2,$$

where the summation is over ten-year intervals. The values

$$X(t) = \hat{\alpha} \exp(\hat{\beta} t) = \exp(-24.170 + .02216t) \qquad (13\text{–}9)$$

are the *fitted values* of $X(t)$. $X(t)$ and $\hat{X}(t)$ (along with values for a model not yet discussed) are compared in Table 13–2.

Discussion.   In Example 3 we found the best model (by our criterion) in the model universe under consideration, the model which comes closest to explaining the actual process $X(t)$ under the stated assumptions. We may be satisfied with the specified universe, and therefore, with the model given by (13–9); it would be foolish not to ask ourselves if we are satisfied. However,

TABLE 13–2.   COMPARISON OF $X(t)$, $\hat{X}(t)$, and $\hat{X}'(t)$[a]

t	$\hat{X}(t)$	$X(t)$	$\hat{X}'(t)$
1790	5,370	3,929	10,593
1800	6,702	5,308	12,518
1810	8,364	7,240	14,794
1820	10,439	9,638	17,484
1830	13,029	12,866	20,662
1840	16,261	17,069	24,419
1850	20,294	23,192	28,858
1860	25,329	31,443	34,104
1870	31,612	39,818	40,305
1880	39,454	50,189	47,632
1890	49,241	62,980	56,292
1900	61,455	76,212	66,525
1910	76,700	92,228	78,620
1920	95,727	106,022	92,913
1930	119,473	123,203	109,805
1940	149,110	132,288	129,767
1950	186,099	141,718	153,358
1960	232,263	180,007	181,238
1970	289,879	208,615	214,187

[a] In thousands.

it is much more likely that we will look at Table 13–2 and wonder if we went astray, if we were deluded into thinking that our model universe was comprehensive. Of course, it should not be rejected out of hand, it should instead be enlarged or compared with other universes that are deemed reasonable a priori; that is, those which could be endowed with some prior probability. We will return shortly to this point and to relate Example 3 to the next example.

Example 4

Consider again the population growth of the United States given in Table 13–1. Suppose again that population increases exponentially according to (13–7), but now error is assumed to enter additively by way of $\varepsilon'(t)$, thus:

$$X(t) = \alpha \exp(\beta t) + \varepsilon'(t), \qquad (13\text{–}10)$$

where the $\varepsilon'(t)$ are normally distributed with zero mean and constant variance and are independent.

This example differs from the last in a pragmatic way: the maximum likelihood values of α and β cannot be found easily since differentiating the likelihood function leads to equations that cannot be solved explicitly. Oliver (1970) describes an iterative solution and cites references for its derivation. I used a different iteration (which I do not advertise because it converges too slowly to be of much use) to obtain the fitted values

$$\hat{X}'(t) = \hat{\alpha}' \exp(\hat{\beta}' t) = \exp(-13.718 + .01670t). \qquad (13\text{–}11)$$

$X(t)$ and $\hat{X}'(t)$ are compared in Table 13–2.

Examples 3 and 4 Discussed

In each of these two examples we reduced a model universe to just one model, $\hat{X}(t)$ and $\hat{X}'(t)$. Each universe is a model of the same process; how do the universes compare? The answer may provide a basis for deciding between $\hat{X}(t)$ and $\hat{X}'(t)$. It may lead also to a new and "better" model, but for now we confine our attention to $\hat{X}(t)$ and $\hat{X}'(t)$.

On examining Table 13–2 it is not too difficult to favor $\hat{X}'(t)$ as a model of U.S. population growth. However, I took considerable liberty in comparing the models in terms of "population" instead of "log population." Had I done the latter, $\hat{X}(t)$ would of course look better than $\hat{X}'(t)$. It should be clear that if one is predicting and interested in getting "close" to population and has to choose between $\hat{X}(t)$ and $\hat{X}'(t)$ he should choose the latter, whereas if he is interested in getting "close" to log population he should choose the former. An important question is: Does $\hat{X}'(t)$ look as bad in the universe of Example 3 as does $\hat{X}(t)$ in the universe of Example 4? Since this question is too loose to have a definite answer in its present form, consider instead the following tighter formulation.

Let U and U' denote the universes of Examples 3 and 4, and let U_0 and U_0' modify them in the following way. U_0 contains only the two models $\hat{X}(t)\,\varepsilon(t)$ and $\hat{X}'(t)\,\varepsilon(t)$; and U_0' contains only the two models $\hat{X}(t) + \varepsilon'(t)$ and $\hat{X}'(t) + \varepsilon'(t)$, where $\varepsilon(t)$ and $\varepsilon'(t)$ are as defined earlier. Assume that (the prior conditional probabilities) $P[X(t) = \hat{X}(t)\,\varepsilon(t) \mid X(t) \text{ in } U_0] = P[X(t) = \hat{X}(t) + \varepsilon(t) \mid X(t) \text{ in } U_0'] = 1/2$, so that the candidate models are equally likely in both U_0 and U_0'. If U_0 is the correct universe, then (sparing the details and using maximum likelihood estimates for relevant variances) the posterior probability of $\hat{X}'(t)$ is

$$P[X(t) = \hat{X}'(t)\,\varepsilon(t) \mid X(t) \text{ in } U_0, \text{data}] \doteq e^{-32} \doteq 10^{-14};$$

and if U_0' is the correct universe, then the posterior probability of $\hat{X}(t)$ is

$$P[X(t) = \hat{X}(t) + \varepsilon'(t) \mid X(t) \text{ in } U_0', \text{data}] \doteq e^{-92} \doteq 10^{-40}.$$

Of course, in each case the other model has the remainder of the probability. The latter number reflects the apparent inappropriateness of $\hat{X}(t)$ in U' (cf. Table 13–2), while $\hat{X}'(t)$ is not quite as inappropriate in U.

The magnitude of these two probabilities suggests the incompatibility of U and U': any model—specified by a pair (α, β)—which is reasonably likely in one universe is extremely unlikely in the other. If $(X(t) \text{ in } U)$ and $(X(t) \text{ in } U')$ are deemed equally likely a priori and if the relevant priors are uniform, then the point of maximum posterior probability in this combined universe occurs at $\hat{X}'(t)$, so it would be selected according to our criterion. (I do not mean that this is obvious, only that it is true.) Before concluding that something is special about either $\hat{X}'(t)$ or U' it should be remembered that our criterion was chosen more for convenience than relevance. Other criteria will usually lead to a different model, typically one between $\hat{X}(t)$ and $\hat{X}'(t)$. One such criterion is the one which selects the model corresponding to the expected value of the posterior distribution, a more relevant criterion for most purposes.

What is, or should be, of interest to the scientist are the posterior probabilities of $(X(t)$ in $U)$ and $(X(t)$ in $U')$. In light of the incompatibility of U and U' these are about the same as the corresponding prior probabilities (for most priors on α, β, and the relevant variances). This phenomenon occurs quite frequently, even though seemingly sufficient evidence is at hand to indicate the correct model, and is usually disconcerting until it is realized that none of the candidate models (or universes) is correct. For the examples under discussion this is most dramatically seen by making plots of the residuals $\log X(t) - \log \hat{X}(t)$ and $X(t) - \hat{X}'(t)$ as is done in Figure 13–3. Each of the corresponding error terms $\log \varepsilon(t)$ and $\varepsilon'(t)$ was supposed, as part of the respective universe, to be normal and the errors *independent* for any two (or more) values of t. On the basis of Figure 13–3 this assumption is difficult to accept for either error term; the errors seem too systematic, as any measure of serial correlation would belie.

FIGURE 13–3. PLOTS OF LOG $X(t)$ — LOG $\hat{X}(t)$
AND $X(t) - \hat{X}'(t)^a$

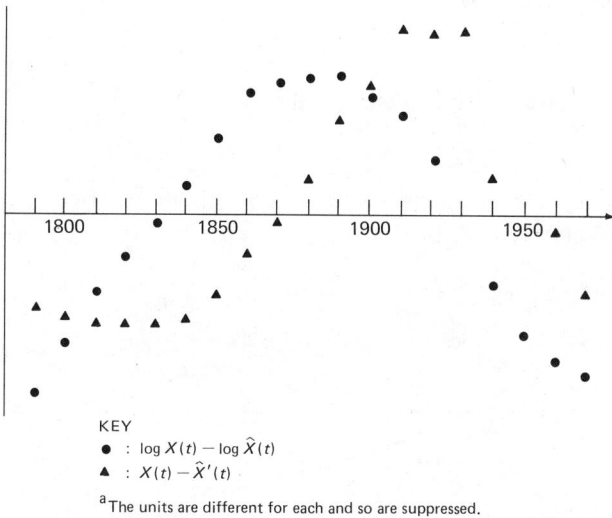

KEY
● : $\log X(t) - \log \hat{X}(t)$
▲ : $X(t) - \hat{X}'(t)$

[a]The units are different for each and so are suppressed.

(I feel obliged to make an incidental comment here. Many users of regression techniques incorrectly feel confident in their model if they obtain a large multiple correlation coefficient, a number which has practically nothing to do with the implicit probability assumptions.)

With Figure 13–3 in hand, the scientist's task becomes more interesting. Directions in which to look to find "better" models readily suggest themselves, but this will not be pursued here. These new models can then be compared with the old models and with each other using scatter plots and posterior probabilities.

The examples given thus far have not illustrated very well how probabilities associated with subsets of a universe change. As noted, the posterior probabilities associated with universes U and U', regarded as subsets in their union, of Examples 3 and 4 are essentially the same as the prior probabilities. This is not the case in Example 5. While it has the flavor of a textbook example, nothing like it can be found in existing textbooks. The problem is fundamentally similar to that of a "hypothesis test," and existing texts have an entirely different approach; as mentioned previously, the crucial difference is that hypothesis tests do not associate probabilities with the truth of the hypotheses. The example will use slightly more sophisticated statistics than required until now; some readers will want to skip it. A political background is added for spice; the problem is a fundamental one.

Example 5

Suppose that there are two existing theories about the length of time t (in days) between revolutions in a certain country. Theory 1 says that time t has the probability density

$$f_1(t \mid \lambda) = \lambda e^{-\lambda t}, \qquad \text{for } 0 < t; \tag{13-12}$$

and Theory 2 says that it has the density

$$f_2(t \mid \lambda) = \lambda, \qquad \text{for } 0 < t < 1/\lambda. \tag{13-13}$$

The parameter λ is meant to be the same in both theories and represents the (daily) revolution rate. $f_1(t \mid \lambda)$ and $f_2(t \mid \lambda)$ are compared in Figure 13–4.

FIGURE 13-4.

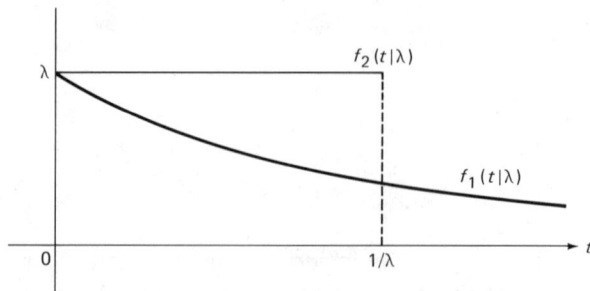

As always we specify a universe imagining that it is the last word, that no theory other than Theory 1 or Theory 2 is correct. An individual model in the universe is determined by a value of λ *and* the specification of whether the density is $f_1(t \mid \lambda)$ or $f_2(t \mid \lambda)$. To be specific, assume that Theories 1 and 2 are equally likely a priori—that is, before we observe any revolutions—and that the prior density of λ is proportional to $1/\lambda$ for $\lambda > 0$ (that is, the prior for $1/\lambda$ is uniform). The latter assumption means that smaller values of λ are considered more probable than larger values; it is made mainly for mathematical convenience.

Suppose that we observe the times prior to n revolutions and denote these (supposedly independent) times $t_1, \ldots, t_n$. We propose to find the posterior probabilities of Theories 1 and 2—that is, the probabilities that the true density of t is $f_1(t \mid \lambda)$ and $f_2(t \mid \lambda)$—and the posterior density of λ. Accordingly, we need the likelihood functions of λ for both theories:

$$L_1(\lambda \mid t_1, \ldots, t_n) = \lambda^n \exp\left(-\lambda \sum_1^n t_i\right), \qquad \text{for } 0 < \lambda,$$

$$L_2(\lambda \mid t_1, \ldots, t_n) = \lambda^n, \qquad \text{for } 0 < \lambda < (\max_i t_i)^{-1}.$$

Using Bayes's theorem,

$$\begin{aligned}
Q_1(t_1, \ldots, t_n) &= P(\text{Theory 1 is correct} \mid t_1, \ldots, t_n) \\
&= KP(t_1, \ldots, t_n \mid \text{Theory 1 is correct}) \\
&= K \int_0^\infty L_1(\lambda \mid t_1, \ldots, t_n)\lambda^{-1} d\lambda \\
&= \frac{K(n-1)!}{\left(\sum_1^n t_i\right)^n} \\
&= KK_1,
\end{aligned}$$

$$\begin{aligned}
Q_2(t_1, \ldots, t_n) &= P(\text{Theory 2 is correct} \mid t_1, \ldots, t_n) \\
&= KP(t_1, \ldots, t_n \mid \text{Theory 2 is correct}) \\
&= K \int_0^{(\max_i t_i)^{-1}} \lambda^n \lambda^{-1} d\lambda \\
&= \frac{K(\max_i t_i)^{-n}}{n} \\
&= KK_2.
\end{aligned}$$

Therefore,

$$K^{-1} = K_1 + K_2 = (n-1)!\left(\sum_1^n t_i\right)^{-n} + \frac{(\max_i t_i)^{-n}}{n}, \qquad (13\text{–}14)$$

and the required posterior probabilities are determined by

$$Q_1(t_1, \ldots, t_n) = \frac{K_1}{K_1 + K_2} = \frac{n!}{n! + \left(\sum_1^n t_i \max_i t_i\right)^n}. \qquad (13\text{–}15)$$

Suppose that three revolutions are preceded by 3, 24, and 5 days of peace (read in another time unit if you do not like "days"). Then (13–15) yields

$$Q_1(3, 24, 5) = \frac{3!}{3! + (32/24)^3} = \frac{81}{113} \doteq .72.$$

To see how this probability is affected by further observation, suppose that a fourth revolution occurs and that $t_4 = 4$. Then, (13–15) yields

$$Q_1(3, 24, 5, 4) = \frac{4!}{4! + (36/24)^4} = \frac{512}{539} \doteq .95.$$

If instead, $t_4 = 24$ then (13–15) yields

$$Q_1(3, 24, 5, 24) = \frac{4!}{4! + (56/24)^4} = \frac{1944}{4345} \doteq .45.$$

Obviously, Theory 1 explains the case (3, 24, 5, 4) better than it explains the case (3, 24, 5, 24) when it is compared to Theory 2. The reader is invited to investigate further the relationship between the two theories by, for example, finding times $(t_1, \ldots, t_n)$ for which (13–15) is as large as possible or as small as possible for fixed n.

The posterior density of λ depends on the posterior densities of λ in Theory 1 and Theory 2. These are

$$g_1(\lambda \mid t_1, \ldots, t_n) = K_1^{-1} \lambda^{n-1} \exp\left(-\lambda \sum_1^n t_i\right), \qquad \text{for } 0 < \lambda,$$

(a so-called gamma density), and

$$g_2(\lambda \mid t_1, \ldots, t_n) = K_2^{-1} \lambda^{n-1}, \qquad \text{for } 0 < \lambda < (\max_i t_i)^{-1}.$$

Using an elementary conditional probability relationship, the posterior probability of λ is seen to be

$$g(\lambda \mid t_1, \ldots, t_n) = g_1(\lambda \mid t_1, \ldots, t_n) Q_1(t_1, \ldots, t_n)$$
$$+ g_2(\lambda \mid t_1, \ldots, t_n) Q_2(t_1, \ldots, t_n)$$
$$= \begin{cases} K\lambda^{n-1} \left[\exp\left(-\lambda \sum_1^n t_i\right) + 1\right], & \text{for } 0 < \lambda < (\max_i t_i)^{-1} \\ K\lambda^{n-1} \exp\left(-\lambda \sum_1^n t_i\right), & \text{for } (\max_i t_i)^{-1} < \lambda, \end{cases}$$

where K is given by (13–14). In the case $(t_1, t_2, t_3) = (3, 24, 5)$,

$$g(\lambda \mid 3, 24, 5) = \begin{cases} K\lambda^2 (\exp(-32\lambda) + 1), & \text{for } 0 < \lambda < 1/24 \\ K\lambda^2 \exp(-32\lambda), & \text{for } 1/24 < \lambda, \end{cases}$$

where $K = 1{,}327{,}104/113$.

The posterior density $g(\lambda|3, 24, 5)$ is a maximum at $\lambda = 1/24$; therefore, in the combined universe of Theories 1 and 2 (according to our criterion) we would say that the revolution rate is one every 24 days. However, if we had decided (not on the basis of the probability .72, I hope) that Theory 1 is correct, then we would say that the revolution rate is one every 16 days, since $g_1(\lambda|3, 24, 5)$ is a maximum at $\lambda = 1/16$. (I note in passing that the posterior expected value of λ in the combined universe is $275/3616$—one revolution every 13.5 days—and in the universe of Theory 1 is $3/32$—one every 10.7 days.)

Summary

In this section we have been concerned with the changing probability assessments of models and sets of models in a model universe. The universes in the examples have of necessity been modest. A scientist should build into his universe as many models of a process as he can. His universe should be dynamic, new models added that seem suggested by accumulating data, and old ones discarded (unless there is room to keep them) as their posterior probabilities get small enough. This statement seems obvious, really, and in fact should describe whole sciences, as well as individual scientists. But scientists as well as individuals become enamored of particular models, models that could quickly be weeded out by Bayes's theorem. People are terribly conservative information processors—there is no room for emotion in Bayes's theorem. Of course, prior probabilities are emotional, but no scientist should impose his personal probabilities on users of his research. Rather, he should let his conclusions depend on the prior probabilities of the user so that conclusions can vary from user to user. This means that even in the healthiest of sciences there will probably not be a consensus about the appropriateness of the various candidate models. However, a healthy science will have dynamic scientists (in the above sense) and, therefore, will itself be dynamic.

EMPIRICAL MODELS

Until now we have been concerned with, broadly speaking, the problem of selecting a model from a specified model universe. We have been imposing a particular sort of probabilistic structure in the form of a model universe, which may be quite general, and discussing how the probabilities associated with individual models change as data accumulate. Imposing a model universe not only restricts the probabilistic structure to a particular type or set of types, it also restricts the variables under consideration to a specific set. This restriction may not be too constraining if the scientist displays sufficient imagination in naming the variables to be considered, but then he is left with the not so trivial task of saying how they interact. In any case, no scientist can be certain of the sufficiency of his imagination.

A number of methods (factor analysis, etc.) have been originated, mainly by social scientists, to serve to indicate a subset of variables which seem to be important in the system, or process, under consideration. A purpose of these methods is to decrease the number of variables in the system to a more manageable number without losing much model-building ability. Using terminology developed in previous sections, the model universe contains all models of a particular type (e.g., linear) which use a sufficiently small number of the total number of variables (subject to certain constraints). The end result is (usually) a model given explicitly in terms of the variables in this manageable subset.

Recently, a number of methods has been put forward which do not single out variables but let the user see how all the variables interact with each other in the data at hand; the end result is a set of relevant variables, but it is not necessarily a subset of the original variables. (I say "recently" to stress that the methodology is in its infancy. The fact is that there is a long tradition in the social sciences for such methods, methods where the object is to exhibit the data so as to facilitate seeing what there is to be seen.) The two most important and widely known such methods are cluster analysis and multidimensional scaling, the application of either of which is more of an art than a science. I will not describe these methods in great detail, instead the reader is referred to Dollar and Jensen (1971) for the former and Kruskal (1964) for the latter, both of which contain additional references. Incidentally, Dollar and Jensen also compare cluster analysis and factor analysis.

I will give a brief description of each method and illustrate each by example. Many times someone has data, but not a single notion of what the data might be trying to say. He would like to see a few answers before he formulates the questions. For such a person one of these methods can be an invaluable aid. They are mainly learning tools; if you try to argue a point using them, you will have to say something like: "As any idiot can see. . . ."

It would not be exaggerating much to say that there are as many different techniques of cluster analysis as there are technicians. However, all clustering techniques are alike in one respect: their common objective is to place objects that seem similar on the basis of a number of observable characteristics (variables) into the same group, or cluster. Most such numerical classification techniques have their origins in biological taxonomy, where the objects are usually individual specimens and the clusters are species. Techniques differ in their treatment of the number of objects per cluster, number of clusters, and the measure of similarity of objects. The effect of a cluster analysis is to reduce the set of variables to just one, the variable which designates into which cluster each object is classified. However, more variables are usually needed if the clusters are to be described or characterized.

Example 6 illustrates a technique of cluster analysis. The example was selected randomly, though, of course, the data are real.

Example 6

Consider the seven major Soviet industries listed in Table 13–3. An "object" is an industry. (There is nothing peculiar to the example about industries; some readers may wish to substitute other meanings for the symbols given in the table.) Table 13–3 gives the output of each industry for four years spaced in a forty-five year period as a percentage of the 1958 output. Suppose that the similarity of the industries is based on the table, so that we are really comparing the growths of the respective industries; a more comprehensive comparison of the industries would include other characteristics as well. We wish to group the industries into clusters of similar industries. A straightforward way of doing this made up for the occasion will be described.

TABLE 13–3.   SOVIET INDUSTRIAL AND MINERAL OUTPUT[a]

Industry	YEAR			
	1913	*1940*	*1955*	*1958*
Coal (C)	6	33	79	100
Oil (O)	8	28	63	100
Steel (S)	8	33	82	100
Pig Iron (I)	11	38	84	100
Electric Power (E)	1	27	72	100
Motor Vehicles (M)	0	28	99	100
Tractors (T)	0	14	74	100

SOURCE: *Encyclopedia Americana* (1962 ed.).
[a] Percent of 1958 output.

As a measure of the dissimilarity $D(C, O)$ of the coal and oil industries, for example, take the sum of the absolute differences in relative outputs over each of the years: 1913, 1940, 1955; that is,

$$D(C, O) = |6 - 8| + |33 - 28| + |79 - 63| = 23.$$

Computing the dissimilarities D for each pair of industries in a similar way yields the dissimilarity matrix given in Table 13–4. As a measure of the appropriateness of cluster systems which contain n clusters take the sum σ_n over all clusters of the dissimilarities D for all pairs of industries in the same cluster; we wish to find the cluster system with smallest σ_n. For example, the cluster {C, O, S}

TABLE 13–4.   DISSIMILARITY MATRIX

	C	O	S	I	E	M	T
C	0	23	5	13	18	21	30
O		0	24	32	17	34	33
S			0	10	23	20	35
I				0	29	26	45
E					0	18	16
M						0	29
T							0

would contribute $D(C, O) + D(C, S) + D(O, S) = 23 + 5 + 24$ to the σ_n of any cluster system containing it. It should be evident that such a measure tends to make the size of the clusters uniform. Those cluster systems of n clusters with smallest σ_n are given in Table 13–5 for each possible n, together with the corresponding σ_n. For $n = 4$ two cluster systems have the smallest σ_n and are both shown.

TABLE 13–5.   SYSTEMS OF n CLUSTERS WITH SMALLEST σ_n

n	Clusters	σ_n
7	{C}, {O}, {S}, {I}, {E}, {M}, {T}	0
6	{C, S}, {O}, {I}, {E}, {M}, {T}	5
5	{C, S}, {E, T}, {O}, {I}, {M}	21
4	{C, S}, {E, T}, {I, M}, {O}	47
	{C, M}, {E, T}, {I, S}, {O}	47
3	{C, S, I}, {O, E}, {M, T}	74
2	{C, O, S, I}, {E, M, T}	170
1	{C, O, S, I, E, M, T}	501

Much of the art involved in cluster analysis comes interpreting Table 13–5, and perhaps selecting an appropriate n, though detailed interpretations will not be attempted here. (Some science is available to help interpret Table 13–5; as a function of n, some values of σ_n are smaller than would ordinarily be expected, and may indicate some sort of "natural" clustering.) However, two characteristics of the results listed in Table 13–5 seem obvious to the least artistic among us, and are far from startling. First, the growths of the coal, iron, and steel industries seem similar, and unlike the growths of the other industries. Second, the growth of the oil industry seems unlike that of the other industries; it does not fit comfortably into any cluster. Now I do not advertise these observations as truths, I only say that on the basis of a little evidence they look like statements to investigate if you are looking for truths.

Discussion

The clustering technique of Example 6 was used because of its simplicity, and not because it is recommended for any purpose. It has some versatility in that two objects in the same cluster in the preferred n-cluster system can be in different clusters in the preferred $(n - 1)$-cluster system, but this kind of versatility causes complications for computational algorithms. (If the $(n - 1)$-cluster system can be constructed from the n-cluster system, then only $n(n - 1)/2$ such systems need be considered.

While cluster analysis is a single-variable method, multidimensional scaling, as the name implies, is a multivariable method. Its objective, however, is much the same; namely to associate objects with similar objects based on a number of observable characteristics. The objects are placed in a space of fixed dimension k in such a way that they are near objects that are similar and distant from objects that are dissimilar. The k dimensions can be thought of as corresponding to the k most important variables. Since the placement of the objects depends only on the data, these variables will not necessarily be identifiable, that is, obviously related to the observable characteristics. The arrangement of the objects suggests which variables are related to particular directions in the space, and how strong the relationships are. These directions may not be orthogonal, and each may suggest more than one variable.

A measure of the dissimilarity (or similarity) of all possible pairs of objects is required. The objects are placed in k space so that the interobject distances correspond as closely as possible to the interobject dissimilarities. If there are more than k objects, then an exact correspondence would be most unlikely, and for many more than k objects a reasonably good correspondence would be an indication that there are no more than k variables which are important (since in this case any of the objects could be nearly reproduced only using k dimensions).

Example 7 illustrates the technique of multidimensional scaling and facilitates comparisons with cluster analysis.

Example 7

Consider again the seven Soviet industries of the Example 6. The "objects" are again the industries. In a typical multidimensional scaling problem, the dissimiliarity between any two objects will depend on more than one characteristic; however, for simplicity assume that the measure of dissimilarity between industries depends only on the growths of the industries and is given by Table 13–4. Let the (Euclidean) distance in k space between coal and oil, for example, be denoted $R(C, O)$. To obtain a particular configuration of the seven industries in k space we will minimize the sum s_k of the absolute differences between dissimilarity and distance for each of the twenty-one pairs of industries; $s_k = \Sigma \mid D - R \mid$. In some problems the number of dimensions k will be dictated, in others various values of k should be tried; we first try $k = 1$, then $k = 2$.

The linear configuration of the seven industries with smallest s_1 is pictured in Figure 13–5. The distance matrix for this configuration is given in Table

FIGURE 13–5.

13–6a and subtracted from the dissimilarity matrix (Table 13–4) in Table 13–6b. The value of s_1 for this configuration is the sum of the absolute values of the numbers in Table 13–6b; $s_1 = 169$. The signs of the numbers in Table 13–6b indicate characteristics of this example that will be further evinced when we examine the case $k = 2$. For example, it is evident that oil does not fit at all comfortably in the same dimension with the other industries.

TABLE 13–6.

		(a) DISTANCE MATRIX ($k=1$)						(b) DISSIMILARITY MINUS DISTANCE MATRIX ($k=1$)					
	C	O	S	I	E	M	T	C	O	S	I	E	M	T
C	0	10	3	8	22	31	41	0	13	2	5	−4	−10	−11
O		0	13	18	12	21	31		0	11	14	5	13	2
S			0	5	25	34	44			0	5	−2	−14	−9
I				0	30	39	49				0	−1	−13	−4
E					0	9	19					0	9	−3
M						0	10						0	19
T							0							0

The relationship between single-dimensional scaling ($k=1$) and cluster analysis is evident upon circling the clusters given in Table 13–5 on Figure 13–5. This relationship is illustrated particularly well in the 2-cluster and 3-cluster systems.

Before attempting to interpret Figure 13–5, it will prove advantageous to consider the case $k=2$.

For $k=2$, the configuration of the seven industries with smallest s_2 is pictured in Figure 13–6. Again, Table 13–5 should be reexamined in view of Figure 13–6. The distance matrix for this configuration is given in Table 13–7a

FIGURE 13–6.

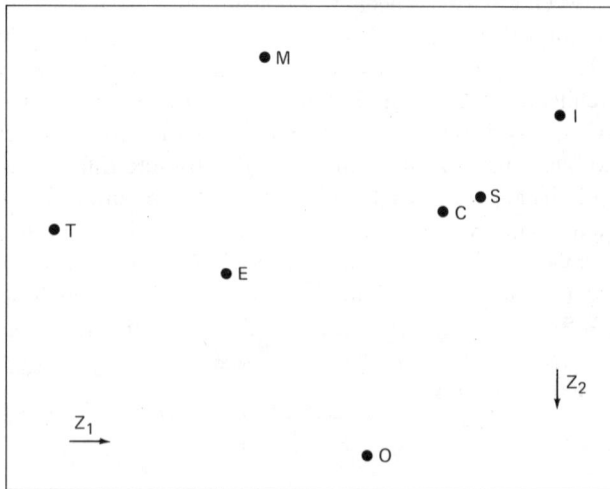

and subtracted from Table 13–4 in Table 13–7b. For this configuration $s_2 = 22$, which is a substantial reduction from 169, the miminum s_1. Actually, this reduction is not too surprising when it is realized that there is a three-dimensional configuration for which Table 13–4 is the distance matrix, that is for which $s_3 = 0$. Of course, this will not be true in general; the dissimilarity structure

TABLE 13–7.

	(a) DISTANCE MATRIX ($k = 2$)							(b) DISSIMILARITY MINUS DISTANCE MATRIX ($k = 2$)						
	C	O	S	I	E	M	T	C	O	S	I	E	M	T
C	0	21	4	13	19	19	32	0	2	1	0	−1	2	−2
O		0	23	32	19	34	32		0	1	0	−2	0	1
S			0	10	22	21	36			0	0	1	−1	−1
I				0	31	25	43				0	−2	1	2
E					0	18	15					0	0	1
M						0	30						0	−1
T							0							0

in this example is so very simple. Nevertheless, the introduction of the third dimension does not represent as much of an improvement as does the introduction of the second dimension ($s_2 - s_3 = 22$ and $s_1 - s_2 = 147$).

Part of the art (and the fun) of multidimensional scaling is labeling the dimensions, the empirically important variables, for the indicated configuration. Because of the dissimilarity structure in this example, such a variable is bound to depend on industrial growth, though we could call it by any name we please. I have labeled two directions in Figure 13–6 z_1 and z_2. The reader is invited to name these variables, or those for some other labeling. I submit the following: z_1, "rapid early growth," and z_2, "rapid recent growth." If it were true that industries with large z_1 have small z_2 (those that bloom early do not bloom again), then one variable would probably be sufficient in describing an industry, and s_1 would be substantially lessened. However, such is not the case, particularly for the oil industry. The oil industry, which has a moderate z_1 and large z_2, was uncomfortable in one dimension but has found a home in two dimensions.

A word is in order about practical approaches for finding configurations of objects that fit well into many dimensions. Any multidimensional scaling involves iteration. The algorithm used in Example 7 was made up for the occasion and is not available in computer program form, but there are programs available for related algorithms (Kruskal, 1964).

SUMMARY AND CONCLUSIONS

The probabilistic nature of stochastic model universes can be applied to accumulating empirical evidence to modify the probabilities that the individual models correctly describe a process, correct relative to the other models. Models or sets of models can thus be discarded from the universe as their probabilities become sufficiently small and new models incorporated. Bayes's theorem is essential for evaluating these probabilities.

Cluster analysis and multidimensional scaling can be used to help ascertain the character of relevant variables by displaying the data in clusters or in multi-dimensional space.

To most readers the fourth section will seem completely unrelated to the second and third sections. It seems unrelated to me as well. Perhaps it does not deserve to be called "statistics." Though it is true that the methods discussed in the fourth section have only recently been developed and widespread use of Bayes's theorem is hardly a few years older, the fact is that it is not easy to use a particular configuration of objects in k space, for example, in an inference argument. One rather suspects when he notices something peculiar about a configuration that it means something, but what device can be used to set down a reasonable universe which includes that something? And how are probabilities to be assigned to the members of the universe? These and related questions may be answered soon; however, even if they never are answered, the techniques described in the preceding section (and similar techniques) may endure for what they are today.

BIBLIOGRAPHY

Alker, Hayward R., Jr. "Statistics and Politics: The Need for Causal Data Analysis." In Seymour M. Lipset, ed., *Politics and the Social Sciences*. New York: Oxford University Press, 1969.

Anscombe, Francis J. "Topics in the Investigation of Linear Relations Fitted by the Method of Least Squares." *Journal of the Royal Statistical Society*, Series B, Vol. 29 (1967), pp. 1–52.

Dollar, Charles M., and Jensen, Richard J. *Historian's Guide to Statistics, Quantitative Analysis and Historical Research*. New York: Holt, Rinehart, 1971.

Edwards, Ward, Lindman, Harold, and Savage, Leonard J. "Bayesian Statistical Inference for Psychological Research." *Psychological Review*, Vol. 70, (May 1963), pp. 193–242.

Halmos, Paul R. *Naive Set Theory*. New York: Van Nostrand, 1960.

Kossack, Carl F. "Statistical Analysis, the Computer, and Political Science Research." In Joseph L. Bernd, *Mathematical Applications in Political Science*, Vol. II. Dallas: The Arnold Foundation of Southern Methodist University, 1966.

Kruskal, J. B. "Nonmetric Multidimensional Scaling: A Numerical Method." *Psychometrica*, Vol. 29 (June 1964), pp. 115–29.

Morrison, Donald F. *Multivariate Statistical Methods*. New York: McGraw-Hill, 1967.

Raiffa, H., and Schlaifer, R. *Applied Statistical Decision Theory*. Boston: Graduate School of Business Administration, Harvard University, 1961.

Chapter 14
Data Analysis, Process Analysis, and System Change

RONALD D. BRUNNER
AND
KLAUS LIEPELT

Much current attention in the social sciences generally, and political science particularly, is focused on an array of descriptive statistical tools used as a means of constructing empirically based theories. To a considerable extent this attention has been narrowly limited to consider cross-sectional, comparative studies to the relative exclusion of longitudinal, time-series ones. This chapter examines both theoretical and practical results of making this methodological choice. To facilitate the discussion, a simple macro theoretical model—originally constructed by Paul A. Samuelson to describe the multiplier and accelerator in a national economy—is presented. Differences between a model's structure (its several elements taken together in systematic ways) and the behavior it is capable of producing (the time series generated by it) are drawn to make the point that qualitatively different behavioral outcomes may be generated by a simple model merely by changing the values of its initial parameter values. To pursue this point, survey data collected in a German public opinion poll are relied on to indicate the limitations of conventional descriptive statistical methods in learning about the underlying structural configurations responsible for the observed behavior. A strong argument is made to adopt the process—or contextual and longitudinal—observational perspective.

Among students of comparative politics, and particularly those who adopt the macropolitical perspective, there exists a growing interest in *change* as an

Reprinted from "Data Analysis, Process Analysis, and System Change," *Midwest Journal of Political Science*, Vol. 16 (November 1972), pp. 538–69, by Ronald D. Brunner and Klaus Liepelt, by permission of the Wayne State University Press. The initial version of this chapter was presented at the American Political Science Association meetings in September 1970. We wish to thank Garry D. Brewer and Steven Coombs for many productive conversations about the material presented here; The Institute of Applied Social Research (Infas) at Bad Godesberg, Federal Republic of Germany, which provided survey data; and the Center for International Affairs at Harvard University and the Institute of Public Policy Studies at The University of Michigan, both of which provided research support. Responsibility is ours alone.

487

approach to the understanding of political systems. Perhaps the most comprehensive introduction to the approach is Samuel P. Huntington's survey and analysis of the study of political development.[1] Huntington both documents and advocates increasing attention to the investigation of change in the components of political systems. In essence, his contention is that this "change to change" promises to avoid the conceptual difficulties stemming from the use of the "Great Dichotomy"—modernity and tradition—and from the use of the concept of political development in other than an evaluative sense. Robert Burrowes discerns a shift, particularly in the past five years, from a cross-national comparative approach to increasing concern with longitudinal questions.[2] Whereas cross-sectional data and statistical techniques are appropriate for the former, he advocates the use of longitudinal data and techniques for the latter.

While this "change to change" promises conceptual payoffs and suggests the reorientation of data and techniques, it also sharpens the contrast between two epistemological viewpoints regarding the nature of political systems. One is a data analysis viewpoint found in many cross-national quantitative studies in comparative government. The other is a process[3] viewpoint consistent with, but largely implicit in, many theoretical and case studies. At a more or less philosophical level, the two viewpoints provide different answers to one of the most basic questions of comparative government: In what respects are nations the same, and in what respects do they differ? At a more practical level, the viewpoints suggest different and often conflicting theoretical inferences from data or statistical summaries of data in the study of system change. As attention is focused on system change and as data are integrated into this approach, the differences between the viewpoints and their practical implications must be explored and taken into account. This chapter is an initial step in these directions.

The differences between the two viewpoints are elaborated in the next section, which uses a model of considerable historical importance in macro economics to explore the complex relationship between a system of theoretically relevant processes and data on the behavior of the system. Subsequently, the section entitled "An Example: The NPD" uses a study of the right-wing NPD (National Demokratische Partei Deutschlands) in the Federal Republic of Germany to illustrate with real data some of the points made in the section on viewpoints. The remainder of the chapter focuses on the adequacy and inadequacy of conventions of evidence—both data analysis conventions and the emerging conventions of process analysis—which have been used to make

[1] Samuel P. Huntington, "The Change to Change: Modernization, Development, and Politics," *Comparative Politics*, Vol. 3 (April 1971), pp. 283–322.

[2] Robert Burrowes, "Multiple Time-Series Analysis of Nation-Level Data," *Comparative Political Studies*, Vol. 2 (January 1970), pp. 463–80.

[3] For present purposes, a process may be conceived as a stable relationship through which a change in one or more input variables produces a regular and predictable change in an output variable.

theoretical inferences from data or statistical summaries of data. The conventions of data analysis considered here are shown to be largely fallacious under reasonably general conditions.

CONTRASTING VIEWPOINTS

Let us begin with a consideration of a classic study in Keynesian economics, Paul Samuelson's study of the interactions between the multiplier analysis and the principle of acceleration.[4] Unlike real-world systems, the mathematical system on which this study is based is completely known, and the behavior of the system has no stochastic components. This enables us to explore with confidence the general nature of the relationship between processes in the system and the system's behavior.

The Multiplier-Accelerator

Following Alvin Hansen, Samuelson specified an economic system consisting of five components:

Y_t, additions to national income;

C_t, private consumption expenditure induced by previous public expenditure;

I_t, induced private investment;

α, the marginal propensity to consume;

β, the relation, giving the ratio of induced private investment to changes in induced private consumption.

Variables are denoted by the time subscript t. Parameters, which are assumed to be constant over time, have no time subscript.

The relationships among the components of the system were given in the three equations below. Equation 14–1 is merely an accounting identity[5] that defines additions to national income Y_t as being equal to the sum of induced private consumption C_t, induced private investment I_t, and a constant level of governmental deficit spending denoted by 1. Equation (14–2) is a mathematical representation of a process hypothesis known as the multiplier analysis: The current level of induced private consumption C_t is determined by the level of additions to national income in the previous period Y_{t-1}, and is equal to a proportion α of that level. Equation (14–3) is a representation of another

[4] Paul Samuelson, "Interactions Between the Multiplier and the Principle of Acceleration," *Review of Economic Statistics,* Vol. 21 (1939), pp. 75–8.

[5] An accounting identity, unlike a process hypothesis, is a convention that is true by definition.

process hypothesis, the principle of acceleration: The current level of induced private investment I_t is determined by the change in consumption $(C_t - C_{t-1})$ and is equal to a multiple β of that change.

$$Y_t = C_t + I_t + 1 \qquad (14\text{--}1)$$

$$C_t = \alpha Y_{t-1} \qquad (14\text{--}2)$$

$$I_t = \beta(C_t - C_{t-1}) \qquad (14\text{--}3)$$

We may define the *structure* of this or another class of systems as the set of components (variables and parameters) and the set of relationships among these components. Together they constitute a *theory* of the systems. A *model* of any one of the systems is the general structure with the magnitudes of the variables and parameters specified to represent a particular time–space *context*. The *behavior* of a model is the set of time series of the variables that are produced as the model operates through time.

Hansen had previously calculated time sequences for the variables in this system using various magnitudes for the parameters α and β. In effect, he deduced the marginal behavior of several hypothetical economic systems having identical structure but different parameter values. The results, similar to those graphed in Figure 14–1, were surprising and somewhat confusing. In some cases a constant level of governmental deficit spending caused the variables to increase asymptotically toward constant levels. These levels are 2.0 and 1.0 for Y_t and C_t, respectively, in Figure 14–1a. (I_t is constant and equal to zero because $\beta = 0$, an important restriction considered below.) In other cases Y_t, C_t, and I_t oscillated, but each oscillation was smaller than the previous one, and the variables converged to constant levels. These levels are 2.0, 1.0, and 0.0 for the three variables, respectively, in Figure 14–1b. In other cases, as in Figure 14–1c, the variables oscillated, but each oscillation was larger in magnitude than the previous one. Finally, in some cases the variables increased smoothly, approaching a compound interest rate of growth, as in Figure 14–1d.

Hansen's surprise and confusion derived in part from the fact that the multiplier and the accelerator were already well-known hypotheses in macro. economics. Indeed, it was known that the model sequences in Figure 14–1a (the special cases where $\beta = 0$) were typical of the behavior of the multiplier alone and that this asymptotic form of behavior was the only form the multiplier could produce. Yet the multiplier, in conjunction with the accelerator, produced four qualitatively different forms of behavior! It was the *interaction* between the two hypotheses that turned out to be important. Thus, in principle, a system of this type may produce forms of behavior that go beyond the forms produced by its individual relationships.

Using the mathematical technique of difference equations, Samuelson resolved the confusion by proving that the system can produce these four and only these four qualitatively different forms of behavior over time depending on the relative magnitudes of α and β, but independent of the initial levels of the

FIGURE 14-1. BEHAVIOR OF THE MULTIPLIER-ACCELERATOR

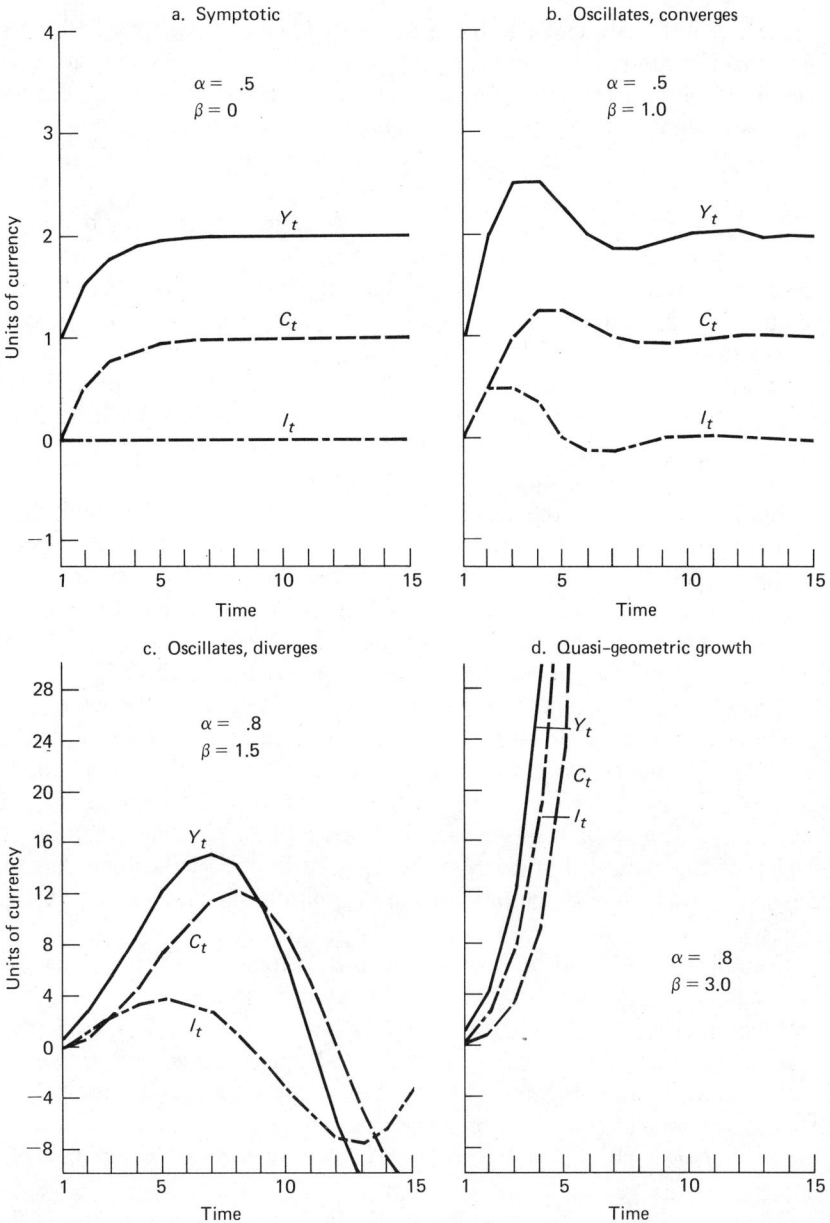

a. Symptotic

$\alpha = .5$
$\beta = 0$

Y_t

C_t

I_t

Units of currency

Time

b. Oscillates, converges

$\alpha = .5$
$\beta = 1.0$

Y_t

C_t

I_t

Time

c. Oscillates, diverges

$\alpha = .8$
$\beta = 1.5$

Y_t

C_t

I_t

Units of currency

Time

d. Quasi-geometric growth

Y_t

C_t

I_t

$\alpha = .8$
$\beta = 3.0$

Time

variables. There is, of course, a quantitatively unique pattern of behavior for each unique combination of α, β, and initial levels of the variables.[6]

[6] Discussions of the multiplier-accelerator and its solution can be found in Samuel Goldberg, *Introduction to Difference Equations* (New York: Science Editions, 1961).

Process Viewpoint

Perhaps the easiest way to interpret the behavior of each model is to view it as a manifestation of a feedback system adapting or responding to a shock or disequilibrium (externally generated by the constant level of governmental deficit spending). Each response is qualitatively constrained by common structure and quantitatively constrained by response parameters unique to each model.[7]

Every feedback system has at least one set of components and relationships that senses some disequilibrium, produces a response to it, and provides a circuit or loop by which the consequences of the response feed back to change the magnitude of the disequilibrium. In the multiplier-accelerator, the component that senses disequilibrium is the expression $(C_t - C_{t-1})$, the rate of change in consumption. The response is the level of induced private investment I_t, which affects Y_t directly through equation (14–1) and C_{t+1} indirectly through equations (14–1) and (14–2). The subsequent magnitude of the disequilibrium then becomes $(C_{t+1} - C_t)$.

Within each system, the magnitude and persistence of the disequilibrium, as well as the variance through time it generates in all three variables, depends upon the magnitudes of the parameters representing the specific context. Where $\alpha\beta$, the gain across the loop, is less than 1.0, as in Figures 14–1a and 14–1b, there is a secular decrease in the magnitude of $(C_t - C_{t-1})$, as well as in the rates of change of Y_t and I_t. The variables approach equilibrium, the state in which their rates of change are zero, because the response parameters are not large enough to sustain or increase the disequilibrium induced by the constant level of governmental deficit spending. Where $\alpha\beta$ is greater than 1.0, as in Figures 14–1c and 14–1d, there is a secular increase in the absolute magnitude of $(C_t - C_{t-1})$, as well as in the rates of change of each of the other variables. Because of the parameters, each response contributes in the long run to increases in the absolute magnitude of the disequilibrium motivating subsequent responses.

Another relationship between α and β determines whether the pattern of variance through time is complicated further by oscillations. If $\alpha > 4\beta/(1 + \beta^2)$, as in Figures 14–1a and 14–1d, the disequilibrium $(C_t - C_{t-1})$ remains positive (even if it approaches zero), and there is no oscillation. However, if $\alpha < 4\beta/(1 + \beta^2)$, as in Figures 14–1b and 14–1c, the disequilibrium in induced consumption oscillates between positive and negative values. The combination of parameters is such that each response to a positive disequilibrium contributes eventually to the generation of a negative disequilibrium, and vice versa. In short, given the processes in the systems, the diversity of behavior across systems and through time reflects parametric constraints on the ability to adapt to

---

[7] Adaptation and constraint figure prominently in Herbert Simon's important concept, artificial behavior, which means man-made rather than natural behavior. See his book, *The Sciences of the Artificial* (Cambridge, Mass.: The MIT Press, 1969).

disequilibrium in consumption induced by the constant level of governmental deficit spending.

Despite this diversity in behavior, there exist a few simple processes underlying the behavior of all four systems, and these processes can serve as theoretical explanations of their behavior. Given the cross-system differences in the parameters α and β, the processes in the systems' common structure explain and can reproduce the behavior of the four systems exactly. For example, the expression $\beta(C_t - C_{t-1})$ explains and can reproduce the value of I_t regardless of the time period or the particular system chosen. Thus, the processes are accurate, parsimonious, and general explanations of system behavior both in the cross-system context and within each system through time. Stated another way, all of the information on system behavior in Figure 14–1 (the magnitudes of three variables in four systems at thirteen or more points in time) is contained in the three equations stating the processes and the accounting identity, the eight parameter settings, and the initial values of the three variables. From the viewpoint of the social scientist seeking a theoretical explanation of this diverse behavior, success could be measured in terms of the extent to which the processes are clarified.

Data Analysis Viewpoint

In a manner more or less conventional in comparative government, one could attempt to interpret and explain the variance (or diversity) of the systems' behavior by applying statistical techniques like correlation and regression to the behavior graphed in Figure 14–1. Part of the variance is interpreted as systematic variance arising from some functional relationship between two or more variables and reflected in the form of the statistical model. Another part of the variance is interpreted as unsystematic variance arising from the multiplicity of unknown or unmeasured variables affecting the responses of units of observation; "a basic and unpredictable random element in human responses . . ." and errors of observation or measurement.[8]

The cross-system approach uses systems at a point in time as units of observation and focuses on the explanation of variance across systems. To illustrate, suppose we correlate I_t and C_t using the regression equation $I_t = a - bC_t$ at any cross-section in time except $t = 1$. This is, of course, both the simplest and a rather common form of regression equation. Consider first a sample of multiplier-accelerator systems at least one of which is in *disequilibrium* and which have different propensities to invest (i.e., different values of β). The product-moment correlation r between I_t and C_t across such systems would be less than one, and the single estimate of b in the regression equation would have no necessary relationship to any one of the several β's in the process relationships. Moreover, the magnitude of the correlation and the estimated parameter

[8] J. Johnston, *Econometric Methods* (New York: McGraw-Hill, 1963), p. 6.

can be expected to vary from one cross-section to the next. Among other things, the statistical model misconstrues some of the variance through time in individual systems as cross-system variance, and assumes one parameter value measuring the impact of consumption on investment for the sample as whole when there are in fact four values—one for each system in the sample.

Consider next a sample of multiplier-accelerator systems each of which is in equilibrium. The sample might include Figures 14–1a and 14–1b, where equilibrium is closely approximated by $t = 15$ and where β equals 0 and 1, respectively. The product-moment correlation produced by the estimation of the equation at a cross-section is still less than one, and the estimate of b still bears no necessary connection to the β's. However, in this sample, as opposed to the first, the magnitude of the correlation and the estimated parameter will be stable from one cross-section to the next because the variables are in equilibrium. The statistical model has no opportunity to confuse longitudinal and cross-system variance because the former is not present.

Unexplained variance indicated by less than perfect correlations often would be attributed, as we have seen, to errors in specifying the regression equation (particularly variables left out of the regression equation), to the influence of stochastic factors in the system, and to observation errors. Yet the latter two sources of variance do not exist in these four hypothetical systems, and there is *no* cross-system regression equation that can be expected to produce a correlation of one for these samples. Given the stated conditions, a generalization based on cross-sectional correlation-regression analysis such as this is general only in the sense that a summary is general: it is derived from a number of cases, but cannot be expected to reconstruct any one of them with complete accuracy. Attempts to increase accuracy by grouping cases into more homogeneous subsamples for separate analysis or by estimating a separate regression equation for each cross-section make the generalization less general and less parsimonious. Such generalizations have little meaning apart from the description of the particular context from which they are derived. They have the properties of descriptive summaries, whether or not they are called hypotheses or theoretical statements.

The longitudinal approach uses states of a system at successive points in time as units of observation and focuses on the explanation of differences through time. Let us again use the regression equation $I_t = a + bC_t$ for illustrative purposes. If applied to the behavior of a system in disequilibrium, the regression equation can be expected to produce results similar to those in the cross-sectional analysis. For example, for the time series of C_t and I_t graphed in Figure 14–1c, the time-series correlation and the slope b are positive for the period $t = 1$ through $t = 5$ in which both variables are increasing, but are negative for the period $t = 5$ through $t = 8$ in which I_t turns downward and C_t continues to increase. Both the correlation and the slope should approximate zero for the period $t = 1$ through $t = 8$. The statistical model attributes variance in I_t to C_t when in fact variance in I_t was produced by $(C_t - C_{t-1})$. Thus, as before, the statistical results are less than perfect and vary with the context, in this case the time period selected.

If applied to the behavior of a multiplier-accelerator system in equilibrium, the correlation regression analysis is of no help because there is no variance across time; consequently, the values of parameters and the associated correlations are undefined. However, if we impose a small stochastic component on the time series for C_t and I_t in Figure 14–1b after about $t = 15$, where the variables closely approximate equilibrium, the values of the statistics are defined. The longitudinal analysis would produce a correlation and a regression slope of approximately zero, even though a process relationship exists between the two variables.[9] The statistical results would be subject to slight variations arising from stochastic components.

With one exception, any form of the regression equation can be expected to produce similar results. The exception is the form of the regression equation that coincides exactly with the process relationship. In the case of the accelerator, this form is $I_t = b(C_t - C_{t-1})$. The intercept in this regression equation has been forced to zero and the independent variable is a transformation of two consecutive values of C_t. The fitting of the regression equation to the time series would explain all variance and the estimate of b would equal β for the system in question regardless of the time period selected.

In short, for generalizations based on correlation-regression analysis to have the same desirable theoretical properties as the process relationship, the regression equation must reflect the form of the process which generated the data. Stated positively, an understanding of process is a prerequisite to the theoretical use of correlation-regression techniques as tools in the study of feedback systems. Stated negatively, the imposition of misspecified regression equations—those that do not reflect the underlying processes which produced the data—on variables not in equilibrium leads to unstable statistical results of descriptive and heuristic utility only. Theoretical progress in the study of system change requires more than a shift to longitudinal data and data analysis techniques.

Organized Complexity[10]

The multiplier-accelerator analysis suggests that systems having common structure and unique parameters are *organized* and *complex* in specialized senses of these terms. They are *organized* in the sense that the interaction of processes

---

[9] The process relationship would signal its existence with a positive correlation if the exogenous level of governmental deficit spending were increased.

[10] The term *organized complexity* was introduced by Warren Weaver in "Science and Complexity," *American Scientist,* Vol. 36 (1948), p. 539. Its meaning as used in this chapter was developed in *Organized Complexity: Empirical Theories of Political Development* (New York: The Free Press, 1971), by Ronald D. Brunner and Garry D. Brewer. See also Herbert Simon, "The Architecture of Complexity," in his *The Sciences of the Artificial,* p. 86, for a rough definition of a complex system.

can produce very diverse and perhaps unexplained behavior which need not be attributed largely to stochastic components or measurement error. They are *complex* in the sense that complete knowledge of the structure, parameters, and initial conditions of even a small feedback system does not in itself imply either a qualitative or quantitative understanding of its behavior, as Hansen discovered when he began calculating time sequences; and that given data on the behavior of such a system, it is not a trivial task to clarify its structure, as indicated by the application of regression equations to the behavior of the multiplier-accelerator models. In short, complexity refers to the "gap" between knowledge of the structure and information about the behavior of a system.

Intellectual "jumps" from data on behavior to theoretical structure, and vice versa, require some conventions of evidence, and in particular some rules and procedures for making theoretical inferences from data or statistical summaries of data. The major practical implication of the process viewpoint on the nature of systems—which entails the viewpoint that such systems are organized and complex—is that the conventions of data analysis are largely fallacious and other conventions are needed to perform their functions. These points will be elaborated in a later section.

The major implication of a more or less philosophical sort lies in the answers to the basic question of comparative government: In what respects are nations the same, and in what respects do they differ? The process viewpoint on the nature of systems assumes that countries are similar to the extent that the processes in each country are the same and different with respect to the parameters governing the operation of the processes in each country and the initial conditions in each country at the start of the analysis. Hypotheses are statements about process expressed verbally or mathematically. At least some of the diversity we observe in the behavior of a sample of countries can be attributed in principle to differences in parameters exacerbated by systemic intractions even if the processes in each country are assumed to be the same. In contrast, the conventional data analytic viewpoint assumes that countries are similar to the extent that they conform to the cross-national regression line (explained variance) and different to the extent that they deviate from it (unexplained variance). Hypotheses are often, although not always, statements about variance and covariance expressed as regression equations or their verbal equivalents. To the extent that such hypotheses are provisionally accepted, unexplained cases tend to be attributed to stochastic factors and measurement error.

AN EXAMPLE: THE NPD

Now let us turn to a real-world example, the temporary electoral success of the right-wing NPD in the Federal Republic of Germany in 1966 and 1967. We will draw heavily from an earlier analysis by Klaus Liepelt.[11] The purpose is to illustrate concretely the points made in the last section and to provide the basis for reconsidering in the next section the relationship between processes in a system and the system's behavior.

Some Statistical Results

The results of interest here concern the possible impact of private economic expectations on potential support for the NPD. To ascertain private economic expectations, each respondent was asked if he thought his economic situation in the coming year would improve or worsen. To ascertain potential support for the NPD, each respondent was asked whether he would possibly vote for the NPD or had already done so.

The individual level, cross-sectional results were based on the combined samples for November and December of 1966 and are summarized in Table 14–1.

TABLE 14–1.   PRIVATE ECONOMIC EXPECTATIONS AND POTENTIAL SUPPORT FOR THE NPD: THE INDIVIDUAL-LEVEL RESULTS FOR NOVEMBER–DECEMBER 1966[a]

		ECONOMIC EXPECTATIONS		
		Improve	*Stay Same/DK*[b]	*Worsen*
NPD	Yes	12% (32)	10% (80)	18% (93)
Potential	No/DK[b]	88% (226)	90% (743)	82% (428)
Support	Total	100% (258)	100% (723)	100% (521)

Source: Probability sample of the Institute für Angewandte Sozialwissenschaft (Infas) in Bad Godesberg, Federal Republic of Germany, November–December 1966. Percentages have been reported in Liepelt, *op. cit.*, p. 257.

[a] $b = -.0514$; $r = -.075$; $r^2 = .006*$ (statistically significant at the .05 level).

[b] DK indicates "Don't know" responses.

Overall, potential support for the NPD was about 6 percentage points higher among those with pessimistic expectations than among those with optimistic expectations. In other words, those who thought their economic situation would worsen were more likely to support the radical right-wing party. Among respondents whose objective economic situation suggests economic vulnerability, the corresponding percentage point difference was larger: It was 29 percentage points for the self-employed and unemployed, and 22 percentage points for employees in small businesses. For employees in large businesses, the difference was only 1 percentage point. Among respondents with organizational ties to the unions or the Catholic Church, or both, the percentage difference in potential support between the pessimists and the optimists also tended to be small or even

[11] Klaus Liepelt, "Anhänger der Neuen Rechtspartei," *Politische Vierteljahreschrift*, Vol. 8 (July 1967), pp. 257–71. (Translated in Chapter 3 of this book.)

negative. It was −3 percentage points for union members, 8 percentage points for practicing Catholics, and 3 percentage points for union members with Catholic ties.[12] While a moderate correlation may exist within the first two of these mutually exclusive groups, the overall statistical relationship is not strong. Using the frequencies corresponding to the percentage data in Table 14–1, coding the categories of economic expectations as 1, 0, and −1, and coding potential support for the NPD as a dummy variable, the product-moment correlation between the two variables is −.075. It turns out that private economic expectations explain in a statistical sense only about six-tenths of one percent of the variance across individuals in NPD potential support.

The individual level, cross-sectional analysis can be extended using as yet unpublished cross-tabulations from the same source for each of the five months in the period November 1966–March 1967.[13] The results are summarized in Table 14–2.

TABLE 14–2.   PRIVATE ECONOMIC EXPECTATIONS AND POTENTIAL SUPPORT FOR THE NPD: INDIVIDUAL LEVEL RESULTS FOR MONTHLY CROSS-SECTIONSª

Month	Economic Pessimists % NPD Supporters	Stay Same/DK % NPD Supporters	Economic Optimists % NPD Supporters	Pessimist– Optimist Difference (%)	b	r	R^2
Nov. 1966	19 (246)	11 (396)	14 (119)	5	−.0333	−.065	.004
Dec. 1966	17 (275)	9 (427)	11 (139)	6	−.0404	−.085	.007ᵇ
Jan. 1967	11 (254)	7 (444)	4 (178)	7	−.0385	−.102	.010ᵇ
Feb. 1967	10 (156)	5 (473)	4 (209)	6	−.0247	−.068	.005ᵇ
Mar. 1967	13 (122)	7 (477)	11 (165)	2	−.0058	−.013	.000

SOURCE: Probability samples of Infas, November 1966–March 1967.

a Figures in parentheses in the second, third, and fourth columns give the number of pessimists, stay same/DK's, and optimists from which percentage of NPD supporters is calculated.

b Statistically significant at the .05 level.

The variability of statistical results from one cross-section to the next is rather small in absolute terms. The difference between pessimists and optimists in potential support for the NPD ranges from 7 to 2 percentage points in January and March, respectively. The regression slope ranges from −.0404 in December to −.0058 in March. The correlation varies nearly an order of magnitude from −.102 to −.013, in January and March, respectively. The variablilty of statis-

---

[12] These groups were isolated through the use of a program which divides and subdivides the total sample according to variables which maximize the between-group differences in a dependent variable—in this case potential support for the NPD. The program is similar to the Automatic Interaction Detector developed at the Institute for Social Research at The University of Michigan.

[13] The cross-tabulations for August, September, and October of 1966 were not available at the time these calculations were made.

tical results may reflect misspecification of the implied regression equation or stochastic components in the system's behavior or measurements of its behavior. However, the relationship is statistically significant in December, January, and February, but not in November and March.

The analysis of system change focused on aggregate results over time, rather than differences between individuals at a cross-section in time. It was based on the percentage potential support for the NPD and an index of private economic expectations for each of eight months from August 1966 through March 1967. The index is the difference between percentage optimistic and percentage pessimistic of the total (including "Don't know" responses) in each monthly sample. The results were presented graphically and are reproduced in somewhat revised form in Figure 14–2. The overall statistical relationship is quite strong: The correlation between the index and NPD support across the eight months is −.869, and the correlation across the seven first differences (or monthly changes) of the variables is −.795. The regression slopes for raw variables and first differences are, respectively, −.250 and −.283. Both relationships are statistically significant at the .05 level.

The analysis of system change can be extended to include the period from April through November 1967 using unpublished data from subsequent monthly surveys not available at the time Liepelt's article was written. The two variables for each monthly sample as a whole are graphed in Figure 14–3. In this period the correlation between the index of economic optimism–pessimism and potential support for the NPD changes by .648 to −.221, and the correlation between the first differences changes by .761 to −.034. The regression slope for the raw variables changes by .173 to −.077, and the regression slope for first differences changes by .272 to −.011. Neither relationship in the second period is statistically significant. In terms of correlations, regression slopes, and statistical significance, the changes from the first period to the second are rather substantial.

Unfortunately, the corresponding within group results can currently be calculated only for the last five months of the first eight-month period. This of course reduces the degrees of freedom and makes the results for this period statistically less stable. Whatever the reason for the instability, the changes in results from the first to the second period are rather large. For the raw variables, the correlation changed as much as 1.16 (from −.797 to +.364) within the union–Catholic group, and the slope changed by as much as .469 (from −.398 to +.071) within the group of employees in small firms. For the first differences of the variables, the correlation changed by as much as 1.442 (from −.702 to +.740) within the group of employees in small firms, and the slope changed by as much as .741 (from −.788 to −.047) in the group of employees in large firms. In the first period all correlations and slopes within the six groups for both raw variables and first differences had negative signs, but in the second period there were as many positive as negative signs. The raw variable and first difference relationships were statistically significant at the .05 level within the union group in the first period, but were not in the second. No other relationships were statistically significant.

Both the cross-sectional results and the longitudinal results vary with each

FIGURE 14-2. PRIVATE ECONOMIC EXPECTATIONS
AND POTENTIAL SUPPORT FOR THE
NPD: SYSTEM CHANGE RESULTS FOR
AUGUST 1966 TO MARCH 1967

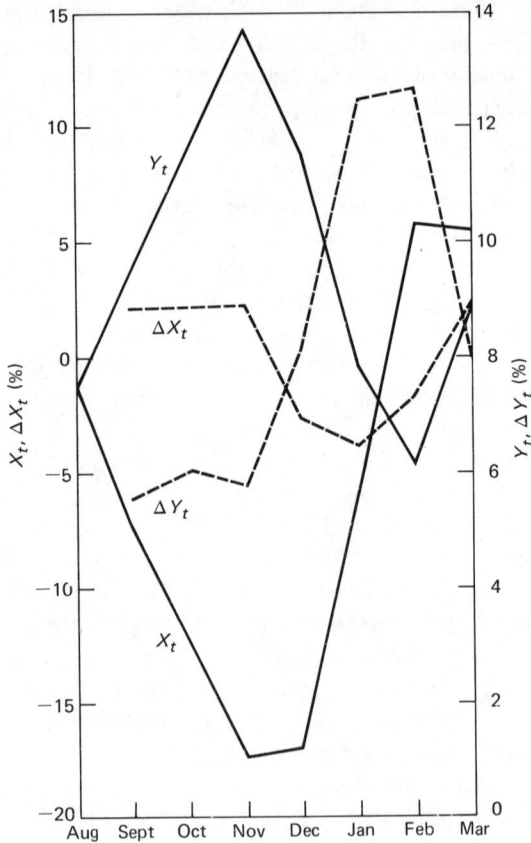

$$\widehat{Y}_t = 8.320 - .250\, X_t \qquad r = -.869 \quad r^2 = .755^a$$
$$\Delta\widehat{Y}_t = .381 - .283\, \Delta X_t \qquad r = -.795 \quad r^2 = .632^a$$

where

  X_t is the index of economic expectations at t
  Y_t is potential support for the NPD
  $\Delta X_t = X_t - X_{t-1}$
  $\Delta Y_t = Y_t - Y_{t-1}$
  $\frown$ indicates the regression prediction.

Source: Liepelt, op. cit., p. 261.

[a]Statistically significant at the .05 level

change in context: From cross-section to cross-section, from individual to aggregate level, from time period to time period, and from group to group. In some cases the changes in results are quite large in magnitude and entail changes in the positive or negative sign of the coefficient and in statistical significance.

FIGURE 14-3. PRIVATE ECONOMIC EXPECTATIONS
AND POTENTIAL SUPPORT FOR THE
NPD: SYSTEM CHANGE RESULTS FOR
APRIL 1967 TO NOVEMBER 1967

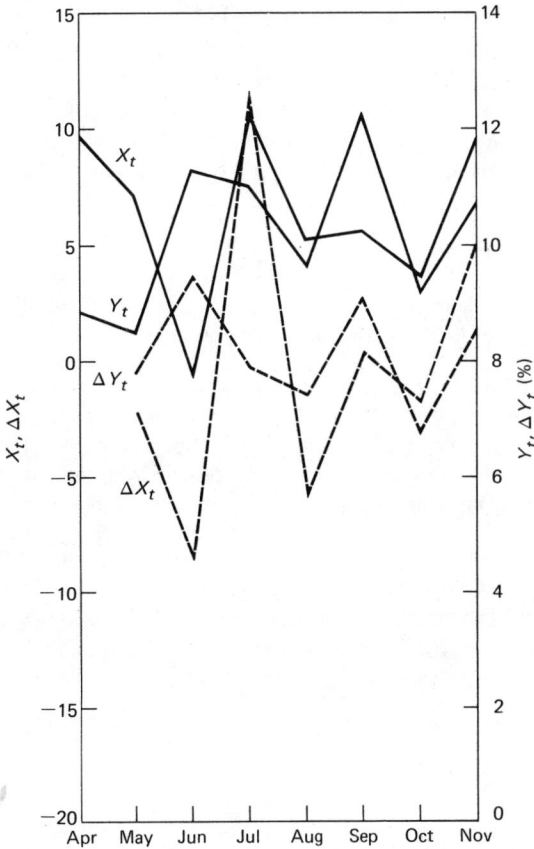

$$\widehat{Y}_t = 10.664 - .077\, X_t \qquad r = -.221 \quad r^2 = .049$$
$$\Delta\widehat{Y}_t = \quad .271 - .011\, \Delta X_t \qquad r = -.034 \quad r^2 = .001$$

where

X_t is the index of private economic expectations
Y_t is potential support for the NPD
$\Delta X_t = X_t - X_{t-1}$
$\Delta Y_t = Y_t - Y_{t-1}$

⌢ indicates the least squares prediction

Source: Probability samples of Infas, April through November, 1967.

The variance and covariance theorems underlying the well-known ecological fallacy (and related fallacies) constitute one approach to understanding the variability of results.[14] Unlike the approaches considered in the next section, this approach does not provide a refutable explanation based on hunches about the nature of a particular system or class or systems that generated the data, but rather an "explanation," which is true by definition, based on statistical statements that apply equally well to any set of interval data, however generated. For example, covariance *within* a cross-section is always equal to *total* covariance in several cross-sections taken as a whole minus covariance *between* the cross-sections. One fallacy lies in making inferences that assume information about the between or trend variance and covariance having information only about the magnitude of the variance and covariance within one cross-section. Within cross-section and between cross-section variance and covariance are equal and presumably lead to equivalent inferences only under unusual conditions. The equality of within and between variance and covariance must be demonstrated in each case, rather than assumed.

Nevertheless, there apparently exists some hope that cross-sectional results can be generalized to statements about change over time without examining trend data. For example, Robert Burrowes has written that,

a question that confronts the user of cross-sectional techniques is that of whether it is ever appropriate—and, if so, when—to base inferences regarding change over time on the analysis of data collected on a single time point. . . . The question is of basic importance, and deserves far more attention if longitudinal inferences drawn from cross-sectionally collected data are to be taken with any degree of confidence.[15]

If inferences are based on variance and covariance, and if within cross-section variance and covariance must be demonstrated, rather than assumed equal to trend variance and covariance, then data over time must be used to determine whether "inferences drawn from cross-sectionally collected data are to be taken with any degree of confidence."

Elements of a Process Theory

Let us turn to some other results of the NPD study which, taken together with the results just considered, play a role in Liepelt's contingent forecast of possible changes in the West German political system. First, through several

---

[14] See W. S. Robinson, "Ecological Correlations and the Behavior of Individuals," *American Sociological Review,* Vol. 15 (June 1950), pp. 351–57. Robinson's argument is generalized by Hayward R. Alker, Jr., in "A Typology of Ecological Fallacies," in Mattei Dogan and Stein Rokkan, eds., *Quantitative Ecological Analysis in the Social Sciences* (Cambridge, Mass.: The MIT Press, 1969).

[15] Burrowes, *op. cit.,* p. 468. See also E. Kuh, "The Validity of Cross-Sectionally Estimated Behavior in Time Series Application," *Econometrica,* Vol. 27 (April 1959), p. 211: "What should be stressed . . . is that cross-sections cannot be used to make time series predictions unless a systematic relationship between the cross-section and time series estimates has been firmly established."

indirect questions, authoritarian political predispositions were found not only among supporters of the NPD, but in the middle and opposite end of the political spectrum as well. For example, at least 56% of the supporters of the CDU, FDP, and SPD felt that national socialism also had a good side, suggesting a latent threat to democratic government. Second, while only 38% of the NPD potential supporters were willing to acknowledge the similarity of the NPD's current aims to those of the Nazis, 75% of the rest of the sample did. The relatively small percentage among NPD supporters may suggest a fear of social sanctions for openly acknowledging active support of nationalistic-authoritarian aims through support of the NPD. Third, in a survey after the state elections in Hesse, only about 15% of SPD and CDU supporters personally knew someone who had voted for the NPD, and only about 37% of the NPD voters knew someone else who had voted for the NPD. This suggests that the "spheres of social contact" of major party supporters and NPD supporters were quite distinct, and that for nearly two-thirds of the latter, voting for the NPD was essentially an individual act lacking the personal confirmation and reinforcement attending votes for the major parties.

These results, together with some verbal process hypotheses, were used to make some projections about possible developments in West German politics. It was felt that if there were a period of social uncertainty and economic pessimism, the number of potential supporters of the NPD would increase. To the extent that the number of supporters increased and the period of uncertainty and pessimism continued, the NPD supporters would realize, through mass and interpersonal communications processes, that neighbors, friends, and colleagues held similar sentiments. Consequently, they would become less inhibited by the hypothesized norm constraining the open expression of nationalistic-authoritarian views. Given the widespread existence of authoritarian predispositions, the diffusion of the NPD's nationalistic-authoritarian views through communication processes would generate additional support for the NPD from the ranks of those who previously identified with the major parties. In short, there may exist conditions and processes capable of amplifying through feedback the strength of the NPD and of establishing it and the views it represents as legitimate features of the political landscape, no longer dependent on economic dissatisfaction.

Of the barriers believed to check the formation of a new party system with a strong radical right, three are related to the material considered here. First, ties to the unions and the Catholic Church tend to insulate voters from radical right influences. Voters in these social contact spheres and organizational communications networks are so strongly integrated into, and identified with, one of the major parties that a new ideology or organization has little room to develop among them. Second, where these ties do not exist, the concentration of business into large firms tends to encourage political pragmatism among employees. The third, and most important, inhibiting factor is a favorable economic situation. If the democratic parties can succeed in stabilizing the situation so that individuals do not have to worry about their jobs and income, there is little reason to turn to the radical right.

CONVENTIONS: INDIVIDUAL RELATIONSHIPS

Theoretically productive confrontations between hypotheses about the structure of a system and data on its behavior require some conventions of evidence to distinguish valid and fallacious conclusions. Drawing on the material presented in the two preceding sections, we consider such conventions for individual relationships in this section. In the next section we consider such conventions for systems of relationships.

Data Analysis Viewpoint

The conventions of evidence in data analysis that can be brought to bear on the problem of making theoretical inferences are well-known and relatively simple. Regarding the question of the existence of a relationship, one convention is simply to scan all the correlations produced from a data set and to pay attention to those which are relatively high and to ignore those which are relatively low: The decision rule is that a weak correlation signals a relationship that doesn't exist or is not worth worrying about. Of course, what is a high correlation for one person may be a low correlation for another: The standard is largely subjective. Another convention is provided by statistical significance tests, which give the probability that a correlation could have been obtained by chance if the real correlation were in fact zero. If this probability is sufficiently low, the null hypothesis of zero correlation is rejected: The inference is that the relationship may exist. If the probability is sufficiently high, the null hypothesis is not rejected: The inference is that the actual correlation could be zero and the obtained correlation a result of chance.

Regarding the question of the form of a relationship, several conventions similar to those above have been used. One convention holds that to choose among alternative regression equations, each having a different functional form, one examines the proportion of variance R^2 explained by each, or the statistical significance of each. The alternative with the high or statistically significant R^2 is provisionally accepted, and the alternative with the low or statistically insignificant R^2 is rejected. Another convention holds that to choose among alternative independent variables, one incorporates the variables into a single equation and estimates the parameters. If the estimated parameter associated with one independent variable is significantly different from zero, and the parameter associated with the other variable is not, the first variable is chosen over the latter.[16]

---

[16] Arthur S. Goldberger, in *Topics in Regression Analysis* (London: Macmillan, 1968), Chapter 9, considers the question of choice of functional forms in the context of regression analysis. He asserts (p. 125) that "Unfortunately, no clear-cut answer to these questions exists." He goes on to advocate tests of the significance of regression coefficients and goodness of fit as measured by R^2 to choose among functional forms.

Analyzed in terms of these conventions, the statistical results relating economic expectations and support for the NPD give rise to inconsistent "theoretical inferences." Table 14–2 indicates that the magnitudes of the individual level, cross-sectional statistics vary with the cross-sections, and that R^2 is statistically significant in three cross-sections but is not statistically significant in the other two. Having results only for January 1967 and applying the statistical significance convention vigorously, one would conclude that a relationship exists. But having results only for March 1967 and applying the same convention, one would conclude the opposite. Apparently, according to this convention, a relationship exists in December, January, and February, but not in November and March. Similarly, Figures 14–1 and 14–2 and the system change analysis indicated that the correlations and their statistical significance vary from the first eight-month period (August 1966 through March 1967) to the second eight-month period. Applying either the high R^2 or the statistical significance convention to the results for the first period, one would conclude that a relationship exists. But applying either convention to the results for the second period, one would conclude the opposite. Apparently, according to these conventions, the relationship exists in one period but not in another. Put another way, the results have only descriptive, rather than theoretical, significance. Without going into alternative regression equations and alternative independent variables, it is clear that the statistical results produced by simple statistical models and these data are sufficiently unstable to make inferences about the form of relationships dependent upon each particular context.

The previous discussion of the multiplier-accelerator system suggests an explanation for the instability of the results: The variables are not in equilibrium and the statistical models imposed on them are misspecified. The models adapted to the various contexts are, of course,

$$Y_{i, t} = a + bX_{,i\,t} \quad \text{and/or}$$

$$\Delta Y_{i, t} = a + b\Delta X_{i, t},$$

where $X_{i, t}$ is a measure of economic expectations and $Y_{i, t}$ is NPD potential support, i refers to a unit of analysis and Δ indicates the first differences of the variables. The search for a third variable to generate stable statistical results and consistent inferences might be a necessary, but surely not a sufficient, step. Whether the underlying process which generated the data is best represented as a two-, three- or more variable relationship, the choice of the form of a statistical model is a choice about the form of a hypothesized process that cannot be sidestepped by the uncritical use of standard statistical models.

One might be tempted to resolve the problem of inconsistent "theoretical inferences" by rejecting the particular form of the regression model used to generate statistical results instead of rejecting the conventions of evidence. However, the choice is not "either–or" but "both–neither." As our exploration with the multiplier-accelerator demonstrated, if the statistical model is accurately specified, then variance explained and statistical significance will tend to be high and stable within limits imposed by stochastic factors. However, if the model is misspecified and the variables in question are in disequilibrium, then variance explained and statistical significance can be expected to be unstable (high or low, significant or insignificant) depending upon the nature of the misspecification and the particular context to which the model is applied. In short, under conditions of disequilibrium, the conventions produce consistent inferences only if the model is accurately specified. Under conditions of equilibrium, the statistical results are stable and the conventions produce consistent inferences whether or not the model is misspecified. But accurate specification is the question at stake in theoretical work, and not an *a priori* assumption. If accurate specification cannot be assumed, then neither can the utility of the conventions of evidence considered here.

While conventions of evidence and the statistics generated by a misspecified regression equation constitute an insufficient basis for making theoretical choices, the statistics themselves may be of heuristic value in formulating hypotheses about the underlying mechanisms that could have produced the data. For example, in Figures 14–1 and 14–2, the mean of the index of economic expectations increased from -6.0% to $+6.5\%$ from the first period to the second, while variation in the index decreased to almost one-sixth of its previous level, and variation in potential support for the NPD decreased to almost one-fourth of its previous level. One of many possible hypotheses suggested by these results is the following: If there exists some unknown tolerable level[17] of economic optimism–pessimism above which there is no felt pressure to translate economic pessimism into support for an extremist party, and if the level of support depends in part on the difference between this tolerable level and the actual level of economic pessimism, then the correlation between expectations and support can be expected to decrease as expectations increase. At or above this tolerable level, variance in support would depend upon other factors.

Process Analysis Viewpoint: Toward Alternative Procedures

In 1948 Warren Weaver[18] contended that scientists had not yet developed the techniques and procedures necessary to cope successfully with problems of organized complexity. Applied to problems of testing empirically the form of individual relationships in political systems construed as organized complex systems, this assessment still appears to be largely correct. In this study we can only suggest two approaches that might eventually lead to the development of more appropriate techniques and procedures.

One approach is suggested by our previous discussion: Explore the relevance of the *instability* through time of statistical results (particularly regression

---

[17] This is not a particularly strong condition. It asserts, basically, that a norm is used to evaluate the actual level of economic optimism–pessimism.

[18] Warren Weaver, *op. cit.*

coefficients in time-series applications)[19] as a criterion for rejecting alternative process hypotheses expressed as regression equations applied to different contexts. These contexts *should* include different time periods in which the variables are not in equilibrium. The contexts *might* include different countries or different geographical or functional groups within countries (e.g., the socioeconomic groups in the NPD study). Instability in results that could not be explained by chance or group differences might be an important signal that the hypothesis is incorrect. To the extent that the form of the equations must go beyond the simple linear additive models (so familiar in comparative government) to forms which have complex expressions on the right-hand side of the equation, this approach might be very inefficient. Each of a large number of plausible or possible equations might have to be tried, even though subsets of the equations might have certain properties in common. A more efficient procedure might exclude whole subsets by testing for the appropriateness of a common property. In this way, intermediate results—properties that cannot be rejected—might be cumulated.

A second approach is to adapt the strong inference[20] version of scientific method to problems of organized complexity. Strong inference emphasizes the construction of tree-like structures showing contingent relationships among the logically possible or theoretically plausible combinations of alternative properties of a particular relationship. The alternative properties apparently must be mutually exclusive and exhaustive. For example, the independence or interdependence of some aspect of the behavior of individuals might be proposed as alternative properties having different consequences for the form of an aggregate relationship. As a second step, strong inference emphasizes the design of an "experiment" in which patterns found in a set of data indicate absence of one of the properties. The third step is to check for the existence of the pattern. We know of only one system change study in the social sciences which conforms to the logic of the strong inference method.[21]

---

[19] Regression coefficients are less sensitive to random measurement errors than correlation coefficients. See Hubert M. Blalock, Jr., *Causal Inferences in Non-Experimental Research* (Chapel Hill, N.C.: University of North Carolina Press, 1961), p. 147. Moreover, such regression coefficients can often be given cultural interpretations. Part of what is meant by cultural differences is the differential propensity to respond to a given stimulus within different groups. The prevalence of cultural differences and the need to disaggregate by cultural groups are suggested by Lucien Pye's observation that ". . . in no society is there a single uniform political culture." Lucien Pye and Sidney Verba, eds., *Political Culture and Political Development* (Princeton: Princeton University Press, 1965), p. 15.

[20] John Platt, "Strong Inference," in his *The Step to Man* (New York: Wiley, 1966).

[21] James S. Duesenberry, *Income, Saving, and the Theory of Consumer Behavior* (New York: Oxford University Press, 1967 ed.), pp. 1–6. For illustrative purposes, it might be useful to reconstruct the logic of this study in highly simplified form.

The Keynesian consumption function assumed that every individual's level of consumption depends only on his absolute income and, therefore, is independent of the income of others. An alternative hypothesis is that one's level of consumption depends on one's relative income and is therefore dependent on the income of others. "Because [household] budget studies show that high income groups save a higher proportion of income than low income receivers, it follows that the aggregate savings ratio will rise with [aggregate] in-

Neither approach to the development of the necessary scientific tools will resolve all uncertainty. Both require genuine creativity in the generation of productive hypotheses. Both will give misleading results if the dependent variable reflects the impact of variables not incorporated into the relationship. Moreover, from the process viewpoint there exists a reasonable expectation that the extension of time series to include ever more recent time periods may provide clues requiring the modification or rejection of the functional forms which were consistent with the data from earlier periods. Data for some periods may not contain enough information to distinguish alternative hypotheses even if the hypotheses are directed to the right question. The basic uncertainty, however, is the modifiability of individual and aggregate behavior which may be reflected in changing parameters or changing relationships over time. On the other hand, by monitoring a set of variables over a long enough period of time, we may be able to discern enough clues to produce a reasonably reliable and stable characterization of the process underlying behavior.

The development of a set of procedures or conventions of evidence relevant to problems of organized complexity would be an important contribution to the study of system change in so far as it purports to be theoretical. Regardless of the merits and limitations of the approaches suggested in this chapter, the first step in the development is the recognition that we presently lack the required tools.

CONVENTIONS: SYSTEMS OF RELATIONSHIPS

Data Analysis Conventions

Regarding the question of the existence of a system of relationships, there does not appear to be a set of procedures sufficiently widespread to justify calling them conventions. There is, however, at least one example of the use of multiple regression addressed to this question. Each of four variables—urbanization, literacy, media participation, and political participation—was taken in turn as a dependent variable with the other three variables as independent variables. The multiple correlation coefficients for the four equations as applied to a cross-sectional sample of at least 54 countries ranged from .91 to .61. The conclusion was that "The size of these coefficients demonstrates that the relationship be-

---

come . . . [p. 2]," *if* the assumption of independence is correct. But this contradicts aggregate statistics which "do not show any tendency for the proportion of income saved to rise with income [p. 2]" over the period 1869–1927. In other words, the Keynesian independence assumption, the household budget data, and the aggregate time-series data taken together are inconsistent, and Duesenberry rejects the independence assumption. The two sets of data are consistent with the assumption that one's savings (income minus consumption) depend on one's relative position in the income ranking. What distinguishes this study from many quantitative studies in comparative government are the clear understanding that the goal is to clarify the qualitative form of a function, the creativity and care taken to derive empirical tests from the hypotheses, and the fact that these tests themselves depend only on the stability or instability of the savings ratio, rather than on some particular magnitude.

tween the four sectors *is* systemic." [22] Given our previous discussion, it should be clear that under reasonably general conditions—disequilibrium and model misspecification—the size of the multiple correlation coefficients could vary considerably from one cross-section to the next and through time. The conclusion about the existence of a system aside, the stability of the statistical result on which it is based assumes either that the model is accurately specified to represent the processes which produced the data or that the variables are in equilibrium.

Regarding the question of the form of a system of relationships, the procedures and conventions associated with the causal modeling technique introduced by Simon and developed by Blalock[23] are most common in comparative government. Basically, hypothesized causal relationships are expressed as a system of linear equations. Assuming that the error terms in each equation are uncorrelated with error terms in the others, predictions can be derived about the pattern of correlation coefficients (or the pattern of zero and non-zero partial regression coefficients) to be observed if the hypotheses are correct. If the predicted pattern is not observed, the model is rejected.

That the *pattern* of correlation coefficients is no more immune to the instabilities arising from misspecification and disequilibrium than individual coefficients has been shown in a simulation experiment.[24] Using a twelve-equation model of modernization and mass politics disaggregated into rural and urban sectors, and random variations in two sets of inputs reflecting Turkey in 1950 and the Philippines in 1951, respectively, time-series behavior for twenty-five hypothetical countries resembling Turkey and twenty-five hypothetical countries resembling the Philippines were generated. The model contained no stochastic factors, and measurement error was limited to insignificant rounding errors.

Two equations in the model which generated the data were selected. The first equation represented a process hypothesis indicating that the level of government expenditures in sector i at time t (denoted by $G_{i, t}$) depends partly on support for the government in sector i at time t (denoted by $V_{i, t}$), according to a "pork barrel" rationale. The second equation is an accounting identity indicating that $G_{i, t}$ is one component of aggregate income in sector i at time t (denoted by $Y_{i, t}$). In order to permit the derivation of a predicted pattern of correlation coefficients via Simon's technique, these two equations were simplified to produce the causal model

$$V_{i, t} = e_1$$

$$G_{i, t} = b_1 V_{i, t} + e_2$$

$$Y_{i, t} = b_2 G_{i, t} + e_3$$

---

[22] Daniel Lerner, *The Passing of Traditional Society* (Glencoe, Ill.: The Free Press, 1964), p. 63.

[23] The technique is discussed in Blalock, *op. cit.*

[24] See the section on "Methods" in Brunner and Brewer, *op. cit.*, and particularly note 140 on p. 176.

and the error terms e_1, e_2, and e_3 were assumed to be uncorrelated. If the model is correct, then the prediction (ignoring subscripts) is that $r_{VY} - r_{VG} r_{GY} = 0$. The results obtained from correlations among the variables in eight different contexts in the simulation experiment are summarized in Table 14–3.

TABLE 14–3.   APPLICATION OF A CAUSAL MODELING TECHNIQUE TO
SIMULATED DATA

	SAMPLE BASED ON TURKISH INPUTS		SAMPLE BASED ON PHILIPPINE INPUTS	
	$(N = 25)$		$(N = 25)$	
	Predicted	Actual	Predicted	Actual
Rural sector ($i = 1$)				
$t = 5$	0.0	.168	0.0	.394
$t = 10$	0.0	.490	0.0	.106
Urban sector ($i = 2$)				
$t = 5$	0.0	.062	0.0	−.165
$t = 10$	0.0	.069	0.0	−.066

Adopting the arbitrary criterion that an absolute difference of greater than .100 between predicted and actual results is cause for rejection, then the model would be rejected in five of eight contexts. In short, the results are unstable and the inferences inconsistent. The problem cannot be attributed to *gross* misspecification of the causal model (the variables are in fact directly linked in the simulation model), to changes in the structure of the simulation model across samples or across time (this remains constant), to changes in parameters across time (these also remain constant), or to stochastic factors (these have been eliminated). The problem lies most directly in the misspecification of the form of the linear causal mechanisms and in the disequilibrium of the variables. Misspecification gives rise to error terms in the linear causal mechanisms, and since the simulation model has several feedback loops, the errors are correlated. The problem lies indirectly in the need to simplify the hypotheses in the system in order to facilitate derivation of a predicted pattern of correlation. It was concluded that "In general, causal modelling . . . of this type is limited by the need to assume simple linear causal mechanisms and to assume that errors in these mechanisms are uncorrelated. If the mechanisms are too complex or if the errors are correlated, predictions about the pattern of correlation coefficients cannot be derived." [25]

Process Analysis Conventions

As we found in the multiplier-accelerator example, relationships for which individual behavior is well known may produce very different and surprising

[25] *Ibid.,* p. 176. James S. Coleman notes that the use of this causal modeling technique with cross-section data assumes either implicitly or explicitly that the causal processes have resulted in an equilibrium state. See his article, "The Mathematical Study of Change," in Hubert M. Blalock and Ann B. Blalock, eds., *Methodology in Social Research* (New York: McGraw-Hill, 1969), p. 444.

behavior when allowed to interact as a system. If a theory suggests that several processes are operating in the real-world system or systems in question, then it also suggests that the behavior produced by these systems and reflected in time-series data may exhibit important interactions. Furthermore, the nature and effects of the interactions may be different from system to system even if the processes in the systems are identical. Consequently, in order to test the deductions from system theories, we must incorporate differences in parameters and initial conditions (the state of the system at the time when analysis begins), deduce the time series for each individual system, and then compare the generated and historical time series. A prerequisite for making the necessary deductions is the translation of a verbal or correlational understanding of the relationships into mathematical forms.[26] For sufficiently small and simple systems, powerful mathematical techniques like the technique of difference equations used by Samuelson can be employed.[27] For larger, more complex systems, it is necessary to abandon mathematical techniques and deduce behavior for each set of inputs by performing a sequence of numerical calculations. This, of course, is simulation. Unlike causal modeling, simulation techniques do not force one to make gross simplifications in order to deduce testable results.

Although the variables and processes in the study of the NPD in its present form are not sufficiently well defined to specify a mathematical version, it is worthwhile for illustrative purposes to suggest a direction that might be taken. First, the model should be disaggregated by social groups because the response parameters governing the assumed relationship between economic expectations and NPD support, as well as other components, appear to differ in magnitude from group to group and because much of the theory focuses on interactions between groups. Second, variables defined for each group should include economic expectations, party support, latent authoritarianism, and a norm inhibiting the expression of authoritarian views. Parameters defined for each group should include the response parameters in some as yet unspecified economic expectation—NPD support relationship, and the minimum tolerable threshold of economic pessimism. It would be necessary to define variables representing the relative discontinuities in communication processes between and within groups. Third, with the exception of economic expectations (which may be exogenous in a first approximation), the processes in the model should produce changes in each of the variables. Obviously, alternative ways of specifying the theory in its present form and a number of possible extensions beyond the aspects considered

[26] Deductions from verbal or correlational statements of theory tend to become indeterminant very quickly as the number of statements increases and to the extent that the correlations are low. For a discussion of the problems of making deductions from axiomatic theory ("the greater A, the greater B; the greater B, the greater C; therefore, the greater A, the greater C") see Herbert L. Costner and Robert K. Leik, "Deductions from Axiomatic Theory," *American Sociological Review*, Vol. 29 (December 1964), pp. 819–35.

[27] To the extent that the achievement of an elegant mathematical solution precludes the study of all but small and uninteresting system change models, mathematical techniques are diversionary.

here exist. But even these few comments suggest a system much more complex than the multiplier-accelerator.

If an acceptable mathematical representation of the theory could be specified, it could then be used in an attempt to reproduce or explain the time-series data. Departures between deduced and historical time series could serve as a test of the theory and as a means of locating those formulations which need revision. These tests, however, are generally more sensitive to the location of variables left out and to problems in the overall loop structure of the model than to errors in the precise form of individual relationships. Even where accurate historical time series are partially lacking, it can often be shown that specifications which seem logically consistent and empirically plausible in the initial statement of the system are inconsistent or implausible when required to operate within the context of the system as a whole. Up to a point, scientific progress can be made without entirely accurate and complete data. Such a model could also be used to explore the magnitude or duration of pessimistic economic expectations necessary to generate self-amplifying increases in support for the NPD.

Some may consider these research directions to be exciting possibilities. Any excitement, however, should be tempered by the awareness that there is a number of unanswered questions concerning the use of mathematical models and computer simulation in political science, and the experience of other disciplines in the use of similar methods is not particularly helpful in answering them. Econometricians, for example, often appear to state relationships rather haphazardly and focus most of their time and energy on exploring the statistical properties of their parameter estimators. As we have seen, the adequacy of parameter estimates depends on the extent to which the stated relationships reflect the processes which produced the data. Perhaps the econometricians' allocation of attention is not altogether inappropriate since Keynes seems to have been remarkably successful in clarifying some important macroeconomic processes. Given the state of political science, however, it seems clear that process clarification and not parameter estimation is the first order of business.

SUMMARY AND CONCLUSION

This chapter contends that if theoretical progress through the use of data is to be made in the study of system change, more than a shift to longitudinal data and techniques is required. The multiplier-accelerator example demonstrates that even in the absence of observation errors and stochastic factors, systems having identical processes can exhibit very diverse behavior (or variance, to use the statistical term) both across systems and within systems through time, depending upon the particular space–time context examined. If a statistical model like regression applied to behavior of this type is misspecified in the sense that it does not accurately reflect the form of the process which generated the data, and if the behavior of the system is not in equilibrium, then the regression model will misconstrue the amount and sources of variance explained and unexplained in the dependent variable, and the statistical results can be expected to be unstable across contexts. Such instability is illustrated in the NPD example. The statistics associated with the regression model will be of primarily descriptive and heuristic, rather than theoretical, significance.

Given this result, conventions of evidence in data analysis relying on results such as statistical significance and goodness of fit are largely fallacious as means of rejecting or failing to reject hypotheses of theoretical significance. Such conventions can be expected to produce consistent inferences only when the form of the equation used to estimate regression and correlation coefficients is not misspecified or when the data to which it is applied are in equilibrium. For the case of equilibrium, the inferences generated by the use of these conventions may be wrong even if they are consistent across contexts. For both the case of equilibrium and the case of disequilibrium, an inference about misspecification is the objective of the analysis in so far as it purports to be theoretical, and accurate specification cannot be assumed a priori. Alternative conventions more appropriate in terms of a process analysis, rather than a data analysis, epistemology are not yet well developed.

While these are negative conclusions, there are also some positive implications of this exploration into the study of system change. First, the goal of theoretical work in comparative government should be the clarification of process relationships.[28] This is *not* a novel suggestion. Several years ago Norman Jacobsen suggested that political scientists return to process analysis, "the tool which Bentley fashioned." [29] Herbert Simon has written:

The notion of substituting a process description for a state description [that is, a description of a system at a cross-section in time] has played a central role in the development of modern science. Dynamic laws, expressed in the form of differential or difference equations, have in a large number of cases provided the clue for a simple description of the complex.[30]

As indicated in this study, process relationships are not only a prerequisite to the theoretical use of statistics. They suggest also a means of reconciling the diversity we observe between systems and within systems over time with the scientific assumption that both order and the possibility of useful general explanations exist. With an understanding of processes, we should be able to bridge the gap between the structure and behavior of organized complex systems.

Second, given that statistical tools are not so powerful for theoretical purposes as the current conventions of data analysis suggest, theoretical efforts will

---

[28] Sidney G. Winter of the Institute of Public Policy Studies, The University of Michigan, has criticized the orthodox theory of the profit maximizing firm from a process viewpoint in his paper, "Satisficing, Selection, and the Innovating Remnant," *Quarterly Review of Economics,* Vol. 85 (May 1971), pp. 237–61.

[29] Norman Jacobsen, "Causality and Time in Political Process: A Speculation," *American Political Science Review,* Vol. 68 (March 1964), pp. 15–22.

[30] Simon, *op. cit.,* p. 117.

be considerably facilitated by increased attention to existing theoretical and case studies emphasizing process and to nonstatistical uses of mathematics. Our verbal literature both stimulates creativity and disciplines the range of speculation in the clarification of individual process relationships in system theories. New scientific procedures are required to clarify further the forms of these individual process relationships using time-series data. Mathematical representations of system theories are necessary to deduce their consequences for purposes of evaluating the theory as a whole and for attempts to explain or predict the behavior of individual systems over time.

Third, monthly survey data of the kind collected by Infas and used in the NPD study are extremely useful in the study of system change where mass publics are concerned. The data help in inferring process relationships, in defining the appropriate disaggregations, and in testing and evaluating individual relationships and whole theories. Given these purposes, crossnational surveys of, say, twelve countries at one cross-section in time are much less useful than are surveys of two countries at six successive cross-sections in time.

In a larger sense, the implication of this chapter is that we should take each shift in substantive interests as an opportunity to reconsider and modify our methodological conventions and points of view. While we cannot expect them to be entirely satisfactory at any point in time, we can at least reappraise them at appropriate intervals and undertake the necessary adjustments.

Indexes

Name Index

Ackoff, Russell L., 355
Adams, Richard, 190
Adelman, I., 213
Aitken, Hugh G. J., 358
Akzin, Benjamin, 285
Alchian, A. A., 354
Alker, Hayward R., Jr., 104, 159, 161, 292, 447, 464
Allison, Graham T., 357
Almendinger, Vladimir V., 294, 459
Almond, Gabriel, 6, 163–64, 278
Althusser, Louis, 127
Amis, Kingsley, 298
Anderson, C. Arnold, 353
Anderson, Charles W., 362
Ando, Albert, 328
Aldrain, Charles F., 28, 32
Angell, R., 25
Anscombe, Francis J., 463
Anton, Paul, 292
Apter, David E., 28, 94, 96, 163
Aquinas, Thomas, 346
Aristotle, 346
Arnold, T. W., 286
Aron, Raymond, 291
Arosemena, Carlos J., 179, 185
Arrow, Kenneth J., 24, 28, 355
Artle, Roland, 299
Ascher, William, 21, 300–1, 303
Ashby, W. Ross, 163, 351
Ashton, E. G., 287
Asimov, Isaac, 291
Augustine, Saint, 346
Averch, Harvey A., 162, 297

Babson, R., 305
Barber, B., 285, 295
Barghoorn, Frederick C., 95
Barnes, J. A., 163
Bass, Jerome R., 95
Batchelor, James H., 360
Bator, Francis M., 355
Bauer, P. T., 359
Bauer, Raymond A., 292–93
Baumol, William J., 354

Bayby, F. L., 291
Bayes, Thomas, 465, 469–70, 479, 485–86
Beard, Charles A., 89
Bell, Daniel, 284, 287, 295
Bellamy, Edward, 298
Bellman, Richard, 291, 297
Bennis, Warren G., 295, 351
Bentley, A. F., 513
Berelson, Bernard, 290
Berger, Morroe, 95
Beria, L., 278
Berke, Joel S., 360
Berlin, Isaiah, 92
Bernstein, Jeremy, 291
Berry, Brian J. L., 211, 212, 230
Berry, Donald A., 22, 265, 437, 462
Bertram, Christoph, 287
Binder, Leonard, 94
Bisco, Ralph L., 294
Black, C. E., 162
Bloc, Marc, 92
Bloomfield, Lincoln P., 287, 297
Blumenstock, Dorothy, 25
Bobrow, Davis B., 95
Boguslaw, Robert, 298
Boulding, Kenneth E., 285, 292, 295, 355
Bowman, Mary Jane, 353
Braibanti, Ralph, 26, 353
Brandt, Willy, 147
Braybrooke, David, 354, 356
Brech, Ronald, 287
Brewer, Garry D., 1, 21, 165, 296, 301, 327, 362, 439
Bronowski, Jacob, 346
Bross, I. D. J., 355
Brown, Lawrence, 352
Brown, W. O., 93
Browning, Rufus P., 352
Bruce, R. D., 292
Bruchey, Stuart, 90, 92
Bruner, J. S., 25
Brunner, Ronald D., 1, 21–22, 165, 301, 327, 437, 487
Brzezinski, Zbigniew, 358
Buckeley, Walter, 351

517

Bullock, Allan, 92
Burack, Arnold B., 287
Burns, Arthur F., 293
Burrowes, Robert, 488, 502

Cady, John F., 94
Caiden, Naomi, 359
Calder, Nigel, 286
Caldwell, Lynton K., 358
Campbell, Donald T., 362
Carlisle, N. V., 287
Caro, Francis G., 360
Carter, Gwendolyn, 93
Carter, Launor F., 162
Cartwright, D. P., 29
Castillo, Ramón S., 117
Cetron, Marvin J., 291
Chambers, R. J., 361
Chandrasekhar, S., 290
Chapman, Brian, 358
Chapple, Eliot D., 361
Cherry, Colin, 28
Churchman, C. West, 24, 28, 354–55
Clapham, Christopher, 32
Clark, Colin B., 289
Clarke, Arthur C., 285
Clarke, I. F., 287, 298
Clarke, John I., 231
Cleveland, Charles E., 43
Cline, Howard F., 94
Cloward, Richard A., 361
Cohen, Morris R., 92
Coleman, James S., 32, 94, 161, 163, 353
Collingwood, Robin G., 92
Conley, Ronald W., 361
Converse, Philip E., 294
Coombs, C. H., 269
Cooper, Sophia, 293
Corpuz, O. D., 94
Crane, Dwight, 297
Crecine, J. P., 161, 447
Crotty, James, 297
Crozier, Michel, 357
Cutright, Phillips, 104, 162

Dahl, Robert A., 15, 24, 28, 254, 356, 361
Dahrendorf, Ralf, 205, 298
Dalkey, Norman C., 293, 299
Danelski, David J., 163
Danskin, J. M., 297
David, Paul T., 295, 299
Davies, James C., 108, 187
Davis, Kingsley, 250

Debbins, William, 92
Debreu, Gerard, 357
de Chardin, P. Teilhard, 285
Deemer, Walter L., 296
Deese, James E., 42
de Jouvenel, Bertrand, 284–86, 295, 298
DeLand, E. C., 460
Delaney, William, 27, 357
Denton, F. H., 162
de Solla Price, D. J., 295
de Tocqueville, Alexis, 108
Deutsch, Karl W., 92, 161–63, 191, 286–87, 292
Deutsch, Morton, 352
DeWeerd, Harvey, 297
Dollar, Charles M., 464, 480
Dollard, John, 296
Dorfman, Robert, 355, 361
Dorn, H. F., 296
Dorsey, John T., Jr., 27
Downs, Anthony, 287
Dror, Yehezkel, 21, 286, 357–58, 366–68, 371
Dublin, L. I., 307, 312–14, 316, 324
Ducoff, Louis J., 288
Duncan, J. W., 292
Duncan, Otis Dudley, 284
Dunham, Vera, 25
Durasoff, Douglas, 20, 167, 169, 170–72, 268

Easton, David, 164, 189
Edel, Abraham, 28
Edelman, Murray, 24
Edwards, Ward, 356, 465
Einaudi, Luigi R., 184
Eisenstadt, S. N., 162–63, 356
Eldridge, H. W., 288
Ellul, Jacques, 285, 291
Erhard, Ludwig, 147
Erikson, Eric H., 93, 96
Erlich, Alexander, 358
Etzioni, Amitai, 351
Evan, William M., 162, 296, 352
Ewald, William R., 299

Fainsod, Merle, 358
Fairweather, George F., 352
Feldman, Arnold, 105
Feldstein, Martin S., 362
Feller, W., 354
Festinger, Leon, 29, 249
Fischer, David H., 92

Fisher, Franklin M., 328
Fisher, J. C., 291
Fitch, John S., III, 20, 164–65, 173
Foltz, William J., 162
Foster, George M., 163
Freedman, Ronald, 290
Freeman, Howard E., 351
Frey, Frederick A., 96, 164
Friedland, William H., 32
Friedman, Milton, 400
Friedmann, John, 200, 204–5, 208–10, 216, 226
Friedrich, Carl J., 27
Froman, G., 289
Frondizi, Auturo, 122, 123

Gable, Richard, 27
Gabor, Denis, 285, 298
Gadamer, Hans-Georg, 299
Galbraith, J. K., 305
Galtung, Y., 285
Gannet, H., 307–8, 319
Gardiner, Patrick, 92
Gasteyger, Curt, 287
Geertz, Clifford, 289
George, Alexander, 25, 96, 364
George, Juliette, 96, 364
Germani, Gino, 119
Gillespie, R. W., 288
Gilmore, Robert, 94
Gilpin, Robert, 357
Golay, Frank, 359
Goldhamer, Herbert, 296
Goldrich, Daniel, 191
Goldsen, J. M., 287
Golemblewski, Robert T., 352
Gordon, Theodore J., 299
Gould, Peter, 231
Gouldner, Alvin, 351
Gouschev, Sergi, 298
Greenberg, Emile, 295
Greenberger, Martin, 287
Gross, Bertram, 292–93
Gross, Neal C., 266, 353
Grundy, Kenneth, 28, 32
Gurr, Ted R., 294
Gustafson, James, 24
Guttentag, Jack L., 293

Haas, Ernest B., 287
Hackett, Anne-Marie, 288, 358
Hackett, John, 288, 358
Hagen, Everett E., 288, 358

Hägerstrand, Torsten, 297, 352–53
Hajnal, John, 296, 325
Hamilton, Herbert, 352
Hansen, Alvin, 489, 496
Hanson, A. H., 359
Hanssmann, Fred, 354
Harman, Harry H., 47
Hauser, Philip M., 27, 290
Haveman, Robert, 359
Hawkes, Nigel, 297
Heilbroner, Robert L., 287, 295
Helmer, Olaf, 291, 294, 297–99
Hempel, Karl, 274
Herz, John H., 286
Hickman, B. G., 296
Hill, Laurence S., 299
Hillegas, Mark R., 298
Hirsch, W., 285, 295
Hirschman, Albert O., 161, 195, 354–58, 436–37
Hitch, C. J., 354
Hoagland, Hudson, 290
Hockett, Homer Carey, 92
Holland, E. P., 288
Holmberg, Allan R., 26, 353, 444–45
Holton, G., 292
Hopkins, Frank S., 286
Hopkins, Raymond F., 20, 167–69, 244
Hoselitz, Bert F., 358
Hsia, Ronald, 289
Hughes, H. Stuart, 92
Huntington, Samuel P., 162, 287–88, 351, 358, 488

Ibarra, Velasco, 174
Iklé, Fred C., 364
Illia, Auturo, 122, 125

Jacobsen, Norman, 513
Janowitz, Morris, 27, 357
Jantsch, Erich, 291
Jaspers, Karl, 287
Jennings, John B., 362
Jensen, Richard J., 464, 480
Johnson, E. A. J., 230
Johnston, F., 293
Johnston, John J., 93, 174, 179
Jungk, Robert, 285
Juvilier, Peter H., 358

Kahn, Herman, 284–86, 298
Kant, I., 346
Kapinga, M. E., 265
Kaplan, Abraham, 24, 28–29, 161, 355

Karlsson, Georg, 353
Karpat, Kemal H., 93
Katz, Daniel, 29
Katz, Elihu, 352–53
Kazin, Alfred, 298
Kecskemeti, Paul, 364
Kelly, R. Gordon, 286
Keniston, Kenneth, 300
Kenyatta, Jomo, 19, 31, 36, 39
Keynes, J. M., 289, 512
Khrushchev, Nikita, 278–79
Kidd, Charles V., 291
Kiesinger, K. G., 147
King, Martin Luther, 32
Kirby, Robert, 296–97
Kirst, Michael W., 360
Klein, Burton H., 357
Klein, Lawrence, 289
Klemm, Frederich, 291
Klyuchevsky, Vasily, 96
Koehler, John E., 21, 162, 369–70, 396
Kogan, N., 364
Kogiku, K. C., 289
Kolers, Paul A., 42
Korbel, John, 289
Kossack, Carl F., 464
Kruskal, J. B., 480
Krutilla, J. V., 354–55
Kuhn, Thomas S., 102, 161, 351
Kuznets, Simon, 199

Lakoff, S. A., 350
Landsberg, H. H., 291
Langer, Walter L., 364
Lanusse, General, 125
LaPalombara, Joseph, 27, 95, 162, 356
LaPorte, Todd R., 287, 291, 449
Lasswell, Harold D., 2, 4, 12, 24–26, 28,
    285–86, 288, 292, 294–95, 299–300, 302,
    343, 350, 353, 355, 360, 363–64, 436–
    37, 439, 441, 446–47
Latham, F. B., 287
Lavin, M. M., 297
Lawrence, J. R., 354
Lazarsfield, Paul F., 254
Lederberg, Joshua, 291
Leff, Nathaniel, 27
Leites, Nathan, 24
Lenin, N., 258
Leontieff, Wassily, 289, 327
Lerner, Daniel, 25, 94, 163, 176, 206, 285,
    331, 350, 446
Lervins, Leon, 288

Lev, Daniel S., 95
Levin, H. J., 290
Levin, Martin L., 352
Lévi-Strauss, Claude, 127
Lewis, Bernard, 94
Lewis, John P., 230
Lewis, R., 293
Lewis, W. Arthur, 358
Leys, Wayne A. R., 24, 355
Lien, Arhtur P., 292
Liepelt, Klaus, 22, 29, 128, 437, 487, 497,
    499
Lieuwen, Edwin, 177, 179
Lilley, S., 285, 295
Lindblom, Charles E., 15, 24, 354–56, 359
Lipset, Seymour M., 95, 104, 112
Lompe, Klaus, 295
Lotka, A., 307, 312–14, 316, 324
Lovewell, P. J., 292
Lynd, Robert S., 350

Maas, Arthur, 356
Mabogunje, Akin L., 223, 228
Machlup, Fritz, 357
Macridis, Roy C., 93
Maddison, Michael, 286
Magsaysay, Ramon, 342
Maisel, Sherman J., 294
Malenkov, G., 278
Mamalakis, Markos, 127
Mannheim, Karl, 247, 298, 448
Mannoni, O., 164
Margolis, Julius, 359
Martin, Henry W., 358
Marx, Fritz Morstein, 27, 247
Marx, Karl, 108
Mason, Edward S., 288
Mayer, J., 290
Mazlish, B., 96
Mboya, Tom, 36
McAlister, John T., 94
McKean, Roland, 354
McLaughlin, Milbrey W., 360
McLean, H., 96
McLuhan, Marshall, 286
Means, R. L., 24
Menderes, 342
Menzel, Herbert, 353
Merkx, Gilbert, 19, 97–99, 103, 165, 186
Merton, Robert K., 25, 163
Mesthene, Emmanuel G., 290
Meyer, Donald, 96
Meyerhoff, Hans, 11, 90, 92

Meynen, Wicky L., 353
Michael, Donald N., 299
Miller, S. M., 351
Millikan, Max F., 358
Modigliani, Franco, 292, 295–96
Montgomery, John D., 27, 162
Moore, Barrington, 127
Moore, W. E., 298
Morgan, George A., 299
Morris, Charles W., 25
Morris, Cynthia Taft, 213
Morrison, Donald F., 464
Mudd, Stuart, 290
Muller, H. J., 92
Mumford, Lewis, 298
Mus, Paul, 94
Myrdal, Gunnar, 203–4, 356

Nagel, Ernest, 161
Namenwirth, J. Zvi, 25
Needler, Martin C., 94, 96, 178, 180
Nelson, Richard R., 291, 356
Neustadt, Richard, 363
Newall, Allen, 161
Newcomb, Theodore M., 249
Newell, Allen, 296
Newman, Peter, 296
Nordlinger, Eric, 92
North, Liisa, 185
Novick, David, 356, 361
Nye, J. S., 27
Nyerere, Julius, 19, 31, 37, 39, 254, 261, 263

Odinga, Oginga, 36, 220
Ogden, C. K., 298
Ongania, Juan Carlos, 125
Orcutt, Guy H., 289
Osgood, C. E., 25
Outka, Gene H., 24
Ozbekhan, Hasan, 291, 294

Paloczi-Horvath, G., 287
Panofsky, Hans, 294
Papanek, Gustav F., 288
Pardee, F. S., 291
Park, Richard L., 359
Parker, S., 293
Parsons, Talcott, 252
Pascal, Blaise, 346
Paxton, E. W., 297
Pearl, Raymond, 307, 309–12, 314–15, 318, 323
Peck, Merton J., 357

Perón, Juan, 19, 114–16, 118, 122–23, 125
Pirro, Ellen B., 19, 29–31, 42
Piven, Frances Fox, 361
Plato, 32
Platt, John Rader, 350
Pool, Ithiel de Sola, 25, 28–29, 361
Powell, G. Bingham, Jr., 6, 163, 278
Pressman, Jeffrey, 359
Prest, A. R., 354
Price, Don K., 351
Pritchett, H. S., 307–8, 322–23
Prothro, J. W., 25
Pye, Lucien W., 93, 97, 163, 248

Quade, Edward S., 297
Quant, R. E., 355
Quillan, Ross, 42

Raeff, Marc, 96
Raiffa, H., 269
Ramsay, Paul, 24
Rathjens, George, 287
Ravetz, Jerome R., 350
Redfield, Robert E., 190
Reed, L. J., 290
Rein, Martin, 358
Reiner, Thomas, 299
Rescher, Nicholas, 294–95
Reynolds, Clark W., 416
Richards, Audrey, 94
Riddell, J. Barry, 231, 242
Ridker, Ronald G., 362
Riggs, Fred W., 94, 272–73
Riker, William, 193
Rivkin, Arnold, 27
Rivlin, Alice M., 289, 351, 361
Robinson, Richard D., 95
Rogers, Everett M., 286, 353
Rokeach, M., 293
Rosberg, Carl G., 32, 94
Rosenbloom, R. S., 360
Ross, Harry, 298
Rossi, Peter, 361
Rothchild, Donald, 27, 32
Rothenberg, Jerome, 354, 361
Rourke, Daniel L., 299
Rowse, A. L., 92
Runion, H. L., 25
Russell, E. J., 290
Russell, J. R., 360
Russett, Bruce M., 104, 286, 292, 296
Ryan, Bryce, 353

Samuelson, Paul A., 175, 487, 489, 511
Sarbin, T. R., 249
Sayeed, Khalid Bin, 27
Sayles, Leonard R., 361
Scherer, Frederic M., 357
Schlesinger, Arthur, 89
Schon, Donald, 361
Schramm, Wilbur, 163
Schubert, Glendon, 163
Schultz, Theodore W., 352
Schultze, Charles, 359
Selznik, Philip, 360
Shapley, Lloyd, 357
Sharp, Walter, 95
Sherif, M., 249
Sherwood, Clarence C., 351
Shils, Edward A., 96, 285
Shubik, Martin, 165, 296, 302, 328, 343, 346, 447
Siffen, William J., 94, 162
Simon, Herbert A., 15, 161, 296, 356–57, 449, 513
Singer, J. David, 25
Sloane, C. S., 307–8
Smith, M. G., 27
Smith, Nicholas M., Jr., 28
Smith, Thomas C., 94, 362
Snyder, D., 293
Soedjatmoko, 93
Soja, Edward, 20, 166–67, 197
Speier, Hans, 296
Spengler, Joseph J., Jr., 27, 355
Spier, L., 355
Stalin, J., 277–78
Steiner, George, 299
Stekler, H. O., 289, 297
Stepan, Alfred C., III, 95
Stone, Philip J., 29
Suchman, Edward A., 360
Sundquist, James L., 361
Suyin, Han, 288

Taubman, P., 289
Teitz, Michael B., 361
Theil, Henri, 296
Theobald, Robert, 287
Thomas, Clayton J., 296
Thompson, James D., 359
Thompson, W. S., 307, 311–14, 316
Thrall, R. M., 269
Tilman, Robert O., 95
Tinbergen, Jan, 296, 354, 397
Tinker, Irene, 359

Titmus, Richard M., 361
Tobin, James, 27, 166–67, 354
Tobin, Richard, 20, 197
Tugwell, Rexford G., 287
Turner, Frederick Jackson, 89, 95
Turvey, R., 354
Tversky, A., 356

Ul-Haq, Mahub, 289
Uriburu, General, 115

van den Berghe, Pierre, 204
Vassiliev, Mikhail, 298
Verba, Sidney, 163
Vernon, Raymond, 413
Vickers, Geoffrey, 285, 295
von der Mehden, Fred R., 362

Walker, Jack L., 352–53
Wallich, M. A., 364
Walsh, C., 298
Ward, Robert E., 93
Waterson, Albert, 358
Weaver, Warren, 506
Webber, Melvin, 299
Weiker, Walter F., 95
Weiner, Milton G., 294, 297
Weiner, Myron, 95, 162
Weiner, Norbert, 295
Weingartner, H. M., 292, 296
Whelpton, P. K., 307, 311–14, 316
White, Leonard D., 161
White, R. K., 25
Whitson, William A., 96
Wholey, Joseph S., 362
Wiener, A. J., 284–86
Wildavsky, Aaron, 357, 359
Winks, Robin W., 92
Winter, Gibson, 24, 355
Wirth, L., 355
Wittfogel, Karl A., 93
Wittgenstein, Ludwig, 102, 127
Woodruff, C. E., 307–8
Woodruff, Philip, 96
Wright, Christopher, 357
Wright, Quincy, 352

Yanaga, Chitoshi, 358
Young, James Sterling, 91, 95
Yrigoyen (also Irigoyen), Hipólito, 116–17
Yule, G. U., 29

Zolberg, Aristide, 32

Subject Index

Africa
  East Africa Common Market, 79
  leaders, 19, 219–21, 227
  Sub-Sahara, 33
  tropical, 198
"African Socialism," 32
"Africanization," 29
Allocation of attention, 3
Alternatives, 17–18, 21, 26, 345
  approach, 345, 350
  "cool and hot" development strategies, 364–66
  estimation of, 17, 347, 353–56
    a priori social-ethical assessments, 348
    Bayesian statistics, 347
    benefit analysis, 348
    extrapolation, 347
    forecasting, 347
    market research, 347
    model construction, 347
    resource analysis, 347
    survey techniques, 347–48
  evaluation, 17–18, 21, 348–49, 360
  factors conditioning present practices, 367
  goals of those participating in the context, 367
  goals' trade-off issue, 18, 26
  implementation, 17–18, 348, 359
  invention, 17, 345–57
    creativity, 346–47, 351
    innovation, diffusion, 351
  policy-oriented research, 347
  policy space, 347
  power and wealth as values, 365
  recommendations, 367
  respect revolution, defined, 366
  selection, 348, 356
  termination, 17, 349–50, 362
  trends, 367
Analytic techniques
  cross-national comparative, 488
  cross-sectional analysis, 487
  longitudinal, time-series analysis, 487–88
Approaches

bureaucratic, 7
chartists and fundamentalists, 328–29, 340, 343
crises of development, 7, 12
cybernetic, 7, 16
elite, 7
policy, 1, 17, 19
political-cultural, 7, 341
stages of development, 7, 12
structural-functional, 7, 341
Argentina, 19
  cycles of rebellions, 112, 118, 124
  histories of, 107–10
  social classes of, 120–21
  "The Permanent Crisis" in, 118, 123
Artificial intelligence, 15
Arusha Declaration, 37, 59, 80

Bayesian statistics, 462–84

Case studies and descriptive histories
  long-run, contextual, empirical political histories, 98
  perspectives contexts, 93
  rebellions, 97
    cycles and, 113
    military, 115–16
    party, 115
    regional, 115–16
  spatial and temporal resolutions, 93, 97
  time-series data, 98–100, 113
    analysis, 112–13
    quality, 100
    relationships, 113
    reliability, 100
  verbal, descriptive-historical, 94
Complex social problems, dealing with
  approaches
  of policymakers, 440
  of researchers, 440
Comprehensiveness, 2
Conditions
  analysis, 169
  approaches
    communications, 163, 166, 170

contextual policy, 159–60, 168, 174
cybernetic, 161, 163
as intellectual approaches or orientations, 159
bureaucracy, 162
comparison, 169
conditions-oriented work, 160, 162
cross-sectional context, 168
decision-making systems, 170
development "crises," 166
diffusion of an innovation, 166
government change in Latin America,
   193
individual and aggregate behavior, 168
   elite, 168
   goals, 168
information, 170
institutions, 170
Latin American coup d'etat, 164, 173–74
methodological problems, 168
military in Latin America, 177
mobilization, 166
models and model-building, 161, 165,
   169
normative issues, 167
organizational behavior, 169
policy questions, 167
political culture, 161, 163, 191
political parties, 162
political roles, 167
   behavior, 167
   expectations, 167
   orientations, 167
problem-solving orientation, 165
   alternative projections, 165
   conditions, 165
   formal model, 166
   goal clarification, 165
   model-building, 165, 169
   trends, 165
projections, 167
revolution of rising expectations, 187
scientific description and orientation,
   168–69
set theory, 170
simulation model, 175
   computer simulation, 176
social mobilization, 191
space and time, 167
structural analyses, 13, 169
structural-functionalism, 161, 163
structure and behavior, 13, 160, 170, 174
suboptimize, 159

support concept, 188–90
systematic description, 169
systems, 161, 164
time series, 168
trends, 159, 165–66, 168
Content analysis, 30
   application of, 45–47
   conceptual, 42
   machine content analysis, 84–86
   problems and decisions, 80–81
   The Pirro African Dictionary, 42–43
      list of categories, 43
Contextualism, 4–6, 16, 22, 197

"Decision seminar"
   advantages and disadvantages, 343–44,
      448–50
   forecasting, 444
   multiple methods used, 443
   of political development, 444–48
      SEADAG (Southeast Asia Develop-
         ment Advisory Group), 445–46
      Vicos project, 444–45
      Yale development decision seminar,
         446–48, 460
   problem-solving orientation, 442
      conditioning, 442
      expectations, 443
      future outcomes and projections, 442
      goals, 442
      trends, 442
   strategies to manage complexity, 450–
      60
      measurement and display, 456–60
      perceptual insights, 451–53
      problem identification, 453–54
      problem space, 454–56
      the policy phase, 456
   theory of, 441
Decisionmaking
   under uncertainty, 26
Demands, 13–14
Developmental construct, 12, 294, 299–300

Events
   contemplation of, 3
   manipulation of, 3

Factor analysis
   applications of, 47–58, 216–19
Forecasting, *see* Projections
Formal models
   data analysis conventions, 508–10

data analysis viewpoint in, 493–95, 504–6, 513
organized complex systems, 495–96, 513
process analysis conventions, 510–12
process theory, 502–3
process viewpoint in, 492–93, 506–8, 513
variance and covariance theorems—ecological fallacy, 502

"Garrison State Hypothesis," 12, 294, 299–300
Geographic concepts
circulation system, 197
diffusion processes, 197
growth poles, 197
networks, 197
primate city, 197
Geography
discipline of, 197
mathematical and statistical modes of analysis in, 197
German NPD (National Demokratische Partei Deutschlands)
age and sex of NPD voters, 132
economic expectations and the NPD reservoir, 147, 150
estimate of NPD gains through worsening of economic expectations, 148
NPD's future, 152
NPD's potential, 129, 511–14
by income and economic expectations, 146
NPD's reservoir
and economic expectations, 144
socioeconomic profile of, 136
and the traditional parties, 140, 496–99
opinions, attitudes, and party preferences, 151
party political history of the mobile segment of the electorate, 142
party support in socioeconomic groups, 139
political elections of 1966–67, 101, 130
political origin of the NPD voter potential, 141
prior election behavior and party preference (1966), 143
structure of the potential NPD voters in the federal district, 134
supposed grounds for NPD successes, 149
Goals, 2, 8–11, 19, 23

abstract principles, 9
agenda, 9
change in, 9
"cool" and "hot" cultures, 11
and elite behavior, 27
idealist versus realist, 9–10
methodological techniques to study, 28, 30
political development as overriding, 38
symbols and, 31
Growth poles, 214–25, 219, 222, 227

Historical-descriptive research, see Trends

Kenya, 29
contextual setting, 35–36
contribution of political ideas to policy, 73–77
geographic analysis of, 217–20
speeches by presidents of (listing), 39–41
and Tanzania, 33
Kenyatta, Jomo
speeches of, 39–41

Levels of resolutions
spatial and temporal, 89

Methods
analysis
cross-sectional, 106, 436–37, 487
longitudinal, 100, 436, 487–88
process styles of, 437
comparative, 105–6
"decision seminar," 436, 439–61
limitations, 100
multiple, 6–7, 18–19, 22
perspectives, 21
alternatives, 435
conditions, 435
goals, 435
projections, 435
trends, 106, 435
problem-oriented aspect of the policy approach, 435
Mexico
fiscal policy, 401–4
political cycle in, 404–7
information and policy making in, 422–30
adequacy of available information, 422–25
short-run policy and growth, 428-30
use of information, 425–28

monetary policy, 407–22, 430–32
  excess demand for funds, 407–13
  model of, 413–22
  spending and stability in, 400–7
Model assessment
  empirical models, 478–84
  procedures for, 470–78
Modernization policy making, 372
Modernization processes and problems, 371

NPD, see German NPD
Nyerere, Julius
  speeches of, 39

Organized complexity, 495–96, 513
  modernization and mass politics, 331–32, 338
  real-world systems, 341

Partial order and political systems, 268
  partially ordered set (poset), 268–69
  Soviet style systems, 268, 276
  "succession crisis," 276
  Thailand, 273–76
    bureaucracy, 268
    politics, 272
Policy
  analysis, 6–7
    intellectual tools for, 2
    level of spatial detail, 99
  sciences, 372
Policy and the future
  methods to study, 327, 341
    extrapolation versus process models, 327
    See also Developmental construct
  system properties influencing
    Ando-Fisher theorem, 328, 336–40
    connectedness, 334, 336–37, 341
    structure and behavior, 329
Political ideas, 32–34; see also Content analysis
Political roles, 244
  concepts of, 28
  deviance role, 263
  elites, 31, 244, 248, 256
  expectations, 246
    role expectations (norms), 247–48
  institutionalization among roles, 262
  political behavior, 244
  political culture, 244, 246
  political roles, 245

structural-functional, 244
  Tanzania, 245
Political symbols, 25
Political systems, 279–80
Preference recognition and specification, 26
Primate cities, see Spatial development dynamics
Problem orientation
  concept described, 1–22
Projections, 16, 21, 283–302; see also Policy and the future
  alternative projective methods, 17, 283–84, 302
    cohort method, 312, 314, 320–21
    component method, 311, 320–21
    extrapolation, 292–95, 302
    games, 283, 294, 296–97
    group judgment techniques, 283–84, 294, 299
    logistic model, 320, 323
    planning, 283–84, 299
    process models, 283–84, 292, 294, 296, 302
    scenario writing, 283, 297
    simulations, 283, 294, 296
    utopia writing, 283, 294, 298
    See also Developmental construct
  in complex systems, 283
  conditioning factors, 283
  costs of inaccurate projections, 304
  economics, demography, and technology, 289–92
  evaluation of, 315
  length of, accuracy and plausibility, 322
  logistic law of population growth, 309
  need for accurate projections, 303
  normative, 285
  planners as specialists, 283, 325
  political forecasting, 285–86
  in problem orientation, 3
  problem-solving approach, 283, 300
  "quality of life," 292
  scientific models, 283
  social indicators, 292
  specialists in, 16–17
  technological, 285
  trend information, 295
  "utopians," 284

Rebellions
  cycles of in Argentina, 107–11
  Davies hypothesis on, 108, 110

Regional development theory, 200–2
  deviation-counteracting systems, 201–10,
    225–27
  differentiation of the system, 202
  equilibrium models, 202
  political participation, 207
  regional growth, 207, 211
  structural functionalism, 202
Role process, 248, 250
  role behavior, 248, 250
  role expectations, 248
    of elite, 260
  role orientations, 248, 250

Samuelson's multiplier-accelerator anal-
    ysis, 175–76, 489–91, 494–95, 512
Sierra Leone, 197–98, 231–32
Social process, basic elements in, 4–6
Spatial development dynamics, 198–208
  as means to organize society, 198
  backwash effects, 203, 207, 216, 239–
    42
  core and periphery, 205–8, 214–16, 226–
    29
  disequilibrium, 208, 210, 229
  equilibrium, 200, 208, 213, 216
  level of analytic resolution, 197
  modernization surface, 213–16, 221–27,
    231, 237–39, 241
  primate cities, 201, 203, 211, 214, 226–
    27
    rank size, 211, 213
  spatial system, 209, 216, 221–29
    locational patterns of economic ac-
      tivity in, 209
    political organization in, 209
    settlement patterns in, 209
    sociocultural patterns in, 209
  spread effects, 203
  See also Growth poles
Specialists, 3, 14–16, 27
  deformations of specialization, 16
Statistical reasoning
  Bayes's theorem, 465, 469–70, 479, 485–
    86
  in model assessment, 465–70

Truman-Dewey election in 1948, 470
Structural formation, see Spatial develop-
    ment dynamics
Structural solidification, 236

Tanzania, 29
  contextual setting, 36–37
  contribution of political ideas to policy,
    73–77
  and Kenya, 33
  speeches by presidents of, 39–41
Temporal sequencing concept, 91
Trends, 2, 11, 19, 89
  class distinctions in, 96
  conditioning factors, 98
  cycles, 98–99
  graphical displays of research results, 98
  illustrative cases or descriptive histories,
    91
  individual level detail, 96–97
  institutions as focus, 95
  literature on, 91–96
  multiple perspectives and interpretations
    of events and related sequences, 89
  overview, 91
  philosophical studies, 91
  projective, 98
  purposes, 89–90
  selectivity and interpretive limitations of,
    94
  theoretical and methodological works,
    91
  thresholds, 98

United Nations Economic Commission for
    Latin America (ECLA), 109, 119
Urbanization, 200–25
  preindustrial, 212–14

Values
  and symbols, 28–29, 33–35
  collective or mass, 27
  Lasswell's category, 4
  methods to study, 42–46
  See also Goals